The New
Question Box

Catholic Life for the Nineties

Catholic Press Association Book Awards 1992

First Place

Popular Presentation of the Catholic Faith

The New Question Box — Catholic Life for the Nineties by Father John J. Dietzen, Guildhall, wins first place.

There seems to be nothing about the faith that Father Dietzen does not treat somewhere in this compellingly readable book. A well laid out question-and-answer form, with questions divided into subject categories, make this a book one can dip into or (very tempting!) read from cover to cover.

Father Dietzen combines impressive knowledge with deep pastoral sensitivity. Long may he and his writing continue to inform and inspire seekers about the faith.

Editors and reviewers say . . .

"... up to date, which is a great blessing because of the many changes in all areas of church life since the 1960s... avoids the extremes of either excessive liberalism or excessive conservatism..." — *Msgr. Charles Diviney, reviewing for Catholic News Service*

"... clarifies religious dilemmas for readers with succinct ease... much like a rewarding chat with a good friend who also happens to be a caring pastor... no curt answers, but a lot of patient, understanding, loving ones..." — *Catholic Digest Book Club*

"... especially noteworthy for its contemporary flavor... We recommend it highly." — *Ligourian*

"... answers are helpful and encouraging to Catholics who want to be faithful to the religion to which they belong, and to their own consciences..." — *Chicago Catholic*

"... it speaks to the average Catholic and answers questions in a straightforward manner, with clarity and sensitivity..." — *Father David W. Givey, editor, Catholic Standard and Times, Philadelphia, Pa.*

"Father Dietzen not only offers us a solid approach to questions in a most difficult time, but he does it with the approach of a pastor who deals with people and not just theories..." — *Msgr. Robert G. Peters, publisher, The Catholic Post, Peoria, Ill.*

"... does his rsearch well, and his answers are concise, plain and to the point... when people are obviously in pain and their questions show it plainly, he is gentle and sympathetic in his approach." — *St. Anthony Messenger*

John J. Dietzen

The New
Question Box

Catholic Life for the Nineties

- Enlarged
- Documented Sources
- Current Code of Canon Law

Guildhall
Peoria, Illinois

Cover design by Ann Aspell

Library of Congress Cataloging in Publication Data:

Dietzen, John J., 1927-
    The New Question Box
    A collection of writings from the author's syndicated column
the Question Box
    Includes index.
    1. Catholic Church — Doctrines — Miscellanea.
    I. Question Box. II. Title.
BX1754.3.D52 1983 230'.2 83-18540
ISBN 0-940518-07-4 (pbk.)

Printed in the United States of America
First printing, July, 1981
Second printing, January, 1982
Third printing, enlarged and revised according to the 1983 Code
of Canon Law, November, 1983
Fourth printing, revised, February, 1984
Fifth printing, revised, October, 1985
Sixth printing, March, 1986
Seventh printing, revised, October, 1986
Eighth printing, revised, November, 1988
Ninth printing, revised, January, 1991
Tenth printing, revised, November, 1992

Guildhall Publishers
Peoria, Illinois
61651

PREFACE

Question and Answer columns have been popular in the Catholic press in the United States since the turn of the century. This book is proof of their continued success.

"The New Question Box" by Father John J. Dietzen — a collection of such columns syndicated by Catholic News Service — won the 1992 Catholic Press Association Book Award for the best popular presentation of the Catholic faith.

The author is a priest of the Diocese of Peoria, and surely the dean of the question-and-answer columnists of all time. The former associate editor of The Catholic Post, newspaper of the Diocese of Peoria where his column first appeared more than two decades ago, he has been in pastoral work since 1973 and now heads Holy Trinity Parish in Bloomington, Ill. His column appears in more than 50 newspapers in the U.S. and Canada.

More than 10 years ago, responding to many requests to publish his work in book form, Father Dietzen put together questions and answers that dealt largely with the then still "new" liturgy that had evolved since Vatican II. Catholics then were still concerned about women wearing hats in church, whether confessionals should be done away with, and if people were permitted to drink from the chalice.

The answers to those questions became obvious in the intervening years, and a whole new genre of questions surfaced. Today people are asking about AIDS, about abortion and euthanasia, about unmarried couples living together, and many other complex questions about marriage, divorce and annulment procedures. Questions about Scripture, the sacraments, the Mass, and the wide spectrum of lay ministry and other parish involvement are included in the author's voluminous mail.

These concerns of Catholics reflect not only the changes in our society, but also their own abiding desire to live according to the teaching of their faith. And often the questions seem to point to the future — questions asked in the 1940s were almost omens of the changes called for by documents of the Second Vatican Council.

Whatever meaning sociologists and church historians might derive from question and answer columns, they are for the average reader an excellent source of information. To that end, the various editions of The New Question Box have been revised over the years to reflect the evolving thought and practices of our faith, and to keep the contents of the book up to date. A major revision came in 1983 when the text was revised to conform to the new Code of Canon Law.

The long hours and scholarship required to research and write the column that appears in today's Catholic newspapers under various headings are, for the author, a labor of love for the Catholic faith and for his readers. His column, syndicated since 1975, covers a wide range of topics, and he draws his answers from many sources — papal encyclicals, Vatican documents, bishops' pastorals, the Code of Canon Law and the Bible — and he enjoys a wide circle of authoritative sources he calls upon to provide definitive information on difficult subjects.

Ordained in June, 1954, he has served as family life director for his diocese, as retreat master and lecturer on a wide range of topics, and as a board member of The Catholic Press Association. In addition to his parish work, Father Dietzen now also serves as co-chairman of the Respect Life Board of the Peoria diocese, and as chairman of the Catholics for Life Department of the Catholic Conference of Illinois.

We are pleased to present this 1992 edition of The New Question Box and look forward to living out its subtitle, "Catholic Life for the Nineties." Readers should also welcome this book for the answers it provides to their questions, and for the sense of courage, confidence and peace of heart and mind that a knowledge of their faith can bring.

Guildhall, 1992

INTRODUCTION

In April, 1947, explorer Thor Heyerdahl set sail from the west coast of Peru to begin what was to be one of history's most famous voyages. Hoping to explain the puzzling presence of apparent South-American cultures in the distant south Pacific, he and his companions struggled to bring their tiny balsa raft, Kon-Tiki, into the offshore Humboldt Current. Their theory, which proved correct, was that once they entered the current there would be no turning back. It would carry them irrevocably thousands of miles across the Pacific to the islands of Polynesia. This now-famous migration is an appropriate image of the Catholic Church and much of the rest of Christianity since Vatican Council II (1962-65).

In previous editions of this book I have indicated that a major purpose in writing it, and the column in which most of the questions and answers first appeared, was to assist Catholics in understanding, adapting to and spiritually profiting from the changes in our faith that followed the Council. There was, to be honest, much naivete in those years. Some foolishly thought that the world's bishops made a big mistake in those four years and that sooner or later we would return to "normal". Certain others were just as wrong. Claiming enthusiastic embrace of the Council's work, they perceived it as calling primarily for procedural changes: reform the Mass according to its ancient traditions; establish broader ecumenical inter-action with fellow Christians and those of other world religions; revise our Eucharistic and sacramental liturgies so people might better participate in them and be formed by their spiritual power.

Twenty-five or more years later we have accomplished those procedural changes to a significant degree. As we have begun to live them, however, we find ourselves increasingly forced to acknowledge that these changes are only the beginning. They are externals, important externals surely, whose more profound and far-reaching function is to point Catholics toward a renewed understanding of the relationship we believers in Christ should have with the worldwide human family.

Few serious historians or theologians today would question that the bishops of Vatican II launched our ecclesiastical raft to where there is no turning back, into a current leading us more and more to acknowledge that the predominant model for the Church in our age must be that of a Servant People, a bringer of healing and hope. Peoples of the world are wracked by the fear and often reality of famine, terror, war, suppression of human rights, torture, nuclear holocaust and, worst of all, hopelessness. The Church cannot stand outside looking in. "Today especially," as the American bishops have said, "the Church presents herself as a pilgrim of hope."

We are I believe only beginning to understand the magnitude of that call by the Holy Spirit and what it will demand of us. To move from an image of Church which in the minds of many seemed to be identified with social prestige, power, and even material affluence is not easy. To this day some Catholics, laity and clergy, seem to measure the Church and even its ministers by such signs.

Nevertheless, in our own country and in Catholic communities around the world, it seems the Church increasingly sees itself otherwise, as pilgrim sharer in the world's suffering, and bearer of hope and compassion. This movement grows perhaps most of all out of the Council's insistence that, always recognizing the need for proper roles of governing and teaching charisms in the Church, the Holy Spirit is at work inspiring, moving, and energizing all the People of God to be the Lord's faithful "witnesses to the ends of the earth." (Acts 1:8) Such a vision brings all elements of the Church to a greater unity and closeness, closer to each others' suffering and closer to their Catholic experiences and insights.

Thus as we move toward the close of the third decade after the Council, the purpose of *The New Question Box* remains the same, though happily on a deeper, more challenging, and more hopeful level. This latest edition will, I hope, make easier a joyful dedicated living of our faith in that same spirit. It is therefore written from a pastoral viewpoint, responding to some large and small questions facing the Church and the whole People of God today, especially in daily life and practice where all holiness and goodness ultimately lie. Where necessary, historical background on questions of conscience, belief and practice attempts to deepen understanding of how and why the Church reached the positions it assumes today.

Perhaps an image even more apt than Kon-Tiki for the Body of Christ today is that of a growing child. Once conceived, and unless it is violently destroyed, human life too possesses a persistence, an irrevocability. There is no turning back. Yet it needs to be nurtured, cared for, and treasured as a gift. We are like that today as a Church, individually and collectively. A great gift of life has been placed into our hands and, like the loaves that fed the multitudes, the Lord expects that none of it be wasted.

I have tried here wherever possible to assist and encourage that perspective, that frame of mind by which the Catholic Christian can function with fidelity to the teachings of the Church and to his God-given intelligence, common sense and faith, and with confidence that any risks are taken in the security of the enduring love of a faithful God.

Again I offer my profound gratitude to those whose professional competence and advice have contributed to the preparation of *The New Question Box*, and to the thousands of correspondents and many friends whose questions, insights, criticisms, and inspiring living of the Christian life have made this book and the column possible. They, their crosses and their hopes, have a special place in my heart and in my prayers.

John J. Dietzen
November, 1992

TABLE OF CONTENTS

munion — Communion in the hand — Communion after remarriage — Easter duty — Communion for mentally handicapped — Communion for infants — Communion for semicomatose — Communion before Mass — Communion at home.

Chapter V: **Baptism and Confirmation**   235

Qualifications for godparents — Orthodox godparents — Protestant godparents — responsibilities of godparents — delaying baptism — churching of women — number of sacraments — place for baptism — baptism without permission — parents' responsibility — stillborn children — validity of Protestant baptism — children of unwed mothers — limbo — Confirmation sponsors — Confirmation name.

Chapter VI: **Marriage and Family**   269

Marriage vows — purposes of marriage — permanence — marriage as sacrament — banns — preparation for marriage — homosexuality — pre-marital sex — living together without marriage — interfaith marriage — promises in interfaith marriage — children of interfaith marriage — children and the Mass — responsibilities of parents — honor due parents — Catholic marriage in Protestant church — in vitro fertilization — children and cults — theology of marriage — divorce and Communion — Sanatio in Radice — impotence — Dispensation from Form — physical abuse in marriage — ministry to divorced — Natural Family Planning — birth control — Onanism — sterilization — sterility — marriage of cousins — alcoholism — infidelity — polygamy and church law.

Chapter VII: **Divorce, Annulment, Remarriage**   357

Marriage regulations — Pauline Privilege — Privilege of the Faith — excommunication — sacraments after divorce — Defect of Form — "Catholic divorce" — remarriage after divorce — marriage cases, procedures — diriment impediment — marrying "out of" the church — marrying divorced non-Catholics — Roman Rota — annulments — annulment cases — children in annulment — counseling after annulment — divorce and the Sixth Commandment.

This book is dedicated with affection and gratitude to my family, those who have always been and those who have become my family through the years, and to the thousands of readers whose questions, insights and searching faith are a continuing source of admiration and inspiration.

The Bible

Church and sacred Scripture

A priest we know has said some things recently I would like to understand better. He said the church existed before the Bible, at least before the New Testament. I realize this is true. But today, he added, we can do without the Bible, but we cannot do without the church. This is more than my understanding of our faith can absorb. Could you tell me in more detail what he meant?

As you say, the church certainly existed before the New Testament was completed. Many Christians were born, lived and died before the last book of the Bible was even written somewhere at least 60 or 70 years after Jesus died. The Bible was not solidified in its present combination of books until centuries later.

The statement that the church could do without the Bible is, in my view, at least ambiguous. In a way, of course, he is right. Theoretically the church could do without the Sacraments of Baptism, Penance, Holy Orders and possibly even the Eucharist. Who are we to say that the church could not have been formed in a variety of other ways than Jesus actually arranged?

The church which really exists, however, is unthinkable without all of these elements and it is just as unthinkable without the Bible. Surely, the living community of faith with its leaders (particularly the pope and other bishops) will be the living carrier of the message and life of Christ to the world until the end of time. There is one sense, then, in which this living family of Christ will always be the final interpreter of the biblical word of God. It is equally true, however, that Scripture enshrines the teachings of the Lord and of the apostles with a special clarity and universality, so that it will be for all time the norm against which the church measures all its actions and its faith.

Whatever we propose as "might have been," the real church would soon be lost without Scripture. This is why the church has always venerated the Bible just as she venerates the body of Christ. "From the table of both the word of God and of the body of Christ she unceasingly receives and offers to the faithful the bread of life, especially in the sacred liturgy" (Dogmatic Constitution on Divine Revelation of Vatican II). The council document goes on to say that "all the preaching of the church must be nourished and ruled by sacred Scripture."

With this view of Scripture, it is impossible to understand how the church could get along without it. As that same constitution of the Vatican Council says, "It is clear that sacred tradition, sacred Scripture and the teaching authority of the church, in accord with God's most wise design, are so linked and joined together that one cannot stand without the others. All together and each in its own way under the action of the one Holy Spirit contribute effectively to the salvation of souls." (No. 10)

Biblical literary forms

I am sick and tired of hearing that the Bible is full of allegories and parables. If the word of God does not suit your 20th-century ungodly lay and scientific concept of the world and of God, don't snipple here and there to your liking. Don't you believe the Bible is the word of God?

I'm sorry you are sick and tired of hearing it, but the plain fact is that much of the Bible is made up of allegories and parables — and poetry, fictional short stories, speeches, fables, and numerous other forms of literature.

You are, of course, free to believe what you wish about the Bible, even take it as word-for-word history if you can figure out how to do that. But the church's teaching is clear: The "truth" the Bible expresses is to be found in the meaning that the sacred writers intended when they wrote that particular part of Scripture. And to arrive at that truth, one must investigate whether that writer was producing straight history, a fable with a moral lesson involved, poetry, or another kind of writing. Only then do we discover most accurately what God is saying to us.

I like the example of George Washington and the cherry tree. The "truth" of that story is not in the facts of the plot, but in what it says about George. Should a scientist some day prove there never was a cherry tree at Mount Vernon, our answer would be, "so what?" The story is not about a cherry tree, but about the honesty, integrity and nobility of the character of our first president. Furthermore the man who thinks it is a tale about cherry trees and horticulture will miss the whole point.

Similarly the man who thinks, for example, that the story of Jonah is mainly about man-swallowing whales and storms at sea will miss the real "truth" of the story which the author intended — that God's love for mankind is universal, and the many other revelations which that book so enchantingly unfolds. In that particular instance, it makes not one whit of difference whether the whale carried our hero around for three days or whether there even was a Jonah in the first place.

As Vatican Council II teaches, it is in all these ways, including some sections of straight history, "that the books of Scripture must be acknowledged as teaching solidly, faithfully and without error that truth which God wanted put into the sacred writings for the sake of our salvation" (Constitution on Divine Revelation, paragraph 11).

The acceptance and proper understanding of the written word of God is naturally of primary importance to Catholics. If you're really interested in what the church teaches on the subject, read the Constitution on Revelation which I just quoted, or the encyclical *Divino Afflante Spiritu* of Pope Pius XII (1943). Any priest should be able to help you find at least one of these.

Bible only for experts?

You mentioned that in reading the Bible it is important that we have some idea of what the writer intended when he wrote a particular book, and how the people understood it then. How can an ordinary person be expected to know all this? Shouldn't we read the Bible unless we do know these things?

Reading the Bible in a spirit of prayer and faith in God's word is always good and fruitful. In fact, someone who approaches Scripture with this attitude will reap far more benefits than one who has a lot of technical knowledge about the Bible, but no faith.

However, at least a little information about the background of the Bible and its books can make the reading of Scripture more beneficial and prevent much confusion and misunderstanding. Very little of the Bible is "straight" history as we think of it. Most of it is poetry, parables, personal or community reflections on memorable events, legal documents, visions or other manifestations of what were interpreted as God's reactions to human happenings, prophecies veiled in extremely mystical symbols — and even efforts by ancient theologians to put together in a cohesive way this whole series of revelations and experiences.

Since, in addition, all of what is now in the Bible was handed down by writing or word of mouth during a period of thousands of years, it's obviously an advantage to know, for example, what *kind* of writing each book was meant to be, and even to know some of the historical circumstances of the time. A parallel might be a 1935 newspaper being read today by an older man and a high school freshman. The paper would be far more intelligible and significant to the man who experienced those years than to the 14-year-old who knows only the words he sees on the paper.

Difference in Bibles

Could you please tell us the main difference between the Catholic Bible and the King James version? I know there is

a difference, but why do some people of other faiths say that Bibles are all the same?

There are today only two major differences between what we might call Protestant and Catholic Bibles.

First, Catholic Bibles contain all or part of several books in the Old Testament that do not appear in the Protestant biblical tradition. These books are Tobias, Judith, Baruch, First and Second Maccabees, Ben Sirach (Ecclesiasticus), Wisdom, and parts of Daniel and Esther. For reasons we won't go into here, biblical scholars refer to these as the deutero-canonical books, because of varying positions among Jews of the Old and New Testament periods concerning them

The second major difference is that Protestant Bibles generally do not include much in the way of footnotes, explanations or introductions. The Protestant tradition that the Holy Spirit alone guides each individual in his or her reading in Scripture has caused publishers of Bibles to shy away from anything which in their view would put some sort of human intervention between the reader and the Holy Spirit.

Catholic Bibles have not hesitated to include such materials, giving background to entire books or passages, describing the audience to which the book was addressed, and so on. More and more Bibles published under Protestant auspices tend to include similar notes to assist the readers in understanding what the biblical writers were dealing with.

Apart from these, there is generally no great difference between Protestant and Catholic Bibles. In past centuries, certain biblical passages were translated quite differently, colored by doctrinal positions of the two groups. The science of choosing and translating biblical manuscripts, however, is now so highly developed that any slanting of translations in this manner is simply out of the question for reputable biblical scholars of any faith.

New translations of the Bible are, of course, underway all the time. The King James version, published in the Protestant tradition, is simply one of the early English translations (1611), which, however, retains much of its popularity because of the exceptional style and language which have made it a classic of English literature.

More modern versions, and there are several excellent ones, are naturally easier for most of us to understand and are in many instances more accurate translations. The most authoritative current English translation in the Catholic tradition is the New American Bible, prepared under the auspices of American and other English-speaking bishops.

In the Protestant tradition there is The English Bible, and some other excellent ones, notably the New Revised Standard Version.

All of these, of course, are published in a wide variety of sizes, editions, and so on; but the titles I have mentioned, among others, indicate the actual biblical translations contained in the books.

Were Adam and Eve real?

My son came home from high school the other day and said his teacher told them Adam and Eve never existed. This goes down to the fundamentals of our faith, doesn't it? Did they, or didn't they? If there were two people who started the human race, how do we explain the different races — Chinese, Negro, etc.?

We don't know (and probably never will) whether or not there were two original human beings from which all the rest of us descended. And if there were, we surely do not know their names.

One thing is certain: We will never find out from the Bible. Holy Scripture simply was not written to pass on to us such details of anthropology as this. Whether there were two "first parents" or 200, or exactly where they came from, has little to do with the spiritual and theological intent of the biblical story of Adam and Eve — which was put together in the form we have it only a few hundred years before Christ.

That story, which we find in the first chapters of Genesis, is meant to convey to us some of the most important truths of our faith — that the world, including the human family, owes its existence to the one true God; that this world as it came from God was good and was meant for mankind's happiness; that whatever misfortunes there are on earth come from man's own stubbornness and sinfulness; that even in the beginning God had a plan to eventually save man from his sinfulness, and so on.

I don't know why this should be so "fundamental" for your faith. The great facts about God and our relation with him are the real message of Holy Scripture. As for the rest, scientists generally agree that any certainty about such things that happened way back in the dawn of history, tens or hundreds of thousands of years ago, is well nigh impossible.

The position of the church on this subject was made clear in the encyclical *Humani Generis* of Pope Pius XII (1950). In it the Holy Father insisted that the theory that there were more than two "first parents" of the human race should not be taught as an established fact. And that's where the matter stands.

Concerning the origin of the races, neither the Bible nor Christian revelation gives us much to go on. Some of the more fundamentalist Christians profess to see hints in the Scripture about how some of the races started. But the church's position, once again, is that this type of question must be answered by the sciences of anthropology and paleontology, not by theologians or Scripture scholars.

Many Adams, many Eves?

You say we may accept the possibility that there were more than one Adam and Eve who originated the human race. I have no big problem with this, but do have two questions. How do you explain scriptural references such as St. Paul's remark, "Through one man (Adam) sin entered the world" (Romans 5,12)?

And isn't it true that many church councils, such as the infallible Council of Trent, and several church documents refer to Adam as "the first man?"

One critical point to remember in considering both your questions is that neither Scripture nor the council you mention were addressing themselves at all to the question of polygenism (that is, whether there were many first parents). Therefore one must be careful in claiming they answered a question that, up to that time, had never even been approached seriously, if at all.

To your first point, preachers and other orators quite commonly use the device of referring to well-known historical characters to make a point, with absolutely no intention of declaring judgment on the actual existence of these characters. When a priest in a homily, for example, refers to the Prodigal Son or the Good Samaritan, he is not professing a belief that these particular individuals of Jesus' parables ever really existed. They fit the point to be made, and that's all their mention really means.

Jesus did this, St. Paul did it, and conciliar decrees and other official church documents do the same. As mentioned above, these documents were not directly concerned with polygenism. But if reference to the scriptural story of creation helped explain or support their teaching, they rightly had no hesitation in using it.

In *Humani Generis* Pope Pius XII explained some doctrinal and scriptural problems with polygenism (some of which have been resolved in the last 30 years, incidentally), and says that no Catholic should hold that opinion (polygenism) as a fact since "it is not apparent" how this opinion is compatible with certain Catholic beliefs.

Humani Generis labels the belief in more than one Adam and Eve a conjectural opinion. It does not call that opinion erroneous or heretical.

By the way, there is no such thing as an "infallible council." A particular truth may be taught infallibly. But the fact that some truths are taught solemnly in a conciliar or papal document doesn't mean that everything is, even if it's in the same sentence.

Does Bible give earth's age?

I am a sponsor in our parish catechumen class. A priest told us in one session that someone once determined from the Bible that the earth was only about 6,000 years old. I find that fascinating! But he had no further details. Have you heard of this?

It is fascinating, especially in light of the information we have today about the history of the earth and of the human race. Your priest might have been speaking of at least two people. During the 17th century Archbishop James Ussher of Ireland, after much careful adding up of figures from the Book of Genesis, determined that the world was created in 4004 B.C.

Some time later, a Dr. John Lightfoot of Cambridge University, England, claimed to prove that the exact moment of the creation of Adam was "October 23, 4004 B.C., at 9 o'clock in the morning." I suppose there is someone somewhere who still believes that. To my knowledge at least, even those who reject any evolutionary explanation of the creation of the world would find it difficult to swallow those figures.

Age of the human race

Last week's newspaper had a story about some people finding human skeletons that are supposed to be over three million years old. I don't know that much about the Bible, but a friend and I were discussing the article and she said that, according to the Bible, the whole world is only about 6,000 years old. I'm sure we don't believe that. At least I don't. But what can you say to someone like that? Is there any reason we can't believe that the human race is three million years old?

You raise a lot of big questions. Answers will vary greatly depending on one's understanding of the Scriptures, of religion, of God — and even of science.

There is absolutely nothing in our Catholic faith that would prevent us from accepting any age for the human race. The Bible was never meant by God to be a course in archeology, paleontology, or even of history, in our usual understanding of that word. It is a story of God's saving plan for mankind, wounded and crippled by his own selfishness and pride, and how that plan unfolded. It is a book of faith, not of technical information.

This goes especially for the first 11 chapters of Genesis, which "cover" the whole history of the world up to God's call of Abraham as the father of the Hebrew people somewhere around 1800 B.C. The great Jewish theologians who put those stories together (creation, the flood, etc.) several centuries before Christ, had many ancient myths and legends to go on, but basically they knew even less about the details of the origin of the world than we do.

This bothered them not in the least. Their purpose, under the inspiration of God, was to make believers, not scientists, out of their people.

There's no reason at all you cannot believe men and women were strolling the earth three million years ago — if you're satisfied with the scientific evidence.

To the other part of your question: If someone insists that every fact, figure, name and event in holy Scripture is technically, scientifically, and historically accurate, don't waste your time arguing about such things as the age of man. You're simply on different wave-lengths about the meaning of biblical truth.

Old Testament view of God

In the books of Moses God is portrayed as a tyrant who has all the personal characteristics of some of the Roman emperors. Certainly God, who started the universe, is all powerful. But to portray him as was done in the books of Moses and other places in the Old Testament is an insult to the intelligence and greatness of God. Don't you agree?

It seems to me you are limiting yourself by a very simplistic view of revelation. The fact is that, in revealing himself to them, God does deal with men and women at the level where they are. To do anything else would do violence to the free response which God continually invites from his people — an invitation and response which must change as people themselves change.

From your knowledge of history you must be aware that sensibilities develop and grow in human beings. Placing men and women in public stocks on the town square was thought to be an act of unusual kindness in the early days of our own nation, considerably more humane than the public whippings generally acceptable before that.

We have seen advances in understanding human dignity even within our own church in 2,000 years. Suicide, for example, was looked upon quite differently in the times of the early martyrs than it is now.

Bishop Eusebius of Caesarea, the most renowned historian of the early centuries of Christianity, tells us that in his own time (third and fourth centuries) those who ended their own lives rather than participate in the gruesome cruelties of the arena were themselves honored as martyrs.

Surely this view of taking one's own life is not consistent with later Christian understandings of suicide.

At this very moment, Christian churches and perhaps our entire Western civilization are experiencing a new level of sensitivity and awareness about human dignity, which makes us seriously question many past assumptions about "just war" and capital punishment.

I think we should not be too hard on Moses or other ancestors whose images of God and man appear so foreign to us. After all, while he is continually pulling us ahead in new ways, God seems always to have a great deal of patience with us where and as we are.

The church's stand on evolution

What is the church's stand on evolution? Our pastor is teaching it at the seventh and eighth grade level. Even if he is right, does he have the right to instill evolution in the minds of our children at that age? Doesn't he need permission to be teaching evolution in our Catholic schools?

If by evolution you mean the theory that human life (and most other life on this earth) evolved or developed in some manner from other living beings — as distinct from having been created immediately by God "out of the slime of the earth" — the church has no doctrine on it one way or the other.

Our faith teaches that the world, including human beings, was created by God, and that the existence of each human soul results in some way from a particular act of his creative powers.

Beyond this, how God actually created our human bodies, whether in an instant or in stages and processes that extended over thousands of years is not a question which our Catholic faith has ever addressed. Nor does it affect Catholic doctrine.

Nor can one appeal to the Bible for an answer. As I've explained before, the Scriptures (at least according to the Catholic understanding of them) have no intention of answering such scientific or technical questions.

The great faith declarations of Genesis — that God created the world and all that exists by his own creative, loving power; that creation as it comes from the hand of God is all good; that even after mankind's fall God calls him to renewed unity with his Creator and with his fellow human beings, and so on — none of these stand or fall on how exactly God created the human family.

As far as the church is concerned, it is not a religious question but a scientific one. This is true even though some supposed experts of the past, who were often no better scientists than they were theologians, claimed that the theory of evolution spelled the death of the Bible and of Christianity.

Personally, I'm convinced that the evidence from biology, paleontology and related sciences make at least some form of evolution the only reasonable position to hold.

But one is free to hold otherwise if he thinks the scientific evidence leads elsewhere. Either way, one may be a good Catholic in no conflict with the doctrine of the Catholic Church.

Evolution and the soul

I enjoy your question column each week, but one you had recently on evolution puzzled me. You said that one is free to hold at least some belief in evolution and still be a good Catholic in no conflict with the doctrine of the church.

Animals do not have souls, right? But human beings do. So how can we have evolved from apes, gorillas, monkeys, or so-called missing links? Aren't they animals?

As you correctly point out, there is something that makes us human that cannot be explained by the material part of us that might be derived from other living beings through some sort of evolution. This non-material, spiritual element that is essential to our human personality is what Catholic tradition, following the terminology of one Greco-Roman philosophy, has called the soul.

Since this soul has no parts, one cannot break off a piece and pass it on in the way our parents, for example, pass on the material for our bodies from their own.

This is one reason the church has taught, and still teaches, that while our bodies may evolve from other bodies, the spiritual part of us could only come into existence through a direct creative act of God. Each of our souls comes, as it were, fresh from the hand of our Creator.

Tradition has seen at least hints of this teaching in Holy Scripture. For example, at death "the dust returns to the earth from which it came, and the spirit returns to the God who gave it." (Ecc.12:7) And, "We have had our earthly fathers (literally the fathers of the flesh) to discipline us and we respected them. Should we not then submit all the more to the Father of spirits and live?" (Heb. 12:9)

In our own time this position on evolution was repeated by Pope Pius XII in his encyclical *Humani Generis* (1950). The teaching of the church, he says, "does not forbid that, in conformity with the present state of human sciences and sacred theology, research and discussions on the part of men experienced in both fields take place with regard to the doctrine of evolution, inasfar as it inquires into the origin of the human body as coming from pre-existent and living matter — for Catholic faith obliges us to hold that souls are immediately created by God."

Noah and the Ark

During my young years I thought that everyone and everything perished during the great flood except Noah and his family and animals (two of each). His family and the animals survived because he took them with him on the ark. Now my granddaughter, who taught Bible school at her Catholic Church, tells me the story of the great flood and Noah was only a myth, or words to that effect.

We cannot read stories of the Bible, especially those which go back tens or hundreds of thousands of years into prehistory, as if they were written by modern scientists or historians. Just as Jesus used parables (which are fictions to convey a truth he wanted to teach), other parts of the Bible can do the same.

Except for those Christian groups who are biblical literalists (meaning that they accept every part of the Bible as literally true, as if they were scientific and historical documents in our modern sense of the word) almost no one today would, for example, view the story of Noah and the Ark as literally and historically accurate.

This by no means says that the story is not true. The truth of the story is not in whether or not the details are accurate, but rather in the knowledge it reveals to us of God's power, man's capacity for both good and evil, God's desire to forgive and save us, and so on. Sometimes, in fact, when we concentrate too much on the technical details of stories like Noah, we tend to miss the real message which God is telling us if we listen in the right way.

A point you mention in your question is one proof that the Noah story was never intended to give intricate details. You note that Noah took two of each animal into the ark with him. This is true according to one part of the flood story (Genesis 7, 8-9). Later on, however, we are told there were seven pairs of clean animals taken into the ark (Genesis 7, 25). This seeming contradiction obviously posed no difficulty for the writer who finally put the story together as we have it, because his purpose was not to count animals or days of rain. Under the inspiration of the Holy Spirit, he had a far more profound message than that.

Did Abraham commit adultery?

I don't understand the story in the Bible about Abraham. He had a wife, Sarah, but he also had a son (Ishmael) by a slave girl before the son of his real wife. Now, wasn't Abraham committing adultery?

If you check the book of Genesis (chapter 16), you'll note that the slave girl, Hagar, was actually Abraham's concubine. In the Old Testament, however, a concubine was more than simply a mistress in our sense of the word. She was an actual wife, but of some lower status than the wife (or wives) who enjoyed the full legal status of wife.

The possession of concubines seems to have constituted a

kind of transition practice between polygamy (having more than one wife), which was quite common in the ancient world, and monogamy (one wife). No one seems very sure of the exact difference between a wife and a concubine. Probably much depended on the particular time and culture. But having children by concubines was considered completely proper and legal.

The practice continued for centuries after Abraham, who lived about 1700 B.C. In fact, among the Jews as well as other ancient cultures (and in some localities even into modern times) the best barometer of a man's wealth was the number of concubines in his harem. About 925 B.C., a major indication that King Solomon was the richest man in the world was that he had 700 wives and 300 concubines — which has got to be some kind of record! (see I Kings, chapter 11)

Egyptians and the Exodus

Our local newspaper contained a story recently about a new theory concerning the death of the Egyptian soldiers when the Jews were fleeing Egypt in the Exodus. According to the scripture scholar, a tidal wave caused the death of the soldiers. Since this happened centuries before the biblical story, the implication as we gather it was that the Bible story could not be true. Could this have happened the way the newspaper described it?

The newspaper was speaking, I assume, of a theory advanced during the past few years by Dr. Hans Goedicke, a world-renowned scholar of Egyptian history and professor at Johns Hopkins University.

Briefly, his theory is based on an ancient description of an Egyptian military disaster which occurred apparently in the year 1477 B.C. According to the story, a huge tidal wave came in from the Mediterranean Sea and caused the death of hundreds of travelers. Goedicke proposes that these travelers were the escaping Hebrews and that the soldiers killed in the disaster were the pursuing Egyptian army.

Many theories about the exact nature of the escape of the Hebrew people are compatible with what we have in the Scriptures. Even so, however, Goedicke's theory has been severely attacked by, I believe, the vast majority of other scholars who have commented on it.

Based on what we know from Scripture and elsewhere (the "Song of the Sea," for example, in Exodus 15 is believed to be the oldest passage of the Bible, written very close to the time of the Exodus), the new theory would place the Hebrew-vs-Egyptian event too far north, too unlike what we are pretty sure happpened according to biblical evidence, and at least 200 years earlier than other available information would indicate for the Exodus.

There's no problem of "faith in the Bible" here one way or the other. But the theory you ask about is a long way from causing any serious problems with the traditional Bible story.

Does Israel belong to the Jews?

In connection with the present fights between the Jews and the Arabs, the claim has been made by the Jews that the land of that area belongs to them. They say God gave it to them. Do you agree? How could they claim such a thing?

In the Old Testament, as God formed Abraham and his descendants into his "Chosen People," he is believed to have particularly destined them for the territory which we now know as the state of Israel. The cohesiveness they would develop in relation to this land would be an important part of the many ways God would develop the theological and social conditions necessary to prepare for the coming, and for the work, of Jesus.

Some (most?) Jewish people feel this Divine plan still gives a foundation for their claim to the land. My conviction, and, I believe, the position of any official statements by the Catholic Church, is that the Old Testament theological claim has little or no relevance to the present situation. Settlement of the problem must be on the same basis of political and social justice as might lead to the solution of any other such dispute — and that would include consideration of the history involved during the past 2,000 years as well as in the time before Christ.

Why are things "unclean"?

The more I read the book of Leviticus the more confused I become. Why are perfectly normal functions and things considered unclean? Where did all these strange laws about food, lepers, death, and so on originate?

According to Jewish law, contact with four categories of things rendered an individual unclean, that is, unfit to participate in any worship. These four categories include leprosy, dead bodies, certain foods that were labeled unclean, and sexual functions. Nearly anything that had to do with sexual intercourse, sinful or lawful or not, was considered unclean.

This uncleanness was not necessarily something spiritual, and generally had nothing to do with holiness. In fact, usually it could be taken away by simply washing oneself. But the system was severely adhered to among the Jews. We learn from the Gospels that at least some groups of Jews, such as the Pharisees, insisted on the most rigid observance of all such laws, a position for which they are frequently attacked by Jesus.

No one has ever been able to give a satisfactory explanation of the origin of these Hebraic regulations. It seems clear that they relate somehow to similar laws observed by pagan cults among whom the Jews lived, but every explanation suggested appears to have as many arguments against it as for it.

Jesus' primary objection to the whole system centered on its focus on externals. As he said, it isn't what a man eats or what he touches that really counts, it's what is in his heart and what comes out of that heart that determines how good a person he is.

Circumcision

Circumcision puzzles me. I understand the medical reasons why circumcision may be recommended. But what could circumcision possibly have to do with religion?

The Bible says that Jewish men were to be circumcised. And the Bible says Jesus was circumcised. Is there any reason?

Not too many years ago I would have had to say no one

knows the answer to your question.

Perhaps that is still true, but there is the possibility of an answer in what we have learned from some ancient inscriptions discovered in the last few years.

It is quite possible that circumcision is closely related to human sacrifice, a practice apparently widespread in some ancient cultures of the Middle East.

A few years ago archeologists in the Near East discovered a text supposedly written by a priest of the Phoenician culture. According to this writing a god named El, to prevent destruction of his city, sacrificed his son to his father, a god named Heaven.

El then circumcised himself and commanded that all his followers should themselves be circumcised to avoid destruction of the city.

The rite of circumcision, in this tradition at least, seems to be a substitute and symbol for human sacrifice, a part of the body is substituted for the whole.

Ancient cultures saw an intimate relationship between the individual and the entire tribe or community. Thus the fact that this sacrifice involved part of the organ of procreation proclaimed that the whole nation or clan, present and future, was consecrated to the god it worshiped.

In this context it is easy to see why the descendants of Abraham came to view circumcision as a fitting and necessary expression of their covenant with the God of Israel.

Why did God choose the Jews?

Some of us think the Jews must accept Christ before they can rightfully return to their homeland. Others believe the Jews will go to what is now Israel and later accept Jesus as Son of God. Doesn't their return have any connection to the Bible? Where can I find a passage that says the Jews will go back before they have changed and have recognized Christ as Messiah?

We look in vain in the bible for answers to questions like this. We cannot answer political and territorial questions of 1992 on the basis of biblical texts, certainly not in isolation from the social and political realities of the intervening 2,000 years. At least this is the way the church views its relations to Israel and the Middle East.

There seems to be, however, a theological and spiritual assumption in your letter that is well worth looking at since it misses an awesome truth of our faith and does considerable injustice to God. If any truth comes through to us in Scripture, it is that God's love, his favor, his covenant is not conditioned on any actions of ours, individually or communally.

You seem to say that the reason certain "blessings" have been withheld from the Jewish people is that they haven't straightened themselves out with God. The Scriptures, both Old and New Testament, speak entirely the opposite. God's covenant of love, his loyalty, is simply a given. When he does venture a reason for choosing the Hebrew people, that reason seems to be that they were of all people the least deserving Maggot and worm, he calls them (Isaiah 41:14), stiff-necked, never satisfied. In fact, among the major evidences of the truth of the Old Testament as God's revelation is the consistently unlovely picture the Hebrew authors paint of their own nation, their own people. No people is that hard on itself without some overpowering spiritual motive.

Yet God never withdraws his pact with them. The lovely story in the book of the prophet Hosea is only one of hundreds of ways God declares that however disloyal and adulterous his people may be, tossing their love out to any other "husband" who comes along, he's always there, faithful and calling them back.

It seems to me this truth of our faith needs much repeating today. My mail reveals a readiness in many Catholics and other Christians to proclaim what God and the church ought to do to people who don't shape up to their satisfaction. We need at bare minimum to admit that when we fall to this temptation we have to that degree fallen from Christ's view of things.

In the Gospels we never find our Lord telling anyone: Go get your life straightened out and then we'll talk. He never approves evil, and obviously has quite clear principles about the kind of life he expects from his followers. The disciples discover this often, for example when Jesus insists on the unique power of the cross (Jn 12) or when he catches them trying to maneuver themselves into high places and chastises them sharply (Mt 20). But first and always he loves them as they are, no strings attached, unconditionally. He knew he could do a lot of new things with people if they responded to his invitation to intimacy.

In the Gospels this is a consistent major accusation of the religious leaders against Jesus: He is a friend of sinners and eats with them (see, for example, Matthew 9:11 and 11:19). In their view, he should have at least imposed a "reform program" before he allowed them to get too close. The fact that he did not was a main reason for his rejection and death. All this is simply part of our Catholic faith and tradition. We need to remember it. Perhaps it doesn't fit with the way we think things "ought" to be. But as God tells us often enough, his ways are not ours, nor is his justice our justice.

Who is Yahweh?

I recently purchased a prayer book that often uses the word "Yahweh" for God. I see this word many times today, but I went to 12 years of Catholic school and never heard it once. What does it mean and why is it used so much now?

The word "Yahweh" represents the best effort of modern Scripture scholars to reproduce the most holy Jewish title for God. In ancient Hebrew tradition, this sacred name was never used except in solemn ceremonies.

According to the major biblical tradition, it is the name God gave himself when he spoke to Moses in the burning bush in Exodus, Chapter 3.

The word already was used, however, in some parts of the earliest chapters of Genesis. In whatever way it originated, the word seems to come from the Hebrew verb "to be" and generally is translated as something like "he who is" or "I am he who is" — expressing the total superiority of this living God over all creation.

Instead of the forbidden word "Yahweh," Jews usually referred to God in their daily conversations and prayers by the word "Adonai," Lord. In Hebrew writing, when they wished to refer to God, the consonants of Yahweh were used (YHWH) with the vowels for Adonai (aoa). This indicated that the word "Adonai" should be used in the reading.

However when the earliest English Bibles appeared, the translators made one word out of that combination, ending up with the hybrid "Jehovah," a word which really never appeared in any language.

Yahweh is a strange word to us, even though we use the first part often in our Catholic worship. The word "allelluia" literally means "praise to Yahweh" or "praised be God."

While the precise pronunciation for it is lost somewhere in history because of the Jewish prohibition against saying it aloud, it does hold an honored place in tradition as the unique name for the one living God of Israel and of Christians.

Should people fear the Lord?

Aren't we supposed to be trying to love the Lord? If so, why do we keep suggesting that the way to love the Lord is to fear him? A short time ago two different responsorial psalms said we are to fear the Lord and that salvation comes to those who fear him. How can you really love someone you are afraid of?

The expression "fear of God" in both the Old and New Testaments does sometimes mean the kind of fear you speak of, an anxiety and perhaps even dread of God's judgment and justice. Many of Jesus' parables, for example, such as that of the rich man and Lazarus, recommend something of this kind of prudent apprehension over the account we will be required to give to God for our lives.

Mostly, however, when Scripture speaks of the "fear of the Lord" it means a kind of marveling, reverential fear. Perhaps the words "awe" or "wonder" would say it better for us.

It may help if we realize that for the Jews, to "fear the Lord" signified the totality of their religious beliefs and activities in relation to God, including their worship. This ties into another saying we hear several times in the Old Testament: The fear of the Lord is the beginning or the foundation stone of wisdom.

In the Bible, wisdom always represents the highest activity of a human being. Putting it briefly, it meant seeing things (at least as much as is possible for us) from the perspective of God, from the perspective in other words of the fullest reality, and then applying that perspective to one's moral and spiritual life.

Thus, Psalm 111's declaration that the fear of the Lord is the beginning of wisdom might be paraphrased (far less poetically) this way: Recognizing with awe the truth that God is Lord and Creator and we are his creatures is the first step to understanding and living in harmony with reality.

The great tragedy of Adam and Eve as with all sinners is that they forgot that truth at a crucial moment. (See Genesis 3:5)

This is the kind of fear of the Lord Isaiah ascribes (11:3) to the coming Messiah, and which we believe to be among the gifts of the Holy Spirit.

Composition of the New Testament

To settle an argument, how long did it take to write the New Testament?

If you're talking about the actual writing and putting together of the books of the New Testament as they are in our Bible, the earliest was the first letter to the Thessalonians, written around the year 50 or 51, about 20 years after Jesus' death.

The Gospel of Mark, the earliest of the four Gospels, dates from perhaps the year 65, though all the Gospels made use of documents, liturgical rites, and other traditions which existed in the Christian communities before that date.

The last books were probably the three letters of St. John and the book of Revelation, all of which were probably written sometime around the year 100, or later.

Thus, the basic composition of all the books covered a period of somewhere around 50 years.

Who wrote the Gospels?

During a sermon on the radio, a Protestant minister said that the Gospel of John was not written by the apostle John the Divine, and that Catholics and Protestants agree on this. Don't we have to believe that the New Testament was written

by the apostles? If not by them, then who did write the Gospels?

It has long been known by Scripture authorities of all Christian faiths that several books of the New Testament were not actually written by the persons traditionally thought to be their authors. The Gospels of Matthew and John are almost certainly two New Testament books of this nature.

There's nothing surprising here. In ancient times a literary work commonly bore the name of the person out of whose teaching the work was formed, even if the man himself did not write it — or perhaps was no longer even alive. The book would still be recognized (and even named) as the teaching of that particular "master" or famous person, though developed, edited, and expanded upon by others perhaps over a period of many years.

This, of course, has no bearing on whether or not the books of the Bible were inspired. The church has never made doctrinal declarations about the authors of the books which make up the Bible.

Interpreting the Gospels

Last Holy Week the Gospel of Mark about the denial of Peter was read at Mass. In the gospels of Matthew, Luke and John, the denial of Peter was three times, but in Mark two times.

The Gospel of Mark confuses the readers. Why not correlate the three into one gospel so as to have the true meaning?

All the gospels speak of Peter's three denials, including the Gospel of Mark (14:68, 70 and 71).

Your question, however, raises a significant point that occurs frequently in the mail I receive. Perhaps it is one aspect of the conviction among many Catholics and other Christians that everything in religion should be black and white, without ambiguity, including the Bible itself. Any evidence that this is not always so is met with disbelief, if not (as apparently in your case) confusion.

The problem you experience is not uncommon. When we

read the New Testament, especially the gospels, we easily tend to think we are reading a life of Christ much like any modern biography. We feel that the first job of Matthew, Mark, Luke and John was to get the facts straight or, as you say, "correlate" the different accounts to get to the "true meaning."

We know, however, that the gospels were never intended to be that. Aside from the fact that scientific historical scholarship as we are familiar with it is a relatively modern invention, details of fact were of no critical concern to the gospel writers. Their intention was rather to explain the meaning of the message of Jesus, what he stands for and what his followers are expected to be.

Since that is what the evangelists set out to do, we are doomed to failure if we expect something else. Evidence for the truth of what I am saying abounds in the New Testament.

We know, for example, that the Eucharist, or the Breaking of the Bread, held a high place in the minds of early Christians. One would assume that at least here they would have their "facts straight."

Yet the quoted words of Jesus in the institution of the Eucharist at the Last Supper are different in all three synoptic gospels (Matthew 26, Mark 14, Luke 22, John does not refer to the Eucharist at all at the Last Supper, at least in this direct way).

The differing readings perhaps reflected variations in the liturgy from one place to another in those early decades of the church. Whatever the reasons, the gospel writers had no problem adding or subtracting ideas they thought necessary to express what they wanted to say about Jesus.

What I am saying is not a minority opinion of a few biblical scholars. It is the official position of the Catholic Church about the formation and character of the gospels.

In 1964 the Pontifical Biblical Commission issued an instruction on the historical truth of the gospels. From the many things handed down to them, says the commission, the gospel writers "selected some things, reduced others to a synthesis and explained yet others as they kept in mind the different situations of each of the churches.

"They selected the things which were suited to the varying situations of Christian believers and to the purpose they had in mind, and adapted their narration of them to the same situations and purpose. . . . The truth of the story is not at all affected by the fact that the evangelists relate the words and deeds of the Lord in a different order and express his sayings not literally but differently, while preserving their sense."

Thus, as the instruction indicates, the first principle of the church in interpreting the Scriptures is: Seek out the meaning intended by the evangelist in narrating a saying or a deed in a certain way or in placing it in a certain context. What did the writer intend to say? That is the first question to ask.

If the evangelist or any other Scripture author intended to give us poetry, or a fable, or a short fiction story, we will miss the whole point if we try to read and understand that poem or parable or novella as a historical document.

Insofar as the gospel authors knew about each other's writings, as Luke and Matthew seem certainly to have known about the earlier Gospel of Mark, they obviously had other concerns besides meshing their facts.

Their message was much bigger, much different and much deeper for their readers than that.

Who were Joseph's parents?

We know the parents of the Blessed Virgin Mary were named Joachim and Anna. Have we ever learned the names of the parents of St. Joseph?

Outside of Scripture, Christian tradition gives us no information at all about the parents of St. Joseph.

In fact the Bible itself is no help. Two different fathers are listed for St. Joseph in the Gospels. In Matthew (1:16), the father of Joseph appears with the name Jacob. In Luke (3:23), Joseph is said to be the son of Heli. However, neither genealogy intends to give a complete line of descent. Matthew obviously wanted to emphasize Jesus' descent from King David and Abraham; Luke's concern is Jesus' human descent from Adam.

In either case we cannot tell how close the relationship was between one of these two "fathers" and Joseph. One may have been his real father. More likely they were both ancestors a little further back.

About Joseph's mother, not even Scripture gives a hint.

Mary's pregnancy

I'm still confused about that part of the Bible concerning the birth of Christ. It deals with the problem Joseph had when he found out that Mary was with child. Apparently it was perfectly all right with everyone that Mary was going to have a baby before she was even married. It seemed to be no problem for St. Joseph either after he found out it was somehow God's doing.

Were unwed mothers that common in those days too?

The explanation really isn't all that complicated. You've certainly heard that in ancient times (in fact, up to the present day in some places), marriage consent was given not only by the bride and groom, but by the families involved. This promise of marriage often took place at a formal, though not necessarily elaborate, ceremony. Sometime after this consent came the actual nuptials — when the groom officially took the bride into his home.

Jewish custom at the time when Joseph and Mary were married seems to have followed something like this procedure. First came the betrothal, which included the consent of all concerned and the giving of the dowry to the groom by the bride's parents. Later came the marriage celebration, with the marriage feast Jesus later referred to often in his teachings and to which he compared the Kingdom of God.

Bride and groom might be together as husband and wife immediately after the betrothal, or wait until after the nuptial ceremony. St. Luke and St. Matthew seem to say that it was during the period between these two events that Mary became pregnant with Jesus. It would not have been at all unusual.

Was Mary a virgin?

I have always thought it was Catholic teaching that Jesus was born of Mary while she was still a virgin. Now I hear that some top theologians deny this. Is this true?

No, it is not true. There is no ranking Catholic theologian that I know of who denies what we call the virgin-birth of

Jesus, though many aspects of this teaching remain profound problems in Catholic as well as Protestant scholarly circles.

One of these is, for example, the problem of just what the church's official declarations about the virgin-birth (in the various creeds for instance, and in some of the ecumenical councils) actually meant. Usually such declarations are intended to combat some erroneous teaching of the time; so a knowledge of just what the church was trying to refute is essential in order to understand the precise meaning of these doctrinal statements.

As with the Bible itself, it is misleading and dangerous to approach church documents for answers to questions which were not even being addressed at the time, or which these documents did not intend to address.

Interestingly, while many passages in Scripture support the teaching of the virgin-birth of Christ, some others seem to create a problem about it. Large parts of the early church seemed to have been unaware of any doctrine about the virgin-birth even many decades after Jesus died. Outside of St. Luke's story of the conception and birth of Jesus, practically all the New Testament is silent about a virgin-birth tradition.

As you can see this becomes quite involved and deserves a great deal of open study. But again, no top theologians are "denying" the virgin-birth of Christ. They do often insist, as we would expect them to, that they have no fear that honest discussion of the virginal conception of Jesus will lead to a traumatic choice between modern scholarship and teachings of the church.

Isaias and the Virgin Birth

I have been told that there is no support in the Old Testament for our belief that Jesus was conceived and born of a virgin. However, we were taught in the past that the passage from Isaias 7 refers to Christ and Mary when it says, "The Virgin shall be with child, and bear a son." Can we or can't we use that to help prove the virgin birth?

It is true that the church often uses this text of the prophet Isaias in connection with the virginal conception and birth of Jesus. As so much of this magnificent biblical book (really the "book" of Isaias is at least two books) Isaias 7:14 gives us rich insights into the significance of the coming of the Savior.

However, several things prevent these words from being a "proof" of the virginal conception of Jesus.

First, the original Hebrew of Isaias, written about 600 years before Christ, does not say virgin, but young girl — "almah." When it was translated into Greek a few hundred years later, the Greek word "parthenos" was chosen — which usually does mean virgin. It was this Greek translation, for instance, which was quoted in the Gospel according to Matthew in the story of the infancy of Jesus (Mt. 1:23).

Because the prophet did not actually use the word virgin, most modern translations working from the original texts use the words maiden, or young woman, in this passage. The New American Bible which you quote does say "virgin," but a footnote explains the confusion over the exact meaning of the sentence.

Furthermore, there remains real uncertainty whether Isaias himself intended these words as a prophetic reference to the coming Messiah. He may have meant them to refer to specific persons he was dealing with politically at that time in his life. At any rate, the text apparently was not understood by anyone in reference to the Messiah, or to virginal conception, until its use by St. Matthew.

Did Jesus really exist?

I am a college student studying the poetry of T. S. Eliot. One of his works is said to parallel the story of Christ's death and resurrection.

A commentator points out that during the 19th century anthropology began to demonstrate that many concepts held to be Christian were actually ancient ideas whose origins were buried deep in prehistory.

My question is: Did Jesus Christ really exist as a historical person? I know that a lot of stories in the Old Testament are perhaps legends but the question of Christ as a real, actual, historical person versus Christ as a myth or symbol is far more

important. I hope you can shed some light on this for me.

First, no reputable historian today would argue that the historical Jesus of Nazareth did not exist. The evidence is simply overwhelming, more so now than a century ago when many historical and anthropological resources available to us were still unknown.

Our knowledge of ancient cultures and literature has multiplied geometrically in the past 200 years. We are now aware of numerous narratives from ancient pagan cultures which parallel biblical stories, and in some ways the story of our Lord and of our Christian faith.

This will not surprise or threaten us if we keep in mind a few important facts.

In the first place, Jesus, his teachings and his church in many significant ways flow (as he himself insisted) out of the religion and culture of the ancient Hebrews which themselves often paralleled the religious cultures of surrounding peoples.

Both in his teachings and in his own life, Jesus dealt with and lived in relation to profound human needs, hopes, loves, failures and possibilities. Far from being startled, one would expect that much of what he said would echo mankind's ancient wisdom as it confronted these same realities and reacted to them in religious ways.

There is really no problem in saying that Jesus, his person and his life, is a "myth" in the strict sense of the word, something that goes to the heart of all human experience, and reflects what is universal in mankind's relationship to creation and the creator.

The problem comes when we say that Jesus is "nothing but" a myth. He is that but he is much more. It is not a question of either-or but rather both-and.

He does reflect the longings and religious instincts of many cultures of the human race; in him, however, God the creator himself enters directly into human history through the incarnation of the second person of the Trinity.

It is because Jesus Christ is both God and a full member of our human family, like us in everything except sin as the letter to the Hebrews says, that he is able to be our Lord and Savior in a way that people before him could at best only dream of or hope for.

The name of Jesus

My question is about Jesus. Is this his first or his last name? We usually refer to him as Jesus Christ, but I've read some spiritual books that call him Christ Jesus, or even other forms of Jesus. Why are these different names used?

First, let's look at those two names themselves. The name Jesus is one form of several similar Hebrew names (Joshua, Yeshua, etc.), all of which loosely mean "Yahweh (God) is Savior," or "the salvation of Yahweh."

Luke tells us that this is the name given our Savior at the annunciation to Mary. It is also the name told to Joseph: "You are to name him Jesus because he will save his people from their sins." (Mt. 1:21)

The name Christ is not a last name in our sense of this word. It is rather the English (and Latin and Greek) equivalent of the Hebrew word "messiah," the anointed one — that is, the expected one who would be chosen or anointed by God as the king and Lord who would save his people.

Our word "christening" is still used occasionally for baptism, since anointing with oil is part of that ceremony.

We find all combinations of those names in the New Testament. Jesus is there, of course, though Our Lord is referred to by that name alone very few times.

Jesus Christ occurs several times though the English often quite correctly renders the second word as an adjective, "Jesus the Christ." The reversal of those names also appears a couple of times, as in "There is no condemnation now for those who are in Christ Jesus." (Rom. 8:1)

By far the most frequent designation for Our Lord in the New Testament, however, which appears dozens of times, is simply the name Christ. The use of this title as a proper name for Jesus became common very early after the resurrection.

All of these are still perfectly proper, though the form "Jesus Christ" is found most often in more formal literary or liturgical works.

What does "Son of Man" mean?

Our group has been discussing the way Jesus in the Bible calls himself the Son of Man. We are puzzled.
Obviously he is referring to himself. But why doesn't he say Son of God? Or does he do this more than we realize? We'd appreciate your explanation.

Your question is a larger and more important one than I suspect you realize. The answers can tell us a great deal about how Jesus saw himself and his mission, and what he considered most necessary for us to know.

Whatever responses we are able to give raise perhaps as many questions as they answer; but they reveal much about the Gospels.

As you indicate, the title Son of Man occurs often in the four Gospels, a total of 82 times. Remarkably, it is used all those times only by Jesus himself.

Its first and most basic meaning is the obvious one: He is a man, truly a human being. ("Son of" is a typical Hebrew expression meaning that one is a member of that particular group or species. See for example Psalm 8.)

There is more to it, however, as our Lord uses the phrase. It has overtones of Jesus as Messiah, "one like the son of man coming on the clouds of heaven" (Daniel 7:13). In the only New Testament use of the title outside the Gospels, Stephen refers to this text before his martyrdom (Acts 7:56).

Another meaning is evident from the numerous times Jesus refers this title to himself in the context of his passion and death. As the Suffering Servant of Yahweh (Isaiah) it is precisely as man, a member and representative of the human community, that he sees himself undergoing his redemptive suffering and death.

John adds another dimension to the title. In that Gospel the Son of Man is spoken of as one who existed before his appearance on this earth (cf. John 6:62). The pre-existence of this "Son" does not appear in the other Gospels.

Obviously, Son of Man is a title Jesus considered significant to express who and what he was, and is, as our Savior.

Son of God, on the other hand, is a title Jesus claims for

himself very rarely, though it occurs over 70 times in the Gospels, mainly the Gospel of John.

In light of the first century church's developing theology, it reflects the unique relationship Jesus had with the Father.

This unparalleled relationship, a kind no one else possesses, is what enables Jesus to be mediator between us and the Father. It gives his saving actions their power to redeem the world.

Thus, to answer one part of the question I believe you're asking, even when the title Son of God is used in the New Testament it is not in the doctrinal sense we later Christians might assume.

It refers more to Jesus as Savior than to his divine nature as the second person of the Trinity. Speaking technically, the title Son of God in the Gospels, and the rest of the New Testament, is soteriological rather than metaphysical.

The Gospels, in other words, are more concerned with revealing to us the Lord Jesus as Savior of the world, sent by the Father, than with theological terminology.

Development of Christian dogma about the Trinity, and its implications about the divinity of Christ, would come fully into its own only much later, in the third, fourth and fifth centuries.

The subject is well worth discussion by your group, or any group interested in searching the Gospels for a deeper understanding of Jesus and his mission, and how that mission is shared by the church, his body on earth today.

Was Jesus born on Christmas?

One night our study club realized that no one knows exactly when Jesus was born. How did we come to celebrate Dec. 25 as the anniversary of his birth? Do we know what year he was born?

Strange as it seems, we have no idea of the date of Christ's birth. The Gospels are absolutely no help on that. From information given especially in the Gospel of Luke, scholars generally believe that Christ was born between the years 8 and

6 B.C. Though our present calendar was supposedly based on the year of Christ's birth as the year one, the science of historical scholarship was not sophisticated enough for them to come to as precise a determination as we are capable of, thus the difference of six or eight years.

Numerous theories have been put forward through the last 2,000 years to explain Dec. 25 as Christmas Day. The most likely one, however, the one most generally accepted by scholars now, is that the birth of Christ was assigned to the date of the winter solstice. This date is Dec. 21 in our calendar, but was Dec. 25 in the Julian calendar which predated our own, and Jan. 6 in the Egyptian calendar. This latter date is still followed by some Eastern-Rite Christian churches.

The solstice, when days begin to lengthen in the northern hemisphere, was referred to by pagans as the "Birthday of the Unconquered Sun." During the third century, the Emperor Aurelian proclaimed Dec. 25 as a special day dedicated to the sun-god, whose cult was very strong in Rome at that time. Even before this time, Christian writers already had begun to refer to Jesus as the Sun of Justice. It seemed quite logical, therefore, that as Christianity began to dominate the religious scene in the Roman Empire, the date of the "new-born sun" should be chosen as the birthdate of Christ.

Were there Magi?

At Christmas time, a priest speaking on television said maybe there were no Magi who came to the crib of Christ. This story is in the Gospel. What does the church say about our belief in the Three Kings? Is it possible that the story did not really happen?

First, we're not speaking here about anything which is part of our required belief as Catholics or Christians. Particularly does it not involve any belief in "three kings." The Gospel of Matthew, the only one that tells this story, does not call them kings, nor does it say how many there were. Eastern Catholics, for example, traditionally speak of 12 kings, not three.

The answer to your question involves many technicalities of biblical interpretation referring to the literary form, or style of writing, used in this Gospel. We are fairly certain, from careful study of the Gospel and other documents written about the same time, that Matthew contains several examples of what is called "haggadic midrash" — that is, stories that are used to spin out and clarify the meaning of a particular event or teaching.

Such stories were intended to convey as clearly as possible the truth of the mystery being considered. They were not meant by their author to be taken literally, in our sense of the word, and were quite common among Jews as effective teaching tools.

One may believe that the story of the Magi happened exactly as it is described in the Gospel, or that it is partly made up but based on some actual journey of Magi to Jerusalem about the time of the birth of Jesus, or even that the story is legendary and intended to call attention to the fulfillment of the prophecies referred to by Matthew.

Any of these understandings is compatible with the Catholic understanding of the meaning and divine inspiration of the Bible.

Did Jesus know he was God?

Recently in a homily I heard a priest comment that "according to scripture scholars Jesus came to the realization that he was God over the course of his life."

I heard the same idea about a dozen years ago in a theology class at a Catholic college. The reaction was: "If Jesus didn't know for sure that he was God, why should we follow his teachings?"

What is the official church teaching on this matter? Why do we stress the humanity of Jesus?

Your question involves one of the two pivotal mysteries of our faith. (The other is the Trinity.) We believe that Jesus is truly God and truly human.

How can one person combine in himself all the attributes

of an infinite God and at the same time all the attributes (except sin) of a very finite human nature? That is mystery. It is the question Christians have wrestled with since the beginning and which we continually attempt to understand further, always realizing that a full explanation is beyond the reach of our intelligence. I surely do not pretend to know the answer.

Whatever we say must respect both of those natures or we undermine an essential of what we mean in professing Jesus as Savior. We cannot deny any facet of God as present in Jesus. On the other hand, our faith and the New Testament itself affirm that Jesus was not just dabbling here and there with being human. He possessed a perfect human nature, including a real human mind and a real human will, with all that those things necessarily imply.

Some people, and some theologians in the early centuries especially, have spoken of Jesus' mind in such a way that it nearly destroys the humanity of that mind. They seem to say that, particularly in a crisis, he possessed a kind of trap door that connected his mind to God's, in effect making his mind not human but divine.

How far can one go with this without ultimately claiming that Jesus did not really, but only seemed to, have a human intelligence, a human nature?

Even the New Testament seems to be clear about the distinction. Luke tells us that as Jesus lived in the home of Nazareth he "progressed" steadily in wisdom and age and grace before God and men" (2:52).

Hebrews tells us, among many other statements regarding the nature of Jesus, that he learned "obedience from what he suffered" (5:8).

From the tone of your letter you might well remark: How can one say those things about God? We don't know. But obviously Luke and the author of Hebrews felt comfortable saying them about Jesus.

We must be extremely careful that our ways of speaking do not imply a denial of the divinity of Jesus. We must, however, be just as careful not to say anything that would imply a denial of his genuine human nature.

It is not a matter of "stressing," but admitting that he was truly a human being as well as truly God.

As I said, the union of those two natures in our Lord is a mystery. We may try to delve into a mystery, but we must never attempt to solve it by taking part of it away. This we would do if we denied something in Jesus that is necessary for a true human nature.

As for the reaction of the students as you report it in your question, the mystery of the incarnation always has been a stumbling block to discipleship with Jesus. And I don't imply agreement with everything any priest says about Jesus when I say that.

Each of us confronts an enormous test of faith, however, when we meet the full implications of that mystery. For some today, as for the people of his home town when he came back to visit, he is still "altogether too much for them."

Did Jesus learn?

I read recently some ideas that I think strange.

I wonder if it is right to say "Jesus learned obedience through suffering." Wasn't he born obedient? When the devil tempted him on the mountain for 40 days, wasn't he being tried for weakness? It seems to me that our Blessed Lord died giving glory to God his Father, who is our Father. Jesus didn't have to learn obedience; he was God!

The quote you give did not originate with a modern writer. It is straight out of the letter to the Hebrews in the New Testament. It is, in fact, only one of many statements in that letter and elsewhere in the Bible which stress a truth many Catholics have a hard time believing — that Jesus was really, truly human, with all that implies in body and spirit.

From my own experience, it seems that the denial of the humanity of Jesus is easily one of the most serious errors of faith in our day. For historical reasons, we have so concentrated on the fact that he is God that we have greatly underplayed the truth that "He is like us in everything except that he did not sin." (Hebrews)

The remarks in Scripture about Jesus growing, learning, suffering, crying, struggling with weakness and fear, and so on, were as vital to the early Christians as they are to us. These

Christians realized, as we should also, that our belief that Jesus is truly human is just as important as our belief that he is God. If either were not true, his saving life, death, and resurrection would be only an empty gesture. If, for example, Jesus is only God and not man, it might prove God's benevolence toward us, but we would not be the saved people we believe we are. Jesus could only accomplish salvation, as we believe in it, by being fully and actually one of us.

St. Luke's Gospel tells us that Jesus grew in wisdom and overall manliness in the sight of God and man. As Hebrews puts it, Jesus is able to be the compassionate and effective priest he is because he once shared our weakness, and was himself "made perfect" and "learned obedience" through the things he suffered.

The quote you give simply repeats, therefore, what the Bible says about Jesus' humanity, a most important truth if we are to appreciate properly the mystery of the Incarnation and his role as our Savior. All passages about Jesus going through the same processes of development and struggle as the rest of mankind (as long as we eliminate any moral weakness or sin) simply reflect this essential element of our faith. We not only can believe it, we must believe it, if we are to be faithful to our Christian traditions.

We do not, of course, ignore the obvious problem of how these human conditions coexist in a person who is God. How can God learn, or be puzzled, or tired? For that matter, how can God be born, have his diapers changed, be hungry, and die? This is the heart of the mystery of the Incarnation — that Jesus, our Savior, is both God and man. We cannot allow ourselves to resolve that mystery by denying it.

Jesus: true God and true man

The other day a priest referred to Jesus as a human being, as you did in one of your columns. I've always been taught that Jesus is one being, one person, the second person of the Blessed Trinity, that he is indeed not a human person, but a divine person. I accept fully and unconditionally the mystery of the Incarnation and all that the church teaches about the two natures and wills.

Years ago, a Sister gave the comparison of a king who fought with his soldiers, himself wearing the uniform of a private. He was a real private without in any way renouncing his royalty. Briefly, he was a soldier like the rank and file, and at the same time a king. This seems an apt comparison, doesn't it?

Only up to a point. The comparison has too many similarities to an ancient heresy called Docetism, which cropped up in the early centuries of the church. Named from the Greek word, "dokesis," meaning an appearance or something imagined, Docetists asserted that Jesus was not really human. He seemed to be a man, through some sort of illusion, but he really was not.

Thus, the king in your comparison was not really a private; he only appeared to be. It seems to imply, therefore, that when God came to earth, he was not really a human being, not really a man; he only appeared to be. And that is absolutely not what we believe about Jesus.

The popularity of that kind of comparison, and the discomfort many Catholics and other Christians still demonstrate when someone insists that Jesus was and is completely, perfectly human, seem to indicate that the Docetists' concern remains quite alive in the church. Isn't it totally beneath God's dignity — almost blasphemous — to believe that God, without ceasing to be God, literally became a human being?

The answer of our Catholic faith is, loud and clear, "No." In some mystery of providence, God found it fitting to his plan of creation — and to his plan of revealing his eternal love for us — that the second person of the Trinity become a member of the human race.

This is precisely what the church means when it says that Jesus is one person, the divine person of the eternal word of God, with both a divine and human nature. He is completely and totally God, and he is completely, totally man.

Are they real words of Jesus?

Our Catholic newspaper had a recent article about a new book identifying the real words of Jesus in the gospels. I

thought we already have the words Jesus spoke. Or aren't we supposed to believe the gospels when they tell us Jesus said something?

First, I should correct your word "identifying." With no tape recordings or video tapes of Jesus, and only comparatively few and often conflicting records such as the gospels to go by, it is all but impossible to identify with certainty the exact words of Jesus. Almost always, the best we, or the experts in biblical research, can do in such questions is say that the evidence points to this or that reading as more probable than another. Much research of this type is going on, by the way, and it can add immeasurably to our understanding of Jesus and his life and message.

We are able here barely to touch on your assumptions about what Jesus says in the gospels, but a few reminders may help. First, even the gospels themselves, as we have them, often differ significantly in their quotes of Jesus. For example, the Lord's Prayer is different in Matthew and Luke (and both of them differ from the one we use); and the words of the institution of the Eucharist at the Last Supper differ from gospel to gospel.

Second, most ancient texts from which our modern bibles are translated have nothing like quotation marks, or even periods. Punctuation of the kind and complexity we use was unheard of. In those manuscripts, phrases and sentences simply run into each other, on the assumption that the reader will make sense of the words. When a verse reads, "Jesus said such and such," did the author mean that to be a direct quote, or rather simply the idea that Jesus expressed, what we would call an indirect quote? The answer comes down finally to an educated judgment by the person doing the translating.

Third, and perhaps most important, the people who listened to Jesus, and those who eventually put the gospels and other scriptures into the form we have them, weren't nearly as interested in such grammatical details as we are. The precise words that were used, or the syntax, were far less significant than the meaning. For them, the more important concern was that the mind and teaching of Jesus be faithfully passed down,

and then translated from a form of Aramaic (the daily language of Jesus, though he probably knew some Greek and
Latin) to Greek, and eventually to other languages.

The book you mention will contribute much to our
knowledge of the New Testament and what Jesus actually
said and did. However, the gospels as we have them contain their own spiritual power as the Word of God. The most
important traits we bring to them are openness to that Word,
and faith.

Jesus' brothers and sisters

**Did Jesus have any earthly brothers and sisters? If he did,
as the Gospels say, does this mean that Mary and Joseph had
other children as husband and wife?**

Perhaps the text most commonly brought forth to claim
that Mary had other children is Matthew 12:47, which speaks
of some of the disciples as "brothers" of Jesus. Brother in
conversation may often refer to a close friend, or fellow
member of a group. Brother as a title, however, as here,
seems nearly always to have meant a blood relative. After
careful study of all the other possibilities, it is now thought
quite possible that those named brothers and sisters of the
Lord were children of Joseph from a previous marriage of
Joseph, who was of course assumed to be the natural father
of Jesus.

As unfamiliar as this may sound to us, there is nothing
in the Gospels or in official Catholic teaching to contradict
or object to this possibility. Interestingly, Christian popular
devotion seems to have a long held assumption that Joseph
was somewhat older than Mary. If that is true, a previous
marriage could be one of the reasons.

This theory would, of course, in no way reflect negative-
ly on the church's doctrine concerning the perpetual virginity
of the mother of Jesus, and that she had no other children.

I would note also that I am speaking here about official
Catholic doctrine. Private revelations to saints or other vi-
sionaries about details of St. Joseph's life may be fascinating
and may arouse the piety of some. They are not, however,
a necessary part of Catholic belief; an opinion which

disagrees with such revelations is not thereby suspect or somehow less Catholic.

Jesus and his Father

I have a Scriptural question. In the Gospel of Mark (13:32) Jesus says something I do not understand about his relationship to the Father. We know Jesus and the Father are one with the Holy Spirit. Yet Jesus says that no man and no angel, not even the Son (meaning apparently himself) knows the hour of the passing of heaven and earth. How could Jesus say something like that?

We find numerous remarks like this in the Gospel which seem to be incompatible with the fact that Jesus is the second person of the Trinity and therefore shares in all the knowledge of God.

No full answer is possible since we are dealing here with the mystery of the Trinity itself and of the Incarnation. Two general directions of answers, however, are possible.

First, Jesus could be speaking here solely in the context of his human nature, which is limited, as is all human knowledge and understanding. How human limits coexist with divine omnipotence and infinity is, of course, the mystery of the Incarnation.

Another explanation can be that Jesus is speaking not so much of his own personal relationship with the Father, but rather of his mission to reveal to mankind all the truths regarding God that would contribute to the development of our relationship with him here and in eternity. This may be one reason why such seeming contradictions appear often in the Gospel of John, which was written rather late and therefore is able to reflect much more the Christ who is the Risen Lord and head of the church, as distinct from the Jesus who walked the earth with the apostles. In fulfilling his mission as Lord and Savior, Jesus knows much which he cannot tell us — not because of some unworthy jealousy on the part of God, but simply because we could not grasp such knowledge or use it creatively even if it were given to us.

Jesus certainly made clear that he considered it part of his own responsibility to determine how much of what he knows of the Father he should make known to us.

Lord's Prayer reworded?

A column in a Catholic paper suggested that we change the wording of the Our Father. Isn't the way Christ said it (Matthew 6:9-13) good enough?

I'm afraid you are under several misconceptions concerning the Our Father. First of all, no one knows for sure what exact words Our Lord used when he gave us what we Christians commonly call the Lord's Prayer. Jesus did not speak English. What we have are translations from the Aramaic that Jesus used, or even translations of translations.

Since any good translation from one language to another involves a translation not merely of words but of ideas, the exact wording of something like the Our Father might differ greatly according to who is doing the translating. The various English editions of the Scriptures do differ greatly from each other.

As it is, the form of the Lord's Prayer we Catholics are accustomed to is different from the one you refer to in the Gospel of Matthew — and even more different from the form given in the Gospel of Luke (Luke 11:2-4).

Leaders of all Christian churches acknowledge the desirability of a common text, but it's easier said than done. Since all Christians know the Lord's Prayer if they know anything, emotional and devotional ties to the words they are accustomed to are very strong.

What about the addition to the Our Father?

I am a eucharistic minister in a nursing home. In our prayer service I always use the Our Father. One non-Catholic resident who often joins in our prayers asked why we do not add "For thine is the kingdom, the power and the glory forever and ever."

The sentence you ask about — ending the Our Father — began to be used in the Christian liturgy very early in the Christian era, probably because the formula had been common in Jewish worship for centuries.

Eventually some perhaps overzealous copiers of the Scriptures (this was long before the printing press) began adding these words after the Lord's prayer in Matthew (6:9-13) as a gloss — a marginal "interpretation" or pious note, inserted sometimes possibly just to break the monotony of a tedious job.

In later centuries many glosses, including this one, found their way into the bible text itself. This was the situation when the King James Authorized English translation was published in 1611.

Since this version of Scripture was in general use by Protestants for more than 300 years and since it included this one-sentence addition to the Lord's Prayer, the addition became part of what is often called the "Protestant Our Father."

As scholarship developed, however, it became clear to all that this addition was not really part of Scripture, but was inserted afterward. Therefore, Protestant Bibles after the King James version, including the most recent, have eliminated the sentence from the scripture text, mentioning it at most in a footnote as an unauthentic addition to the biblical text.

Bible translations under Catholic auspices never included the sentence. Thus, since it is not actually scriptural, it has not been part of the "Catholic" Our Father.

We do, of course, continue the ancient liturgical tradition even today by saying this prayer of praise together at Mass shortly after the Our Father.

Why didn't Jesus cure more people?

Why didn't more people request cures of Christ who apparently never refused such requests? It seems to me that the path to his temporary home would have been thronged with people who heard of this miraculous healer.

Blind people, crippled, all sufferers have some faith that someone, somewhere, can cure them. Apparently Christ never failed to cure those who approached him. A really successful healer in San Francisco would crowd the town very quickly. Why were there any sick left in Israel?

As you might suspect, you are not the first to be puzzled

by this question. Through all the centuries since Christ, Christians have noted and meditated on the fact that if Jesus cured one person, he could have cured everyone.

Furthermore, since his powers of healing were not limited to time and space, he theoretically could have cured everyone in the world and put an end to all human suffering.

The fact that he did not eliminate all pain and evil from our human condition certainly cannot be attributed to his lack of power, or to his lack of compassion and love. He overwhelmingly showed both of these, most of all by his own suffering, death on the cross, and resurrection.

It seems clear, then, that the healing miracles of Jesus had other larger purposes beyond the relief of pain. For one thing, Jesus saw his healing actions (and other physical miracles such as giving back life to those who had died) as signs of his supreme power over all evil.

To him they were witnesses to the fact that neither physical suffering nor the worst of human sinfulness could ever be larger than the power of good, the power he embodied as God. On occasion he makes this connection quite explicitly, as in the healing of the paralyzed man in Luke, Chapter 6.

Another conclusion Christians have drawn from Jesus' approach to human suffering is that he did not come to take it away, but rather to give it meaning — or at least to help his people understand that there is a need for it. It is as if he said:

"If I don't take away all your suffering, it is not because I cannot do so, or because I do not love you enough. Buried deep inside the nature of mankind and inside the human heart, there is the mystery that fulfillment — perfection — comes from the passage through death to life. The best I can do is tell you this, show you that it applies even to me, and then ask you to follow me and trust me."

If this answer does not sound as final and perfect as you would like, we must remember that we are dealing here with one of the oldest questions human beings have wrestled with: Where does evil (physical and moral) come from, and why is it here? Among the many reasons for Christ's miracles, one is that they were his way of helping us deal with this question. If he could not give us a perfectly satisfying answer, he at least helps us to see that in the mystery of God's providence there is an answer, an answer that is revealed, if only dimly, most of all in his own death and resurrection and in our following of him in this paschal mystery.

Reconciled before Communion

A Sunday Gospel says, "If your brother has anything against you, leave your gift at the altar and first go and be reconciled with your brother." Does this mean that if a person has truly offended another person and has not apologized in any manner, he must first be reconciled before going to Holy Communion?

This passage is one of many in Scripture which makes clear that our relations with those around us hold a primary place above our actions and prayers of worship. There is no question that we tend to minimize the impact and importance of that truth, which is probably why Jesus stresses it as he does, especially in this part of the Sermon on the Mount. (Matthew 5 to 7)

For one thing, our public actions of worship, especially the Mass, are signs of our shared brotherhood as children of the Father, and as brothers and sisters of Jesus. Deliberate hurt, or arousing anger in our brother, makes that act of worship a lie unless it is repaired beforehand by some effort at reconciliation.

Furthermore, we know that our relations with our family, friends and acquaintances constitute the only real barometer of our friendship with God himself. Jesus tells us this in so many words, as does St. John when he says that the way we know we have "passed from death to life" is that we love our brothers. (1 John 3)

Obviously, the degree of necessity for this reconciliation before Communion will vary with circumstances. But the urgency of the principle Jesus gives is quite clear.

Treat others like outcasts?

My family had quite a discussion on the meaning of the Gospel one Sunday. What is the interpretation of the passage

where Jesus speaks about attempting to correct our "brother" by ourselves or with a few others, or finally by the church itself. If he doesn't listen, we are told to treat him like a "Gentile or a tax collector."

This passage occurs in a section of St. Matthew's Gospel in which Jesus describes several aspects of his Kingdom as embodied in the church, that is, in the assembly of his people on earth. Gentiles were non-Jews and therefore heathens as far as the Jews were concerned. Tax collectors, and especially publicans, were in those days considered (often rightly) as sinners, extortioners and traitors. Both groups were held in contempt as outcasts, people to be avoided.

The seemingly harsh words of Our Lord must be understood in relation to what immediately follows. Jesus says that when two or three are gathered in his name, he is there, and will grant whatever they ask. Part of his point is that the spirit of charity, prayer, and trust in him should hopefully prevent any conflict from reaching the point of division which it might reach if approached with only a cold, legalistic attitude.

Another factor in understanding the passage, forgiveness, comes up in the very next verse. Peter asks Jesus if one must forgive his brother up to seven times, which Peter obviously considered as excessively generous. Jesus replied that our forgiving, without demanding undue retribution or revenge, must be unending, at least if that's the way we want God to treat us.

When is Christ with me?

Please explain to me the remark of Christ, "Wherever two or more are gathered in my name, I am there." Why wouldn't he be with me when I am alone?

I suggest you read the whole 18th chapter of the Gospel of Matthew from which your quote comes. In a series of parables and admonitions, we find strong reminders of Jesus' plan that his followers should not be hordes of isolated individuals somehow faithful to him, but rather of an assembly, a "church" of people mutually interdependent and helpful.

This community of believers was to constitute their home, the place they went for assistance, support, and even for the forgiveness of their sins (18:18).

The intent of Our Lord's remark is obviously not that one should never pray alone. He himself often went off by himself to speak with the Father. Rather, the saying affirms that a special and powerful presence of Jesus as Savior occurs when even a few of his family of believers gather together in prayer. That group becomes, as it were, a "little church," or perhaps better, they represent — and in some unique way share in — the power of the whole church at prayer.

Call priests "Father"?

Some Protestant friends have told me many times that one of the things we Catholics do wrong is to call our priests "Father." This is against the teaching of the Bible, according to them. How do we explain what we do since it does say in Matthew 23:9, "Call no one your father on earth, for one is your father in heaven."

The practice of using the title "Father" is not new. It goes back to the earliest centuries of Christianity and has been in use ever since, though the name is traditionally applied more commonly to monks than to secular priests. Protestants abandoned its use gradually after the Reformation.

The reasons for calling the priest "Father" are simple and very natural. He is the usual minister of those sacraments that, in the name of Christ and his church, give us the new birth and life of grace — baptism, the Eucharist, penance and so on. By his continuing care, instruction, and support, he nurtures the life of God which we share as Christians in a manner parallel to the role of our natural fathers.

For this reason St. Paul does not hesitate to call himself the father of his Christian converts. "Although you may have 10 thousand others to teach you about Christ," he told the Corinthians, "remember that you have only me as your father." (1 Cor. 4,15 — Living Bible translation)

He also twice calls Timothy his son because he had brought

Timothy's family to the faith of Christ. (Phil. 2,22 and 1 Tim. 1,2)

Understood literally, this section of the Gospel of Matthew would mean we were forbidden to call our natural fathers by that name, or to call our instructors teachers. The whole context makes clear that Jesus was not hung up on the word father or teacher, but that he condemned the practice of some leaders in heaping titles on themselves out of pride and self-importance. As one of the most respected Protestant biblical commentaries remarks, "If one takes this command literally, the titles 'doctor' and 'professor,' as well as 'rabbi' and 'father' are forbidden to Christians in addressing their leaders." (Interpreter's Bible; volume seven, on the Gospel of St. Matthew)

The "unforgivable" sin

In the Gospel of St. Matthew (12,31), Jesus speaks of a sin "against the Holy Spirit" which will never be forgiven in this world or in the next. What is this unforgivable sin?

St. Augustine, St. Thomas Aquinas and many others believed that by the "sin against the Holy Spirit" Jesus meant the sin of final unrepentance, which is the refusal to repent of one's rejection of God through a serious sin, even at the moment of death. This probably is still the most common view since it is a total, final rejection of all the helps the Holy Spirit offers us to turn away from evil and toward God.

Perhaps another way of saying the same thing is that anyone who deliberately and maliciously refuses the helps which the Holy Spirit gives to keep us from sin in the first place, sins against the Holy Spirit. As St. Thomas says, many gifts of the Spirit are meant to help us avoid sin in our lives. The gift of hope keeps us from despair. The gift of fear of the Lord keeps us from presuming in the wrong way on God's mercy and love, and so on.

All these gifts, he tells us, are effects of the Holy Spirit within us. When we refuse to hope, when we refuse to acknowledge the majesty and power of God in our lives, we, in effect, tell the Holy Spirit we don't need him, and we're in deep trouble. Repentance is impossible because when we're in that frame of mind there cannot be even enough humility for us to admit that we have sinned and need repentance at all.

Whatever the meaning of this Gospel passage may be, the one all-essential truth to remember is that, if we have sinned, God our Father is always there with open arms to receive us back to him, and the Holy Spirit is always ready to help us go there.

What do Christ's sufferings lack?

St. Paul says somewhere we should make up in our sufferings what was lacking in the sufferings of Christ. I thought Christ's atonement was sufficient and superabundant. He did it all! How could we add anything to that?

The passage (Colossians 1:24) has puzzled Christians for centuries. Taking for granted, as you said, that our Lord's sacrificial death and resurrection was absolutely and totally sufficient for the redemption of the world, two sorts of explanation seem most common.

One relates this verse to the context in which Paul speaks of his own role as a missionary of the Good News of Christ. Each new receiver of that message, and each suffering Paul undertakes for the sake of the people and the church, moves the church that much closer to its fulfillment in the preaching of the gospel to the whole human race.

Another interpretation addresses the sufferings themselves, sufferings of Paul and other Christians until the end of the world. Jesus makes clear that the sufferings of his followers, the church, are *his sufferings*. Those who persecute His disciples persecute Him! (Acts 9:4) Thus the fullness of our Lord's saving work, the completion of the mission given him by the Father, will arrive only when the last "daily cross" of which He spoke has been borne faithfully by each disciple and by the community of believers, His Body on earth.

What was "lacking in the sufferings of Christ" was thus not an insufficiency in his redemptive actions. Rather, that work would not attain its complete effect until all his disciples have carried their cross with him.

Did Jesus rise from the dead?

**I find it hard to believe a recent column in our local paper.
In speaking of a seminar by Bible experts, the author says
that most New Testament scholars do not believe Jesus rose
bodily from the dead. According to him, "One Catholic seminary instructor says he does not know of any credible Bible
scholar who would hold for a bodily resurrection of Jesus."
I believe many people would like to know if this is true.**

People who make these kinds of accusations may be operating out of thoughtlessness or a superficial knowledge of the
subject, but they are certainly totally mistaken. Sometimes they
have not even read the writings they condemn.

Any Christian is aware that the resurrection of Jesus from
the dead is the core of our faith. As St. Paul says, if Jesus
has not risen, we Christians are to be pitied. On the other
hand, any thoughtful reader of the Gospels is aware of several
major puzzles presented by the different stories we are given
of the resurrection and events which followed.

Clearly, our Lord's resurrection was not simply a "return
to life" as he possessed it in human form before his death.
He was seen and not recognized by his closest friends, and
then recognized (Jn 20:14). He appeared and disappeared in-
stantaneously (e.g. Lk. 24). And the Gospel stories themselves
differ considerably with each other on many details of the
events on the first Easter Day and the days following. St. Paul
himself, who tells us he had seen the risen Lord, in comparing our resurrection to that of Jesus says that what dies is
a physical body, but what is raised is a spiritual body, im-
perishable, glorious and undying (1 Cor 15).

One of the obvious tasks of biblical scholarship is to compare and analyze in every way possible all of this New Testament information and theology, and develop possible explanations of that information in the context of traditional Christian faith. With very rare exceptions, those solutions in our
century do not include denying the bodily resurrection of our
Lord.

As one of numerous possible illustrations, we might refer
to what is probably the most prestigious and scholarly one-

volume English commentary on the Scriptures, the New Jerome Biblical Commentary, compiled by major Catholic Scripture scholars in the English-speaking world. In a brief but weighty section on the resurrection of Jesus, four of these theologians, whose names are familiar to any serious student of the Scriptures, clearly defend the bodily resurrection of Jesus. They strongly reject the rationalistic and liberal criticism of the 19th century which in one way or another attempted to discredit the resurrection.

Their own position is obvious throughout, perhaps most explicitly in the context of these various "qualities" of the risen Lord. "If the New Testament," they write, "stresses that what was seen was a radically transformed Jesus, it was Jesus who was seen," the Jesus with whom the disciples had walked, talked, ate and lived during his public life. Among some circles it is considered cute and "avant garde" these days to discredit genuine scholarship of any kind, including biblical studies. Unfortunately, sometimes honesty and truth get buried in the process. When you see these extravagant kinds of statements, don't panic. Try to check them out at least a bit. Does the author really know what he is talking about? And does he want to convey the facts honestly? "Don't believe everything you read" is still good advice.

Did Jesus despair on the cross?

In the Gospel of St. Matthew, Chapter 27, Jesus cries out on the cross, "Eli, Eli lama sabachtani" — that is, "My God, My God, why have you forsaken me?" In what language did Jesus speak? Is it possible he said rather, "My God, where are you?" The Jesus I know would never say he was forsaken since he loved and trusted his Father throughout his life.

This passage has puzzled Christians for centuries. At least two points may be helpful in understanding it.

There is no doubt that Jesus did suffer much of our common human experience of desolation, grief, aloneness, and possibly even bafflement at the time of his Passion. It was an agonizing torture so severe that it caused a bloody sweat and brought him close to a feeling of almost total dereliction. We say "close" because in the cry itself is the expression of profound faith in the midst of all the pain — "My God, My God!"

Second, this exclamation of our Lord has long been seen as possibly a wrenching prayer using Psalm 22, one of the graphic passages in the Old Testament which in an uncanny manner parallels the suffering of Jesus on the cross. The words we are considering are the opening words of that psalm. The same psalm is quoted just a few verses before this passage of Matthew (verse 43), and the following verses about Jesus' thirst recall the later words of that same psalm, "My throat is dried up like baked clay, my tongue cleaves to my jaws . . . they have pierced my hands and my feet."

If it is true that Psalm 22 was involved in this cry, as many Christian writers and biblical scholars believe, the words become one of the most powerful acts of faith, love and victory ever uttered by Our Lord.

Why keep the Commandments?

If a person has to keep the Ten Commandments to get to heaven, why did Jesus Christ die on the cross and shed his blood for us?

Romans (3:24) says we are "justified freely by his grace through the redemption that is in Christ Jesus." Isn't it by the blood of the Lord, and not by the observance of the law, that we are forgiven our sins and have eternal life?

You're right. We do not keep the law of God and Jesus Christ in order to "buy" God's love and our sharing in his life. These are free, totally unmerited gifts.

Jesus does tell us, however, what we must do because we are his disciples, part of his family. Several times he corrected his followers when they tried to act, or even prompt him to act, against that lifestyle. (See, for example, Matthew 7:21, 19:17 and chapter 25, and John 9:21.)

In other words, there are certain ways we Christians do things. And Jesus tells us we must operate our lives freely according to that way or we just won't fit into the kingdom.

Does God punish us?

**I am a teacher. While my subject is not the Bible, I do
receive a lot of questions about the Scriptures. One of my
class pointed out that the Book of Exodus says, "I the Lord
your God am a jealous God inflicting punishment for their
father's wickedness on the children of those who hate me,
down to the third and fourth generation."**

**Does this mean my son and his children will be punished
for what I do?**

One of the fascinating phenomena in the Bible, particularly
as we go through the history of the Old Testament, is the
gradual purification and elevation of mankind's understanding of God, and of humanity's relationship with God.

This is true even, perhaps especially, among the Jewish people from Abraham to Christ. More than once, for example,
we read how in war the Hebrew armies annihilated their
enemies, men, women and children, and even the dumb
animals. This was said to be done with the blessing and
sometimes at the command of God himself.

Every Christian, and probably most pagans today, would
find such vindictive slaughter utterly appalling and thoroughly
at odds with every Christian principle.

Even in later centuries of the Old Testament, during the
period before the coming of Christ, such an attitude toward
one's enemies is considered incompatible with a proper
understanding of God and his love for all people.

A similar development occurs in the subject you mention.
Among many cultures, including the ancient Jews, a theory
prevailed that guilt and innocence, holiness and sin, were
tribal. If the patriarch sins, all the tribe are enemies of God
— or the gods. If the patriarch is good and just, the entire
tribe shares his holiness regardless of the behavior of any
individual.

Denial of this type of tribal identity occurs more and more
frequently as time goes on in the Old Testament. Perhaps the
most dramatic refutation of this attitude is the prophet
Ezekiel, whose awareness of and reverence before the majes-

ty and infinite holiness of God is surpassed by no other prophet.

At one point (Chapter 18) he describes the erroneous understanding of God expressed by an old saying, "Fathers have eaten green grapes, thus their children's teeth are on edge."

So ingrained was the tribal concept of guilt that Ezekiel had to defend himself (and God) against the accusation that treating people individually was unfair. The Lord is forced to say, "Is it my way that is not fair, or rather is it not that your ways are unfair?"

Before we too easily judge such ancient ideas harshly, we might ask ourselves how often we have heard others, or perhaps ourselves, remark in the face of a tragedy to a loved one, "What have I done to deserve this?"

Unfortunatey we still tend to make God in our own image and likeness, which may be the reason the image of a vengeful God, half-judge and half-executioner, dies very slowly in the human heart.

Slavery in the Bible?

Is it true that the Bible accepts the idea of slavery? St. Paul has been quoted that Christians should submit to slavery and not try to change things, as if he were really in favor of it.

Not everything that we see people doing in sacred Scripture, even very holy people, represents the highest ideal of human activity.

The Old and New Testaments unfold the gradual understanding by men of the full implications of God's Word as he reveals it to us. Obviously, this understanding even now has a long way to go.

It is true that early Christians were a lot more tolerant of slavery and other social evils than we would be. Perhaps it is better to say that they accepted it as a fact of life that could not change quickly, and they tried to live with it, being as faithful to the ideals of Christ as they could.

Gift of tongues

What is the gift of tongues? Do you believe in it? What

do you think of the Pentecostal Movement, where people are supposed have the gift of tongues?

The gift of tongues is one of the special manifestations of the presence of the Holy Spirit in an individual or group by which the individual (or group) speaks in a language that no one present could understand without a corresponding gift for "translation." It was not uncommon even in the early days of the Christian Church; St. Paul treats the subject at some length in 1 Corinthians, chapter 14.

There is some dispute whether the gift of tongues as experienced then and apparently in a number of instances today is a miraculous ability to speak a foreign language (which could have some missionary symbolism), or an ecstatic expression of syllables totally meaningless to anyone except another person similarly inspired to "interpret" the tongues. Maybe it is a combination of both — or even two separate gifts entirely.

There is no question that speaking in tongues may be a special gift by which the Holy Spirit makes his presence and power evident in a group. One difficulty, of course, as St. Paul points out, is that self-deception is quite easy. An individual, or others, may believe he is speaking in tongues when the vocal expressions result only from a hyper-emotional state. The test of genuinity, according to Paul, is whether the experiences increase faith, serve a constructive purpose, and bring peace to the group rather than confusion.

Participation in charismatic (sometimes called Pentecostal) prayer activities seems to have helped many to a better life of faith and closeness to God. Supposedly, the gift of tongues has been experienced in some (relatively few?) charismatic meetings, but it is by no means essential or common to them.

The millenium

What is the meaning of the passage in the book of the Apocalypse that says the reign of Christ will be 1,000 years? Does this mean anything at all to us, or does it really mean that his reign in the world is 1,000 years?

One is bound to be hopelessly confused about the book of Revelation if he forgets that this is a book of visions and extremely complicated and often totally mystifying symbols. Several groups, some quite large, in the history of Christianity took that passage (Revelation, chapter 20) quite literally. They believed in an actual millenium (from Latin "mille anni," 1,000 years) during which Jesus would reign, and then take the saved into heaven after the final defeat of the devil.

Among ancient people large numbers were frequently symbols of an unmeasurable, infinite time. Perhaps the idea of a final 1,000 years is based on a non-biblical book called the "Secrets of Enoch" in which the world is described as 7,000 years old — with the present time being the final 1,000 years.

With few exceptions, millenarists became rare after the first thousand years came and went after Christ, and it became evident that there must be another meaning to the passage.

Armageddon

A member of another religion mentioned to us about a battle of Armageddon, which is supposed to happen at the end of the world. She said it is in the Bible, but didn't explain any further except that they believe it will be a terrible conflict to separate the good people from the bad. Do you know what she was talking about?

The book of Revelation (chapter 16) speaks of a battle in the last stages of the world involving the devils and the kings of the world — "the great day of battle of God, the sovereign Lord." This event is to occur at a place called Armageddon.

As with so many parts of this highly symbolic book of visions, it is not easy to place what is said in any kind of clear historical or geographic context. The usual interpretation is that the word comes from the Hebrew "har Mageddo," or "mount of Mageddo." Mageddo was an ancient fortress-city of Palestine, overlooking the main pass through the Carmel mountain range. Thus it occupied a key position along the primary military and commercial route between Egypt and the rich countries of the Fertile Crescent.

Mageddo was captured and recaptured numerous times in

its long history, and became somewhat synonymous with a battlefield. For this reason, it would be a likely symbol for the "ultimate conflict" between God and his friends, and the followers of the devil.

The end of the world

When will the world end? Does the church teach anything about it?

The thousands of false predictions which have excited the world at one time or another ought to convince us, even if nothing else does, that God hasn't let us in on his plans for the date of the end of the world.

Whether it is 100 or 100,000 years away, we don't know. The Bible, at best, only speaks of situations which will be present before the end of the world. Even then, it is usually hard to discover what the Scripture writers really mean.

However, those who parade around with signs declaring "The end is near" do have a point. Neither Scripture nor the church is concerned with satisfying our idle curiosity, but rather with reminding us that the day we leave this earth, not the day it burns up, is the end of the world for you and me.

Fundamentalists and Bible Interpretation

I enjoy discussing matters of our faith with others, but I find talking with fundamentalists frustrating. One said he takes the Scripture as it stands with no interpretation; this according to him is how the Holy Spirit guides us, all in plain black and white. No scientific or historical discovery should have any significance in all this, according to them. Does the Holy Spirit really influence us this way?

Two thoughts might be helpful. If by interpretation we mean choosing one explanation, meaning or reading of the sacred texts over another, then it is utterly impossible to read the Bible intelligently without interpreting it.

Let me suggest just two of numerous possible examples of

what I mean. Mark's Gospel says Jesus was baptized by John the Baptist (Mk 1:9); but Luke has John in prison when Jesus came to be baptized (Lk 3:20-21). Which is right? Luke says Joseph and Mary lived in Nazareth before Jesus was born. Matthew clearly assumes that they lived in Bethlehem, and only "went and dwelt in a town called Nazareth" after their return from Egypt (Mt 2:23). Since both cannot be right, in each of these instances what reasons does one offer for accepting one meaning or explanation over the other? That is interpretation, at least of some sort.

It helps also to remember that a major difference between traditional Catholic Christianity and fundamentalism is our attitude toward the created world. Christian tradition from the beginning has taken creation very seriously and sacredly. Whether it is material (bread, wine, water, oil, words, actions) or spiritual (our minds and wills, our passions and emotions), we believe that all creation, rightly used, can be a channel of God's power and grace. The more exclusively other-worldly approach tends to consider things of this world, especially as they are affected by human action, unworthy of God. None are capable of being sacraments, points of contact between God and ourselves through and in which God can work his love.

For us, to reject science, history, discovery is to reject the Holy Spirit. To accept what we learn with our minds, enlightened by faith, honors the God who made us and the Spirit who enlightens us. In other words, we believe that to use what we have been able to learn about the times in which the authors of Scripture wrote, what problems they faced and what they meant to say is affirming, not denying, the Holy Spirit. Everything is obviously possible for God. We believe, however, that the normal and ordinary way the Holy Spirit works in us, individually and as community, is not by shining a mysterious light into our eyes or by some other miraculous intervention. Rather, when we do our best to use well the gifts he has given, his power is at work immeasurably in ways we cannot even imagine (Eph 3:20), enriching our minds and wills as we reflect on him and try to love him more deeply.

As you suggest, this approach to creation and to the Scriptures will not always result in the black-and-white, us-against-them type of answers we might sometimes desire.

We believe, however, it is still the best way to honor God and to respect this world which has come from his creating hand.

Catholics, Fundamentalists and the Bible

I am having some difficulty with a fundamentalist. Could you give me the passages in the bible where Jesus instituted the seven sacraments?

Many Catholics (and most other Christians) who involve themselves with fundamentalist, literalist, cultic Christian groups find themselves confused and embarrassed when they are aggressively confronted with the question: Where do you find this or that in the bible? They panic and run to their priest, or to me, and say: We must be wrong because I can't find this belief in scripture!

The truth is that we, and all Christians, have many important beliefs that are not found in the bible. Jesus did not write a bible, nor did he tell his apostles to write one. He founded a *Church*, a community of believers to which he promised his Spirit, with whom he promised to remain and to keep in the truth until the end of time. (See Matthew 28 and John 15 and 16.) Out of that community of believers came the bible. It is part of Christian tradition, not apart from it. Thousands of Christians were born and died before all the New Testament was even written. They received their faith not from a "book," no matter how sacred, but from the group of those who were Christ's disciples long after he died, the group we call the Church. To put it bluntly, we do not believe, and Christians never have believed, that everything we believe, all the doctrines and truths of our faith, are explicitly in the bible.

Just to be clear, we do believe whole-heartedly that the bible is the Word of God. We believe that nothing the Church believes or holds as revealed by God can ever *contradict* the holy scriptures. That is what the Church means by saying that the bible is the norm of faith for all time. We must always measure our beliefs and practices against that Word. Nothing we believe can ever contradict or deny it. But we believe, as the Church has believed since the beginning of Christianity, that the Holy Spirit guides us, in our Christian belief and life, above all in and through the community of faith, not exclusively by the book which that community of faith produced during the first hundred years of Christianity.

I said above that all Christians hold beliefs, essential beliefs, that come from outside the bible. That includes even the most fundamentalist "bible-Christians." For example, when such Christians point to the bible and say: "You must accept this because it is the word of God," ask them how they know that book is the word of God. Because the book says so? Anyone can write a book and declare in it somewhere that it is the word of God. But that declaration doesn't make it such. Even for Christians who "accept nothing that isn't in the bible," the most basic of all their beliefs, that the bible is the divine word, must come from outside that book. It must be authenticated by someone, or some group, that points to it and says: This is God's word; accept it and believe it. Of course, the community that points to the book and authenticates it in the power of the Spirit is that very community of faith that Jesus founded and promised to be with, the community we call the Church.

So don't panic when asked these kinds of questions. If anything, the thing to panic about is that perhaps you do not know enough about your faith to really explain what and why you believe what you do; you need to study! I'm not trying to dodge your question about the sacraments. I'm just saying, as you should, that I will not be drawn into trying to justify my own Christian faith in a way that I don't accept in the first place. Neither should you.

The Church

People of God

Why is there now so much talk in the Catholic Church about the "people of God?" I presume the phrase means to include us. Is it the same as "the church?" If so, why not just say so?

The term "people of God" — used quite prominently by Vatican Council II — is a much broader name than "church," particularly if we mean it in the very limited sense of Roman Catholic Church.

The phrase comes from the Old Testament, where the people of Israel frequently are called the people of God: that is, a group set apart by God as recipients of special blessings from him.

In the New Testament, the death and resurrection of Jesus and the proclamation of this great event by the preaching of the Gospel gave rise to a new "people of God," brought together not by their own initiative, but by God's own action. (The Greek word for church, "ecclesia," means literally a group called out, or called apart.)

The church, in the sense of the recipients of God's saving work in the world through Christ, obviously can be looked at in different ways. As any mystery, no one description or definition can convey the entire meaning. The phrase, "Mystical Body of Christ," for example, as generally understood focuses on the more *specific* claims an individual may have for union with Jesus, such as baptism, membership in the "organized " church, explicit belief in certain doctrines, and so on.

"People of God," however, focuses rather on the more *general* claims that give to mankind a right to God's mercy and other blessings — the Incarnation, and the death and resurrection of Jesus. This seems to be the reason for the increased use of that name today, especially since Vatican II, which clearly preferred "the people of God" to other titles, such as the "Mystical Body of Christ."

Priesthood of the laity

I became a Catholic three years ago. They told us we would continue learning for many years since there was time during those months to discuss only a small part of Catholic beliefs. I am finding this true. Recently a longtime Catholic gave me a book that speaks of the "priesthood of the laity." We never talked about that, and none of my other books mention it. Can you help?

The response involves some knowledge of the use of the words "priest" and "priesthood" in the New Testament. The Greek word for priest, "hiereus," is never used in the New Testament to designate an official of the church. It is applied to Jesus himself in the Letter to the Hebrews. Sometime afterward, probably around the year 200, it began to be applied to Christian bishops and later to presbyters or elders. I'm sure you understand that the priests referred to in the Gospels, for example, are priests of the Old Testament, not of the Christian church.

In the latter part of the first century, some decades after our Lord's death and resurrection, the whole Christian people are called by St. Peter "a chosen race, a royal priesthood, a holy nation, a people of his own" (1 Pt 2:9). At a certain period in our century it was not uncommon to find this reality expressed as "the priesthood of the laity."

That is not an accurate phrase, however, since Peter's words apply not to the laity but to all Christians, regardless of their official status or ministry in the church. The priesthood he speaks of, which is to announce the praises of God, do good works by which God would be glorified and offer spiritual sacrifices acceptable to God through Jesus Christ (1 Pt 2:5,9, 12) is one shared by all faithful followers of Christ. The more limited sense of an ordained priesthood identifies a particular role that the ordained fulfill, especially in the eucharistic worship of the Christian community.

"The one, true church?"

Can we as Catholics still say that the Roman Catholic Church is the one, true, Catholic and apostolic church? And that we alone possess the truth?

Understanding these qualities in a very carefully defined way, as the church understands them, the answer would be yes. However, I'm afraid that in the sense you mean (and as many Catholics and most Protestants probably think the church means them) the answer would have to be no.

When we call the Catholic Church "true," for example, it certainly does not mean that we believe that we alone possess the truth. Catholic theology not only holds that other churches can profess and teach truth, but also that the Holy Spirit is working within them in a real way with his light and love. This is especially true in Christian churches, but can be true of other religions as well — most certainly and obviously, of course, of the Jewish faith, which shares many essential traditions with Christianity.

Any sincere Catholic does believe that in the Catholic Church there are certain channels of truth and grace and intimacy with Jesus that normally are not present in the traditions, liturgy, and life of other churches. If he did not believe this, one would assume he would belong to another church — or none at all. The same would presumably be true, of course, of any sincere Methodist, Baptist, or Lutheran — for the same reasons.

Our beliefs in this matter were stated well and often in Vatican Council II. We believe that "the one true religion subsists in the catholic and apostolic church"; that truth imposes its demands on the human conscience "by the power of its own truth" and not by coercion, and that the Spirit's gift of truth must be honored wherever it is found. (See the Declaration on Religious Freedom, Art. 1, which is quoted here, and the Decrees on Ecumenism, Art. 2, and on the Church, Lumen Gentium, Art. 15.)

Didache

What is the Didache, which you mention sometimes in your column? Where can I obtain a copy? I am interested in the travels and teaching of the first apostles.

The complete text of the Didache is available now in the Ancient Christian Writers series (vol. 6, Paulist Press). But don't expect it to add much to your knowledge of the travels and teachings of the individual first apostles. This isn't what the document is all about.

The full name of the work is "The Teaching (didache) of the Lord to the Gentiles Through the Twelve Apostles." Written in Greek, it apparently originated in Syria in the first half of the second century A.D., somewhere around the year 125. Despite the name, its 16 chapters contain much more than a list of apostolic teachings. Included among other topics are sections on church structure, some sacramental liturgies (including a remarkably familiar description of what we now call the liturgies of the Word and the Eucharist at Mass), and even policies concerning charitable and social works of mercy.

The Didache was almost completely unknown until little more than 100 years ago, in 1883, when a metropolitan of the Greek Orthodox Church published an 11th century manuscript. Since then the document has become the major source of information about the early church in the generations immediately after the first apostles.

Accepting the changes

I converted to the Catholic faith about 35 years ago. Since then, so many of the things I identified with the church at that time have changed. It's hard, not only for me, but even for some of my friends who were born Catholics. How do

we keep our balance in all these changes, especially the differences in Catholic teaching, and learn to take things in stride?

This question is among the most common I receive, and one of the most difficult. For one thing, any answer must be a quite personal one. Much depends on one's own temperament and faith.

The first requirement is a positive and hopeful attitude about the revolutionary developments going on around us. It seems clear that mankind is on the threshold of a new age; its life on earth — socially, politically, economically and even religiously — will be drastically changed from what we have known. Such a time in history always brings confusion, false starts, tentative hopes and many frustrations, as well as widely conflicting views on how to move into this future creatively without losing what is good from the past.

It shouldn't surprise us that Christians, including our Catholic Church, share in this turmoil and suffering. In fact, it would be cause for alarm only if the church (and that means you and I) were placidly going its own way, not being involved and hurting with those pains and fears that today tear at men's hearts.

In spite of the suffering and upset that accompanies it, this process of change and new birth has been a positive and incredibly revealing experience for the church, and it can be a beautiful and rewarding experience for us, too, if we let it.

The differences you mention are surely real. The difference between the way previous councils (for example, Trent in the 16th century, or Vatican I in the 19th century) talked about such things as the church, God, man and his human sacredness, and the meaning of the Incarnation of the Word of God, and the way Vatican Council II discussed them, is unprecedented in the church. This development has pointed the way toward a vastly enriched approach to prayer, to faith and hope, and to love of God and the world.

These happenings in theology and other areas of Catholic life are not a denial of what was taught in the past; they reflect rather a growing awareness that there is room for many more varieties of approach to the great mysteries about God and man than we once thought. The life of the church, as any other life, is not simply a handing down of neatly tied truths and practices. It is a continuing, adventuresome opening up to truth as the events of history and the grace of the Holy Spirit reveal it to us.

There's risk in all this, of course, and that's where the scope of one's faith comes into the picture. It becomes, frankly, a question of whether one really still believes in God — and of how big a God (and church) one believes in. We Christians know that, by his coming as man, Jesus embraced this poor earth and all creation — including the persons, events and processes of today. We believe that by his resurrection and exaltation with the Father, he is vitally present — today as in the past — as healer and savior, and that he already stands at the end of history as the Lord and Victor-King for all his people. This is the absolute heart of the matter.

It seems to me that God is much more honored by our keeping our eyes and our work focused on that great fact of his lordship, than by our being picky and fearful that every change (or every new weird idea, for that matter) signals the imminent collapse of the church or of God's influence in the world.

To paraphrase a recent bumper sticker, I don't know about yours, but my God isn't cringing in the corner — and neither is my church.

I hope this approaches a helpful response to your question. Work hard for those things we Christians stand for — justice, truth and down-to-earth love for God and our fellow man — and then learn to be a little serene and enjoy the excitement. I have a feeling that's somehow what Jesus is doing, so why shouldn't we?

Was Vatican II a first?

I recently read a remark by a prominent writer that the second Vatican Council was actually the first really ecumenical council. I understood that there were many before this one. What did he mean?

It's true that there were many ecumenical councils before Vatican Council II. It's also true, if one wishes to be geographically and numerically literal, they were not truly ecumenical — that is, world-wide. Possibly the most significant council in modern times, for example, at least in its long range influence on Catholic life and belief, was the Council of Trent. It started in 1545, after eight years of agonizing preparatory work, with only 25 bishops and four cardinals at the opening Mass. Dragging out for 19 years, with 25 separate sessions, it never enjoyed — for various political and religious reasons — the presence of more than a small minority of those eligible to attend.

More recently the first Vatican Council opened in 1869 with about 700 bishops, out of about 1,050 eligible, on hand, and 500 of these were from Europe. At some sessions, only around 100 bishops were present.

During Vatican II, however, about 2,900 bishops and prelates were invited. Over 2,500 attended the opening in 1961 and 2,400 the closing in 1965. Based on numbers and on areas of the world represented, it was by far the most "ecumenical" council in history.

It is not primarily numbers or geography that makes an ecumenical council. The other councils were ecumenical insofar as their actions were at least accepted and approved by the Bishop of Rome, and were applicable to the whole church.

Next ecumenical council?

When was the last Ecumenical Council before the one a few years ago? When will the next one be, and do you think it will cause as much confusion as the last one?

The last Ecumenical Council before Vatican II (1962-1965) was Vatican I (1869-1870). Since these councils are called only when the need arises, the next one may be 10 or 100 years from now.

As for confusion, the next one will likely be similar to most past ecumenical councils; as much will depend on the preparation and renewal that happens before it, as what happens during it. Ecumenical Councils are not known for their settling effect on the life of the church, at least at short range. They usually deal with major historic challenges facing the Catholic people, so one would not expect them to be characterized by tranquility and lack of controversy.

Theology or dogma?

Our study club had a disagreement over something in the book we are discussing — a reference to the "theology of St. Paul." Some of us found no problem with the words, but others claim the phrase is misleading. There is, after all, only one theology that is true, isn't there — at least only one that we as Catholics can accept?

I think you are getting theology mixed up with dogma. They're two very different things.

Theology can mean any development or discourse on ideas relating to God. More specifically, however, it is an organized *system* of thought which tries to synthesize the truths we have about God from reason or from revelation. It is simply some individual's, or group's, insights on how the various doctrines of Christianity, for example, hang together, how they fit in with other aspects of human life and knowledge, and so on.

In that sense, there are many "theologies" which are perfectly respectable and acceptable in Catholic tradition, even though they may profoundly disagree with each other. St. Augustine, for instance, developed a theological system which St. Thomas Aquinas often radically disagreed with in his own theology 800 years later. Today nearly 800 years after St. Thomas, theological systems frequently take basically different avenues toward explaining the meaning of Christian truths than he did.

St. Paul was a man of incredible faith and insight who developed his own theology, putting together the teachings he received from Christ, and enriching his and our understanding of them.

At different times in Christian history, other "schools" of theology placed their emphases quite differently than he did. A good example is the place Paul gives to the Resurrection as the central event establishing Jesus as the Son of God with the power of the Savior. During perhaps most of the centuries since Paul, the theological tendency has been to identify this key event as the Incarnation itself, rather than the Resurrection.

Such differences may appear academic, but they have significant implications in the direction of Christian spirituality and belief. Many "difficulties" with modern theology, for example, result from the fact that it leans heavily toward the Resurrection emphases of St. Paul — which, however, vastly enriches our understanding of the real meaning of the Incarnation of the Son of God.

What are theologians trying to do?

Maybe you can tell me what the theologians are trying to do, destroy the church? As far as I can see, all they are doing is undermining the faith of good people.

This considerably abbreviated query was preceded by several other obviously rhetorical questions concerning current developments in the church. Perhaps this final comment wasn't really meant to be answered either. But its spirit is evident often in letters that cross my desk.

Theology is a highly specialized and intricate science, and theologians are nothing but specialists in that field. Through the centuries, the church has depended heavily on the research and writings of trained experts in this science — theologians like St. Jerome, St. Thomas Aquinas, St. Augustine, St. Alphonsus Liguori, and thousands of other great and lesser lights. Most of them, incidentally, were "prophets without honor" through much of their own lifetime.

When I say the church has depended on them, I include bishops and popes. While they are the official teaching body in the family of Christ, bishops are rarely theologians with highly advanced training, particularly in the critically important fields of scriptural and doctrinal theology, or in specialized technical areas of ethics.

Of its nature, theology is a speculative, open-end science. Part of its business is to be at the cutting edge of Catholic thought as the church's understanding of Jesus and his message develop through the ages. As with mothers, fathers, or priests, there are capable and less capable ones. A theologian may be right or wrong, or in between. His expertise may be in one field rather than another. Above all, his theories and opinions are only as good or as bad as his reasons for them.

When anyone condemns or ridicules "the theologians," therefore, I can't avoid the suspicion that he has never seriously studied what specific theologians have to say on a subject, or he is seeking someone to blame for things he doesn't understand or approve of. Or possibly both of these.

Blanket blaming of parents, teen-agers, intellectuals — or theologians — for our discomforts and crises is a cop-out, and rarely contributes anything toward our understanding or the search for truth.

Is it a 'new' church?

You responded to a comment about changes in the Catholic Church.

The current Catholic Church is administered by liberal clerics. No Vatican Council required these changes, only a group of liberal bishops. Today our churches are good replicas of Protestant churches. The Mass is a horror. Nothing can take the place of the Tridentine Mass, and no group of liberal clergy can change my mind.

Liberals have provided a mass of shallow rationalizations to support their unnecessary changes. In view of the decree by Pope Pius V that the Tridentine Mass never be legally revoked or amended, how can anyone recognize the validity of the new order?

I remain and always will remain a Catholic as I have been taught. I accept no rationalization for unnecessary changes. You and the other priests are always on the defensive about this.

First of all, what you see as defensiveness on the part of some priests is, I think, rather a deep frustration. A major responsibility of priests (and other pastoral ministers) in these years is to help people bridge the transitions that are being asked of them today. We take that responsibility seriously. To see people deliberately close their minds and hearts to the tremendous opportunities the church offers them today to greater holiness and fidelity is not something we take lightly.

I was raised back in the "old church," and we priests had to go through the same process of study, prayer and (I hope) openness to the Holy Spirit as did other Catholics to understand where the Spirit is leading us as the people of Jesus Christ. I know as well as the next Catholic or other Christian that to be asked by anyone, including God, to take up anchor and move where we have never been before is painful. But the fact is he did just that with Mary and all the saints, and he does it with us.

Name calling may help us feel good, but it is no substitute for plain thinking, or facts. A little knowledge of history is a big help. Several subsequent popes decreed changes in what is called the Tridentine Mass right up into our own century, resulting in the Mass we had before Vatican II. (See questions on this subject in the next chapter.)

In fact, the "new" Mass we have today is far more traditional in the church than the pre-Vatican II Mass.

You say you will always be a Catholic as you were taught. In what catechism did you learn that one pope may be accepted at the rejection of others? To say acts are "irrevocable" is routine in official church documents. Pope Pius V changed such irrevocable acts of popes before him, as he had every right and responsibility to do as he saw necessary for the church. Are we to say that as of the beginning of this century Jesus betrayed his promise to be with his church always, and to give it the guidance of the Holy Spirit? If not, then we must believe that John XXIII, Paul VI, John Paul I and John Paul II, and the bishops who are with them, deserve our respect and obedience every bit as much as any pope who has led and served the church in the past. I believe that the Catholic Church, and most other Christians, are moving with great faith and courage — and truth — into an age of enormous challenges. Recent synods and other events in the church prove that our Holy Father and the vast majority of bishops of the church believe the same — and believe that Vatican Council II provided the greatest impetus for this movement.

I know there is much pain and stumbling and bruising along the way. But I truly feel sorry for those who are unable or unwilling to make the journey.

What is the Magisterium?

I am a fairly recent convert to the Catholic faith, but I keep coming across a word in our Catholic paper which I never heard during my instructions. What (or who) is the "magisterium?"

The word "magisterium" comes from another Latin word, "magister" (teacher); it means the power, or duty, of teaching and leading.

Before Our Lord died, he promised his followers that the Holy Spirit, whom he would send, would bring to their minds all that he had told them. Magisterium is the word we use to indicate the authority and responsibility the church has in fulfilling that promise of Christ, the responsibility and charismatic power to be the faithful interpreter of God's word to mankind. It is, in other words, the human instrument Jesus uses to keep his people from serious and dangerous mistakes in their understanding of God and of man's salvation.

This responsibility is personalized and focused in the Holy Father, and in the bishops of the world together with him — a tradition we Catholics believe continues the pattern set by Jesus in placing this responsible authority in Peter, and in the other apostles with him. Because they are in this way the official interpreters and guardians of revealed truths, the bishops and the pope are also often referred to as the church's Magisterium.

This duty is, of course, not carried out in a vacuum. As Pope Paul VI noted some years ago, the Magisterium reveals no new truths, but is to be a "faithful echo" of the Divine Word and of Holy Scripture. In this, pope and bishops need the input, support, and assistance of all others in the church. These would include laity and clergy — who, by the witness of their daily lives help toward a deeper understanding of the teachings of Jesus — theologians, other teachers, and so on.

The Magisterium is one always-living way Our Lord honors his promise to his followers, to "keep them in the truth."

When does the pope speak infallibly?

According to Catholic teaching, when does the pope speak infallibly? Is it in an encyclical, or what? Could you give an example of such a teaching?

While he was still here on earth with his disciples, Jesus told his followers that he would be with them always and that the Spirit he would send would keep them always in the truth.

It is our Catholic belief that this promise is fulfilled in part by the fact that, under certain conditions, the Holy Father, as the focal point of Catholic unity and faith, is invested in a special way personally with this promise of Jesus to keep the church free from error.

This unique certitude of truth — infallibility — is present, we believe, when the pope speaks precisely as chief shepherd and teacher of the church on matters of divine faith or morals, and clearly intends to use the full powers of his role in the church in that solemn manner. This, we believe, is the service he is called on to offer his fellow Catholics as chief bishop in the church.

The infallible nature of a teaching depends not on the type of document in which it is included, but on the intention of the Holy Father made clear in the statement itself. Theoretically, it could be on the back of an envelope.

The latest doctrine considered to be taught with such infallibility was that of the Assumption of Mary, declared by Pope Pius XII in 1950. The last one before that, in 1854, concerned the Immaculate Conception of Our Lady.

Toward the end of a long encyclical, (Munificentissimus Deus), analyzing the long history of the doctrine of the Assumption through the centuries, Pope Pius defined the teaching with these solemn words:

"We have poured forth prayers of supplication again and again to God, and have called upon the Spirit of Truth. Now, for the glory of Almighty God, who has lavished his special affection upon the Virgin Mary; for the honor of her Son, the undying King of the Ages and Victor over sin and death; for the increase of the glory of that revered mother; and for the joy and exultation of the entire church:

"By the authority of our Lord Jesus Christ, of the Blessed Apostles Peter and Paul, and by our own authority, we pronounce, declare, and define it to be a divinely revealed dogma that the Immaculate Mother of God, the ever Virgin Mary, having completed the course of her earthly life, was taken body and soul into heavenly glory."

Infallible teachings

In a discussion on Catholic beliefs, we tried to think of some "infallible" teachings by the Holy Father, but couldn't think of any except the one you mentioned. Could you help?

I'm afraid not — at least not very much. With all the talk and controversy about papal infallibility, one would expect to be dealing with a long list. In fact, it is generally agreed that the defined Catholic doctrines that are such because of a properly "infallible" papal statement total — believe it or not —*two!* They both deal with the Mother of Jesus: the definition of Mary's Immaculate Conception by Pope Pius IX in 1854, and of her Assumption into heaven after her life on this earth, by Pius XII in 1950. (It is possible that another statement of Pius XII concerning the matter and form of the sacrament of holy orders would also fall into this category.)

Both of these truths were, of course, celebrated and accepted in Christianity as much as 1,000 years before these dates.

Pope speaks for all Christians?

Some time after the pope's 1987 visit to the United States, a friend showed me a newspaper quote from a Protestant bishop saying that the Holy Father "speaks for all of us in his moral message to the world."
What did he mean? Surely he is not saying that his denomination accepts the pope as head of the church.

In my 34 years as a priest I have read about and participated in numerous dialogues with clergy and other leaders of Christian churches.

I have a strong impression that increasing numbers of both

non-Catholic and Catholic Christians feel the need for someone who at least in essentials can speak in the name of the
worldwide Christian community.

Such individuals believe that, while we have our internal
differences as Christians, they are relatively insignificant in
the face of the cosmic evils that threaten human society —
massive starvation, wholesale terrorism and other disregard
for human life, the threat of nuclear destruction of life on
earth and so on. The Christian message to the rest of the world
and even to ourselves is severely handicapped by the fragmen-
tation and bickering between Christians.

Many Protestant leaders who would never consider calling
the Holy Father "head of the church" nevertheless speak of
him as the only person in sight who can speak to the rest of
the human race as something like a world leader of Christians.

In that sense he may be, and in fact often seems to be, a
moral spokesman even for many who are not Catholic. That
he would be recognized officially as such is not likely in the
foreseeable future.

Popes elected by people?

**A book used by our study club has a section on the popes.
The comment is made that they were formerly elected by the
people. Can you enlighten us? We all assumed that the popes
were chosen by the bishops or clergy before they were chosen
by the cardinals.**

Your book is right. During most of the history of the
church, most bishops, including the bishop of Rome, were
chosen in some way by the people.

During the first ten centuries, the choice was made by a
commonly accepted procedure involving the clergy and laity
of each particular diocese. Civil leaders had an increasingly
larger hand in the choice, sometimes simply picking a person
they felt would be favorable to their own policies. Thus, the
emperor of the Holy Roman Empire was for centuries the
most powerful factor in the choice of the pope.

Only in 1059 did Pope Nicholas II place the election of the
pope in the hands of the cardinals. (Cardinals as we know

them did not, in fact, exist in the church much before this time.)

The Third Lateran Council (1179) decreed that a two-thirds vote of the cardinals is required for election of the pope. Pope Gregory X, to further lessen political influences on papal elections, ruled in 1271 that the cardinals should be isolated under lock and key during the proceedings — a provision all but ignored in many elections since then.

In 1945, Pope Pius XII revised the procedures, requiring a two-thirds majority plus one for election.

In 1975, Pope Paul VI again revised the procedures somewhat, but did not substantially change the policy for papal elections today.

Predictions about popes

Does the Catholic Church believe in sayings of soothsayers or prophets concerning who will be elected pope and how long the popes will live?

An article in our paper pertaining to the prophets who foretold about the popes said one pope would die very soon after being elected (Pope John Paul I), and the next pope's name would have a "V" in it. (In Polish the present pope's name is pronounced with a "V.")

One prophet said we would have three popes after John Paul I, and the other said four popes. How true are these prophecies?

The so-called prophecies of Nostradamus and St. Malachy have long been discredited. At least they were written long after some popes they claimed to foretell. Early "predictions" are relatively plain. But later ones get fuzzy.

Like the daily newspaper horoscopes, we can read almost anything into them if we want to.

Malachy's prophecy

What is the Prophecy of St. Malachy? Supposedly it foretells a terrible time for the church during the rest of this century. Is it supposed to be true?

One is tempted to say that anyone could foretell a "terrible time" for the church almost any time and he'd probably be right. Sorry to disappoint you, however. The famous Prophecy of St. Malachy can hardly be said to have even that in its favor.

The prophecy that bears his name was supposedly written by Bishop St. Malachy of Ireland, who died in 1148. It pretends to designate 111 successors of Pope Celestine II, who lived about the same time as St. Malachy. These successors are not mentioned by name but by short "verses" said to characterize the man or his time as pope. The first 60 or so are quite clear, and bear a remarkable resemblance to the popes they refer to. After that, however, the prophetic verses become so general many of them could refer to almost anyone at any time.

With a brief Latin phrase that professed to characterize each pope or his reign, the prophecies presumably extended to the end of the world. The phrases are extremely cryptic; it takes a good deal of imagination to pull some meaning out of them for most of the popes.

According to the alleged predictions, only two popes remain after the present one, ending with Petrus Romanus (Peter of Rome) who is to preside over the destruction of Rome and the end of the present age.

The whole "prophecy" is, in fact, an elaborate and imaginative forgery. St. Malachy, who was bishop of Armagh, Ireland, truly did live and had an illustrious career. He died, however, more than 400 years before his supposed prophecy first appeared in Europe.

The author must have had a bit of fun composing this interesting historical and literary curiosity. But it is a fake.

Forgery or not, however, it seems to be "rediscovered" about every 10 or 20 years.

Secret teachings?

In your answer about papal infallibility, you mentioned that the doctrine most recently considered taught with such infallibility was the Assumption of Mary in 1950.

When making a retreat about a year ago, the retreat master

told us that the pope had defined the doctrine that John the Baptist was born without original sin. This happened about six or seven years ago and it was all kept low-key by Rome. Is this true?

No, it is not true. I am sure you misunderstood the retreat master somewhere along the line.

My mail indicates a huge misconception by many Catholics of the teaching role of the pope and of the bishops, something which we shall probably have to come back to.

Speaking directly to the point you make, there would be no reason whatsoever for an important doctrine of the church to be kept low-key. The very purpose of proclaiming any belief, whether with the character of infallibility or not, is to make it known to the world and especially to all Catholics.

In the Gospel of Luke (1,44) we read that at the presence of Mary, the baby (John the Baptist) in the womb of Elizabeth "leaped with joy." Based on this passage, it has long been a pious belief among many Christians that John received the gift of sanctifying grace before he was born. This is not, however, and never has been, an official teaching of the church.

A woman pope?

A friend of mine was raised a Catholic but no longer attends Mass or any church service. He told me that a woman was declared pope sometime in the church's past. Her name was Katherine.

I know that a woman cannot become a priest, much less a pope, at least not legally. But could a woman be named pope incorrectly? Did this happen?

The legend of Popess Joan (not Katherine) pops up regularly, especially in certain anti-Catholic tracts which usually speak as if they have discovered something new. Perhaps your friend has encountered one of these.

The story of Popess Joan is a weird tale which first appeared in the 13th century, nearly 300 or 400 years after she was supposed to have lived. She disguised herself, so the story goes, so effectively that she became a priest, a cardinal in the Roman

Curia, and finally pope. She reportedly reigned for two-and-one-half years as Pope John Angelicus, sometime between the years 800 and 1100.

Her sex was discovered when she gave birth to a child during a papal procession near the Colosseum. The legend is given no credibility whatsoever by historians.

Any married popes?

A book we are discussing refers to the fact that some popes have been married, but doesn't go into detail. Is this true? Have we had married popes?

Of course we have had married popes, beginning with St. Peter, though we don't hear anything about his wife after the references to her mother in the Gospels. (See, for example, Mark 1,30)

The same is true with certain other popes. Records are sparse, so we know little about their married life before or after they became head of the church. We do know that one married pope, St. Hormisdas (514-523), was the father of another pope who was a saint, St. Silverius (536-538).

To my knowledge, the last married pope was Adrian II (867-872). At least for a while after being named pope he apparently lived with his wife and family at the Lateran Palace in Rome, even though an unmarried clergy was by this time rather common in the Western church.

Maybe this was just part of his "liberalism," which he demonstrated in other significant ways during his brief pontificate. For example, against great opposition from those Catholics who wanted to preserve the Latin language and customs, he approved the new Slavonic translation of the liturgy which Saints Cyril and Methodius had just composed for use in some of the Slavic nations.

Anti-popes?

A magazine article I read referred to someone as a possible "anti-pope" and implied that he would not be the first one in history. Were there really anti-popes? I thought there could only be one pope at a time.

It has happened more than once that strong political or religious factions in the church have not liked the man chosen as pope — or perhaps thought he was chosen unlawfully — and so picked their own man and called him pope.

These are complicated messes usually, and difficult to untangle. While there is technically only one pope at a time, historians sometimes have a hard assignment sorting out which is which.

A classic example was during a considerably hairy time for the church in the third century when Pope Callixtus and a very popular anti-pope, Hippolytus, spent a good deal of their adult lives condemning each other. Yet today both of them are honored as martyrs and saints.

There hasn't been an anti-pope, by the way, for over 500 years.

American pope?

Do you think there will ever be an American pope? I think we should strive for this.

No one knows, of course, if or when there will be an American pope. But my guess is as good as anyone else's, and my guess is that it will be a long time before an American is elected to that office.

The church in the New World, especially in North America, is still relatively young. We were officially a "mission country" until just a few decades ago. In the eyes of Europeans, particularly those in leadership positions of state or church, we are still somewhat of an upstart in relation to their part of the world where Christianity has been present and operating (well or ill) for 1,500 to 2,000 years.

That kind of long tradition, or lack of it, inevitably weighs heavily in the feelings and minds of those who do the choosing.

A second reason is more subtle, but in some manner tied to the first. Many attitudes toward authority, law, and even religion itself, that are typically American, or at least are considered so in other countries, are still somewhat "maverick" positions in Catholic tradition. Some of these are more liberal or permissive than older Catholic countries are used to. By general admission, for example, our bishops and our experience in the United States relative to other Christian churches contributed heavily to the more open and accepting stance toward those churches at Vatican Council II.

Some American traditions are more conservative or strict, as, for example, our understanding of the function of law and regulations and how they are to be made and observed. Anyone familiar with European attitudes in these areas of life realizes the significant differences between here and there.

Don't hold your breath. Even if we want an American pope, and I'm not sure we do, we'll probably have to live through a few more Italians — and maybe Spaniards, French, or Germans, not to speak of Poles — before we get one.

Why pope lives in Italy

Why is it that the Catholic Church has a pope who lives in Italy? Couldn't we just as easily have a leader who lived in the U.S.A. or in China?

There's nothing to prevent a non-Italian from being pope, nor is there anything that says the pope has to live in Italy. As you must know, there have been popes of other nationalities. And during one period of nearly 100 years, all the popes lived in France.

However, no matter who he is or where he lives, the pope holds that position because he is the Bishop of Rome.

To discuss fully why this is so would take many books. Briefly, the Bishop of Rome has held the position of preeminence among other bishops in the church from its earliest years, since this is where St. Peter (whom we consider the "first pope") spent the last part of his life and where he died.

We possess letters and other indications that, even before the last of the twelve apostles died, the Bishop of Rome was recognized as the authority over all other areas of the church. Probably the most significant and famous of these is the letter of St. Clement, the third pope after Peter, to the Church of Corinth, Greece, in the year 95.

Of course, other more specific ruling and teaching prerogatives that we attach to the Holy Father's position developed in Catholic doctrine and practice in later centuries.

English pope?

One of our newspapers just finished an interesting series of articles on the papacy. They had a lot of information about the election of a pope. Have they ever elected an English-speaking pope?

Many popes have been fluent in the English language. I suspect your question is whether a man from an English-speaking country has ever been chosen head of the church.

The only one so far was Adrian IV, who was pope from 1154 to 1159 during one of the most difficult periods of change, religiously and politically, in the church's history.

Born of very poor parents apparently, Adrian's name was Nicholas Breakspear. He was born in Hertfordshire and after some difficulties with his superiors in the Augustinian order, he successfully completed several delicate diplomatic missions requested by his predecessor, Pope Eugene III.

All other popes have been from the continental nations of Europe, except possibly a few early ones — notably, of course, St. Peter.

Are bishops divine?

My husband says that when bishops are consecrated that they take on divinity which makes their opinions and decisions the same as those of Christ. Is this true? He says even when bishops are wrong in their decisions according to people, they are still right in God's eyes. Do bishops believe this?

No, Virginia, bishops do not become divine. In fact, God himself is likely happier than anyone that he is not a bishop. He probably couldn't take the hassle.

Did early Christians have priests?

In a Bible discussion group recently, we talked about the

priesthood. Someone said she thought the Bible said nothing about priests — meaning priests as we know them in our church.

Is this true? Didn't the early Christians have priests?

The New Testament speaks of three main ministries in the church: bishops, deacons and presbyters (elders). The exact function of these ministers, especially of the presbyters, is not perfectly clear, although the bishops clearly have the predominant supervisory responsibility.

The Greek word for priest, "hiereus," is not used in the New Testament at all to designate an official of the church. It is applied to Jesus himself in the Letter to the Hebrews. In a couple of other places it refers to Christians in general to describe their special character as the people of God.

There is some likelihood that the presbyters performed certain functions which we relate to priests, although their ministerial relation to the church is far less clear than that of the bishops and deacons.

The word "hiereus," priest, only came into use in the Christian Church about 150 years after Jesus' death and resurrection as the Eucharist came to be more and more recognized as a renewal of the sacrifice of Calvary, as well as a meal. In the religious traditions of that time, a sacrifice was offered by a priest. Thus Christians began to refer that title to their minister who presided at the Eucharist.

Can a priest marry?

We recently received word that a close friend who is a priest is planning to marry. This disturbed me greatly because I believed that the priests who did this were not good priests anyway, and I always thought he was a good priest.

What is his status in the church now? What should be our attitude toward him? Can we in good conscience retain his friendship?

Many Catholics still do not realize that it is possible for a priest to be released from his promise not to marry. Unlike marriage, whose nature and permanence are established by

God himself, the celibacy of the priesthood is something the church could change and has changed in various ways through the centuries.

Jesus established the priesthood to serve his people in various ways, but he never made it his absolute rule that priests could not be married. In fact, married priests have been common in some parts of the world since the beginning of Christianity.

If a priest simply ignores the solemn promise he has made to remain unmarried, it would be wrong. It is entirely possible for him, however, to ask for and receive a release from that promise; in that case, he could marry and remain in perfectly good standing in the church as a layman.

Without his telling you, there's hardly any way you can know what his status is now, since these matters are naturally handled very privately. If you are a close friend, ask him. I think it is only fair that you should know, as it inevitably affects your feelings toward him.

Whatever the answer is, it doesn't mean he was not a good priest. If he did abandon his promise of celibacy without a dispensation, he possibly cut corners and neglected prayer a lot more than he should have, but God is the judge of that.

As for continuing your relationship with him, it can never be anything but right to be a friend to anyone — a thoughtful and honest friend. Try to understand and have the courage to be, and say to him, what you believe is best for him and for the others you must think of.

Ordained after sex change?

If a woman has an operation to change her sex, can she be ordained a Catholic priest? One priest I asked about it said no, because his/her baptismal certificate would indicate the child was female. Another told me there were a lot of technicalities involved. Do you know the answer?

The present canon law of the church requires that one be a member of the male sex to be ordained to the priesthood (CCL 1024). Thus, the critical question is: How does one decide whether an individual is a man or a woman? — a question, one might imagine, that caused little loss of sleep for canon lawyers, at least up to our own day.

The baptismal record might be one way, but it could be objected by some that the sex identity evident in infancy did not reflect the real psychological make-up of the child.

One might ask how the psychology of the person matches up against a description of male or female characteristics. But many psychological experts, unable to integrate into their doctrines the general common sense of human experience, aren't able to agree that there even are such characteristics.

A more physical criterion would be genetic analysis. Every cell of the human body carries a sex-signature in the genes which identify that person as physically male or female. No "sex-change" operation changes that genetic identity.

Administration of sex hormones and cosmetic surgery may modify external sex characteristics to some extent, but not to a degree significant enough to influence a decision like this.

If the question ever arises, the answer to whether such a person could be ordained to the priesthood would, of course, come from the Sacred Congregation for the Discipline of the Sacraments. For the above reasons and others, I would give about 1,000 to one odds the answer would have to be no.

Active married priests?

Because of some actions that have taken place in our area recently, a number of us Catholics wonder about the rule that forbids priests to marry. Can priests now marry and still be active priests? Has there been any change in the church on this matter?

No, there has been no change. The church's policy and practice that its priests be unmarried is the same now as it was before Vatican Council II.

Through a process called laicization, a process handled directly by the pope and his administration in Rome, priests may ask that they return to the lay state — in other words they become again, in effect, laymen in the church. For awhile during the past 15 years or so, this process was simpler and faster than it had been. Pope John Paul II temporarily halted it, however, pending study on how such cases should be dealt with in the future.

Just as a baptized man always remains baptized even if he later ceases to call himself Christian, a man is always an ordained priest even after he is laicized. For several reasons, the church does not allow him to serve as a priest (celebrate Mass, hear confessions, etc.) except in the most serious emergencies, such as if a dying person needs the sacraments.

While a celibate priesthood remains the rule in the Latin Rite, certain other rites of Catholics had, and still have, married priests. Generally these rites are smaller and in other parts of the world, so the ordinary American Catholic would never encounter them.

Why no more monsignors?

Why is it that priests no longer seem to be named monsignors? Is there a new ruling on this?

The rank and title of monsignor is probably best described as a remnant of the times when much more importance was placed on honorary titles in the church.

Today when the church is trying to simplify its life in many ways, it seems to be attempting at several levels to deemphasize positions which are purely honorary in the sense that they have no necessary relationship to the individual's official ministry in the church.

The word "monsignor" incidentally, which means "my lord," is still in some countries the title given to bishops.

As the saying goes, some of my best friends are monsignors, but I suspect that even though some monsignors are still being named, they will be an increasingly lonely breed in the church at least in the foreseeable future.

Why are there some married priests?

We were recently told again that a married former Methodist minister has received permission from the Vatican to prepare for the priesthood in a diocese of our country. Please

explain the difference between the Vatican's granting permission to this man to prepare for the Catholic priesthood and refusing this same permission to properly motivated Catholic laymen. The only difference I can see is that he was a Methodist minister for 10 years before becoming Catholic. If his conversion is the only reason for the Vatican's permission, I'm surprised that lay Catholics are not raising howls of protest.

The policies regarding acceptance of married converts to the Roman Catholic faith as candidates for the priesthood are still in their infancy. Factors which must be considered differ with each group and, of course, with each individual. Some basic directions, however, seem to be emerging.

The largest number (about 50) of married Roman Catholic priests in our country are former Episcopal priests. Their situation is unique. As with the Oxford movement in England during the last century, today's Episcopal priests who leaned toward the Roman Catholic Church generally felt that they should remain within the Anglican tradition and work toward corporate reunion with Rome.

Later, many of these decided to apply individually for acceptance into the Roman Catholic Church as married candidates for ordination. They were formed within the Catholic "system," they argued, embraced Catholic tradition and doctrine, and thought they were Catholic except that they were not in union with the pope. Some of this group, especially those who desired corporate reunion of the churches, even accepted the primacy of the bishop of Rome.

The Congregation for the Doctrine of the Faith, it seems, accepted this line of reasoning, recognized that these Episcopal priests and their families were acting in good faith and approved their reception into the Roman Catholic Church and eventually ordination as married men. They were, in other words, dispensed from the promise and commitment of celibacy. These same arguments would not apply to formerly ordained Methodists or Lutherans who are now Catholics. Obviously, their relationship to the Catholic Church and tradition is quite different. Why would they be accepted as married candidates for the priesthood? Why would lifelong Catholics not be accepted?

The answers to the first question are not clear. Perhaps part of that answer lies in the apparent response to the second. People who are raised Catholic are presumed to know and be committed to the Catholic Church's discipline that married men are not ordained to the priesthood. By entering a marriage in the church, therefore, the church assumes that they have made this choice of the marriage sacrament over the priesthood.

The same would apply in the other direction. By choosing to be ordained a priest, a man raised in and committed to the Roman Catholic tradition is assumed to have made the choice of the sacrament of holy orders rather than the sacrament of marriage. There is at least some evidence that this distinction underlies the difference between decisions made for "born" Catholics and those made for converts to our faith. Normally, no convert to Roman Catholicism, from the Episcopal or any other faith, is considered a candidate for ordination if that individual had once been Catholic, later entered another faith and is now returning to the Catholic Church.

One of the converts, however, who is now a married Roman Catholic priest, was actually baptized Catholic. But since he was raised from infancy in another faith, it was decided that he did not grow up with the usual knowledge of Catholic beliefs and discipline. He could therefore be honestly in good faith about the possibility of being married and a priest at the same time.

It is worth remembering that the first Episcopal priest was ordained in the Roman Catholic Church under the new "policy" relatively recently, on June 29, 1982. The implications of that event and others since, and yet more still under study, are only beginning to be explored. Where they might lead us, if anywhere, no one can yet say for sure.

What is 'incardination'?

We recently received a new associate pastor at our parish. He was incardinated into our diocese.

What does that mean? I thought once you were ordained you remained within your diocese. What would prompt such an occurrence? What are the procedures?

You are correct in that every diocesan priest is incardinated (affiliated) with some diocese, to serve under the bishop of that diocese.

However, sometimes family, health or other reasons make it desirable for a priest to move from one diocese to another. This is arranged through and with the two bishops involved and of course in consultation with the priest himself.

This may occur not only after ordination, but while the student is still preparing for the priesthood.

Priests' wills

I would like to know why priests, monsignors and bishops do not leave their bank accounts, etc., to the church. Please don't tell me they do. Maybe a few, but many very wealthy ones have passed away in my time and not even a tenth of it went to charity. I fully intend to leave my God more than any relative. I am just a lay person and can't understand our leaders' attitude. I can give three very good examples with clippings.

I agree with you on one thing: Priests and bishops do have at least as great a responsibility as anyone else to provide for a just and charitable use of whatever they leave behind at death — just as they should during their lives.

I believe I'm fairly well acquainted with a significant number of priests, and in general with what they do with their money before and after they die. With almost no exceptions, I'd have to say my experience doesn't jibe with your interpretation.

Maybe our difference is partly in your remark about three "good examples with clippings." You surely are aware that for a variety of reasons many individuals, clergy or laity, arrange for the disposal of their money after death in ways that are nearly totally private, and for this reason never show up in "clippings." I know personally of at least two recent instances, one involving a priest of extremely modest means and another where the priest had a good amount of money from his family, in which these priests left generous gifts to parishes, Catholic education programs, or missionary work, but did it in ways that do not show up on wills or other public documents. Few knew about it except the individuals or institutions involved.

When we start judging other people (and usurp a prerogative God has wisely reserved for himself), chances are better than even that we'll arrive at some unbalanced or unjust conclusions.

We priests probably should be more aware than we often are that such things are publicized more now than formerly, and that our leadership in this matter should be more visible than it is.

Physical handicaps in the priesthood?

A friend of mine was told that the Catholic Church would not ordain a man if he did not have all five fingers on his right hand. Two other priests said they had never heard of the situation.

I know of one priest ordained when he was paralyzed and in a wheelchair. Why should having all one's fingers determine whether you are allowed to serve God as a priest?

According to church regulations, a physical defect such as you mention could be an impediment to ordination. The reason for this, insofar as it applies at all today, seems to be simply to assure that a priest be capable of performing his liturgical and other duties in a proper and seemly manner.

As long as a man is able to perform duties to which the bishop might assign him, dispensations related to physical defects are regularly given. There are, after all, far more important qualifications for the priesthood than the number of one's fingers.

Former priest receives sacraments

About five years ago a young man near our small town was ordained a priest; there was a big celebration with all the trimmings. Now this priest is married and can receive the sacraments.

Our daughter married a divorced man about a year ago. He is a wonderful man and they have a child. When he was

in his teens, he got a girl pregnant. Her mother said he had to marry her or pay for an abortion. So he married her and they lived together for three or four months before they were divorced.

I would like to know how that fallen-away priest can receive the sacraments and our daughter cannot. This hurts very much.

She is too shy to talk to a priest. When she was little, the priest always scolded the children and she has been afraid ever since.

First, let's talk about your daughter. If you have related all the basic facts accurately, this case should unquestionably be presented to your diocesan tribunal with a petition for annulment of the first marriage, and the sooner the better. Regardless of her shyness, urge her to speak with a priest she can feel reasonably comfortable with.

If she cannot do that, at least help her write to the diocesan tribunal (I'm sending you the address privately) and ask them for help. The priests there will be happy to help all they can, I'm sure, and will advise your daughter concerning further steps that should be taken.

Considering your concern for your daughter, I understand your feelings about the priest. Remember, however, that the rule that a priest may not marry, as serious and as significant as it is, is made by the church. The church can, therefore, dispense from that rule, as it does when it "laicizes" an ordained priest. The permanence of marriage, however, is outside the power of the church to change.

Hence, while he has failed to follow through on his commitment to the priestly ministry, the man you refer to should not be labelled a "fallen away priest." That implies a judgment which none of us has the knowledge or the right to make. Apparently he followed all the procedures the church requires in changing to his present state of life.

"Resigned" priests and Mass

This question caused quite a disagreement at our study club: When a priest leaves the priesthood, can he still offer Mass and hear confessions? I am a convert to the Catholic faith

and I remember the priest saying "Once a priest, always a priest." But some of my friends disagree.

When a person is baptized, he is, as you know, established in a permanent basic relationship and identity with Jesus Christ — an identity that will always be there. No matter what good or evil he may do in the future, he remains a baptized Christian with all that implies.

Something very similar happens when a man is ordained to the priesthood. When he receives this sacrament, he is established in a new and special relationship to Jesus and his church which involves certain functions and responsibilities in the service of other Christians and of all people.

The "power" to fulfill these services — for example, offering the sacrifice of the Eucharist or administering the Sacrament of Penance — is, therefore, never lost. Some old catechisms used to say that the Sacraments of Baptism, Confirmation and Holy Orders "placed an indelible mark on the soul." The phrase is a poor one because it can be so easily misunderstood in a variety of ways; but it does carry the message that something permanent happens in our relationship to God and our fellow Christians when these sacraments are received.

Hence, personal priestly powers to fulfill these services are never lost. However, a man who has "left the priesthood" may not normally offer Mass or hear confessions. For excellent and obvious reasons having to do with the spiritual good of all, the church forbids such a man to exercise these functions except in extreme emergencies — for instance, if a dying person wished to go to confession or receive the Eucharist and no other priest were available.

Priests in ties?

In newspapers and magazines we see a lot of priests, especially theologians, in non-clerical dress. Father Hans Küng is one that we never see in a collar. What's happening? Are they still priests?

Yes, they are still priests. And as far as priests' clothes are concerned, there isn't that much happening.

Clergy dress is a very mixed bag. Much depends on where and when the priest happens to live. For centuries priests and bishops wore no distinctive garb at all, even when celebrating the liturgy. Later, liturgical vestments developed, and even later, the clergy's daily wear was "clerical" only in that it reflected the fact that many of them were either monks or professors.

The Council of Trent (in the 1500s) simply said clergy should wear clothing "comformable to their order, that by the propriety of their outward apparel they may show forth the inward uprightness of their morals." No color or style was required. A rule made for the American Church in 1884 and theoretically still in force required that priests wear a Roman collar with a dark coat that reached the knees!

In recent decades, while American priests were in Roman collar, priests in Germany quite properly wore white shirt and tie. (The Protestants wore the Roman collar.) And in Italy, priests wore a black cassock everywhere, except, I presume, in bed.

In my own diocese, our regulation is that "lifestyle, dress, leisure activity and public behavior should be left to the mature judgment of priests themselves."

By no means do I imply that some sort of distinctive dress is not valuable or appropriate. But don't be too quick to jump to conclusions because of what you see.

History of celibacy

In light of the present controversies concerning celibacy in the priesthood, I have two questions. Do we have any examples of a celibate life in the Old Testament? And when was celibacy for the priesthood made mandatory in our church?

To my knowledge, the only major Old Testament figure who was celibate was the prophet Jeremiah, who lived around the beginning of the destruction of Jerusalem and the Babylonian exile (sixth century B.C). He was told by the Lord (Jer. 16:1-4) not to marry as a sign to the people that children then being born would die in the tragedies to come.

The very idea of a celibate life for men or women was generally repugnant to the Hebrew culture as it was to most cultures at that time. For a woman to be unmarried and childless was shameful. For men and women, marriage and a house filled with children was seen as a mark of God's blessing.

The first general law in the Western church obliging the clergy to a celibate life did not appear until the later part of the fourth century. This occurred through the decrees of several popes beginning with Pope Damasus (366-384) and numerous local councils in Africa and Europe.

During the next 700 years the marriage of priests, deacons and bishops was unlawful in the Western church. The movement toward a clerical celibacy finally culminated for the universal church in the 12th century at the First and Second Lateran Councils when such marriages were considered not only illicit but also invalid.

Much later, at the Council of Trent in 1563, the law of clerical celibacy was reaffirmed. However, against enormous opposition, the council firmly declared that priestly celibacy was a matter of church law, not divine law. This means that the church could change its legislation concerning celibacy and priests would no longer be obliged to observe it. The church did this for deacons at Vatican Council II when it instituted a married permanent diaconate.

The road of clerical celibacy has been rocky through the centuries, particularly in the early Middle Ages and again in the period before the Protestant Reformation. Rocky or not, it seems clear that the church is not prepared to alter easily a practice which has been so intimate a part of its life for the past 17 centuries.

When did the Roman collar begin?

What is the origin of the Roman collar for clergy? When and where did its use begin? I am a priest and have looked everywhere for the answer, without success.

I am not surprised you found the search difficult. Throughout the centuries right up to our own time, regulations and customs concerning clerical dress differed enormously from one time or place to another, and usually are hard to trace.

For at least the first five centuries of the church there were no special, specific rules for clergy dress. What customs existed then, and for a least 1,000 years after, usually were based more on the cleric's occupation (teacher, philosopher) or more specific vocation (monk, hermit, ascetic, and so on) than on general church law.

Even the Council of Trent in the 16th century simply required "that (Catholic) clerics always wear a dress conformable to their order, that by the propriety of their outward apparel they may show forth the inward uprightness of their morals" (Session 14). Later in that same century Pope Sixtus V designated the cassock as fulfilling the "propriety" of Trent, and apparently intended to require clergy always to wear this robe in public. Until recently, the cassock still was the usual street dress of clergy in Italy and, to a lesser degree, in Spain and France.

The Roman collar never was used in the United States or in England until the 1800s. You may recall seeing portraits of early priests or bishops with a kind of white "choker" around the neck. About the middle of the last century, Bishop (later Cardinal) Nicholas Patrick Wiseman decreed several ways in which his diocese in England should imitate the Italian (Roman) Church, including that priests must wear the Roman collar. Another significant innovation of Bishop Wiseman, incidentally, was that priests should be called Father. Before that the title was used, if at all, only in reference to members of some religious orders, such as Benedictines and Franciscans.

In the United States, the Council of Baltimore (1884) ruled that in public, priests should wear the Roman collar, along with a dark coat that reached to the knees.

As I indicated, one finds significant differences from country to country. In England both Catholic and many Protestant clergy wear the Roman collar. In Germany, among many other countries, the custom was, and still seems to be, that Catholic priests for the most part wear a dark suit and tie. If one sees a clergyman with a Roman collar, there is a good chance it will be a Lutheran pastor. Present canon law merely requires that clergy "cultivate a simple style of life and are to avoid whatever has a semblance of vanity," and are to "wear suitable ecclesiastical garb in accord with the norms issued by the conference of bishops and in accord with legitimate local custom." (Canon 282 and 284)

Illegitimacy and priesthood

Many years ago I read that a boy born out of wedlock could not be a candidate for the priesthood in the Catholic Church. Is this true? This boy I know was adopted by a Catholic family when he was about 3 months old.

In the former Code of Canon Law illegitimacy was among the "irregularities" that prevented reception of holy orders.

This law did not intend to punish anyone; it was simply one manner in which the church attempted to protect the dignity of its public worship.

Even then, there were procedures that were in fact not at all uncommon to allow the ordination of an illegitimate child.

The new (1983) Code of Canon Law does not include this obstacle to holy orders. It is, therefore, no longer in effect.

Priesthood after annulment?

If a man is divorced and has been granted an annulment, is it possible for him to become a priest or a brother? Does it matter if there are children from this marriage?

If an annulment is granted, it means that no marriage existed between those two people. From that viewpoint, at least, no impediment exists prohibiting ordination to the priesthood or entry into the religious life.

You would not be the first one to whom this might happen. I am acquainted with both men and women who have entered the religious life following an annulment.

All natural obligations which a parent would have for his or her children would need to be assured before any church superior would consider an individual for ordination or entry into a religious community.

Care for minor children is obviously a top priority. Expectations would be different, of course, for children who are grown and living independently.

You would need to contact a bishop or religious superior to check out further requirements.

Duties of permanent deacons

Since 1971 a number of men have been ordained permanent deacons in our archdiocese. Please enumerate the duties they perform in church as permanent deacons. This point is not clear to many Catholics. Do the deacons receive remuneration for acting in this capacity?

Before I answer your question directly, it should be noted that liturgical functions of the deacons, especially at the celebration of the Eucharist, are intended to be a climax and a symbol of the other services they render to the community outside of the liturgy. This important point is made constantly by those who work in the training and supervision of the deacon programs.

The following liturgical functions are assigned to deacons by the church:

1. to function as deacon at celebrations of the Eucharist,

2. to function as celebrant of the Sacrament of Baptism (anyone may administer the Sacrament of Baptism in emergencies; deacons are officially appointed ministers of that sacrament by the church),

3. to take Holy Communion to the sick in their homes, hospitals and other health care facilities,

4. to serve as celebrant of Benediction of the Blessed Sacrament (this includes wearing the proper vestments, exposing the Blessed Sacrament, and giving the blessing with the sacred vessel containing the Eucharist),

5. to serve as celebrant at wake services for the dead and at graveside burial services,

6. to officiate at marriages,

7. to administer the sacramentals of the church according to the rite indicated by the church, including blessing religious articles, and the blessing of throats on the Feast of St. Blase, and

8. to bless and distribute ashes on Ash Wednesday.

The new Book of Blessings (1984) indicates a number of blessings at which a deacon may preside. It adds that whenever a priest is present, it is more fitting that he preside and that the deacon assist by carrying out those functions proper to the diaconate. (n. 18)

Deacons may also preach at celebrations of the Eucharist and other ceremonies. However, this function as well as the faculty to officiate at marriages must be explicitly granted to them by the bishop of the diocese.

Many, perhaps most, of the permanent deacons receive no regular pay for the services that they give. Policies concerning remuneration are established by the diocese and the institution in which the deacon serves.

Was Mary a "priest?"

Why do women want to say Mass when Christ's mother didn't? Our Blessed Lord chose 12 men, and not one woman, to be his apostles. Are they in their right minds?

I've heard a lot of arguments for or against ordination of women to the priesthood. But yours is a new one to me. My first reaction is: How do you know Mary never presided at the celebration of the Eucharist — or "said Mass" — with the early followers of Christ? My guess also would be that she did not. But the Bible tells us not a word about what she did or didn't do after Pentecost. The clergy structure of the church developed slowly after Jesus' death and resurrection and if any women were considered as possible leaders in the celebration of the Eucharist, Mary could have been high on the list.

As for the apostles, Jesus excluded not only women but all non-Jews from that core group of leaders. In the Jewish male-oriented culture in which he lived and worked, it would have been socially unthinkable for him to have named either a woman or a Gentile as an apostle. Yet when the time and cultural situation allowed — which was very soon after his death — Gentiles were allowed into the priestly function of the church.

Women's role in church

Women in the Catholic faith are encouraged to participate in church activities which include serving on school boards, parent-teacher organizations, parish councils, liturgy committees, and other planning groups.

Others play a vital role in religious education as nuns, CCD teachers, or just plain Mom. Women have been the backbone of many right-to-life groups. They are also asked to be readers at Mass and distribute Communion.

And yet, our daughters are not permitted to serve Mass. What is the reason? Does the church really teach that women are inferior? (One priest I asked said that was nonsense; but I wonder.) Perhaps this restriction was reasonable in the past, but it certainly does not make sense today.

Yours is a difficult question to deal with because the picture of the ministry of women in the church is thoroughly confusing.

The law, of course, is clear: Women are not eligible for ordination to the diaconate or the priesthood, or for installation into the ministries (formerly minor orders) of lector (reader) or acolyte. Other liturgical regulations, however, allow women, at least in some circumstances, to perform nearly all the functions of both reader and acolyte, except what we would call serving Mass.

In his Apostolic Letter on the reform of Minor Orders (Aug. 15, 1972), Pope Paul lists the duties of reader: reading the Scripture and responsorial psalm, presenting the intentions of the prayer of the faithful, directing singing and other participation by the faithful, preparing other Scripture readers, and "instructing the faithful for the worthy reception of the sacraments." All these can be and are done by women.

Acolytes serve as special ministers of the Eucharist, and as assistants to the deacon and priest during the Eucharistic Liturgy. They may also expose the Blessed Sacrament for adoration, and instruct others in their function in the liturgy. Again, of these four acolytes' duties, church law now allows two of them, the first and fourth, to be performed by women.

No one, to my knowledge, has given any reason this should be. If closeness to the Eucharist is the criterion, distributing Communion seems of higher dignity than bringing the wine and water and holding the paten.

Concerning the inferiority of women, there are some embarrassing theological traditions that must be faced, because they cannot help but influence attitude and regulations about women's role in the liturgy.

For example, one of the latest comprehensive series of Latin theology textbooks was published only within the past few decades by an American theologian. The volume on the Sacrament of Orders reflects a long theological trend when it says that women should not be allowed to have the office of teacher because of their "natural condition of inferiority and subjection." Being weaker, they "are inept for the heavy labors of the social and ecclesiastical life." (!!) Their moral feebleness "is manifest in the lightness of judgment, in credulity, and in the fragility of spirit by which she is less able to reign in the passions, particularly concupiscence."

This was written in 1962, but the idea is not new. St. Thomas Aquinas said several times that women are by nature mentally and morally weaker than men, and that women are naturally subject to men.

No wonder so many Catholics feel an urgent need for some rethinking of the position and role of women in the church.

Past views on women

In speaking of how much we have to overcome regarding the role of women in the church, you explain that St. Thomas Aquinas wrote that women are all inferior morally and mentally to men. One friend who is supposed to know a lot of theology told me he does not believe St. Thomas would ever say anything like that. Can you tell me where remarks like this are found?

Anyone at all familiar with the history of Christian thought would know that statements along these lines are not unusual. To place the question in proper context, however, we need to understand two historical facts of life.

First, for much of the history of the human race, up until very modern times in fact, prevailing biological teaching was that in human procreation women provided only a "nest" and growth material for new life. The only "active" part was the male seed which totally determined the nature of the new person.

Furthermore, it was believed that if the male seed was perfect, a male was born. If it was significantly defective, a female baby resulted, whose physical, mental and moral prowess would inevitably be less than a man's.

Second, again until fairly recent times (indeed theologians are still wrestling with how this attitude fits with what we know about human activities) in anything having to do with physical processes like generation of the species, these processes as they occur in animals, and "why" animals do them, were generally considered to provide the best insight on how and why they should happen in human life. Particularly did this affect Christian moral viewpoints on the purposes and moralities of sexual activity between men and women.

Knowing this helps us understand, even if we cannot agree with him, that St. Thomas (who died in 1274) was simply reflecting the best science of his day when he said that a woman is a misbegotten or defective male. (*Mas occasionatus* I,99,2 ad 1; all references that I give here are to the *Summa Theologica*.)

"The active power which is in the male seed is intended to produce a perfect image of itself, a masculine sex," he said. "When a female results it is either because of a weakness in this active power or because of some indisposition of the materials, or even from a change produced by an outside factor — for example, from south winds, which are humid." (!!) (I,92,1 ad 1) St. Thomas, incidentally, received that idea about the south winds from Aristotle.

Clearly such erroneous biology easily leads to other equally bizarre conclusions. Thomas says, for example, that women need the virtue of sobriety more than men "because there is in them a greater proneness to concupiscence . . . sobriety is more required in women because there is not sufficient strength of mind for them to resist these concupiscences." (II,II,149,4)

These supposedly scientific conclusions led to spiritual implications as well. A woman cannot be validly ordained to the priesthood, said Thomas, regardless of her qualifications, since "no status of prominence can be signified in the feminine sex, because woman has the status of subjection, and so cannot receive the sacrament of orders." (Supp. — 39,2)

Similarly, a woman should not baptize, even in an emergency, if there are men around to administer the sacrament. (III,67,4c)

Unfortunate and faulty as one might find statements such as these, it seems to me one should hestitate in condemning too heartily Thomas and other great thinkers who accepted what was almost universally believed to be scientific fact. It illustrates, however, the kinds of baggage we need to sort out to understand better the relationship of men and women in human society and in the church. Ultimately the answer for us appears in the fundamental equality between men and women as taught by Jesus and the rest of the New Testament, a position these theologians found almost impossible to integrate with what they "knew" to be scientifically true.

Finally, to prove that the theologians of no particular religious denomination hold a monopoly on being occasionally wrong, I offer the classic analysis of Martin Luther (*Table Talks*) on the place for women:

"Men have broad shoulders and narrow hips, and accordingly they possess intelligence. Women have narrow shoulders and broad hips. Women ought to stay at home; the way they were created indicates this for they have broad hips and a wide foundation to sit upon."

Altar girls

Is it permissible now for a parish to have altar girls at Mass? A parish in our area has had altar girls for a long time, and I know the bishop is aware that this is going on.

It is definitely still against the regulations of the church for girls or women to function as servers at Mass. The ruling was reiterated by the Vatican in the past few years. As I remarked above, this regulation is understandably confusing since nearly every other ministry at Mass, except that of deacon and priest, can now be filled by women as well as men.

I suppose you are right in saying the bishop is aware of the situation. But don't draw any conclusions from that. One day Pope John XXIII was asked how he managed to deal with the overwhelming responsibilities of the papacy. He said, "I try to see everything, overlook much, and change a little." Most bishops with whom I am acquainted try to follow that wise philosophy.

Women counselors in the church?

Don't you think we need women counselors in the church? No matter how hard a priest may try to listen to a woman's problem, especially a marital one, he will ultimately dismiss it as trivial because he cannot understand the importance of it to her.

The first important requisite for effective counseling is at least some degree of competence — that is, the ability to identify a problem when someone presents it, and to have some clear ideas on how to treat the problem or help the client to handle it. It also includes an awareness of one's limitations in providing assistance or therapy, and how and when to guide a client to appropriate further assistance.

Most priests today are very much aware, perhaps far more than most lay people are, that ordination of itself does not carry with it this kind of competence, especially for more complicated personal or family pathologies, which is why a large number of priests continue their studies to increase their ability in this phase of their work.

Much depends on the individual you consult — his kindness and understanding and your confidence in him. Perhaps your first mistake, therefore, was in failing to search around for a priest you would have reason to believe had some kind of experience, competence, and wisdom you could trust.

While a qualified counselor of either sex (whether married

or unmarried) ought to have sufficient basic insights to help an individual of the other sex, it can easily be that for some individuals the most help will come from a counselor of the same sex, if for no other reason than that client feels more comfortable with the arrangement. At any rate, most counseling services, including Catholic social agencies, generally try to staff both men and women, who are available if you ask.

How do I join the Church?

I am a 17-year-old Protestant. However, I feel that I belong in the Catholic Church. I have been reading about the church and have been going to Mass. I am writing for advice. How should I act when I go to Mass? Should I recite the creeds and prayers along with the church members? Should I speak to the parish priest about this? How can I be absolutely sure that I am ready to become a Catholic and how do I go about joining?

I have thought and prayed about this for over a year and feel sure God is supporting me. All signs show me that He is. My heart also tells me that I'm headed in the right direction. I am anxiously awaiting your reply.

Your letter was a cool breeze on a warm day. As a Catholic who loves our church and our faith a great deal, I'm always greatly pleased when someone like you wants to share it. And I'm happy for you. Obviously you even now feel God working in your heart through the contacts and experiences you have already made with the Catholic faith.

My first advice is that you talk with a priest, or perhaps to a Catholic friend who might lead you to a parish program for someone like yourself. While we are always pleased that someone wishes to join our faith, we are concerned, as you obviously are, that this decision be made with sufficient understanding of what it means to be a Catholic. Our "faith" is not simply a list of doctrines we accept. It is a way of life based on friendship and intimacy with Jesus, a special kind of relationship to ourselves, to God, and to others. This relationship is enlightened and supported by the scriptures and by our shared life of prayer and worship and service.

Every Catholic parish has some process, some program, to help people know when, as you say, they can be sure they are ready. For more and more parishes today that journey of faith involves what is called the Rite for Christian Initiation of Adults (RCIA). Over a period of several months you will pray and learn, share your faith and doubts and questions with others, and have plenty of time, guidance and companionship as you weigh the decisions you will need to make.

In the meantime keep going to Mass every Sunday. Listen and participate attentively. You may stand, kneel, join the prayers; in fact you are welcome to do whatever everyone else does, except receive Communion. As you probably know, that should wait until you finally become a Catholic. Please talk to someone about your desires soon, if you have not already done so, and get moving with your plans. Good luck. I'm sure many others who read this will join me in praying for you and wishing you well.

Want a "Christian community"

What advice would you give to parishioners who want very much to have Christian community in the parish, but because of circumstances, it is not available, nor is communication whereby the situation might be reversed.

A living Christian community is obviously not something that is "available" or not, in the same manner as a parish school or boy scout troop might be available. A genuine community is a warm and personal thing, a gradual growth that involves shared and deeply felt faith, goals, experience, loves, hopes and even failures and disappointments.

I presume you mean, therefore, that as you see it the machinery for sharing in this kind of Christian community is simply not present, at least for some significant number of parishioners. In this case several questions might be asked.

Are you sure that what you desire *can* be done, legally, within the present church regulations concerning the liturgy, the parish, or other elements involved?

Are you sure that any significant number of parishioners really want the things you (perhaps very correctly) believe the parish should provide? Chances are good that in any parish many members have only the foggiest notion of what the words "Christian community" mean in the first place, and couldn't care less whether or not any more changes are thrust upon them. Since priests, like everyone else, differ temperamentally in their inclinations as leaders or followers, perhaps your job at the moment is to talk around, test your ideas with other parishioners, and see if you and they might share the same needs and suggestions — and then take them to the parish priest. I know of no priest who is on principle opposed to what might make better Christians and Catholics out of a significant part of his parish, though it is painfully obvious that he and his parishioners may often be poles apart in their view of what constitutes a "good Christian," or a good Christian community.

Finally, you might ask yourself: How far is it to a church that better meets the spiritual needs of my family, as I see them? In all fairness, it must be acknowledged that Catholic Church law is extremely permissive in the leeway it provides individuals as to where they will worship and hear the Word of God — and hence where they will find their "Christian community."

Belonging to a parish

I live in one state and work in another. I am registered in the parish where I live. Three years ago I decided to go to Mass every morning. The only church I could attend and still make it to work was close to my job. After three years I'm beginning to wonder which church is really mine.

Since on weekdays no collections are taken, I have not been contributing to that church. I give my fair share to my home church but cannot afford to give anything more.

Should I quit my church and register in the one I attend on weekdays?

Many Catholics find themselves in your situation. They belong to one parish but for various reasons attend another through the week.

Don't worry about it. I'm sure the priest at your workday

church is pleased to have you there. If you wish to do so occasionally, give a little something to show your appreciation for the opportunity to attend Mass there. But nothing more is really required.

A more important point is that perhaps you need to reflect with some seriousness about what it means for you to be a member of a parish. It seems you may be among those Catholics who feel that "belonging to a parish" means hardly more than where you go to Mass and place your envelope in the Sunday collection.

If everyone acted on that principle no parish would be worth much. Church law defines a parish as a "specific (stable) community of Christian believers" (canon 515). If that means anything, it means that every parish is a fellowship of believing Catholics who help each other and the rest of the community to live out the Gospel of Christ together.

Are you single, married, a parent? Whatever your present state of life, the priests, staff and probably many other people in your parish are trying to serve you and everyone else, liturgically and in other ways. They need your help.

As a general rule, the pastor in the parish where you reside is primarily responsible for you. For a serious enough reason, however, you might register in another parish.

I suggest that you pick out the one where you can honestly expect best to dedicate and use your talents and make it, in fact, your parish.

Can we change parishes?

My husband and I have some serious problems with our parish. In some ways we enjoy it, but we feel we and particularly our children are missing some awfully important things in the church today. Part of it is the liturgy, but it goes beyond that to a spirit that we seriously feel is just not where the church is today.

We really want to do what is right, but are not sure where we stand as far as parish membership is concerned.

Is it possible to join another parish? We certainly will appreciate any help you can give us.

Your concerns are vital ones for many in the church today.

The solution is not easily arrived at, but there are a few thoughts that may help.

For centuries a "Christian community" meant a small area in which a group of people lived and did nearly everything together, including prayer and worship. Our Catholic traditions and laws concerning parishes developed in such situations.

In today's mobile society, however, it is often hardly more than a legal fiction to say that members of the parish are "neighbors." A person's community is more likely to be based on his work, education, recreation, social life, and even on his religious and apostolic activities, including the liturgy.

Today the church allows wide varieties in parish liturgies. The spirit of parishes will differ depending on how both priest and people understand the church and what they believe a Christian community should be.

Current regulations of the church seem to recognize all these kinds of factors. Parishes are indeed generally territorial. This means that the local parish priest is responsible for the care of all the faithful in that territory. Church laws spell out those responsibilities and the care with which pastors must carry them out. (See for example CCL nos. 515-519.)

However, the faithful themselves also have rights which are relevant here. They have the right to present their desires and needs, especially their spiritual needs, to their pastors. (CCL no. 212)

According to their knowledge, competence and position, they have the right and sometimes the duty to make known their views concerning the good of the church not only to their pastors but also (with respect for the common good of everyone) to others in that parish community or elsewhere. (CCL no. 212)

They are obliged to assist in the necessary works of the church — its worship, its apostolic mission, its charities, the care of its ministers, and its care of the poor (CCL no. 222)

They have a right to the spiritual helps of the church, especially the Word of God and the sacraments, and a liturgy carried out as the church allows and prescribes, to help them pursue their proper form of spiritual life and to grow in Christian and human maturity. (CCL nos. 213, 214, 217)

Clearly, good and faithful Catholics might well perceive these rights and duties (among others also specifically pointed out in the law of the church) quite differently from the pastoral vision and style they experience in their own local parish. The difference may be such that they feel they cannot honestly and charitably fulfill these obligations and rights in that particular parish community.

For these reasons, the church's policies and attitudes are much more flexible than formerly.

In a sincere concern for the health of the whole church family, however, it seems to me a Catholic should preserve some sense of responsibility toward the people of the parish in which he lives, even though he may join and participate in another parish community.

Changing religions?

Not long ago a friend of mine, a "born" Catholic, formally converted to Judaism. He did this after years of reflection and, I assume, prayer.

We could say, I think, he knew more clearly than most what he was doing. He had postgraduate degrees in biblical studies and taught for many years at Catholic schools, including on the college level.

He did it deliberately and seems at peace with his conversion.

My question is this. It seems to me there are two possibilities. In leaving Catholicism for Judaism he was either following God's grace or he was moving against it.

If the second, he resisted grace more or less consciously, in which case the church would probably term him an apostate. Or, he acted without being aware of what he was doing. Neither of these seems warranted by the facts.

That leaves the other possibility, that he was responding to some divine initiative which was "calling" him out of Catholicism and into the Jewish faith. That fits the facts better but it doesn't seem to fit orthodox Catholic theology to me.

My question: Is there any way for an orthodox ecclesiology to accommodate the possibility of God calling someone away from the church to another religious position? Put another

way, can a Christian truly know and accept Jesus as Lord and Savior and then be called by grace to disaffirm this?

I suppose one could make the argument that strict, traditional, orthodox Catholic Christian ecclesiology would find it difficult or impossible to explain that kind of movement of faith.

However, in spite of the firmness of our faith in the teachings of Christianity, orthodox theology always recognizes its limitations. Most particularly it recognizes that the ground gets very shaky and dangerous when one begins to set limits on what God can, or particularly what he cannot, do.

God has revealed to us many truths, especially in and through Jesus Christ, which we must accept totally and according to which we must live. But he never told us that he has revealed everything of his plans and his ways of action.

Often and in various ways he has said just the opposite. The words of Isaias, "My ways are not your ways," says the Lord; "As high as the heavens are above the earth so far are my ways above your ways," are repeated one way or another countless times in both the Old and New Testaments.

Jesus says, to give just one example, that there are many things he could tell us, but our minds and understandings are just not able to grasp them.

I do not imply approval of what your friend has done. I simply note that there are too many secrets about God and about that particular person's relationship to God, of which we are too ignorant to make any spiritual judgments.

Our task is to be faithful to the love God asks of us as individuals and as a church. Without denying or belittling any of our own beliefs, we must ultimately admit that the goodness or sinfulness of your friend's decisions are a matter between him and God.

Religious life for divorced

What opportunities are there in the church for a divorced Catholic man or woman who would like to dedicate his or her life to God.

What you suggest is not at all impossible.

Each Religious congregation or order, however, has its own regulations and procedures in such matters. Anyone interested in such work should contact the desired Religious community, and ask the possibilities of working with them in their apostolate.

Religious communities

I am aware there are numerous different orders of priests, such as Jesuits, Franciscans and Oblates, and other orders of Sisters. I'm curious as to how many there are, their names, and why there are so many.

After a bit of research, I'm not sure anybody anywhere knows how many orders (or congregations or institutes) of Religious men and women exist in the world. Just one reason is that, while there is a central agency in the Vatican dealing with this part of the church's life (Congregation for Religious), Religious communities may spring up and flourish under the authority of local bishops long before they appear on any kind of permanent and centralized list where they might be counted.

Hundreds of religious institutions of men (groups which live a more or less common life under rules to which they commit themselves) are part of today's church, along with probably a few thousand institutions for women.

All such orders developed in response to what their founders perceived as needs of the church at that time — prayer, preaching, teaching, care of the sick, missionary work, and so on. Some have continued for more than a thousand years; others gradually died out as the need for them declined or as responsibility for those needs was assumed by others.

According to the Official Catholic Directory published by P. J. Kenedy and Sons, Sisters from approximately 360 different Religious congregations presently serve in the United States, though the motherhouses (headquarters) of many are located in other countries. Included in this group are close to 50 different Franciscan orders. Some have hundreds of members, others less than a dozen.

Also in the United States are nearly 100 Religious orders

of priests, comprising 40 percent of all the priests in the nation. The others are diocesan (secular) priests, who are ordained for service in their respective dioceses. Twenty-four additonal Religious orders in the United States are composed entirely of brothers, having no priest members at all.

As you can see, the lives and apostolates of Religious men and women in the Catholic Church are enormously widespread and varied. And this says nothing of the several hundred Protestant Religious congregations in our country and in Europe, some of which have contributed immeasurably to the efforts toward Christian renewal during the past 40 years.

For more specific information, you could write directly to a particular Religious order, or to either the National Sisters' Vocation Conference, 1307 S. Wabash Ave., Chicago, Ill., 60605, or the Conference of Major Superiors of Men, Suite 601, 1302 18th St., N.W., Washington, D. C., 20036.

Which convent to enter

The priest in our parish asks us often to pray for vocations to the Religious life. I believe my daughter may be interested in entering a convent, but I'm at a loss about which ones I might suggest.

What would be a good traditional convent for her to write to? Restoring sensible habits that distinguish Sisters would be a great incentive for young women, I'm positive.

Let's not get into a discussion of nuns' habits at this late juncture. My only question might be: Does your daughter have the same attitude about Sisters' habits and lifestyles as you have? What kind of Religious community might she herself be interested in investigating?

One thing is sure. There is enough variety in congregations of men and women today to suit anyone who is serious about dedicating his or her life to Our Lord through religious vows and service. Please suggest that your daughter write to the vocations director, in care of the chancery office of your diocese, express her thoughts and hopes as clearly as possible, and ask for advice. I'm certain she'll receive all the assistance she needs.

Handicaps to vocations?

Must a person have a personal reference or sponsor to enter a Religious order? My brother tells me that if someone has a physical illness this is a sign that the individual doesn't have a vocation. What about handicapped men and women who are otherwise healthy?

Religious orders of men and women vary greatly in the types of work they do in the church. Mental and physical qualifications would vary accordingly. A foreign missionary needs certain different abilities than a high school teacher, and both of these would differ from a more contemplative order which demands its own physical and mental qualities.

Some illnesses or handicaps would naturally make life in a Religious community difficult or impossible. But orders exercise such variety of service today that it is entirely possible yours would not rule out the Religious life.

My suggestion is that you write to a priest, Brother, or Sister whom you know — perhaps in the Religious order that you are considering — and ask their advice. You don't lose anything by trying, and with some asking around, and with some prayers, you may find just what you're looking for.

Why don't Sisters wear habits?

The nuns in our parish, as most nuns today, no longer wear their veils and habits. But I have seen some Sisters recently who have and wear the full religious garb. Why is this? A Protestant friend asked me and I don't know the answer.

Within rather broad regulations supplied by the church, "Religious are to wear the religious garb of their institute, described in their proper law, as a sign of consecration and a witness of poverty."(CCL 669)

Some groups of Sisters still adhere to the traditional style habit, or something quite close to it. Others provide for considerable flexibility for their members as to color, style, and so forth. Without getting involved in the wisdom or propriety of the presence or lack of changes, this is at least the reason for the differences you note in the types of dress worn by women in Religious orders.

Of course, rules concerning dress, no matter how carefully and prudently drawn up, are not always respected by all Sisters — or Brothers or priests for that matter. So it may not be fair to blame everything you see on the whole church, or on the community to which an individual belongs.

Will there be Sisters much longer?

With all the changes and confusion in the Religious life, do you think the Sisters will be around much longer?

Yes, I think Sisters will be around for a long time. There has been, and will always be, an important place in the church for the witness of the celibate life for men and women, and of those with life commitments of Christian obedience and poverty. They help us to carry (as good husbands and wives do in their vocations) important and unique messages of God's love and fidelity that men will always need.

In June, 1983, Pope John Paul II wrote to the American bishops of the need for pastoral care of Religious men and women. Among the essential elements of the religious life, he noted, are consecration to Jesus Christ, apostolic works, personal and liturgical prayer, public witness, a government calling for religious authority based on faith, and a special relationship to the church. These elements, said the Holy Father, make the religious life a great gift of God to the local church and to the church throughout the world. They are however, lived in different ways from one institute to another.

Ever since Abraham, God's will has been worked out through man's humble, prayerful, and patient willingness to change. There's no reason it should be different for Sisters.

Secular institutes as a vocation

I read your column from a single woman inquiring what vocation might be open to her and other single Catholics. Perhaps you could have mentioned the secular institutes. There are over 160 in the world, and we have a National Conference of Secular Institutes in the United States.

I am grateful to the spiritual director of the Don Bosco Volunteers, a secular institute for women, for reminding me of this relatively new Catholic vocation. The roots of such a vocation go back several centuries, but the institutes were officially recognized only in 1947 by Pope Pius XII. Secular institutes have since been praised and encouraged by other popes. Pope John Paul II noted in 1988 that members "offer proof that temporal realities, lived with the power of the Gospel, can give life to society, making it freer and more just."

The present Code of Canon Law defines a secular institute as "an institute of consecrated life in which the faithful, living in this world, strive for the perfection of charity and endeavor to work for the sanctification of the world especially from within" (c. 710).

Depending on their particular constitutions, this vocation is open to single lay people or sometimes to diocesan priests or deacons who feel called to a more intense consecration of their lives to God. A booklet, "The Consecrated Woman," explaining the Don Bosco Volunteers and giving information on secular institutes in general is available by writing to this institute at 202 Union Ave., Paterson, N.J. 07502. Other information is available from the U.S. Conference of Secular Institutes, Box 4556, Washington, D.C. 20017.

Quick conversion?

I am upset about a person who was just converted to the Catholic faith. Her ideas of the faith are very different from what I feel a convert should have.

The short classes and the idea of receiving baptism, Holy Eucharist and confirmation all in one was just beyond me. The ceremony took about half an hour and it was over so quickly that no one, least of all the new convert, understood what was going on. They were even told, as I understand it, that premarital sex is all right if the couple is planning to be married soon. How do you explain all this?

You would have to talk with the convert or, maybe even better, with the priest involved, for specific answers to some of your questions. However, I think a few considerations would be helpful for you.

First of all, when you hear something that bizarre about what some priest or other teacher is supposed to have said, it is vital to get the facts before making any judgments. I am quite certain there is no class for converts that teaches what you indicate.

As I said, if you really are concerned and particularly if you are involved personally with the individuals, go to the source and learn what was actually said.

Are you certain that the convert really did not understand what was going on when he or she was received into the church? Most catechumen classes today are very thorough in the training and preparation of men and women for entry into the church. It is not done haphazardly or lightly.

One of your remarks that makes me wonder if perhaps you may be out of touch with what is going on in the church in preparation of converts is your concern about receiving the Sacraments of Baptism, the Eucharist and Confirmation at one time. These are the three sacraments of Christian initiation. For years now the proper procedure for receiving adults into our faith is that these sacraments are given together.

This presumes, of course, that the reception of the catechumen into our faith is done during the Sacrifice of the Eucharist, at which time the new convert would naturally receive Communion for the first time. Earlier in the Mass the Sacrament of Baptism is administered and the officiating priest administers the Sacrament of Confirmation to the convert.

This all constitutes one part of the Rite for Christian Initiation of Adults, the official guide for preparation and reception of new members into our faith.

Please do some reading about this, or ask a priest or one of the new converts to explain exactly what preparations they experienced for reception into the church. I believe it would be enlightening and expand your own understanding and appreciation of your faith.

Catholics and cults

My friends and I are more and more confused by an increasing number of organizations and movements we are supposed to join to be active and better Catholics.

Some make us suspicious, especially one or two groups tied to appearances of the Blessed Virgin Mary, or so they say.

Some others look good. Others scare us because they claim we cannot become "good, loyal Catholics" except the way they tell us.

Sometimes they sound awfully narrow. We've had priests involved in some of them and have been told they are the only priests we can trust to hear our confessions or give us advice. How can we tell what to think?

Your concern is a healthy one. Apparently it is shared by many Catholics these days. I might suggest a few basic guidelines from our Catholic tradition.

First, however, we must remember that ours is a big church. Historically, when it is at its best and most alive, there's always room for a whole rainbow of ways for people to pray, to think, to live out their faith and grow in holiness.

Just because something does not appeal to us or may even seem a little far out doesn't mean there is anything bad about it. Without respect and room for these differences and honest varieties within the appropriate framework of faith, the church stagnates.

But to your question. One danger sign to look for is any position which rejects what the church is doing and teaching today. Many groups, for example, some of them, as you say, related to alleged supernatural apparitions, refuse to accept the teachings of the church since the Second Vatican Council. In their opinion these teachings and practices conflict with what they see as the "golden age" of Pope Pius V and the Council of Trent in the 16th century.

We believe on the contrary that the same Spirit who was with the church in the past is with it now.

Another large, red warning flag is any claim that this or that group is the "elite" of the church, that they are the real and genuine Catholics, that anyone not with them or who sees things differently from them is somehow a second-level Catholic.

I, too, have known some who have their own priests who are supposed to be, for one reason or another, the only ones who "understand" them and are good enough to minister to them.

These types of organizations (one might sometimes even call them cults) have been around since the beginning of Christianity. We read about them already in the New Testament.

It seems to be a common temptation for any religious society. In my 34 years as a priest, I have led or been involved with dozens of spiritual and apostolic movements. All of them have accomplished much good.

But nearly every one went through a stage when it needed to fight the temptation to consider itself something like an eighth sacrament, to believe no one is a genuine, full Catholic until he or she has done their "thing," or seen things their way.

Of course, groups and societies who pursue this course always have the highest motives — to "purify" the church and so on. But, unchecked, such attitudes often have led to gross intolerance and arrogance. When sufficiently large, they have caused enormous personal injuries, persecution and hurt to the body of Christ through the centuries. But still they surface every generation or so.

The sacraments, the Gospels and the basic prayer and spiritual efforts taught in continuous church tradition still are quite sufficient to make good, loyal and complete Catholic Christians. One archbishop noted this a few months ago, specifically in connection with one of the several dozen alleged apparitions current today. But his remark is valid in other matters as well.

"One can become a saint," he wrote, "and fully participate in the life of the church, without giving credence to such apparitions; they are not part of the deposit of faith. In fact, basing one's piety on them can often be narrow and illusory."

The third and best criterion of all in evaluating the genuineness of these movements and societies is the old standby: What are their fruits, their results? Are they bringing to the

Catholic community (parish, diocese, universal church) greater hope, unity, charity, kindness, peace and other fruits of the Spirit listed by St. Paul? (Galatians 5:22).

Or do they seem to be causing mistrust, secretiveness, elitism, hostility and bickering, division and oppression?

You can guess which ones St. Paul and Christian tradition recommend.

Converts and the knowledge of faith

How are convert parents to help their children through a Catholic grade school when they themselves are still learning? I took instructions more than 10 years ago. What I learned then was not all retained and I can't remember being taught such things as May Crowning or first confession and First Communion (child style).

I feel that to be better Catholic parents we need to be better educated. Our priest is old-school in his ideas. I know from retreats I've been on that there are different ways of believing. My fear is not to know enough about my religion to answer my children's questions. If you can understand my feelings on this matter enough to make a question out of it, I would be grateful.

You ask some good questions which obviously express the concern of thousands of other Catholic parents as well.

In all our classes and programs for people preparing to enter the Catholic faith, we attempt to prepare them for the very frustrations you feel. Even most lifelong Catholics don't realize how the "feel" for numerous practices, devotions, feasts and customs has become part of their bones through the years.

An inquiry class cannot possibly cover all these points. To be perfectly honest, they must be lived through perhaps several times and not just learned about if one is to really understand them.

Several remedies are available to you. The first and perhaps most important is to give yourself the opportunity to experience as many as possible of the things you hear about in your parish or elsewhere that will acquaint you with the daily lifestyle of being a Catholic.

This doesn't mean you must accept or even like everything

you see. Ours is a big church with a long, rich, and profusely varied tradition. All of the tradition is good, but everything cannot be for everyone.

The Eucharist, the sacraments, fidelity to the Christ who reveals himself in the Gospel — these are the essentials. Ways of prayer, preferences in liturgical celebrations, customs which bring the great themes of our faith into our home, these will vary from one person to another, one home to another, and for that matter from one parish or diocese to another.

So be patient, but give yourself a chance.

Another help for "born" Catholics as well as converts is to have a good Catholic dictionary in your home. Some excellent ones are on the market, briefly explaining most points of Catholic history, belief, and practice you could ever want to know about.

Also, take advantage of every opportunity your parish gives you to cue in on what is happening to your children. Every good parish and school has numerous sessions for parents, especially at times like first confession, First Communion and confirmation.

Finally, don't be surprised at all at your need to know more. In today's church, a constant effort to keep up on what's happening, and why, is absolutely essential for any priest or parents who don't want their children or parishioners leaving them behind.

The church is not a museum, but a community of living believers who face in each generation the responsibility to reapply the Gospel and the traditions of the church to new experiences and new demands.

History proves that sometimes the church as a whole tends to forget this. For a long time, for example, the church seemed to act as though it could live and teach in the 19th and 20th centuries pretty much as it did in the 15th century — a neglect that helped make Vatican Council II, which Pope John intended to move the church toward dealing more realistically with modern society, such a jolt for the Catholic world.

Individual Catholics can do much the same. The assumption that what one learned 30 years ago will do for the rest of one's life, if it was ever valid, surely isn't valid today.

Unless we are to be strangers to the church our children will live in and that we ourselves will be a part of 30 years from now, consistent, prayerful reading abut how and why this church is trying to meet the challenges of today's society is absolutely necessary. Many Catholics feel alienated and frustrated these days because they haven't realized this. The Holy Spirit will keep you moving in the right direction with your children.

The Baltimore Catechism

The Baltimore Catechism we hear so much about — where did it come from? And why isn't it used as much in religion classes as it used to be?

The Baltimore Catechism was the result of the desire of the American bishops in the last century to have a concise summary of Catholic doctrine. It was written at their request in 1885, after the Third Plenary Council of Baltimore, from which it receives its name.

One of the many so-called "national catechisms" having the same purpose, it followed basically the tradition and format of the famous Roman Catechism written by three Dominican theologians after the Council of Trent, around the year 1565. This Roman Catechism, by the way, was not meant for general use by the faithful, but only as reference material for "pastors and others who hold the office of teaching."

For several centuries after that, such catechisms largely replaced Holy Scripture and a living liturgy as a primary means of transmitting the faith. Biblical research, and its practical application in the understanding of Christian life and belief, was minimal in the church for various reasons. Official rites, the Mass and sacraments especially, also became less meaningful and useful as a help to teaching a living faith.

More recently, as a result of the unprecedented expansion of knowledge about Holy Scripture, and of the liturgical renewal of this century, many varieties of catechetical books are based more on the Bible and on a re-vitalized liturgy. For this reason, these books are increasingly relied on for catechism courses and other types of religious formation of young people and adults.

Who wrote the Baltimore Catechism?

I am a CCD teacher and we still often use the Baltimore Catechism in our parish. A magazine article we were given spoke of "the theologian who wrote the Baltimore Catechism." This is very misleading. The Baltimore Catechism was written and approved by the American bishops, who said it should be used in all religion classes.

Actually, the American bishops said the doctrine in the catechism should be the foundation of religion teaching; they never suggested even at that time the book be used in all religion classes.

The theologian you speak of was Father John McCaffrey, a highly respected expert in theology who served as personal theologian for several bishops at the various Councils of Baltimore in the latter part of the last century. Apparently at the bishops' request, Father McCaffrey drew up the catechism. After some revisions, it was eventually adopted as the "Baltimore Catechism."

Why no catechisms?

Why does there seem to be a general rejection of "catechisms" today? We learned our religion from catechisms, but you can hardly find one anywhere these days, at least any that satisfy me now.

Your questions concern many others than yourself, though perhaps not so much now as a few years ago. There are at least two quite important reasons that religious educators, priests, and others, rely less on the old-style catechisms than they once did. First, the simple, often one-sentence responses to the great questions about God, man, life and eternity, often implied that these few words wrapped up all that the church knows or could know about the questions. Human language is always limited and very incomplete when it comes to topics or questions like these. The new Universal Catechism, scheduled to be issued in 1992 or 1993, shows much more sensitivity to these realities than most previous catechisms.

Second, and this is closely related to what I've said already, most answers to man's religious searching are open-ended; they're always subject to new insights, further enrichment and adjustment, even to the point that the emphasis in former answers may be found not nearly as accurate as ones later arrived at. This is true even — perhaps, especially — of our Christian faith. As it lives out its life on earth through the ups and downs of history, the church will be expanding and growing in its understanding of Jesus and his teachings until the end of time.

Coming back to the faith

How does a person who has been away from the church for years redeem himself and get back to the faith? Or is that even possible? It would be like starting all over again — relearning prayers, how to act at Mass, and all that.

How does one make a confession after all these years? I could never remember all the sins since my last confession.

Believe me, it is not nearly as complicated or as difficult as it appears to you now. In fact, if you have decided that you wish to return to full practice of your faith, the hardest part is already over.

Make an appointment with a priest you have confidence in, perhaps one that you have had occasion to see is considerate and thoughtful, and ask his help. It isn't at all necessary that you even know him now. He will guide you. If you are ready and have made all the decisions necessary, it may all be done in one visit with him — except for catching up, as you say, on a lot that you may have missed through the years. But with your good will, that will come. The important thing is to take the first step.

What does excommunication mean today?

One reads in history about persons and groups being excommunicated or place under interdict. We read little about it happening in modern times.

What does present canon law have to say about excommunication and interdict? In what circumstances are these measures applied?

Excommunication and interdict are two of the sanctions, or "punishments," which Christian people have applied to those who seriously violate the Christian or Catholic rule of life.

In practice, for the average Catholic both of these sanctions are basically the same. In either case, the individual is forbidden any liturgical ministry in the Mass or other public worship of the church and may not receive or celebrate any of the sacraments. Other consequences refer mostly to those who hold some public office in the church.

The occasional need of the Christian community to isolate gross offenders from participation in community activities dates all the way back to biblical times. The Gospels and the Letters of the New Testament refer on several occasions to situations in which the offender should be expelled from their midst. (See, for example, I Corinthians, Chapter 5)

Excommunication and other sanctions were far more significant and powerful, of course, in past centuries when the church and at least some civil governments had a far more intimate relationship than they have today. Partly for this reason, church laws regarding these sanctions were in the past far more complicated and severe than they are today.

Our present Code of Canon Law provides automatic excommunication for only seven serious offenses in the church: desecration of the Blessed Sacrament; laying violent hands on the pope; absolving an accomplice in sin; a bishop consecrating another bishop without a mandate from the pope; direct violation of the seal of confession; procuring a successful abortion; rejection of the church through apostasy, heresy, schism.

However, it must be noted that many circumstances, such as the age of the individual (no automatic excommunication applies to an individual under the age of 18), fear or ignorance that might have been involved and so on, affect whether or not the excommunication or other sanction actually was incurred.

It also is important to remember that application of such severe sanctions, whether in the New Testament itself or in the church's law, are intended both for the good of the community and for the direction and healing of the one who has sinned against that community.

No excommunication, interdict or other sanction is ever permanent and irrevocable. It always includes the invitation to repentance and return, and holds out promise of forgiveness from God and the Christian community, the church.

It should be obvious from what I've said that, while our present laws are much simplified, this part of the church's legislation remains quite involved because the church wants to make them applicable only in the most serious cases and only when absolutely necessary for the common good of the Catholic people.

Specific cases should be taken up with one's parish priest or confessor.

Does it cost money?

Doesn't the Catholic Church want converts? My daughter-in-law had been married before. She decided on her own to take instructions to become a member of the Catholic faith. They informed her there would be a charge for the paper work, but isn't a total of about $200 just a little steep? I was a convert 27 years ago, and if they had charged like that, I would have said "forget it."

There is no charge at all for anyone entering the Catholic faith. Any minor expenses for some books or other materials are usually absorbed by the priest himself, or the parish.

The figures you gave indicate that some sort of marriage case, possibly an annulment, was processed for your daughter-in-law so she could marry your son. Depending on the kind of process required, the figure you give, perhaps somewhat less or a little more, would be the normal offering requested. Some of this would pay expenses in your own diocese; some, again depending on the type of case, might pay for stages of the case handled in Rome.

Admittedly this may sound steep but even most Catholics have little idea of the average amount of hours and days, including usually professional consultation with psychiatrists or medical doctors or others competent in the fields involved in a particular case, that are required at all levels to complete an annulment procedure. In other words, whatever money is given is by no means a gift to one or another priest who works on the case. It simply pays basic expenses of the offices and personnel whose services are needed before the final decisions are made, sometimes a year or more after the original petition.

Furthermore, no one is denied these services simply because they cannot pay for them. Provisions are made in every diocese and in Rome for the waiving of these charges when necessary. In some cases, as in our own diocese, the bishop authorizes that these be paid out of parish funds if the individuals are too poor to give the stipend.

Do I give enough?

I am deeply hurt by some people in our church who think I don't give enough money in the collection. I almost died three years ago and cannot work as hard as I used to. I do try to give what I can to poor people. I know some people laugh at me when I give 25 cents a week in the collection, and 25 cents in the poor box.

I am old and spend a lot for medicine, but I feel I spend more money on poor people in a month than those who laugh at me spend in a year. What can I do?

If 25 cents is all you honestly feel you can place in the collection basket each Sunday, please don't be embarrassed. Many other parishioners, especially older ones, are in the same position you are. I really doubt that anyone is laughing at you for what you are doing, but if anyone ever says anything to you, ask them to read Mark 12:41.

If it is any consolation to you, I know other pastors agree with me that the ones who disturb us most (because they are grossly unfair to the rest of their parish) are those who totally ignore their responsibility to share in accepting the financial responsibilities of the parish by giving absolutely nothing.

Others, of course, are in nearly the same category, giving only a token of what they could and should give. Obviously you are in neither of these categories.

Incidentally, please don't let yourself into the same trap you dislike in others. There's no way you can possibly know how much these other people give to the poor in one way or another. Do what you can, and leave them and their responsibilities for God to judge.

Denying services to non-contributors?

Do parish priests have the right to deny parish privileges such as baptism, marriage and funerals to parishioners they feel are not contributing enough money to the parish?

Every Catholic has an obligation — and it is an obligation — to contribute his fair share to the best of his ability toward the financial responsibilities of his particular parish community. Parish priests almost always give every benefit of the doubt in making allowances for families and individuals who cannot give as much as they would like to give. To arbitrarily cut people off from the services of the church would unquestionably be wrong.

However, this is not the whole story at all. People who continually ignore their financial responsibility to the church, who place a very low priority on carrying their fair share of the burden with other members of their parish, not infrequently manifest some poverty of faith in other ways as well.

As we will discuss in the chapter on Baptism, certain basic requirements of commitment to the Catholic faith, including some assurance that the parents intend to raise their children as Christians and Catholics, is absolutely required before baptism can take place. Similarly, couples may come to be married and demonstrate such immaturity and ignorance of their religion and of the meaning of the sacrament of marriage, that the priest may seriously question whether this boy or girl should (or even could) enter a valid marriage in the church.

In other words, a priest has no right to baptize or marry people simply because they present themselves for these sacraments. If any requirements are lacking, he has a responsibility to refuse or at least delay the ceremony until the situation is changed. In such instances, the individuals involved may protest that they are being discriminated against for financial reasons, when both they and the priest know the facts are otherwise.

Polish National Catholic Church

I was baptized in the Polish National Catholic Church, but made my First Communion and was confirmed in the Roman Catholic Church. Since my marriage years ago in the Roman Catholic Church, I have practiced my faith. My problem is my family doesn't know that background. Should I be rebaptized, or can I "go to the grave" without their knowing?

In the latter part of the last century, certain groups of Polish immigrants in the United States experienced severe disagreements with other priests and bishops, especially concerning the ownership and operation of their parishes.

As a result, first in Illinois and then in Pennsylvania and elsewhere, around the turn of the century these conflicts evolved into the schismatic movement which would become the Polish National Catholic Church.

In its beliefs and particularly in its worship, this church is very similar to ours, at least as we were before Vatican II.

There's no question of the validity of your baptism; you do not have to be baptized again. In fact, even a formal confession of faith, which would usually be asked of one joining the Roman Catholic Church would seem to be superfluous, given your background.

For your peace of mind, perhaps you could talk with a priest privately and take his advice.

What is the Hebrew rite of the church?

Can you explain what the Hebrew Rite of the Catholic Church is? I have heard that this is a way for Jews to remain Jews and still become Catholics. How can this be?

There is no such thing as a Hebrew Rite of the Catholic Church. An intriguing suggestion has been made in recent years from some private sources that the formation of such a rite be considered, but no serious study of the matter has been made, to my knowledge, by any Catholic authorities.

The proposed rite would function much as other non-Latin rites of the church (Byzantines, etc.) Ultimately subject to the Holy Father, they would have their own patriarch in Rome or Jerusalem. All Hebrew Roman Catholics would be eligible to join the rite. Jewish feasts would be observed in a manner compatible with Catholicism; the rite would have church buildings in harmony with its own traditions, and eventually a Hebrew liturgy would be prepared and used.

In other words, the purpose would be that Catholics of Hebrew descent might maintain their racial and cultural identity for themselves and their children, removing what is presumed to be some of the main objections Jewish people have to becoming Christians and Catholics.

The idea is innovative and interesting. No one knows yet how acceptable the proposal might be to Jewish men and women who may be inclined toward the Catholic faith, or to the church officials.

Catholic Church and the UN

Has the Catholic Church ever condemned the United Nations? How can so many priests and bishops defend it?

Catholic leaders, especially those who speak officially for the whole church, have consistently promoted the existence and growth of the United Nations (UN) and urged that its international authority be strengthened.

Since the UN was founded, Popes Pius XII, John XXIII, Paul VI, and now John Paul II, have recognized its limitations and weaknesses, but insisted it is still the best hope for world peace and order. This position is confirmed by the encouragement and support the church has offered in all the major agencies of the UN since World War II.

The Mass
Eucharistic Liturgy

The word "Eucharist"

I'm in the dark about the word "Eucharist." It is used a lot today both for Holy Communion and for the Mass. Why can't we simply say Mass and Communion?

The word "Eucharist" comes from the Greek word "Eucharistein," to return thanks. It is one of the most ancient designations for the Eucharist among Christians, since that was its primary purpose — to remember what God has done for us in Jesus Christ, and thank him for it.

That name is clearly much more specific and meaningful than "the Mass," which is simply an English corruption of the Latin words which formerly ended the Mass, "Ite missa est."

The church is, of course, returning to use of the word in many ways. Our celebration of Mass is divided, for example, into the Liturgy of the Word and the Liturgy of the Eucharist.

The long prayer which the priest says, and to which the people respond, which contains the narration of the institution of the Eucharist is called the Eucharistic Prayer. It begins with "Let us give thanks to the Lord our God," to which the people respond "It is right to give him thanks and praise."

Why are Masses different?

It used to be that we could attend Mass at any church and it was the same at all of them. Now it's different at all of them. Why?

Also, why don't they all use the same books so as to be uniform?

Part of the answer to your question becomes evident if we recall a little history about the Mass.

During the first 15 centuries of the church's life, the Mass was not the same in all the churches. Especially in the first several centuries, the celebration of the Eucharist was just that — a celebration. Actions, words, music and whole atmosphere of the Mass were different according to who was there, the condition and circumstances of their lives, and so on.

For a variety of reasons, the Mass gradually ceased being an event that the people participated in as members of the Body of the Risen Christ. It became rather a sacred ceremony carried out by the priest that the rest of the people were simply required to *watch* reverently.

By the time of the Council of Trent in the 1500s, much of the early history of the Mass which we are aware of today had been completely lost. The bishops at that council, however, were faced with numerous attacks against the Mass and the Eucharist from leaders of the new Protestant Reformation. They understandably responded to these attacks by taking one form of the Mass — the form used in Rome at that time — and declaring it the *only* form of the Mass allowed in the Western Church. Every action and prayer was spelled out in minute detail. No options were offered. No variations were permitted.

Long before the Second Vatican Council, church leaders were aware that this kind of frozen liturgy was blocking the growth of real liturgical prayer and worship and that something had to be done to loosen things up. The purpose wasn't variety for variety's sake. It was to enable people of different ages and times and temperaments and circumstances to make the Mass a genuine, living worship-celebration of their Christian life.

The variations you speak of are now specifically allowed and suggested in the official instructions on the Mass. Numerous options for Scripture readings are offered. Several prayers or exhortations are accompanied with the notation that the priest should "use these, or similar words." Wide leeway is given in such things as music and actions. The Sign of Peace, for instance, is to be given "according to local custom."

When you're present for a Mass that is different than you're used to, why not relax, try to get into the spirit of it and share in it as well as you can? A little giving in, and trying to share what others are feeling could be a real act of charity toward those around you as well as to yourself.

Multi-cultural liturgies

I have read that the church is allowing awfully strange customs at Mass in foreign countries — Hindu ceremonies in India, tribal dances in Africa, and even ancestor worship in China. I know things are changing, but will the Mass be the same from one place to another at all any more?

The Mass will always be the same in its essentials — the renewal of the offering which Jesus made to the Father on Calvary, and the Communion of his body and blood as the sign and source of the one Body of Christ. In other words, it will always be a sacrifice, and a sacred meal.

Apart from these essentials, however, eucharistic worship will depend on the culture, customs, language and temperaments of the people who offer it.

Certain historical circumstances have caused most of us to think of the Mass as unchanging and "universal" in the wrong sense. Enormous and irreparable damage has been done to the cause of the church because of small-mindedness and short-sightedness in this matter. A few hundred years ago, for example, an imaginative missionary effort that might have brought all of China into Christianity collapsed because officials in Rome insisted on such things as that all Masses be in Latin, that priests must wear Western-style dress and vestments, and so on.

This attitude, long in disrepute, was officially put down by Pope Pius XII. When the church attempts to call a people to a better way of life under the inspiration of the Christian religion, he said in one of his encyclicals, "she does not act like one who recklessly cuts down and uproots a thriving forest. She grafts good stock upon the wood so that it may bear even better fruit." The policy of using anything in local cultures, even religious customs, that can conceivably be meshed with Christian beliefs is now well established.

Chinese, incidentally, do not "worship" ancestors. They have traditionally a remarkable reverence and honor for them. A misunderstanding of this custom has been another costly mistake for the church.

Why Call Mass a Memorial?

Why are priests now calling Mass a memorial? Isn't it still true that the Mass is primarily a sacrifice? My interpretation of "memorial" is for someone who is deceased. Certainly Christ lives! We receive the living risen Christ. Isn't this a downgrading of our belief?

It is true we often refer to the Mass as a memorial carried out "in memory of his death and resurrection" (second Eucharistic Prayer). However, this designation for the celebration of the Eucharist is not new. It goes back to the earliest records we have of prayers offered at the Eucharistic celebrations.

Obviously, the word memorial in this context does not mean something for the dead. It simply means something done in memory of someone or something. In fact, this is the reason Jesus himself gives us in the gospel for the celebration of the Eucharist, "Do this to remember" me and what I have done for you.

In the Mass the entire purpose is to remember what Jesus has done in his sacrificial death and resurrection, to give thanks for it (which is what the word Eucharist means), and then to renew our offering of this eternal sacrifice of Jesus to the heavenly Father.

Far from being downgrading, remembering — with thanks and praise — is what the Eucharist is all about.

Sunday Mass useless?

I have several friends, both Catholic and non-Catholic, who

think weekly Mass is useless. One of them says it is better to go to Mass three or four times a year when he really gets something out of it than to go every Sunday just because it's the law. I guess I don't agree with it, but I don't know why. Doesn't that attitude really make sense?

That attitude would make good sense if the Mass were just another of several optional prayer services. It doesn't make sense, however, if one understands the focal position that the Eucharistic Sacrifice and sacrament hold in the life and actions of a Christian.

We might start with the fact that the requirement of weekly sharing in the Eucharist (or if you prefer, "going to Mass every Sunday") isn't something new. Way back in the early years of Christianity, centuries before there were any "church laws" in our sense of the term, participation in the Sunday Eucharist every week was expected, in some ways more urgently than it is today. We have documents that reflect early Christian policy if one of their number deliberately failed to be present for the Eucharist for two or three weeks running; they were considered as no longer members of the church, no longer Christian!

If this appears severe, it obviously means that they believed something about the Mass that we have lost through the centuries. For them, it wasn't a matter of committing a "mortal sin" by disobeying a law about Sunday Mass. It was simply a conviction that one could not really understand and believe what the Mass is all about, and then fail to be there for even a few weeks.

Today the church is trying hard to help us reclaim that conviction — that the sacrifice and table of the Eucharist, sharing in the offering of Christ to the Father, and receiving together his body and blood in Communion, is the *key* and indispensable way Jesus intends to unite men and women with himself and form them into his family until the end of the world.

In other words, Mass is where, above all, we learn the spirit and message of Jesus. Through reflection on the words of Scripture and through the language and actions of the liturgy of the Eucharist, it is where we continually identify ourselves as his members, acknowledge who are our brothers and sisters because of him, and assure each other of our mutual encouragement and support. In that larger sense, even in a church with 500 persons, the presence or absence of one really affects everyone — including the individual himself.

If this way of speaking about the Mass sounds strange, it is unfortunate. Perhaps it is one of the prices we have paid for coming to see missing Mass on Sunday as a mortal sin because it is against a law of the church. The fact is that, even if there were no such law, presence at the Sunday Eucharist would still be "required" simply because one is a member of the family of Christ, simply because one is a Christian.

Catching up with the church at Mass

For reasons I won't explain, I was out of the church for nearly 25 years. Just came back to confession and Communion several months ago and I never realized how much I missed it.

I'm trying to catch up, but one thing that bothers me is that the Mass is not in Latin the way I remembered it. I enjoy your column and hope you can help me understand.

I'm happy for you. Obviously you consider the church your home and I welcome you back.

Your letter intrigued me. About 1970, when I began writing this column, questions like yours concerning our vernacular liturgy were frequent. Now, more than 20 years later, I realized as I read yours that it's been many years since the last such question.

I believe the reason is rather simple. The vast majority of Catholics have become so accustomed to participating and praying, by both listening and responding in their own language, and to the insights of faith they receive in this way, that they can hardly imagine the Mass otherwise. This is why, with almost no exceptions, every effort to "revive" the Latin Mass as the norm for public worship has folded quickly.

Increasingly my own conviction is that if Vatican Council II had accomplished nothing else, hearing God's Word and offering the Eucharist in the language of the people would have made it worthwhile. From there, the Holy Spirit can keep our vision clear and lead us to whatever is good.

Perhaps a few thoughts may help you understand all the above and see an answer to your question. Take our Eucharistic Prayers, for example. They are, of course, as are all other parts of the Mass, first and pre-eminently our worship of the Father in and with Christ. But they are also a "school" in which we encounter week after week the essential truths and challenges of our faith. The Trinity, the incarnation, the redemptive, forgiving mission of Jesus; the meaning of Christ's eucharistic presence as in every age he forms his church into "one body, one spirit" in him (Eucharistic Prayer II); the Communion of Saints; the pastoral structure of the church expressed by explicit petitions for, and in union with, the pope and local bishop in every eucharistic prayer; the "royal priesthood" (1 Pt. 2:9) of all the faithful assembled, the "we" who "offer to you, God of glory and majesty, this holy and perfect sacrifice" (Eucharistic Prayer 1); the Second Coming — it's all there and more!

And it's all in the great Amen, and in the Communion we receive to seal again our part in the new covenant with him who initiated it.

Add to this the creed we profess and the Word of God we hear and reflect upon, and it's no wonder that the celebration of the Mass is "for both the universal and the local church, and for each person, the center of the whole Christian life" (General Introduction of the Roman Missal, No. 1).

It's also no wonder that from the earliest decades Christians viewed weekly sharing in that Word and Eucharist as the life breath of their faith. A believer could not drink in those words and actions, and respond to them year in and year out, without their taking deep root in the heart. And people are, indeed, to "drink them in," be immersed in what is going on. Each celebration, the church says, should be "planned to bring about conscious, active and full participation of the people, motivated by faith, hope and charity" (General Introduction of the Roman Missal, No. 3).

The point is that ordinarily all this could not conceivably occur without the intimacy and immediacy of communication in one's own language. This is precisely what most

Catholics have now come to discover from their own experience.

After trying all kinds of substitutes for centuries, including eventually vernacular translations of the missal (which were on the Index of Forbidden Books until 1897), the church has returned to its ancient tradition of celebrating the eucharistic mysteries in the language of the people who are there.

I hope these ideas help you and others like you who missed a lot. Give yourself time and take the effort to discover what that "conscious, active and full participation" can do.

Mass on Sabbath day

A few weeks ago I saw a reference to the obligation of hearing Mass on Sunday, tying it to the commandment to keep holy the Sabbath day. Is this really a law that not even the pope could change?

The commandment to "keep holy the Sabbath day" could never be interpreted as a commandment referring to Sunday Mass. For one thing, the Mass was still many centuries in the future when Moses received the Ten Commandments. For another, the Sabbath day — from the Hebrew verb "sabat," rest — was Saturday, the seventh day of the week, not Sunday.

Christians have, of course, celebrated Sunday as the Lord's Day from the earliest centuries, but the obligation to attend Mass on Sunday, as we know it, is comparatively recent. That obligation, as it now exists in church law, could be removed or modified by the church itself.

Sabbath changed to Sunday?

Why was the Sabbath changed from Saturday to Sunday, and is there a chance it might be changed back someday? The Seventh Day Adventists are passing out pamphlets dealing with this subject, and they are so convincing that I've decided to go to Saturday evening Mass until this is explained.

The very early Christians changed the "Sabbath" day to Sunday for a variety of reasons. First, the fact that the resurrection of Jesus is recorded in Scripture as occurring on the first day of the week certainly had much to do with the fact that this seemed the most appropriate day to celebrate the Eucharist to commemorate that event. The first Christians also made a point of changing their days of observance (including fast days) from those prescribed by Jewish law to emphasize their departure from traditions and customs of the people of Israel.

When the Seventh Day Adventist Church was formed about the middle of the last century, the four men and one woman who became its nucleus were somehow convinced that Saturday, not Sunday, should still be the "holy day" of the week. It is one of the lesser ways the teachings of that church depart from general Christian tradition. There's no reason whatsoever to suspect this Sunday tradition will ever change.

Which day is the Sabbath?

We commonly refer to the Sabbath as the seventh day of the week. The Bible does not say this. It does say many times that the Sabbath is the seventh day after six days of work.

There is a big difference in these two sevens. The seventh day of a calendar week is one set date each week, but the seventh day after the beginning of the first day of work can be any day of the week.

The Bible does not speak of any consecutive seven-day cycles up to the time of the Israelites' first Sabbath. Therefore, we know that before this time, there was no standard weekly calendar used such as the one in use at Christ's time.

Though God commanded a Sabbath rest day, he did not necessarily mean the seventh day. Thus, Sunday-keeping saints have not gone to hell for not keeping Saturday.

You may be right. I'm not sure how practical your suggestion is, however. No matter how theoretically correct you are, I don't believe the argument will carry much weight with people who believe we must observe the Sabbath on Saturday.

I believe you would find it difficult to discover evidence that observance of a seven-day week came after the Jewish regulation of rest on the seventh day. Long before the observance of the Sabbath rest was an established regulation among the Hebrews, a seven-day week was not all uncommon in several Near Eastern cultures, including that of the Jews. Apparently this resulted from the division of the lunar month (28 days) into four sections, though other cultures, such as the Greeks and Romans, divided the lunar month into three sections of roughly ten days each.

It is entirely possible that the Hebrew tradition of six days work and one day rest developed out of the context of the seven-day week, the last day of which would be a day of recuperation from labor. In other words, the history of the Sabbath may be a fascinating study, but it doesn't offer much ammunition against Sabbatarians (those who insist on Saturday as the holy day). Our reasons for observing Sunday as the Christian holy day arise from entirely different sources.

A sin to skip Mass?

Has the church changed its rules on attending Mass? Is it still a mortal sin to miss Mass on Sunday? We have relatives who go only when they feel like it. Their excuse is that there is no more sin since Vatican II.

I am sometimes tempted to believe that one of the biggest mistakes the church has made is to make it a "law" that we must go to Mass on Sunday. Letters like yours always sharpen that temptation.

For yet far too many Catholics, the obligation to participate in the Mass each Sunday is in somewhat the same category of church law as abstaining from meat on the Fridays of Lent, or even of attending Mass on holy days of obligation. It obscures the whole tradition of our Christian faith on the significance of the Sunday Eucharist for us Christians.

To speak of the presence or absence of a church regulation as a primary motive for participation in the Sunday Eucharist radically misses the point. In early Christian times, centuries before it was a church "rule," participation in the Eucharist each week was considered automatic.

Assuming one was not ill, only two reasons could explain

an individual's routine absence. He had either decided he did not wish to be a Christian any more, or his knowledge of the faith was seriously deficient and more instruction was needed.

Sunday Eucharist, in other words, constituted the life breath of the Christian person and community. Both the New Testament and the earliest Christian writings point out this truth. (See, for example, Acts 20:7, "On the first day of the week, when we gathered for the breaking of the bread . . .")

The church has begun to realize in the past few generations that many, maybe even most, Catholics have lost touch with this essential Christian tradition, if indeed they were ever aware of it. To participate in the Sunday Eucharist because "I have to" may be normal at certain stages of growing up. A Catholic adult at age 30 or 50 should have moved beyond that.

To answer your question directly, the law is still there and perhaps is still necessary for most or all of us to have the opportunity to grow to a fuller appreciation of this central part of our faith.

The code of canon law recalls our tradition: "Sunday is the day on which the paschal mystery is celebrated in light of the apostolic tradition and is to be observed as the foremost holy day of obligation in the universal church." It then provides, "On Sundays and other holy days of obligation the faithful are bound to participate in Mass" (canons 1246 and 1247).

Vatican Council II did not and had no intention to minimize the essential role of the Sunday Eucharist in the life of the church.

Sunday Mass still obligatory?

I've heard in recent years that one need not go to Mass on Sunday unless it is "meaningful." Attending Mass is only a matter of "substantive" obedience, it is said. If you're not getting out of it what you think you should, don't go, and don't worry about it.

A short time ago, however, I read again that we may miss Mass only for a serious reason. Has that teaching changed? I'm a convert, so I don't know a lot of things.

Attendance at the Sunday Eucharist is a serious obligation

for Catholics for reasons that far transcend the fact that it is a church law. This obligation binds us unless we are excused from it for a proportionately serious reason.

What, precisely, such a reason would be must be determined ultimately by the individual himself in the light of his overall respect for and observance of this obligation. "Substantive" obedience to the Sunday Eucharist regulation simply means that when one is otherwise faithful to that responsibility, he need not worry or feel guilty when, on occasion, something — a vacation, unusually exhausting work, and so on — makes it exceptionally difficult or inconvenient to get to Mass.

The question of attending Mass only when one "gets something out of it" is another matter. Contrary to what certain psychological experts seem to tell us, there is nothing wrong at some point in our lives in doing something because someone says we must. It is an essential part of our maturing process to act in certain matters simply because someone important to us (parent, teacher, priest, church) says, "It's good for you. Do it." We all go through this. It's one of the steps we take toward making values our own — or, if you wish, doing a thing because "I get something out of it."

Surely there's something spiritually incomplete in a 30 or 50-year-old Catholic who hasn't long ago passed the point where he goes to Mass only because the church says he must. His problem isn't, however, that he once went for that reason. Every child or teen-ager has gone or will go to church for that reason somewhere along the line. The mature adult's tragedy is that he was never helped to grow beyond it, a description which sadly fits too many Catholics today.

Saturday Mass limited?

I have heard that a Catholic may fulfill his Sunday Mass obligation on Saturday evening only if he cannot get to Mass on Sunday morning. Is this true? If so, it's news to me.

It's news to me, too. The Vatican's Instruction on Eucharistic Worship which deals with this privilege places no such restrictions on one's right to fulfill the Sunday obligation on Saturday evening.

The Code of Canon Law (CCL 1248) simply says: Anyone satisfies the precept to participate in the Mass by assisting wherever it is celebrated in the Catholic rite either on the day (Sunday or holy day) itself, or in the evening of the preceeding day.

Sunday Mass age limit?

Is there a regulation stating that persons over the age of 59 are not obligated to hear Mass on Sundays and holy days? A friend of mine contends that there is.

Many older people may be so handicapped or otherwise unable to get to Mass that they would often, or perhaps most of the time, be excused from Mass. The obligation to participate in Mass on Sundays is a serious church law, but anyone is excused on a given Sunday for serious reason.

There is, however, no age limit on the Sunday Mass regulation for a Catholic, once that individual has reached the age of reason.

Sunday Mass where?

Our family has attended Mass quite regularly outside our own parish. Someone recently told me this was against the church's regulations. We know what we must do if we want our children to grow up with a love and appreciation for the Mass and their faith. But out of curiosity, is there any church law on this subject?

Church law provides that one's Sunday obligation may be fulfilled anywhere the Mass is legitimately and properly celebrated "according to the Catholic rite." (CCL 1248)

Aged and Sunday Mass

I am 81 years old and was told by a priest that I was excused from Sunday Mass if I didn't feel up to going.

Also, someone told me I never had to go to confession, and I could receive the sacraments. Is this true?

At your age, you certainly are excused if you do not feel

comfortable going on any particular Sunday. In fact, if you cannot go without danger of getting sick, or serious danger of perhaps falling and hurting yourself, you are completely excused from Sunday Mass.

Your priest was right. God does not want you endangering yourself to attend Mass. Keep up your prayers and go to Mass when you can. That is sufficient.

The only time one must receive the Sacrament of Penance before Communion is when he or she is conscious of a deliberate mortal sin. I am sure it is all right for you to go to Communion whenever you have the opportunity, even if you do not get to confession.

If you are unable to go to Mass for a few Sundays, or even longer, please call a priest in your parish and ask him to bring you Communion. Many parishes also have special ministers of the Eucharist who might bring Communion to your home each Sunday. If the priest himself comes sometime, perhaps you could use that opportunity to receive the Sacrament of Penance.

Saturday Masses elsewhere?

My wife and I both belong to a church and a diocese which do not have a Saturday night Mass.

When someone from our parish attends a Saturday night Mass in another diocese, and comes home Sunday, is he obligated to attend Sunday Mass in his own church to fulfill his own Sunday duty?

As I'm sure your pastor would agree, the laws of the church on this matter are very clear. If you are a visitor in another diocese, the laws of that diocese regarding such things as Sunday Mass apply to you. Therefore attendance at a Saturday evening Mass in that diocese would fulfill any obligation for the Sunday Eucharist that you have. You would not be required to attend another Mass the following day.

I must confess that I am extremely uncomfortable answering your question this way. Our weekly celebration of the Eucharist is such a beautiful and important thing in our lives as Catholic Christians that it is a shame to have to reduce it to such details of obligation as this.

The purpose of the church in allowing the fulfillment of this responsibility in a Saturday evening liturgy was to provide a broader opportunity for observance of the Lord's Day. Such a regulation certainly makes sense, especially in light of the church's celebration of Easter itself (after all, each Sunday according to Christian tradition, is a "little Easter") which is anticipated by evening Masses on Holy Saturday.

Thus, a solid Christian tradition lies behind the opportunities given by the church for uniting the hours of Saturday evening to the celebration and observance of the Lord's Day.

Hour for Saturday Mass

What is the earliest hour of the day on Saturday that I may hear Mass and fulfill the Sunday obligation? Some churches in our area have Mass at 4 p.m., and I have heard that this is too early.

It is the responsibility of the bishop of each diocese to determine the time on Saturday afternoon when "Sunday obligation Masses" may begin. In most dioceses it is 4 p.m. or 4:30 p.m., but you would have to ask your parish priest what the rule is in your own diocese.

Normally it is safe to say that any parish Mass regularly scheduled on a Saturday afternoon is intended to be within the guidelines set by the bishop for fulfilling one's Sunday obligation.

Shopping for Saturday Mass?

Does a Saturday Mass which doesn't have the Sunday liturgy — such as a wedding, funeral, or jubilee Mass — still fulfill the Sunday obligation? There seems to be a difference of opinion on this.

I hate the thought of "shopping around"; it certainly seems to negate the spirit of the Mass. But that's what I feel like I'm doing when I must check with the priest first to see if the Mass "counts" or not. This problem also came up in the last Easter Vigil.

You're really asking three questions, so let's take them one at a time.

1. The Instruction of the Vatican on Eucharistic Worship of May 25, 1967, which provides for anticipating the Sunday Mass obligation on Saturday evening, says that when a parish Mass is scheduled on Saturday for that purpose, the liturgy for the Sunday should be celebrated. It does not, however, make the actual Sunday liturgy a *condition* for fulfilling the Sunday obligation. Thus, a Catholic could fulfill that obligation, if he intends to do so, regardless of which Mass is offered — presuming, as you said, that it is within the required time period for your diocese.

This is similar to a Mass on Sunday itself. We all know that even if one attends a wedding, anniversary Mass, or special parish feast day Mass on Sunday, he still fulfills the obligation to attend Mass. There is no indication that the church intended to make the Saturday evening privilege more strict.

However, each bishop, as the chief liturgist in his diocese, has the responsibility for establishing specific regulations for that diocese, including setting the time when Saturday Masses in anticipation of Sunday may begin.

2. How about the "shopping around?" Differences of opinion are possible on Saturday Mass as on many other subjects. If you come to a decision in good conscience, however — perhaps on the advice of a priest whom you consider competent — that is sufficient wherever you go. Whether a Mass "counts" or not does not depend on the opinion of the parish priest who offers it.

3. All of the above is irrelevant to the situation on Holy Saturday. The Mass at the Easter Vigil is liturgically *the* Easter Mass even more than the one following morning.

Masses said for the people?

When I was younger I was always told that Sunday Masses were said for the people who attended. The collections paid for the Masses.

Today you go to church and Mass on Sunday is being offered for somebody who has died or for an anniversary. I don't think this is the way it should be. I still think the Sunday

Masses should be said for the people. Can you tell me if things have changed?

Your question reveals some confusion about a number of things. But it also reveals that you have some good Catholic instincts, because the church has rules that provide for exactly what you think should be.

Pastors of parishes (and also bishops, incidentally) are obligated by church law to offer the Eucharist every Sunday and holy day, and a few other special days, for the intention of all the people committed to their care, not just those present at the Mass.

This responsibility usually is refered to as the "Missa pro populo," or "Mass for the people." By our church regulations, it is an obligation in justice that the priest or bishop owes to his people.

However, this obligation binds only pastors, so there could be other Masses on a given Sunday that are offered for other intentions and would be announced this way in the parish bulletin, for example.

In fact, regulations in some dioceses provide ways in which even the pastor would be able to offer the Eucharist for other intentions as well, provided he has fulfilled his obligation for his people.

One final point. The collections at Mass do not, as you seem to indicate, provide a stipend for this Mass for the people. Collections provide for the financial needs of the parish. The pastor receives no stipend for the Masses he offers for his people.

Televised Mass and Sunday obligation

If the pope's blessing with a plenary indulgence can be obtained by all who followed the rite on television or radio, why can't the obligation of Sunday Mass be fulfilled by watching a Mass on television at home on Sunday morning?

For that matter, why can't we confess over the telephone?

The answer is basically simple: The Mass is not a private prayer; receiving a blessing is, even though there are public and communal aspects to any blessing given, for example, by the pope to the world.

Many Catholics still do not realize that the obligation concerning Sunday Mass is not to hear or watch someone else do something, but to be there to do it oneself, and share it with our fellow Catholics. The Eucharist is an action, a celebration, of the Catholic community and cannot be substituted for by seeing a television program.

If one cannot be present for Sunday Mass with one's parish or other community, a television or radio Mass may assist in uniting one with it in spirit, or in realizing one's desire for union with Christ in the Eucharist. But such listening or viewing is never a substitute for being there.

Confession, too, is a personal dialogue and presence with the Catholic community on earth as represented by the priest. This personal confrontation with the people of God, with the priest as their ordained representative, is essential to the sacrament.

With our understanding of the sacraments, televised or telephoned confession could not fulfill the requirements for the sacrament of forgiveness of sins.

Which holy days

I and a few of my friends would like to know why some states observe holy days and others do not. I thought all holy days, not just a few, were to be observed by all Catholics. Can you explain this?

Several factors may explain why certain holy days are observed in some places and not others.

First, 10 holy days of obligation are prescribed for the universal church: Christmas, the Solemnity of Mary the Mother of God on Jan. 1; the Ascension; the Assumption of Mary, Aug. 15; All Saints Day, Nov. 1; the Immaculate Conception, Dec. 8; Epiphany; the Feast of St. Joseph, March 19; Corpus Christi; and the Feast of Sts. Peter and Paul, June 29.

Of these, only the first six have been celebrated traditionally as holy days in the United States. This is still true.

As many other countries, we transfer the feast of Epiphany and Corpus Christi to a Sunday near those feasts.

In addition, the conference of bishops (for example, the bishops of the United States) can abolish certain holy days of obligation for their region or transfer them to a Sunday with approval of the Holy See (Canon 1246).

In yet other cases individual bishops, for a reason that serves the spiritual good of the faithful of the diocese, may dispense them from observance of a particular holy day.

Most of the time, these will explain the differences you find. Certain other factors, such as the ethnic background of a particular part of a country or the world, also may affect which feasts are observed as holy days.

Holy day Masses

When a holy day of obligation falls on a Monday, are vigil Masses for that holy day permitted on Sunday? May a person go to Mass twice on Sunday — once for the Sunday, and once for the holy day?

Masses are permitted on the evening before the holy day regardless of the day of the week, if, of course, the bishop has approved such Masses for that diocese.

The character and discipline of our observance of holy days of obligation certainly leaves much to be desired liturgically, particularly when the holy day falls on Saturday or Monday.

The complications over which Mass to attend for which obligation can become almost ludicrously legalistic. According to current church legislation, however, it is possible to do as you say — attend Mass on Sunday morning for your Sunday obligation, and in the evening for the holy day of obligation.

One might also attend the evening Mass on Sunday for the Sunday obligation, and attend Mass the following day for the holy day.

It is certainly more appropriate to attend these respective Masses with the appropriate readings and prayers (Sunday Mass for Sunday, and holy day Mass for the holy day), but this is not actually required for fulfilling the obligation for either Sunday or holy day Masses.

As I mentioned, the bishop of each diocese determines

whether there will be evening Masses in anticipation of Sunday and holy days, and at what time those Masses may be offered.

"Far out" liturgies

I've heard several times about so-called "far out" liturgies. What are these "far out" Masses?

Obviously the phrase isn't a technical one and doesn't appear in any official church documents. So it might mean a lot of things.

For some people, a Mass with guitar music, or with a lady lector or Communion minister, is far out. A large group of Catholics still believe that our new English Mass is itself far out, if not downright heretical, and that the Holy Father has betrayed the church by allowing it.

More commonly, however, "far out" means a liturgy that violates serious regulations of the church concerning the Mass and the sacraments. Church authorities — ultimately, the bishop of each diocese — have the responsibility of seeing to it that a spirit of decency, dignity, and reverence is preserved in all official worship. This doesn't mean that they can arbitrarily impose their own likes and dislikes on everyone else. Nor can they in justice refuse to permit perfectly legitimate varieties in the liturgy, not recognizing that genuine differences in personality, background, and age, ought naturally to be reflected in the way people worship.

It does mean, however, that all — priests, especially — have the responsibility to observe those basic regulations by which the church attempts to keep ceremonies of the worship of God from becoming cheap, tawdry, and sometimes offensive displays.

For example, certain rules exist concerning the dress of the priest and the place for the offering of the Mass. They are intended to be observed in all but the most grave circumstances. Therefore, to offer the Holy Sacrifice in shirt sleeves around the kitchen table would certainly be unlawful, would seem to demonstrate some lack of community consciousness and concern — and by almost every definition would be "far out."

Mass in a private home?

If Communion can be brought to a sick person, why can't Mass be offered for them at home, too? My father is confined to a wheelchair except when he goes to the doctor. Would it be possible for a priest to have Mass in his home sometime? It would mean very much to him and to the rest of us.

More than once during recent years, the church has indicated that bishops may allow Masses outside of churches or chapels — in homes, for example. One of the many different circumstances in which such Masses are explicitly approved is the gathering of family and friends in the homes of the sick or aged who cannot otherwise participate in the Eucharistic Celebration.

Some rather obvious regulations are indicated for such celebrations to preserve the propriety, serenity, and sacred character of the Mass. (See the Instruction for Masses for Special Gatherings, May 15, 1969.)

Home Masses for the sick, and for other gatherings and events, are not uncommon in our country. In most dioceses, Mass may be offered in homes at the discretion of the pastor of the family in whose home the Mass is to be celebrated.

Mass stipends and intentions

During the Mass in our parish, and I believe in other parishes in our area, the priest reads the petitions presented after the gospel. He concludes these petitions with, "and for John or Jane Doe for whom this Mass is being offered."

We as a family look forward to participating in the Sacrifice of the Mass. But when the priest says the Mass is "being offered for John Doe," I wonder, is the principle purpose for the parishioners being there to offer it for John Doe? Would it not be more appropriate for the priest to say, "For John Doe, who is remembered at this Mass"?

Also certain names appear repeatedly in the church bulletin listing Masses for the coming week. One may get the impression that these people are going to get to heaven in a hurry. How about deceased persons who have no one to offer Masses for them?

For well over 1,000 years, Catholic people have had the custom of Mass offerings for the church's ministers and other needs of the Christian community.

Along with this custom, however, the church has carried on an almost continuous struggle to avoid any semblance of commercialism about the Mass, and misunderstandings about the meaning of such offerings.

Language which is at least open to misunderstanding has not been uncommon; the example you give is a good one. Among our primary beliefs about the celebration of the Eucharist is that its reach and intentions are as broad as the first offering of that sacrifice by Jesus on Calvary.

As our Eucharistic Prayers make quite clear, every offering of this sacrifice includes not only the whole church but the whole human family, living and dead. Even should he wish to do so, no priest could narrow down that worldwide embrace as Jesus renews his sacrificial offering in the person of his church on earth.

When a priest accepts a Mass offering he accepts, according to church law and our traditional theology, the responsibility to include that intention in his prayers at Mass. This is the meaning of the church's law which states, "It is lawful for any priest who celebrates or concelebrates Mass to receive an offering to apply the Mass according to a definite intention." (Canon 945)

For this reason, a statement that the Mass is "being offered for" an individual, or to include that name specifically in the prayers for the dead during the Eucharistic Prayer, is generally considered inappropriate since it places undue attention and emphasis on that particular intention rather than on the entire church.

Obviously, therefore, no one "buys" major ownership, as it were, in a particular offering of the Eucharist. If any announcement of the special intention is to take place, perhaps your suggestion is a good one liturgically and theologically, "John or Jane Doe is being remembered at this Mass."

What I have said above should respond to your other question about apparent advantages of the rich over the poor in the celebration of the Eucharist.

Several stipends for Mass?

Is there a church law that forbids two or three intentions at a Mass? I think most people would not object to two or more intentions for a Mass rather than wait two or three years before having the Mass said.

I understand your concern. In fact, every Mass is offered for many intentions, including all the living and all the dead. The Eucharistic Prayer, for example, at each Mass makes that clear.

However, if you're talking about Mass stipends, the present law of the church is clear. Only one stipend or offering may be accepted by a priest for any one Mass.

Canon 948 says, "Separate Masses are to be applied for the intentions for which an individual offering, even if small, has been made and accepted."

In other words, what you are suggesting is, at least lawfully, out of the hands of individual priests. The reason, which is obvious, is to avoid abuse in offering and accepting Mass stipends.

Mass for homosexuals

In a recent issue of our diocesan newspaper, I read that an archbishop celebrated a Mass to mark an anniversary of the local chapter of Dignity, an organization of Catholic homosexuals.

In Romans, St. Paul condemns this kind of lifestyle. Who is right, St. Paul or this bishop?

Bishops (as well as the rest of us) will differ widely in their judgment on the most appropriate and helpful ways to be a true pastor for such groups, who certainly need a particular kind of guidance and spiritual assistance. Bishops must, of course, be concerned to some degree about misunderstandings that may come from their actions, though it is clear that some people will take amiss almost any public apostolic work toward homosexuals and certain other groups.

As the archbishop said, Catholic homosexuals are still

members of the church; as such they need and deserve prayer, direction and support for whatever spiritual conversion is required of them. These needs must be met as generously as possible by their bishops and by other ministers in the church.

Pius V's Mass trampled?

Would you please explain why the Latin (Tridentine) Mass of Pope St. Pius V was not translated into English or other native tongues, rather than trample it underfoot? I understand, and know there was a curse also, that no one could ever change the Mass. If they did they would suffer the curse.

At the Second Vatican Council, the bishops of the world laid down the rules for the revision of the Mass. These requirements are found in the Constitution on the Sacred Liturgy, "Sacrosanctum Concilium."

The revised missal, they said, should be drawn up so that both texts and rites "express more clearly the holy things they signify"; that the several parts of the Mass should be clear as to their nature and purpose, and how they are connected together; that the active participation of the faithful be more easily accomplished; that the "treasure of the Bible be opened up more lavishly so that richer fare may be provided for the faithful at the table of God's word"; and that a rite for concelebration by many priests be incorporated into the new missal.

In other words, just as Pius V saw the need for action in his day, Paul VI, along with the rest of the bishops, felt strongly that the so-called Tridentine Mass lacked too many of these elements to serve well the liturgical and spiritual renewal of modern Catholics.

It is more than a little sad, and a testimony to the shallowness of faith of many Catholics, that the eucharistic altar, the great sign of Catholic unity, should become the stage for belligerence and even rejection of the authority of Jesus in the person of the Holy Father and others who have the responsibility of guidance in the church. The fact that some can even speak of a "curse" for revising the Mass is further evidence that their understanding of the Mass is one step above superstition. It also proves they know nothing of the history of the church or of the liturgy.

When Pius V issued his edition of the Roman Missal, he pleaded that it be an instrument of liturgical unity and a witness to purity of worship in the church. Paul VI did the same when he issued the current one after Vatican II. The "legitimate variations and adaptions" allowed for in the new rite were themselves a basis for hope, he said, that the revisions "will be received by the faithful as a help and witness to the common unity of all."

Every sincere Catholic will do everything possible to make that happen.

Are Latin Masses allowed?

Will you please explain the present ruling of the church concerning Latin Masses? Some priests have told us they are not allowed. A group in a nearby city, however, advertises that they have "the old Latin Mass" every Sunday.

If Latin Masses are possible, why don't more churches have them?

According to present regulations for the celebration of the Eucharist, the language of the Mass should normally be that of the people who are attending, in other words, the local vernacular tongue.

Why don't more churches have Latin Masses using the new eucharistic rite? The answer is simply that the majority of Catholic people just do not seem to be enthused about the idea.

During recent years, numerous parishes have decided to schedule a regular Latin Mass at the request of some Catholics who express a nostalgia about the way things used to be. At first, memories of beautiful Latin chants, hymns and high Masses may attract a fair number of Catholics. In a short time, however, nostalgia wears thin and the people realize that their appreciation of the Mass and the importance of their personal participation has changed and grown considerably since the old days. The limitations of a Eucharistic Liturgy in a foreign language, even in the new rite, appear quite clearly and the Latin Mass experiment is abandoned.

I'm among those who profoundly miss many moving aspects of our liturgical heritage which we are gradually losing (at least for a time) because of our change from the Latin language to the vernacular. The opportunities for a common worship with our fellow Catholics from other countries when the occasions arise, as they do more frequently now than formerly, is another reason for keeping in touch with our Latin liturgical traditions.

I firmly believe, however, that the instincts which guided the bishops at the Vatican Council and which have guided church authorities in liturgical reforms since then are unassailable. Any foreign language, including Latin, simply cannot today be a vehicle for the primary purpose of the Eucharist as the church sees it: to offer the fullest worship to our Heavenly Father and to be the primary expression of our unity with Our Lord, and through him, with each other as his church.

Tridentine Mass on Sunday?

Is it a sin to attend a Tridentine Mass?

I'm not sure what you mean. I don't suppose it's ever a sin to pray or participate in prayer, anywhere or any time, unless the situation would imply some outright contempt for God or the church.

Are you asking: Can one fulfill his or her duty to share in the Sunday Eucharist by attending a Tridentine Mass? That's a whole other question.

First of all, the real Tridentine Mass — the one approved in 1570 by Pope Pius V shortly after the Council of Trent — hasn't been used exactly as he prescribed for nearly 400 years. Just 34 years after it was promulgated, Pope Clement VIII instituted some changes, approving what he said was now the new definitive edition of the missal.

(If anyone printed or sold a missal different from this one, he was to be excommunicated, his press and books confiscated and pay a fine of 500 gold ducats!)

In spite of Clement's warnings, however, his revisions were of course only the first of many approved by later popes.

The last edition of the missal for the Roman rite Mass before Vatican II was published in 1962 incorporating all the previous changes, including those of Popes Pius XII and John XXIII. This missal (and only this one) was the one later approved by the Congregation for Divine Worship for limited use in some circumstances.

When Mass is celebrated from this missal, it must, of course, be totally in Latin, with no mixture of English, as was permitted in later missals.

I go through all this because it affects the answer to your question. Canon law (CCL 1248) provides that one fulfills the duty of participating at Mass on Sundays and holy days by assisting at any Mass celebrated in a "Catholic rite."

The only Catholic Roman rite Masses approved by the church for public worship are those according to the missal approved by Pope Paul VI in 1969, and, under limited and clearly defined conditions, the 1962 missal described above and approved by Pope John XXIII.

Obviously, you cannot be expected to know all this and appraise every Mass before you attend. It is, however, the serious obligation of every priest to celebrate the Eucharist only in accord with rituals officially established and approved by responsible authorities in the body of Christ.

One of the conditions, incidentally, which must be present before a bishop may grant permission for a Mass with the 1962 missal, is that the priest and people who make the petition have no ties with groups which call into doubt the lawful force and doctrinal soundness of the form of the Mass approved by Pope Paul VI in 1969.

This latter form is the one in general use today.

Why was Mass in Latin?

A recent issue of our Catholic paper quoted a cardinal about some of the changes in the church. According to this article, he said that before Vatican Council II "our historical sense was somewhat blunted," giving as one example the lack of awareness that the Mass had not always been celebrated in Latin.

I never thought of this. In what other languages has the Mass been celebrated before the changes we have today?

I agree totally with the cardinal's assessment. Judging from my own experience and from my mail through the years as author of this column, the greatest single reason for rejection and lack of understanding of the current developments in the church is the ignorance of so many Catholics of even a basic knowledge of the past centuries of our history as a church.

Without a sense of history, one easily falls in the trap of assuming that what has been since we were born has always been. As one woman said to me not long ago, protesting our use of English at Mass: "If Latin was good enough for Jesus, why isn't it good enough for us?" The fact that Jesus and most of the early members of our faith quite possibly didn't even know Latin, didn't phase her, if indeed she ever considered it.

To answer your question, the Mass, even before Vatican II, has been celebrated in numerous languages. In the beginning, of course, the language of the liturgy was almost certainly Aramaic, used by Jesus and the disciples and early Christian converts.

Before long, however, the common liturgical language was Greek, the tongue most commonly known in the world before Christianity first spread. Numerous other languages such as Syriac, Arabic and Coptic, one of the few "relic" languages of ancient Egypt, have been and still are used in the Catholic churches of the East.

Apparently during the third century, the Roman church began to adopt Latin as its quasi-official tongue. This was understandable for many reasons. At that time and for nearly the next thousand years, every literate person understood Latin. Civil and church business was conducted in Latin. It was therefore natural that the liturgy should be in Latin.

At the time of the Council of Trent (mid 1500s) and for years after, use of local languages during the liturgy was considered "Protestant." To suggest a greater openness to vernacular languages (as many did at Trent) was to become suspect of disloyalty or heresy.

Even during these centuries, however, many languages — Armenian, Greek, German, Chinese, Mohawk Iroquois in the United States, and others — were officially approved from time to time.

The move to return to local languages for our liturgy developed slowly over the past 100 years or so. The rationale for that development has been explained by recent popes and, in several places, by the bishops of Vatican II. In that council's Constitution on the Sacred Liturgy, the bishops expressed their desire to change those features which may have "crept in which are less harmonious with the intimate nature of the liturgy" or which have grown less functional.

Among these was the language itself. Texts and rites should be restored, they said, "so that they express more clearly the holy things which they signify. Christian people, as far as possible, should be able to understand them with ease, and take part in them fully, actively, as befits a community" (No. 21). Christians always insisted that their liturgical rites be in a language that conveys the reverence and mystery of what we celebrate. Experience proves that this can be accomplished with careful and dignified use of the language of the people.

Latin wasn't a dead language

In your answer about the Mass in Latin, with all your jargon you did not mention the real reason the Mass was in Latin.

No one who presents himself as an authority on the Catholic faith with a question and answer column could possibly be unaware of the fact that the "dead," and therefore unchanging, Latin language was deliberately adopted so the church's dogma would be uniformly interpreted around the world; so that the words of Christ would remain free from the vagaries of local semantic influence and trendy philosophical interpretation. You know this. It demands further response.

I don't know where you received your information, but it is grossly inaccurate. As I explained above, in the very early centuries of the church, the typical language for liturgical and certain other Christian usage and activities was Greek. As the church, particularly in Europe, became more involved and even identified with Roman, and therefore Latin, culture, Christian authorities gradually realized that to continue Greek as the "official" language of the church would be to lose effective touch with people for whom Greek was more and more a foreign language.

In the West, as distinct from the Eastern or Oriental churches, almost anyone who could read and write at all knew Latin. It was the language of commerce and most social intercourse.

This is why, in the fourth century, perhaps most significantly under the influence of Pope Damasus, Latin gradually became the language most commonly used by the church, even in the liturgy. With the dissolution of the Roman Empire in the fifth century and later, local cultures and languages in both southern and northern Europe began to predominate until eventually Latin itself became a dead language.

How and why it continued to be the official language of the church in most of the Western world until our own century is another story. It is well worth remembering, however, that Latin became the "Catholic" language not because it was dead, but because it was one people could understand.

Why is priest "presider"?

Recently, prior to the beginning of Mass, I've been hearing an announcement which conveys that Father Doe is the "presider for the Mass," rather than the customary "celebrant of the Mass."

In the lexicon of the church, are these two phrases synonymous, or is the sacramental priesthood being confused with the priesthood of the people?

The designation of the priest as presider or presiding priest is used for at least two good reasons which tie closely together. First, the priest is not the only celebrant of the Eucharist. It is quite proper, and in fact necessary if we are to remain faithful to Christian tradition, to say that the entire community gathered around the altar in faith is celebrating that faith by hearing God's Word and by offering the Eucharist.

This reality is made clear countless times in the liturgy, especially in the eucharistic prayers. The first eucharistic prayer (the so-called Roman Canon, which was the only one used for some centuries before Vatican II), for example, makes abundantly clear that while the priest is doing the speaking, he is acting and speaking for all.

"All of us gathered here before you . . . offer you this sacrifice of praise," it says.

"Father, accept this offering from your whole family," it repeats later.

And, "We, your people and your ministers . . . offer to you, God of glory and majesty, this holy and perfect sacrifice."

Second, therefore, the priest is appropriately and accurately described as the presider at the celebration, the one who, as the dictionary says, occupies the place of leader and directs the proceedings.

The General Instruction of the Roman Missal makes clear that this is precisely what the priest was ordained to do. "Within the community of the faithful a presbyter also possesses the power of orders to offer sacrifice in the person of Christ. He presides over the assembly and leads its prayer, proclaims the message of salvation, leads the people in offering sacrifice through Christ in the Spirit to the Father, gives them the bread of eternal life and shares it with them.

"At the Eucharist, he should serve God and the people with dignity and humility. By his actions and by his proclamations of the word he should impress upon the people the living presence of Christ" (No. 60).

In the liturgy and theology of the church, the sacrament of orders gives the priest a leading and indispensable role in the celebration of the Eucharist. In fulfilling that role, however, he is not doing something for the community, as the word celebrant might seem to indicate.

He is doing something with that community, of which, before he is a priest, he is also a member through baptism.

Thus, while there is nothing wrong with the word celebrant as long as it is properly understood, designating him as the presiding priest describes much more accurately and fully his true role in the eucharistic liturgy.

A 'new Mass'?

We were taught that nothing could be introduced after the death of the last apostle. How can there be a "new Mass"?

I cannot believe you were taught that nothing new could be introduced after the death of the last apostle. If that were true we would still be offering the Eucharist — or "hearing Mass," if you wish — in Greek or Hebrew with everyone sitting, or more probably standing, around the dining room table.

Since the church is not a museum, but the living, breathing body of Christ, it has changed much. Many of our beliefs and practices developed and changed in varying degrees over the past 2,000 years.

The same is true with the Mass. It has undergone hundreds of changes through the centuries. The form of the Mass most of us older Catholics grew up with was simply one of the many the church has experienced throughout its life.

Our present ritual is, therefore, only one in a long series of "new Masses" in the church's history, though it has many more similarities to the "old Mass" of the early Christians than any other format the Mass has enjoyed during the last 1,000 years.

Masses for the dead

When someone dies and has received all the rites of the church, and we know that he or she has led a good Christian life, what do you think of having Masses offered for the deceased? If we believe in God's mercy and love, do you think that year after year we should continue to offer and have Masses said for them?

There are many reasons why Masses may be offered for a deceased person. First, as all prayer, the intention may be to ask God's blessing and grace on that person during his or her life. Strange as it sounds, we know that God is not bound by the limits of time. Past, present and future are all now to him. And we can put ourselves in that sphere of reference of eternity in our prayers.

The church in fact does this all the time; in the funeral liturgy, for example, and in some anniversary liturgies years after the individual is deceased, the prayers ask God to give that individual the blessing of a holy and peaceful death.

Another reason is that, as long Christian tradition teaches, our prayers and other good works can truly help those who have died in any satisfaction for sin that may be due. Exactly how this works out in God's providence we naturally do not know. But it is still valid and solid Catholic belief.

Finally — and this is far more common than we might think — our Masses and prayers can simply express thanks and praise to God for the life of a person we have loved and still love. I know many men and women who firmly believe their loved ones are in heaven and who may even pray to them as among the saints of God, but they still have Masses offered for them. Obviously, these Masses are simply expressions of their faith and hope — a part of their remembering, and of their joy over the happiness of someone they love.

"Privileged" funerals and weddings?

I've been to many Catholic funerals and weddings. Frankly, I am mystified often by the differing numbers of priests attending such events. At certain ones many priests are present; at others not even the pastor is there to officiate. How do you explain this different kind of treatment for different people?

As pastor of a fairly large parish, I am sensitive to the concerns you bring up. I know that no matter how simple and often obvious the answer, misunderstandings inevitably arise and rash judgments too often result.

Usually, the answer is quite obvious when one knows the background of the individuals involved. With almost no exceptions, the explanation is simply that the individual has worked (often in a very quiet way) in agencies or institutions that would involve contact with many priests. Or it may be that the family itself includes some priests, or just close friends who are priests.

Many such details would, of course, not be familiar to persons who do not know the family intimately.

As for which priest performs a wedding or funeral, in most parishes, I believe, that depends simply on which priests are free to do so, and who is able to work best with the family in making arrangements for the wedding or funeral. I have always found people thoroughly understanding and thoughtful in such situations.

Mentally handicapped at Mass?

Often when I attend our parish Mass a group of mentally handicapped teen-agers is present with a person in charge. Why do these poor people have to attend Mass? Surely they do not understand what is going on and are not interested in being at church.

Do they have the obligation to attend Sunday Mass?

In my opinion you vastly underestimate the ability of many mentally handicapped people to understand and participate in the liturgy, or other activities for that matter.

A group from our local association for retarded citizens regularly attends Mass in our parish. In addition, I frequently celebrate Mass myself with a number of mentally and physically handicapped children and adults. My experience is that, while their intellectual grasp might not equal that of others, their joy, their awareness of the presence and love of God and their simple human warmth are unmistakable.

True, much of this results from the unusual degree of tenderness and care given them by their parents and family, and from the love of the many remarkable people who volunteer to help them. But it's real nonetheless.

Such children probably would be excused from Sunday Mass. By no means does it follow, however, that they cannot receive much from, and offer much to, those who celebrate the Eucharist with them.

Must priest offer Mass?

At our parish there are five Masses on Sundays and three

priests in the parish. How many Masses is a priest allowed to say in one day?

Also, isn't it a rule that a priest must say Mass every day?

According to general church law, priests are allowed to offer no more than one Mass each day, though bishops can permit them to offer two Masses on special feasts and Sundays when necessary.

The basic principle in all such matters is that the reasonable needs of the people must be met, especially where Mass and the sacraments are concerned. Thus it is not at all uncommon for priests to offer two Masses on weekdays — for example, when a funeral Mass must be added to the daily Mass schedule.

Many priests also must frequently offer three Masses on Sundays to fulfill a minimum schedule of Masses in a parish church. Priests properly avoid this as much as possible but sometimes, in light of the disproportionately small number of priests available in a given parish, it must be done if the priests wish to give appropriate service to the people.

The church has no strict law about when a priest is required to offer Mass, but certainly urges very frequent celebration of the Eucharist. Canon law says, "Remembering that the work of redemption is continually accomplished in the mystery of the Eucharistic Sacrifice, priests are to celebrate frequently; indeed daily celebration is strongly recommended, since even if the faithful cannot be present, it is the act of Christ and the Church in which priests fulfill their principal function." (CCL 904) Obviously, in fulfilling his responsibilities to the people of his congregation, any priest in a parish will celebrate the Eucharist almost every day, under normal circumstances.

Candles at Mass

We have been involved several times in arrangements for Mass in church and elsewhere. I know at one time the candles used in the liturgy were to be blessed and contain at least 51 percent beeswax. I understand this is no longer true, but a priest I asked said he wasn't sure. May candles used at Mass

be of other materials? And how many should there be at Mass?

The General Instruction of the Roman Missal, found in the front of the official Sacramentary ("missal"), contains the basic instructions for the celebration of the Eucharist.

These regulations simply state that candles are required "to express devotion or degree of festivity." The candles may be placed on the altar or around it in such a way, however, that they do not block the view of what is happening on the altar. (no. 269)

There are no specific regulations, therefore, about the content or number of candles. These should be appropriate to the solemnity of the celebration and the design of the sanctuary area.

Chalice

Is it true that the chalice at Mass doesn't have to be gold or gold plated any more?

Until recently, the rule was that at least the inside of chalices and other vessels used to hold the consecrated wine and hosts at Mass had to be gold plated.

According to present regulations, such sacred vessels should be of some material which would be considered locally as having some value and appropriate for sacred use. Ebony or other hard woods are mentioned as examples of appropriate material.

Incidentally, the regulations as to the shape of the vessels are broader also. It is required only that they have a form that is in keeping with the local culture and with their purpose in the liturgy.

Unconsecrated chalice at Mass?

Recently a priest offered Mass in the home of a friend. The friend wanted the priest to use a cup that belongs to their family as a chalice, but the priest refused. He explained he could use only a consecrated chalice. I thought this rule had been changed. Has it?

There are some changes in the rules about chalices, but the priest was correct. Only blessed chalices should be used for offering the Eucharistic Sacrifice. The reasons for this are clear; anything used this intimately in the Eucharist should be reverently cared for and not be put to common use.

It is true that now chalices probably become "blessed" simply by being used for the offering of the Eucharist. But once they are so used, they should remain set apart for that purpose thereafter. The intention to devote a chalice and/or paten exclusively to the celebration of the Eucharist is expressed by a special blessing by a bishop or priest during or outside of Mass. (See the *Rite for the Dedication of a Church and Altar*, 1977.)

If the occasion arises again, and if the cup meets the necessary qualifications, perhaps your friends would be willing to give the vessel to the priest or to the parish church to be used as a chalice.

Bread for the Eucharist

What is the church's canonical position on bread to be used for the celebration of the Eucharist in the Latin Rite? Are you aware of any suitable and acceptable recipe for homemade altar bread other than the traditional hosts?

Also, if you would, what are the sources for this information? I believe that not only I, but many other Catholics will be helped by knowing where we are on this.

I cannot respond to your question honestly or intelligently without first explaining that we have two seemingly contradictory sets of regulations for eucharistic bread.

Our church has insisted increasingly during recent decades on the vital importance of signs in the celebration of the liturgy, especially the other sacraments and the Eucharist. These signs — oil, water, bread, wine, gestures, words — are of the essence of the sacraments and should reflect as fully and genuinely as possible the reality they purport to be. Dirty water or gummy oil, while perhaps valid for the sacraments, is grossly inappropriate.

Thus, speaking of the Eucharist, the church has insisted

that the bread for the Eucharistic Celebration "appear as actual food" (General Instruction on the Roman Missal, no. 283). In other words it should look and taste like bread people really use.

On the other hand, the tradition of the Latin Rite, at least for many centuries, and the present regulations of the church indicate that no other ingredients are to be added to the wheat flour and water in the making of the bread.

To my knowledge, and I've had much correspondence about this in recent years, I know of no one who has been able to make bread that way, have it come out looking more like recognizable bread than our customary hosts, and still be serviceable for Communion use.

One is reminded of the little boy who was asked if he believed that the bread had become the body of Christ. He replied, "I believe it is the body of Christ, but I don't believe it was bread."

Early in 1978 the American Bishops' Committee on the Liturgy presented a canonical position paper to the appropriate congregation in Rome searching for some leeway by which unleavened bread could be prepared with a few additives that would make it appear more like real bread.

The following year Cardinal Francis Seper, the late prefect of the Congregation for the Doctrine of the Faith, responded that "it would not be appropriate to accept the suggestions" of the paper for some additions to the material for eucharistic bread.

On May 23, 1980, an instruction by another Vatican office (the Congregation for Sacraments and Diving Worship) repeated basically the same instructions. Thus, these regulations presently govern the Latin Rite Church in the preparation of eucharistic bread.

As you imply in your question, quite different regulations apply to the Eastern Rite Churches.

A final note: The communications from the Vatican congregations, particularly the letter from Cardinal Seper, speak only of "lawfulness and desirability" of different bread materials.

Bread with additions to the wheat and water, therefore, would be valid but not lawful for eucharistic bread.

Are altar stones still required?

A parish in our city recently built a new church. Formerly each altar where the Holy Sacrifice of the Mass was offered had to have an altar stone with the relics of one of the saints. But we noticed this otherwise beautiful altar did not have one. Are such relics required anymore? If not, why not?

No, altar stones with relics are no longer required. In fact, unless understood correctly, they are not even permitted.

In the early church, the Eucharistic Sacrifice was often offered over the tombs of the martyrs since they were in a special way witnesses to Jesus Christ by their willingness to die for him. Later the practice developed of having a martyr's body, or part of it, placed in the table of every altar as a continuation and reminder of that tradition.

As time went on — and the architecture of churches and altars became more imaginative — the altar began to lose its identity as "the table of the Lord." It sometimes seemed to become overpowered below statues of angels and saints or other structures.

We don't need to get any more detailed about that trend, but the church clearly, in its present reform of the liturgy, is trying in every possible way to make the altar table the central and prominent feature of a church building, as it should be. The Introduction to the Rite for the Dedication of an Altar (promulgated on the authority of Pope Paul VI in 1977), requires that the altar be constructed away from the wall so the priest can easily walk around it, and that it be in a central location where it will draw the attention of the whole congregation. In any new church, statues, pictures of saints or relics may not be placed on or over the altar.

In other words, the altar is dedicated to God, and the meaning of the practice of dedicating altars to God in honor of the saints must be made clear to the people with this in mind.

The Instruction provides for a continuation of the tradition of placing relics of martyrs or other saints "in" the altar, but only under the following conditions:

1. Relics intended for such placement must be of such a size that they can be recognized as parts of human bodies.

Tiny relics of one or more saints should not be used.

2. Great care must be taken to be sure the relics are authentic. It is better for an altar to be dedicated without relics, than to have relics of doubtful credibility.

3. A reliquary must not be placed on the altar, or in the table of the altar (as altar stones used to be placed in a niche in the table of the altar). It must be placed beneath the altar, as the design of the altar might allow.

The Code of Canon Law (CCL no. 1237) provides that such depositing of relics should be reserved to fixed altars, that is, altars which are attached to the floor so they cannot be moved.

Requirements for liturgical music

The priests in our parish have begun to ask us not to sing or play some music we have used for years. They say it isn't liturgical. It seems to me that if we have done it and it makes people happy, there's nothing wrong with it. How can priests act this way? Is there anything we can do?

The size of a really adequate answer to your question would be staggering, far beyond the scope of this column. Your concern is far too important, however, not to respond to at least in some way.

My first reaction to your letter (which was considerably longer then the part I quoted) is that your parish is lucky to have the priests you describe. While individual judgment always enters into music, it sounds as if they know what they're doing.

The fact that a musical composition sounds passable and that it makes people — choir or congregation — happy, does not by itself make it sacred music. As Pope John Paul said two years ago, "It cannot be said that all music becomes sacred from the fact and at the moment in which it is inserted into the liturgy."

The church has very explicit and clear criteria on what music may be used in liturgy, and also how it should be used. These criteria appear in our own time in the section on sacred music (Chapter 6) of the Constitution on the Liturgy of Vatican Council II, and in numerous documents by the U.S. bishops and others.

Briefly, any music must meet three tests before it may be used in the Eucharist or other official liturgies.

1. The first is artistic: it should be basically good music, in both composition and performance.

In my judgment, of the three tests this is the one most offended against in many parishes. Whether traditional or modern, organ or guitar, choir or folk-group, music does not become appropriate for the liturgy simply because the notes hang together and the composer or performers have a well-intentioned heart.

2. Second, music must be liturgically correct. That means, among other things, that the music must fit the liturgical seasons and feasts and must give opportunity for the whole congregation to participate in those parts of the Mass which are theirs.

A solo "Our Father," for example, or a response to the Preface ("Holy, Holy, Holy") sung by a folk group alone, would offend against this requirement.

3. Third, the music must be pastorally appropriate. That doesn't mean it has to be something the pastor likes, but that it be music which will help this particular congregation at this particular time pray and worship God well together.

Lots of concerns enter here: the musical experience and proficiency of the people; the economic, social and family cares they bring to that celebration of the Eucharist, and so on.

Obviously, few parishes measure up fully to all of these requirements all or even most of the time. But as St. Augustine once remarked about liturgical music (1,600 years ago — it's no new problem): "Do not allow yourselves to be offended by the imperfect while you strive for the perfect."

What can you do? If you're serious about your interest, get a copy of the booklet, "Music in Catholic Worship," by the American Bishops' Committee on the Liturgy. A good study of this very readable document is a bare minimum for any competent Catholic musician or music director.

It's available from USCC Publications, 1312 Massachusetts Ave., N.W., Washington, D.C., 20005.

Keep familiar songs in liturgy

Perhaps you'd comment about how we are subjected to so many new songs in church during the year. The amount is unreal. We hardly have learned one when another comes along. We're senior citizens and like to sing, but seldom will they keep a song around long enough to do it well and enjoy it.

What happened to the old policy of repeating songs that we learn? We know the melody, we know the words, and we can enjoy them.

Your feelings are, I'm sure, shared by a multitude of others and they deserve to be seriously considered.

Two fatal dangers lurk in any liturgy planning. One is to have everything always new, the other is to have everything always old. Real liturgy, whether it is family, patriotic or religious, always has a core that remains the same. An individual family may have its own traditional and consistent manner, for example, of celebrating birthdays. In the Mass we have a basic core of actions and words that we call the Liturgies of the Word and Eucharist.

Even outside that core, however, there needs to be a degree of continuity and familiarity, or as you say, enjoyment. Some ability to be comfortable and free in singing chants or hymns is absolutely essential for genuine individual and community worship. I believe most mistakes and frustrations with our liturgical worship are caused by forgetting that truth.

The other kind of error, always having everything the same, can be just as disastrous to active and intelligent prayer. Even within a good and healthy family birthday "liturgy," the celebrant still may choose the meal or the color of the cake.

Well-prepared and musically decent new hymns, used long enough for people to come to enjoy praying with them, are also essential for any community that wants a living liturgy. Obviously there can be no strict rules about this. So much depends on the nature of the worshiping community. Its age and culture, even its understanding of and commitment to good liturgy, all enter the picture.

What is essential is that everyone be sensitive to both sides of the scale. If you feel one or other of these considerations is lacking in your community, you have every right to surface your concern and request whatever insights might be offered by those responsible for the liturgies and other services in your parish.

When to kneel or stand?

Our parish is quite traditional. Recently we visited another parish where the congregation only stood or sat. There was no kneeling during the entire Mass. This upset me. There seems to be no humility while standing during every part of the Mass. What is the right thing to do?

The regulations of the church on this subject are simple. Generally, people are to stand from the prayer over the gifts (said by the priest just before the preface of the Eucharistic Prayer) to the end of Mass. Exceptions are that they should sit after Communion if there is a time of meditation, and they should "kneel at the consecration unless prevented by lack of space, large numbers or other reasonable cause" (General Instruction of the Roman Missal, 21). In 1969 the American bishops adapted this ruling for the United States, providing that people should kneel from after the Sanctus (Holy, holy, holy) acclamation until after the Amen at the end of the Eucharistic Prayer (Appendix to the General Instruction, 21).

It may help your blood pressure if you remember that many liturgical practices, even those which we often consider absolutely essential, differ immensely from time to time, and even more from place to place. For many centuries Christians never knelt at Mass. When larger churches and basilicas were built, standing was the normal posture through the entire Mass. In fact, in Rome and other ancient and modern cities, numerous Christian churches still do not have seats, let alone kneelers.

Even to this day, all four major Eucharistic Prayers refer to the people as "standing" around the altar (using the Latin "circumstantes," those standing around; or the verb "astare," to stand near). I don't wish to demean the idea or practice of kneeling at Mass, but it's worthwhile to keep things in perspective.

Even in the Western world, kneeling and genuflecting have

been part of the Mass for only a few hundred years. Before that, kneeling was primarily a sign of penance and contrition. During one period of the church's history it was forbidden to kneel during Mass, and standing was obligatory on Sundays and during the Easter season. As the missal says, "A common posture observed by all is a sign of the unity of the assembly and its sense of community. It expresses and fosters the inner spirit and purpose of those who take part in it" (General Instruction on the Roman Missal, 20).

Cultural customs and traditions can never be ignored. The church's general practice and the American bishops honor those traditions in attempting to preserve that "sense of community" in action. But the history of cultures and of our church proves that in itself one posture is not necessarily better or more reverent or humbler than another.

Bow or genuflect?

A couple of times recently, I have seen people — in one case, a priest — bow toward the altar and the Blessed Sacrament instead of genuflecting. Can you tell me why they do this? Shouldn't we genuflect if we really believe in the presence of Jesus in the Blessed Sacrament?

Genuflection — bending one or both knees as an act of reverence — happens to be the act of reverence Catholics of our time and country are most accustomed to, but a profound and devout bow can be just as reverent. Until perhaps 300 years ago, bowing was the common way of showing reverence to the Eucharist, or to the crucifix. It was considered quite proper, in fact, for young girls to curtsey to the Blessed Sacrament.

Our practice of genuflection derives mainly from practices of imperial Rome and the later courts of Europe.

Entrance procession exalts priest?

At a recent meeting one of our liturgy leaders stated she would like to do away with the entrance procession at weekend Masses. She thinks it makes the priest look like an emperor and appear better than everyone else.

She would like the priest to sit somewhere in church and just walk up and start Mass. She has seen this done somewhere and liked the way it looked. I have checked all liturgy documents I can find and do not see this mentioned as an option. I think most people feel the entrance procession gives dignity that the liturgy should have. Can you tell me if it is permissible?

I too have seen what you describe. In my view, however, it entirely misses the real purpose of the entrance procession and song in our liturgy. This same misunderstanding is reflected in the opening instructions one still occasionally hears from cantors: Let's stand and greet our celebrant as we sing hymn 91, "How Great Thou Art." The procession and song are not to greet or honor the celebrant, however great he may be, but to further unite the minds and hearts of the assembly and begin their community worship of God. Having ministers simply pop up to perform their liturgical functions misses a golden opportunity (if the entrance rite is done well, of course) to add dignity and focus to what is about to take place.

These are not simply my ideas; it is the ancient understanding of the entrance rite reflected in many present liturgical documents. Our major guide to the celebration of Mass puts it as well as any. After the people have assembled, it says, the entrance song begins and the priests and ministers come in. "The purpose of this song is to open the celebration, deepen the unity of the people, introduce them to the mystery of the seasonal feast and accompany the procession" (General Instruction of the Roman Missal, 25).

I really need to say something about another facet of your question. Of course the priest is no better than anyone else. But as you say, most people knowledgeable in their faith are aware that the ordained priest is not merely one who happens to walk up and start Mass. He has a unique function as leader of the community's eucharistic worship. As one who is sacramentally designated to act in the name of Christ and his body, the church, the priest has as his primary duty the proclamation of the Gospel of God to everyone (Vatican II, Decree on the Ministry of Priests, 4). Priests "exercise this sacred function of Christ (announcing the divine Word to all) most of all in the eucharistic liturgy" (Constitution on the Church, 28; Decree on Priests, 13).

This is not the time to prolong that point, but I believe we badly need to avoid falling into a trap here. Some priests today seem to feel that they exalt themselves by belittling the non-ordained, especially lay people — the "you can't do what I can do or be where I can be" syndrome. In the other direction, however, one finds some lay people who apparently feel that minimizing the role and ministry of the ordained is somehow a path to "equal status."

It seems to me that this is at very least not helpful. As we struggle to recognize and utilize more perfectly the gifts of each of us, our common dignity and equality before the heavenly Father is too well affirmed and proven by our faith for us to allow ourselves to resort to such tactics.

Why does priest kiss the altar?

We have a question about kissing the altar. Why is this done by the priest? Some do it after the last blessing at Mass and some do not. Is there some reason?

For us Catholics the altar is not only a piece of furniture. It is loaded with all kinds of precious symbolism.

Along with the pulpit, where the Word of God is proclaimed, it is the focal point of our meeting with God the Father in and through Jesus Christ. If the liturgy of the Eucharist is the central event which brings us to the Father "through him (Christ), with him and in him," the altar around which this happens holds for us a place of primary honor and dignity.

The General Instruction of the Roman Missal explains: "The altar, where the sacrifice of the cross is made present under sacramental signs, is also the table of the Lord. The people of God is called together to share in this table. Thus the altar is the center of the thanksgiving accomplished in the Eucharist."

The church extends this thought even further by referring to the altar not only as the place of renewing the sacrifice of Jesus, but as Jesus himself. He is the "altar" in which the sacrifice of the new covenant took place, and in whom that sacrifice is continually reoffered until the end of time.

The fifth Easter preface to the Eucharistic Prayer proclaims, "As he gave himself into your (the Father's) hands for our salvation, he showed himself to be the priest, the altar and the lamb of sacrifice."

This is why the church sees the altar (not the crucifix, or even the tabernacle to reserve the Blessed Sacrament, which should be apart from the altar) as the central and focal point of those buildings where we gather to celebrate the Eucharist.

It is also why tradition has called for the bishop, priest and deacon to venerate the altar, usually with a kiss, at the start of each Mass.

Instructions for the Mass are clear about the priest and other ordained ministers kissing the altar at the beginning of the eucharistic celebration, as they enter the altar area. (General Instruction of the Roman Missal, Nos. 27 and 85)

As for the end of Mass, kissing the altar is either not mentioned at all (No. 57) or is called for "ordinarily" (No. 141). Obviously the priest is given leeway here, depending on circumstances.

Reverence for Gospel

Just before the reading of the Gospel at Mass, the priest touches his head, his mouth and his breast. Then most of the people do the same. What does this mean?

The priest and people are (or should be) making a small sign of the cross on their forehead, their lips and breast. The action is a prayer that the Good News of the Lord which they are about to hear may be always in their minds, on their lips and in their hearts.

Sing the Alleluia

Recently I began working with a liturgy planning group in our parish. We need information about the Alleluia. Some feel it should never be used unless it is sung at Mass. Others say it is better to say it than not have it at all.

A book called the Lectionary is the official ritual of the church for the Liturgy of the Word at Mass. It contains the Scripture readings and provides for those parts of the Mass related to these readings. According to the Lectionary, "the Alleluia or the verse before the Gospel must be sung, and during it all stand. It is not sung by the cantor who intones it or by the choir, but by the whole congregation together" (no. 23). Other liturgical documents, for example the decree of the Congregation for Divine Worship governing chant at Mass (1972, No. 7) always assume that the Alleluia is sung. The instruction of our American bishops' Committee on the Liturgy, "Music in Catholic Worship," says, "If not sung, the Alleluia should be omitted" (no. 55).

The reason for emphasis on singing the Alleluia is twofold. First, the dignity and reverence due the proclaiming of the Gospel calls for special attention. This is also why incense and lighted candles are often used at the Gospel book at that time. In addition, the word "alleluia," which loosely translated means "praise to Yahweh," is the great acclamation of joy and praise to God in both the Old and New Testaments. Reciting the Alleluia would be the liturgical equivalent of reciting instead of singing "Happy Birthday to You" at a birthday party.

Holding hands at Our Father

At some of our Masses we have held hands during the Our Father. Now someone tells us this was forbidden several years ago. Is this true?

Not to my knowledge. In 1975 the Sacred Congregation for Divine Worship was asked whether the congregation might hold hands during the Lord's Prayer instead of offering the Sign of Peace. The answer was a strong no. "The Sign of Peace is filled with meaning, graciousness and Christian inspiration," it said. "Any substitution for it must be repudiated." A concern was implied that this liturgical gesture of joining hands is not in the rubrics of the Mass. But the question and answer was directed at considering the practice a replacement for the Sign of Peace (Notitiae 11, 1975, 226).

Hear or read Scripture?

Our parish has booklets for people to use at Mass. Until recently our booklets had the readings from the Bible that are read in Sunday Mass. Now they do not.

For those of us who were raised with the notion that the ideal was to use a missal and follow the priest at Mass, it certainly is puzzling when we're told we should not be reading at Mass, even the readings from the Bible.

The main reason for our puzzlement is that we have forgotten that *hearing* the Word of God is a liturgical act, an act of public worship. When the Mass was in Latin, meaningful hearing of the Word was, of course, impossible. So after English translations of the Mass became permissible around the beginning of this century, we fell back on following what the priest was saying by reading the English version.

When the lector (reader or priest) proclaims the Word of God at the celebration of Mass, he performs an act of worship; and we perform an act of worship with him by *listening* attentively and prayerfully to that Word. Thus, the church's directives discourage whenever possible the printing of the Scripture texts in Mass booklets.

Obviously, this doesn't mean that private reading of Scripture is unimportant or discouraged. It's simply that the solemn proclaiming of the Word during Mass is not the place for it.

In fairness, I believe two things should be provided before the Scripture texts are taken out of the hands of the worshipers. First, the church ought to have a decent and adequate public address system. Second, the lectors should be trained to read the Scriptures clearly and intelligently so they can be easily understood. Until these two qualifications are met, it's probably better to have the printed texts in hand. But even then we should try to wean ourselves away from reading to listening whenever we can.

Can women be lectors?

Is it true that women are now allowed to be lectors (readers) at Mass? If so, why are there so many churches where only men have this privilege? We are in a small parish and have

some women lectors. Visitors from other places, however, sometimes tell us that they do not like the idea, and that only men are allowed in the sanctuary.

According to present liturgical regulations, except for functions reserved to priests and deacons, women have almost the same right to liturgical ministry as do men. This includes leading the singing, directing liturgical participation, acting as commentator, reading Scripture, and serving as special ministers of the Eucharist. One exception is actual assistance at the altar as a server.

By decree of the Congregation on Divine Worship, only those qualifications may be required of women as are required of men — worthiness of life, and so on. The same decree also requires that when women do read the Scripture, they do so where the other readings are proclaimed so that a single place is reserved for all biblical readings. In other words, it is no longer stipulated, as it once was, that women remain outside the sanctuary. Whatever a woman does, she should do in the most appropriate place.

The American bishops emphasized the same thing in a 1971 statement on the liturgy: "In the liturgical celebration, as in other facets of the church's life, there should be no discrimination or apparent discrimination against women."

The exercise of the ministry of reader by women is provided for in the present Order of the Mass (1969), the Instruction of the Congregation for Divine Worship of 1970, and the above-mentioned liturgical instructions issued by the American Bishops' Committee on the Liturgy in 1971 — among numerous other documents.

Sign of the Cross

Very few priests begin or end the homily with the Sign of the Cross. As I remember it used to be done all the time. Any reasons for the change?

This may appear a trivial question to some, but there's a reason for whatever change has taken place that might help our appreciation of that part of the Mass.

Often in recent decades and centuries, the sermon was considered a separate kind of oration or instruction inserted in the middle of the Mass. Too frequently, it even had nothing to do with the Scripture readings of the day.

Today the church emphasizes the continuity that should be evident between the readings, the Creed or Prayer of the Faithful, and the Eucharistic Prayer. Anything that does not reflect that continuity — such as the Sign of the Cross or other words which would indicate that something new is now going to begin — is discouraged.

The Sign of the Cross by which the celebrant begins the Mass and proclaims that it is for the honor of the Trinity covers the entire celebration, including the homily.

Difficulties with homilies

How does one tell a Catholic priest his homilies are as boring as hades? Does an adult congregation have to be told that an Epistle to the Phillippians was written to the people of Philippi?

For attention-getters do we have to be shown an apple or a banana? On various Sundays we have had a man's hat, a flashlight, a picture of a lamb "who also looks like a victim," and U.S. currency ("money to burn").

I'd like to bet $10 that for most priests who read this, the first gut reaction will be: You're damned if you do, and damned if you don't.

I realize what you're saying, having been subjected myself to some awfully condescending and childish talks in my life. But with all the wailing about the quality of unprepared homilies today, I think you have to at least give your priest credit for trying.

As a parish priest who wants to meet the minds and hearts of a whole rainbow of people on Sunday mornings, I can assure you that any priest who exercises the time and ingenuity on his homilies that yours does would welcome greatly whatever critiques and suggestions you might offer.

I and most other priests, I believe, deeply appreciate such reactions from our parishioners. Feedback on his homilies is one of the things a priest needs most and receives least. Sometimes it is difficult to implement these suggestions for one reason or another, but we're grateful for them anyway.

So tell the priest how you feel. He may or may not be able to do anything about it, but I bet he thanks you.

Is Creed necessary?

A young priest who has been in our area for about five years never says the Profession of Faith, neither the Apostles' nor the Nicene Creed. I have asked him why he does not do this, even on Sunday, and he says the Creed is reserved for special occasions. However, it is not used even on Christmas or Easter.

As a Catholic I feel I have not fulfilled my Sunday obligation if I have not attended a complete Mass. Could you please explain the policy concerning the Creed.

The presence of a Creed does not determine the validity of one's participation in the Eucharist. The praying of the Profession of Faith is not an essential part of the Mass on Sunday or any other time.

The official instructions for the Mass, however, provide that the Creed be recited by the priest and people at least on all Sundays and special feasts. There is no liturgical basis whatsoever for neglecting that part of the Mass on a regular basis.

"Maker" or "creator"?

What is the reason for changing the word "creator" to "maker" in our Profession of Faith at Mass? The word "maker" has a downgrading and untrue implication of the beginning of the world. Why the change in the Nicene Creed?

The change was made because the word "maker" is a more exact translation of the Nicene Creed, both in the original Greek and in the Latin versions.

The creed which resulted mainly from the first ecumenical council which took place at Nicaea in Asia Minor, uses the Greek word "poietes." The usual Latin translation of that is "factor." Both words literally mean maker rather than creator.

As long as we're on the subject, this same reason explains some changes in the wording of several parts of the Mass during the past 20 or 30 years. The new wording is simply a more exact translation.

I get some questions, for example, asking why in the same creed we now say "we believe" when the Latin of the so-called old Mass said "credo," I believe.

The reason is that the most authentic texts of the Council of Nicaea use the plural both in Greek and in Latin for that verb. "We believe" is a more correct translation, therefore, than "I believe."

"The Spirit, the Lord"

In the Creed at Mass, why do we say we believe in "the Spirit, the Lord?" What is the significance of this, since that title is always reserved for Christ? Are there other creeds or liturgical books where the Spirit is called Lord?

In the church's tradition, the title "Lord" (in Greek, "Kyrios") does most often refer to Jesus, but not always. Christ enjoys that title most appropriately as the God-Man, the unique mediator between God and creation, and therefore Lord of the world.

The title has also been used for the Holy Spirit, however, since he shares in the divine nature of the Father and Son, and therefore in all the prerogatives and attributes they have as God.

The church in the East (Constantinople), with its heavily Spirit-oriented mysticism, speaks of the Spirit as Kyrios more than does the West (Rome), and usually relates this title to the Third Person's work as Giver and Generator of life. Some early Eastern forms of the Apostles' Creed, as well as the Creed of Nicaea we use at Mass, illustrate this tradition.

The reference to the Holy Spirit as Lord was not in the original Creed of the Council of Nicaea; it was added by the Council of Constantinople half a century later.

Jesus' words at Mass?

The words of consecration in our "new" Mass are different than they were in my English missal in the old Mass. How

can this be? Isn't the Consecration supposed to contain the words that Christ used at the Last Supper?

Jesus obviously never spoke English, so any words we have can be only a translation, an effort to put the meaning of what he said into another language.

If you look at the Gospels, and at St. Paul's description of the Last Supper in the Letter to the Corinthians, you will find that even they differ in the words they ascribe to Jesus in the institution of the Eucharist. The reason is that the exact words of Jesus were not that important to the writers of the Gospel, who probably reflected the words used in the Eucharistic Liturgy at the time and place that particular part of the New Testament was written.

It's the same today. In the Eucharistic Prayer, which, as the name implies, is essentially a prayer of thanksgiving and remembrance, the important thing is that the words give the meaning that Jesus intended, as this meaning is handed down to us in Scripture.

Shed for all — or many?

At the Consecration of Mass, the English translation heard in our churches says that the blood of Christ "will be shed for *all* so that sins may be forgiven."

How can they possibly come up with this? In the gospel of Matthew it says that at the Last Supper Jesus said all should drink of his blood "which is being shed for *many* unto the forgiveness of sins."

My question is, who made this diabolical mistake by inserting the word *all* instead of many as the gospel says?

I can go you one better. Even the present Latin text of the Mass says "pro multis" which literally means for many, but which is translated in the English as "for all."

Judging from my mail, a lot of people who don't like the changes in the church complain about this, urged on sometimes by priests or others who don't know their Bible very well.

The English translation is a proper one, which is clear (if not simple) from the original languages involved.

The Greek text of Mark and Luke for these verses from the Last Supper uses the words *hyper pollon* ("for many"). Matthew uses a different preposition in the text you mention, but the meaning is the same.

However, in these passages, as we know from a study of the texts, there are many semitisms — that is, ideas written in Greek in the gospels but based on previous texts written in a semitic language, in this case either Aramaic or Hebrew.

The significant factor is that Hebrew and Aramaic have no word for "all." Hebrew *rabbim,* which means "many," also sometimes has the meaning of "all" — "the many who form the whole." Numerous examples of this appear elsewhere in the Bible, both in the Old and the New Testaments. To cite just one example, in Matthew 20:28 where Jesus says he gave his life for the ransom "of many," the meaning is clear that he gave it for all mankind, not just some.

We know, furthermore, that this all-inclusive meaning of "many" was well understood by early Christians. John's gospel, for instance, while it devotes five chapters to events at the Last Supper, gives no description of the institution of the Eucharist on that night, as do the other gospels. John's main eucharistic texts are in chapter six where Jesus "foretells" that he will give his disciples his flesh to eat and his blood to drink. There, in the climactic phrase, Jesus declares that the bread he will give is his flesh "for the life of the world" (John 6:51).

The same meaning is kept, by the way, in Spanish ("por todos"), Italian ("per tutti"), French ("pour la multitude") and other languages.

Our English words at Mass, therefore, far from being diabolical, are the most accurate translation of this important passage that biblical scholarship can give us.

What is "epiklesis"?

I have a new missal and find it very helpful in understanding many things about our parish Mass. Several words, though, I can't understand. What is "epiklesis?" It is there several times but never explained.

I imagine you find the word in the explanation of the Eucharistic Prayers, or perhaps alongside the four Eucharistic Prayers themselves.

"Epiklesis" is a Greek word that means an invocation, or more literally, a calling-down. It is the name given to that part of the Eucharistic Prayer in which God the Father is asked to send down the Holy Spirit on the bread and wine that have been placed on the altar that these may become the body and blood of the Lord, and that the spiritual effects of the body and blood will be received by those who offer it.

From earliest times these solemn prayers of thanksgiving, which we used to call the Preface and Canon of the Mass, and which form the heart of our Eucharistic Liturgy, have contained such an invocation under this title.

Doxology or Amen?

I travel a lot and would like to know which is right: Should the people say the "through him, with him" prayer with the priest at the end of the Eucharistic Prayer, or not? In some places they do, and in others they do not.

The prayer you speak of, which is known as the Doxology — literally "prayer of praise" — at the end of the Eucharistic Prayer of the Mass should not be said by the attending people, but only by the priest. The people's part is the solemn response, "Amen," which should normally be sung, or at least recited fully and solemnly by all present.

While it is considered avante garde to say the entire Doxology together, the practice rather betrays an unfortunate ignorance of the majestic significance of the great prayer "Amen." This word goes back centuries, even to the prayer of the Jewish people in the pre-Christian era. It means: "All this is true, we believe it." In other words, it is a profound and reverent affirmation of all that was just said and done. As such, it is a magnificent conclusion to the Eucharistic Prayer by all present who share in the offering of that Eucharist.

In the book of Revelation (Rev. 3:14), Jesus himself is called "the Amen, the faithful witness" of the Father, the one who reflects and affirms perfectly all the father wishes to be and to say to mankind.

Considering the half-hearted, timid manner with which most congregations respond with this great "Amen" at Mass, whether it is sung or recited, it is understandable that many feel the whole Doxology should be said by everyone just to keep that entire solemn moment from falling flat. But that is not the way it should be.

Kiss of Peace

How and why did the practice of the Kiss of Peace or shaking hands at Mass originate? Do you think Our Lord shook hands with the apostles when he said, "My peace I leave with you, my peace I give you?"

How can this practice be avoided by those who find it obnoxious?

The Kiss of Peace is among the oldest rites connected with the Mass. At least five times, the New Testament speaks of Christians greeting each other with a "holy kiss" or a "kiss of love." It is probable that already this ceremony was part of the liturgy. We know for sure that by around the year 150, the kiss as an expression of unity and peace among Christians constituted a regular part of the Eucharistic Liturgy.

For centuries the Pax (Peace) as it was called was exchanged by everyone at Mass. Toward the late Middle Ages, the practice began to be observed only by the attending clergy, and other signs (embraces and so on) often substituted for an actual kiss. This continued until our present time when the kiss, or sign, of peace is once again prescribed in some manner for all the faithful. The church's official Order of Mass states that just before the breaking of the bread in anticipation of Communion, "all exchange the sign of peace and love, according to local custom."

Thus, in spite of your misgivings and suspicions, the sign of peace has deep roots as a fitting external expression of the Christian meaning of the Mass and Holy Communion. In the beginning, the rite took place early in the Mass, but soon found its way to the time around Communion, the sacrament which we still refer to as "the sign of unity and the bond of love."

If we really believe that in receiving the Eucharist we share the table and the meal which Jesus provided to express and build our family unity as his brothers and sisters (and therefore as brothers and sisters of each other), doesn't it seem rather bizarre that anyone would consider it obnoxious to reach out and touch another in a gesture of charity and unity just before going up the aisle with him or her to receive the body of the Lord?

The church's long adherence to the Kiss of Peace as a significant element of the Mass might reasonably suggest that anyone who finds that part of the Mass annoying lacks something fundamental in his understanding of what the Eucharist is all about.

Peace sign obnoxious?

Some time ago your column included a question on how the practice of shaking hands at the Sign of Peace can be avoided "by those who find it obnoxious."

You didn't answer the question. Some of us do find it obnoxious to submit to that gesture. Our dislike has nothing to do with understanding or not understanding the Eucharist. If the Sign of Peace is so deeply rooted in the liturgy, why did not the American church discover it before 1965?

I can only strongly disagree with you. Dislike and rejection of that part of the Mass unquestionably has a good deal to do with understanding or not understanding the Eucharist.

One may question, as many do, whether a handshake or a hug is the most appropriate sign of friendship and love in our country.(What would we put in its place?) But that some appropriate external expression of affection and unity is proper sometime during the Mass cannot be denied by anyone who understands that the Eucharist is the sign of the bond that unites us as followers of Christ.

I don't presume to judge anyone's conscience on this or any other subject. Many of us, after all, did grow up in a climate that saw the Mass solely as a prayer, totally personal between the individual and God. We do not easily move beyond such training.

The fact is, however, that such a view of the Mass is, at best, grossly incomplete. It was precisely to help us broaden our understanding of the Eucharist in our Catholic lives that the church introduced (or reintroduced) elements of our Eucharistic Liturgy which remind us that the Eucharist is first and above all a community worship — the worship of people who are together precisely because they are brothers and sisters of Jesus Christ, and therefore of each other.

A handshake, an embrace, or a kiss, may not be the best possible sign of peace. Imperfect as they may be, however, they carry a message that we need to understand if we are to celebrate the Eucharist together as Christ intended it to be celebrated.

Finds handshake painful

Concerning your answers about being rebuffed at the Sign of Peace, has any priest considered the many thousands of people who have arthritis or other ailments of the hands? I have a severe disease and have had two fingers amputated, and a possible third later on. It can be very painful for many of us, and if it's a man with a hearty handshake it can hurt for a couple of hours. We may look healthy, but if we look down when the priest announces the Sign of Peace, this could be the reason.

Your point is a good one we might all keep in mind. Everyone should be alert and thoughtful of this possibility. In these instances the individual can express the sign of peace with a smile or a word.

Permission for the Sign of Peace

In several churches pastors do not permit any Sign of Peace whatsoever, and it happens only when a visiting priest has not been warned. How does this fit in with submission to authority and the concept of community that, as I understand it, is the reason for the Sign of Peace?

If one takes the liturgical instruction book literally, there is no specific gesture required for the Sign of Peace. The official guide for the ceremonies at Mass state that after the celebrant has said, "The peace of the Lord be with you always," and the people have responded, "And also with you," the priest "may add: Let us offer each other the sign of peace. All exchange the sign of peace and love, according to local custom."

However, this is not the whole answer to your question. A statement on the Sign of Peace by the United States Bishops' Committee on the Liturgy notes that "the re-introduction of the kiss of peace within the Mass was not perhaps preceded by sufficient catechesis covering its history, significance and use." We still suffer from this lack of understanding, which affects both priests and laity. It is not helped at all by the tragic decline in appreciation of the place of symbol in liturgical ceremonies, a decline which has occurred for many reasons over the past few hundred years.

Many priests and lay people are still suspicious of any close personal interaction with another at Mass. They feel safe with words, but not with actions which might give expression to those words. So they are not comfortable with this exchanging of a sign, or kiss, of peace, even though it is simply an effort to express externally what will happen a few minutes later when those same people will share in eating the body of Christ.

While not absolutely commanded, therefore, the Sign of Peace is more than an incidental or optional part of the Eucharist. These words from the bishops' statement may help to explain why:

"The liturgical renewal has recognized the value of the assembly and its right to participate actively in the liturgy. The (Vatican II) Constitution on the Liturgy, in indicating the various forms of the real presence of Christ, emphasized his presence in the assembly itself.

"In view of this providential re-evaluation of the liturgical assembly . . . it is clearly stated that, at the invitation addressed to the faithful, all exchange the sign of peace according to local custom. It is not a peace that moves out from the altar, a clericalized peace, but a community peace exchanged among those in whose midst is the real presence of Christ the Lord."

Why strike your breast?

Why do some Catholics strike their breast at the "Lamb of God" part of the Mass? What does this signify? Should it still be done?

Striking one's breast with the hand or even with a stone is an ancient symbol of repentance and sorrow.

The reason seems to be that since the heart is considered in our culture the focal point of feelings, striking the heart signifies that we are "broken-hearted" about what has been done. In fact, our word "contrition" comes from the Latin phrase "contritus corde," which literally means "crushed in the heart" or "broken-hearted."

Striking the breast as a symbol of our need for God's forgiveness can still be a significant sacramental action. The present Order of Mass, for example, at the Penitential Rite near the beginning of Mass, provides that when the Confiteor is used, people strike their breasts at the words, "I have sinned."

Sacred vessels

During the past weekend I attended Mass at the parish church of my son and his family.

Toward the end of Mass, instead of washing the chalice and dish himself, the priest let the servers take the chalice to the side table where the servers washed them.

This is a new one on me. Isn't the priest the only one who is to wash the sacred vessels any more?

Concerning the washing of the chalice and other sacred vessels after the distribution of the Eucharist, the General Instruction of the Roman Missal states: "After Communion the acolyte helps the priest and deacon to wash the vessels and arrange them. If there is no deacon, the acolyte takes the vessels to the side table where he washes and arranges them." (n. 147) While this refers directly to those installed formally as acolytes, the Instruction also provides that laymen, even if they have not received institution as ministers, may perform all functions below those reserved to deacons. (n.70)

It is at least proper and necessary that anyone caring for sacred vessels be mature and properly trained for a dignified and correct exercise of these responsibilities.

Even when the priest or deacon washes the vessels after Communion, this should be done if possible at the side table of the sanctuary or later in the sacristy. (n.120) Normally the priest or deacon should not purify the chalice and other vessels while standing at the center of the altar.

Bells during Mass?

Can you tell us whether or not bells are to be used at Mass? Our former pastor discontinued them and we thought sure our new pastor would start them again. But he says we don't need them anymore. If they were important and nice to have in the past, why not now?

It seems clear, at least from my own mail and contacts, that the use of bells at Mass is gradually disappearing. Which, just by the way, is somewhat strange.

The former instructions for Mass instituted by Pope Pius V in July, 1570 (and revised by later popes), did not even mention bells; yet, by this century Catholics often considered them nearly an essential part of the Mass. On the other hand, present instructions (since 1970) say bells may be used at certain parts of the Mass; yet they are now heard less and less.

To answer your question, good reasons lie behind the change, but as is always true with folk customs, they're not easy to untangle. Perhaps the best I can do is give a little background.

The ringing of bells during Mass apparently began in monasteries during the Middle Ages. Only choir monks attended the conventual (community) Mass in mid-morning. Others out in the field followed the progress of the Mass through the chapel bell.

One event which occasioned increased use of bells was the introduction of the elevation of the Host and chalice after the Consecration, around the year 1200. These elevations came to be seen (even in our own time) as the main part of the Mass. Some fervent Catholics even moved from church to church just to watch the elevation. Bells were rung to express elation and to let everyone know "Jesus is now here" and all present could look at him.

In 1972, the Vatican congregation responsible for liturgy related the use of bells to the level of liturgical education in the parish. Where this education has been adequate, it noted, there is no need for this kind of signal. If sufficient liturgical instruction is in fact lacking, bells should be rung at least at the two elevations to elicit joy and attention. (Notitiae, 1972, 343)

As I indicated above, one reason for bells during the long period when the people were primarily passive at Mass was to express joy over the Lord's presence. The people were to be attentive and reverently silent.

Two things, at least, have changed this. We have a deeper awareness than did the people of those days that, while Jesus does become present to us in a new way under the form of bread and wine in the Eucharist, he doesn't come fresh, as it were. As we gather to celebrate that Eucharist, we *are* the body of Christ long before he becomes present to us as our food and drink, and as our sacrifice to the Father.

Also, we now express that joy over the Lord's Eucharistic presence with our own voices, especially in the acclamation after the Consecration, and in the great Amen at the end of the Eucharistic Prayer. As in many other ways in the liturgy, we do ourselves what we formerly could only watch — or listen to — someone else doing.

Crossed arms at Communion

Please explain something I have seen in two churches recently. At Communion time some people come up with their arms crossed. The priest does not give them Communion, but says a prayer. What is this all about?

The practice you describe is observed in a number of parishes today. Any Catholic who is not receiving Communion, young children, and people of other faiths who wish to do so, approach the communion station with the rest of the congregation. As they reach the priest, they cross their arms over their breast as a sign they do not wish to receive Communion.

The priest or other eucharistic minister places his or her hand over the head or shoulder of the individual and says a brief blessing or prayer; it is simple and unformalized, for example: May Jesus our Savior keep you always in his love. Amen.

The priest and people who take advantage of this opportunity see several good points to recommend it. Perhaps most of all it gives Christians of other faiths, who cannot, of course, normally receive Communion at a Catholic Eucharist, a way of sharing in the Communion part of the Mass in some manner.

Numerous non-Catholics are present in some churches each Sunday. Some are alone, some have come with Catholic spouses and some may be non-Catholic husbands and wives. Most of these participate fully in the Mass in every other way through the responses, the Sign of Peace, and so on.

While we cannot invite them to the Eucharist itself, we can do more than ignore them after the buildup of the Eucharistic Prayer by allowing them to share some expression of our care and our common Christian identity during this intimate part of the Eucharistic Celebration.

Others point out that it can be a reverent and humble way to acknowledge our religious divisions, and our prayer that the Holy Spirit will heal the divisions of the family of Christ on earth.

It also allows children who have not yet made their first Holy Communion to share this time more closely with their families. I have found it tends to increase their interest and desire for full sharing in the Eucharist when that time arrives.

To my knowledge, two main objections have been offered against this practice. It has been suggested that having people come forward for a eucharistic blessing confuses the liturgical sign of the reception of the Eucharist, thus reducing the significance of receiving Holy Communion itself.

The objection would seem to be logical, but having experienced this practice for several years in our parish it seems that's not what happens. If anything, it increases the awareness of the great privilege and reality of receiving the Eucharist, whether the individuals are children, adults who are preparing to embrace the Catholic faith, or others who for one reason or another cannot or do not receive the Eucharist.

Liturgy scholars with whom I have discussed the matter see no reason to object to the practice.

A more practical objection is that people who become accustomed to the practice in one parish will be confused or embarrassed when their request for a eucharistic blessing is not recognized or accepted in another.

This obviously becomes a serious concern for any thoughtful pastor. Whether or not this disadvantage outweighs the advantage is, of course, a matter of pastoral judgment to be determined by the parish priests and others responsible for the liturgy.

One should remember, too, that some Oriental rite Catholics routinely approach Communion with arms crossed this way, a fact which might cause a bit of confusion in some parts of the country.

It is interesting that Pope John Paul II has himself given such a blessing: In June, 1989, on a visit to Sweden, he gave the blessing to Lutheran Archbishop Bertil Werkstrom of Uppsala and Lutheran Bishop Henrik Svenungsson of Stockholm when they joined the Communion line at his Mass in Stockholm; the pope even recalled the event with feeling in his general audience talk more than a year later, on Jan. 23, 1991.

The real presence after Mass

Please explain how and when the church came to the conclusion that the real presence of our Lord continues at a time other than the actual celebration of the Eucharist. It does not seem to be logical or to be the purpose of the sacrament for the Lord to continue to be present outside of the sacrifice of the Mass.

The real bodily presence of our Lord in the Eucharist under the appearance of bread and wine is of course one of the foundational truths of our faith, from the early Christian communities on. Perhaps our strongest evidences of this fact in the New Testament come from St. Paul; for example, his declaration that the cup we bless and share is the blood of Christ, and the bread we break and eat is the body of the Lord (1 Corinthians 10:16), and St. John's Gospel. This Gospel, written probably toward the end of the first century, reveals the clear belief of Christians at that time about the identity of the eucharistic species as the body and blood of the Lord. (see especially John 6)

It seems clear that from those earliest decades the Christian communities understood that this real presence of the risen Lord in the eucharistic bread and wine endured after the Eucharistic celebration itself. This celebration took many forms, including some incidentally that did not include what we call the words of consecration in the institution narrative of the Mass. An example is the Eucharistic Prayer contained in the "Didache," The Teaching of the Twelve Apostles written in the first part of the second century, one of the most valuable documents we possess from early Christianity.

Whenever the Eucharist was celebrated, however, it was assumed that union with that eucharistic community could be enhanced by receiving the sacred species later if necessary. Somewhere around the year 150, the Christian philosopher and martyr, Justin, writes of the worship service which Christians celebrated each week on "the day of the Sun." He describes the reading and reflection on the Scriptures, prayers, the Eucharistic (thanksgiving) Prayer and Communion, and then tells how portions of the bread from that Eucharist were taken to those who were absent.

We know that it was quite common for deacons and others to take Communion to the sick, prisoners, and others who were not able to be at the community celebration. This belief has been consistent in the church ever since. A good example is the Communion service during the liturgy of Good Friday. Since about the year 800, Communion has been received in this ceremony using hosts consecrated at a previous Mass. (See the chapter on Ecumenism for additional information on Christian beliefs about the Eucharistic presence of our Lord.)

Holy Communion

Communion under both species necessary?

Several Protestant friends have asked me a question I can't answer. At the Last Supper, Jesus commands us to take and eat his body and drink his blood. Why don't we do that? Please don't tell me that's changing; it doesn't explain why it was not done up to now. And don't tell me it's not practical or convenient. If this is what Jesus wanted, who are we to say it's too time-consuming?

Your question is a good one, and frankly I'm not sure there is an answer that will satisfy your friends. As usual, however, a little history on the subject puts it into better perspective.

For most of the history of the church (about 12 centuries), Communion under both species was standard at Mass. Much theological and spiritual significance was placed on the symbolism of receiving the Lord in Communion under the form of both bread and wine.

Even during this time, however, all the way back to the earliest years, Christians clearly understood that one did not have to receive both forms in order to truly receive the living Lord. Never was there some sort of gross supposition that in the bread one received the dry body of Christ, which later became alive with the blood when one drank from the chalice.

Communion under one species was, therefore, not at all unusual from the beginning. The Eucharist would be taken to the sick at home, for example, under the form of bread alone, and no one doubted that the individual received the whole sacrament. Infants or young children, and the sick who could not swallow food, were given Communion only in the form of wine.

Around the 12th century, a few groups began to claim that one did not truly receive the Eucharist unless one received the form of both bread and wine, a trend which prompted the church to look more favorably on Communion under one species. Later on, as some Protestants began to push the idea that the whole Christ is not present under only one species, the church increased its emphasis on the ancient truth: Anyone who receives only the form of bread or wine receives the living Christ in Communion.

For this reason, church law eventually went so far as to forbid the people to receive from the chalice at Mass. Thus, the practice of receiving only the Host became common not to deny that both species was the ideal, but simply to make clear the rejection of the error that demanded both species.

Today, of course, the danger of that doctrinal error is long past, so the church has resumed its insistence that receiving under both species is the ideal, symbolically whole way to receive the Eucharist. The point appears numerous times in official liturgical documents. It appears at least twice, for example, in the General Instruction of the Roman Missal which says the people "should be urged" to take part in Communion under both forms, "which brings out the sign of the eucharistic meal more fully."

The major instruction on the liturgy of September, 1970, repeats that Communion under both kinds "is the more perfect expression of the people's participation in the Eucharist."

From all this at least two points seem clear. First, anyone who says we must both eat the bread and drink from the cup in order to truly receive the Eucharist contradicts the belief and practice of Christians from the beginning.

Second, anyone who believes that Communion by bread alone is the normal way of Catholics, and that Communion also from the chalice is merely a dispensable liturgical frill, is out of touch with the long eucharistic tradition of the church, not to speak of present liturgical directives.

For us Catholics (and one would hope for all Christians),

it comes down to this: Jesus, living in his church, is the best interpreter of those teachings and commands assigned to him in the Gospels.

Intinction

Your column in our Catholic paper said in relation to the different ways of receiving Communion under both species, that "intinction is a liturgically correct method of distributing Holy Eucharist."

In training to become a eucharistic minister in our diocese, I was told this form of receiving the Eucharist is not acceptable. Some documents were apparently cited in support of this. I would appreciate your clarification on this matter.

The church's instructions concerning the Mass provide for three alternate ways to receive Communion under both species besides the most obvious and common way of drinking. (General Instruction of the Roman Missal, 240,252) One is from a tube or straw, which is generally silver. Another method is with a spoon. The pieces of consecrated bread would be laid into the wine and dipped onto the tongue with a spoon. This method is common in many Eastern Rite churches. The other is the one you indicate.

I know of no official document which forbids Communion by intinction — dipping the Host in the cup and then giving it to the communicant. It is still theoretically an acceptable way of giving Communion.

However, at least two things urge strongly against its use. First, it is a much less appropriate and symbolic way of receiving under both species than actually drinking from the cup. More seriously, distributing Communion by intinction removes the option of receiving Communion in the hand. A Host that has been dipped into the chalice could only be placed on the tongue of the recipient.

Thus, practically speaking, the training and information you received was correct.

Communion from the cup

I cannot understand why Catholics do not always receive

Holy Communion from the chalice as well as the Host. Why is the blood of Christ not as important as his body, when he gave both at his supper and said we should have both to have eternal life?

I'm a convert to the Catholic faith and trying hard to understand some of these things.

Speaking strictly and theologically, we receive the whole living, risen Jesus Christ whenever we receive Holy Communion, whether we receive that Communion under the form of bread by itself, wine by itself, or both together. I'm sure you realize that Jesus is not somehow divided up in the Eucharist, with half of him under the form of bread and the other half under the form of wine. The words "eating" and "drinking" express two ways we can make our eucharistic communion with him; but we receive Jesus, whole and entire, either way.

On the other hand, Communion under both species is much more than a mere liturgical frill. This manner of receiving Communion sacramentally expresses the reality of the eucharistic meal with far greater richness than Communion under one species alone.

The General Instruction to the Roman Missal puts it very well: "The sign of Communion is more complete when given under both kinds — bread and wine — since in that form the sign of the eucharistic meal appears more clearly. The intention of Christ that the new and eternal covenant be ratified in his blood is better expressed, as is the relation of the eucharistic banquet to the heavenly banquet...The faithful should be urged to drink from the cup, for this brings out the sign of the eucharistic meal more fully." (240 and 241)

Thus, it is good to take advantage of any opportunity to receive under both species. Just keep in mind that when we receive only the bread, or only the cup, we are "eating his body and drinking his blood" since we receive the living, risen Lord.

AIDS from the Communion cup?

As a health-care worker I occasionally care for AIDS patients. These patients are usually in isolation.

I know there have been no documented cases of AIDS pass-

ed by tears or saliva, but the Communion cup frightens me in this respect.

I was excited about receiving Communion under both the bread and the wine when it began. However now my husband asks me not to take the wine and he doesn't either due to the threat of AIDS. Has this problem been considered in parishes?

More than a year ago (in 1987) I responded to a similar question. At that time I quoted the best authorities in the country supporting the opinion that no evidence exists indicating that AIDS may be contracted through something like a common communion cup. That position seems to be even stronger now.

As most people are aware, acquired immune deficiency syndrome (AIDS) is caused by a virus which invades, among others, one group of cells vital to the body's system of defense. The virus destroys virtually all these cells. Infections and other problems, which we would normally fight off easily, become devastating and eventually fatal.

The methods by which the disease is transmitted from one person to another are commonly known. Scientists agree that what is called casual contact is not among them. In April, 1987, the Health Letter of the Harvard Medical School strongly rejected the theory that people who live in the same household as an AIDS patient, using the same utensils, linen, and so on, may communicate the disease to others in their community. "Studies of household contacts have not found any evidence of transmission," it said. Certain types of sexual relationships and people who share drug needles run high risk, according to the document. Apart from this, "those whose physical contact with others is non-sexual have virtually no risk of getting the disease."

Later, a Federal Center for Disease Control spokesman whom I consulted confirmed to me that no evidence exists linking transmission of AIDS from one person to another with the types of contact connected to drinking from a common communion cup.

During 1988 the Surgeon General of the United States attempted to put the best current knowledge together in an informative brochure on AIDS, which he sent to every household in the country.

"You won't get the AIDS virus," said the study, "through everyday contact with the people around you in school, in the workplace, at parties, child-care centers or stores.

"You won't get it by swimming in a pool, even if someone in the pool is infected with the AIDS virus. . . . You won't get AIDS from saliva, sweat, tears, urine or . . . a kiss. . . . It can't be passed by using a glass or eating utensils that some-one else has used."

To be sensitive and alert to the dangers of AIDS only makes sense. The best scientific research available, however, still in-dicates that using a common communion cup at Mass is not one of those dangers.

Daughter doesn't like wine

Our five-year-old daughter doesn't like to receive Commu-nion under both species. She doesn't like the taste when she drinks from the chalice, or even when the Host is dipped in-to the wine. Would it be offensive to ask the priest to use another kind of wine?

First, good for you for having a five-year-old who goes to Holy Communion. We presume, of course, that she knows what she is doing. Certainly most five and six-year-olds, especially those in good Catholic homes, have the capacity to understand all the eucharistic theology the church requires of them for receiving this sacrament.

As for the wine, she's not alone. It can bother adults, too, including some priests. There may, in fact, be medical reasons involved, such as diabetes, which could prompt an individual not to want even the small amount of wine received at Communion.

It's surely all right to mention it to the priest if you wish. Communion under both species is optional even when it is offered at a particular Mass. Your child should know that she may pass up drinking from the chalice and still receive the entire sacrament, the living body and blood of Christ.

Diabetics and alcoholics

Your answer directed to the 5-year-old's dislike for the wine flavor when she receives Communion from the cup alarmed

me. You point out that Christ's body and blood are present in both Host and chalice. However, once bread and wine are consecrated, the Host cannot be dipped in "wine."

No one need receive under the appearance of wine, but only alcoholics should avoid it (due to taste and odor). No diabetic, for example, could be harmed by drinking the blood of Jesus.

It is common in Christian tradition to refer to the eucharistic species as bread and wine when the context shows clearly that the consecrated body and blood is intended. This occurs over the centuries in poetry, prayer and theology.

Even one of our Eucharistic Prayers (IV) speaks of the Sacred Species as "this bread and wine." So we need not be oversensitive about the terminology.

As for alcoholics and diabetics, the Precious Blood of the Eucharist not only tastes, looks and smells like wine, it has all the chemical qualities and effects of wine. Some diabetics are very understandably warned by their doctors not to drink from the cup at Communion time.

Communion at home

Q. Is there a rule about what to have ready when the priest or Communion minister comes to my home for Communion? Also, can I go to Communion on Holy Thursday and Good Friday?

The official ritual of the church for Communion outside of Mass says that when Communion is given anywhere outside of a church "a suitable table is to be prepared and covered with a cloth; candles are also to be provided" (No. 19). This would, of course, include at home.

The same ritual says that people who are sick may receive Communion any time on Holy Thursday and Good Friday. On Holy Saturday it may be received only as viaticum, that is, if the person is dying" (No. 16).

This is indicated also in the Sacramentary for the liturgy of those days. The introduction to the Good Friday celebration notes: Holy Communion may be given to the faithful only at the celebration of the Lord's passion, but may be brought at any hour of the day to the sick who cannot take part in this service.

Selection of eucharistic ministers

What are the rules for selecting lay people to be eucharistic ministers? Some believe there are guidelines and others believe it is more or less up to the pastor. If there are norms for selecting these lay people, what are they?

The norms for special eucharistic ministers were established by Pope Paul VI in 1973 in his instruction on facilitating reception of Communion, *Immensae Caritatis.*

In this instruction the pope designated that such ministers should be chosen in the following order: reader, student of a major seminary, male Religious, woman Religious, catechist, man or woman. However, this order may be changed according to the prudent judgment of the local bishop.

In practice, most bishops in our country and others have not demanded this absolute preference of men over women or Religious over lay people. As the pope indicates, however, the decision is up to each bishop.

Beyond this, Pope Paul states that "a special minister of Holy Communion must be duly instructed and should distinguish himself or herself by Christian life, faith and morals, striving to be worthy of this great office; cultivating devotion to the Holy Eucharist and acting as an example to the other faithful by piety and reverence for this most holy sacrament of the altar. Let no one be chosen whose selection may cause scandal among the faithful."

Several methods are possible to keep the final choice from being an arbitrary one on the part of the pastor. All parishioners may be invited to volunteer, for example, or suggestions might be sought and tabulated from members of the parish council or other significant organization.

Can women give Communion?

I was in a church for Sunday Mass and saw a woman helping to distribute Communion. Since when is this allowed?

At least since April 30, 1969, and in some places in the world before that. On that date, the Vatican instruction entitled *Fidei Custos* provided for the authorization by the local bishop of certain individuals to help distribute Communion in parishes or other institutions where the priest for some reason needs such help.

Frankly, I'm surprised you have only recently encountered the practice. The qualifications for such ministers of Communion are that they be "mature Christian persons of excellent character, who take their faith seriously and live a Christian life." There is no requirement as to sex.

Dislike eucharistic ministers

Dear Readers:

I received a letter from a lady who said that if she had to receive Communion from a lay person she would not receive at all. Return mail, much of it more than a little emotional, proved two things: that the church of the past 75 years or so succeeded remarkably in instilling practices aimed at reverence for the Holy Eucharist, and that this very success has created enormous confusion, and plain error, in the beliefs of many Catholics.

The following excerpts represent recurrent themes in the protests mailed to me, and my responses.

From Missouri: You mention that the church has excellent historical, theological and liturgical reasons for allowing lay persons to distribute Communion. Whatever that means, if they exist in the 1980s, they also existed in the 1920s and 1930s, if Jesus is really present in the Eucharist. If touching the Host in the 1930s was such a serious matter, why can everybody handle it now?

In all the responses, this was the most common error — confusing belief in the real presence of Jesus in the Eucharist with practices or regulations which often governed our attitude toward it. I, too, was raised with the strong admonition that to touch the Host, or even the chalice unnecessarily, was a serious sin.

What we did not realize was that these policies (insofar as they were "rules" at all) were only church rules, and were in fact observed only in certain parts of the world even at that time.

Therefore, the church could change them, as it changed the Lenten fast and Friday abstinence.

From Delaware: I will not go to Communion to a lay person. He's no better than I, so why can't I give Holy Communion to myself?

You are able to give Communion to yourself, if you choose to receive Communion in your hand. However, a eucharistic minister — priest, deacon, or lay person — will still distribute it to you.

From Florida: All the reverence we had for the Host is gone. It seems to be only a piece of bread. Is the church drifting back to the days of Martin Luther?

The church introduced the current eucharistic practices for the very reason that it senses a need to safeguard truths about the Eucharist that have been lost in recent generations. When it allows a layman or woman to give Communion, as it did for centuries in the past, the church in no way implies a lessening of its belief in, or its reverence for, the eucharistic presence of Our Lord.

Martin Luther, incidentally, believed firmly in the real presence of Jesus in the Eucharist until he died.

From Iowa: These two fantastic fingers of the priest were the next thing to God. And now anyone can give Communion? No way!

As gently as I can, I have to say this understanding of the priesthood borders on superstition. A priest is not ordained, nor are his hands (not two fingers) anointed with oil, to qualify him to give Communion, but to designate and empower him to preside at the celebration of the Eucharist — or offer Mass, if you will — with his Catholic Christians.

Fast before Communion?

What exactly is the present rule for the fast before Holy Communion? Are the rules the same for the entire world?

At the end of the third session of the Second Vatican Council in 1964, Pope Paul considerably simplified the eucharistic fast. According to this 1964 decree, persons should fast from food and liquids, including alcoholic liquids, for one hour before receiving Communion (not, therefore, one hour before the Mass at which they receive).

Water does not break the fast, and may be taken anytime. The same goes for medicine.

The reason for this regulation is simply to aid in preparing oneself spiritually and mentally for participating in the offering of the Eucharist at Mass, and for receiving it in Communion.

Basically, this regulation applies to the whole church, though there are some variations in different parts of the world.

Communion fast for the sick

My aged aunt is staying in our home. Is the fast before Communion to be the same for her as for the rest of us? Or is she excused?

The general rule is that we should fast for one hour from solid food and beverages, with the exception of water, before going to Communion. The ancient tradition of the eucharistic fast, which this continues, is one way we express and increase our devotion in receiving this sacrament.

However, because of their special needs, the discipline is considerably relaxed for the sick and aged, as well as for people like yourself who take care of them.

Thus, the period of the eucharistic fast is reduced to "about a quarter of an hour" for:

1) the sick, in hospitals or at home, even if they are not confined to bed;

2) those of advanced age, even if not bedridden, who are confined to their homes or a nursing home;

3) sick or elderly priests; and

4) persons who care for the sick or aged, and any family of the sick or aged who wish to receive Communion with them, when they cannot conveniently observe the one hour fast. (Rite for Holy Communion and Worship of the Eucharist outside the Mass, no. 24)

The Code of Canon Law says simply that the sick and aging and those who care for them can receive the Eucharist even if they have consumed something during the preceeding hour. (CCL 919)

Obviously, the intention is that the sick should be given every possible opportunity to receive Holy Communion.

Medicine, of course, never breaks the Communion fast for anyone.

Communion with wine for sick

I am a eucharistic minister and take holy Communion to elderly and ill people in their homes. Often, people become too ill to be able to take even a small piece of the host. Is the church giving any thought to allowing eucharistic ministers permission to give a sip of consecrated wine to these people?

What you suggest is already quite common. Many seriously ill patients, even some who are not terminal, are unable to swallow even the smallest piece of anything solid. The church provides explicitly for these people in its instructions on care for the sick. According to the Ritual for Pastoral Care of the Sick, sick people who cannot receive Communion under the form of bread may receive it under the form of wine alone.

If the wine is consecrated at a Mass not celebrated in the presence of the sick person, the consecrated wine is kept in a proper vessel and placed in the tabernacle after Communion. The precious blood is carried to the sick in a vessel which is closed in such a way as to eliminate all danger of spilling; something like a small medicine bottle is generally used. If some of the precious blood remains after Communion it should be consumed by the minister, who should also see to it that the vessel is properly washed (No. 74).

Perhaps even some deacons or priests, are not familiar with this provision. It would be enlightening, I think, for all ministers of the sick who at any time might administer the Eucharist to have a copy of this ritual and read carefully the general introduction and the introduction to the many forms that sacramental care of the sick might take. Inexpensive paperback editions are easily available.

How often to receive Communion?

A recent homily in our parish left several of us perplexed. The priest emphasized that we should not go to Communion each time we go to Mass. We should not go to Communion sometimes, he said, so that others who do not go will feel more comfortable. Also, we should not give our children the example of going each time; they should see us go to Mass without going to Communion.

To be honest, these statements hurt us deeply since we go to Communion often and hope our children will want to go also. To us, not going to Communion is like going to a banquet and then not partaking in the best part. I hope you can clear this up for us.

Like you, I find it hard to understand those kinds of statements, assuming, of course, that you are reflecting accurately what the priest said.

It is true that some priests (and lay people) feel for some reason that many Catholics go to Communion today when they should not. I have, in fact, heard similar ideas expressed by some of my priest friends in Europe. After remarking on the difference between their Sunday Masses, at which perhaps half the people receive Communion, and our own, where almost everyone receives, they revealed their suspicion that if American Catholics were as spiritually honest as they should be, fewer of them would be going to Communion so often.

I am fully aware that the consciences of some Catholics have become dulled to the point that they see no conflict between seriously sinful lives and receiving Holy Communion. But I fail to understand how anyone might claim that half, a quarter, or even five percent of our people are walking around in mortal sin. It seems to me this would involve, among other things, some very rash judgments.

Another explanation is possible. There is still more than a little touch of Jansenism loose in the Catholic Church. Jansenism, a heresy quite strong in Europe and America into our own century, taught that few people are worthy to receive Communion more than once or twice a year. That attitude deeply infected Catholic spirituality, and traces of it remain to this day.

Fortunately for all of us, none of whom would ever be worthy to receive under such severe restrictions, the church has long since rejected Jansenism as a distortion of the function of the Holy Eucharist in our lives. Put simply, this sacrament is meant to be food and strength for our pilgrim journey in this life; it is not offered as a reward for a holy and sinless life.

I'm with you. Parents, priests and teachers must help children develop a healthy and delicate conscience about sin and its relationship to the Eucharist. But we must also help them understand that the Eucharist cannot be simply an occasional or incidental element in either the Mass or in their own lives.

We have no doctrinal or psychological basis for assuming that deliberately refraining from receiving Holy Communion will help us effectively fill either of these responsibilities.

Communion more than once a day

Can a person receive Holy Communon more than once a day without special permission?

The church's regulations did once provide that Communion be received only once a day. Several years ago, however, those rules were considerably relaxed, allowing Communion more than once on a number of specified occasions.

As a practical guide, there are two categories of such occasions. The first would be special ritual Masses — weddings, funerals, Masses for baptism or anointing of the sick, etc. One might, for example, attend a wedding on Saturday morning and then attend an anticipated Sunday Mass the same evening. Holy Communion may be received both times.

Also, if someone serves a ministerial role such as lector at a second Mass, he or she may receive Communion again.

Another possibility, though not very common, would be when one fulfills two Mass obligations in one day. For example, if a holy day falis on Saturday, one could attend Mass for the holy day Saturday morning and an anticipated Mass for Sunday on Saturday evening, and receive Communion at both liturgies.

The Code of Canon Law simply says that anyone who has received the Eucharist may receive it again on the same day only during a Eucharistic celebration. (CCL 917) In 1984 the Vatican Commission for Interpretation of Canon Law ruled that even at Mass Communion should not be received more than twice a day.

It will help to understand these policies if one is aware of two concerns the church considers in such matters. First, and most basic, is that the normal practice should be that (unless there is a serious sin) one receives the Eucharist whenever one participates in the Mass. This is I believe fairly well understood by most Catholics today. Reception of Communion is an integral part, not an optional extra, in the celebration of the Eucharist. While this is true for everyone, it is particularly applicable to those with official ministerial roles for that liturgy.

On the other hand, the church knows from experience that some Catholics are tempted to treat sacred things, even the Mass, in a superstitious manner. I once knew a lady who proudly and piously claimed she attended 11 Masses — at least the "essential parts" — every Sunday.

To prevent people from collecting Communions in a similar fashion was one reason for the church's stricter once-a-day rule in the past, as well as for the clear, if broader, policy today. It trusts that peoples' deeper and fuller awareness of the meaning of the Eucharist will discourage any abuse and at the same time prompt them to receive Communion whenever it is appropriate — even more than once a day.

First Communion before confession?

My grandchildren attend a parish in our city where children cannot go to confession until after they receive first Communion. I think that is wrong. How can the teachers and priests there do that?

I have come to believe just about anything is possible, but I seriously doubt that any parish follows a policy that forbids first penance before first Communion. It would be extremely difficult to defend such a position.

Recent documents from Vatican congregations remind us that "When he arrives at the age of discretion, the child has the right, in the church, to receive both sacraments (penance and Eucharist)." There should be no "general rule" anywhere requiring reception of Holy Communion before the first reception of the Sacrament of Penance. (On First Confession and First Communion, from the Congregations for the Sacraments and Divine Worship, and for the Clergy, March 31, 1977)

This means that as a child reaches the age of reason, he has a right as a Catholic to be instructed at his own level about the sacrament of forgiveness by his parents or teachers, and he has the right to an opportunity to receive this sacrament.

Perhaps that parish, as many or most other parishes, provides assistance to children and parents to prepare for both penance and the Eucharist, and then urges parents to present their children when they are ready for either one. In other words, in those parishes children are not *required* to receive the Sacrament of Penance before first Communion.

Children do have a right to receive the Eucharist as soon as they are aware of the basic doctrines and have a desire to receive. There's the famous story of Pope St. Pius X (called "the Pope of the Eucharist") who offered Mass one day for a group of pilgrims. While giving Communion, he came to a six-year-old boy whose parents said, "Holy Father, he is not yet old enough to receive." The pope turned to the boy, held up the Host, and said, "Who is this?" The child answered, "That is Jesus."

"He knows enough," said the pope, and gave the boy his first Communion.

The traditional discipline of the church, stated in the Council of Trent and re-stated in present law, requires sacramental confession before Communion only when one is conscious of a grave (mortal) sin. (Canons 916, 988, 989) How this traditional Catholic discipline applies to children receiving first Communion is affected by another law which says parents and pastors should "see that children who have reached the use of reason are correctly prepared and nourished by the divine food as early as possible, preceeded by sacramental confession." (c. 914)

Many customs developed concerning the sequence of these two sacraments during recent centuries, especially in light of the practice of very infrequent Communion in the time of the Jansenistic heresies and after. Many Catholics still alive remember when even outstanding members of the Faith received Communion two or three times a year, and confession automatically preceded Communion every time. Naturally, first Communion would be no exception.

As the congregations indicate, children have a right to both penance and the Eucharist, and this right must be honored in accord with solid traditional doctrine of the church concerning these sacraments.

Can infants receive Communion?

Our new Catholic neighbors have several children, teen-agers and up.

Their mother told me the other day that all their children received First Communion when they were infants, before they came to this country. How is this possible?

If her children did indeed receive Holy Communion as infants, I suspect that this family is a member of one of the Eastern-Rite Catholic Churches, a suspicion which is strengthened by the fact that you say they came from another country. For many centuries, in fact up until about the year 1200, babies were given Holy Communion immediately after baptism, at which time they were also confirmed. In other words, the three sacraments of initiation — baptism, confirmation, and the Eucharist — were commonly ministered all at one time. Certain Eastern churches continue that custom.

When you have a chance, check with your neighbor. If her husband belongs to an Eastern rite, chances are that so do all the children (CCL 111), in which case they would receive their Christian initiation according to that rite.

Communion for semi-comatose

Can a semi-comatose person receive Communion? My son was in an accident which resulted in a badly broken leg. Three

months later he had surgery to remove the body cast, and something happened. He can open his eyes and move his head. He hears, but we do not know if he understands, though we feel he does.

Doctors say he has brain damage, but we will not know how much he can understand until, or if, he comes out of the coma.

As his mother, I feel he should be given the benefit of the doubt that he knows what is going on, at least to a degree, but just cannot communicate his feelings. Why should a young man be denied Communion this way? Those I talk with all seem to give me a different answer. The situation has been going on for nearly a year.

Not having talked with any of the priests or doctors involved, I can answer only from the information you give. Judging from what you have described, I feel as you do, that there is some reason to suspect your son might have enough consciousness to be aware, at least to some degree, that he is receiving Communion and that there's nothing lost in trying.

I'm assuming from your letter that he does take some food or drink through the mouth. The Eucharist should never be administered intravenously but, if he can eat or drink anything, he could receive the Eucharist.

As you hint in your letter, it is by no means an unusual medical experience for a patient to be able to hear and understand certain things without being able to respond in even the slightest way — a hand squeeze, a blink of an eye, and so on. This fact, of course, remains unknown until the patient recovers fuller consciousness.

I suggest you sit down again with one of the priests who knows the situation and discuss it thoroughly. Your son's tragedy must be a terrible suffering for you as well as for him, and I'm sure any priest will be willing to do all he can to help you both.

What is spiritual Communion?

What exactly is a spiritual Communion? I am a convert, and an older Catholic tells me that we receive the same graces

from this as from actually going to Communion. Is this true?

A spiritual Communion is a conscious, serious internal act of desire to receive Holy Communion, or more specifically, to have the union with Our Lord that normally accompanies the proper reception of this sacrament. It can, of course, be made in one's own words or thoughts, and those who prayerfully desire Communion with Jesus in this way enjoy the blessings and helps of the sacrament itself.

One hears less about spiritual Communion today because of the comparative frequency with which the Eucharist is actually received at Mass. Spiritual reception of Communion began to be quite common 800 or 900 years ago when Holy Communion was received rarely, perhaps only a few times during one's lifetime. Older people still alive today can remember when the majority of Catholics received Communion once or twice a year. In this kind of atmosphere, formal spiritual Communions could naturally play a much larger role in one's spiritual life.

Such Communion "by desire" is still good, of course. But much of its spiritual significance is absorbed today by the richer understanding of the sacrifice of the Eucharist, and its proper influence in our daily prayer and work.

Particles of the Eucharist

Isn't there danger of desecrating the Host from particles falling on the lips, hands, clothing, pews, or floor after Communion? What should one do about such fears?

It is Catholic doctrine that Jesus Christ is present in the Holy Eucharist as long as the reasonable appearance of bread and wine is there. The traditional theological phrase is that Christ is present "under the species of bread and wine." The Latin word "species" means "that which can be seen," or "that which makes manifest."

Thus, when the "species" of bread or wine are no longer there, as for example in almost microscopic crumbs, the Body of Christ is no longer present. The church wants us to deal with the sacraments with the eyes of faith, but also in a common sense, human manner. Don't worry about tiny particles that "may" have fallen and adhered to clothing or fingers. This kind of scrupulosity is unnecessary and actually distracts from the attitude of love and devotion that should surround our reception of the Eucharist.

Communion in the hand

I was taught in a Catholic school that the priest's hands and his right thumb and forefinger were especially blessed for handling the Body of Christ and dispensing Communion. If this is so, how can nuns and lay people be allowed to give Communion?

I am still not sure about the idea of receiving the Body of Christ in my hands. It seems to me it should be placed on one's tongue. Can you clear this up? I don't necessarily dislike it. I just don't understand.

Contrary to what many Catholics report they were taught, it was never true that the priest's thumb and finger were anointed in order that he might "handle the Body of Christ." The symbolism of placing oil on a person, whether at baptism, confirmation, or ordination, is not intended as a particular sanctification of that part of the body. It signifies that the entire person is consecrated and dedicated to an exalted position as a member of the family of Christ.

Jesus himself is said to be anointed by the Father; in fact, that is the meaning of the word "Christ" — one who has been christened or anointed to a role and mission of particular dignity.

Certainly a focal part of that mission for the ordained priest is to preside at the Eucharistic Liturgy and make possible for the rest of the Christian people, and celebrate with them, the unbloody renewal of the death and resurrection of Our Lord. The anointing, however, is not directly related to giving Communion any more than it is to the forgiveness of sins, or any other priestly function. This point is particularly clear from the fact that for 1,200 years or so, it was common for any

Christian to give Communion to any other Christian. People took Communion in their hands at Mass, gave it to each other, and even took the Eucharist home to family or friends who could not be present at Mass.

Within the past few centuries, in an effort to counteract certain heresies which denied the real presence of Jesus in the Eucharist, the church gradually built up the detailed prohibitions we learned about not touching the Host. When I was small (in the 1930s), we were taught that it was seriously sinful to touch not only the Host itself, but even the chalice, paten, or ciborium in which the Host and consecrated wine were contained.

We now know, however, that such prohibitions did not reflect (as we then assumed) what the church had "always" done, and that they involved nothing essential to Catholic doctrine or practice.

You are never, of course, forced to receive Communion in your hand if you do not wish to do so. There's always the option to receive either way. Frankly it seems to me that the hand is no less holy than the tongue. The incredible fact is that Jesus gives us his body and blood as our spiritual food and drink in the first place. From that viewpoint, at least, to make a big deal out of which part of our body touches the Host first appears to me to be supremely ridiculous.

How Communion in the hand happened

Why did the American bishops set such a bad example for American Catholics by voting for Communion in the hand in 1978?

At the pope's Mass at St. Mary Major on New Year's Day, the same year, there was no Communion in the hand. Don't the American bishops follow the example set by Christ's highest representative on earth?

The rule of the church is that if two-thirds of the bishops of a nation vote to do so, they may request permission from the Holy Father for the option of Communion in the hand in their country.

Italy's bishops have not asked for or received permission

for Communion in the hand. Thus, when the pope, as Bishop of Rome, declines to give Communion in the hand, he is not necessarily attempting to set an example for anyone, including other bishops. He is simply observing the law which is at present in effect for all Italian dioceses.

Bishops in the United States (and 60 or 70 other countries) have asked for and received permission from the pope for the option of receiving the Eucharist in the hand.

Communion in the hand in Rome?

I read with interest your answer that Communion in the hand is not allowed in Rome. A few years ago, I made a pilgrimage to Rome with the retarded and handicapped. We celebrated Mass in the North American College, in St. Peter's Basilica and in St. Paul's Outside-the-Walls.

If Communion in the hand is forbidden in Rome, somebody should tell the priests who are distributing Communion, or else a lot of good priests will be going to hell. Only a purebred ostrich could say that this practice is forbidden in Rome.

I didn't say it wasn't done in Rome. I said the bishops of Italy had not approved it.

If "good priests" are going to hell for giving Communion in the hand, legally or not, there isn't much hope for any of us. I'm counting on God having a better set of priorities than that.

Communion by which hand?

In receiving Communion in the hand, must everyone put the Host in the mouth with the right hand regardless of whether he or she is right or left-handed? This seems like a worthless question, but in traveling around the country I get conflicting regulations about it.

Isn't it possible for a lefty to get confused and drop the Host? I know one priest who says all must use the right hand.

The policies established by the American bishops for Communion in the hand are clearly stated in the small booklet, "The Body of Christ," published in 1977 by the National Conference of Catholic Bishops, and prepared by their committee on the liturgy.

The booklet is, by the way, an excellent brief summary of the history, theology and practice of our devotion to the Eucharist, and its celebration in the Mass.

This instruction says, "In receiving Communion in the hand, the faithful approach the priest or the other minister of Eucharist with one hand resting on the other, palm up. Everyone ought to have his or her hands uncovered, with no other objects in them.

"The hands should be extended sufficiently outward and upward so it will be evident that the person wishes to receive the consecrated bread in his or her hand. . . . After the priest has placed the consecrated bread in the hand, the individual steps to one side and communicates himself or herself.

"Only then does the individual move to receive from the cup (if the consecrated wine is offered) or return to one's place."

Clearly, nothing is said about which hand. There is nothing more sacred about the right hand than the left.

I believe, however, something further needs to be remembered. Beyond the minimal requirements offered here by the bishops to assure reverential and orderly approach to the Eucharist, this whole concern over precisely how one must receive Communion in the hand, and insisting that one procedure must be used, is a good example of the kind of worship of rubrics that got the church so far off the track in the past.

The sacred reality which we are dealing with and celebrating, and the relationship with God that we are expressing through that celebration, get lost behind all the worry about externals.

The devotion the church calls for certainly would include approaching thoughtfully, responding "Amen" prayerfully, accepting (not grasping) the Host, and consuming it reverently. This much every priest has a right to expect and encourage.

Whether one receives Communion in the hand or on the tongue, it seems to me these necessary attitudes can be crowded out by a lot of personal and arbitrary rules.

Communion after remarriage

If even non-Catholics can go to Communion sometimes in our church, why is it that divorced people cannot? We are members of the church, we believe in the Eucharist, and we're trying to do what's right. It hurts very much not to be able to receive the Eucharist, and we need it maybe more than the others do.

I hope you are aware that simply being divorced is no obstacle to Holy Communion. I assume from your letter that you are remarried; but if you are not, there is nothing preventing your reception of Communion if the usual other conditions are fulfilled.

If one is divorced and remarried, it becomes an entirely different problem.

By present church law, it is true, divorced and remarried Catholics are unable to receive the Eucharist. Without getting too complicated, it must be noted that the church is seriously concerned about moving toward a more understanding and open stance in relation to such Catholics. It recognizes the difficulty and delicacy of the effort to accomplish this without compromising its belief in the permanence of marriage, as well as its convictions about the Eucharist being a sign of unity and faith which has, at least to some degree, been broken by the individual's remarriage in contradiction to the laws of the church.

It seems to me we are experiencing an increasing awareness of the need to recognize that at least many divorced and remarried Catholics are in the present circumstances of their lives still members of the church who spend themselves generously for their spouses and their children. They are doing all they are morally capable of doing to live as good Catholic Christians.

The American bishops acknowledged the urgency of this question and the possibility of its being resolved when they requested the removal of excommunication for divorced and remarried Catholics. The church cannot recognize the second marriage as valid, they said, nor does their move concerning excommunication "of itself" (an important phrase) permit remarried Catholics to receive Communion. This "most difficult question — return to full eucharistic Communion — can be resolved," explained the bishops, "only in a limited number of instances, depending on particular circumstances."

Clearly, much more reflection on the subject can be expected. In the meantime, I suggest you take the bishops' advice to remarried Catholics: "Take the next step by approaching parish priests and diocesan tribunals to see whether their return to full Eucharistic Communion is possible."

(Quotes are from the statement of the American bishops when they petitioned the pope in May, 1977, to rescind the excommunication of divorced and remarried Catholics which had been in force in the United States since 1884.)

Rash judgments about remarried

You stated that by present church law, divorced and remarried Catholics are unable to receive the Eucharist. You give the impression that this is just church law.

I thought it was divine law that we had to be in the state of grace to go to Communion. People who were validly married, got divorced and are now remarried are objectively in the state of mortal sin. That condition lasts until they are willing to give up their sinful relationship. How can you say such people may at some time be able to receive Communion?

You are right in everything you say. You omit, however, some critical additional truths which you have apparently forgotten.

One essential requirement for a serious (mortal) sin is that the individual deliberately remains attached to that sin, or deliberately remains in a sinful situation from which he is morally capable of removing himself. Those last nine words are important. They mean that the person must have not only a theoretical possibility, but a real honest-to-God choice available for getting out of the situation that is objectively sinful. If he does not have such a choice, it cannot automatically be declared that he is in what you call the "state of mortal sin."

The very case you protest, in fact, that of a divorced and remarried Catholic, might present one of the more apt examples of such a condition. Let's suppose a Catholic woman is divorced and remarried contrary to the laws of the church. Fifteen years later, she knows she has done something wrong and wants to do everything possible to get straight with God. By now, however, there are four growing children living in what appears to be a good home with a reasonably happy and stable mother and father. By every human appearance and judgment, at least, the children are dependent upon both parents for the right fulfillment of their basic social, physical, psychological and perhaps even religious needs.

I know of almost no moral theologians and very few, if any, parish priests who would claim that this woman has a serious moral obligation to break up her home, take her children (if she can) and divorce her husband so she can get back to Communion. In fact, most agree today more than ever that the very suggestion of such a solution is grotesque.

(I will not discuss here such solutions as a brother-sister relationship between the husband and wife, which are increasingly recognized as having limited validity in such situations. At any rate, they are private matters between the couple and are therefore irrelevant as to how that marriage looks to outsiders.)

From this it should be obvious that to view all couples in a divorced and remarried relationship as living in mortal sin is plain and simple rash judgment. Admittedly not all such relationships are the same or equivalent to the one example I give, but this type of situation is by no means uncommon.

We should be careful not to pass judgment. It is well to remember Christ's words: "Be compassionate, as your Father is compassionate. Do not judge, and you will not be judged. Do not condemn, and you will not be condemned. Pardon, and you shall be pardoned." (Luke 6:37)

The absolute prohibition against divorced and remarried Catholics receiving the sacraments is a church law, or, if you wish, the church's interpretation and application of a divine law. In taking this stand, the church must consider many factors, such as preserving clearly its teachings on the permanence of marriage, and the meaning of the Eucharist as an expression of faith and unity with the church.

The fact remains, however, that this prohibition is perfectly open to change or mitigation by the church, with no violence done to divine law concerning the Eucharist.

As for those of us who are not directly involved in a situation like this, we should remember that every case is different and there may be many aspects of a case that for reasons of justice or privacy cannot be explained to anyone else. In other words, we ought to just plain mind our own business and remember that God is perfectly capable of watching out for his own interests.

It should be enough for us to hope, and be thankful that a fellow Christian may be able to work out something that can give peace of soul to himself and his loved ones.

Easter duty

Is the obligation of the Easter duty (going to confession and Communion between the first Sunday of Lent and Pentecost) still in effect? We hardly ever hear of it in church any more. What happened to that very strict ruling?

Basically the obligation of annual Communion during the Easter time still exists. According to church law, all the faithful who have received first Communion should receive the Eucharist at least once a year. Unless something serious stands in the way, this should be done during the Easter time which, as you mention, lasts from the beginning of Lent to Pentecost. (CCL 920)

The obligation for the Sacrament of Penance during that period is still as it always has been, binding only if it is necessary for an individual to be able to receive the Eucharist.

You may understand why we do not hear much about it anymore if we recall the obligation of yearly Communion began in a period of great decline in the practice of receiving the Eucharist. By the 12th and 13th centuries when this regulation was first mentioned for the whole church, even priests and Sisters of many strict Religious orders considered Communion five or six times a year as more than enough. Laymen might go years without the Eucharist.

It took centuries for that to change. Actually it was not until Pope Pius X early in this century decreed early and frequent

Communion that the shift to even monthly Communion gradually became accepted and widespread. Today practically everyone who considers himself a practicing Catholic already receives far more than once a year — which is the reason not much is said about the Easter duty anymore.

The Code of Canon Law (CCL 989) states that all who have reached the age of reason are obliged to confess any serious sins once a year. In this law, however, as in past similar statements, the church does not intend to impose a new obligation for confession, but simply to prescribe a time within which mortal sins should be confessed so that, if for no other reason, the Eucharist might be received. Thus, the law does not apply to anyone who is not aware of an unconfessed mortal sin.

It bears repeating, though, that this law deals with the minimum required. By no means does it recommend receiving the Sacrament of Penance only once a year, or only when one is conscious of serious sin. The healing, forgiving and strengthening powers of this sacrament are such that it should be, in some way, a regular part of our spiritual lives as Catholics.

Treating people with compassion

Could you please tell us confused Catholics whether the church requires one to be in the state of grace before taking Holy Communion? I continually see hundreds go to Communion, but only tens go to confession. Am I to assume:

1. Confession is no longer required after mortal sin before receiving Communion.

2. People go to Communion knowing they are not in the state of grace.

3. The rules have been changed by the church concerning confession, Communion and grace.

4. The church quietly is closing its eyes and saying little or nothing, as in our parish.

My suspicions are strengthened by the once or twice a year drives to get people to the confessional, while never mentioning weekly or monthly confessions or the need for them.

I understand your question, and am sorry that a preoccupation with the numbers of people that go to Communion as opposed to those going to confession troubles you so. Times when pastors published the number of Communion wafers dispensed and the number of people who went to confession, or who attended novenas or offered spiritual bouquets of certain prayers, are long gone.

Of course church rules have not changed about either sacrament, and of course the church is not "quietly closing its eyes" and saying nothing. I would suggest, as gently as I can, that you might be leaning toward rash judgment of the people you feel "go to Communion knowing they are not in the state of grace."

I might suggest further that you ease up on your worry. God sees what is in their hearts, as he does indeed see what is in yours. Try to see these people in a more compassionate light and make no judgment about the state of their souls. That's up to God alone.

Communion for non-practicing Catholic

My mother, aged 89, is on the verge of death. She is greatly troubled over an incident and I don't know how to console her.

A priest brought her Communion in the hospital. In the room were her daughter-in-law and 22-year-old grandson. The priest offered both of them Communion, and they both received.

The daughter-in-law is a practicing Catholic, but her son (my mother's grandson) has not been to the sacraments for years. He's always too tired and openly says he no longer believes "in that stuff."

Everyone was taken by surprise, but my mother is deeply upset over the incident. Was not the priest imprudent and careless in this case? To my mother, who has a great devotion for the Eucharist, it was a cause of real turmoil.

Perhaps, as you suspect, there was little time for anyone to think and no one should be blamed.

Priests and special ministers of the Eucharist who serve the sick need to reflect carefully on your experience. By no means is it always compassionate to give Communion indiscriminately in such situations. Part of real compassion is always a healthy, sensitive respect for another person's conscience.

Pushing reception of the sacraments on them when they are not ready is as bad as refusing them the sacraments when they are.

A prayerful and thoughtful invitation to people in these circumstances to receive the sacraments is certainly in order, but they should be given the opportunity to decline. This may save the individuals themselves, as well as bystanders such as your mother, a good deal of later remorse and confusion.

When Host is dropped

Does the Catholic Church still have the dry sink where the dropped Host was put directly into the ground? It seems now the priest picks it up and keeps on going.

I remember going anywhere in the United States and the Mass was the same. Now you don't know from one Sunday to another. One time the priest comes from the back of the church, the next from the sacristy. Is this what the church calls keeping up with the times?

It was never suggested, or even proper, for a Host to be disposed of in the sacrarium, which is the proper name for the sink you speak of. Many churches have such a place, leading directly into the ground, to dispose of holy water, for example, which should not be poured into the common sewer.

The consecrated Bread and Wine, however, are never treated that way, as long as the appearance of bread or wine is still present. If the priest does not feel comfortable distributing a Host to someone after it has fallen to the floor, he may keep it and consume it himself later.

The rest of your concerns are further evidence that, for many people, the biggest problems with the "new church" are not doctrine or even moral teaching, but practices that they have become comfortable and familiar with. That isn't all bad, of course, because many of our happy memories and emotions are connected to those practices.

It helps, however, to keep an open mind about them, and try to understand why some things today are done differently than we recall. You mention, for example, the priest often coming to the altar from the back of church. This form of entrance, if it is done well, adds much dignity to the Mass. It emphasizes the solemnity of what is about to begin, and it places proper importance on the various roles that will be played by ministers in the procession — the reader of the Word of God, for instance. It also provides a better framework for the song which should normally open the liturgy.

I can only urge you to try to participate in your heart, as well as in your actions, in what is happening. It will be good for your faith as well as your nerves.

Communion for mentally-handicapped

A child in our neighborhood is attending school for the retarded and cannot remember her prayers, so she never made her First Communion. She is 12 years old. May she receive Communion when she attends Mass on Sunday with her guardian?

The more basic question is why she has not made her First Communion. Mentally handicapped children often cannot memorize prayers. By no means does it follow that he or she cannot grasp enough of the meaning of Communion to receive this sacrament.

If she is attending school, she surely is able to achieve some knowledge of Jesus and understand that she receives him in Communion.

I hope you will encourage her guardian to talk with a priest. If someone can pray very simply with her and help her understand at her own level what she is doing, she should be receiving the Eucharist regularly.

Communion before Mass

Do the new rules of the church forbid the priest to give out Communion before Mass on weekdays?
I go to weekday Mass frequently and see many parishioners leave before Communion. Sometimes they stay for Communion but leave right afterward. I hate to see them miss Communion.

For a long time, including the time many of us were growing up, most Catholics had largely lost awareness of the intimate connection between Holy Communion and the Mass. At best they were considered as two separable events. The important thing was to receive Communion; missing the rest of the Mass seemed not all that significant.

This attitude is a gross distortion of the meaning of the Eucharist, and the church is trying hard to correct it. The proper time to distribute and receive Communion is at the appropriate place in the Mass, and this should be the normal procedure in every parish.

When an individual cannot receive Communion at Mass, however, whether because of age or illness or for other reasons, yet wishes to receive Communion, the priest should see to it that the person has the opportunity.

The practice instituted by a parish will depend much on the local community, how many churches and other Masses are available, and so on. In our parish, for example, during Lent we schedule three Masses each day, plus an early morning Communion service for those who cannot come to Mass.

If an individual simply cannot be present for Mass and receive Communion at that time, he should explain the situation to his parish priest. In such circumstances, church regulations present no obstacle for a priest to give Communion outside of Mass.

Communion should be ministered

As a parish priest I see conflicting practices concerning Communion under both species. I've seen the chalice left on the altar; each person came, picked up the chalice and drank from it. At other times, Communion ministers have given the chalice to the people.

Do you know if both of these practices are correct? What is the rule?

The chalice should never be left on the altar for each individual communicant to pick up and drink. The theology and entire symbolism of the Communion rite require that the Eucharist be "ministered" to the individual communicants.

Regulations on giving Communion are clear on this. It is no more correct to receive Communion from the chalice this way than it would be to receive the Bread by just picking it up from the ciborium on the altar.

The church is so conscious of the need for ministering the Eucharist that it provides an emergency procedure when not enough ministers are present at a particular Mass. When sufficient eucharistic ministers are lacking for some reason, the priest may "appoint a suitable person who in case of genuine necessity would distribute Communion for a specific occasion." ("Immensae Caritatis," 1973, instruction of the Sacred Congregation for Divine Worship) A brief commissioning ceremony for that particular situation is given in the same document.

Just as the minister of the Host holds the Host and says, "The Body of Christ," the minister of the chalice presents the cup to the communicant and says, "The Blood of Christ." The communicant answers, "Amen."

Eucharistic para-liturgies

This summer I attended a charismatic meeting and liturgy at a retreat house in our diocese. The basket of hosts was passed around. One lady in our group was not Catholic, so I passed the basket to a Catholic. Another Catholic lady took the basket and handed it to the non-Catholic who took it and received it at Communion time. She also drank the wine from the chalice.

Has the church given its approval for this?

According to your description of the ceremony, I wonder if perhaps this was not a celebration of the Eucharist but rather what is called a para-liturgical service. Such a service is not an actual liturgy in the official Catholic sense though it may have many similarities to the Eucharist.

I have been present several times at a "sharing of the bread and wine" ceremony which is obviously intended to recall the Last Supper, but which everyone present understands is not a real Mass.

If the ceremony you attended was an actual Eucharistic Liturgy, there were a lot of serious problems about it. First of all, a non-Catholic member of the group unquestionably should not receive the Eucharist under these circumstances. If the priest in charge knows it is being done, he should kindly but clearly explain the Catholic teaching and policy about Communion of non-Catholic Christians at a Catholic Mass.

I also have serious concerns about the whole liturgy you describe, again assuming it was a valid Eucharistic ceremony. The bread should under no circumstances be "passed around" as you describe it either before or after the Eucharistic Prayer. Communion should be distributed by the priest or other eucharistic minister in the proper way for the symbolism for the Eucharist to be fulfilled.

The same goes for drinking from the cup.

Catholics should not receive Communion at an official eucharistic or "Last Supper" liturgy in a Protestant church. Again, however, sharing the bread and wine at a para-liturgical devotional ceremony with people of other faiths is certainly permitted.

Obviously at least a few people in the ceremony you attended were confused. Whoever is in charge of such a ceremony should make clear to everyone for the sake of their own consciences the precise nature of that ceremony.

Ministering the Eucharist

I am a special eucharistic minister. During a recent workshop we were told that when we give Communion we should look at the person, smile and say "the Body of Christ," then wait until the person says "amen" and give the host.

One priest, however, says we should not even have eye contact. He quoted someone who said, "Look at the host. You came to receive the Body of Christ, not to visit with the celebrant. The gift is more important than the one who delivers it."

Liturgical regulations require that Communion be "ministered," not just picked up from the altar, for example, precisely because this or any other sacrament is not only a transcendent divine activity, it is also a human interaction between two members of the Body of Christ.

We must continually reflect both of those realities, Pope Paul VI said, "if we wish to keep the celebration of the sacraments from deteriorating into an almost superstitious formalism" (Address to Rome priests, 1970).

Any eucharistic minister, priest or otherwise, always should be keenly conscious of a truth that has awed theologians from the early fathers of the church on: The person to whom we are ministering the Body of Christ is already the Body of Christ, both individually and ecclesially.

The church itself is present already both in the minister of the sacrament and in the recipient, says the Rite for Anointing the Sick (No. 40).

St. Augustine, commenting on the "tremendous import" of St. Paul's words that we, though many, are one bread, one body, says to his people, "By the grace of redemption, you are already that which you receive" in the Eucharist. In Communion, in other words, the Body of Christ gives the Body of Christ to the Body of Christ.

In light of truths like that, how can we possibly pretend detached uninvolvement when we invite a fellow member of our faith community to one of the greatest experiences of faith either of us can ever make?

Perhaps a core of the problem is that last statement about the gift being more important than the one who delivers it. Who, after all, is the one who "delivers" it if not Christ himself?

That also is a truth held most sacred in Christian tradition. Jesus Christ is present in the sacramental liturgy in the person of his minister, says Vatican Council II, quoting Augustine, "so that when a man baptizes it is really Christ himself who baptizes."

"Rightly then," the council continues, "the liturgy is considered as an exercise of the priestly office of Jesus Christ" (Constitution on the Liturgy, No. 7).

Thus perhaps the best question a minister of the Eucharist might ask is, How would Jesus himself do it if he were the one standing here in his own physical person?

I can't believe he would do it without visibly expressing in some genuine way the warmth, joy and intimacy of life he shares with the one standing before him.

Give name before Communion?

Some priests and special ministers of Holy Communion use the name of the communicant before saying the Body of Christ or the Blood of Christ. I have done this myself at retreats where I know the names of everyone. I do not feel it is pastorally appropriate at a parish Mass where the priests or ministers do not know the names of all who will receive Communion. It seems to create an "in group" and "out group" and thus to be divisive at the very time we should be most united. I find it especially "cruel" at a school Mass and only a few in each class are named, usually the more popular and endearing children.

What is the official stand on this, or what seems appropriate to you as one aware of pastoral practice on a far broader scale than I am? If at any time we ought to be treated alike and no distinctions made, it is at Communion. I have also seen priests carry on conversations with people who approach them for Communion, even stoop down to speak playfully to children while holding the Communion plate in the other hand. Any comment on that?

Apart from the general and specific liturgical principles concerning integrity of the liturgy text, I know of no regulation that would directly govern this situation. Some feel these principles are broad enough to accomodate the practice you speak of; others do not.

Directives which guide our behavior as liturgical ministers indicate that we are not to minister the sacraments like robots. Along with the other sacraments, Holy Communion should be administered in a human, friendly, warm and responsive manner, consistent with that sense of dignity, reverence and, as you well note, impartiality, which should always characterize any minister of the liturgy.

It seems to me the practice of giving names at Communion goes a little over the edge of inappropriate familiarity and camaraderie at Communion time. Be that as it may, it certainly too often goes over the edge of inappropriate partiality. It may perhaps be appropriate on certain special occasions. As you indicate, however, the wrong impression can easily be, and I know for a fact sometimes is, conveyed. Obviously, nothing should happen during Mass, most particularly at Communion time, which appears to give recognition and affirmation to one group to the exclusion of others. Almost inevitably this is what happens when peoples' names are used at Communion, particularly in a parish or other broad community Mass. This is the main reason I never do it, and appears to be the reason you as a pastor are also sensitive and concerned about the practice. The same ideas are relevant to the last part of your question. This type of interplay does nothing for the sanctity of the Communion rite.

In an increasing number of parishes and dioceses in the country young children and others who are not receiving Communion, non-Catholic spouses and parents for example, may approach the Communion minister with arms crossed over the breast to receive a brief blessing. This means a great deal spiritually to a lot of people. This simple ceremony, however, should be brief and straightforward. It should never degenerate into the kinds of things you describe. I have a suspicion that what you observed was not this type of Communion blessing. Those I have seen always reflected an obviously sincere dignity and reverence.

Baptism and Confirmation

Qualifications for baptism sponsors

I have several questions referring to Catholic baptism. Must there always be two Catholic adults to act as godparents, or is one Catholic adult and one non-Catholic sufficient? Or is either one required to be a Catholic? Is there any age requirement?

How can a priest from one parish tell me one thing and a priest from another say something different? Isn't the purpose of godparents to assure a Catholic education if something happens to the parents?

The rules of the church in these matters are very clear. At least one Catholic sponsor is required at a Catholic baptism.

According to the Rite of Baptism, the requirements for a single sponsor are mainly that the sponsor:

1. be mature enough to take the responsibility to testify to the faith of an adult convert, or to profess with the parents the church's faith when a child is being baptized;

2. be able to help the parents as necessary to bring up the child as a good Christian;

3. have received the Sacraments of Baptism, Confirmation, and the Eucharist; and

4. Be a member of the Catholic Church who is living a life in harmony with that faith and with the role of sponsor.

5. Be at least 16 years of age, unless an exception is made for a special reason.

6. Not be the father or mother of the one to be baptized. (CCL 874)

If there is only one sponsor, that sponsor may be a man or woman, regardless of the sex of the child. If there are two, it should be one of each sex. (CCL 873)

When only one Catholic sponsor is assigned, a baptized non-Catholic Christian may stand in place of the second sponsor. However, this non-Catholic is not a godparent in the canonical sense of the word; he or she is officially referred to as a "Christian witness" to the baptism.

Since all the above is explicit Catholic policy around the world, you shouldn't be receiving conflicting information from priests. Perhaps some of them are not familiar with church regulations on the subject, particularly in the Introduction to the Rite of Baptism itself and in the Directory for Ecumenical Matters of May 14, 1967.

Though parents do hold the primary obligation for the religious upbringing of their children, baptismal sponsors are by no means without their own responsibilities unless the parents die. The baptism ceremony, in fact, directly asks the godparents if they are willing to help the parents in their duties as mother and father. This help may be given in various ways: by moral support to the parents, by staying close to their godchild in showing interest in his spiritual development, by perhaps a small gift on the anniversary of birth or baptism, and so on.

The Introduction to the Rite of Baptism beautifully states that the godparent is added spiritually to the immediate family of the one to be baptized and to represent Mother Church. As occasion offers, he will be ready to help the parents bring up their child to profess the faith and to show this by living it.

Baptism sponsors

I could not believe what I read in your column concerning requirements for sponsors at confirmation and baptism. In the 1920s when I was a child, I was called by the priests next door to us to be a godmother for a dying baby, or for a baby whose parents knew no one to stand up at the baptism.

The priest assured me I had no obligation. It was an act of love and compassion. In the 1950s I was sponsor for a poor litle girl who knew no one to be her sponsor. The priest said,

"God will give you graces." According to what you say, I could never have been a sponsor in those situations.

You were surely generous and thoughtful to offer your help and support in these situations. I'm sure the priest appreciated it, as I have when similar situations arose in my own pastoral ministry.

The responses I gave reflect the procedures for the sacraments defined by the church for normal circumstances. Even today the church leaves much up to the judgment of the people involved in emergencies or in the special types of cases you describe.

I think we must remember, too, that the situation today is vastly different than it was in the 1920s or 1950s. In those days the assumption was much more common, whether or not it was actually justified, that parents would exercise their responsibilities amidst a relatively supportive community of relatives, friends and others of their faith. These so-called support groups often made the obligations of godparents much simpler.

However valid these assumptions may have been previously, the church today — both clergy and laity — recognizes that such close supportive relationships are simply not available to most families. It is this awareness which prompts the church to be far more concerned about and to examine more carefully the intentions and commitments of parents and sponsors in the sacraments of Christian initiation.

Godparent by proxy

We have a baptism coming up in our family. The ones we would like as godparents cannot be at the ceremony since they will be in the military in Germany at that time. Is it possible to have a proxy godparent who would stand in for them?

Previous church law (before 1983) explicitly mentions the possibility of proxies at baptism. But no longer. Neither official liturgical books nor other church laws now provide for official "proxies" at baptism.

This does not necessarily mean that godparents must be present at the baptism ceremony. While the ritual calls for certain responses from godparents during the baptism, their primary responsibilities toward the child (or adult) can be accepted and carried out without their physical presence at that time.

Even if not present, they must fulfill all requirements for baptism sponsors, and the baptizing minister must have absolute assurance that they intend to accept and fulfill their obligations to the child. Their names will be recorded in the parish baptism record.

Sponsors are not required, of course, for validity of baptism. The introduction to the baptism rite for children says: Each child may have a godfather and godmother. Canon law states that insofar as possible the one to be baptized is to be given a sponsor.

Thus, as long as the actual sponsors are qualified and explicitly committed to their responsibilities, there seems to be no reason against another one or two people standing in for them at the ceremony itself, even though they would have no official designation as proxies.

Can Protestants be godparents?

May two people who belong to a Protestant religion be godparents at a Catholic baby's christening? I am friendly with a couple whom I would like very much to be sponsors for my baby.

Someone told me that is not possible but that I could have one of the friends be a godparent as long as the other person is a Catholic.

Your friend is correct. According to the requirements of the Rite of Baptism, a sponsor for a Catholic child must be a practicing Catholic who has received the three sacraments of initiation.

When one considers that the responsibility of the sponsor is to encourage and give good example to the baptized child in living his or her Catholic faith faithfully and generously, it is obvious that only a practicing Catholic could fulfill that responsibility in an appropriate manner.

Only one Catholic sponsor of this kind is necessary, though

there may be two. A second "Christian witness" to the baptism may be a baptized Protestant who would, of course, accept the responsibility of guiding the newly baptized child in leading a good Christian life.

Orthodox godparent

A friend of mine who is Russian Orthodox was recently godmother for her Catholic friend's baby. Is this permissible?

As I explained earlier, in place of a second Catholic baptismal sponsor, a Christian of a Protestant denomination who may be a relative or friend of the family may serve as a Christian witness of the baptism with a Catholic sponsor. A Catholic, incidentally, can do the same for a member of a Protestant denomination. In both cases, of course, the responsibility for the Christian education of the person baptized belongs to the godparent who is a member of the church in which the person is baptized.

An even closer participation is permitted when the person to be baptized is a member of one of the separated Eastern churches, which would include the Russian Orthodox. A member of one of these churches may be godparent, together with a Catholic godparent, at the baptism of a Catholic infant or adult. (Directory Concerning Ecumenical Matters of the Secretariat for Promoting Christian Unity, May 14, 1967, no. 48)

Your friend therefore acted quite properly in being godparent at the baptism, at least according to the regulations of our church. In all such instances the individuals involved from other faiths should be sure that their action is not contrary to the regulations of their own church as well.

Are godparents obsolete?

Recently, I was godmother for a relative's baby. I was disappointed at the baptismal ceremony. As godmother I had no part or say while the baby was being baptized. The mother and father held the infant and stood in the center while the godparents were standing beside them.

I don't see why godparents have to be chosen since they are not doing their traditional part.

Apparently you have not had an opportunity to attend a baptism for a good many years. Throughout the renewed ceremony for baptism, the primary responsibility of the parents in the training and education of their children is emphasized far more strongly than in the older rite.

As you indicate, the parents now hold the child and they make the primary promises for the Catholic upbringing of the child who is baptized. Don't you agree that this is precisely the way it should be?

It may be true that in the ceremony itself godparents take a less active role, though there are several actions and promises that involve them personally. Their primary function always has been, and still is, to support and assist the parents in every way possible as the child grows toward full Christian manhood or womanhood.

If anything, a thoughtful and faithful godparent means more to parents than ever before. Heaven knows, mothers and fathers today need all the help they can get in giving example, support and guidance to their children in the critical years of development. Godparents who take their responsibilities seriously are badly needed by both parents and children.

Maybe you did not get to hold the baby at baptism. I hope you remain conscientious about the much bigger responsibility that is still there.

Changing sponsors

Some time ago you replied to a question about whether a child's godparents can be changed.

I call to your attention a 1984 statement from the Roman Congregation for the Sacraments concerning substitute godparents. It may be helpful to your readers.

I am grateful to the chancery official who referred me to this document. It may indeed be enlightening and helpful when a child's godfather or godmother has either died or has proven for one reason or another unwilling or unable to serve appropriately in that role.

When a godparent abandons the Catholic faith, for example, the child's parents might understandably wish another person to become godparent, one more likely to care for the child's spiritual welfare should the parents die or become incapacitated.

The Congregation for the Sacraments has acknowledged that very possibility, stating that the bishop of a diocese may officially designate a *substitute* sponsor, whose name could be inscribed on the official baptismal register. This ruling has been sent to bishops in both the United States and Canada. (Reply of November 13, 1984; in 1985 Roman Replies of the Canon Law Society of America.)

There may on occasion be good reason for this kind of official change of godparent. However, as I explained previously, a loving, concerned friend or relative can usually do just as much good for the child without going through all this formality.

Must child wait for baptism?

We have a dear friend, a boy nine years old. His parents do not want him baptized until he is old enough to decide for himself if he wants to be a Catholic.

If he were baptized by a Catholic priest, would he automatically become a Catholic? I always thought this didn't happen until after instruction, confession, and first Communion.

When a child is born and baptized into a Catholic community (whether baptized by his parents, a priest, or someone else), that child is considered a Catholic, though of course he may repudiate that faith and that church later in his life.

If, as you say, the boy's parents do not intend to raise him Catholic, much the same answer would have to be given here as in other similar questions.

Illegitimate child's father

Our unmarried teen-age daughter had a child more than a year ago. Our pastor, a Catholic social worker, and a lawyer

said the father's name need not appear on the birth certificate or the baptism certificate.

We moved shortly before the baby was born. The parish priest at the new church insisted that our daughter name the biological father or he would not baptize the child. She was upset, but wanted the child baptized so she named the father.

This still upsets her and she would like to have this man's name removed from the official church record. The biological father was not Catholic and has, in fact, never even seen the child.

You had the correct advice in the beginning. The father's name definitely does not need to appear on the birth certificate or the baptism certificate. To my knowledge, all states require the name of only one parent on the birth certificate.

Neither is the name of the child's father required on the baptism record. In fact any name could be given, which could easily result in serious injustice to innocent people, so in such circumstances the father's name should never be on a baptism record.

There really appears to be only one thing that can be done and that is to write to the bishop and explain the situation. It is possible, however, that at this time even the bishop could not have the name removed.

For others who might sometime be in this unfortunate situation, the name of the father need never be on the birth certificate or the baptism certificate. Indeed, such information can very legitimately be refused.

Blessing after childbirth

What has happened to the "churching of women" ceremony? Years ago in my parish it was given often during the year, but no parish that I know of does it now. Is it still given anywhere?

Part of your answer lies in the history of the ceremony. The churching of women, or the Blessing after Childbirth, apparently entered Christian practice as a carryover from the Jewish ceremony of purification. Under Jewish law, a number of actions incurred a certain spiritual contamination or uncleanness. Among these were any actions involving sexual functions, legal or illegal. A woman was unclean after childbirth, for example, seven days if the child were a boy, and 14 days if the child were a girl. (See Leviticus, chapter 12) This uncleanness was formally removed by an appropriate rite of purification. (The purification of Mary after the birth of Jesus is still celebrated by the church as part of the Feast of the Presentation on Feb. 2.)

In its Christian form, the ceremony took more the theme of thanksgiving to God for the safe birth of the child and petition for God's blessings on the mother and child.

One reason the blessing after childbirth is not more widespread among Christians is that many of its features, prayers and blessings are already implied or included in the rite of baptism. The newly revised baptismal rite contains numerous references to the parents and to what is in their hearts and prayers concerning their new child.

The new Book of Blessings (n. 236) includes a blessing for mothers unable to be at their children's baptism so they might "benefit from the blessing that in the rite of baptism prompts the mother and all present to thank God for the gift of the newborn child."

How many sacraments?

A few of us Catholics are in a discussion group with some Protestant couples. A question came up recently about the sacraments. Where do we get seven sacraments? If Christ instituted them, why do the Protestants recognize only two?

There was no actual enumeration of seven sacraments until more than 1,000 years after Jesus' resurrection. During those centuries, however, the Christian church recognized that among all the religious ceremonies, some rites carried with them in a special way a contact with Christ and his life, and were connected with times in the lives of Christians — birth, life, growth, worship, forgiveness, sickness and death.

As early as the year 200, the theologian Tertullian wrote about the special goodness of those marriages which the church blesses and seals and which the heavenly Father ratifies.

Around 1150, another noted theologian, Peter Lombard,

researched all this Christian experience and came up with a list of seven sacraments in what approached our "scientific" sense of the word. This list was accepted by St. Thomas and other theologians. There really was no serious disagreement about it until the Protestant Reformation nearly 400 years later. Interestingly, while the Western (Latin) and Eastern churches fought violently over many matters of faith, this is one thing they agreed on.

The reasons most Protestant churches acknowledge only two sacraments (baptism and the Eucharist) are complicated. Mainly it is because these two are (even in our Catholic doctrine) the focal sacraments of the Christian life and because they are more obviously founded on explicit texts of the Gospels. However, it might be noted that some Protestant communities do increasingly provide rites for other sacraments. Some Lutherans, for example, celebrate a rite for confession, and Anglicans for the anointing of the sick.

The list of seven sacraments was defined as a matter of Catholic faith by the Councils of Florence in 1439, and Trent in 1547.

Baptism at home?

My husband and I are expecting the birth of our second child. My husband is not baptized but is deeply religious and attends Mass with the family each Sunday. He feels unable at this time to join the Catholic faith because of personal reservations; I respect his wishes.

We were left with little feeling of celebration after our first child's baptism three years ago. We are becoming more active in the parish, but our Catholic friends are scattered all over the city.

We asked the priest who married us, a close family friend for many years, if he would baptize our baby in our home. He agreed, pending approval of our parish pastor.

Our pastor, however, says that a baptism can only be conducted in the parish church except in an emergency. Every priest we asked seemed to have his own personal opinion, but none seemed to know the rules of the church or where to find them. What is your opinion?

For us Catholics, our community — or parish — church holds a place of special reverence. It is more than simply a handy building in which to do our religious business. It is literally the home of a parish family, a group of believers who together share their faith in their worship of God, in the celebration of the Eucharist and the other sacraments.

A church building, is, therefore, a sign and symbol that reminds us of many things about our religion, not least of which is the responsibility we have for each other in developing and supporting the faith we share together. Admittedly no parish does this perfectly, but it is what we are about and what we aim at trying to be with and for each other.

This explains the church's centuries-old bias for locating important events of our faith in the community's special place of worship. This same conviction is behind its present rules for the celebration of baptism.

These rules are really not that hard to find; they are in the Introduction to the Rite of Baptism for children which I would assume any priest, certainly any parish, owns. The regulations that bishops, priests and others are expected to follow are contained there.

According to these guidelines, "so that baptism may clearly appear as the sacrament of the church's faith and of admittance into the people of God, it should normally be celebrated in the parish church." The bishop, after consulting the local parish priest, may permit baptisms to take place at a baptismal font in another church or public place of worship within the parish boundaries, but in these places also it is the normal right of the parish priest to celebrate baptism.

The Rite of Infant Baptism states: "Outside a case of necessity, baptism is not to be celebrated in private homes" without the bishop's permission. (n.12) Except in an emergency or some other pressing pastoral reason, baptisms are not to take place even in hospitals. When such an emergency occurs, the parish priest is responsible for being sure that the parents are "suitably prepared beforehand."

Most priests with whom I am acquainted try to be as considerate and permissive as possible in such situations. However, they do have a responsibility to consider the faith of the individuals involved and the faith of the whole parish family, and to respect the church's instructions for the administration of the sacrament.

Your priest friend will surely be welcome at the ceremony. I hope his presence and the increased familiarity you have gained with some of the people in the parish will help make the baptism of your new baby the joyous celebration it should be for everyone.

Is infant baptism wrong?

Our newspaper had a short article about baptism. Apparently there is a new ceremony for baptizing adult converts. But the article quoted some Catholic authority that infant baptism is wrong and that we shouldn't do it any more. Is this true? Surely we aren't going to stop baptizing babies now!

There is a beautiful new rite for initiating an adult into the Christian faith which includes, of course, the Sacrament of Baptism.

I have read quotes of the remarks probably referred to in your letter concerning this new rite. The introduction to the ceremony indicates that this rite is the norm for all initiations into the church. One noted liturgical scholar has, it seems, interpreted this to mean that anything except adult baptism is abnormal. According to the quote I have seen, he said, "The normative nature of adult initiation means that departures from the norm, while necessary for serious reasons, are always abnormal. Hence, indiscriminate infant baptism, while common, is abnormal and should be stopped."

Infant baptism of the children of Christian parents has been a practice of the church almost since its beginning. The psychological and spiritual community of the family as Christian people was recognized very early. Even though the child was too young to believe on his own, his parents knew they were a "new creation."

Their Christianity was not an incidental frosting on their personality. They believed, as St. Paul said, that for them "To live is Christ." It was only natural, therefore, that their child share from its earliest days in their faith and love — and their baptism.

True, in our earliest records, as in Acts 2, perhaps only

adults were baptized, though we can't be sure of that. Very soon afterward, however, infants were apparently included, at least as whole families were brought into the church, which seems to have been rather common.

All Eastern and most Western churches consider infant baptism as coming from the very beginning of the Christian era. The great theologian Origen, for example, about the year 280, and St. Augustine (about 400) considered infant baptism a "tradition received from the apostles." St. Irenaeus (about 180), a close friend of St. Polycarp, who in turn knew St. John and the practices in the time of the apostles, took it for granted that infants and children should be baptized along with adolescents and adults.

Not only has the church embraced this practice through the centuries. The discoveries of modern psychology concerning the deep spiritual and religious involvements between parents and children seem only to strengthen the wisdom and validity of that tradition.

If, then, our author means to say that the practice of infant baptism in itself is abnormal, I believe he must yet bring forward a good deal of evidence and argument if he expects to make his case.

If, however, by "indiscriminate infant baptism" he simply means that we should not pour the baptismal waters over everyone that comes along, I can only agree with him. But I don't know many priests who do that.

Child of non-Catholic widow

Our son joined the Army Medical Corps and while in the service married a non-Catholic girl from the South. A child was conceived and was born eight months after our son died.

When I asked his wife if she would have the baby girl baptized, she asked, "What's that?" After I explained, she said her parents had recently joined a Protestant Church and there were no Catholics in their area of the state. But she consented for us to have the baby baptized.

Our parish priest then told me the mother would have to promise to raise the child Catholic before he could perform the ceremony. As a CCD teacher, I teach that when you are

baptized you become a child of God. An innocent baby receives all these graces and I believe this rule should not apply in these certain circumstances.

The priest said he believes as I do, but has to obey the rules. Please give your views on this.

Apart from a danger of imminent death, no child should ever be baptized in the circumstances you mention. At least three weighty considerations are involved.

First, the baptism would place serious religious obligations on the mother which she is at present apparently unwilling and almost certainly unable to fulfill. Several times the baptismal rite emphasizes that the parents (and godparents) must realize their duty to raise the child in the faith and church in which that child is being baptized, and they profess that they intend to fulfill that responsibility. Not being Catholic herself, and isolated from any significant support from Catholics, she is right in being reluctant. It would be totally unfair to place that burden on her.

Second, the Sacrament of Baptism does bring with it many precious gifts of identity with Jesus and his Mystical Body on earth. Our concern over the importance of baptism, even for infants, is most legitimate. However, the Catholic church does not teach that God's love and life and promise of saving grace are denied to the unbaptized.

To the contrary, as Vatican II noted, we believe that the Father's providential care and Christ's redeeming love are at work in all people. Baptism is important in Our Lord's plan for us but we mustn't panic if someone is not baptized.

Finally, baptism might place the child in some jeopardy later on because of her relationship to many church laws. For example, with no chance of being raised Catholic, even the validity of a future marriage (according to Catholic marriage legislation) may be in doubt, through no fault of her own, if she is baptized a Catholic in the present circumstances.

Baptism is a great and powerful sacrament. But it isn't magic; the church's guidelines for it are intended to keep it in proper perspective. The priest was right in his advice to you.

Baptized without permission

My husband became a born-again Christian about two years ago and is deeply involved in the Charismatic Movement.

Friends of ours who are Christian Scientists had a baby recently. My husband baptized their baby without their knowledge.

I feel that he disrespected their personal beliefs. I think they should know, but have mixed feelings about telling them. Your opinion would be appreciated.

Your husband is apparently operating out of a very superstitious understanding of the sacraments.

Be that as it may, he surely acted against the rights of the parents and the child in this circumstance. No child should be baptized in such a situation unless his or her parents agree and intend to raise the child as a Christian. Even then, they should be directed to a priest or another Christian minister for the proper preparation, performance, and recording of the baptism.

I see no good that could come from your telling the parents at this point. You might wish to inform them if, in the future, they plan to have the child baptized, but probably it could cause only hard feelings if you told them now.

Baptism without father's consent

My daughter is married to a Moslem. He refuses to get married in the Catholic Church. They now have a baby and my daughter wants him baptized.

Is there a way that my daughter can receive the sacraments and baptize the baby without his consent? Someone told me it can be done.

It is possible something might be done to help your daughter in this circumstance and that the child might receive the Sacrament of Baptism.

Exactly how this might happen must be worked out between her and the priest in her parish, or perhaps with the advice of another priest in her area with whom she may be acquainted.

Please urge her to talk with her priest as soon as possible and follow his counsel.

Should priest delay baptism?

During the last few years I've heard of priests hesitating or even refusing to baptize children. Recently my nephew told me that when he and his wife took their first child to the priest for baptism, the priest gave them a hard time. He told them he would have to talk to them a few times about their own practice of the faith before he would baptize the baby.

I don't know what my nephew will do, but I do know that other parishes do not hold up baptisms like this. Isn't there a church law that says children are to be baptized as soon as possible after birth? Does the priest have any right to postpone baptism this way just because the parents don't go to Mass as often as they should?

The heart of your question and of the priest's approach with your nephew lies in the last phrase of your last question. Whenever a Catholic couple (or the Catholic partner in an interfaith marriage) is seriously deficient in the practice of religion, the parish priest has not only a right but an obligation to delay the baptism of their child until he can help the parents straighten out their own faith.

True, the church does insist on the parents' obligation to have their children baptized "within the first three weeks" after birth. (CCL 867) The law assumes, however, that the parents are practicing Catholics prepared by their teaching and example to bring their children up as good active Catholic men and women.

Thus the same law requires that immediately after birth, or before, the parents go to their parish priest to request the Sacrament of Baptism for their child and to be properly prepared for it.

The church, in fact, insists that a priest cannot lawfully baptize a child unless he has a solidly-founded hope that the baby will be raised properly as a member of the Catholic religion. If evidence for this hope is lacking, he should delay the baptism and explain to the parents why this is being done. (CCL 868)

The Introduction to the new Rite of Baptism emphasizes the point. At least twice during the ceremony, Catholic parents openly proclaim that they accept and believe the faith in which that child is being baptized, and that they are willing to give the example and teaching necessary for that child to be raised in the faith, and so on. Under any normal circumstances, this promise cannot be made by supposedly Catholic parents unless they themselves are faithful to the practice of their faith, and are not simply bringing that child for baptism out of a sense of family tradition or a vague feeling that "it's the right thing to do" — which is often true today with parents who do not go to Mass regularly or otherwise are weak in their beliefs, or are not very faithful in practicing what they say they believe.

Obviously the church is concerned that parents not be placed in the position of making a profession of faith that they do not honestly and fully believe. Thus, the parish priest is directed to work with the parents who are not yet ready to profess that faith completely and to assume the responsibility of educating their children in the faith, and then to decide upon the right time for the baptism.

I realize that such regulations may startle many Catholics. But being realistic, we are in a situation different from the one we were in when the church instituted the practice of almost automatic baptism of children of baptized Catholic parents. Frankly, in this as in numerous other aspects of our faith, the church today is trying to pull us (both clergy and laity) away from viewing the priest as simply the administrator of a religious club, who is there to respond and satisfy religious needs, as it were, on demand.

Anyone who knows the history of the church of the past two or three hundred years is aware that by automatic baptisms, first Communions, and so on, whole populations of people were left at an almost primitive level of Catholic faith. One generation of baptized non-practicing Catholic parents followed another. Few, if any, were required to deal honestly with their own need for God, and to open themselves to the possibility of growth to anything like a full Christian Catholic life. As someone put it well, a church which never says "no" to parents who are seriously deficient in their belief and practice of their faith will never allow them to become deeply believing parents.

I believe your nephew and his wife are fortunate to have a priest who is trying to help them question seriously who and what they are as Christians, and to be certain in their own hearts that the baptism of their child will be what it was meant to be, a genuine recommitment of all their family to their Catholic faith.

"Immediate" baptism?

How can you be so stupid? In spite of what you say, no priest has any right to refuse or delay to baptize a baby any time.

Whatever happened to original sin? How can you condemn a baby for something it didn't do?

No priest better ever hesitate to baptize a grandchild of mine just because his parents don't go to Mass the way they should, or I'll give him a piece of my mind.

I must admit a number of people wrote protesting what I said in that column, but you have an unusually delicate way of expressing the point.

To answer the question implied by your letter, there has been a change in the church's attitude toward baptism of children. The assumption that parents are practicing Catholics, and that the child is actually being baptized into a genuine Christian community which includes the child's family, is no longer possible. It is too often contradicted by the facts.

Baptism of a child (or an adult) is not an individual matter between the person and God. It is an action of the whole Christian community welcoming that child as part of a family that belongs to that Christian community, and it is the child professing its belief (through its parents and godparents) in that community, and wishing to become a part of it.

This is not something incidental to baptism; it is essential to it. Admittedly it is an aspect of baptism that was not stressed in the past because it didn't need to be. Today the situation is quite different. A highly respected canon lawyer made the point succinctly a few years ago at a meeting of the Canon

Law Society of America. Speaking of the right to baptism (and the other sacraments of initiation, the Eucharist and Confirmation), he said, "Surely human beings have a right to enter that community and participate in it. But they have no right to enter it to destroy it. The community itself has the right of self-preservation and growth. It has the right to be what God intends it to be. And this right of the community conditions the right of individuals to enter it." In other words, before an individual is baptized, the parish — and the whole Christian community — has a right to know that the commitments made in that ceremony are honest.

This is not only for the good of the community, but also for the good of the child. You may have forgotten that in baptism the individual baptized makes some awesome promises to participate as a full active member of the Christian community as he grows in that community. It is totally unfair for parents to commit a child to that kind of responsibility when they have no intention of properly assisting that child to grow in that community and enable it to fulfill those promises honestly and sincerely in later years. Parents who do not practice their faith have no right to make commitments on the part of the child that they are not willing to help that child fulfill. It's basically as simple and as direct as that.

We still believe in original sin, but the baby is in no way being condemned for something it didn't do. The church has never taught that unbaptized children or adults will lose their soul, or will even be through no fault of their own deprived of the presence of God in eternity. We know that Jesus commands baptism for his followers and that this is the normal way for entry into the kingdom. God never assured us, however, that he has revealed all his plans to us, or that he does not have ways of bringing his life and grace to human beings in other ways than through baptism. Certainly the church has never taught, for example, that unbaptized pagans who possibly never even heard of God or of Jesus are automatically deprived of eternal salvation. It has, on the contrary, always taught that God has ways which man does not know, and these are his own secrets to reveal or not as he wishes.

He gives his church the responsibility of directing its own

life in a way that will help that community to remain faithful to what he commands and to the lifestyle that he has revealed, including procedures for administering and receiving the sacraments.

The shift in the church's perspective is solidly established in our present legislation and policies concerning the sacraments. In addition to numerous references to this policy in the Introduction to the Rite of Baptism itself, the Congregation for the Doctrine of the Faith (June, 1970) insisted that a well-founded hope for a Christian education of a child must be present or the child should not be baptized.

In other words, the church is making every effort to lead us to a richer and fuller understanding of the church as the family of Christ, and how all of her activities, most especially the sacraments, must reflect that vision.

Parents' responsibility at baptism

Your answer about possible hesitation to baptize babies has me really disturbed.

I have a grandson a year old who has not been baptized, but my hands are tied. The infant's father, my son, has become one of the hordes who have ceased attending Mass.

He's in a mixed marriage but there's no interference from his wife. He was educated in Catholic schools through college. I feel a condition such as this needs deep consideration before a decision to delay baptism of the baby. It could mean complete severance from the church. Why don't you consider this?

I certainly do consider it, and any priest who has to deal with this kind of situation considers it very carefully. Receiving people into the church, whether infants or adults, is one of the greatest joys of the priesthood. We do not lightly pass up that opportunity.

We do have, however, an obligation to the Christian Catholic community and to the parents of children who are presented for baptism. We must not perpetuate a lukewarm or non-existent connection with the church by supposedly Catholic people simply because they want a baptismal ceremony.

Somewhere along the line, parents of children must decide where they stand with God and with their religion. We do them no service by pretending that being half in and half out is no problem as long as they come around to the church for big moments in their lives.

I, and other parish priests, do not simply refuse to baptize people. We spend many hours and sometimes weeks working with parents, trying to help them to come to a decision about whether they can honestly present their children for baptism and commit themselves to the kind of life that will be necessary if their children are to be raised as Christians and Catholics.

Frankly, from my experience, I believe the likelihood of greater severance from the church is most remote. By our working with parents in this way, many parents have come to realize that they must stop playing games with their faith and with God and lay their life on the line as Catholics and Christians. Others have not come to this conclusion yet, but I have known no one who has ended up more separated from the church than they were before.

Understanding, and the proper kind of encouragement, incidentally, from grandparents and friends can be a great assist to fathers and mothers who are contemplating the baptism of their children, and prompt the kind of personal commitment this ceremony will demand from them.

Are stillborn children saved?

Last month I gave birth to a stillborn baby. The doctor said he died about twelve hours before birth. The nurse asked if we wished the baby baptized; we said yes and assume this was done.

We are confused. What is the church's teaching on this kind of baptism?

We had a simple graveside service, but I just couldn't face being there. Is it appropriate to have a memorial Mass for our baby? He was certainly not guilty of any sins.

We feel our family can never be complete since David will always be missing. My husband and I feel so sad. We are getting little in the way of answers and comfort.

The tragedy you have suffered is one of the most difficult parents ever face. I know you must hurt deeply and, as you say, the hurt will never completely go away.

That is always true in the death of someone we love; but there is a special pain when a baby dies as yours did.

Maybe it will help a little as time goes by to keep a few things in mind.

The sacraments, including baptism, are for the living; they really cannot be received by someone who has already died. If there is any doubt whatsoever, the baptism may be administered just in case.

However, that is far from the whole story. Jesus told us clearly that baptism is the sacramental or "sign" way by which people enter into his community of faith.

Christians have always pondered the exact meaning of this, since it is clear that many people die without baptism, often without hearing of God or Jesus. If God loves all people equally and wishes them to have the grace of redemption, how does that come about?

The possible explanations offered by theologians through the centuries have been numerous. But one principle endures in theological tradition: Considering God's obviously universal intention for the salvation of the human race, the gift of his redeeming love is offered in a genuine way to anyone who does not place a personal obstacle in its way.

This would apply to children such as your son. How God might accomplish this, he has not told us, as he has not told us many details of his salvation plan.

My own conviction, similar to that of some major theologians through the centuries, is that God sees the child of a family such as yours as a Christian part of a Christian family.

Without becoming too involved, the explanation is basically this: The Christian (and Catholic) identity which you and your husband have is not plastered on your "natural" life like frosting on a cake. You are not some sort of neutral person with a veneer that we call "Christian." You are Christian people; your "personality" so to speak, is itself Christian.

Thus, neither would your child be something neutral to which some day this "veneer" called Christianity might be added. Had he been born, baptism would have signaled and brought about his participation in this visible church on earth. But the grace of baptism does not come in one magical moment, as our belief concerning the death of a catechumen, to cite one example, proves.

A catechumen (one who is preparing to enter the Christian faith) is considered a member of the church and has a full right to Christian burial at Mass, even though a baptismal ceremony was never performed. The same can apply to children who die before their parents are able to have them baptized. (CCL no. 1183)

That policy indicates, at least, the grace of baptism is working long before the pouring of the water.

One might add that God's creation of us is itself, in the light of the Incarnation, an act of the redeeming, salvific will of God.

Although the church's teaching on this matter is far from definitive, certainly this much is true. God loves your child as much as he loves you; Jesus died for him as much as for any of us; your baby is in the Lord's loving and redeeming care. While your child will never be with you again on earth, he will always be part of your family; the full joy of that relationship is something you and we can look forward to.

I will pray for you, as I'm sure many readers of this column will also.

Parents left the church

My son, an excellent Catholic before this, married a non-Catholic divorced woman who had two children, and they had two sons of their own.

My son is willing to have his sons baptized, but won't raise them as Catholics, and he doesn't go to Mass even on Easter and Christmas.

I am wondering if it would be all right to have the children baptized in some other religion. That way they would at least be Christians.

A child should not be baptized into any Christian community unless at least one of his parents is committed to that faith and intends to raise and educate the child in that religion.

Merely having children baptized does not make them Christian unless they are entering a Christian community (their family and a larger Christian community) that will nurture that Christian faith and make it a reality in their lives as they grow.

From your letter it seems obvious that your son and his wife do not consider themselves Catholic. In fact, unless you have omitted something important, it doesn't seem that they have any religion at all. Arranging for the children to go through a baptism ceremony will not solve either their parents' problems or their own.

Baptism and remarried parents

I have a niece who was married to a non-Catholic boy in a big church wedding. They were divorced after a year, and she wanted to marry a Catholic. The priest told her nothing could be done. So they got married by a justice of the peace.

I know their marriage is not valid according to the laws of the Catholic Church. Now they are expecting a baby. Will their child get to be baptized as a Catholic?

As has been stressed in previous pages, being baptized as a Catholic means much more than simply that a priest performs the ceremony. The newly baptized commits himself personally or through parents and godparents to a life of faith, worship and mutual support within the Catholic community. His fellow Catholics oblige themselves to the same for him.

At least twice during the baptism ceremony, the parents formally and explicitly profess that they understand and accept this belief of what is being done, and they promise that they will assist their child in fulfilling that responsibility through the coming years. Also, immediately prior to the solemn profession of faith before the pouring of the baptismal water, parents receive the serious admonition: "This is the faith of the church. This is the faith in which these children are about to be baptized."

Are the parents you describe able to make such a promise? It is entirely possible that they can if they themselves are committed to living as full a Catholic life as circumstances permit. One point in their favor is that they both have at least some Catholic background and roots in the Catholic faith. That doesn't remove all the problems, but it does give them a bit of a head start in a difficult task.

The final decision, of course, rests with the parents and with their parish priest.

Parents married out of church

Our family needs your advice. May a Catholic couple be godparents for a child whose parents are not married in the Catholic church?

Before any child is baptized, the general law of the church as well as the instructions for the Rite of Baptism require that the priest have some assurance that the child will be helped to grow up educated and trained as a member of the Catholic faith. This is a serious obligation for parish priests.

Under some circumstances, it is possible for a priest to judge that all necessary conditions are present for the baptism of a child whose parents are not married in the Catholic church. The assumption would certainly be, however, that at least one of the parents is Catholic and gives evidence of the necessary intentions for such a baptism.

Normally you should be able to assume that if the baptism is taking place in the Catholic church, all the requirements are present and you would be free to act as godparents. In fact, in such a situation, particularly if the child's family is close to you, you may be able to bring a significant amount of faith and support to them in the Catholic raising of their child.

If you have any other specific doubts, I suggest you talk with the parish priest who is planning the baptism with the child's parents.

Children of unmarried mothers

I have a friend whose daughter is pregnant and not married. She and her boyfriend do not wish to marry until they finish high school in about a year. Can she have the baby bap-

tized in the church without being married? Also, can she give the baby the father's name even though they are not married?

It is possible for children of unmarried mothers to be baptized. As for any other baptism, however, several requirements (which I have explained before) must be met before the priest could baptize the child as a Catholic.

I would strongly advise your friend's daughter to think twice before naming the baby after the father. They're still very young and much can happen in the next year, or before they decide finally whether or not to marry.

To answer your question, however, the laws are generally very liberal about names. One may choose nearly any name one wishes for himself or for a child as long as the choice does not injure the rights of others.

State laws do differ in a few instances, however, so the girl involved should check with a lawyer and with the boy involved before she acts.

Validity of Protestant baptism

In your question column you stated that long before Vatican Council II the Catholic Church accepted baptism of certain Protestant churches, including the Disciples of Christ.

I was baptized in 1962 in the Catholic Church. Either you or the priest who baptized me are misinformed. In spite of my insistence that I was baptized properly previous to 1962, I was required to receive conditional baptism. This caused a hurtful situation for me and my family.

Several people wrote after that column appeared with stories similar to yours. I believe you would encounter a much different situation if you were joining the Catholic Church today.

The statement to which I referred, which assumed the validity of baptism of most Protestant congregations, appeared in a reply from the Holy Office, Dec. 28, 1949.

It resulted not only from a better awareness by the Catholic Church of baptism in these other churches, but also to at least some degree from a more developed theology and practice concerning baptism in some of the Protestant denominations.

The development in understanding has increased enormously since that time, of course, making conditional baptism (or, as it is sometimes erroneously called, rebaptism) of converts to our faith relatively rare.

Most times today if a convert has belonged to one of the major Protestant denominations, conditional baptism is given only if the fact that the person was baptized is uncertain, or if the individual himself or herself has a serious reason to doubt the validity of the previous baptism.

Present regulations of the church, in fact, forbid conditional baptism of converts without a reasonable doubt and serious investigation of the previous baptism. (Rite of Reception of Baptized Christians into Full Communion with the Catholic Church, no. 8.) See further details on Protestant baptisms in the next chapter.

Saint's name for Baptism?

Is it any longer required to have a saint's name for Baptism?

The Rite of Baptism does not require the parents to choose the name of a saint for their child.

However, the tradition of naming children after one of the saints is still good and admirable. Among other things it is one way of reminding them that they are part of a long Christian line, and puts them early in touch with the heroes of our faith.

Limbo

I was speaking with a recent convert to the Catholic faith about Limbo, and she said she had never heard of it. Don't they teach that any more? Don't we believe that that is where children go who are not baptized?

One objection to older approaches to teaching Christian doctrine (which the church is trying to correct today), is that all teachings were often presented as of equal importance and certainty. Thus, some Catholics suspected that the entire doctrinal structure of the church was collapsing when meat was allowed on Friday.

The teaching about a "Limbo" for infants is a good example. It revolves around a question about which we still know very little: what happens to an infant who dies without baptism?

For centuries there apparently was not much concern on the subject. It was simply assumed that God took care of these children in his own way. Some theologians held that such unbaptized infants suffered some pain of sense, but by the 12th or 13th centuries that idea was widely rejected.

A few centuries later, Limbo was a subject of some heated debate. The heretical sect called Jansenists taught that, according to God's revealed doctrine, all infants dying without baptism are condemned to the fires of hell. In 1794, Pope Pius VI condemned this teaching. One may believe in a Limbo — a place of happiness that is not heaven, and which has no suffering — and still be a Catholic, he said. This is the only mention of Limbo in all the major official documents of the church.

God's plan for infants who die without baptism is one of many subjects he has not told us much about. They certainly do not suffer the painful separation from God that is the result of serious personal sin. Does God, as some theologians hold, give a dying infant a moment of awareness in which he or she can make a decision for God? Or does God in some way accept the faith of the child's parents — or the faith of Jesus in his church — as the faith of that child, sufficient for salvation?

We simply don't know. We are certain only that God, in his clear love and desire for the salvation of all mankind, has arranged some plan for fulfilling that desire through the merits of Jesus our Savior.

A Limbo of natural happiness for infants is, therefore, something Catholics may believe. It is not a necessary part of our faith.

Enrollment for baptism?

Friends of ours had a child several months ago and asked to have him baptized. As they explain it, the priest told them he could not baptize the baby since neither of the parents is a practicing Catholic. (The husband is not Catholic; the wife is, but admits she doesn't go to church very often.)

However, the priest told them he would enroll their baby, and perhaps baptize him later. I've never heard of that. What does it mean?

As I explained above, the church has pointed out numerous times during the past generation that children should not be baptized in the Catholic Church unless there is solid reason to anticipate they will be raised as Catholics. Normally this means at least that one of the parents, if not both, are practicing their Catholic faith.

In 1970, the Sacred Congregation for the Doctrine of the Faith repeated this position. If neither parent is a practicing member of the church, and (as would usually be true in this case) there are not sufficient reasons for the priest to proceed with the baptism, one option open to him and the parents is the following:

A priest may "enroll" the child (presumably as a member of the parish, and as a candidate for future baptism) with a view to its being baptized later; he would then meet with the parents several times to prepare them for the responsibilities assumed in the baptism of their child. (Notitiae 1971, 69)

Some, though relatively few, parishes now follow this procedure. Apparently your friends' parish is one of them.

Can only a bishop confirm?

I read with interest your answers to questions in our paper. Born and raised a Protestant, I desired for a long time to be a Catholic and converted in 1976.

The priest in the parish gave me instructions for about six weeks, then administered the rite of confirmation. Since that time, some close Catholic friends have wondered whether a priest can give confirmation, or can only the bishop do this? Now I am not sure if I am truly a Catholic. Am I?

No need to worry. If you followed the instructions and procedures your priest suggested, you are a full-fledged member of the Catholic faith.

Until a few years ago, the Sacrament of Confirmation was ordinarily administered only by a bishop. Now, however, a parish priest may administer this sacrament in several circumstances, one of which is the reception of an adult convert into the church. After the baptism (or after the profession of faith if the person is already baptized), the rite of reception into the church calls for the priest to minister confirmation to the new Catholic.

This proper procedure seems to be what happened in your case.

Responsibilities of sponsors

I have heard that it is now possible for the same person who was sponsor at baptism also to be sponsor at confirmation. Is this correct? And does the confirmation sponsor have to be a Catholic?

According to the revised regulations concerning confirmation, it is not only permissible but desirable that the godparent at baptism also be the sponsor at confirmation if he or she is present for the ceremony. The reason is obvious. The responsibility assumed by the sponsor at confirmation is the same as that of the sponsor at baptism, that is, to help the candidate for the sacrament to live up to his baptismal promises under the influence of the Holy Spirit. Having the same sponsor on both occasions emphasizes this responsibility more effectively.

There may, however, be a different sponsor for confirmation.

Included among the qualifications for the sponsor are that he be spiritually qualified, that he be sufficiently mature to undertake the responsibility involved, and that he be a Catholic who has already received the three Sacraments of Baptism, Confirmation and the Eucharist.

Confirmation name needed?

Our daughter will be confirmed soon and nothing has been said about a confirmation name. Is it still proper to have a special name at that time?

It is no longer required to have a confirmation name different from the one given at baptism. The use of the person's baptismal name is allowed at confirmation since this better expresses the close relationship between these two sacraments, both of which are part of the process of Christian initiation and commitment.

Candidates may choose a new name for confirmation if they wish. I'm sure this will be explained in your parish.

Supplying ceremonies

I have a 23-year-old daughter, partially handicapped mentally and physically, who was born with hydrocephalous. When she was in the hospital she was confirmed by a Ukrainian priest. Now she wants to be confirmed by a bishop, have a sponsor and pick a confirmation name like her brothers and sisters.

Could she possibly be confirmed the next time this sacrament is scheduled at our parish?

The Ukrainian (sometimes called the Ruthenian) Rite is among those rites in full communion with our church, under the pastoral jurisdiction of the bishop of Rome. Probably the one who confirmed your daughter was a priest of this rite.

If so, the confirmation she received was almost certainly a valid sacrament. If it was she would not be confirmed again since, like baptism, this sacrament is not repeatable.

Even so, however, there are simple ways in which she could share in the solemn ceremony of confirmation. She could choose a confirmation name, which she had not the opportunity to do previously, and someone close to her could serve as sponsor.

Such participation might be compared to "supplying the ceremonies" for baptism after a baby, for example, has been privately baptized in an emergency. The child may be brought to church later and the entire solemn rite of baptism is celebrated, with the sole exception of the pouring of the water.

Considering the spiritual significance such a celebration would apparently have for your daughter and your family, I feel certain your parish priest and your bishop would be anxious to work something out along these lines.

You must talk with a priest in your parish, however, first to ascertain the above facts, and then to explore possibilities appropriate for your daughter and for the parish community.

Just for the record, some branches of the Ukrainian Rite are not Roman Catholic but Orthodox. The chances that the priest who confirmed your child was from one of these branches are slim, and in any case would not change what I said above.

Parents sponsors?

In your column you once said that parents could be sponsors for confirmation. They have served as such in our parish for several years, but now our pastor said that, according to the bishop, parents should not be sponsors now. Who is right?

The Introduction to the Rite of Confirmation expresses the preference for the godparent of baptism to be the confirmation sponsor. Or another person may be chosen. In this same paragraph the document says, "Even the parents themselves may present their children for confirmation." (n. 5)

In light of this, it was often judged, particularly before the new Code of Canon Law, that parents may be sponsors. But the words don't say that. Parents may be "presenters", not sponsors.

The new Code of Canon Law requires confirmation sponsors to fulfill the conditions given for sponsors at baptism (CCL 893). Fathers and mothers are prohibited from serving as baptismal godparents (CCL 874).

The situation is somewhat confused since no confirmation sponsor is absolutely required in the first place. The confirmation ritual and canon law, respectively, specify that "ordinarily" and "insofar as it can be done" a sponsor should be chosen for the candidate. So there may be no sponsor at all.

At any rate, the present law of the church on confirmation sponsors is the following: (1) The baptism godparent is preferred. (2) Another person may be chosen. (3) In either of these cases, or if there is no sponsor, a parent may "present" the individual for confirmation.

Confirmation sponsor

I have a niece who lives with her father, who is divorced and remarried. I believe this girl will ask me to be her sponsor at confirmation. Would it be all right if I accepted?

The problem is that she often does not go to Mass and there are things I could not change; nor could I be responsible for her being brought up as a Catholic.

One can never be sure as a sponsor, or even as a parent, how children will turn out in their religious practices and convictions. But a situation such as you describe surely prompts more than the usual concern by someone asked to be sponsor.

I suggest you first have a little talk with the priest in her parish to find out what the children are being told about the relation of confirmation to their future lives as Catholics, and what else is expected of them as candidates for this sacrament.

Then talk with your niece. Depending on her age, you may be able to help her begin to make some realistic, personal decisions.

If her relationship to the church is as tenuous as you indicate, and continues that way, it would not seem to make much sense for you to commit yourself (which is what you do as sponsor) to help her to do something she doesn't want to do in the first place.

What the sacrament would mean to her then I don't know; but it could be unfair and perhaps meaningless for her to ask you to be her sponsor under these conditions.

Marriage and Family Living

Origin of marriage vows

Would you know where the words of the marriage vows originated: "I take thee . . . till death do us part." Did they come from Christ or officials of the church?

The language of the marriage vows did not come from Christ. In fact, the words or actions by which marriage consent is expressed by the bride and groom have varied greatly from one time to another, and even today from country to country and from one Catholic rite to another.

The only essential in our Christian context is that the couple declare to each other in some external way their intent to join now in a permanent marriage union with faithfulness to their spouse. This declaration may be in words or, as in some rites, almost entirely in symbolic actions — such as drinking from the same cup, conferring of the wedding rings, etc. The significance of these actions is as clearly understood by all the participants as words would be.

Form of marriage vows

Our family attended a wedding last Saturday in which the wedding vows were ones I have never heard before. The couple said something rather long about their love and how they wanted to live together for life, but none of us remember hearing any other vows.

My daughter will be married in October. Is it possible now

for a couple to use their own words and make up their marriage vows?

The ritual for marriage in the Latin Rite of the church contains one form of consent at a wedding: "I, Joseph take you, Jane, to be my wife. I promise to be true to you in good times and in bad, in sickness and in health. I will love you and honor you all the days of my life."

Instead of a statement by the couple, the priest may put this vow in the form of a question: "Do you, Joseph, take Jane . . . ?"

In November, 1969, the American bishops approved a second form with which we in the United States are more familiar: "I, Joseph, take you, Jane, for my lawful wife, to have and to hold, from this day forward, for better or worse, for richer, for poorer, in sickness and in health until death do us part."

If the couple prefer, this form also may be put as a question asked by the priest.

One of these forms must be used at all marriages of Catholics in the United States; a couple therefore are not free to compose their own vows, nor does any priest have a right to compose his own.

The reasons for this should be obvious when we realize that marriage vows (anytime, but in a special way between two Christians) are not a private affair between the couple; they have importance and implications for the whole community.

The U.S. Bishops Committee on the Liturgy explains it this way:

"While the couple may well find language of their own to express very profoundly the consent and covenant which they undertake, this is a central ritual and ecclesial act and they have a responsibility to the community of believers assembled, that is, the church before which they manifest their consent, to use language clearly and certainly conformable to the church's faith and understanding of the sacrament."

In practice, this requirement works no hardship whatsoever on the couple, since there are numerous chances for them to express their faith and understanding of their vows during the wedding ceremony.

One of the most obvious and frequently used is the opportunity for the couple to compose their own prayer to be recited together, or separately, either shortly after they declare their vows or during the meditation period after Communion.

This may be, incidentally, what you heard the couple say.

If a couple unexpectedly employs other language of consent or commitment than that provided in the rite, no matter how appropriate that language may be, the presiding priest should see that one of the approved forms is used also.

He might do this very simply by using one of the two question forms I mentioned above. (Bishops' Committee on the Liturgy Newsletter, August-September, 1981.)

Required marriage instructions

In connection with the approaching marriage of a relative, I was told that there would be no instructions for the couple by the priest.

With so many marriages ending unhappily or in a divorce, I find this hard to believe. Aren't priests required to give some sort of instructions or help to people before and after they are married?

By church law, parish priests are under heavy obligations in this part of their pastoral life. The Code of Canon Law (CCL 1063) binds a pastor to see that his parish community assists all the faithful of that community in preserving and increasing the holiness of Christian marriage.

He is to accomplish this in several ways: by instructing children, young people and adults on the meaning and duties of Christian marriage and parenthood; by preparing brides and grooms before their wedding concerning the holiness and responsibilities of marriage; by a meaningful celebration of the marriage liturgy, bringing out how the couple signify and participate in the unity and fruitful love of Jesus and his church, and by helping married couples themselves protect and increase the holiness of their family life.

The parish priest is not required, of course, to provide all this instruction and assistance personally. The range of areas in which the couple needs assistance is vast. It involves instruction and counseling on finances, interpersonal communications, in-laws, sexual expression of their love, the care and upbringing of children, and numerous other elements of life that are significant in the early years of their marriage and throughout their married life.

Most parish priests today rely heavily on Pre-Cana Conferences, Engaged Encounters and other excellent programs for those preparing for marriage, and a whole range of aids for husbands and wives in their service and love for each other and their children.

Pre-marriage requirements

Different rules for different churches in the same city have always troubled me. But recently this affected me personally.

Our daughter was to be married to a Protestant boy. We tried to have a Catholic wedding, but there was no way because no one would allow it without the required pre-marriage conferences.

My daughter and I were in a local florist shop before the wedding, and a lady friend of mine told me that her son's wedding was arranged with only three week's notice. She said they were allowing her son and daughter-in-law to take the pre-marriage course at a later date after the wedding. None of the priests in our parish suggested this. Please explain how this was allowed to happen.

The purpose of the pre-marriage conferences which are required in most dioceses of the United States today is to help a couple evaluate their strengths and weaknesses, and to assist them in the final decision concerning their marriage. It makes little sense to do this sort of reflection after marriage, even though the ideas may be helpful to a couple any time.

The priest in your parish followed the regulations for your diocese, and from what you reveal in your letter concerning your daughter's faith and maturity, my first reaction is that he acted quite correctly.

It is possible that under certain circumstances, in the judgment of the priest involved, some preliminaries required in an area or diocese may be dispensed with. Perhaps the priest in the other parish followed proper procedures in doing what he did also.

Your letter emphasizes the urgency of following diocesan guidelines in these matters to prevent confusion by everyone involved. If you want a fuller explanation of why the priest in your parish made the decision he did, and another priest made a different decision, ask them. They will explain the reasons to you.

Preparing for marriage

My daughter and her fiance attended Sunday afternoon classes with other couples at a distant church. These classes were boring because my daughter took college courses which covered all segments of married life.

My daughter's friend was just married a couple of weeks ago at our parish. She told my daughter that she would never go through again what she and her fiance had to with our parish priest. The marriage talks were very dull. The 100 or more questions they were asked to answer were personal and none of his business.

If my daughter refuses to answer these questions can our pastor refuse to marry them?

All dioceses in our country now have some form of required preparation programs before marriage. In more and more places these programs take two forms. One is some type of premarriage class or series of conversations with trained married couples about various aspects of early marriage. These "classes" of course take many forms, from a series of lectures in a Pre-Cana program to weekend Engaged Couples Encounters. Understandably, the quality of these programs varies from time to time and place to place, depending on leadership and participants. Not everything will appeal to everyone. I have found, however, that much depends on the attitude of the people attending. Usually couples who attend with an open mind and who feel they still may have something to learn find these courses useful in some way. At least they appreciate the church's concern for every possible care to prepare the bride and groom for a good and happy marriage.

The other element common to most marriage preparation requirements is an instrument to help the couple evaluate their agreements and strengths and weaknesses in important aspects of the early years of marriage.

Some couples naturally profit more than others from such programs. But, in my experience, all of them, including those most highly educated, recognize full well why the church expects couples preparing for marriage to participate in them. They are grateful that everyone involved, including the parish priest, is concerned enough and loves them enough to want to help. I am not aware of the specific program in your parish. It seems to me, however, that what I have said may help to put the experience of your daughter and her friend in some proper perspective.

"Promises" in a mixed marriage

Your answer concerning the marriage of a Catholic with a non-Catholic sounded so simple.

Why didn't you mention that the Catholic party must sign a statement that the children of that marriage must be raised Catholic? Some young people are surprised to learn that such papers must be signed before the marriage can take place before a Catholic priest. If one of the parties does not agree to this, the marriage cannot take place.

What you say is true, and I adverted to it briefly in my answer. But obviously the matter needs a little more explanation.

Formerly, both the Catholic and non-Catholic partners signed promises to raise the children Catholic. This practice was changed by Pope Paul VI in a document on interfaith marriages ("Matrimonia Mixta") in 1970.

While the procedure is different, the intent of the church is the same: to prevent at least as much as possible any serious harm to the marriage because of religious differences between the husband and wife. Let me explain.

The procedure today is this: The non-Catholic partner signs or promises nothing. The Catholic partner signs two statements. The statements are basically as follows:

1. I reaffirm my faith in Jesus Christ, and intend to continue living that faith in the Catholic Church, and

2. I promise to do all in my power to share my faith with our children by having them baptized and raised as Catholics.

The non-Catholic partner is not asked to sign or promise anything. The priest who is helping the couple arrange for the wedding is required to sign a declaration that the non-Catholic partner has been informed of this affirmation and belief of the Catholic.

Normally, the priest will also explain what these beliefs mean to the Catholic, and how such beliefs affect the Catholic's life, and then urge the couple to be sure before their marriage that their respective faiths and convictions can be preserved and honored in their marriage.

Several points need to be noted about the "promises" made by the Catholic. First of all, they add absolutely nothing to what a Catholic already believes if he or she is truly Catholic. When an individual presents himself to a Catholic priest for marriage as a Catholic in the Catholic Church, the priest and the church have the right and obligation to assume that that individual is a Catholic — which means there are some things that person is honestly convinced of and adheres to as his personal faith.

Among these are the two statements given above. Any Catholic who does not hold these as basic beliefs is either grossly ill-informed about his religion, or is very shaky in his faith.

Why then are the declarations asked at all? One reason is as a reminder. But more importantly, they are meant to help the couple identify any differences in their religious beliefs or expectations from the marriage, so that these differences can be dealt with and resolved before the marriage takes place.

In other words, while the church knows what a good and knowledgeable Catholic believes, it does not pretend to know the religious beliefs of the non-Catholic. It presumes, however, that the non-Catholic has some beliefs about God, family, marriage, and other religious matters. And it is concerned that these beliefs of the two people be confronted by them before the marriage so that any critical differences may be ironed out.

Ultimately, of course, this must be done by the two people

themselves, acting from the base of their own convictions. They must be sure that any conflicts of belief (for example, about their own personal religious obligations, the baptism and education of their future children, and so on) can be resolved without either of them being asked to compromise what their conscience tells them are serious moral obligations before God.

If such resolution proves impossible, the couple could not, of course, enter the marriage with a good conscience.

The entire procedure is simply another expression of the church's loving concern for the faith and conscience of the Catholic, first of all, but also of the non-Catholic, whose convictions are, one would hope, just as serious to him as ours are to us.

Interfering in interfaith marriage

What do I say to a 33-year-old daughter who is married to a non-practicing Jewish man? She was raised in the Catholic faith, was a CCD teacher and so on, and then "love" came along. Since they started courting, his mother became interested again in the Jewish faith. As a result, they could not be married in the Catholic Church because of Jewish law excommunicating anyone who takes part in a religious ceremony of a Christian faith.

They were married in a local hotel with my parish priest present to give the blessing, with permission of our bishop. At the time, when I discussed children with her, she said they would raise the children in both faiths, which to me is a contradiction.

I feel she is setting our Christian heritage back 2,000 years. My priest tells me, in the name of ecumenism, that it is her decision and to stay out of it. She is expecting her first child and I feel that since it is my grandchild I do have the right to say something.

First of all, I hope whatever you do will be more in the name of common sense than ecumenism. You do, of course, have the right to say something, but it may not be anywhere near as much as you would like. Tell her (and you only need do it once) exactly how you feel very clearly, and why. Then stay out of it.

Obviously her faith means something to her or she would not have gone through the process of obtaining a dispensation from the form of marriage, which she obviously did. This allowed the marriage to take place before someone other than a priest. If you act in haste and say things you would be sorry for later, you could alienate her and her family completely and not be able to be present as a grandmother.

Don't worry. It is not within her power to "set Christianity back 2,000 years." It all comes down quite simply to one fact. You must live with the results of your Christian upbringing, and your daughter must live with hers. Keep your own faith, recognize your limitations, and above all be as certain as you can that whatever you do is done with unselfish love for her and her family.

Banns of marriage

Are the banns of marriage announced any more? I know of several marriages of friends where they were not given in church at all. Will they be announced only if the family asks for them, or what?

The banns of marriage are announcements of an intended marriage with the intention that anyone aware of impediments to that marriage will make that fact known. While the former canon law required them, their importance has been less stressed in recent years than in the past, perhaps because our population is much more mobile than formerly; people who know the bride and groom are likely to be spread out much more. Also, the testimonies of family and friends required before marriage are more extensive than they used to be.

The present law of the church does not require banns, but does provide that bishops' conferences may include them among appropriate inquiries which are to precede marriage. (CCL 1067) Our American bishops do not prescribe them at this time.

Can cousins marry?

Would you please explain what relatives are forbidden to marry, and how this is figured? A cousin of mine is engaged

to another cousin, actually a second cousin. I didn't think this was permitted in the Catholic Church. Many people do not know relatives farther back than grandparents or second cousins.

You are referring to an impediment to marriage that in our church law, and in many state laws, is called consanguinity — which literally means common blood.

There are two kinds of consanguinity. One is the direct line, meaning the relationship between an individual and his or her parent or grandparent.

Such a direct line relationship is, of course, a serious impediment to marriage and, since it is not simply a church law, no permission (dispensation) for a marriage between two such people is possible.

The other kind of consanguinity is indirect or collateral. This is the relationship, for example, between brothers and sisters (second degree), first cousins (fourth degree), and so on.

According to general Catholic Church law, any collateral relationship, up to and including fourth degree (what we usually call first cousins), is an impediment to marriage. (CCL 1091)

As with the direct line, no dispensation can ever be given by the church for a marriage between brother or sister. In the other cases, however, the church, through the bishop, can (and fairly often does) dispense for a serious enough reason.

Marriage between first cousins, for example, is far more common in some cultures of the world than it is in our own. In such situations, dispensation by the church for those marriages are also relatively common.

The church's laws forbidding marriage within certain degrees of consanguinity are, of course, based on social and health reasons which are rather obvious. While a few ancient cultures apparently allowed some type of marriage relationship between brother and sister and even between parent and child, some of these relationships were forbidden by every major code of law with which we are familiar, even those which predate the Jewish law of the Old Testament.

Incidentally, yours is one part of the country (Pennsylvania) in which there are relatively large numbers of Oriental Rite Catholics. Laws which govern these branches of our church vary somewhat from our Latin Rite canon law, particularly in the method of computing degrees of relationship. But, in practice, the impediments and the possibilities are similar to those I have explained.

Breaking an engagement

I just broke my engagement to a fine man who was generous in every way except one. He hates children. I want children when I get married and told him so, but he has a peculiar outlook on having a family.

Can you give me a few reasons why a man should say awful things about children? Otherwise he has a nice personality. But I had to give up the thought of marrying him.

I can think of a number of reasons that a man might not want children, either because of some unfortunate experiences in his background or simply because of his general attitude toward life.

Whatever the reason, you are fortunate in having the wisdom and courage needed to end the engagement. A lot of men and women would not have sufficient conviction of their own principles to make such a decision, or in many cases they entertain the vague hope that "something will work out." It rarely does.

I hope your experiences will support others in thinking clearly about what to expect from their marriage, and in having sufficient strength of conviction that they will not deliberately settle for such major compromises even at the beginning of their married life.

Is pre-marital sex wrong?

I am a Catholic dating a Protestant girl. We are in our 20s and considering marriage in the future, maybe in two years.

I have never had an affair with anyone, but is it wrong to have sexual relations with the one you intend to marry?

I have never felt this way about anyone before. My girl says she loves me very much and would like to marry some day. We have talked of having sexual relations, but I'm really con-

fused. I do want to marry her, but I also want to do what is right.

We need an answer that will help us both. I know one of your answers may be that if you love each other enough you will both wait. We both want to be sure.

Catholic moral teaching remains and is likely to remain that sexual relations before marriage are wrong. Within the limits of our space here, I can mention only a few, but I believe very important, thoughts that may help.

First, you must realize that your desire for sexual union with the girl you love is not only normal, it is the way you ought to feel about her. Any man or woman who plans to marry and doesn't strongly want sexual intimacy with his or her partner is in trouble. They need either a medical examination or psychiatric counseling — or a serious re-examination of their choice of partner.

Such a desire is, however, no basis all by itself for judging whether sexual intercourse is morally right or wrong for you. As all Catholic-Christian moral doctrine, this teaching of the church was not pulled out of thin air. The church simply confirms by its own insight and belief what is common human experience — complete sexual intimacy between people who are not married is hurtful in serious ways that are usually not even dreamed of beforehand. And it is therefore sinful.

The total giving of themselves that sexual intercourse involves implies an acceptance of responsibility and permanent, committed trust of another that you are simply not able at this point to profess honestly. No matter what you say you mean to each other, you do not have the assured and promised commitment to one another that marriage, and only marriage, brings with it.

The vows you one day profess (if you marry each other, and that's still a big "if") will not be a mere legal formality to make official what was already there before. As your family and friends and church will witness by their presence, the promises you make on that day will make your relationship for the first time more than just a private arrangement between the two of you. Only then will you have established the kind of permanent, public responsibility to and for each other that makes sexual intercourse an honest, truthful expression of what you are together.

Contrary to what one regularly hears today, there is no evidence whatsoever that sexual intimacy before marriage increases the chances for a happy union after the wedding. If anything, the contrary is true, for some very practical reasons.

Many of the joys, adventures and excitement of sexual experience and fun can easily (much more easily than you might believe) become old hat. There may possibly even accompany this experience at least some sense of guilt. Sexual intimacy can thus become seriously blunted in its potential for helping couples in working patiently and tenderly through the tensions, uncertainties and new responsibilities of the first years of marriage.

Sexual intimacy also tends to become almost obsessive, especially when divorced from other needs and responsibilities which accompany normal daily married life. Once sex is begun, it can become a kind of hovering presence for a young man and woman. When they meet for a date, they know how the evening will end. All ingenuity in finding and learning other ways of having fun together, in communicating their hopes and concerns and ideals, even in exploring how they can make some gift of themselves to others who need them — all this easily becomes crowded out and ignored. Sex is always available, and it requires little in the way of thought, personal effort or unselfishness.

Your ideals and your love for each other are obviously deep. I hope you will keep them that way and always think through your moral decisions in this light. The payoff in happiness and peace of mind will be worth whatever it costs.

Living together before marriage

I have accepted most of the changes in the Catholic Church and feel they were for the betterment of all concerned.

However, something has recently occurred in our church which is beyond comprehension. A Catholic young lady and a Catholic man, living together for at least the last eight months, finally decided to marry. Banns were published in the church bulletin and they were married in a Catholic church

on Saturday evening with all the church's matrimonial services. They lived together up to the time of the services.

**Is living together before marriage now acceptable? Please
explain if this is a customary procedure.**

Living together before marriage is definitely not acceptable
in Christian morality. It is a hurtful, sinful situation, regardless
of how the couple involved may view it at the moment.

On the other hand, a man and woman have a right to marry
and Catholics have a right to a Catholic marriage ceremony.
I believe, however, that the solemnity and public character of
that marriage rite must be determined by balancing the rights
of the rest of the Catholic community — the right not to have
the marriage ceremony subjected to ridicule and reduced to
meaningless gesture. These are delicate pastoral decisions, to
be worked out in close consultation with the bride and groom
and all concerned.

Engaged couple shares bedroom

**When a couple is engaged, one set of parents of the cou-
ple see no wrong in the couple moving into the boy's bedroom.
The other parents believe this is seriously immoral. In this
case, doesn't the parish priest have the obligation to tell the
couple and the condoning parents that it is wrong, and to help
guide them back into the Christian lifestyle — instead of condoning it?**

I understand your hurt, disappointment and frustration over
what this young couple is doing. In addition to being wrong,
this kind of arrangement makes difficult if not impossible the
real joy and mutual support that the discoveries of living
together can bring when accompanied by that special commitment and covenant as husband and wife.

The trust and faithfulness these discoveries help build in
the context of marriage pay rich dividends in future years.
You want this, of course, in the fullest degree possible for your
son or daughter.

You wonder what you can do. At this point, not very much,
at least in the light of the few details you have given. Obvious-

ly, no parents have any obligation to condone or allow such an arrangement in their home. Nor should they.

As for the other parents' feelings, or the priest's, have you discussed this with them? And I mean personally? Much misinformation and misunderstanding in situations like this result from second or third-hand sources, however reliable you think they should be.

Talk to all the individuals involved. Don't be ashamed of your position or hesitate to enforce it. At the same time, make your love and care for these young people as clear as you can. Remember, God is their judge, not you.

Parents respond on live-ins

Dear Readers:

A mother wrote saying that her daughter had moved into an apartment with a young man. She asked for help on how to deal with the situation. How could she keep the door open and still make her own feelings clear? Should her daughter's friend be invited to family functions?

I indicated some of the many factors that need to be considered in coming to a good decision, and also invited readers who have faced such decisions to write to me of their experience. The response was overwhelming, not only in volume but in the evidence it gave once again of the faith in God and of the beautiful, almost primitive, parental instinct of love and protection that guides good mothers and fathers.

First, by far the majority insist that parents have a right and responsibility to make clear they believe that what is being done is wrong and why; but absolutely no shunning, no keeping them out of family gatherings, even if that means inviting the live-in partner also and showing basic Christian kindness to him or her as well. Everyone who mentioned the subject agreed that the couple should not be permitted to share a bedroom in the parents' home.

Not more than 1 or 2 percent of the parents pushed a hard-nosed approach: These "children" made their choice; they're out and they can come back when they change their ways. None of this group, incidentally, gave evidence in their letters to me of having faced the situation personally. There was much difference of opinion about under what circumstances parents should visit the other home. Many made the point, however, that parents should offer no support, financial or otherwise, to the upkeep of the couple's home.

Some of the most encouraging and inspiring notes were from adults now happily in good and strong marriages (with their former live-in partner or someone else) who expressed their gratitude for their parents' patience, faith and goodness during a period they know now was a tremendous test of those parents' love. These children, now with children of their own, admit they would never have kept their faith, or perhaps their emotional balance, if their parents had not stayed with them.

For the moment I will allow one Rhode Island couple to speak for nearly 300 others who expressed similar convictions.

"First and foremost we have to remember that our children, a gift from God, pass through us. We do not own them. Second, we are admonished by God not to judge or we will be judged. So at this point, it is obvious we do not have much control except perhaps a negative approach like shunning them, which I think is against all Christ's teachings.

"The answer sounds simple, but it is not, because of the heartbreak that comes from watching those we love do harm to themselves and others . . . The true solution is to do and accept the above, having faith that God will see us through, keeping the doors open and encouraging love and communication, with the understanding between God and us that he will make the final judgment and enlighten us and our children to understand our responsibilities."

Be tough on live-ins

I am a regular reader of your column and a disgruntled Catholic. With responses such as the one you set forth (see above) dealing with live-in sin and immorality, it is no wonder that the youth of our country have lost all sense of sin. You almost condone the immorality of cohabitation outside of marriage. It is priests like you who are diluting the meaning of the priesthood. I have had experience of a couple living together, but I did not water down the morality of the church to please the sinners.

It's about time priests starting preaching the moral principles and teaching of the church for a change, and stop promoting all the crackpot teaching of post-Vatican II theologians. It's high time you priests in the modern church got with it.

Many parents have written or phoned me since that column, thanking me for the help it was to them as good Catholics in attempting to deal with an extremely complicated and painful family situation.

You are asking me to answer a question that was not asked. The parent who wrote knew very well the situation was morally wrong; I agreed with her. She wanted to know not whether the couple should be doing it or not, but rather how do good parents handle the situation with charity and fidelity to what they believe, and with honesty to everyone involved. This obviously was also the concern of the hundreds of parents who wrote to me, and whose responses I attempted to summarize.

You apparently had your own way of dealing with the problem. Other parents have different methods and follow them without any denying or watering down their convictions about the moral character of what their children are doing. The parents who approached the situation more tenderly and patiently than it seems you did are not morally corrupt, and it is wrong and rash for you to imply that they are. The fact that many of their children are now in good marriages and raising good Catholic families says a lot for the validity and goodness of their methods.

Marry "in the church"?

My daughter plans to marry a divorced Protestant. He was baptized in the Baptist Church. Since they were told that they cannot marry in the Catholic Church, should my daughter obtain special permission from the bishop in order to marry in a Protestant church?

Is it possible that a priest can be present at the ceremony and give them some special blessing?

When the priest said your daughter and her fiance cannot marry in the church, he meant that they cannot be married according to the laws of the church, not simply that they cannot have the ceremony in the church building. A dispensation from the bishop to marry without a priest, in a Protestant church or elsewhere, is possible only when a couple are free to marry each other validly within the framework of Catholic marriage laws.

Therefore, without a declaration of nullity or other procedure (which apparently your parish priest considers unlikely) no such permission could be given, nor would a priest be present.

As a possible help to others, I should point out that your question, and your daughter's situation, is just one more illustration of the need to consider these facts of life before, not after, a person gets seriously involved with another with the possibility of marriage. The church's basic teachings and regulations concerning marriage are clear, long-standing, and readily available for the asking.

Therefore, if an individual's Catholic faith is considered personally valuable and essential, some principles and rules for personal guidance on dating and courtship must be set for oneself long before things have come to the point of planning the marriage.

What about a garden wedding?

My daughter wished to have a garden wedding performed by our parish priest on a Sunday. I received a reply that according to diocesan policy, sacraments should be performed in a sacred place, a church, and further that weddings may not be performed on Sunday. Is it unfair to call this arbitrary?

A friend just returned from a Catholic wedding on Sunday in another diocese. My brother in California said that Catholic garden weddings are commonplace out there.

Was Pope John's "throwing open the windows of the church" only so much press?

Let's take your questions one at a time. First, the general law of the church requires that a marriage between Catholics or between Catholics and a baptized non-Catholic be celebrated in a parish church, unless specific permission is granted by the bishop for marriage in another place.

If the non-Catholic party is not baptized the marriage can be celebrated either in church or some other suitable place. (Canon 1118)

As I have explained previously in this column, the church has tremendous respect for our church buildings as sacred places where particularly sacred events in our Catholic life should take place. Marriage of Christian people is one of them.

Thus, not only because it is an act of worship, but because a marriage is a solemn action that should not be trivialized in any way, a parish church is unquestionably the preferred location. Exceptions are allowed especially when at least one of the parties has so little connection with or respect for religion that this negative attitude would be harmful to a ceremony in church.

As the Code of Canon Law which I quoted makes clear, bishops can make exceptions; the usual policy, however, is the one followed by your own bishop.

While customs differ from country to country, Sunday weddings, while not unheard of, have been and still are strongly discouraged in most of the United States. First of all, Sunday responsibilities of priests in most parishes are already quite heavy, if not often exhausting. For this reason, and because of tight Mass schedules, it would be asking more than is normally possible for the priest to give the kind of attention, care and liturgical prayerfulness a couple deserve at their wedding.

More important, the church is if anything more insistent than it has been for many centuries on the importance of participation in the parish Sunday Mass by all members of the parish community. Anything which would detract from that, or seem to "substitute" for it is generally discouraged.

Priests who are sensitive to this concern will, apart from emergencies or very special circumstances of course, avoid even home Masses or other special group Eucharists on Sunday.

Thus, while no universal law of the church prohibits it, your diocese is only one of the many adhering to the policy that marriages should be scheduled on days other than Sunday.

As a pastor, I realize these policies sometimes seem inconvenient and arbitrary. But most of the time they are not. When Pope John XXIII "threw open the windows" it was to better help us identify, nourish and in some cases protect the most sacred traditions of our faith.

Proper concern for how and where we celebrate the Eucharist and other sacraments is one of the ways we try to do this.

Still have nuptial Masses?

I seldom see a reference to a nuptial Mass any more. Does it still mean a regular Mass centered around a wedding? Does it have to be performed in the morning? And do both parties have to be Catholic?

Nuptial Masses are generally referred to today as simply the Mass on the day of marriage. The wedding ceremony takes place after the Scripture readings and homily, but most of the variable parts of the Mass such as the prayers, Bible passages, prayers of the faithful, and so on, center on the theme of marriage.

According to general church regulations, wedding Masses may take place any time of the day or evening, but individual dioceses may have local rules limiting this in some way. In many parts of the country, for example, wedding Masses are not allowed on Sundays without special permission from the bishop.

Marriage ceremony without Mass

Our daughter plans to marry soon. She informs us that they want a wedding in a large church in our city, but she and her fiance want no Mass because they do not practice their faith.

She already set a date with the pastor of that church to be married there, but did not tell him there would be no Mass. Will the priest perform the ceremony without a Mass? I'm sick at heart and don't know how to handle this. Would it even benefit the couple spiritually if they had a nuptial Mass feeling as they do?

As you must be aware, it is not unheard of today for couples, both of whom come from Catholic homes, to approach the time of their marriage having very little faith in the church or sometimes even in God. They may be good young men and women otherwise, but are perhaps going through a religious crisis that they probably should have dealt with in adolescence.

When this happens, as you suggest, it often does seem more proper and honest for the couple to have a marriage ceremony without the Eucharist, which for them in this circumstance would have little or no meaning. In fact, many priests speak to couples about this option when it is clear the couples hold little interest in having a nuptial Mass.

My own approach, and I think that of most priests, is to use the time available before the marriage to discuss with the couple the need for making some firm decisions at this juncture of their lives about what life, God, the church, the sacraments and the Eucharist mean to them, if anything. With responsibilities for each other and perhaps soon for their children, they no longer have the luxury of floating aimlessly in these critical areas of a mature life.

I have no idea, of course, what the policy of that particular pastor is. I would urge your daughter to meet with him soon and level with him about her feelings and plans.

A sacrament without believing?

I am greatly disturbed by an answer you gave about marriage. You said that non-Catholics are considered to have a sacramental marriage if they are validly baptized Christians.

Is this true if they do not believe the marriage is a sacrament? And suppose the ceremony is witnessed by a clergyman who also does not believe it is a sacrament? You seem to answer in the affirmative.

If this is your belief, it would seem to make the sacraments simply magic. I suggest you reconsider your answer to a very serious question.

The answer I gave is correct according to present Catholic belief and practice. The questions you raise are, however, truly serious and are, in fact, being studied intently by theologians and canon lawyers.

The position of the church concerning sacramental marriages is loaded with some critical problems. According to our theology, marriage is the only sacrament that individuals can receive not only without knowing it, but even without believing in it — in fact, even deliberately rejecting a belief in the sacramentality of their marriage. Your question pinpoints the precise situation in which such an anomaly might occur.

At least part of the solution seems to lie in a clarification of the meaning of the word sacrament. That there is a significant and profound difference between a marriage of non-Christians and the marriage convenant and life of two Christians who meet and live with each other as committed members of the family of Christ, would not be denied, I believe, by anyone. As St. Paul said in the Letter to the Ephesians, the marriage of a man and woman who are already brother and sister in the family of Christ is itself a sign — a sacrament — of the love that flows between Christ and his church.

So the church is attempting to polish its understanding of Christian marriage.

The problem, incidentally, arises not only in the type of situation you describe. A similar question must be asked of a marriage which involves an individual who calls himself a Catholic but whose beliefs and practice of the faith are nearly non-existent. How realistic or honest is it to call such a marriage a sacrament — that is, a proclamation and commitment to living out their faith as members of the body of Christ?

Your question is an excellent one. Frankly, I'm surprised more people don't ask it.

Why marry before a priest?

I understand that now a Catholic girl can be married in a Protestant church by the boy's minister. I thought it had always been necessary for a Catholic to be married by a priest to be validly and truly married in the eyes of the church.

The rule you mention was the one most of us grew up with, but your feeling is a good example of how easily we believe something has "always" been simply because it's the only way we've known. This danger applies particularly to disciplinary laws of the church, which is what is involved here.

Although Christians were urged from early days to be married in their religious (Christian) family before a priest, no rule said all Catholics *had* to be (for validity) until 1563. For technical reasons even that rule didn't apply to most of the United States or to some other parts of the world. Thus, a marriage involving a Catholic could be performed by a minister or judge and be recognized by the church.

In the U.S., only since 1908 have all Catholics been bound by the requirement to be married before a priest, a law which the church is relaxing in some instances now, as you indicate in your question. However, even today a dispensation is always necessary from the bishop in order for that marriage to be valid according to Catholic Church law.

Dispensation from Form

A devout Catholic friend of mine is marrying a Jewish girl in a civil ceremony presided over by a justice of the peace.

I've spoken to two priests on his status with the church after his marriage, and received two different answers. Will he or will he not be a Catholic in good standing after this ceremony?

It is clear from my mail that many Catholics remain confused about this.

First of all, the law requiring Catholics to be married before a priest is a church law, not a law given by God. Through many centuries the church accepted civil marriages as valid for its members as well. At the same time, the church always insisted on the special sacramental character of marriages between two Christians, and urged that this sacramental character be honored in the way the marriage took place.

The rule that Catholics must exchange their consent before a priest in order that their marriage be valid has existed for the universal church only since the early part of this century.

Pope Paul VI modified this rule several years ago. Bishops may now dispense Catholics so that they may be married by someone else, a minister of another church, justice of the peace, and so on. This is referred to officially as a dispensation from the form of marriage. (CCL 1127-2)

The petition for such a dispensation is made by the couple through the priest who is arranging the marriage. The priest explains to the bishop the reasons he feels such a dispensation might be granted, reasons such as avoiding family alienation, a close relationship or friendship with the non-Catholic minister, and so on.

Unless such a dispensation is asked of the bishop and granted by him, any marriage of a Catholic with another Catholic, or with a person of another faith, that does not take place before a priest is still invalid according to Catholic Church law. (CCL 1108,1117)

Catholic marriage in Protestant church?

Recently a Catholic friend of ours was married to a divorced man in his Presbyterian church by a Presbyterian minister. We understand that a Catholic priest attended and blessed the couple after they were married.

Does the Catholic Church recognize this marriage as valid and can she receive the Sacraments of Penance and Communion? If so, we would like an explanation.

The situation you describe is entirely possible within the

legal framework of the Catholic Church, and (except for being married in the Protestant church) the possibility is by no means new in the Catholic Church.

There are two ways the second marriage might take place in light of his previous union. First, there could have been an annulment of that first marriage. This means, as is discussed more at length elsewhere, that some impediment existed from the beginning of that first marriage so that in the eyes of the church, and possibly of the state as well, there was never a marriage at all.

The other way is through a process called Privilege of the Faith. This process is similar to the Pauline Privilege (see 1 Corinthians, chapter 7) which would allow a second marriage in certain circumstances when it would be helpful to the faith of one of the parties. Privilege of the Faith cases are used to dissolve the marriage of a baptized Protestant (or sometimes Catholic) and a non-baptized person so that the partners in that marriage may marry again.

Neither annulment nor Privilege of the Faith cases are new in the church, though the average Catholic doesn't even hear about them until it involves a friend or member of the family. The marriage you speak of quite probably involved one of these processes and therefore was perfectly legitimate according to Catholic marriage laws. There is no reason the Catholic wife could not receive the sacraments.

Most Catholics surely know by now that a marriage of a Catholic and a Protestant can take place before a Protestant minister, provided the proper permission (technically called a Dispensation from the Form of Marriage) is obtained from the local bishop. When this happens it is quite common for the Catholic priest to share in the ceremony. I myself have done it several times when members of our parish were married in the church of the Protestant spouse.

Non-Catholic marriages are valid

I am a widowed Catholic who married a twice-divorced Protestant in a civil ceremony.

He was baptized and married in the Lutheran Church. I was informed by my parish priest that my marriage could not be blessed nor could I receive the sacraments unless my husband pursued a petition of annulment.

If the church, in fact, does not recognize marriages performed outside the church, why is it necessary to have a marriage annulled which, in the eyes of the church, was never performed in the first place?

It is my understanding after speaking with others during my travels that this ruling is not consistent nationwide.

What is your opinion?

You are mistaken, as are apparently countless others both Catholic and non-Catholic, in your assumption about the marriage of Protestants or others who are not Catholic.

It is true that every baptized Catholic who has not formally rejected the Catholic faith must be married before a priest (or bishop or deacon) to be truly married according to the laws of the Catholic Church.

That rule does not apply to those who are members of another faith, or who have no religion at all. If neither marriage partner is Catholic and both are free to marry (if neither has a previous marriage, for example), the Catholic Church recognizes this union as a true, valid marriage.

If two Buddhists marry, for instance, before a Buddhist monk, we acknowledge that as a real marriage, uniting the two people in a marriage bond.

Even more, if both non-Catholic partners in a marriage are validly baptized Christians, such as two Lutherans or Methodists, we Catholics view that union as not only a valid marriage but a Christian sacrament.

Hundreds of Catholics, and others who become involved in a serious relationship with Catholics, cause themselves much pain because they do not remember this simple but essential truth. Most priests with even a little parish experience have had at least one couple approach them to be married with the nonchalant remark, "He was married before, Father, but it doesn't count because he's not Catholic."

The church honors every marriage, Catholic or not, as a sacred union that cannot be simply brushed off.

Thus, any previous marriage by one of the partners planning a wedding must be dealt with in an appropriate way by the church before the forthcoming marriage could take place.

There is nothing at all new in the above regulations and policies of the church. In this matter there is no difference between one part of our country, or the world for that matter, and another. They are provisions of the theology and law which govern the Latin-Rite Church.

Is marriage by Protestant minister a sacrament?

My question concerns an answer you gave about the marriage of a Catholic to a Protestant in a Protestant church and by the Protestant minister.

If the clergyman performing the marriage is not Catholic, will the marriage be a legal and valid marriage only, or will it be the Sacrament of Matrimony.

My Catholic niece is marrying in the Methodist Church under a situation which is painful to our family since there was no dispensation obtained, as far as I know.

According to our traditional theology as well as the present canon law of the Catholic Church, any valid marriage between two baptized Christians is a sacramental marriage. The special relationship with Jesus Christ which comes through baptism makes the marriage union of those two people special also.

Scripture tells us that every marriage on earth reflects in some way the relationship of fidelity and love between God and his people. For Christians this symbolism goes a giant step further in its symbolizing the redemptive love of Our Lord for his church and through that church for the whole world. St. Paul points up that relationship in his discussion of Christian marriage in Chapter 5 of Ephesians.

From what you tell me in your letter, however, the marriage of your niece is a different case. All baptized Catholics are obliged by church law to be married before a priest unless a dispensation from this requirement is obtained from the bishop.

Any marriage of a Catholic before any other religious or civil official without such a dispensation would not be a valid, true marriage according to the laws of the church.

Power to administer sacraments

In a recent issue of our diocesan paper you answered a question concerning the validity of a marriage performed by a Baptist minister. Assuming a dispensation was given as you stated, does such a dispensation confer upon the minister the power to administer the sacrament of matrimony? Is the Catholic Church acknowledging non-Catholic ministers as equally validly ordained as its own priests with the same powers to administer not only the sacrament of matrimony, but all the sacraments?

Shouldn't such large changes in the church's attitude toward other ministers in matters that affect aspects of our everyday lives be brought out at church from the pulpit, and not left just to the chance that the right question might be asked?

In our church, and generally in civil law, people are not married "by" the person officiating at the wedding. They are married by each other.

Thus, in Catholic theology and practice, the priest does not administer the sacrament of matrimony; the bride and groom administer this sacrament to each other by making and declaring the covenant that unites them as husband and wife.

This is clear in the Code of Canon Law, which states that the couple are married "in the presence" of the priest or other officiating person, and that the officiating minister "assists" at the ceremony (n. 1108).

As for your second point, it might be helpful to remember that priests are often unaware of subjects in which people feel confused or ill-informed until they are asked, which is of course one of the reasons for this column.

Marriage to an atheist?

I met my husband in 1964 and after many ups and downs through several years, we decided to marry. It was then I found out he was never baptized and really seemed to be what he always called himself — an atheist. A nun in my school had said that Catholics cannot marry someone unbaptized, so I encouraged my fiance to join a church, which he did; he was baptized in the United Church of Christ. We took his baptismal certificate to the priest, and were married.

Now I've begun to worry about our marriage, whether it is truly a marriage since I am not sure how much he wanted to be baptized in the first place. Our two children are being raised Catholic. My husband encourages their prayers and participates in the celebration of our Catholic feasts.

What can or should be done to, or with, our marriage? Is it valid? I don't know any priests here well enough to ask.

From what you have told me, there's no question that your marriage is valid.

First, it is possible for a Catholic to marry a non-baptized person. It's done all the time. Under the former Code of Canon Law, a dispensation was required for a Catholic to marry one of another faith, or of no faith. Different kinds of dispensations were needed when the non-Catholic party was baptized, and when he was not baptized. However, to avoid the very problem that bothers you, normally both of these dispensations (technically called, respectively, dispensations for Mixed Religion and for Disparity of Cult) were granted in a mixed marriage. This way, whether the non-Catholic was baptized or not, the marriage was perfectly valid. Since 1983, a dispensation is needed and given only when the non-Catholic partner is not baptized. (CCL 1086)

Continue to receive the sacraments, and be happy your husband takes the supportive attitude he does concerning the faith of you and your children.

Latin-Ukrainian Rite marriage

I am a devoted Roman Catholic going with a girl who belongs to a Ukrainian Catholic Church.

I need to know whether this is a Catholic church. If we are married, will this be accepted by our church without any changes on the girl's part?

The Ukrainian Rite is one of the Eastern churches which are under the pastoral authority of the Bishop of Rome.

Like many Eastern-Rite churches, however, this rite has undergone a tumultuous history and until recently suffered severe pressures and persecution under the Russian Communists in the countries of Eastern Europe. As a result of these centuries-old conflicts and divisions, there are today both Catholic and Orthodox groups using the Ukrainian Rite.

Ukrainian-Rite Catholics are as much a part of our church as are Latin-Rite Catholics, though certain permissions and delegations are sometimes required before a marriage can take place between Catholics of these different rites.

It happens that the church you mentioned (in Pennsylvania) is one of the Catholic churches of the Ukrainian Rite. Your question, however, is a wise one, and should be asked by anyone contemplating marriage with a person who belongs to a different rite. If a Latin-Rite Catholic wishes to marry someone from an Orthodox church, long and complicated preparations might be required before the marriage can take place.

Vows in interfaith marriage

My nephew is marrying a non-Catholic and asked the priest if their marriage ceremony could have two recitations of the vows, one for the priest and one for the Protestant pastor of the bride who will also be present. The priest said this was impossible. I thought this was done often now in other churches, so why can't it be done in our parish?

No, this procedure is never allowed in the Catholic Church, nor in any Protestant church that I know of. For one thing, it could create considerable legal confusion over the marriage that might be detrimental to the new bride and groom.

Both by general church law for the entire world, and by

regulations of the bishops of the United States, it is not permitted to have two separate religious marriage services, or one service which would include both the Catholic and non-Catholic marriage ritual.

You may be thinking of the marriage of a Catholic to a person of another faith (or of no faith) which takes place before a judge or Protestant minister rather than before a priest. As I've explained several times before, it is permitted now, on condition that a dispensation is obtained for such a marriage from the Catholic party's bishop.

Help for inter-faith wedding

I am excited and enthusiastic over the direction my faith journey has brought me, but sad because of the hurt it is causing my family. I am the fifth living member of my family to become an ordained Protestant minister. Six years later, after much soul-searching and prayer, I was released from my ordination. Next Easter I hope to be confirmed into Roman Catholicism. This decision has pained my parents. I feel torn between respect and love for them and my love for the Catholic Church.

While we are not engaged, my special friend and I do plan to marry. Instead of dreaming what colors, flowers and dresses, I have always visualized the music, Scripture and liturgy of the wedding service. Recently my father shared his hurt that he could not lead the marriage vows and could not baptize my children as he had his other grandchildren, though I intend to request that my father participate in the wedding service as much as is allowed.

To assist worshiping Protestants at our wedding, I hope the priest will allow me to type the liturgy from the missal into a bulletin format that could be followed by my family and friends. Is this possible? Do you have other suggestions?

Situations like yours are always and inevitably extremely sensitive and painful. Some claim that if we were able to share the Eucharist, it would solve most of the problem. I seriously doubt that; surely it would not be true in light of the long commitment of your family to belief and service within your Protestant background.

I'm happy you and your friend are concerned to do whatever possible to prevent, or at least minimize, any hurt and disappointment for your families. It will not be possible for you to wipe away all the pain; it is part of the cross we all carry because of the sad division among the followers of Christ. I think your suggestion of a worship aid for everyone to use at the wedding is an excellent one. If you include the words of familiar hymns and prayers it may help your family and friends to realize you have not left as much of your heritage as they assume.

Another suggestion. Protestants usually relate quite easily to our Liturgy of the Word. It is the Liturgy of the Eucharist which confuses them and makes them feel they are involved in something far too "Catholic." Yet nearly every Protestant denomination, certainly including yours, reverences the Lord's Supper, even when not celebrating it frequently.

How about putting something like this in your leaflet for them? "At the Last Supper on the night before he died, our Lord Jesus Christ celebrated a sacred meal with his disciples. He took bread and wine, said 'This is my body; this is my blood,' and told them to eat and drink. He then said, 'Do this to remember me.' Thus, the Lord's Supper (called by Catholics the Mass, or the celebration of the Eucharist) is sacred to all Christians. Catholics obey this command of Jesus each week, but in a special way at the most important times in people's lives. This Eucharist of our Lord Jesus will be part of today's marriage ceremony as we remember and thank God our Father for what Jesus has done for us. We are all invited to unite ourselves, and especially the bride and groom, to Jesus Christ and to share his death and resurrection in our lives."

I have found that some explanation like this does much to help other Christians at least understand what we (and they) are about in a marriage ceremony, even if they cannot fully accept it.

A Jewish-Catholic wedding

You have written often about interfaith marriages, but I

**don't remember your answering a question about something
I encountered recently.**

**There was a Jewish-Catholic wedding in which much of the
Catholic liturgy was omitted. While it took place in the
Catholic Church, there was nothing Catholic about it, no Sign
of the Cross, and the name of Christ was never mentioned.
A Protestant friend who attended made the statement that
it could have been performed in the courthouse.**

**Can you explain why this happened? There was a time when
the Catholic Church didn't sway one inch in this respect, and
now the pendulum has swung completely the other way.**

The kind of wedding you describe always presents a painful pastoral dilemma to the church, to the priest in a parish,
and usually also to the families.

The Catholic is marrying someone who, apart from what
we share in our Jewish heritage, is totally alien to our Christian culture and traditions. By the time they are preparing for
the wedding, there is little chance that their religious differences will affect their plans for marriage one way or the
other.

In such circumstances, the church, through its pastors and
others, attempts to do all it can to strengthen the moral and
spiritual commitments of the couple about their marriage, to
respect the beliefs of both parties and their families, and to
treat the Catholic with the charity and concern that any
member of the church deserves. At the same time, we, the
church, must be faithful to ourselves and not contradict our
own beliefs.

The marriage ceremony you describe represents one pastoral
attempt to respect all these responsibilities. The approach, in
fact, is quite common in the marriage of a Catholic and Jew.
Nothing of our beliefs is denied; the ceremony simply utilizes
those elements of our faith which we hold in common with
the Jewish traditions — which elements are, of course, extremely rich. (The same policy often is followed, incidentally, by priests and other Christians who participate in prayer
at events where both Christians and Jews are present.)

The solution is clearly not ideal for anyone concerned. But assuming the couple are to be married with the blessing of the church, the alternative would be a dispensation from the bishop for them to be married by another clergyman or a civil judge. I imagine you would agree that this would be no improvement over the manner in which your priest handled the marriage.

Wedding in a hotel?

My daughter is marrying a Jewish man and a priest will officiate. The wedding will take place on an island where there is a non-denominational church. If it rains, the alternate place is the library in a hotel.

In requesting the library to be used, the pastor of the parish in which the hotel is located says we have not received permission.

In your article you mentioned that such couples could be married in a Protestant or other church. What is your opinion concerning this?

According to Catholic Church law, as I have explained, the marriage between a Catholic and a baptized non-Catholic is normally to be celebrated in a parish church. The local bishop can permit such a marriage to be celebrated in some other place that would be suitable.

Your daughter's marriage, of course, is to a non-baptized person. Church regulations indicate that these marriages may take place in a church or "other suitable place." (Canon 1118)

The words about a "suitable place" are essential because any marriage is a sacred commitment. While Christian marriage has the special character of sacrament, Scripture makes clear that every marriage, Christian or not, in some way reflects God's love and covenant with our human family, and our responsibilities in that covenant to him in return.

The solemnity of the wedding ceremony, including the place where it is celebrated, must reflect that reality as well as possible. In our understanding, the marriage rite is more than a social event, though others who do not view marriage as we do might consider it almost that.

No special permission from the bishop is necessary for this suitable place, but the local priest or deacon preparing the marriage has the responsibility to be sure the sacred character of the wedding is preserved. I would hope not only your daughter but her Jewish partner wishes to give witness to that understanding of their marriage ceremony.

The above applies, incidentally, to any marriages celebrated by priests or deacons. The same principles would apply generally to a marriage celebrated by another clergyman or civil official after the Catholic partner has received a dispensation from the form of marriage.

"Sanatio in Radice"

When a bishop grants a *Sanatio in Radice*, is a record kept in the bishop's (chancery) office?

Is the couple granted the *Sanatio in Radice* entitled to a copy of the bishop's approval for their personal records, or does this remain in the church records only?

For the enlightenment of those who have never heard of a *Sanatio in Radice*, we'd better explain what it is. This process, often simply called a *Sanatio*, is a validation of a marriage that already has taken place.

The validation is accomplished in such a way, however, that any impediment to the marriage that may have been there is dispensed or corrected, and the renewed consent of the couple is not required. According to church law, it is as if the marriage were valid from the beginning.

Suppose, for example, a Catholic man were marrying an unbaptized woman. Without a dispensation such a marriage would not be valid according to church law. Suppose further that by some oversight (which may have been unknown even by the priest and the couple) the necessary dispensation was never given before the marriage ceremony.

By the process of *Sanatio in Radice* (a Latin phrase meaning literally "a healing at the root"), the necessary dispensation would be given perhaps months later, but the marriage is then considered valid from the wedding day.

To answer your question, a record of such actions is kept in the chancery.

If the couple feels a need for it and they request it, a copy of the record of the action may be sent to them.

Priest doesn't marry you?

An 80-year-old friend told me recently that a relative was married and praised the priest who "married them." I replied that even the pope cannot marry someone; the couple marry each other and the priest simply receives their vows.

Would you please tell me if I'm correct in believing that an ordained priest can administer only six of the seven sacraments?

Technically, you are right. The bride and groom by their exchange of marriage vows administer the sacrament of matrimony to each other; the priest is there as the official witness and representative of the church.

Therefore, in the Latin Rite, ordained priests can administer only six of the sacraments. (In some other Catholic rites priests may marry, in which instance, of course, they would also administer the Sacrament of Marriage.) Thus the expression to be married "before" a priest is theologically preferable to "by" a priest.

Don't get your hopes up though. Your chances of reversing several centuries of English tradition on the subject are somewhat less than promising.

"Unofficial" marriages

Is there any way a couple can be married in the Catholic Church without having the marriage registered with the state? My first husband died and I have been raising our three children on an annuity from his former employer. However, that annuity stops when I remarry.

I have met a fine gentleman who wants to marry me, but he is on a low income and we would need the annuity money for the children. Could we get married without having it "official?"

There's no way you could do that, to my knowledge. Any person empowered to officiate at marriages (clergyman, judge, etc.) is obliged by law to notify the proper state office of the fact of the marriage. This is normally done through completion of the marriage license which the couple must acquire before they can be legally married.

Failure of a priest, minister, or anyone else, to notify the state that he has performed a marriage is a violation of the law for which he may be punished, at least with a fine.

Common law marriage, by which a couple would simply begin to live together without benefit of a properly performed and registered marriage ceremony, is not recognized in most states. Therefore, attempting an "unregistered marriage" could create serious legal problems for the clergyman and yourselves.

Should you still have questions, it would be best to discuss the matter with an attorney, who could also advise you on other serious legalities.

Shower for divorced person?

Recently I was asked to help at a shower for a Catholic bride who was marrying a divorced man. The wedding was to take place in a Protestant church because it couldn't be performed in a Catholic church. I refused. Did I do wrong? Could a Catholic who knew all this attend the wedding in good faith?

A person's decision in a situation like this is never an easy one because it involves so many seemingly conflicting obligations of charity.

Of course you are not acting in true friendship if a friend is doing something you consider seriously wrong and harmful, and yet you pretend that you consider it blameless or a minor matter of personal difference. In the all too common circumstance you face, it is generally easier for a close friend or relative to be involved in such a wedding, and at the same time have the bride and groom perfectly aware that their involvement in no way implies agreement with the couple's attitude toward marriage and divorce, but is simply a gesture of friendship and affection. For a more distant acquaintance it may be more difficult to do this.

In my own experience, I have found that individuals are often confirmed in their easy attitude toward divorce and remarriage by the ready and unquestioning "approval" of their friends and relatives. Some sad, complicated family tragedies have resulted.

Of course, there may be obligations in charity to others, too, such as your family, your children — and not least of all to yourself. You have your own convictions and you don't have to be ashamed of them. It's not hard to feel pressured in such situations today by the claim that everyone has the right to "do his own thing." Fine. But that goes both ways. You have just as much right to do your own thing, even if it means saying, "I don't agree with what you are doing." With a little thought, I'm sure you can make your point with tact and kindness.

I'm sure you are aware that there are circumstances in which a Catholic may quite legitimately be married in a Protestant church. That would seem ruled out by your question, however, if you are sure, as you say, that her marriage "couldn't be performed in a Catholic church."

Sinful to attend anniversary party?

A friend of mine, a divorced Catholic, will be celebrating the 25th anniversary of her second marriage soon. Would it be a sin if I attended the celebration?

Such decisions can cause us concern, but it isn't a question of sin or not. You obviously are giving it serious thought and want to do the right thing.

The question is rather, "What is the better thing to do?" After 25 years, the likelihood that she will interpret your presence as your personal approval of her whole past life is small indeed. It would be considered a gesture of friendliness and love for the couple.

Unless you feel other circumstances involved should strongly influence you, make your decision on the basis of your friendship and support for her.

Should priest have attended?

How would the church view the attendance of a priest at a large reception following a wedding performed by a judge of a Catholic couple, one divorced and the other a widow?

The action taken by this Catholic couple in planning their wedding and reception in advance, being aware of the fact that their wedding would not be sanctioned by the church, their attendance at Mass and receiving Holy Communion on the morning of their wedding is, in my opinion, a source of scandal to the community.

Under the circumstances of the wedding, doesn't the presence of the priest at the reception constitute his approval of the wedding?

It is possible that, for some reason, both individuals were free to marry and that they received a dispensation to be married before a judge. In the circumstances you describe, however, the likelihood of that is quite remote.

If the marriage was invalid according to the laws of the church, as most Catholic people would understandably assume, it would seem that the attendance of a priest at the reception would be at least extremely confusing. Attendance by certain friends, or even a family, might be interpreted a little more easily as simply an expression of friendship — though even that would have to be thought through very carefully beforehand by each individual.

The priest's attendance would normally be interpreted as an apparent celebration and congratulation concerning a marriage that, according to Catholic Church regulations, simply does not exist.

Your comment about their attending Mass and Communion on the morning of their wedding is what makes me wonder if perhaps there was not some permission given for this ceremony. Whatever the policy of your diocese, I cannot imagine a priest sanctioning that kind of contradiction between the individuals' life of prayer and worship and what they professed by their open rejection of church law later in the day.

Approving such a course of action would be no favor even
to the couple being married, who appear already to have an
awfully mixed-up conscience. Ignoring for the moment the
scandal to everyone else, someday they will have to sort out
their beliefs and actions, and straighten themselves out on who
they are and what they believe. Confusing the couple further
by apparent approval of their present action can only hurt
them in the long run, it seems to me, and is surely no favor
to them.

Witness at civil marriage?

**Is it permissible for a practicing Catholic to be the main
witness at a wedding between a divorced Catholic and a Protestant in a civil ceremony?**

**I have heard that this is not allowed by the church, but have
been told that I am misinformed.**

It is wrong for a Catholic to be a witness at a marriage
ceremony which is invalid and wrong according to church law,
as this marriage seems to be.

It is possible, though unlikely according to your letter, that
the marriage will be in accord with church legislation. This
would have required action by a Catholic marriage court
relating to the first marriage, and a dispensation for the new
marriage to take place in another church or court.

If you're not certain, your parish priest can help you find
out.

Nephew married out of church

**My niece's boy is married outside the church to a divorced
girl. They tried to arrange to be married by a priest, but it
took too long, so they were married at her Protestant church.**

**As a Catholic, am I permitted to give this boy and his wife
presents or money for Christmas and their birthdays? I think
a lot of him, and want to be sure I am doing the right thing.**

These kinds of situations always call for difficult and often
painful decisions. While one cannot presume to judge another

individual before God, you obviously believe, based on your Christian convictions about marriage, that the boy has done something seriously wrong.

Surely, if he claims the right to do his thing, you have at least as much right to do yours. In no way should you be expected to deny your beliefs or act contrary to them, or pretend you approve his actions. At the same time, you wish to preserve a good relationship in the family, and to let him know he still has your love.

My own conviction is that in such circumstances much more is gained by honey than vinegar. Give the gifts that you feel appropriate, and make sure he realizes your affection for him.

I think you owe it to him, though, to let him know clearly (and this need be done only once) how you feel about what he has done, especially since there seems to be a respectful attitude toward you as his great-aunt. You should not be in the permanent position of wondering whether he is misinterpreting your actions as an agreement with what he has done.

Should he become angry with you for saying what you think, chances are good this will be because he feels a genuine guilt over his action and resents being reminded of it by someone close to him. If this happens, hard as it may be for you, you will have done a considerable favor for him both psychologically and spiritually.

Impotence: an impediment to marriage

An article I read has me confused. It referred to an Illinois couple who wanted to marry but were refused because the man was impotent. Later the bishop intervened and granted a dispensation so that the marriage could take place in a Catholic church.

Some television reports I heard confused impotence with sterility. I know the difference, but when I was in Catholic high school we learned that impotence was an impediment to a valid marriage. A person cannot make a contract he cannot fulfill.

Impotence is as much an impediment as insanity, close

blood relationship or previous marriage. I would certainly like to have an explanation.

I received many questions on this subject from various parts of the country, partly inspired I imagine by the same newscasts that confused you.

You seem to remember your high school marriage class well, but for those who don't, we should make sure of the difference between sterility and impotence.

An individual is sterile, in the legal sense of the word, when he or she is incapable of parenting a child because of a defect in the natural internal process of generation; in other words, in the elements of that process that are involuntary. A man who produces no sperm, for example, or a woman who has no ovaries, is said to be sterile.

Impotence, on the other hand, is the inability to have sexual intercourse because of some physical or emotional defect.

You are right that impotence is an impediment to a valid marriage. As you know, however, time is not available in high school religion class to examine many details. And one detail is vitally important in this case.

In order for it to be an impediment to marriage, impotence must be absolute in the sense that it is permanent, with no hope of rehabilitation that might in the future make sexual relations possible for that individual.

The bishop and other officials of the diocese involved received medical opinions from some of the best authorities in the country that such absolute impotence is very rare.

Rehabilitative techniques for people who suffer from paralysis-related impotence (as the man did in this case) are improving all the time. All experts consulted suggested that these improvements hold out some hope here. Where there is any such hope, the impotence is legally doubtful and the couple have a right to marry.

This was the final decision made by the bishop. He gave no special permission or dispensation. He simply followed basic principles of our church laws (and, incidentally, of some civil laws) and told the couple they were free to marry in the Catholic Church.

Sex and old age

I have a question we discussed recently. Are sex and intercourse permitted after the child-bearing possibility is eliminated because of age?

I'm amazed how often this question is asked. The answer is yes. The inability to have children is of itself in no way a moral or spiritual obstacle to sexual relations.

Many couples (I would hope most of them) find their sexual relationship full and enriching well into their older years. Not only is there nothing wrong with it; this is the way it should be and what they should attempt to be for each other if possible at any age.

Permanence of marriage

If two people were divorced, one Catholic and one non-Catholic, and they want to marry each other, why can't they be married in the Catholic Church? Why must the Sacrament of Communion be denied the Catholic for life?

A thousand factors may determine whether or not a particular second marriage can be performed in a Catholic church. This answer, therefore, must speak only of general and basic truths; it cannot attempt to explain specifically about your son's marriage.

When two people marry, the presumption of the church is that they are promising and uniting themselves to each other, as they themselves say, for life. This commitment is religious and most serious and binding in conscience. Certainly no one is married in the Catholic Church without being reminded that this is what marriage involves.

When this commitment is broken, the church takes the position that, whatever private and personal justification the individual may give to himself, facts must be accepted and acted upon as they appear in public.

In other words, without judging the person's interior relationship to his own conscience and to God, as far as the church's society is concerned a second marriage cannot take place when one or both partners already have spouses to whom they have united themselves in marriage. The fact that a civil divorce has been granted would not change the matter. (See the next chapter on divorce, annulment and remarriage.)

The same facts explain why such persons should not go to Communion. The church accepts at face value the individual's personal and religious commitment in the previous marriage. In such a presumption, a second marriage would be seriously wrong. And, as you know, continuing to do something one knows is seriously wrong rules out the worthy reception of Holy Communion.

It should be noted, of course, that some couples in such marriage situations sincerely do not believe they are wrong, or find it impossible to get out of the situation without gross injustice to others. Later questions will deal more explicitly with some of these situations.

Polygamy and church law

Recently I read that it was not until the late Middle Ages that a papal encyclical banned the practice of polygamy in the church. Would you comment on the history of polygamous practices in the church prior to its being officially prohibited?

There is no evidence that the Catholic Church, either in its theologians or (even more so) in its official teachings, ever approved the practice of polygamy, that is, one husband having more than one wife at the same time.

Several reasons may explain the confusion you apparently encountered. One is the obvious divine approval of polygamous marriages in the Old Testament. Christian theologians through the centuries have speculated on how that could be.

Some said polygamy is only illicit because of an explicit command by God. A more common position is that having several wives is against the natural law but was permitted in the Old Testament by God for special reasons. In either case, none have defended polygamy as a morally lawful option since the time of Christ.

It is true that several hundred years ago the church made some strong statements against polygamy that might seem to imply this teaching was something new. These Catholic declarations, however, were to repudiate a position held by some of the major Protestant reformers that at very least leaned heavily toward occasional permission to have more than one wife.

The political leader, Philip of Hesse, for example, consulted Martin Luther and Philip Melancthon about his desire to take a second wife. They gave their approval since "what was permitted in marriage in the law of Moses, the Gospel does not take away." The Council of Trent in 1563 strongly opposed that position.

Even into this century some writers unfriendly toward the Catholic Church have claimed that certain popes permitted bigamous unions for some royal officials.

The allegation was repeated several times, for example, that Pope Clement VII declared himself prepared to grant a dispensation to King Henry VIII for bigamy. To my knowledge, however, no historian today seriously embraces that position.

Protestant baptisms recognized

I am a Catholic married to a Lutheran. Our 3-year-old son was baptized in the Lutheran Church. I attend Mass every Sunday and my husband and son attend the Lutheran Church regularly.

I realize that when I married, I affirmed that I would do everything in my power to see that my children would be raised Catholic. After many discussions and much prayer, we are trying to do what is best for all of us.

I pray often that someday we will be able to worship together. I need to know if the Catholic Church recognizes our son's baptism. As guilt overwhelms me, I wonder where I stand with the church. Also, some time ago I read that it's possible that within 10 years Catholics and Lutherans may

have intercommunion. Could this be true?

First, let's talk about your son. There's no reason whatsoever for you to be concerned whether or not he is really baptized. As a Catholic, you wonder what our church's position is on this. It is quite clear.

The Catholic Church recognizes the validity of baptisms in many other Christian churches. There's nothing new about this. Vatican Council II often refers to baptism as one of the sacramental bonds that link us with other Christian churches.

In one place the council says, "The Christian way of life of these (Protestant) brethren is nourished by faith in Christ. It is strengthened by the grace of baptism and the hearing of God's word." (Decree on Ecumenism, no. 23.)

Long before that the church explicitly mentioned Lutherans, along with Presbyterians, Baptists, Methodists, Congregationalists and Disciples of Christ as among those who should not receive even conditional baptism if they convert to the Catholic faith, since there is no reason to doubt the validity of the baptism they received in the church they belonged to before.

As your letter implies, the promise or affirmation made when you were married adds nothing to the responsibilities any believing and committed Catholic has as he or she enters marriage.

Those who take their religious commitments seriously (and for Catholics this would include certainly their beliefs concerning the church, the Eucharist, the sacraments, etc.) have a grave responsibility to do everything possible to provide their children an opportunity for that same relationship to God.

However, sometimes even with the best intentions what one would wish to do is found to be impossible. This is why the affirmation made by a Catholic before an interfaith marriage is worded precisely as you stated: I will do everything within my power to share the faith that I have with our children by having them baptized and raised as Catholics.

From your letter it seems you have taken this responsibility seriously, but because of tragic misunderstandings between you and your husband about the strengths of your personal religious convictions, things have not worked out.

Please try not to feel guilty about this. Whatever mistakes may have been made in the past, you did, and are doing, the best you could, which is all God asks of us.

Be faithful to your own convictions and live your Catholic faith as fully as you can. If you do that as charitably as possible with your family, God will certainly bless your efforts in his own way.

The difficulties you describe are just one more evidence of how seriously couples should take their religious convictions at the time of their marriage. One of the primary purposes of the church's requirements in anticipation of an interfaith marriage is to bring the couple to a serious dialogue about their beliefs in God and their church.

Without a mutual and honest understanding before marriage, there is great danger either that the marriage will be fatally shaken by the differences later on, or one of the parties will be required to compromise what is seen as a weighty responsibility before God — which is where you find yourself in your marriage in relation to your child.

No one today is able to foretell the future of the ecumenical movements of our age. In spite of the increased understanding between Lutherans and Roman Catholics, however, there is no evidence that the intercommunion you speak of is likely in the immediate future.

Are parents still responsible?

Doctrines taught in religion classes of Catholic schools today seem so often to differ with what I and other parents think. Is our responsibility for the Catholic education of our children lessened, since we don't know what's happening?

Absolutely not. While parents, as well as teachers and school officials may often forget it, parents remain the ones with the primary right and responsibility for the growth of their children, and that includes their education. A mother and father no more surrender this responsibility by sending their children to school than they surrender primary obligations for their child's health by sending him to a doctor.

Certainly the faith is "taught" today much differently than when we were in school. (Considering the unspeakable tragedies of the past 30 years, both at home and abroad, by the failures of supposedly religious people, one would think, incidentally, we might welcome efforts at a few changes.)

But, to be frank, why don't you know what's happening? Special programs for parents of students, even series of classes, are common today in Catholic schools and other religious education programs. Annual or semi-annual Masses are scheduled for students and parents to help parents better understand the liturgical implications of the faith their children are building. Attendance at all such activities is typically poor — unattended mainly by parents who openly admit their confusion over what their children are being taught.

Such parents often stay away because they fear they will learn something that will shake them up and make them do some fresh thinking. It may be an explanation, but it's hardly a responsible way to act.

If your school or religion class is doing something you don't understand, ask your child or his teacher to try to explain it more fully. You might even attend a class or two and show them both, at least, that you care.

Honor of one's parents

What is meant by the commandment: Honor your father and mother?

Does this mean that if you are disobedient at home you are breaking the commandment and therefore committing a mortal sin?

Obedience to parents is surely a significant element, but we should not start with that word when we discuss the fourth commandment.

It is worth noting that in both listings of the commandments in the Old Testament (Exodus 20 and Deuteronomy 5) the word honor is used. Thus, obligation to respect and love one's parents, to care for them as necessary, lasts throughout life.

The duty of honor is a serious one. The integrity and strength of family life depends upon this relationship and, by extension, much of the respect for authority in human society grows out of that kind of family relationship.

Obviously obedience is part of this honor and respect when one is growing up under the care of one's parents, who have the primary responsibility of guiding us toward adulthood. When we are young and when we are living within their home, their regulations and commands should be obeyed unless, of course, those commands involve something sinful.

The seriousness of violating this or any other commandment depends on many factors. To neglect one's parents grossly, to refuse continually to show them the respect and love which they deserve simply because they are our parents, to disobey a serious and important rule — all these may be serious sins if, of course, they are fully intentional and deliberate. Most "disobediences" against parents in the normal process of daily living are a long way from this kind of serious sin.

Parents reject daughter

I would like your interpretation of the words "judge" and "condemn" in the following example.

If a girl has been married in an enforced marriage, it is obvious she has committed a sin against purity. If an accusing person (a parent of the girl) states that because she has done wrong she will never be forgiven and may never come home again, and that they never want to see her, is the parent "judging" or "condemning?" Is condemning or judging ever justifiable?

Your statements cry out for comment on a number of aspects besides your actual question. For example, under no circumstance — including pregnancy — is there such a thing as an "enforced marriage." Until the marriage ceremony itself, both partners are entirely free to marry or not. In fact, in some instances the circumstance of the girl's pregnancy might increase the urgency that they *do not* marry, but deal with the situation in a different way. Anyone who encourages such a couple in the belief that they "have to get married" is guilty of a sinful and grave injustice toward them.

Young couples whose sexual activity leads them into an unmarried pregnancy generally never stop to think of the many people they hurt and the lives they distress in addition to their own. Among those who suffer much are, in most instances, their own parents. Even so, I find it difficult to grasp how supposedly emotionally stable parents can react to their child in the manner you describe, though I know from unhappy experience that it does happen. The Gospels, beginning with the Sermon on the Mount, abound with clear statements from Christ that this kind of attitude toward *any* sinner is unjustifiable and sinful.

Any sin committed by the two people may have been repented and forgiven long before anyone knew of the pregnancy. If God has forgiven, by what contortions of conscience could anyone assume the right to withhold forgiveness, to play God in this brutal way? And this at a time when genuine unselfish support and love from the parents may be needed more than ever!

There is, after all, still such a thing as hating the sin — which we must — and loving the sinner, which we also must. Each time we pray the Our Father, we ask God to "forgive us as we forgive" those who offend us. Do the parents or others you describe really want God to treat them as sinners, the way they treat someone else?

Pregnant, afraid of parents

A recent conversation I had with a young Catholic girl disturbed me greatly. The subject was abortion. While she knew abortion was "morally wrong," the young woman said that if she ever became pregnant she would choose abortion. When I asked this college-bound woman why, she responded, "Because my parents would kill me or make me feel so bad I would want to kill myself."

Her parents happen to be very active supporters of the pro-life movement. This made me stop and wonder how many other young women faced with similar circumstances are recommending or having abortions, knowing the spiritual consequence, to escape the wrath or heartbroken reaction of their parents. No unmarried young woman looks forward to facing her parents and saying, "I'm pregnant!" The agony, the fear, the mortification must be terrible for both parties. But mistakes in life do happen and we as Catholics are taught love and forgiveness. I hope these women believe that, and that their parents can find the strength to love by that rule.

Every life is a gift from God. If not for that young woman, then perhaps for some very deserving and loving couples awaiting adoption. Pro-life support should begin at home, not surely by encouraging sexual activity but to discourage hypocrisy, and more importantly, save lives.

Maybe everyone else already knows this. But I had to say it.

Everyone else does not know it. What you have said needs saying more than you know. Thanks for writing.

Children no longer go to Mass

During our 40 years of marriage, my husband and I have had some rough times, but we felt we had a good family.

Three of our children survived. They all had a good Christian education and training. Our sons went to Mass often and served sometimes nearly daily. Our daughter was in the convent nearly 10 years and left. She married, divorced, and is now living with a man. Our children are basically good, but none of them goes to church anymore.

After years of daily Mass and Communion myself, this troubles me greatly. My conscience is really bothered by it and I feel I must have done something wrong. Can you give me any ideas on how to deal with all this?

Your disappointment over your children's religious attitudes and lifestyles is shared by many parents — which is, I realize, no great consolation to a mother and father. I have two suggestions.

We must admit genuinely that there comes a point when children become responsible for their own lives. There comes a time at which parents, after having done their reasonable best for their sons and daughters, allow that responsibility to shift to their children's shoulders.

They need not agree, or pretend to agree, with all those children do. But a great load is lifted once we accept the fact that they are now adult persons in their own right and must answer for their own lives.

Furthermore, parents (and for that matter, anyone who has responsibility for others) should find great consolation in knowing that nothing done out of love for another person is ever lost. From our human experience, and particularly as Christians with the example of Christ before us, we believe in the transforming power of love.

The effects of our loving actions may not always appear in the way, or at the time, we would wish. They are there nevertheless, and will show themselves in times and places we never expect — and perhaps will never even know about.

Even sociologists agree that children possess an uncanny instinct for absorbing and retaining the values they perceive in their parents. Once again, however, these effects may not reveal themselves in manners that will easily lessen the pain of disappointment and sense of failure on the part of parents.

In other words, when our work of being parents and nurturing does not produce the visible results we would wish, by no means does it follow that this work was a failure.

As the first letter of John says in the New Testament, we believe in the power of love — the love God has for us and the love we have, in him, for each other. This means that we do the best we can with our admittedly limited abilities, and then trust that love will accomplish, in its own time, place and manner, everything we hoped for.

Children won't go to Mass

My teen-age children think I'm wrong in forcing them to go to Mass on Sundays. They are 14 and 16, but they say they "don't get anything out of it." We battle every Sunday. Can you help me put the record straight? What can I do?

What record? It's all in your question, and it sounds awfully frustrating and unhappy for both you and your children.

Looking at it only from your direction right now, it's critically important for parents and any others responsible for growing children to keep clearly in mind what they are aiming at, long range, in their religious training.

I'm sure your primary goal is to help your children toward a mature, living faith and trust in God, and a feeling of reverence for the place of the Eucharist in the community of Catholics that will be with them in their adult lives. Your purpose is not simply to be able to congratulate yourself after 20 years that you've been able to get them through those church doors every Sunday morning.

Clearly, the understanding of the Mass and the community of faith that should ideally exist between parents and children have broken down seriously in your home. If, when your children are in their mid and upper teens, you are still forcing and battling over something as central to Catholic life and worship as the Mass, I think you'd have to agree there isn't much likelihood that they are building a faith they will love and be proud of later on.

There is still time for you to reconsider seriously what you really want to achieve in your children in the matter of religion. This may involve asking yourself some pretty brutal questions such as: What does your own faith mean to you, and why are you so concerned that your children share it? Why do you go to Mass yourself?

If you're to be any support and guide to your children, make yourself be very specific in your answers. Perhaps a conversation with a priest or a teacher who deals regularly with teen-age children would help you. It's too bad this wasn't done more thoughtfully before — like 10 or 15 years ago.

More on teen-agers and the Mass

Dear Readers:

My response to the mother who wrote saying that she had a battle every Sunday morning with her teen-age children about going to Mass must have hit many tender nerves. Here's a sampling of readers' reactions:

From Texas: You are wrong in saying something has seriously broken down in a home when teen-age children have to be battled and forced to go to Mass. Catholic education must share in the fact that, of our eight children, only one still practices her religion. You're as frustrated as we are.

From Illinois: Your answer is typical of the parish administrator who can't be bothered with pastoring, who doesn't inquire into the possibility that the "turned-off" teen-ager may be his fault.

From Arizona: I'm not too sure you believe in the laws of the church or the first of the Ten Commandments. I was terribly mixed up, but a true and old-time priest friend told me: "Just remember, Joanne, the things the good nuns taught you."

From Florida: I don't know what ivory tower you've been living in. Children who went to church with enthusiasm in their earlier years seem to undergo a personality change in adolescence. "As the twig is bent by the peer group, so the tree shall grow."

From Ohio: In a good Catholic high school my daughter was taught she did not have to go to church every Sunday. Where have you been? Don't you know what they are teaching these days? Many parents are having the same problem, and it starts at school, not at home!

My only further response to these and others who wrote is that it is useless, and usually grossly inaccurate, to assign blame for the religious floundering of young people today. The parent asked what she could do about the problem, not what churches or schools could do. I tried to answer her.

Home, church and school are closely interrelated, and normally reflect each other. I still believe, however, that the home is the major factor in what a person becomes as an adult —

which may be quite different, incidentally, from what he is as a teen-ager.

As for what is being taught in schools, have you ever gone straight to the teacher involved and asked what exactly is being said and taught? I have, several times. It can be a helpful and sometimes enlightening experience.

Finally, I'd like to pass on what one reader claims would have been the "correct answer" to the question. I disagree with some of it, especially the first sentence, which he himself contradicts at the end. But it makes many good points. Here it is:

"Until large numbers of priests learn to make their liturgies the meaningful and beautiful services they can and should be, there is nothing you can do. Your best efforts are nullified by the lifeless, sterile and cold liturgical services conducted by so many of our priests. You might try searching in your area for a parish where the priest does something more than go through a ritualistic ceremony which not even he seems to believe in.

"So many priests make no effort to turn the child on. Athough they are the celebrants, they refuse to treat the Mass as a celebration. They resent and often refuse to offer the Sign of Peace. They think love is a dirty word when used by one person to another, and are horrified by the idea of a kiss in the sacred confines of the church.

"CCD classes are devoted to catechism-like teachings by rote, with no attempt to understand what their students need and want. They are satisfied with reports to the bishop which show that they do, in fact, have a Mass and CCD schedule. After that, in the words of one priest in our diocese: If they don't come, the hell with them.

"These comments do not apply to all; they do apply very often. Keep trying. In the meantime, don't blame yourself. Do your best to inculcate Christian values in your children; continue to love them, encourage them and pray.

"Because of God's gift of free will, they cannot be forced to be practicing Catholics. Continue to give good example. Let them know that you yourself are aware of their problem, but are trying, through the Mass and sacraments, to stay close to God and his church."

Parents and children at Mass

I implore you to tackle an aggravating problem that pastors and columnists alike are apparently afraid to settle. That problem is lack of common sense among parents of small children at Mass. They fail to exert any control over their loud, fussing kids, even during the homily. Even in most churches that provide quiet rooms, pastors refuse to require parents of small children to use them or not come.

I have changed parishes three times in the last two years because of this exasperation and currently do not belong to any. My concern takes me back to earlier days when children attended Mass in a group under the discipline of a nun who tolerated nothing short of rapt attention.

If you were a pastor who wished to deal with this in a genuinely Christlike manner, how would you do it? Before giving your answer, it might be worth considering a few facts. I agree with you that some parents are not as considerate as they might be when their small children disturb everyone in the vicinity. But they are by no means always the neglectful, inconsiderate parents you seem to assume.

Perhaps more often than not, those parents, sometimes single parents or Catholic partners in a mixed marriage, have exerted more effort and patience and plain determination to be there for Mass than any of the rest of us. They're doing their best, their faith brings them, they're already hassled enough in their lives, they've come to ask the help of God (and perhaps our understanding) and are usually the first to take it personally as just one more put-down if we priests do what you suggest. I know this for a fact from my own experiences with people.

By far more parents of small children are thoughtful about this, and I'm proud of the patience and understanding of the rest of the people in church when things don't always go smoothly. To some this may sound like a stupidly simplistic approach, but my feeling is that it is natural for little children to stew and fuss and sometimes cry. But (unless, of course, they drown out the best part of my homily!) I'd rather have them there than not there, especially if their parents could not come without them.

Nurseries and cry rooms may be some help, though for several reasons I'm not all that sure about cry rooms. Any parish priest will tell you they're not the whole solution. College students in our community often tell us they like to come to our, or other, parish Masses rather than liturgies for students only. With old people and babies and everything in between, Mass is, as one student said, "More the way it ought to be." Maybe she has caught on to something the rest of us forgot.

Children and cults

We are parents who would like your insights about our children and, I guess you would call them, cults or fundamentalist sects. Our whole area has had things happen that really disturb and worry us, not only with collegians and teen-agers but even younger children. Sometimes things are out of hand before parents even know about it.

From my own experiences with families in this frightening kind of crisis, and from research of others, it seems there are at least two absolute essentials for parents to consider. These may provide at least a base for your group's deliberations.

First, we need to be sure that our children have a solid spiritual framework for their lives. Nearly always, cults or fundamentalist evangelicals who labor aggressively and successfully to recruit participants are simply filling a spiritual vacuum in those who become their adherents. Being certain our children (or ourselves) "have the answers" and "know the truths of the faith" is not enough. We must work with them at every stage of development to talk over what their faith means to them in the daily business of living, how it helps to bring sense and understanding and Christian perspective to their routine personal crises and challenges.

This absolutely requires that they be well introduced to the Gospels and are beginning (or are well along the road as they grow) to be aware of a personal relationship with Jesus Christ.

It is especially when these are lacking that cults or revivalist sects of various kinds find fertile and ready ground for their message.

A frequent fatal mistake is to assume that such spiritual movements are happening in our children simply because they go to Mass every Sunday and attend Catholic school or religion classes. (Failure in these, of course, only compounds the problem and for Catholics nearly guarantees a serious religious crisis sometime in the future.) Essential as these fundamental practices of faith are, they cannot produce a vibrant and significant faith life unless that life is actively and consciously nurtured at home, somewhere along the lines I've indicated.

Where is our children's faith? What do they believe? What do prayer, church, Christ mean to them? If we don't bring them to ask themselves those questions, eventually somebody else will. All this implies, of course, that we have developed a level of serious communication with our children, which takes us to number two.

Part of the lifeblood of such cults is a high degree of secrecy. They need to exist in a kind of shadow world. The reason is simple. In varying measure, they depend on and demand, as much as possible, total control of their adherents, far beyond that of other religious organizations.

Therefore, they must attempt to control what their members hear and read and think. Adherents must be insulated as much as possible from outside influences that might introduce "dangerous" ideas or doubts. Secretiveness, concealment of their tactics, their plans, even their membership thus becomes a major strategy, a necessary discipline to which all are gradually introduced. The mass suicide of the "believers" at Jonestown several years ago was one of the more vicious examples in our generation of this type of religious movement. But others less grievous have been, and are, nearly as destructive of peoples' lives.

What this says is, we urgently need habits of trusting openness with our children. If we have from early on become accustomed to discussing faith and God and religion with them, we have a big headstart. When we perceive that they are becoming withdrawn about certain religious conversations or experiences, when we hear remarks like "You wouldn't understand; it's my business," or when they consistently avoid the subject, it is time to be concerned and do something about it. Nothing healthy or good is happening when children, of any age, feel this need to be furtive.

Clearly, such openness between parents and children cannot begin at the age of 16 or 14, or even 10. So both of these suggestions tie closely together. At least this is a start. I wish there was a simpler, easier answer, but I don't believe there is one.

Disappointed parents

If a son has knowingly entered an invalid marriage, are his parents obliged to accept this? Can they refuse to forgive him? Can they receive the sacraments worthily without forgiveness in their hearts?

You are suffering a deep personal tragedy. All good parents want the best for their children and, for mothers and fathers who have a deep religious faith, that means hoping their children will share in the benefits that come from a committed belief in God and his teachings.

You feel that your son has lost all this, at least for the present. I believe you are more hurt and disappointed than embittered or unforgiving. Don't hesitate to go to the sacraments, and keep praying for true peace of mind — and peace with God — for him and for yourselves.

Should affairs be confessed?

My husband and I have been married about 40 years. Before we were married I had an affair that was a very unpleasant situation.

Eighteen months after we were married, my husband, who was in the service, wrote to ask me if I had sexual relations before our marriage. I confessed. He came home permanently about two years later after our second child was born.

When my husband is sober and working, he's a fine person. But when he is drunk, he accuses me of having affairs and other things I would not think of doing. As a child I lived a good Christian life and I still go to Mass and Communion almost every day. Yet he still accuses me of these awful things. I have never cheated on him, and have kept my marriage vows.

When I told my doctor about this situation with my husband, she said he was using me for some guilt he had. This man has never told me in person that he loves me; he has written it, but never said it. Forty years is too long to do this. I need your help or advice on handling this. It's getting too much for me anymore.

Your letter is one more proof of something that cannot be said often enough. Such confessions by husbands and wives generally accomplish nothing except to threaten the atmosphere of that relationship for the rest of their lives.

This is particularly true when one partner prompts, or tries to force, such a confession from the other. So many negative factors are at work here that pushy questioning about such matters offers a quite sufficient reason to wonder about the love or emotional stability of one's partner. A normal person would possibly not want to know such information and even more would not want to inflict the pain that such a confession would cause someone he loves.

These things are and should be kept between oneself and God. You cannot go back and relive your life, but maybe what I've said can help put your situation in a little better perspective.

I agree with your doctor. Your husband's attitude through all these years says something more about him than it does about you. From your letter it seems to me you are handling the situation as well as possible. What you're saying is that his continued lack of consideration, to put it mildly, hurts you deeply. I understand that. But your own persevering patience, love, prayer, and understanding will enable you to go on coping with it.

You cannot do this alone. Friends or counselors whom you can trust are essential. From my mail and my personal experience, however, I can't be too insistent in recommending Al-Anon, a group related to Alcoholics Anonymous but consisting of the spouses and children of people who are addicted to alcohol. Members can help you cope with the Jekyll-Hyde personality your husband displays and help you understand how to depend on God and others for help.

Al-Anon or Alcoholics Anonymous should be listed in your phone book. If not, write to Al-Anon Family Group Headquarters, Box 182, Madison Square Station, New York, N. Y., 10010.

Husband is homosexual

I have been married for 28 years. We have four children, two living at home. My husband has waited until now to begin acting out his homosexuality. I've been suspicious for years, but I love him. My life has been turned inside out and I don't know what to do.

I am deeply sorry for you and your family. It is impossible for someone who has not been through this kind of horrible experience to imagine the devastation suffered by a spouse and children in the face of such revelation.

You ask what to do. First, you have not indicated the ages of your children still living at home, but if they are still minors, or otherwise will follow your suggestions, you need to get them help. This kind of collapse in the sexual structure of their family, and their perceptions of that collapse, require outside professional assistance. You also need such counseling and advice to help you clarify and keep healthy your own emotions and feelings, as well as to understand from your perspective what was going on in your marriage.

Fortunately or unfortunately, such experiences are common enough that support groups exist for just such persons as yourself, and even for your children. And I don't exclude even your married children from the need of some support and understanding. You may call Catholic Charities or any other major social service organization to learn the names of people to contact.

The above must be your first and immediate priorities. I know you love your husband and want to help him. No one can be helped in such circumstances, however, unless he or she genuinely desires help and will work to receive it. Given the years this problem has been going on in the context of an apparently normal family life, I suspect he will not be open to or capable of the kind of radical openness to action that you and the rest of the family would need to put your lives back together. Finally, don't be afraid to talk to your parish priest or another clergyman in whom you can have confidence and ask his help. He may have some helpful insights and at least can direct you to the other kinds of assistance you need.

Wife abused before marriage

My husband and I were married almost three years ago. On the outside, we looked like the happiest couple while we were dating. What no one knew was that he was verbally and mentally abusive to me the two and one-half years we dated. Why I put up with it, I still don't know, other than that I loved him so much and the good times outweighed the bad. Though the abuse lessened quite a bit when we were married, I have been on high blood pressure medication and tranquilizers ever since. I'm only 32 years old.

He is still short-tempered, not understanding, and makes me nervous. I have had every test imaginable; there is nothing physically wrong with me. I have seen several counselors for the past two years and they encourage me to leave him. At first I said it was out of the question because I truly believed that if persons get divorced they will go to hell.

However, now when I look at this more objectively, I do believe I have grounds for separating from him; possibly grounds for an annulment. My husband and I have seen counselors together but they have not helped. I just don't feel like myself anymore, and frankly I don't think I ever will again. I'm a nervous wreck and am not at all the person I used to be. Do you have any advice?

I hesitated to print this letter. I often fear that I will allow my experience as pastor to influence excessively my journalistic judgment as to which letters to use. But I know there are thousands of people who will read and urgently need to hear what you say.

The community life of marriage can be a source of enormous joy and spiritual growth when the two people sincerely love and respect one another, and treat each other with care. But marriage is not a reform school or an institution for psychological therapy. Men and women who marry with the intention of changing radical personality deficiencies in their spouse, who hope "things will get better when we're married," are always tragically disappointed.

I hope engaged couples who find themselves in situations similar to yours will read your letter thoughtfully. The only advice I can give you is to continue the course you are on, and talk to a priest soon about your own spiritual response to this relationship and the options open to you as a Catholic. Good luck.

Husband has been unfaithful

I am reluctant to talk to my parish priest about this problem, but I need help from someone. Two months ago I found out that my husband was involved with a white woman. (We are black.) Later I found out that she is pregnant by him. What do you advise me to do? At this point I'm confused. I can't forgive him and am very unhappy living with him now. He's a truck driver and is away five days out of a week. Of course, he blames me for what happened; he says that I neglected him and that is why he turned to this woman for love and companionship. We have six children, aged five to 16.

Please help me make a decision. I can't do it alone.

I understand how terribly hurt you must be by this tragic action on the part of your husband. Certainly you cannot make a wise decision without sharing the problem and exploring your alternatives with someone you can trust.

On the other hand, it is impossible for me to advise you

helpfully at this distance. So many feelings of all involved must be explored, and so much of the past and present history of your relationship with your husband needs to be considered, that you need someone with whom you can sit and talk out the problem.

Don't be too quick to count out your parish priest as a consultant. I realize the situation is embarrassing to you, but you will not scandalize him and he has probably helped many others in similar dilemmas. Beyond that, try a wise relative or friend, or a professional counselor you can have confidence in. But don't try to go it alone. You need all the support and encouragement you can get from someone who is interested in you and your children.

Abuse ends marriage

I am filing for dissolution of my marriage. My husband and I were married ten years ago and were blessed with two children. We had major problems, particularly in connection with his drinking. I couldn't get him to any counseling; he said the priest who married us told him the marriage wouldn't last anyway.

He threatened me verbally and physically, and even loaded a shotgun which he threatened to use on me. Would this dissolution make it possible for me to be married in the Catholic Church again, should I meet someone I care about?

You are not entirely clear on what you mean by a dissolution. If you are referring to an annulment that might be granted through a Catholic marriage tribunal, there's no obstacle to your marrying someone else once that annulment is declared.

An annulment means that no genuine marriage ever existed between the two people, so there's nothing at least from that direction that would prevent marriage to another.

You never definitely state whether or not you and your husband have a civil divorce. Such a divorce, without action on your case by your diocesan marriage tribunal, would not, of course, allow your remarriage in the Catholic Church.

In addition, tribunals normally do not accept cases for annulment until a civil divorce is final. This policy prevents legal complications which could otherwise easily occur.

If you have not already done so, please go to a priest in your area, explain your circumstances and follow his advice. He will help you through the required annulment process.

Help after divorce

I need your advice desperately. I am a Catholic and my family has been Catholic for generations. About nine years ago I married a non-Catholic man. After seven years of heartbreak and disappointment, I finally got the courage to face defeat and get a divorce. I know I should have done it sooner, but I felt like I failed. Even now, after two years, I feel ashamed of it and hate the word divorce; it's like death.

My former husband did not want to give up his single lifestyle after marriage, like drinking with the boys regularly and coming home when he felt he wanted. A lot of other things were involved, but the hardest part was when I found out after we married that we could not have children. I thought we would adopt, but he absolutely refused. I prayed for a long time that he would change his mind, but he didn't.

I'm going on 34 years old, and if it's God's will, I hope to marry again and have a child before I get older. I do, however, want to marry in the church and with God's blessing. I'm writing to you to say I would like an annulment and I feel I really deserve one. I need your advice on this greatly.

You obviously have been hurt much during the past years and feel frustrated and betrayed. I hope you will be able to find the way toward new hope in your life, and a way to put things back together for yourself.

The first thing you should have, even more than an annulment, and which I am sure you want deeply, is a healing of all these past hurts and some serenity of mind so that you can make a new beginning in your life. I urge you as strongly as I can to search for some assistance to achieve this healing through confidences you can share with a wise friend, or with one of the many groups that are designed to help people such as yourself get a new start, or perhaps both. Many people have suffered the same kinds of collapse you experience and have learned much about how to help others through these same tragedies.

A movement called "Beginning Experience" is gradually spreading around our country to give precisely this kind of support and guidance to divorced, widowed and separated Catholics. You may obtain information about this movement by contacting Beginning Experience, 305 Michigan Ave., Detroit, MI, 48226.

The details you give in your letter make me strongly suspect that the marriage tribunal of your diocese would accept your case to investigate for a possible annulment. This would require, however, that you discuss the matter with a priest in your area who would begin the process.

I understand your reluctance to discuss the matter with a priest who knows your family well. Ask a friend in another area of the city to suggest a priest who may not be an acquaintance of yours, but who would be open to talking with you. Follow his advice. You might also ask him to suggest ways of finding the type of personal assistance I spoke of above.

Formerly married Catholics

A parish in our area has announced a series of meetings for "formerly married Catholics." Isn't this dangerous for the church to give recognition to the divorced and separated? Can a divorced Catholic receive the sacraments?

The church — which means all of us Catholics — has a serious responsibility to provide what assistance we can to those who are trying to adjust to a "single" style of life, and often trying to raise a family without the help of a spouse.

This responsibility has been neglected far too long, perhaps because of this attitude that such Catholics are somehow "untouchables." You must know that with the pressures and conditions of married and family life today, many are divorced or separated through no fault of their own. Some factors in marriage relationships are as much out of one individual's control as the death of the spouse was out of control of a widow or widower.

Furthermore, the end of their marriage does not mean the end of their need to love and be loved — especially, incidentally, by their still-married friends.

When widows and widowers and separated Catholics were relatively few in number, perhaps there was some excuse for not recognizing their special needs and trying to meet them. That is no longer true. Rather than "dangerous," the series of meetings of divorced, separated and widowed Catholic men and women is, if anything, long overdue.

There is nothing in itself that prevents a divorced man or woman from receiving penance and the Eucharist. In certain ways they may need the sacraments more in learning how to move away from their accustomed married life style. The same rules apply to them in this matter as to any other Catholic.

Here as elsewhere, we have no right to judge or condemn, but rather to do all we can to strengthen and heal and support.

Don't blame the church

I brought my family up under strict Catholic teachings and my daughter is a very strict, dedicated Catholic. She now loves and plans to marry a man who has been divorced for seven years.

They explained their situation to a priest who told them they cannot be married in the Catholic Church. This is a great shock to me and my daughter, who thought she would bring her husband into the church and now she is being rejected.

It's no wonder the church is losing attendance. I see Catholics who are divorced and some remarried, and still receiving Holy Communion. Why? Why cannot my daughter at least be married at the side altar?

Any Catholic even minimally educated in the teachings of our faith must be aware of the basic teachings of the church concerning marriage, and therefore aware that he or she is looking at possible big problems when a serious relationship is allowed to develop with a divorced person.

Sometimes an annulment or other procedure may be implemented by which two such individuals might marry according to the laws of the Catholic faith. But the church has absolutely no power or authority before God to do what you are asking, that is, to approve the marriage of a man and a woman, regardless of previous husbands or wives, simply because those two people are in love and want a Catholic wedding.

The priest you mentioned apparently gave good advice. The place where the marriage takes place — side altar, high altar, or park bench — is irrelevant to the validity of the marriage. As long as a former spouse is living, no marriage according to church law is possible without an annulment or other formal procedure which would assure that both partners are now free to marry.

If your daughter does have the strong Catholic roots you seem to indicate, I would strongly urge her to go back to the priest, or to another priest, and ask him to investigate the possibilities of one of these procedures.

Evolving theology of marriage

I am a woman 57 years old, unable to have children. An article I read recently claimed the Catholic Church has taught that marriage relations are allowed only if the couple can and want to have children.

My question may be strange, but even according to the new rules are we not supposed to have intercourse because no children could result, just a union of two middle-age people?

I'm afraid the answer to your question is far more involved than you expected.

The church's theology of marriage and of marriage intercourse developed slowly through many centuries, and is in fact still evolving. It always has seen marriage relations as something good. But in explaining why, it has had to choose between a variety of apparently contrary explanations.

One thing it has acknowledged and adhered to almost exclusively for centuries was that having children is good and having children makes marriage and marriage intercourse good.

Thus at one time, for many centuries in fact, general Christian teaching was that sexual intercourse was sinful when conception was impossible.

Before going further, two facts are significant.

First, throughout history until within the last two centuries, little was known about the biology of procreation. Theologians and scientists commonly believed that the total "seed" of life came from the male.

In intercourse the incipient human being was transferred to the woman's body where it grew until birth.

This obviously affected moral teaching, since any loss of this seed was considered at least in some way homicide.

Second, from the age of St. Augustine (fourth century) again nearly until our own time, the one recognized factor justifying sexual intercourse was the possible conception of a child. This philosophy, which prevailed to some degree all through those centuries, developed in reaction to some of the gnostic and dualist ("spirit is good — material things are evil") theories of those days, which one way or another threatened Christian life and doctrine.

In effect, for this reason and because it always involved a vehemence and delight which "goes beyond the bounds of reason," intercourse could be "justified" only by an intention for procreation.

These points may sound complicated and academic but they carry enormous practical consequences which affect an honest response to your question.

St. Gregory the Great, who died in the year 604, for example, followed the general teaching in his "Pastoral Rules" that married people should have sexual relations only to have children, and added that if any pleasure is mixed with these relations, they sinfully transgress the law of marriage — though the sin was admittedly not serious.

For the same reasons, until the very late Middle Ages prominent theologians and canonists taught that sexual relations were gravely sinful during pregnancy.

Only under the powerful influence of Albert the Great (13th century) did this position concerning pregnancy begin to be reversed. The debate in those days was vehement, since it began a major break with the tradition that no other morally legitimate reason existed for intercourse than the intention to have children.

Even so, as late as the 15th century the famous preacher St. Bernardine of Siena referred to the "modesty" of animals during gestation as an indication that married people should not have intercourse at all during pregnancy.

Only in the last 300 years or so, particularly through two highly respected theologians, Thomas Sanchez and St. Alphonsus Liguori, has the expression of affection and married love been increasingly acknowledged as valid and morally acceptable in intercourse, even when conception of a child is impossible.

All the recent popes, of course, have expanded on this theme, particularly since the landmark encyclical on Christian marriage by Pope Leo XIII (1880).

As the saying goes, this may be more than you wanted to know. Obviously, the history of this subject in the church is enormously complicated, and all kinds of contrary opinions existed at the same time. But the above brief sketch may explain the background of what you read, and why you need not be concerned about your forthcoming marriage.

No "new rules" are needed. The possibility of having children is not a factor which needs to concern you in your marriage relationships.

Natural Family Planning

I want to be a happy wife and mother, but my problem is I feel I have enough children to keep me worrying about their upbringing and making them good Catholics and providing for them. At my age, I'm afraid I couldn't cope with a new baby, and I worry about having babies later in life on account of retardation. I practice birth control, and feel guilt-ridden; but I wonder if the church recognizes this sort of problem. I can't see how an all-loving God could make a good

mother and father burn in hell under mortal sin for doing what they feel is in the best interest of their family life. I'm confused, and have to know.

From your letter, it seems to me that you are asking help not so much directly about birth control as about how to come to a decision that will give you peace of conscience and peace with God. This sort of personal advice is impossible in a column such as this.

I urge you to talk the matter over with a competent priest (or someone else) whom you trust and with whom you feel comfortable. I hope you will do it soon.

If you haven't already, I urge you to look up the nearest Natural Family Planning (NFP) information program in your area. Sometimes not very accurately referred to as the "new rhythm method," NFP is a far more advanced method of family planning increasingly used by people of many faiths and in several nations. It differs radically from the old calendar method of determining fertile and infertile times for sexual intercourse, utilizing several symptoms which occur in the ovulatory cycle as signals helpful to the husband and wife.

The method can be quite successful for the vast majority of normally intelligent and motivated couples.

Most larger communities have centers where instruction on NFP is available. Further information on NFP centers is available from the Couple to Couple League, Box 11084, Cincinnati, Ohio, 45211, and from the Catholic Social Service agencies in many dioceses.

Historical perspectives: The Church and NFP

We are friends with several couples and were recently discussing Natural Family Planning.

One older couple in the group told us they remember when the church condemned any kind of rhythm method for family planning. We younger couples said we didn't believe that, but they insisted.

We agreed to ask you. Is what this couple said true? If so, how do you explain it?

Basically, your older friends are correct, but that is to over-simplify. The subject is a long and complicated one in Christian tradition.

First, let's make our subject clear. We're speaking of any method by which a couple attempt to arrange their sexual relationships in order to avoid pregnancy by limiting intercourse to the infertile times in the "rhythms" of a woman's menstrual cycle. The first people we know of, in our Western civilization at least, to see the contraceptive possibilities in this method were fifth century B.C. Greek physicians. While their timing of fertile periods was seriously mistaken, it was as good as any would be until only about 150 years ago.

The most important early Christian theologian to deal with the subject was St. Augustine, who severely condemned the use of infertile periods to avoid conception. He berated the Manichaeans for telling people to watch "the time after purification of the menses when a woman is likely to conceive and at that time refrain from intercourse," lest a child be conceived. This proves, he said to them, "that you consider marriage is not to procreate children but to satiate lust." It makes "the woman no more a wife but a harlot" ("De Moribus Ecclesiae Catholicae et Manichaeorum," c. 18).

The whole question did not become so relevant morally until the 1840s, when French physician Felix Pouchet was thought to have pinpointed the fertile period more exactly. Soon this raised serious questions for theologians and priests in confession and after much controversy the matter was presented in 1880 to the Sacred Penitentiary (a Vatican agency) for answers. The reply, which one way or another governed most official Catholic thinking on the subject for decades, concluded: "Spouses using the (rhythm) way of marriage are not to be disturbed and a confessor may cautiously insinuate the opinion in question to those spouses whom he has in vain tried to lead from the detestable crime of onanism."

In other words, to suggest limiting intercourse to the infertile periods was apparently allowable if that was the only way to stop people from using other contraceptive techniques. Controversies on the matter pretty much died, however, when the "Pouchet method" proved mostly unreliable anyway.

In the 1920s, scientists in Austria and Japan (Knaus and Ogino) discovered radically new data on the fertile periods, data generally confirmed by today's science and used as the basis for most current "rhythm" programs. This data inspired further questions and development of Catholic teaching on the subject, though some major moral theologians continued to hold that rhythm could only be allowed as the lesser of two evils.

Certain Catholics today attempt to interpret those past positions as not unfavorable to the general use of the woman's sterile period for birth control. There is no question, however, that they were understood commonly by leading Catholic clergy and lay people, theologians and otherwise, as forbidding the practice.

Some of my own friends and later co-workers in family life offices around the country were shocked and scandalized when in 1951 Pope Pius XII completely opened the door to the rhythm method. "Observing the non-fertile periods alone," he said, is entirely moral if there are serious medical, eugenic, economic or moral indications, "which often occur" (Address to Italian Catholic Union of Midwives, Nov. 26, 1951, N. 36). One physician, nationally acknowledged for his expertise on the subject, spoke for many others in the 1950s when he said that any rhythm method is against the natural law, since it intentionally arranges that specific acts of sexual intercourse be rendered infertile, thus separating the husband-wife love aspect of sexual intercourse from its potential to beget children, the same argument St. Augustine used against rhythm 16 centuries earlier.

This controversy over the morality of rhythm only abated, in fact, in face of the mushrooming contraceptive and abortion movements of the 1960s and 1970s. Since then, of course, the door opened by Pope Pius XII has swung wide open to complete approval and encouragement by the church of this form of family planning.

Today the church's teaching is quite explicit. Utilizing the rhythm of the woman's menstrual cycle, by NFP for example, couples may, with sufficient reason, intentionally and morally attempt to arrange their sexual lives so their actions of intercourse will be infertile and not result in pregnancy.

But "each and every marriage act (intercourse) must remain open to the transmission of life." (Pope Paul VI, "Humanae Vitae" 1968, No. 12)

What is Natural Family Planning?

We found your answer, explaining that Catholic church officials formerly said rhythm birth control was immoral, very interesting.

But we were not sure of the connection with Natural Family Planning. The question the woman or man asked was about that, but you did not answer it directly. The NFP couples we know say it is not rhythm but something entirely different. Can you help us?

While the word once referred mainly to a method of counting the days before or after menstruation ("calendar rhythm"), "rhythm" is, in fact, a generic term to designate any method which attempts to avoid or regulate pregnancy by avoiding intercourse when it is thought the woman is in the fertile part of that cycle. The historical perspective I gave in that response applied, as I said, to any method by which a couple attempt to arrange their sexual relationships to avoid pregnancy by limiting intercourse to the infertile times in the "rhythms" of a woman's menstrual cycle.

NFP is one (and most probably the best) of those methods, even though it did not exist, at least under that name, until relatively recently.

Part of the answer to your question lies in the fact that there are two critical elements in the effectiveness of any "rhythm" method. One is the scientific-medical clarification of when the fertile time of a woman's monthly cycle occurs. At various times in previous ages that time was thought to be immediately before or immediately after her "period." We now know that is not true.

Under average conditions an ovum (egg) is released from a woman's ovary about 14 days before the beginning of menstruation and "lives" approximately 24 hours after its release. It is during those 24 hours that fertilization (pregnancy) can take place, if the male's sperm unites with the ovum. The sperm is capable of fertilizing an ovum for about 72 hours, perhaps more. Thus, there are, in very round numbers, about four days during each menstrual cycle when intercourse could result in pregnancy.

The other critical element in the effectiveness of any rhythm method, therefore, is determining exactly when that 24-hour-period occurs, thus providing basic information about when intercourse must be avoided if the couple wishes to avoid pregnancy. Once these core days have been identified as accurately as possible, certain additional factors must be considered to determine finally the "safe" days of that menstrual cycle. Of course, the systems can be used in the opposite way if the couple wishes to have a child. Numerous factors can be tested at home to attempt to determine that time. They include the woman's temperature, identifiable pains or feelings in some parts of her body that consistently accompany certain phases of her cycle, the "thickness" of bodily secretions that vary at different times of the month and so on. Women differ in their cycles, of course. Sickness, tension and other factors also affect any of these physiological events.

Obviously, the effectiveness of any "rhythm" method depends on the motivation and commitment of a couple who want it to work. It takes a good deal of patience, perseverance and discipline to be regular in making these tests and to abide by the findings.

Natural Family Planning combines several of the above criteria. For those couples who are sufficiently motivated and seriously want it to succeed and who are faithful to its regimen, it has a very high rate of success as a method of family planning. NFP training programs are available today in almost all dioceses and major cities.

Billings Method of birth control

Please let me know where I may obtain information on the Billings Method of birth control. I have contacted the local Planned Parenthood Association and they never heard of it.

The so-called Billings Method of family planning (named after Dr. John Billings, who helped develop it), is basically an ovulation detection system of practicing rhythm — though many of its sponsors avoid that word because of deficiencies of other rhythm systems in the past.

The method is relatively new in the way it correlates several components for determining the time of ovulation, and it utilizes much up-to-date scientific information and practical experience. It has proven enormously successful and helpful to thousands of married couples.

In most dioceses of our country the Catholic Social Service or Family Life Office either sponsors Natural Family Planning or NFP centers, or they are at least in contact with NFP counselors. I suggest you call either of these diocesan offices in your area for more local information.

Origin of teachings on birth control

I know there is much controversy about birth control today and the church is officially against it. I'm puzzled, though, on how it came to teach what it does. Was it originated by a pope, or a council, or what? And what is the scriptural basis for it?

Thousands of pages have been written on the questions you ask.

As far as we know, Jesus never taught anything explicitly on the subject of birth control. The church's position on birth control as well as its other moral teachings developed gradually. Questions confronted people at various times and the church responded.

From the time of Saint Paul, Christian teachers placed enormous emphasis on virginity, often even inside marriage. Largely as a result of this emphasis, a number of strange sects arose who attacked marriage from any of several directions. Some were materialistic and sensual; others were quite "spiritual," claiming that marriage, and especially sex, were evil and beneath the dignity of enlightened Christians.

To counteract these groups, the church had to answer the question: If virginity is so ideal, how does the church avoid being in the position of condemning marriage and sexual procreation?

The manner in which Christian teachers and theologians answered this question proved critical and significant in the church for nearly 14 centuries. One option open to them was the one suggested in St. Paul's Letter to the Ephesians: Sexual intercourse is closely associated with married love and is, among other things, important for the growth and development of that love.

However, under pressures from the social structures of the time and from the great emphasis on virginity in the church, and in order to compromise with the contempt for sexuality among these heretical groups, theology and preaching took on an entirely different direction. Sexual intercourse can be good and holy, said Christian teachers. But what makes it good and holy is procreation, the desire for a child. Thus enjoyment of sexual relations, or having intercourse as an expression of love for one's spouse, is sinful unless the couple desires to conceive a child.

Additional support was claimed for this attitude by an appeal to "nature." The obvious physical function of any organ (including sex organs) was considered "natural," entirely divorced from any relation to the whole person. As some of the great early preachers and doctors of the church put it, the natural way is the way animals do it — and animals have sexual union to procreate other animals. Human beings, therefore, should do the same.

St. Augustine, who died in the year 430, crystallized this basic attitude toward sex in his writings. His approach generally predominated in the church until perhaps 150 years ago; contraception was included in the lists of sins (penitentials) drawn up by various theologians since about the eighth century.

Until modern times, official teaching on the subject has been generally informal and local, but has followed the attitude I just explained. In his famous Pastoral Rules, for example, Pope St. Gregory the Great (590-604) taught that married couples may have intercourse to have children, but if any enjoyment is mixed with it, they sin against the "law of marriage."

As anyone knows who has read St. Thomas Aquinas, Chaucer or Dante, this rather severe approach came under considerable suspicion, not to say disregard, through the centuries. Only since the first part of the last century, however, thanks largely to one of the great theologians of modern times (St. Alphonsus Liguori), has respectable Catholic theology accepted the fact that married love and affection possess an essential, even primary, significance in sexual intercourse.

Traditional teaching on contraception has, of course, been adhered to in all papal documents. But the essential role of the love and affection between husband and wife in sexual relations is increasingly emphasized, especially by Popes Pius XI, Paul VI and John Paul II.

Both the Old and New Testaments tell us much about the meaning of sexuality and sexual relationships between men and women. No one seriously claims today, however, that scriptural texts can solve the birth control controversy one way or the other.

Catholic teaching on the subject was summarized and repeated in the historic encyclical letter of Pope Paul VI, *Humanae Vitae* (1968). The Holy Father surveyed the traditions of the church in its respect for the conjugal and parental designs for marriage, noted the many ways nature itself causes "a separation in the succession of births," and concluded by reiterating the position of the Catholic Church: "Nonetheless, the Church, calling men back to the observance of the norms of the natural law, as interpreted by her constant doctrine, teaches that every act of marriage intercourse must remain open to the transmission of human life."(n.11)

Popes, bishops, theologians and others have insisted that people faced with decisions in this matter must be helped with compassion, love, understanding, patience and acceptance. After *Humanae Vitae,* the American bishops, among many bishops' conferences, urged "those who have resorted to (contraception) never to lose heart, but to continue to take full advantage of the strength which comes from the Sacrament of Penance, and the grace, healing and peace in the Eucharist."

We must, therefore, (and I hope do) have the utmost concern and care for the ambiguities and tensions experienced by couples facing sometimes heartbreaking decisions. It needs to be said clearly, however, that, whatever its controversial aspects, the church's position on this subject comes straight out of its reverence and respect for the enormous gift of human life. Obviously the question here is radically different from that of abortion or infanticide, where human life is already begun. Yet, the church firmly believes, as Pope John Paul II has written, "that human life, even if weak and suffering, is always a splendid gift of God's goodness. Against the pessimism and selfishness which cast a shadow over the world, the Church stands for life. In each human life she sees the splendor of that 'yes,' that 'amen' who is Christ himself. To the 'no' which assails and afflicts the world, she replies with this living 'yes', thus defending the human person and the world from all who plot against and harm life." *Exhortation on the Family,* 1981; no. 30)

Purposes of marriage

Your background on the church's position on birth control was very informative.

The natural sex drive and the parent instinct has a beautiful result, a new life. Isn't a secondary but nonetheless beautiful result of sex between husband and wife the relief of the stimulation of the sex urge, resulting in bodily peace, feelings of love and mental balance between the couple? That is, of course, for those who choose the married path of life.

What are the church's views on this?

You stated the church's view beautifully, with one exception. The church would not be so anxious about that word "secondary." The development of married love and peace between husband and wife is more than a secondary purpose of their life together, including the sexual side of it.

In his impressive and historic encyclical on Christian marriage (*Casti Connubii*, 1930), Pope Pius XI taught that the mutual fulfillment and holiness of husband and wife is itself a "primary purpose" of the married state.

Vatican Council II, in all its statements on marriage, avoided the "primary-secondary" approach completely. All essential aspects of marriage — openness to children, mutual affection, sexual relations and the rest — depend on and support one another. "While not making the other purposes of matrimony of less account," says the council, "the true practice of conjugal love, and the whole meaning of family life which results from it, have this aim: that the couple be ready with stout hearts to cooperate with the love of the creator and the savior, who through them will enlarge and enrich his own family day by day." (Church in the Modern World, n. 50)

Pope John Paul expanded on this theme in his exhortation quoted above. "The fruitfulness of conjugal love," he wrote, "is not restricted solely to the procreation of children, even understood in its specifically human dimension. It is enlarged and enriched by all those fruits of moral, spiritual and supernatural life which the father and mother are called to hand on to their children, and through the children to the Church and the world." (n.28)

Shop around for advice?

A person asked a priest, "What do I do if a priest tells me in confession it is wrong to practice birth control?" The priest answered that all priests in the diocese are not well versed in this, and to shop around till he found the answer he wanted. Do you agree with this?

I agree with the first part, but certainly not the second. A Catholic manifests utterly no honesty with God by shopping around to get the answer he has already decided he will accept.

It is quite another thing to look for a priest you consider

compassionate and informed, a priest who knows what's going on in the field which concerns your conscience, and whom you feel you can count on to respect and reflect the teaching of the church as it applies to you, with every possible consideration of your own needs.

To "shop," if necessary, for such a priest is wise. He'll be the biggest help to you in reaching a good decision. Every priest dealing with lay people has a serious obligation to be aware of how his advice is consistent with the basic principles of moral theology, especially as they impose serious obligations.

Lay people, of course, cannot and should not rely solely on a priest for this guidance. They have a duty to make themselves at least minimally knowledgeable about essential factors in any serious decision which, after due prayer and reflection, they must make according to their own well-formed consciences, and for which they will be responsible to God.

Onanism

In your history of the church's teaching about contraception, you failed to bring in the Bible. Look in the book of Genesis about contraception: "A detestable thing, a conjugal blasphemy that offends the highest attribute of the Father, Creation."

First, I'm not sure where you found the quote, but it is not from Scripture. Among a few things wrong with it, creation is certainly not the highest attribute of the Heavenly Father. (His greatest attribute, by his own declaration, is his merciful, forgiving love!)

Scripture was not included in the brief history to which you refer because it has little, if anything, to say directly that is helpful regarding the morality of contraception. Indirectly, of course, it says much about the meaning and value of life, the relation of children to the love and hopes of parents, the lordship and authority of God, the importance of generosity and faith, and so on, all of which play a role in any moral decision including this one.

Presumably your reference to the Bible is to Genesis, chapter

38. Onan's brother had died. According to God's law in the Old Testament, Onan was bound to marry his brother's widow, Tamar, and have children by her if possible. The 'Levirite" law prescribed that these children would legally be not his, but his brother's. For this reason, says Genesis, whenever Onan had relations with his brother's widow, "he wasted his seed on the ground, to avoid contributing offspring for his brother. What he did greatly offended the Lord, and the Lord took his life."

The passage has often been wrongly interpreted as an explicit condemnation of contraception, and even more of masturbation. It is commonly acknowledged, however, that not the "wasting of the seed," but the refusal to observe a most serious family and tribal law was primarily responsible for Onan's condemnation and punishment.

Mother takes pills

I would like to know if birth control pills are against the teaching of the church. My mother has been taking these for quite some time. I found this out when I stumbled onto them. If this is wrong, how should I get her to stop? She is at Mass every Sunday.

Take it easy, now. You're jumping to a lot of conclusions. There are ways, of course, that "birth control pills" could be used wrongly. Perhaps you do not know, however, that there are certain women whose doctors prescribe such pills for perfectly legitimate reasons, many of which have absolutely nothing to do with birth control.

What are usually known as birth control pills are now more properly called by the broad generic name of progestational steroids. They are basically nothing but artificial hormones, hormones which some women need more of at certain times than their bodies produce naturally.

It's even quite common that these medications are needed on the same monthly regimen as they would be if they were being used directly for contraceptive purposes.

If it still bothers you, and you think it could help, why not ask your mother about it?

Sterilization

If a young Catholic woman with three children who has unsuccessfully used the rhythm method had her tubes tied, has she committed a mortal sin? Has her husband sinned, especially if he agreed with her in wanting no more children?

Can she go to Mass and the sacraments? Do you think the Lord tries to understand the reasons why we do what we do? I pray to the Lord for answers, but they don't come very easily. I know many Catholic people hard-pressed for answers and we desperately need help on where to turn. The answers aren't in a Sunday sermon like they might have been years ago. I'm sorry my questions got so long, but many young couples need these answers and I'm number one on the list. I'm 28 years old.

Let's take your questions one at a time. First, and maybe the hardest to respond to: Did you commit a sin?

The Catholic Church teaches that any kind of direct sterilization (such as tubal ligation or vasectomy) is objectively seriously sinful. This means that such an action in itself, considered in isolation (if that were possible) from the circumstances of the individuals involved, is a serious offense against God, our Creator, since it deliberately destroys one of the major functions of our body.

Whether an act of sterilization is subjectively sinful — that is, did the person involved actually commit a grave sin? — is a far more difficult question. Involved here are such considerations as these: Did this person realize fully that the action was seriously sinful for him or her when the action was done? Were there alternatives that the individual was emotionally, intellectually and spiritually capable of choosing and carrying out? Worded more theologically, was the person morally free-willed when he acted as he did? Were there other circumstances present that might diminish full responsibility for any possible sinfulness in what was done?

While these are routine questions in determining moral responsibility for our actions, it is usually hopeless, fruitless and sometimes even harmful to attempt to untangle them after the fact, even for the person directly concerned. Usually the individual has a pretty good idea of how his action fit in with what his conscience told him was right and wrong. Once the thing is done, the right thing is to put the matter in the hands of Our Lord, ask his forgiveness for any sinfulness of which one may be guilty, and then move on.

How about your husband? Certainly, encouraging and assisting another in doing something that is seriously wrong can itself also be seriously sinful. However, the same questions discussed above would apply to him as well as to you.

Can you go to Mass and receive the sacraments? By all means! Not only can you, you should do so. With your enormous responsibilities as a mother and wife, and with your concern over your actions, you need the healing and forgiving love of Jesus which we experience so powerfully in the Sacraments of Penance and the Eucharist. Don't put it off any longer. Go to a priest you feel will be compassionate and honest with you, and talk with him.

Scripture and sterilization

Is there any Scriptural text in either the Old or New Testament which directly or indirectly condemns sterilization of a man or a woman as a means of birth control?

We could never expect to find a text in Scripture directly condemning such an operation. When the Bible was written and for centuries afterwards, sterilization procedures of the kind you ask about were not even dreamed of.

Indirectly, both the Old and New Testaments have much to say, and Catholic theology on the subject draws heavily from these teachings. You are surely aware that the Bible insists numerous times that human life, including one's own, is primarily a gift of God and in his hands, not ours. As St. Paul puts it, "None of us lives as his own master and none of us dies as his own master. While we live we are responsible to the Lord, and when we die we die as his servants. Both in life and death we are the Lord's." (Romans 5, 7-8)

This clearly means more than that we cannot kill ourselves or others. We must respect the limits of our rights over the members of our bodies, and the functions of our life as well — proportionate, of course, to how intimately a particular part of our body is related to the wholeness of our person and our life.

Rarely, if ever, may we look to Scripture for answers to specific cases involving modern technology of any kind. Bioethics, for example, presents us today with baskets full of moral questions which the writers of the books of Scripture could not have imagined. That does not mean, however, that the Bible does not have some very critical things to say on the subject.

Sterility

What would be a wife's position if her husband had a vasectomy operation without her knowledge or approval? Would she be practicing some sort of sinful birth control by having sexual intercourse once she has been informed of the surgery?

Your question might more basically be phrased: May a married couple have intercourse even though they know their union cannot result in children because of a condition of sterility? Such a condition may be present naturally (as when one partner is unexplainably sterile), after a hysterectomy, at a later age when child-bearing years are past, and so on.

No moral obstacle to sexual relations exists in these circumstances. The possibility of the wife becoming pregnant and bearing a child is not a moral requirement for intercourse.

Regardless of how it started, you have a condition of sterility in your marriage which, at least on your part, did not and does not now imply any sinful intention or deliberate wrong action. There is no reason why you would be required to abstain from sexual relations.

However, you cannot ignore another element in the situation. Your married life, including your sexual life, is not carried on as two individuals isolated from each other. Therefore, since the cause of the sterility in your marriage was deliberate, it is important that you help your husband overcome and correct any sinful conscience and any continuing intention of violating his responsibilities in relationship to God in the matter.

"In Vitro" fertilization

Would you please explain the church's stand on "in vitro" fertilization?

It is important first to clarify what we're talking about. "In vitro" fertilization is one of the methods now technologically possible for conceiving a child without sexual relations between a man and woman. In this case the gametes (woman's ovum and the male sperm) are united and conception occurs in a test tube in which also the first stages of growth of the new human life take place. Soon this new embryo is transferred to another environment, usually the mother's (or another woman's) womb for continuing development. Such fertilization is called heterologous if the gametes come from people who are not married to each other. Homologous fertilization means that the reproductive cells come from a husband and wife married to each other.

"In vitro," literally "in glass," fertilization is considered entirely morally unacceptable by the church, basically for at least three reasons. First, from the time ovum is fertilized a new separate human life has begun which has its own growth and dignity. Commercial, scientific and other procedures often performed on lives begun "in vitro" violate the respect and physical and spiritual reverence owed to these lives. Second, "in vitro" fertilizing usually means that a number of zygotes (fertilized ova) are produced; some are utilized by being placed in a womb, all but one or a few of them usually die one way or another. While this may not in some circumstances involve direct killing of human life, it can immorally place new human beings in high risk of death.

And third, this process for initiating human life is seen as a subversion of the dignity and unity of marriage, and of the integrity of natural and necessary parental relationships with children as they come into the world. This aspect of the moral character of "in vitro" fertilization may seem less tangible, but it is an important and profound one. In the tradition and teaching of the church, sexual relations in the context of married love is the only setting worthy of bringing into existence a new human life.

Heterologous fertilization, of course, brings in the additional questions of marriage fidelity and parental identity and responsibility. But even if the fertilization is homologous (husband and wife providing the cells for the new life of their child) it deprives human procreation of the dignity which is proper and natural to it.

The fullest and most current explanation of the church's teaching on these matters is the March 1987 "Instruction on Respect for Human Life in Its Origin and on the Dignity of Procreation," issued by the Congregation for the Doctrine of the Faith. It says of this procedure, "In conformity with the traditional doctrine relating to the goods of marriage and the dignity of the person, the church remains opposed from the moral point of view to homologous 'in vitro' fertilization. Such fertilization is in itself illicit and in opposition to the dignity of procreation and of the conjugal union" (II,5).

Perhaps it needs to be clearly said that when "in vitro" or any other kind of artificial human fertilization does happen, the resulting life is no less human and no less to be accepted and cared for with love. This, of course, underlies the first and second points I made above.

For those of us who were raised when there was only one way for a baby to be conceived and carried to term in the womb of its own mother, it comes as a surprise to know that today there are at least 30 different combinations of methods all this can happen. And each has its own array of religious and human, and therefore moral, questions. It is a continuing and monumental challenge for the church, or anyone else, to address these technological developments honestly and at the same time remain faithful to those values we hold so sacred about human life and relationships.

Widow worries about the past

I have been a widow for many years and something from my past haunts me. I married a man who told me he had a

vasectomy. I married him knowing this and received the sacraments every Sunday without confessing that I was guilty of practicing birth control.

I have confessed this sin since I became a widow. The priest made no comment, gave me absolution and that was all.

What else am I to do? Every time I go to Communion I feel I am committing a sacrilege.

It might have been helpful to you if the priest had explained a little bit. But probably the main reason he did not comment was that there really was nothing to comment about.

Often in the Sacrament of Penance, particularly when dealing with something that is past, it is futile (and probably impossible) to sort out how much guilt there may have been over something done that was wrong. This certainly is true in your case, as the priest probably realized. He knew that to go into the past and try to unravel degrees and qualities of guilt would really serve no purpose.

The only important thing was that you were confessing that, insofar as you were guilty of any sin before God, you were sorry for it. God certainly accepts that, and the priest did too. Whatever sin there may have been is now forgiven because of your sorrow, and through the Sacrament of Penance. It is all past and you are certainly forgiven.

I realize it is easier to say this than to accept it in our hearts. When we feel we have done wrong over a period of time, it is difficult to believe that we can lay it all out before God and know that his love and mercy are larger and stronger than any of our weaknesses.

But that is precisely the message that Jesus gives us and which he carries out through his church in the Sacrament of Penance.

You are perfectly correct in receiving Holy Communion as often as you can. You might make an additional intention in this sacrament and in your prayers asking God for the grace of full acceptance of his forgiving love for whatever wrong intentions or actions there may have been in your past life.

Divorce, Annulment and Remarriage

Summary of marriage rules

I know you receive and answer a lot of questions concerning marriage. Some people divorce and remarry in the church, some cannot, and some have marriages annulled. Frankly it's darned confusing to me, maybe because I've really never seen a list of all the rules in one place. Is it possible for you to tell us what these rules or laws are? I think it would help me and probably many others to understand some of the situations in our families.

Yours is probably one of the most sensible questions I've ever received, and one of the most difficult to answer. The marriage legislation of the church is long and involved, reflecting at once its concern for the sacredness of marriage and its concern for the people in painful or impossible marriage situations.

From my experience, however, the following summary of the church's present marriage laws should go far in answering questions about specific cases, as they would apply normally to our country:

1. Every baptized Catholic who has not formally rejected the Catholic faith must be married before a priest (or bishop or deacon) in order to be validly married according to the laws of the Catholic Church. Without a dispensation from the bishop, any marriage that does not take place this way is not valid in the eyes of the church. (See CCL 1108, 1116, 1117)

2. If neither marriage partner is Catholic and both are free to marry (for example, if neither one has a previous marriage), the Catholic Church recognizes the union as a true, valid marriage. Thus, contrary to what some people still believe, the church definitely considers the marriage between two Hindus, for example, or two Baptists or Lutherans, as real marriages.

3. Furthermore, if both non-Catholic partners in a marriage are validly baptized Christians, the Catholic Church views that marriage as a Christian sacrament. They receive the Sacrament of Marriage and have what we call a sacramental marriage.

Because they are Christians, their marriage carries with it that special reflection of the covenant of love that Jesus has for his people, his church. As the Second Vatican Council put it so beautifully, "Christian partners are strengthened, and as it were, consecrated, by a special sacrament for the duties and dignity of their state . . . The spirit of Christ pervades their whole lives with faith, hope and love."

This unique character of all Christian marriages has special significance in our marriage laws, as the next point makes clear.

4. While the church does claim authority to dissolve certain marriages "in favor of the faith," it considers any sacramental marriage, in the sense explained above, entirely beyond its reach or power to dissolve.

Thus, if it is certain that two people in a valid marriage were truly baptized in any Christian church, there is no possibility of the church's dissolving that marriage to allow either of the individuals to marry again. (Remember that "dissolving" a marriage is different from an annulment, which is a declaration that there was never a valid marriage at all.) This rules out such procedures as the Pauline Privilege or Privilege of the Faith which might be used in other circumstances, and which we'll talk about next.

Remember that in any case involving someone who has been married before and who now wishes to marry someone else in the Catholic Church, all pertinent facts (such as baptism, previous marriages and divorces, etc.) must be substantiated by appropriate documents and, if necessary, by testimony of people in a position to know. This is one way the church attempts to assure that the persons involved do not get into a new situation that will hurt them again, perhaps even worse than before.

The church does, as I said, claim authority to dissolve certain marriages so that the partners may be married again. This is what happens in most situations where a person who is Catholic marries for a second time.

If one or both of the partners in a valid marriage is not baptized (wherever that marriage took place), such a marriage may be dissolved by the church so that a later marriage may be true and valid. This procedure is based on a passage in St. Paul (1 Corinthians 7:12-15) in which Paul discusses marriages and remarriages of new converts to Christianity.

For at least 1,500 years, the church has interpreted this teaching as giving it the right to dissolve marriages of unbaptized people "in favor of the faith" — that is, for the good of their faith.

Such procedures may be of two kinds:

1. Pauline Privilege, named after St. Paul. This method is used to dissolve the valid marriage of two non-baptized persons if one of the partners wishes to become a Catholic and marry a Catholic. These cases are usually decided by the marriage tribunals of the local diocese.

2. Privilege of the Faith. Through this approach, the church dissolves a valid marriage of a baptized person (whether that individual is Catholic or Protestant) with a partner who is not baptized. Here, one spouse is baptized at the time of the marriage; in the Pauline Privilege procedure, both are unbaptized.

Normally, Privilege of the Faith cases are decided by officials in Rome.

Finally, one more word about annulment, which is a formal declaration that what seemed to be a valid marriage was never really a marriage at all. Note carefully that this is different from dissolving a marriage that is truly already in existence.

In most annulment procedures it makes no difference whether the people involved are Catholic or Protestant, baptized or not. What must be proven is that some condition was present in the marriage that made real marriage promises impossible.

One example of such a condition would be if one or both spouses intended never to have any children in their married life. Another example would be an emotional or psychological instability so serious in one of the partners that he or she simply was incapable of genuine, full commitment to the kind of life together that marriage involves.

Annulments are discussed more fully under other questions.

Divorced persons still Catholics

I married a Catholic in the Catholic Church. Five years later I completed instructions and was baptized (but not confirmed). Seven years after that we were divorced.

My question is: In the eyes of the church, was I a Catholic at the time of my divorce? Because I am divorced, am I now a Catholic? I have not remarried. Is it proper for me to go to Mass and receive Communion?

I am continually surprised at the number of divorced (and other) Catholics who feel they are out of the church, or are otherwise somehow second-class Catholics now.

In a word, the answer to all your questions is yes.

There's probably not a parish in the country which can claim to have the kind of assistance and support for divorced men and women that it should have and would like to have. So perhaps some basis exists for the feeling of being "left out" to some degree. But the fact is, a divorce in itself does not remove anyone from full membership in the church.

We Catholics make no secret of our convictions about the permanence and indissolubility of marriage. But it's also obvious that personal tragedies can develop in a marriage which make it emotionally, spiritually, and perhaps even physically dangerous if the husband and wife remain living together. One or both of the spouses has no alternative except to legally separate for his or her own health and the health of any children.

When such separations involve good and sensitive people, they are never an "easy way out." They carry terrible burdens of hurt, fear and frustration which may never be completely healed or forgotten. There's just no way that the church could say to such suffering people "You're out."

Yes, you were a member of the church after you were baptized and you are still a member of the church after your divorce. There is nothing to prevent your receiving the Sacraments of Penance and the Eucharist.

After the breakup of a marriage, unless outright gross infidelity of one kind or another is part of the history, a realistic and helpful assigning of guilt is probably impossible and unnecessary.

For whatever faults there were on your part, ask God's forgiveness, including through the sacrament of reconciliation, and receive the Eucharist regularly. You will need it and all the other help you can get to fulfill your new responsibilities to yourself and others.

Divorced not excommunicated

A columnist in our local daily paper recently discussed the remarriage of divorced Catholics and whether they could go to Communion. Several times she quoted a priest whom she named and identified as a "widely known Catholic authority on separation and divorce."

After explaining that such people were no longer excommunicated from the church, the priest said that Communion is "not a gold star, not a badge for having it all together . . . We say that the meal (Communion) is not supper for those who have it all together, but for those to whom the Lord is reaching out in their struggles. This is not a relaxation of formal rules, but a greater degree of understanding of the Eucharist, that it is a meal of healing, of reconciliation for people trying to do their best under the circumstances."

What is your opinion of his attitude?

Again, divorced and remarried Catholics are no longer excommunicated. That change says nothing about the validity of their new marriage. It simply says that they are still members of the Catholic Church, except that they have done something seriously wrong in violation of its laws and, perhaps in most cases, divine law.

Generally, I must agree with the priest you quote. If one is a Catholic (which a remarried Catholic still is), the only other requirement for receiving the Eucharist is that he or she is not deliberately in the state of mortal sin.

Note that this does not say they have not committed a serious sin. Perhaps they have, if all necessary conditions were present. But being in the state of sin means that one deliberately continues in a sinful situation from which he is morally able to remove himself. This means that the individual is physically and emotionally and spiritually able to remove himself from that situation, and able to do it without causing even more serious harm.

To use an obvious example, a remarried man, for instance, may have extremely serious responsibilities of every kind to his present family. Even though all this may have come about because of a sinful action, those responsibilities are there now. If he simply cannot leave his home without serious physical, mental and even spiritual harm to his present wife and children, I know of almost no one who would claim he must break up that family in order to get himself straight with God.

The illustration points out that such situations are possible and that no one is in the position to judge another.

Your priest's final phrase, "trying to do the best under the circumstances," must be understood seriously and correctly. Like the expression, "follow your conscience," it can mean many things. But understood rightly in the light of the teachings of the church, it summarizes one's responsibilities before God quite well.

Excommunication and remarriage

I still don't understand a few things about the possibility of divorced and remarried Catholics returning to the Sacrament of Communion.

Does the church now consider second or third marriages all right, since these people are no longer excommunicated? If not, how can the church say it is possible for them to receive Communion if they are living in sin?

I realize this matter sounds extremely complicated and confusing to most Catholics.

First of all, be clear on one point. In eliminating the excommunication of divorced and remarried Catholics, the American bishops explicitly stated that their action could in no way indicate acceptance of these second marriages as valid and sacramental. The fact that persons in this situation are no longer excommunicated simply means that they remain members of the church and may share in many ways in its life and worship. (Actually, many remarried Catholics were doing this already, which only increased confusion over the significance of the bishops' action, which they intended as an expression of concern and care for these members of our faith.)

To your second question, it is true that divorced and remarried Catholics are living in an objectively sinful situation according to the church's laws which reflect its beliefs in the permanence of marriage. For this reason, of course, the general rule of the church is that they cannot receive Communion.

However, whether the individuals involved are as you put it, "living in sin" as far as their own souls are concerned, is something only God can know and judge. It is possible they are not, if, for example, they sincerely wish to do everything necessary to get straight with God but find it morally impossible to leave the present spouse without proportionately serious emotional, spiritual, or physical harm to others. This is simply good traditional moral theology.

Applying, then, our traditional theology of the Eucharist, it becomes clear that receiving Communion may be considered in some instances. As the bishops said, the lifting of the excommunication does not "of itself" permit divorced and remarried Catholics to receive the Sacraments of Penance and the Eucharist, but the possibility is not ruled out.

A daughter and her parents' divorce

About two years ago my parents separated. They divorced six months later. My father had another girlfriend (a neighbor) at the time. This woman also had divorced her husband. In the meantime I found out my father has seen other women in the 21 years of my folks' marriage and was dating this woman long before their separation.

I was told yesterday by my father that he plans to marry this woman. I am devastated. He says she is going to convert Catholic and they are going to be married in the Catholic Church. I cannot see at all how this marriage can even take place. Is there something I can do?

I nearly passed by your letter because it involves awfully heavy matters for a daughter like you to be forced to deal with. However, you seem old enough to understand the hard things that need to be said and which may be helpful to many others in circumstances like yours.

Do you know what an annulment is? Briefly, it is a declaration that some circumstances existed throughout the marriage that made a marriage between those two people impossible. It could be that an essential condition for a valid marriage is lacking. For example, if it can be proven that a man had no intention of being faithful to his wife, that marriage would be invalid from the beginning.

We know also that some people, even adults who may say the marriage vows beautifully, and even to some degree live a decent marriage, may in fact be so emotionally immature and unstable that a true marriage covenant with anyone is impossible.

I have only your letter to go on, of course. And in no way do I pretend to anticipate decisions of marriage tribunals. I'm simply trying to help you to understand what may be going on here by telling you that, from what you have said, it is quite questionable whether your father is capable, or has ever been capable, of the genuine commitment marriage requires. The promiscuity you describe during an entire marriage would seem to indicate a terribly dwarfed personality. Such an individual may be sincere in entering a marriage, yet just not possess enough emotional or psychological equipment to commit to the community of life that we believe marriage to be.

From your letter it appears that your father has introduced some sort of case to your diocesan tribunal, though if I were you I would not be too sure until I checked. If he has, the priests and other experts involved must and will make judgments on the information they receive from competent people in and out of the families.

It needs to be repeated that granting an annulment does not automatically allow an individual to enter a new marriage in the Catholic Church. When serious emotional incompetence is established as the grounds for an annulment, the annulment decree insists that no Catholic marriage may take place unless and until appropriate psychiatric therapy has brought that person to a level of emotional maturity sufficient for a real marriage. Otherwise the same problem would make the second marriage as invalid as the first.

I realize this is brief, but it is important for you to know that the officials of the Catholic Church involved in these processes have the same concerns and fears and reverence for marriage as you. They do not take these responsibilities lightly. We hold marriage sacred. It is only because we do honor it as a radical commitment and dedication of one's whole self to another person that cases such as your father's are dealt with carefully and respectfully to everyone concerned.

Your father seems to be a confused and emotionally mixed-up person. If you discover that he has in fact initiated a case with your diocesan tribunal office please feel free to contact that office and talk with one of the priests or other personnel there. As a profoundly concerned daughter, I'm sure they will do their best to help you understand what is going on. In the meantime, continue your prayers and keep your own obviously high ideals. It sounds as if your parents, as well as yourself, will need all the help you can get.

Remarriage after divorce

Is it true that a divorced Catholic couple can remarry (to different partners) in a Catholic church if they are married in a Catholic church the first time? A co-worker has told me that someone in her family remarried that way. I have members in my family who are divorced and would like to remarry in the church. How can some people be allowed and others denied?

If a Catholic couple are married in a Catholic church, there is only one way either of them could marry another partner later on in the church. It would require a declaration of nullity (annulment) for the first marriage, a declaration which must be determined by the marriage tribunal of the diocese where the people live.

To determine whether such a procedure is at all feasible in a particular case, the individual must talk to a priest, explain the situation thoroughly, and he will assist in taking whatever steps are possible.

Sacraments after remarriage

Can a Catholic who has remarried without an annulment receive the sacrament of the Anointing of the Sick? As chaplain of our Catholic medical center, I tell other staff that to receive the Eucharist or anointing the patient must be in the "state of grace." If there is no annulment no sacraments should be administered, except in danger of death.

I am pressured to anoint these remarried people. I feel it more appropriate that confession and the Eucharist be the healing sacraments if the patient is properly disposed to receive them and their marriage status allows it. What do you think is the right course of action?

Some reasons exist in our Catholic tradition for the policy you pursue. We sometimes refer to this sacrament, formerly Extreme Unction, as a "sacrament of the living." This means it is to be received only by someone who is, as you say, in the "state of grace." This "state" is, of course, an internal condition of one's soul, one's personal relationship to God. It is not always or automatically determined by one's external or public status in the church.

Important references to this sacrament might seem to presuppose that one who receives it is in sacramental communion with the church. The decree of Vatican Council II on the liturgy, for example, in its brief outline for reform of rites for the sick, orders that "a continuous rite be drawn up, structured so that the sick person is anointed after confessing and before receiving Viaticum," the Eucharist. (nn. 73-75) This seems to imply that those who receive anointing of the sick should be at least spiritually capable of receiving the sacraments of Penance and the Eucharist.

Canon law, however, says only that "the anointing of the sick is not to be conferred upon those who obstinately persist in manifest serious sin." (1007) This adds another important dimension to the situation.

Those two words, manifest (Latin, *manifesto*) and obstinately (*obstinate*) have a rather heavy meaning in church law. Manifest means that the individual's sin is a matter of some public knowledge. People obstinately persist in serious sin when they stubbornly reject the teachings and laws of the church, and continue in some sinful situation from which they are morally (emotionally, spiritually) and physically capable of removing themselves. All priests with any significant parish experience know that there are people, for example in a second marriage not recognized by the church, who cannot at this moment remove themselves from that situation without enormous injustice to others, particularly their present spouse and children. Such Catholics would not be "manifest" and "obstinate" sinners in the technical sense. Canon law would seem to say they could receive anointing of the sick.

Church law uses the same terminology for those who should not be admitted to Holy Communion (c. 915). The American Canon Law Society, in its massive commentary on the new code, notes that this restriction obviously applies to anyone excommunicated or otherwise separated formally from the communion of the church.

"Other categories of manifest and grave sins are not so neatly discernible," they continue. "The minister cannot assume, for example, that the sin of public concubinage arising from divorce and remarriage is always grave in the internal forum. Any prudent doubt about either the gravity or the public nature of the sin should be resolved by the minister (of Communion) in favor of the person who approaches the sacrament." (The Code of Canon Law: A Text and Commentary; p. 653)

While this last observation throws light on canonical norms for administering the Anointing of the Sick, it should be noted, to avoid misunderstanding, that for ministering the Sacrament of the Eucharist the position in place for the Catholic Church remains that enunciated by Pope John Paul II in his 1981 encyclical on the family. "The church reaffirms her practice, which is based on sacred scripture, of not admitting to eucharistic communion divorced persons who have remarried. They are unable to be admitted thereto from the fact that their state and condition of life objectively contradict that union of love between Christ and the church which is signified and effected by the Eucharist." (#84)

Getting back to sacraments

A mother wrote to you that her divorced and again separated daughter would like to return to the Catholic Church but was afraid she would not be allowed to receive the sacraments.

I hope she accepts your suggestion that she talk with her parish priest and follow his advice.

I am a divorced Catholic who remarried outside the church for the second marriage. The last two years of the second marriage (I am now divorced again) I attended Mass on a regular basis without receiving the sacraments.

Those two years of watching my fellow parishioners receive Communion while I sat were difficult and humbling. I came to realize how much we can take this weekly God-given gift for granted.

After divorcing my second husband I tearfully approached an unfamiliar priest in an unfamiliar city. This priest was literally a godsend to me.

After a long discussion and tearful confession (my first in five years) I started annulment proceedings. The following Sunday I received my first Communion in five years. Before Communion the congregation read aloud "Footsteps." I could hardly see the words on the sheet through my tears.

As I approached Father for Communion he looked at me

and said, "Cathy, receive the Body of Christ." I couldn't even respond as the tears were welling up in my heart again, as they are now reliving that day.

For the past year every time I receive Communion I feel the glory and peace of partaking in this sacrament.

Please tell this young woman and all people in the same situation to continue in their faith by going to Mass, whether or not they are able to receive the sacraments. I pray for them that they may find the peace that I have found through God's grace.

God has given me a very special gift, my fiance. With God's help I plan to finally make a marriage work. I thank him every day. The priest is happily helping us through the preparations and, God willing, will unite us this next summer in the sacrament of marriage.

You give good advice. I'm sure your experience will give hope and courage to many. Thanks for writing.

A misunderstanding

My son married a divorced girl five years ago. At the time they wanted to be married in the Catholic Church but the priest told her she must first sign a paper saying she was not married before. Even my husband would not go along with that.

Now she refuses to allow the three children to be baptized because the church will not accept her and allow her to become a Catholic.

What can be done? My son has spoken to a priest who did not seem able to do anything in their favor.

Somewhere along the line your son and his wife grossly misunderstood either the process the priest was following, or the questions they were being asked. Nowhere in any of its procedures does the Catholic Church ask or encourage any statement that is contrary to the facts as that individual knows them.

At some stages of certain marriage procedures, an individual might be asked if a previous marriage had ever taken place in the Catholic Church. In itself, however, this implies no statement concerning the validity of that previous marriage, since marriages of non-Catholics are recognized by the Catholic Church as perfectly valid, presuming, of course, they are both free to marry.

Your letter gives nowhere near enough facts for me to make even a wild guess at whether a Catholic marriage for your son and his wife is possible. I suggest he lay the whole matter before some priest in his locality and determine if a validation of their present marriage is possible. I hate to see them missing so much spiritually simply because of a misunderstanding.

"Church's laws will change?"

My father is deceased and my mother has married a divorced man who is not Catholic and was never baptized.

I'm not sure whether this man would become Catholic or not. But when they were married the priest told my mother (according to her) that they should go ahead and marry since the church's rules would change in five years.

It's now five years later. What chance is there for her to get married in the church and return to the sacraments?

I am fairly confident that the priest could not have advised your mother to act on the basis of such speculation as a rule change in church marriage laws. Many times we hear, with no deliberate dishonesty at all, what we would like to hear in matters that deeply affect us. My suspicion is that this is what happened to your mother.

Whatever happened five years ago, if the facts you give are accurate, I suggest you ask your mother to talk the matter over thoroughly with a priest first, or, if you would feel more comfortable, you discuss it with the priest yourself first. If your mother's present husband had only one previous marriage, and if there is no other impediment, a procedure exists which might allow the marriage of your mother to be validated in the church.

The procedure is not new, by the way, though it is used more now than formerly.

Is divorce against the sixth commandment?

I am a high school CCD teacher and have a question based on our text. In the teacher's guide on the sixth commandment it lists divorce and unreasonable denial of marital rights among the main sins against this commandment. I don't understand this. I thought divorced people sinned only if they engage in sexual activity with other people or remarry.

First, the basic moral questions to be asked in contemplating a divorce are: What are the real reasons? Is there a genuinely honest cause for what I'm doing? Sincerely responding to these questions is a long way from: "I'm just not interested anymore. I simply want to get out." If you want more detail and depth about what this involves, think about the following. It needs to be said clearly once again: The church does not consider getting a divorce automatically a sin of any kind. We'll discuss this more in a moment. Contrary to what numerous people, Catholic and otherwise, still believe, divorced people are not excommunicated from the Catholic Church. They are not separated from the sacraments, including penance and the Eucharist; and they are not dismissed to the fringes of the church.

However, since the church takes very seriously the sacred obligations of fidelity and permanence that are promised in marriage, we need to address more directly your question about divorce being a sin against the sixth commandment. Every priest with even a few years of parish experience is only too familiar with the thoroughly inadequate manner in which many couples, some Catholics included, prepare themselves for marriage. For this and other reasons, everyone, priests included, is aware today that numerous marriages have over the years become radically dysfunctional. They manifest serious physical or emotional abuse, totally impossible expectations on the part of one or both partners and other evidences of a badly diseased relationship. Of course, this type of condition may exist from the very beginning of a marriage, which is where annulments come into the picture. In these violent circumstances a legal divorce may not only be allowed; it sometimes becomes an outright obligation on the part of the innocent party in order to protect the emotional, spiritual and even physical health of one or both partners and perhaps also of the children. Pursuing a divorce in this kind of situation, which is not nearly as rare as most couples in more stable marriages suppose, is understandably not sinful.

This is not to say, of course, that some grave sinfulness, at least objective sinfulness, is not almost always involved in what leads up to the divorce. That sinfulness may have little to do with the Sixth Commandment or sex. The tragic destructiveness I mention above has much more to do with charity, personal respect and trust, fidelity to promises and plain caring. It is violation of these virtues by one or both spouses, not the legal action at the courthouse, that constitutes the major part of any "sin" involved in divorce.

In Catholic doctrine and law, marriage is a personal covenant commitment between a man and a woman, establishing between them a partnership, a community of the whole of life. Those are awesome words. We need to consider them seriously when we speak of these matters, and not reduce them, and possible sins involving them, only to external omissions. Insofar as they relate to Christian marriage, this applies to the Ten Commandments as well.

Marrying divorced non-Catholics

I am confused about the church's rule regarding a Catholic marrying a divorced non-Catholic.

I can understand a rule against a Catholic marrying a divorced Catholic. But most other religions do not forbid divorce. Therefore, a divorced non-Catholic is acting completely within the laws of his own religion.

Why then should marriage with such a divorced person be against the Catholic Church's regulations?

The institution and covenant of marriage was not made by any individual religion. It was established by God himself, the creator of our human nature.

Certain basic things concerning marriage are, therefore, outside the jurisdiction of any religious group. Any religion, for example, which would presume to declare homosexual marriages to be real marriage covenants subject to all the graces of a sacramental marriage, would be acting far beyond its powers.

In a word, the belief of the Catholic Church is that no religion has any power to grant or approve of divorces in the way they prevail in our society.

Excommunication and Communion

In a recent column about divorced and remarried Catholics, you said that such Catholics are no longer excommunicated. That does not mean, you said, that the new marriage is recognized according to church regulations; simply that the person is still acknowledged as a full member of the Catholic family.

By full member of the Catholic family, does this mean that one may receive Holy Communion? Are they allowed to be practicing Catholics in their parish?

I was widowed several years ago. In dating I meet many divorced men. I would like to marry again but I want to remain in my own church.

One may be a full member of the Catholic Church, not excommunicated, but still not be free to receive the Holy Eucharist. I'm sure you know well that any serious mortal sin by which we break our relationship with God in a radical way keeps us from the communion table until we have repented, been forgiven and given up any sinful situation in our lives.

Unless it takes place within the procedures established by the church, a second marriage after divorce violates a major rule of the church which every Catholic is seriously obliged to follow. This in itself is objectively sinful. It may even be a violation of the law of God itself if the individual remarries, even after a civil divorce, when a previously valid marriage union still exists.

Serious laws by which the church regulates its life and marriage laws are certainly among them, are not just arbitrary "rules of the club." They are the ways the church attempts to be faithful to the Gospel as a community of believers in Jesus Christ. As members of the church, therefore, every Catholic accepts his or her responsibility to share in that mission, and fulfill those obligations as honestly and faithfully as possible. No one pretends to judge how any individual stands in conscience before God. As I indicated, however, such actions are objectively seriously sinful.

I must add that the church (and by that I mean all our fellow Catholics) never just leaves it at that. In many ways, it tries to provide every means possible for people in such situations to return to the sacraments in an honorable and faithful way. Anyone who is divorced and remarried and who wishes to return to a full Catholic sacramental life should talk with a priest in whom he or she has confidence to learn what is possible. Nothing prevents such individuals or couples from participating in almost all other parish activities. They do so in most parishes, including our own.

Marriage to a foreigner

My friend is a Catholic and in love with a man from another country. Some time ago he was married just to remain in the United States. Is there any hope for their getting married soon?

If it can be proven that this man entered into a marriage primarily for the reason you indicate and did not intend a real marriage commitment to his first wife, this fact would be an obvious basis for a possible annulment of his first marriage.

This type of case has become, if not common, at least frequent during the past 15 or 20 years, particularly involving refugees from Latin America and Caribbean nations. But each case must be handled individually by the tribunal of the diocese in which the individuals live.

Please suggest to your friend that she ask her parish priest as quickly as possible for his advice and assistance.

Free to marry again?

I was married twice. My husband in the first marriage, which was in the Catholic Church, is dead.

My second marriage to a non-Catholic was in a judge's chamber. It did not work and we were divorced a short time later. I am under the impression that since my second marriage was not in the church and not recognized by the church, I am free to marry a Catholic and participate in all of the sacraments. I am too shy to face our parish priest about this. But please tell me if I am right.

You are right. As basic as your situation is, I'm surprised how many Catholics continue to be confused about this type of situation.

As a Catholic you were obliged under the laws of the Catholic Church to be married before a priest, or at least have a dispensation from the bishop to be married elsewhere.

Since your second marriage did not fulfill these conditions, you are now free to marry in the Catholic Church. Neither is there any obstacle to your receiving the Sacraments of Penance and the Eucharist.

Married before a judge

My Catholic nephew married a divorced woman and therefore was not married in the church. His wife was married to a Catholic the first time by a judge.

The situation has disturbed my sister immensely. Since she is getting old, she would like to see her son back to the practice of his faith and able to receive the sacraments.

My nephew and his wife go to Mass every Sunday, but it

hurts her, too, that he cannot receive Communion. I'm puzzled why some people who seem to be in the same situation can go to Communion and others cannot.

Your letter left out many details essential for a complete answer. But one detail you do give is very important and should be followed up on if you are sure it is true.

You say that the wife's first husband was Catholic and they were married before a justice of the peace. If that is true, the chance is good that her first marriage was not valid in the eyes of the church, for the simple reason that a Catholic must normally be married before a priest to be validly married.

Are you sure the priest in the parish knows this background? Assuming this was the only marriage the woman had entered before she married your nephew, or that there are no other significant elements in the situation of which you are perhaps unaware, your nephew and his wife might well be able to have the marriage validated in the Catholic Church and he could return to the sacraments.

If they haven't done so already, please encourage them to discuss the situation thoroughly with a priest.

Diriment impediment

Ten years ago when my husband and I were married he had never been baptized. In fact, it is safe to say he is an agnostic, though he told the priest he thought he was baptized when we were preparing for the marriage.

The priest asked him to bring proof of the baptism, but my husband never did. The priest married us nonetheless. My question is, are we rightfully married in the eyes of the church? Several friends tell me that if both parties have not been baptized in some faith, then the church does not recognize the marriage.

It is true that a Catholic cannot validly marry a non-baptized person in the church without a dispensation. Such an obstacle is called a diriment impediment in church law, which means that it not only makes a marriage unlawful, but also invalid.

However, as I indicated, such a marriage may take place validly with a dispensation from the bishop. It is routine that any time no proof of a baptism is obtainable in anticipation of a marriage, the bishop or his delegate automatically grants such a dispensation, if all the other conditions for the marriage are present, of course.

I am confident this is what happened in your own marriage. Whatever dispensation the bishop gave would cover the possibility that your husband was not baptized at all.

If it still bothers you, you might ask the priest who helped you prepare for the wedding. But you really should have nothing to be concerned about.

If spouse is not baptized?

Can a marriage between a Catholic and a non-Catholic be dissolved because the non-Catholic was never baptized?

In his long discussion of marriage and celibacy in the first letter to the Corinthians (chapter 7), St. Paul says that if the non-Christian spouse of a recently baptized Christian is willing to continue living together in harmony, there must be no divorce. If the non-Christian spouse is unwilling, however, the couple may separate for the good of the faith and presumably for the benefit of both.

Since the fourth century — in other words, for about 1,600 years — Christian tradition has (sometimes with considerable hesitation) seen this as a biblical basis also for allowing a divorce and remarriage in the situation you suggest. In church law it is called the Privilege of the Faith.

The procedure is not an overnight one, however, and sometimes can become quite complicated, involving problems of previous marriages, the question of whether or not the husband and wife were baptized Christians, and so forth. Each case is different and is handled separately through agencies set up in the church for that purpose.

If I marry out of the church?

My situation is somewhat different than the one you

discussed recently on divorce and remarriage. I am a Catholic and have never been married, but the man I'm interested in is a divorced non-Catholic. I would like to know, if I enter a marriage of this kind, will the Sacrament of Communion be denied me? He has even mentioned that he would consider becoming a convert if it would help.

The answer to your main question — whether or not you could marry this man according to the rules of the Catholic Church — can only be given after discussing all pertinent details with your priest. So many factors (previous marriages, baptismal status, etc.) are involved that not even a wild guess is possible in this response.

In fairness to yourself, I strongly suggest you keep a couple of things clearly in mind. First, remember that the answer may quite possibly be no. Often an individual pursues a course like this with a vague feeling that somehow "something will work out." Such may not happen, resulting in considerable suffering for yourself and others.

Second, if you do something you believe is wrong, Communion "would be denied" you only by yourself, not someone else as you seem to imply. There is no police force guarding the Communion table. Normally the only obstacle to Holy Communion for a Catholic is a serious offense against God's law that is unrepented and unconfessed. The individual himself is the only judge of that.

Can I remarry?

I have been a Catholic all my life, and am keeping company with a lady, also Catholic. In 1927 I was married by a justice of the peace and later had the marriage validated in the church. We were divorced in 1932.

Since then my first wife has been married eight times. In fact, the reason we separated was that she was running around with other men. I've been told that we could not get an annulment, but I've also been told that anyone marrying that many times is unbalanced.

The lady I'm keeping company with and I would like to be married in the church. We're both in our 70s and nothing

would make us happier than to be married in our religion. What can we do to make that happen?

Getting married eight times, even over a period of 50 years, may well be a symptom of mental or emotional unbalance. At the very least it is a symptom of a pretty shaky idea of the meaning of the marriage promise, and for that reason of a questionable capability for entering into a true marriage with anyone.

In other words, judging, of course, only from the information you offer, this is the kind of case that seems well worth submitting to your diocesan authorities for further investigation. You don't mention who told you an annulment was not possible. If it was not your parish priest or another priest in whom you have confidence, I certainly urge you to discuss the situation with him now.

The fact that all this happened nearly five decades ago complicates matters somewhat, since some of those whose testimony would be desirable have surely died by this time. It's still worth bringing to the priest's attention, however, and let him see what might be done. Good luck!

Married a transvestite

A friend married a transvestite — a person who dresses in clothes of the opposite sex — but didn't find out until after they had been married for some time. She tried living with him, but after a few years she was in such a state the doctor recommended divorce.

She is a good Catholic, but would like to remarry. Could this be grounds to have the marriage annulled? Priests I have questioned doubt it.

It may be possible for such a marriage to be annulled. There's absolutely no way of knowing, however, until the facts are sufficiently investigated.

A major element in the case, of course, is the depth and extent of the psychological illness and incapacity which her husband suffers. In certain instances, this type of person is so emotionally crippled that true consent to marriage, with the relationships and responsibilities this implies, is not possible.

Only appropriate psychiatric and legal consultation can determine that. A decision concerning the nullity of the marriage would then be made based on the results of such investigations.

Suggest that your friend discuss the matter personally with a priest in her area in whom she has confidence and follow the procedure he suggests.

Remarried same man

If I was married by a justice of the peace to a Catholic, later divorced, and then was remarried to the same man by the same judge, can we be married by a priest now? I am a Catholic, too.

If neither of you were ever married except to each other, there is nothing preventing your being married in the church at this time. This assumes, of course, that all the other usual requirements and intentions for a marriage are present.

If either of you have been married to someone else somewhere along the line, that problem would have to be discussed with your parish priest.

Defect of Form

A problem has recently surfaced within our family which has us all puzzled. Our daughter was married by a justice of the peace early last year. The marriage was a tragedy for many reasons and they are now separated. She is filing for divorce.

Our parish priest tells us we must provide copies of baptism, confirmation, and other certificates, and after a hearing she will be granted an annulment.

How can this be? If the Catholic Church does not recognize her marriage and she cannot receive the sacraments in this unrecognized marriage, how can it issue an annulment? We'll appreciate any light you can shed on this.

Your questions reveal a good bit of confusion about annulments. An annulment is simply a declaration (by the church or civil authorities) that no marriage ever existed. Numerous reasons might exist for such a declaration, ranging from purely legal impediments through such conditions as a serious lack of proper intention for marriage, or psychological inability to commit oneself to marriage.

In your daughter's case the annulment would be granted because of what is technically called "defect of form." This means that a Catholic was not married before a priest and therefore, according to church law, the marriage is invalid. One needs to prove that he or she was a baptized Catholic who never formally rejected the church, and that the marriage ceremony never took place before a priest. (CCL 1117) The documents you are to obtain are mainly to substantiate those facts.

It is possible for a Catholic to be validly married before a minister or justice of the peace if a dispensation for such a marriage has been received from the bishop of the diocese. You give no indication, however, that your daughter obtained such a dispensation.

Judging from your letter, there is no reason whatsoever that your daughter is not now perfectly free to receive the Sacraments of Penance and the Eucharist.

Time for marriage cases

Your column is great, and I hope you can help me. Why does a tribunal take so long to decide a privilege of the faith case involving a single Roman Catholic man, aged 57, marrying a divorced Methodist woman, aged 47? A pre-Cana conference priest said six months to a year is possible for a waiting period.

My dear fiance is thoroughly confused, as ordinarily four months is the only waiting time required.

I'm always extremely cautious in making predictions about the time required for completion of a marriage case. To begin with, most cases require a number of testimonies from people familiar with the couple involved; these alone may require several months, depending on the location of the witnesses and their willingness to assist in the case.

Add to this the time required for action by the local diocesan tribunal and possible (as in all privilege of the faith cases, which involve a previous marriage in which one of the spouses was baptized) action by the appropriate officials in Rome, and you are talking about a long time.

The priests and other personnel in the tribunals I know are conscientious, hard working and very knowledgeable people. With almost no exceptions, they are also extremely sensitive to the human realities and pain behind the names on the papers they work with.

Because they are concerned and aware of the anxieties of the people involved, I also have found them most understanding and helpful when anyone asks for information on the status of a particular case.

I hope I don't cause them too much extra work by saying this, but I suggest you ask them for information on the status of your case. This might best be done through the parish priest who is helping you with the case. Failing that, there is nothing wrong with your contacting the tribunal yourself.

What is the Roman Rota?

Our daily paper carried a story not long ago about the Roman Rota. We have also seen it mentioned several times in reference to reform in the church. What is it — and why do some apparently think that it is a problem?

The Roman Rota is the name of the highest standing "court" in the Catholic Church. It goes back about 800 years, and at one time had enormous power. Appeal from its decisions even to the pope himself was impossible without the establishment of a special papal commission.

Today, the Rota hears all types of cases, most of them dealing with marriage, and almost always on appeal from a lower church court. It is made up of about 18 judges (called auditors), who are divided into groups of three to hear and decide cases.

In general, objections to the Rota simply reflect the belief of many that a decentralization of court procedures would be desirable; for instance, it might be arranged that most judicial cases which now must go to Rome for final action would be handled instead entirely within each country.

Among other things, it is argued, such decentralization would reduce considerably the time required (often several years) to obtain a decision from the over-worked offices in Rome.

Annulments explained

In response to a question about annulments, you said:

"If one spouse proves to have an emotional deficiency so serious that a true married life was and is psychologically impossible for him or her, the marriage tribunal would be required to declare that no marriage ever existed even though the couple went through the marriage ceremony, lived together for several years, and had several children in the meantime."

Why don't all the so-called Catholic periodicals get together and submit a proposal to Rome that the phrase, "I take you for richer or poorer, for better or worse, in sickness and in health," be eliminated from the marriage vows?

You are only one of probably many thousands of Catholics who are terribly confused about the meaning of an annulment of a marriage.

It is precisely because the church considers those marriage vows so serious and so essential that it requires couples who enter marriage not only to be sincere, but to have at least a minimum ability to know what the words mean and be able to live by them.

A 12- or 14-year-old girl or boy may love someone very much and be quite sincere in wanting to get married. The church says, however, as do most states and countries, that no matter how sincere such a child may be, he or she lacks the experience of life and the emotional and psychological maturity to realize the implications of those words. He therefore lacks ability to commit himself to a genuine community of life that we call marriage, even though he may say the words clearly and beautifully.

Surely you are aware that this kind of immaturity and lack of capacity for commitment are quite possible in someone considerably older than 12 or 14. These defects, however, are not always easily discernible; they may, in fact, only be evident some time after the couple begins to live together as husband and wife.

It will help, perhaps, if we recall that Religious orders of men and women are allowed to call a candidate to final perpetual vows not only when that candidate has reached a sufficient age, but also only after some years of thought, study and prayer — and after a good while of living the responsibilities that life will require.

Yet we regularly accept young couples for marriage when they have known each other but a few months, and almost nothing is known about whether or not either of them really understands or knows what marriage is all about, or can live up to the responsibilities that marriage entails.

I'm certainly not suggesting trial marriages; in my opinion there is no such thing. Nearly every diocese in the country, in fact, provides an increasing variety of helps to assure a young couple that they are prepared as much as possible for a valid, honest Christian marriage.

I only suggest that given the fact of our upset and confused culture today, we should not be surprised, or for that matter even scandalized, that some number of couples were simply incapable of marriage with each other, and that this fact becomes inescapably clear through proper investigation.

While annulments in the Catholic Church today often derive from this sort of psychological incapacity, other reasons are also possible. Among these would be a clear intention by one of the partners contradicting an essential value of marriage, such as permanence, fidelity or openness to children.

One last remark. I strongly urge you and everyone else to resist the temptation to harsh and rash judgments about annulments and those who receive them. Believe me, annulments are no "easy way out." Behind every one lies a sad story of tragedy, broken hopes, defeat and heartbreak.

But there is another story of faith, love and deep concern for what is right that is able to sustain the individuals involved through the long and often painful annulment process. God is the only one who knows our hearts and he is, after all, the final judge.

Annulment and physical abuse

About five years ago we brought our daughter and her 18-month-old child from Florida to live with us. A neighbor of our daughter had called telling us she had taken our daughter to get stitches in her chin. We didn't realize the situation, but our daughter's husband had been abusing her for over a year. She had tried to stay with him since she felt she should live with her husband.

Now it seems there is no hope for that. We understand that the diocesan marriage court decides if there are grounds for a marriage annulment. Could you suggest what action we might take?

You do not give many details, but I have found that whenever there is serious physical abuse, particularly early in marriage, there are often also other psychological problems that make an annulment at least worth investigating.

Your first move should be to contact your parish priest, explain the situation, and ask his advice. He will guide and help you through the procedures which, as you indicate, are under the responsibility of the marriage court of your diocese. If it is impossible to contact a parish priest near you, you may write directly to the diocesan marriage court and explain the circumstances. I am sure they will help arrange at least an initial interview with someone.

Annulment: no children?

My daughter, a Catholic, has been married to a Catholic man for four years. For two years he gave excuses for not wanting to start a family; then he told her there would be no children in their marriage at all. He has been unfaithful to her and wants to come back but still says there will be no children.

She feels there is no point in getting back together if children are going to be ruled out completely. What can I advise her to do?

In our Christian tradition, in most civil law traditions, and in the laws of our church, openness to at least the possibility of children has been considered an essential element of any valid marriage.

This does not mean that the couple must positively intend to have children. Nor does it rule out the possibility of marriage between a couple who are sterile because of their advanced age, for example.

Openness to the possibility of children does mean, however, that neither of the spouses has a positive intention against children. If either spouse does have such an intention, saying in effect: "I do not want any children in this marriage and do not intend to have any," an essential condition of marriage is lacking in their union.

From what you have told me, that seems to be the clear state of mind of your daughter's husband. This could not be known for sure, however, without the proper kind of investigation.

I strongly suggest you ask your daughter to go to her parish priest or another priest with whom she can talk and explain the situation thoroughly. He will help her pursue the case. If it can be established that her husband has in fact deliberately ruled out an essential element of marriage, the church would declare that marriage annulled — that is, that no real and valid marriage ever existed between these two people.

Is annulment "Catholic divorce?"

A Protestant lady and I had a conversation about a local divorce and remarked that it would be terrible for the children. When I mentioned that Catholics do not believe in divorce, she looked at me and replied, "Yes, I know. You call it annulment."

Another lady remarked, "Divorce or annulment; what's the difference?" Can you give me any help on what to say?

I have dealt with annulments dozens of times in this column over the years. But judging from the number of letters I receive asking almost the same question, the confusion on the subject among Catholics as well as Protestants is obviously extensive.

A good deal of the confusion, in my opinion, results from

the mish-mash program about annulments and the Catholic Church seen on national television. The misleading reporting, misinformation, and outright false statements were so massive and numerous one finds it hard to believe they could all be gathered in one segment of an hour-long program.

Some beliefs and practices attributed to the Catholic Church are so diametrically opposed to the church's teachings, it is difficult to understand how intelligent and educated public figures could honestly present them with a straight face. Even the title, "Divorce Catholic Style," indicated the direction the newsmen were going, and would lead any informed viewer to conclude that their acquaintance with our faith is quite superficial.

Unfortunately, as you indicate, most viewers aren't informed and wrongly assume the editors of these programs are.

There is a huge difference between divorce and annulment. Even complete ignorance of church law and a slight knowledge of civil law will apprise anyone of that fact, since annulment is as much a reality in civil or state law as it is in canon law.

Let's suppose a fairly rich man tires of his marriage and wants to make sure his wife gets no alimony, as she might after a divorce. It is not uncommon in this or other circumstances for the man to petition the court for an annulment, a declaration that for some legal reason there never was a marriage in the first place. This (supposedly) would eliminate any financial claim she might exercise had there been a real marriage and a simple divorce.

One could not, I think, convince that man or his wife or the judge that there is no real and significant difference, but only a semantic one, between a divorce and an annulment.

It is not possible to expand further in this column, but the Catholic Church's understanding of annulment is basically similar to that of civil law. The church does indeed, with Paul in the New Testament, believe that any Christian marriage is a sacrament of the church and is unassailable even by the church. In other words, it cannot be ended by any sort of "divorce."

It also believes, however, that circumstances can be present which might only become absolutely clear years later, but which made a true marriage — that is, a full Christian commitment to a common life of love and all that means in a husband-wife relationship — impossible for those two people.

When it is asked by one of the parties to study this possibility and determine as much as is humanly possible whether or not a real marriage was present, it must in justice respond to that request as fairly and honestly as it can. This is precisely what it does in an annulment procedure.

Where to file for annulment?

I have two questions concerning annulments. Does a petition for annulment need to be filed in the state where the marriage took place? Would the other spouse be contacted or notified of the reasons for the annulment?

Normally the petition for any marriage case, including an annulment, should be initiated with the priest in the parish where the petitioner lives at that time. It makes no difference where the marriage took place.

Unless it is clearly impossible to locate the other partner in an annulment process, he or she is always contacted during the investigations and is notified of the tribunal's action if an annulment is granted.

Concerned about violence

I just finished reading one of your question columns dealing with annulment and the psychological inability of one or both of the spouses to make a marriage commitment. That is where I am. My wife and I have been married almost 17 months, but it really has been rough. At the Engaged Encounter, I told my then fiance that I couldn't make the commitment. There were many tears, but she wouldn't take no for an answer. I felt obligated to marry her.

Every once in a while I'll explode and heap a lot of pain upon her. I never hit her but I have come extremely close. I once dragged her across the room and dropped her. I shook my fist in her face, told her to go back where she came from and threw water on her.

The last time I got mad it was murderous anger that burst

out. It scares me. I've tried to get psychological help, but most people say I have to go with my wife to receive any marriage counseling. She is not open to that and chides me for running to a priest and counselor.

I had previously left a religious order on the grounds that I couldn't decide.

Please pray for us and give us any advice you can.

I have mailed what assistance I could to the man who sent this letter, but it seems to me that a lot of readers need to hear what he has to say. This man, and probably also his wife, are a good lesson for the many Catholics who complain about annulments and say that the church is getting soft.

My experience as a pastor and the mail that comes to me from readers of the question column, prove that this couple is not unusual. Their situation, in fact, is by no means as violent and vicious as some other marriage relationships.

With any sincerity at all, one would have to honestly question whether this couple — this man at least — could possibly be truly married in the sight of God, with a real commitment to the kind of common life and love that marriage promises involve.

The danger in dealing with this subject is that we might seem to imply that any marriage with extremely serious problems between a husband and wife is almost certainly invalid and could be annulled. I want to emphasize that it is not my intention to say that at all. I don't believe it.

Any marriage between two reasonably normal people will encounter occasional and sometimes long-lasting strains, tensions, and differences that will call upon every bit of unselfishness, patience, forgiveness and just plain generous love the individuals can muster. There will be times they might well say they would like out; they just weren't "meant for each other."

These are the times when commitment, grace, perseverance, and keeping a Christian perspective on life are called for and required. These are the times that enlarge the hearts of faithful spouses beyond what they dreamed possible.

In relating this man's feelings, then, I'm not making generalizations, nor am I attempting to anticipate the decisions of a marriage tribunal after its long and careful investigations. I do hope, however, that this sad letter will help us recognize that annulment cases are not only, or even mainly, from people who are just looking for "an easy way out."

Awareness of the daily tragedies of situations like this can help us to be as charitable, forgiving, and supportive as possible to the people in these circumstances and to the church authorities who are trying to help them.

Annulment no privilege

I am not the only Catholic who has been almost destroyed by the decision of the Roman Catholic Church to annul the marriage between a famous public figure and his wife, who bore him three children. How can the church do this when it hurts so many people?

A declaration of annulment is not a "privilege" the Catholic Church chooses to give to one person rather than another. It is a declaration after long and serious study by psychologists and others who are competent to make such judgments, that no marriage ever existed between the two people involved.

Most of the time today this judgment is based on evidence that one or both of the partners in the marriage were, because of serious psychological or emotional deficiencies, completely incapable of real honest marriage consent. This may be true even if several children were born of the marriage during the intervening years.

If the evidence brought forward through painstaking investigation reveals that the husband or wife (or both) were suffering from some emotional or psychological instability so severe that the genuine consent to the common life together that we call marriage was impossible, then the church has no alternative but to declare that marriage invalid.

I sympathize completely with the frustration and pain you feel over these kinds of decisions. That pain and anxiety are understandable in light of the sacredness in which we hold the Sacrament of Marriage.

However, I hope you can understand that it is respect for that very sacredness which prompts the church to require that people honestly know what they are doing before such a union can be a genuine Christian marriage.

In the case you mention and in all other declarations of annulment, the church, after long investigation of all the people involved, comes to the conclusion that there simply was never a marriage.

The hurt in such decisions can be very great. But the answer is to work toward making sure in the future that couples entering into marriage have enough preparation and knowledge to know thoroughly what they are doing so that annulment, or what is called "lack of due discretion," will be less possible in the future.

Furthermore a declaration of nullity makes no moral judgment one way or the other about either of the partners. It simply declares not that the couple would not, but rather that they could not, commit themselves to and live in a true marriage relationship with each other.

Marriage case fees

I have assisted some individuals, divorced and remarried, in going to a priest to seek the possibility of an annulment. I especially am concerned about the fees that some couples have quoted, as much as $300.

There was never a fee several years ago when I was involved in a similar case. Has there been a change? Would you please clarify this for me?

Dozens of hours of work, often including considerable consultation with professional people (physicians, psychiatrists, psychologists and others) are required to complete most annulment processes.

These procedures, with added overhead costs of the offices and personnel involved, can become very expensive.

All dioceses that I know of indicate a fee requested from individuals petitioning an annulment to help cover these expenses. Normally these fees do not cover the total cost, but they help a lot and make such procedures available for as many individuals as possible.

This is the reason for the "fees" you mention. It must be added, however, that these fees are not a "payment" for a favorable decision in a marriage case. Nor are they even a condition for the completion of the case.

In most instances with which I am familiar, fees are normally collected after the decision is made and are, in fact, excused (or sometimes paid by the parish involved) if the individuals are too poor to afford the fee.

I cannot, of course, speak for every diocese but this is the procedure and policy in every place with which I am familiar.

Children legitimate after annulment?

If a man and woman have been legally married for a number of years and an annulment is obtained for whatever reason, are the children born to this couple considered illegitimate?

If the man and woman in question were free to marry in the first place, any children born during their legal union would be considered legitimate by the church even if the marriage was annulled sometime later.

Such a union is called a "putative" marriage; that is, everyone thought it was a marriage and there was no overt reason to think otherwise. The fact that some condition was present throughout the marriage that enabled it to be annulled some years afterward does not change the fact that this couple was thought to be married by everyone, probably including even themselves.

Their children would be considered legitimate for all purposes of church law and, to my knowledge, also of civil law.

It is quite possible, of course, that children could be injured emotionally more or less seriously by the awareness that their parents, at this late date, feel they were never married at all and that such a declaration has now been made by the church or civil law. Legally, however, no stigma whatsoever devolves on the children because of annulment.

Do children prevent annulment?

Where and how do I get information on starting an annulment? A priest told me I have no chance because I have two children. Is this true?

Annulment proceedings should begin with a priest in your area, preferably in your parish, although another priest friend or acquaintance could begin the process.

The priest will then submit your story to the diocesan tribunal which will decide whether there is enough basis for a possible annulment to begin the many steps involved in this procedure. Only after these investigations are completed and evaluated can a final decision be given.

Two children, or 10, are not necessarily an obstacle to obtaining a declaration of nullity. Many circumstances which might be bases for annulment have nothing to do with whether the couple have children or not. If, for example, one of the spouses proves to have an emotional deficiency so serious that a true married life was, and is, psychologically impossible for him or her, the marriage tribunal would be required to declare that no marriage ever existed (in other words, issue a decree of annulment), even though the couple went through the marriage ceremony, lived together for several years, and had several children in the meantime.

During annulment process

I would like your opinion on whether our son may receive Holy Communion. He and his wife were divorced, at her insistence, several months ago. He goes to church regularly, dates occasionally, and has begun a process for annulment of their marriage.

A priest apparently told him that he cannot receive Communion now. This is certainly not what I was taught, and is contrary to what I read in your column. Isn't it possible for him to receive the sacraments unless he remarries?

I suspect either your son or the priest seriously misunderstood the situation. According to the information given in your letter, there is nothing in your son's present life situation that would prevent his receiving the sacraments as a Catholic in perfectly good standing.

Angry over annulment

For the past five years I have attempted to assist a sister

whose 26-year marriage with two children was dissolved by a tribunal on the grounds that they were psychologically incapable of a real marriage commitment. Her spouse was immediately married by a Catholic priest to another woman.

I find it difficult to understand why the church allows her tribunals to dissolve marriages this way. My sister remains single and lonely because she cannot believe the church so easily allows her re-marriage. Please explain this to me.

I have explained annulments and the annulment process in detail often in this column. It is not possible to repeat everything here, but I must point out some major misunderstandings you and your sister seem to have.

An annulment does not "dissolve" a marriage. It is a declaration by competent and highly trained authorities in the Catholic Church that no marriage ever existed between those two people. This has nothing to do with the length of time they were married or how many children they have. It means, very plainly, that some circumstance involved in that relationship made impossible any true marriage commitment in the Catholic and Christian sense of that word between those two people.

The church by no means reaches this conclusion as you say "so easily." Declarations of nullity come only after lengthy and intensive investigations, with every possible piece of helpful information obtained from both parties, their families, and their friends. These investigations along with their interpretation and analysis sometimes take several years. Your sister and you must know this since she was herself part of this process.

If your sister remains unable to reconcile herself to this decision, please ask her to discuss it with a priest in her parish or even with your diocesan tribunal. She clearly needs help to situate herself honestly and comfortably in her present spiritual situation.

Are the rich privileged?

Isn't the Catholic religion the same for all, or do the rich people have more privileges? A book on the Kennedy family tells how Jackie Kennedy was allowed by Cardinal Cushing of Boston to marry Aristotle Onassis after she gave the cardinal some expensive gift. This was after President Kennedy died, and Mr. Onassis had been divorced. I have a dear friend who could not get permission to marry a divorced person. Why the difference?

First of all, church officials who make the final decisions on marriage cases are extremely careful to try to keep their deliberations free of any influence that might arise from the financial condition of the individuals involved.

The Roman Rota, for example, the highest Catholic "court" dealing with marriage matters, publishes a yearly report on the decisions it has made and on the number of those for which no financial compensation was received. Each year it is clear that ability to "pay" has no relationship to the outcome of the case. From my own experience, the same is true of tribunals at other levels.

As we have pointed out, few marriage cases are exactly the same no matter how similar they appear to the outside observer. You and the author you are reading apparently assume the Jackie-Aristotle marriage was approved and blessed by the Catholic Church. This was not the case, since his divorce from his former wife was not recognized by the church. (In fairness, however, it should be said that the marriage laws of the Roman Catholic Church differ in this matter from those of the Eastern Orthodox Church to which Mr. Onassis belonged. It seems that according to his church he was free to marry Mrs. Kennedy.)

As for Cardinal Cushing, there is no record, to my knowledge, that he "allowed" her to enter the marriage. He merely noted that only God knows who is a sinner and who is not, and that the occasion called for an exercise of "charity, love, and mutual respect and esteem." That's still good advice.

Guise of annulment?

Would any priest approve of divorce under the guise of annulment?

No individual priest, even in a marriage tribunal, makes

decisions about annulments. It would therefore be impossible for any parish priest, for instance, to "approve of divorce under the guise of annulment." The investigations and consequent judgments in such cases go far beyond the personal inclinations and feelings of any individual involved in that process.

Annulment delayed

Last December, my boyfriend spoke with the pastor of our Catholic church regarding an annulment of his first marriage. In April he filled out a questionnaire explaining the reasons why the marriage should be annulled and also listed witnesses. This petition was filled out and returned.

None of the witnesses have been contacted after seven months of waiting. I hoped perhaps you could tell us what is causing the delay.

I don't know what might have caused the delay between December and April, but the procedures in such a case do not even begin until the petition is formally presented and a list of witnesses has been provided for supporting testimony.

If you returned the petition form immediately and the parish priest sent it out shortly afterwards, it would not be unusual that some witnesses would not have been contacted at the time of your writing (July). How quickly all this can be done depends on several factors: the volume of cases active in your diocesan tribunal, the location of the witnesses, and the ease with which a parish priest near the witnesses is able to make an appointment with them to complete the necessary forms.

I, personally, am never disturbed when someone with a pending marriage case asks me how it is progressing, whether there is anything else they might do to assist the procedure.

Perhaps an inquiry to your own parish priest would help you to understand how your case is moving. Remember, however, that the final decision on such a case takes a long time, normally considerably more than four or five months.

Annulment — deception?

When my daughter and her fiance were preparing for mar-

riage he said he was a Catholic. No baptismal certificate could be traced, so the priest baptized him just before the wedding.

She had a rough, bad marriage. He smoked a lot of pot and was an alcoholic, as was his mother, who married four men, including one homosexual, in the little time I knew of her.

After one baby died, my daughter had a second child. She wanted her brother to be godfather but her husband insisted on having the man his mother was currently living with — who is, incidentally, also an alcoholic.

We discovered later that my daughter's husband was certainly not a Catholic originally. She is now divorced and, to my disappointment, remarried and expecting another baby. I know it bothers her not to receive the sacraments, though she does go to Mass every week.

I have two questions. Could my son now become the godfather of the first child? And is there some office to which my daughter could go to determine whether she could receive the sacraments? Would it be possible that the first marriage was not valid because her husband was not a Catholic, as he claimed to be?

You and your family have suffered much pain. I hope something can be done to help.

Judging from the facts you give, this case is certainly worth submitting to your diocesan marriage tribunal for study of a possible annulment. The deception and gross personal instability are the kinds of negative conditions the tribunal would wish to examine carefully to determine whether, in fact, a real marriage was psychologically and emotionally possible for your daughter and her husband — in other words, whether the marriage can be annulled.

Concerning the baptism (again assuming your letter contains all the pertinent facts), the man the baby's grandmother was "living with" should never have been allowed to be godfather. A situation such as you describe constitutes a farce of the whole meaning of baptismal sponsors and makes fulfillment of the sponsor's responsibilities nearly impossible. It should have been stopped by either the family or the priest.

Godparents cannot be officially changed, at least without

some complications. But your son would perform an immense service for his sister if he would assume some of a sponsor's responsibilities for the child. I imagine your daughter can use all the support she can get.

Civil record of annulment?

I have some questions about annulments. When the office of a diocese grants an annulment, does the court house remove the record of a marriage from the books, since none actually took place? If children were born during a marriage which was annulled are they illegitimate?

Actions of church tribunals affecting marriages are totally distinct from civil actions and therefore do not affect civil records. An annulment granted by a church body would not be recorded in the court house.

As a practical matter, however, church tribunals never undertake an annulment process until a civil divorce (or on occasion a civil annulment) has been finalized. In other words, a marriage ceases to exist in civil law long before a decree of annulment would be granted by a diocesan tribunal.

Any annulment granted by the church or civil authorities does not affect the legitimacy of children. Children born during a presumed marriage are completely legitimate in both church and civil law even after an annulment.

Need for counseling after annulment

You have written several times that an annulment of a marriage is possible because of the psychological inability of one or both of the spouses to make a marriage commitment.

Any party found "guilty" of such deficiencies by the tribunal, in my opinion, should be refused permission to enter another marriage if these deficiencies make them incapable of honest marriage consent.

However, this is not the case. Once an annulment is granted, both parties are free to remarry with the blessing of the Catholic Church.

It is not true that once an annulment is granted both partners are automatically free to marry in the Catholic Church. True, there is no longer any previous marriage as an obstacle. The church does, however, recognize the very difficulty you raise.

When a serious psychological problem is discovered in an annulment process and there is no evidence that this deficiency has been overcome in the intervening years, the annulment decree itself states that the individual involved may not attempt another marriage in the Catholic church until appropriate psychiatric counseling and therapy is completed.

"Worthy to take up gifts?"

What do you think of divorced Catholics who are now remarried to divorced persons taking up the gifts to the altar at Mass? These people were married in the Catholic Church the first time with a Mass.

I think the proper and Christian attitude in such circumstances is:

1. happiness that the people involved are still trying to keep active in their religion and their spiritual lives, and gaining some consolation and help from their parish in what must be an extremely painful situation;

2. satisfaction that, while these persons may not be free to receive the Sacraments of Penance and the Eucharist, some ways have been found for them to share in the worship of God as much as possible;

3. and, the details of the divorce and remarriage and of how things were worked out for their activities in the parish should not be of excessive concern to you.

No one knows the full background in these cases except the individuals themselves, God, and perhaps to some degree the parish priest. And it is really nobody else's business. Only God knows how guilty of sin a person is in his or her heart for what happened in the past, or how much they may regret whatever wrong has been done.

We should regard these people, then, with the same respect and kindness we owe others — and encourage them to participate in every parish activity that is open to them.

Right and Wrong

Knowing right from wrong

I always thought that when we have to decide whether something is right or wrong, we are supposed to follow our own conscience. However, I mentioned this in a group recently, and the priest said it was not true. According to him, we are obliged to follow the teaching of those in authority, especially in the church. Who is right?

Possibly much of your confusion arises from the fact that the word "conscience" can mean many different things.

You are correct in believing that our personal moral decisions must be made on the basis of what we ourselves honestly believe is right. Whatever another may say or do, God holds us responsible for our moral actions, and that responsibility cannot be shifted to someone else. We must reach our decision and then trustingly be able to stand before God and say, "I may be wrong, but to the best of my ability, I sincerely believe this is what I should do."

What the priest possibly was attempting to tell you was that an honest conscience is not, as many people today appear to believe, a kind of blind instinct or spontaneous feeling. This could come more from selfishness or cowardice than from any good motive.

The church has spoken explicitly on this subject often in recent decades. The bishops at Vatican Council II summarized it well in their Declaration on Religious Freedom (no. 2): "Every man has the duty, and therefore the right, to seek the

truth in religious matters, in order that he may with prudence
form for himself right and true judgements of conscience . . .
In all his activity a man is bound to follow his conscience
faithfully . . . He is not to be forced to act in a manner contrary to his conscience. Nor, on the other hand, is he to be
restrained from acting in accord with his conscience, especially
in religious matters. (nos. 2 and 3.)

A genuine Christian conscience is the product of persevering effort in charity, faith, maturity, reflection, prudence and
prayer. It involves giving proper weight in these reflections to
what our common sense tells us, to the principles given to
us by Our Lord in the Gospels, and to the insights and
teachings presented for the guidance of our Christian lives
by those who have responsibility as teachers in the church.

All of this is required in developing a sincere, adult, Christian conscience, which is the kind of conscience we have an
obligation and right to form and follow.

When is "sin" sin?

**What exactly is meant by the moral principle: Sin is in the
will not in any external act. Over 30 years ago, in a religion
class to youth in their early 20s, a priest recommended that
we memorize that principle as a way to deal with personal
sin. Unfortunately, he didn't explain it. What is the story?**

While there is a proper way that sentence might be
understood, I'm not sure I would accept it exactly as you put it.

It is true that every sin is first and primarily in our will,
not in what we do. The essence of any sin is that it is a
deliberate (that is, freely and consciously embraced by our
free will) act against the law of God.

This means that even before any external action takes place,
our will, which is meant to be turned in love and reverence
toward God, says: "In this I will not obey; in this I want what
I want, not what God wants." When that happens, as Jesus
himself tells us, we have already sinned.

Obviously, the seriousness of the sin depends on how serious
a matter we're dealing with and on other factors. But our experience of sin — our own and others' — confirms that this
is the way sin happens.

Here, as is so often true, the sin of Adam and Eve offers remarkable insight on all the sins of the human family that followed. The Tempter's appeal was not to the enjoyment of the "fruit of the tree of knowledge of good and evil." Rather the devil claimed that only God's jealousy of Adam and Eve was behind his command, and that if they disobeyed God, they then would prove themselves to be God's equal. "God knows well that the moment you eat of it your eyes will be opened and you will be like gods!" (Gen. 3:5).

As always, there was just enough truth to the temptation to make it attractive. By refusing to obey him, wouldn't they prove God was not above them, that they were just as "big" as he was?

The tragedy, of course, was that it was all pretense and lie. They were, after all, not the equal of their Creator. And when they forgot that, their world fell apart.

Thus the core of their sin and ours, the moment when it happens, is when our will says: "Here and now, I come first, not God. It is my will that must be done, not his."

As I noted at the beginning, however, this is not to say there is no sin in the external deed which follows that act of the will. Obviously there is more malice, hurt and destruction (in other words, more sinfulness) in actually murdering someone than in desiring and planning the action without carrying it out.

Incidentally, it is this truth that sin is first and mainly in the will, not in the action, that the church would have us be most concerned about today in the Sacrament of Reconciliation. Deeds are important. But it is the sinfulness in our hearts, the sinful leanings in our will that lead to those deeds, that must be dealt with above all if we are to renew our lives, reduce our faults and grow in holiness.

Making moral decisions

If the church can't or won't say what is a sin, can we ask if there really is any sin? It would seem that everyone, including Hitler, could rationalize their doings.

I am not really sure what connection you are attempting

to make between the church's statements and the existence of sin.

Unfortunately, there is, no doubt, such a thing as sin. The church can and does make absolute statements about sin. However, maybe our expectations of what exactly the church can or should say about God's laws are wrong.

Above all, we cannot think of "the church" as a sort of answer machine for every question about life and morality. The church is a living community of people struggling and working at every point through history to understand and respond to God's laws — especially the primary law of Christ to love God above all and to love our neighbor as ourselves. The bishops and pope have the primary teaching responsibility through the charism of their office, but they, too, are part of this pilgrim church. History has always taught, as it does now, that the black and white answers some people seem to demand are often not possible, or at least that such answers are not at all evident.

Second, we must remember that what we call God's laws often deal with matters of "natural law" — that is, those laws or principles of action that people must follow in order to be truly human, to provide for the right kind of physical, emotional, intellectual and spiritual growth that will make them more perfectly alive and whole as human beings. Among these would be, for example, the principles underlying the Ten Commandments.

As I explained in more detail in the second chapter, the church, again mainly through its college of bishops and the Holy Father, guides us in applying these principles to our daily lives. In carrying out such guidance the church is faced with an ever-changing array of social, scientific, economic, political and psychological realities — all of which in some way affect what is the truly "human" or moral way to act in specific instances.

Our traditional moral principles tell us that circumstances which partially determine what is morally right or wrong change not only from one part of the world or one culture to another. They also change from one time to another.

The classic (but by no means only) example concerns accepting interest on invested money. For centuries the church taught repeatedly that this was seriously wrong because the custom seemed to threaten the economic stability of families and society. One ecumenical council (the Council of Vienne) decreed that anyone who taught that taking interest was not a sin should be punished in the same way as a heretic.

That position gradually changed, of course, as the requirements and nature of large economic systems became evident. The change occurred, however, only at the cost of long confusion and disagreement among bishops, theologians, priests and others about the legitimacy of the practice.

Christ promised us all the guidance we will need to make good, sincere moral decisions. We would do well to remember that promise, and remember that, even in the midst of what seems like confusion, Jesus always keeps that promise. If occasionally there is more gray area than we find comfortable or desirable, perhaps that is his way of telling us to be a little more self-reliant and a little more open to his grace and to the fact that we still have a lot to learn — all of us.

Finally, a key word in your question is "rationalize." One rationalizes morally when he knows what he wants to do, knows his motives are doubtful if not downright evil, and yet fishes around for some phony justification to delude himself and others. This is pure dishonesty right from scratch, and has nothing to do with genuine moral decision-making.

What is obscene?

My question has to do with morality I suppose — the meaning of "obscene." Obscene means something lewd or impure. But now I see it used to describe other things. A remark in our paper said that a recent speech by a high government official was obscene. How do you explain that?

The definition you give is the common one, but it is not the real, basic meaning of the word. The adjective comes down to us from ancient Greek (and perhaps Roman) drama. In many Greek plays, as you know, there were hideous crimes committed: eyes were put out, parents killed their children and vice versa, and the bloodiest monstrosities were perpetrated. However, these were always done *ab* or *ob scaenam* — literally, off the scene, or off the stage, because they were considered too loathsome, too cruel, too de-humanizing to be openly laid out before decent and civilized men.

Thus, whatever is repulsive, cruel, or otherwise excessively shameful in man's dealing with his fellow man, came to be labelled as obscene. Sexual immodesty is, therefore, just one type — and perhaps one of the lesser types — of obscenity abounding in the world.

A good example from Scripture, incidentally, is Isaias' prophetic description of Jesus in his Passion. This future Servant of God, said Isaias, would suffer so violently that he would become as "one of those from whom men hide their faces." In that sense what was done to Jesus, and the whole episode of his subjection to it, was truly "obscene."

Sin in anger?

Is it a mortal sin to use God's name in vain in a fit of anger?

The traditional three requirements for a mortal sin are still good ones:

1. Serious matter — that is, the action must be one which is completely incompatible with a respect and love for God.

2. Sufficient reflection. One must realize when he is doing the action (or refuses to do it in a sin of omission) that if he does what he is contemplating, he is deliberately rejecting God's love and friendship. In other words, he must be fully aware that what he is contemplating is a mortal sin.

3. Full consent of the will. Realizing all this, he still deliberately wants to go ahead and do it anyway. Considering these requirements, it is difficult to see how the action, as you describe it, could ever be a mortal sin.

Alcoholic beverages

By what authority does the Catholic Church approve drinking when the Holy Scriptures are so clear regarding the Lord's attitude toward it? Has no one ever questioned this before? With all the heartache, sin, and irresponsibility that drinking causes, how can one honestly believe that it is approved by the Lord?

Certainly it has been thought of before. A number of Protestant sects, as you must know, consider any drinking of alcoholic beverages a sin.

It is impossible, however, to use the Bible in any way as a basis for this belief. There is no denying that the misuse of alcohol causes enormous suffering and is wrong. Indeed, the Scriptures say as much several times. But Scripture also has numerous good things to say about wine and encourages its proper use for everything from celebrations to bodily health.

There is no scholarly basis whatsoever for saying that the word most often used in the Bible for wine (in both Greek and Hebrew) means anything else than fermented, alcoholic "fruit of the vine." That includes the wine miraculously presented by Jesus to the bride and groom at Cana, as well as the wine St. Paul tells Timothy to take occasionally for the good of his stomach. (I Tim. 5:23)

Defense attorney's duties

Several trials which have been widely publicized — some nationally and some in our area — have made me wonder about what a Catholic lawyer is allowed to do. Many times, from things that come out during a trial, it sure seems to me the lawyer must have known the person who hired him was guilty. Suppose a lawyer does know, is really sure, that a person committed the crime he is being tried for. Could the lawyer take the case and try to get his client off? Isn't it wrong for a lawyer to lie and say things he knows are not true, just because he is the defense attorney?

It is, of course, wrong for an attorney to lie, especially in circumstances such as this. But that doesn't really answer your question.

In our system of justice, a person is legally (even if not morally) innocent until proven guilty. An attorney may take up the legal defense of an individual he knows is morally guilty and attempt to block a conviction.

To accomplish this, the defense attorney may use any legal means that are just. For instance, he may attempt to hide information that would be detrimental to the client and he may attack or take advantage of weak points in the prosecution's case.

At least two actions, however, would obviously be wrong and professionally unethical. One would be an attempt by the lawyer himself to falsify information or documents or lie about the case or anyone connected with it.

The second is where perhaps the greatest danger lies for an attorney who is trying to prove to a jury something he knows is not true. He has no moral or legal right to deliberately attempt to confuse or intimidate a witness into giving testimony that the witness really knows is not true. It goes without saying that the attorney acts immorally in bringing a witness who has the deliberate intention of perjuring himself.

Another consideration is the character of the defendant himself. An attorney would act immorally, for example, if he designedly brought about the freedom of a psychopathic individual who would clearly constitute a menace to people around him, without in some significant way attempting to alleviate that danger.

Gossip

When does an injury to another person by true gossip become sinful? If the information is strictly true and has taken place, where is the injury or the sin?

In my experience as a priest, no crimes of speech (perhaps no crimes of any kind) are more destructive to our social relationships than the one you mention — and the feeling that simply because a thing is true about someone else, we are free to say whatever we like about it, whenever we like, and to whomever we like.

One who thinks and acts this way is grossly in error. When the topic of our loose gossip is true, we're dealing with the sin of detraction and contumely (insult). To lie about others, attributing to them faults and bad actions we know are untrue, is even worse, a sin of calumny or slander.

One commits the sin of detraction when he makes known the faults of another without a very good reason for doing so. It can be a serious moral offense if it does great harm to that other person's reputation by having his or her faults spread about when they otherwise would not be.

The same sin of insult is committed when the other person is refused ordinary decency and respect whether face to face in private, or in public, such as in newspapers or on television.

Even when the other person's faults are public knowledge, it still can be sinful against charity to speak unnecessarily about those faults.

Occasionally there may be good reasons to tell another's faults, to a child's parents, for example. It is grossly wrong, though, to imagine that just because a story about another is true, one is at liberty to spread it around. A person's good name is among his most precious possessions, and the fact that one gets a kick out of being always there with the latest tidbit is no justification for tarnishing that good name. A person's faults are a matter between himself and God. The rest of us should keep our noses out.

Scripture has many strong, condemning words for gossips. In one of the psalms, God doesn't mince words: "The slanderer of his neighbor in secret — him will I destroy."

Already in his own time, St. Paul recognized the poisonous effect of this kind of conversation. He found himself forced to warn against it frequently. His advice to Titus is still valid: "Tell them not to speak evil of anyone." Which means in blunt language: "If you can't say something good about someone, keep quiet."

What is 'usury'?

Is there, or was there, ever a sin called usury?

Yes, there was such a sin, and in fact still could be under certain circumstances.

Roughly speaking, the word "usury," which goes back to ancient Romans, means about the same as our word "interest" — money paid for the loan of someone else's money or other property. The Old Testament broadly condemns this kind of charge to another, with some exceptions.

During Christian times the condemnation continued for the most part. Money was considered a perishable good, like food;

as soon as it was traded for something else, it no longer existed for the borrower. For this reason, St. Thomas Aquinas, for example, taught that it is unlawful to accept money for the use of money, "which is called usury."

One exception was permitted even at that time if the lender suffered a loss or opportunity for profit because of the loan.

Obviously the picture changed considerably with the development of our modern economic systems. Theologians in general, and the church specifically, have for some time held the position that taking of interest for the use of money is lawful, as long as the rate is just and not harmful either to the individuals involved or to society.

Today the term usury refers, even in state laws, to actions which exploit individual needs or financial conditions in order to charge interests which are clearly unjust and destructive of another's ability to live a decent and proper life.

Catholic social doctrine

I have seen many references to "Catholic Social Doctrine." I don't remember anything like this from when I learned the catechism, or in religion classes. What does it mean?

The phrase "Catholic Social Doctrine" signifies the large body of official Catholic teaching dealing with such "social" matters as economic life, rights and responsibilities of private property, political systems and their relationships to the individual citizen, labor unions, war and peace, and many others. These teachings have developed over many centuries, but have been made more specific during the past century, especially in formal teachings of the modern popes.

Pope John XXIII summarized the basics of this complex body of doctrine in one of his great social encyclicals, *Mater et Magistra*. First, he says, all aspects of economic life in a nation must be regulated not for "the special interests of individuals or groups, nor (by) unregulated competition, economic despotism, national prestige or imperialism, nor any other aim of this sort. Rather, all forms of economic enterprise must be governed by the principles of social justice and charity."

Second, all social institutions (governments, welfare programs, international bodies such as the United Nations, etc.) must aim "to achieve in social justice a national and international juridical order, with its network of public and private institutions, in which all economic activity can be conducted not merely for private gain but also in the interest of the common good" of all people.

These principles may sound trite and simple, but their violation lies at the source of most social evils of our age. Major social documents have come during the last century from nearly every pope and from many national conferences of bishops. Some of the most significant of recent popes are the encyclicals *Peace on Earth* of Pope John XXIII (1963), *The Development of Peoples* of Pope Paul VI (1967), and *On Human Work* of Pope John Paul II (1981).

Capital punishment

I have been considering the pros and cons of capital punishment. In my moral reasoning I feel God might be for it.

We on earth must instill some fear. Death that way isn't the worst thing for someone who has killed another, for example, if he dies after repentance.

A hired assassin for the United States is supposedly a moral man. He justifies his killing because a terrorist might kill more people.

Yet I have heard that the bishops of our country are against capital punishment. Can you tell me why?

First, let's separate capital punishment from the kind of self-defense hinted at in the second part of your question about assassins. Defense of oneself when one's life is immediately threatened by another is a different moral question from capital punishment, though some overlap is obviously possible.

The American bishops issued a major statement on capital punishment in 1980, arguing that the imposition of the death penalty is unjustified given the conditions of contemporary society in the United States. Their position has been repeated since then by numbers of groups of bishops, including the

26 bishops of your state (California) as recently as 1985.

Some reasons given by the bishops, which incidentally are echoed by a growing number of Catholic and other Christian theologians, deal with problems inherent in any policy imposing the death penalty:

1. The elimination of any possibility of reform or making compensation;

2. Possibility of a mistake in executing an innocent person;

3. The long and unavoidable delays which diminish the effectiveness of capital punishment as a deterrent and which can produce legal aimlessness;

4. The anguish, even dehumanization, execution brings to the criminal, his family and those who order, perform and witness the execution;

5. The unhealthy publicity and violence in public discussion engendered by the executions;

6. "The not-unfounded belief that many convicted criminals are sentenced to death in an unfair and discriminatory manner: For example, more than 50 percent of those on death row are minorities, virtually all of them poor."

Those are on the negative side. Other reasons deal with important values which would be promoted by the elimination of capital punishment:

1. It would send the message that the cycle of violence can be broken by not taking a life for a life, and that we can find more humane and hopeful ways to respond to violent crime.

2. It would show that we consider each person, even a criminal, as having unique worth and dignity, made in the likeness of God.

3. It would emphasize in another way our conviction that God is the Lord of life.

4. It would follow the example of Jesus who taught and practiced forgiveness of injustice and who came to give his life as a ransom for many.

(The above quote and reasons are from the 1980 statement and the California bishops' statement of September 1985.)

Obviously, the point argued by our bishops and others is that, whatever theoretical reasons might support the death penalty, realities of life in our country today place the morality of such penalties in serious doubt.

Against death penalty?

The bishops seem to think that if a person is poor, a member of a racial minority, or otherwise on the lower levels of the social scale, he has the right to commit any crime he wishes.

In taking their position, the bishops are simply asking for equal justice under the law for all citizens, a right guaranteed by the Bill of Rights. They do not condone any crime, regardless of who the offender may be.

Death penalty a favor?

I hold that the death penalty is good for murderers because it would save them from hell and eternal damnation. The only time a condemned man would examine his conscience is just before he passes on to his reward, and in nearly every case not before.

Once he admits that wrong was done by taking the life of another human being and asks for forgiveness, his soul is not lost but is admitted into paradise. So the death penalty for criminals need not be viewed as cruel or unusual punishment, but as a favor. They will inherit eternal life.

Remarkable! You have just given a perfect reason for hanging at least half the human race. Many non-murderers commit crimes just as serious and just as destructive as murder. Why should they or even lesser sinners be deprived of this potent encouragement to repentance?

What makes you think people become so remorseful before execution? The disciples frequently urged Jesus to force reluctant Jews to accept him through physical coercion. But Our Lord adhered firmly to his conviction and policy that no worthwhile conversion is brought about by violence of any sort. There's no evidence that people are any different today.

What about conscientious objection?

I know the Catholic Church in the United States has a position on conscientious objection. Do these statements of the

American bishops really now give a moral way out of going into the armed forces?

If you're asking whether the position of the American Catholic bishops is that a good Catholic can be a conscientious objector to all war, or to one specific war (such as for example, Vietnam) the answer is yes.

However, you seem to imply that these declarations of recent years suddenly and for the first time make conscientious objection moral. Quite the contrary is true.

The United States hierarchy has made clear that refusal to participate in a war's violence and killing can flow directly from traditional Catholic "religious training and belief." They support this claim from a number of official sources, including positions taken by the entire Catholic Church in Vatican Council II.

Without in any way suggesting that conscientious objection is the only moral position a Catholic might assume, they even urge draft counseling facilities and employment assistance for such objectors.

Just as we esteem those who conscientiously serve in the armed forces, they said, "so also we should regard conscientious objection and selective conscientious objection as positive indicators within the church of a sound moral awareness and respect for human life."

In other words, according to the bishops, the church needs conscientious objectors to get across part of its message for respect for life.

About a decade ago, the world Synod of Bishops in Rome addressed this delicate question. "It is absolutely necessary," they said, "that international conflicts should not be settled by war, but that other methods better befitting human nature should be found. Let a strategy of non-violence be fostered also, and let conscientious objection be recognized and regulated by law in each nation."

Thus, the American Catholic position is not at all radical. It simply says in another way what our bishops insisted on in another pastoral letter to Catholics of our country (1968). Mankind will keep using war and violence to solve its problems until enough young people simply refuse to participate in them.

A few excellent places to find the church's present position concerning war and related questions would be Pope John XXIII's encyclical, *Peace on Earth*; the major statements of Vatican II on war, especially in the *Constitution on the Church in the Modern World,* (no. 80); the address of Pope Paul VI to the United Nations in 1965; the pastoral letter, *Human Life in Our Day,* of the U.S. Catholic bishops in 1968, and their historic pastoral letter of 1983, *The Challenge of Peace.* Any good book store can help you obtain them.

Morality of hunger strikes

I would appreciate your comments on the hunger strikes, particularly in Ireland. Does the church look upon these people as heroes or sinners? Does their cause justify their acts? I think some church authority should speak out on this terrible condition and enlighten all of us concerning this taking of one's own life.

As one might expect, moral theologians and bishops, particularly in England and Ireland, have spoken publicly and strongly on this subject during the past several years.

Theologians who have written about them distinguish between various kinds of hunger strikes. They might be classified into three groups.

First, the hunger striker who does not wish to die but is prepared to accept his own death, if necessary, for the cause.

Second, the hunger striker who wishes to use the possibility of his death to push the other side to give in. This may sound much like the first, but in the second case the death is really accidental and not morally intended.

The third type is the strike which deliberately ends in death. Obviously, this is the most clear and direct case of suicide.

Most moralists and, I believe, all the bishops who have addressed the question, seem to agree that the first category of hunger strike involves indirect killing of oneself and therefore could be a morally acceptable act depending on the circumstances.

The second category, which a group of British theologians refer to as "an exercise in brinkmanship," can also be justified if the cause is proportionately serious and if every other avenue for righting the wrong has failed.

The third category of hunger strike is, however, far less defensible, at least objectively.

Cardinal George Basil Hume of Westminster, England, reflected, I believe, the common teaching of theologians when he wrote in a pastoral letter: "The hunger strike to the death is a form of violence. (It) surely cannot be condoned by the church as being in accordance with God's will for man."

This all sounds very neat but the judgments are not nearly so clear in practice, especially in a country like Ireland where the hunger strike has developed almost into a national institution in the centuries-old struggle of the Irish people for independence from Great Britain.

As one of Ireland's most respected moral theologians notes, the debate even in that country has tended to be conducted in the abstract; theoretical rights and wrongs cannot be isolated from the actual, real life context in which a hunger strike is taking place.

Christian burial for a hunger striker who has died is another matter entirely. The church almost always gives an individual the benefit of the doubt after a suicide.

As the Irish bishops remarked in a 1981 policy statement, "The church teaches that suicide is a great evil, but there is some dispute about whether or not political hunger striking is suicide, or more precisely, about the circumstances in which it is suicide."

In having a Christian burial for an individual who dies in these circumstances, the church clearly implies no position concerning the cause for which the individual died.

It simply accepts that God, and only God, can be the final judge of one's motives and intentions.

What is "immoral"?

I must say something that has puzzled me for a long time. If I sin I would rather sin by loving too much than by not loving enough because God is love. I don't understand the church's stance on categorizing sins.

Sins of sex, we are told, are very wrong in comparison to

lying, gossiping, criticizing. Often sins of sex are the outcome of love which has become inordinate when human weakness and frailty enter.

I have known Religious who were pure as angels, yet displayed a streak of meanness, jealousy and dislike of a particular person, and exaggerated and twisted what they saw into faults, and ran to their superior to tell on others.

Does anything which hurts or destroys a person or reputation in some way flow from some kind of evil?

Yet it seems that the church places these sins in lesser consequence. To me they are worse.

I also have known very good, upright Catholics who are cruel in little ways. They gossip, down others, are arrogant when dealing with less important people, humiliate others and so on. Yet they consider themselves good Catholics because they apparently have come to believe that these things are not as important. I question this.

I am single and believe I am living in a chaste way so I am not trying to justify a way of life. But I do question a lot of things like this that I think are upside down, but which many Catholics believe the church has taught them.

Sometimes people speak to me of someone else, making a remark such as "She (or he) is an immoral person." If I'm feeling more than usually cantankerous, I reply, "You mean she gossips a lot?"

The reaction is usually an expression of dismay which seems to mean, "What in the world has that to do with what I said?"

I would phrase some of your statements a little differently and in such matters we need to be cautious about falling into intolerance and rash judgment. But you make a good and important point.

Beware of judging others

I cannot agree with people who contend that one is free from guilt of sin if he personally feels no guilt and has a clear conscience on the matter.

I'm referring to such serious sin as abortion. As far as I'm concerned, it is childish to base our reactions on personal feelings. Too many have this attitude of permissiveness. They feel, in their particular instance, their actions are perfectly acceptable.

You're probably right in believing that many of us too easily excuse ourselves from moral responsibility even in matters of serious sin. In today's legal and social atmosphere, one area in which this can easily happen is in the direct killing of an unborn human being, which is certainly an enormous and sinful injustice.

However, we must be very careful that we never confuse the objective sinfulness of an action with the degree of guilt an individual has incurred in doing it.

To put it bluntly, there's no way you can possibly know to what degree the person in question is fully guilty of the sin of abortion.

Even the woman herself may find it almost impossible to sort out the motives and emotions and pressures which allowed her to do what she did. At any rate, her guilt, whatever it is, is a matter between her and God.

Admittedly, this is a delicate situation to deal with if a person is trying to be truly helpful to another. An honest acknowledgement and acceptance of one's guilt is always a first necessary step to forgiveness and healing, or it will only rise again to plague her in perhaps much more serious ways later on.

So, gentle reminders of the seriousness of what has been done, of our responsibility for our actions, and of the ready, forgiving love of Christ are always in place. But we should never play God and pretend we know what is really going on in another person's soul.

Wrong for jury to judge?

I am a jury trial judge and must decide which prospective jurors may be excused from serving. Among the frequent excuses is the claim that Jesus said, "Judge nobody and you will not be judged."

Often it is asserted by Jehovah Witnesses, but sometimes also by Protestant ministers. Recently to my surprise, a

Catholic woman told me the same thing. This lady was unique, since many Catholic priests and nuns have served as jurors cheerfully and with dedication. (In our state no one is automatically exempt from jury service. Even former Governor Brown served on a criminal jury two years ago.)

Could you explain just what Jesus meant by this teaching and give me some insight as to what I might reply to people who invoke this passage?

The passages to which you refer (mainly Matthew 7:1 and Luke 6:37) are always interpreted as warnings against harsh and self-righteous criticism of others, not against a clear and open stand on moral issues that affect society.

Jesus himself teaches this attitude, and in this he is in harmony with the whole of Old and New Testament tradition. From the ancient prophets (one might particularly cite Amos, Isaiah and Jeremiah) to the Gospels, God's people have been told they must eradicate the injustices in society that cause injury, injustice and even death to the poor, the helpless and other innocent people.

They must not, in other words, be neutral about what is happening. They are commanded not only to condemn evil done to others, but to do everything possible to eliminate that evil from human society.

Jesus stood clearly in the spirit of that tradition. The Sermon on the Mount, the criterion for the final judgment given in Matthew 25, and numerous other occasions on which the Lord spoke of the responsibility to see that justice is guaranteed for a brother or sister who is suffering unjustly, all indicate that he was not neutral to all this. Nor did he expect his followers to remain simply weeping bystanders.

Obviously, therefore, Jesus did not discourage every kind of judging in the passages your potential jurors invoke. The context shows that while we must not be vindictive and cruel, we must recognize, and help society recognize, and put an end to social injustices that seriously disrupt our human life together.

It may help your jurors also to recognize that, in making legal judgments, we in no way pretend to determine how that person stands personally with God. We have no way of knowing a person's deepest soul and thus no way of knowing whether, or how much, that person is subjectively guilty of sin before God. That surely is not ours to judge.

The purpose of the court is only to determine, under proper instruction from the judge, whether the individual is guilty before the law of the crime of which he or she is accused.

Those are two very distinct kinds of judgments which not only jurors, but the rest of us, too, need to keep clearly in mind.

No more fast and abstinence?

Can you tell me why Catholics don't have laws about fast and abstinence and penance any more? Those laws (of fast and abstinence) always gave us something that other churches didn't have. I think we should still have obligations to do things like that, especially during Lent, so why did the church take them away?

Who says we Catholics don't have obligations to fast and abstinence and other penances anymore? If there is one thing every statement of the church insists on relating to this subject, it is that self-denial — including such things as occasionally limiting the amount or type of food we eat — is a serious obligation for all Christians, and that none of us can ignore that obligation without grave harm to our spiritual health.

What you mean is that the church is usually much less specific about the manner in which we carry out that obligation in our lives, which is a far different thing. In relaxing some detailed regulations about such matters, the Catholic Church, as well as other Christian churches, is simply responding to a very uncomfortable discovery during the past few decades: Far too many Christians so identified their Christianity with the meticulous fulfillment of minute church regulations that they lost contact with how these regulations are related to the basics of their faith in Christ — and thus too frequently lost contact with Christ himself and what he stands for in our lives.

How can we claim to have no law of fast or abstinence or

penance when Jesus himself tells us, "Whoever wishes to be my follower must deny his very self, take up his cross each day, and follow me." Or, "He who will not take up his cross and come after me is not worthy of me." One would be hard put to find a more clear, absolute statement of obligation in any church law, old or new. The New Testament abounds in such passages, either by or in the name of Christ himself.

Friday abstinence

There seems to be a general impression that the law of abstinence from meat on Fridays was abolished.

However, the new code of canon law (1251) states, "Abstinence from eating meat or another food according to the prescriptions of the conference of bishops is to be observed on Fridays throughout the year," except for certain special feasts. This is confusing to a number of us. Is Friday abstinence an obligation or not?

You quote the present law of the Church correctly. Apparently, however, you, and others elsewhere who have discussed this, may not be sufficiently aware of the significance of those words about the "conference of bishops."

The new canon law in this matter repeats briefly some provisions of the Apostolic Constitution of Pope Paul VI on Christian penance (*Paenitemini,* February 1966). The new law must be understood in the context of that document.

In the course of that constitution Pope Paul recalls at great length the importance of bodily penance and self-denial in the Christian tradition, especially the observance of penance involved in the fulfillment of the duties of one's daily life.

The Holy Father then states, "With a view therefore of reminding its children of the precept of penance and urging its observance, the Apostolic See intends to revise the Church's penitential practice in a way suited to the times.

"It will be up to the wisdom and pastoral concern of the bishops to meet and to issue norms, in view of their knowledge of their regions and people, that will serve as an effective means to attain the end proposed."

The Church has no intention to abandon the outward practice of penance, he says later. At the same time other ways of penance are to be considered prescribed by the Church "wherever it may seem advisable to the conferences of bishops to substitute the practice of prayer and the works of charity for the observance of fast and abstinence."

Toward the end of that document the Pope establishes regulations in words similar to those in the new code.

Clearly Pope Paul, and now the 1983 code of canon law, indicate that the former universal law of Friday abstinence for Catholics is abrogated. Conferences of bishops (usually that means the bishops of a particular nation) may adopt that form of penance for their people, or substitute something else.

In November, 1966, the United States bishops responded to Pope Paul's words by establishing the following: Catholics in the United States should abstain from meat on Ash Wednesday and Fridays of Lent, and should fast on Ash Wednesday and Good Friday. Fasting on all other weekdays of Lent is recommended. Finally, "abstinence from flesh meat on all Fridays of the year is especially recommended to individuals and to the Catholic community as a whole."

The American bishops again call attention to the voluntary, though highly commendable, character of Friday abstinence in their 1983 pastoral letter on war and peace. As a tangible sign of their desire to do penance for the cause of peace, the bishops committed themselves to fast and abstain on each Friday of the year. They then invited all American Catholics "voluntarily to do penance on Friday by eating less food and by abstaining from meat" (IV-B-4).

I repeat, however, as recent popes and bishops continually insist, these changes are intended to make us more, not less, sensitive to the need for self-denial in our Christian life. Jesus Himself tells us, "Whoever wishes to be my follower must deny his very self, take up his cross each day, and follow me."

Fast and abstinence rules

Could you define fast and abstinence as to their meaning in the Lenten obligations? Many Catholics differ in their ideas as to what the two words refer to.

The rules are so simple any more, it's hard to see where there can be any confusion worth worrying about. In most places in the United States today, Catholics over 14 years of age must *abstain* from meat (and soup or gravy made from meat) on Ash Wednesday and all Fridays of Lent.

On two days — Ash Wednesday and Good Friday — those over 18 and under 59 should *fast*. This means only one full meal, and only liquids like milk and fruit juices between meals. The size of the full meal, and the two lesser meals, depends obviously on the individual's physical needs.

One is excused from the whole obligation, of course, if his health or work would be seriously affected by this fast or abstinence.

The Lenten emphasis today, as you know, is much more on prayer, the liturgy, good works and voluntary self-denial, than on complicated and severe regulations about food.

You might check with your pastor to be sure of the regulations for your diocese.

Substitute for Friday abstinence?

Is it a sin not to do other penance on Friday now that we have the privilege of eating meat on that day?

No. Eating meat on Friday is not a "privilege" any more than eating it on Tuesday is a privilege.

From the earliest days of Christianity, Fridays have held a special character in the life of the followers of Christ as days of special effort at prayer and some sort of self-denial. Friday commemorated the day of Jesus' death. Christians considered it most appropriate, then, that a special effort be made on that day of the week to attend to his words: If anyone will be my Disciple, let him deny himself, take up his cross daily, and come follow me.

The obligation to heed that command falls upon all Christians — by accepting and carrying the crosses that are ours without looking for them in daily life, as well as in some sort of occasional voluntary penance or self-denial. The American bishops, for example, in their 1983 pastoral letter on war and nuclear armament requested voluntary abstinence from meat on Friday by American Catholics for the cause of world peace.

There is no particular Catholic obligation in our country, or in most others, however, to observe this responsibility on any specific day of the week.

Degrees of wrong in sin

Please help this convert with something that just doesn't seem to add up. Why does the church put marrying outside the church in the same (mortal sin) category as something like murder?

Aren't there degrees of wrongness even among the commandments?

You have some excellent insights on the meaning of sin, and I hope you keep developing them. As you imply, if our life of grace is a relationship with God, that relationship can be affected, even seriously, in varying degrees.

First, you are right (and in total agreement with Christian moral tradition) in seeing degrees of wrongness in acts and intentions which are seriously sinful.

Thus, to say that something is a mortal sin, assuming of course that all necessary reflection and intentions are there, does not imply that it is "just as bad" as any other serious or mortal sin.

We must remember that sin is not measured in pounds or inches. It is an injury, sometimes even a destruction, of our relationship of friendship with God; it involves actions and decisions about things that affect that relationship.

As in other aspects of faith, we learn much about our relationship with God by comparing it with our relationship with another human being. Some things can weaken that relationship ("venial sin"); some actions can destroy it.

A husband, for example, might destroy his relationship with his wife, until repentance and forgiveness follow, by some sort of serious infidelity. He can also destroy it by deliberate vicious emotional abuse that strangles her spirit and perhaps even her sanity. There's no question that the second is more destructive and therefore more sinful.

According to our biblical and traditional understanding of the Christian life, the same is true in our relationship with God. Some wrong actions, serious in themselves, may be objectively less destructive of our relationship to our Creator and Lord than other sins. Certain objectively sinful actions are also more subject to circumstances (fear, lack of awareness and so on) which can diminish or exclude actual personal sin.

In at least one sense, sins which are purely church laws are often, if not always, in this later category. They may undermine, or even destroy to some degree, the social fabric and health of the church as the body of Christ. But they are normally not as immediately and directly destructive of human society and human beings as violations of the ten commandments and other precepts of the natural law.

Sunday rest

What does it mean to "keep holy the Sabbath day" today? I am a senior citizen and try to live by the commandments. I go to Mass unless I'm sick, and say my daily prayers. The problem is that I do some knitting to keep busy.

Several ladies reproach me for this, saying it is sinful to do these things on Sunday. I don't do it for money, but just to relax, and for therapy. Is watching television less sinful than knitting?

You must be aware that the whole "forbidden" work idea developed in a radically different agricultural-labor society. It is futile and misses the point entirely to discuss (as we used to do) whether crotcheting, gardening or changing the oil in the car are allowed on Sunday.

Our aim is rather to have our home and activities reflect, on that day above all, the peace, joy, contentment and love that should be ours because of what Jesus has done for us.

Go ahead and knit — or crochet, or watch television, or do anything else that makes you relax, feel useful or just keep busy, if that is what you like to do. The commandment to keep holy the Sabbath day has nothing to do with these kinds of things for us Christians.

If you go to Mass when you can, and keep up your prayers

and other relationships with God as ou are able, none of these activities is wrong for you on Si nday.

Do them and enjoy them.

Whatever obligations the church has asked us to observe on Sunday are meant as an aid to keeping the spirit of reverent reflection, worship and rest. Vatican Council II calls Sunday "the original feast day" and urges that its observance should always be proposed and taught "so that it may become in fact a day of joy and of freedom from work." (Constitution on the Liturgy, 106)

The Code of Canon Law says almost the same: "They (the faithful) should avoid any work or business which might stand in the way of the worship which should be given to God, the joy proper to the Lord's day, or the needed relaxation of mind and body." (CCL 1247)

Sacraments after vasectomy

Under what conditions could a man receive the Sacraments of Penance and Holy Communion if, after sincere consideration of his conscience, he determined that a vasectomy was not wrong for his circumstances and, in fact, had such surgery performed?

Putting the question precisely as you did, the answer would have to be that nothing prevents such a person from receiving the sacraments. One does not commit a mortal sin unless in doing the action he believes and reflects sufficiently on the fact that here and now he is doing something that is seriously against God's law. Your statement implies that the individual in question is doing just the opposite; as he sees it, he is saying sincerely to God: This is what I believe you want me to do. Such a person is obviously not guilty of sin, and therefore has no reason to mention the fact in confession or to keep from Holy Communion.

The joker in the whole question, of course, is in the words "sincere consideration of his conscience." If you recall another question about conscience, you know that an honest conscience necessarily includes many factors, not the least of which is the moral guidance given by our Christian faith, and by the church.

It also includes at least one most essential "consultation," the one with one's spouse. Even apart from any Christian morality, consideration of such decisions in isolation from, or against the wishes of, one's wife would be in itself a grave offense against justice and charity, whatever else it may be.

"Sincere consideration of one's conscience" with prayer, faith, and trust, is, of course, within the ability of each of us. It seems to me, however, that sometimes some of us are tempted to make it more spontaneous and simple than it in fact is, especially in matters of large, long-range importance. I would suggest that you have not fulfilled that responsibility until you have discussed the subject with a competent priest in whom you have confidence.

After vasectomy

I'm a Catholic who stopped attending the sacraments about five years ago. Two years ago, shortly after the birth of my daughter, I had a vasectomy — not as a protest against the church, but due more to my lack of faith in God's giving me the patience and understanding to raise more than the two children I have.

I've had many sleepless nights since then. I've been attending Mass for the past two years but have not received the sacraments. My children have both been baptized. What can I do now? My wife and I both want to be on good terms with the church and raise our children as Catholics.

Please go and talk to a priest as quickly as possible. Whatever wrong you may have done, there seems to be no reason that you cannot now receive the Sacraments of Penance and the Eucharist. The priest will help you work things out and get back where you want to be.

After a tubal ligation

Does what you said to the man who wanted to get back to the sacraments after a vasectomy hold true for a woman who has had a tubal ligation?

Yes. I remember it was clear in that man's question, and

appears also in your letter, that whatever sin may have been committed is thoroughly repented for, and there is a strong desire to return to the sacraments. In his case and perhaps in yours, part of the motivation was to be a good spouse and good parent.

Endorsing candidates

Is it permissible or proper for a Catholic priest to endorse by name a candidate for public office from the pulpit? To me this is inconsistent with the statement on political responsibility of the U.S. Catholic bishops in 1976.

I presume you're referring to the bishops' plea that all citizens "become informed on relevant issues" and vote freely according to their conscience. Nothing any priest says, of course, can deprive you of that right or obligation.

Promoting (or attacking) specific candidates by name is dangerous, in my opinion, if for no other reason than that it violates the legal prohibition of such electioneering by tax exempt institutions, which includes our churches.

Such siding with one candidate or another from the pulpit is usually (maybe always) counter-productive and can alienate as many as it converts. Catholic people want and deserve to have their churches free of this kind of political activity.

Just as certainly, however, neither the church nor its pastors can allow themselves to be above, or ignore, the political scene. It is their duty to assist their people — from the pulpit or otherwise — in understanding the Christian and Catholic teachings involved in current issues, and to remind their congregations that they are individually reponsible for the moral and social consequences of their political decisions. And that includes the votes they cast.

The bishops themselves and Pope John Paul II teach and operate in this fashion on everything from the death penalty and abortion to human rights and arms sales to foreign countries. As they affirmed during the 1976 presidential campaign, "We are not supporting religious bloc voting, nor are we instructing people for whom to vote. Rather we urge that citizens make this decision for themselves in an informed and conscientious manner, in light of candidates' positions on the issues, as well as their personal qualifications . . . We shall continue to address the issues facing our nation by all appropriate means at our disposal."

It seems to me that's excellent political procedure for all of us to follow.

Priests and politics

I've never heard a good answer to this, and it seems to be getting worse instead of better. Why do so many priests feel they have to demonstrate, march, and get involved in all these political causes? It seems to me they ought to leave that up to us lay people.

When was the last time you yourself demonstrated, spoke out courageously, or in some way, as the saying goes, "put your body on the line" for mankind's great needs like peace, racial and social justice, or feeding the hungry? In all candor, the answer to your question may lie in your answer to mine.

Our individual temperaments, abilities and personal inclinations will determine how we each should fulfill this obligation. One doesn't necessarily have to carry signs to be a good Catholic. But if our Christian and Catholic faith has anything significant to offer in forming policies about these great concerns, someone has to shout it from the housetops — or whatever else is needed to get these ideals out in the daylight and prompt people to consider them.

You'll notice that even the pope and bishops find it necessary today to take "political" positions on matters that were not considered the church's business only a generation ago. If in doing this they seem to be moving too much out of the sacristy, perhaps it's because they're trying to teach us that when it comes to justice, peace, and civic responsibility, our faith demands more, and more specific, things from us than we thought.

Can Catholics join the Masons?

We have been told in recent years that Catholics may join

the Masons if certain conditions are fulfilled. Then a few years ago our local paper reported that the Vatican had reaffirmed its "200-year-old ban against Roman Catholics joining the Masons."

Now I read in our Catholic paper that membership in that organization is permitted only when permission is received from Rome. What is the situation? Are Catholics allowed to hold membership in Masonic organizations or not?

The former (1918) Code of Canon Law stated that anyone who joined the Masonic sect or other society which plots against the church or legitimate civil authority incurred automatic excommunication. Even then, however, that proscription was not in fact as absolute and universal as it was usually understood, for the following reason.

These kinds of regulations come under what might be called the penal laws of the church. And the interpretation and application of penal laws (laws which in some way limit human freedom and apply sanctions) are nuanced and limited by many principles which form part of the church's tradition of jurisprudence.

One such principle is that any regulation or censure which would forbid actions otherwise open to Catholics must be interpreted in its narrowest sense. Such a regulation usually applies, for example, only where the reason for the law clearly exists in a particular situation. Thus, membership in a particular Masonic group would be forbidden only when that organization does in fact oppose the church or government by open prejudice or persecution, undermining civil authority, and so on.

As recently as 1974, the Congregation for the Doctrine of the Faith reiterated this interpretation in a letter to episcopal conferences concerning membership in the Masons. "In the consideration of particular cases," the letter said, "it must be kept in mind that the penal law is subject to strict interpretation. Similarly, it is sound to teach and to apply the opinion of authors who hold that canon 2335 (old code) refers only to Catholics who enroll in associations which truly plot against the church

"Nevertheless, in every case the prohibition remains in effect for clerics, religious, and members of secular institutes not to enroll in any Masonic societies." (prot. n. 272-44)

The statements of the same congregation on February 17, 1981, repeated the position that general principles of interpretation of penal laws should be applied to individual cases.

The later statement to which you refer was a declaration on Masonic association by the same Vatican congregation on November 26, 1983. While the document clearly intends to tighten up the church's position on Masonic membership, it leaves areas of considerable confusion and ambiguity which will probably be resolved only with experience. The declaration, for example, seems to want to stress that nothing is changed, that the church's negative position "remains unaltered" and that joining the Masons "remains prohibited." Yet, as the director of the American bishops' committee on doctrine pointed out, a new regulation seems to be established restricting the power of local bishops. Such bishops, it says, no longer have authority, mentioned explicitly in the 1981 statement, to judge whether a specific Masonic organization could be approved for membership. Apparently even the 1981 statement was understood differently by bishops and by the congregation.

Anyone familiar with the history of Europe and America during the past 200 years is aware that the character of Masonry changes drastically from one place or time to another. Political and anti-religious activities so common to Masonry in Europe and Latin America, have, with some notable exceptions, hardly been evident in most parts of the United States.

Apart from the 32nd degree Southern Jurisdiction of the Scottish Rite, which often has been accused of actions and attitudes prejudicial to Catholics and the Catholic Church, Masonic organizations in the United States generally avoid the more sinister characteristics of international Masonry. In fact, individual American Catholic bishops have publicly praised the attitudes and good works of Masonic groups in several parts of the country.

The new Code of Canon Law does not mention Masons explicitly. It simply forbids Catholics to join any organization which plots against the church. (CCL 1374) However, the major objection of Christians against Freemasonry has been not only its sometimes anti-Catholic and anti-religious activities, but perhaps even more its beliefs and quasi-religious character, many aspects of which seem contradictory to Christian doctrines. It was this in particular which inspired the strongest condemnation yet by American bishops of membership in Masonic organizations. A lengthy report from a committee of the National Conference of Catholic Bishops released in June, 1985, calls Freemasonry "irreconcilable" not only with Catholicism but with all Christianity. "The principles and basic rituals of Masonry embody a naturalistic religion, active participation in which is incompatible with Christian faith and practice. Those who knowingly embrace such principles are committing a serious sin" in professing beliefs which are contrary to Christianity.

The study also describes the "politically reactionary and racist" nature of most U.S. Masonry today. With the exception of one local lodge in New Jersey that admits blacks, it says, "all women, men under 21, and blacks are barred from Masonic initiation in regular lodges."

Local bishops or other church authorities may not make a more lenient judgment or dispense in this matter, according to the Congregation for the Doctrine of the Faith.

Clearly, the prohibition against Catholics belonging to the Masons remains extremely serious. This position, incidentally, is similar to that of many other Christian churches around the world which forbid or discourage affiliation with Freemasonry.

Joining secret societies

I am 18 years old and would like to join the DeMolay. My mother says I cannot join because the Catholic Church does not approve of secret societies, and that the DeMolay is a young men's branch of the Masons.

The boys I know in the DeMolay tell me it is a good Christian group and that none of their secrets are against our church or country. They are only passwords and so forth. They

also tell me that there are a lot of Catholic boys in the DeMolay.

Does the church now allow us to belong to this group and the Masons?

DeMolay is an organization of young men and is related to the Masonic order. However, according to principles of church law, restrictions concerning Masons do not apply to such related groups.

Habit of masturbation

Several years ago because of the incapacitation of my wife, our sex life was over. We still have a warm and loving marriage of over 30 years, but during the last few years I have fallen into the habit of masturbation.

Because I was unable to control this, I no longer received the sacraments and then gradually stopped attending Mass. I despair of ever breaking this habit. A few weeks of control are invariably followed by yet another act or two. Is here an answer for me?

I'm sure there is. The details will have to be wor ed out gradually, but a most important part of the answer is t return to the Sacraments of Penance and the Eucharist. Where there is good will, as there obviously is in your letter, the life and grace available to us in these ways is valuable and powerful.

I suggest you try to find a priest, a confessor, who is willing to take the time and give the attention to assist you. Several explanations are possible for your development of this habit.

Considering your faith and your desire to live a good life, there is serious question about how deliberate and therefore how sinful such actions may be on your part. A kind and willing priest will help you sort this out. Be calm and peaceful about it and trust that God knows where your heart is. I'm sure that with prayer, the Mass and the sacraments, you will find a way to deal with this that will give you peace of mind.

Cloning

Several times in recent years I have read about "cloning,"

and that it is causing a big moral problem. What is it, and what's the problem?

The word comes from the Greek word, "klon," which means a twig or a cutting, and is used to designate a remarkable process which biological science has recently discovered.

It is common knowledge now that every cell in a plant or animal carries that special, unique "genetic code" of that individual. For example, the sets of chromosomes that are in the first cell when the sperm and ovum unite in human reproduction, divide and are duplicated eventually in the billions of cells in an adult body. Certain processes guide some cells to become arms, others to become legs, and others to become blood; but all the original genetic "information" is in each cell.

Not long ago scientists began discovering that it is possible to take a cell from some living organisms and through an extremely delicate procedure, produce a new "beginning" cell that possesses exactly the same genetic make-up as the "parent." This cell would, in effect, grow into an identical twin of the parent body.

Until now, cloning has been successful only with some plants and lower animals. Some scientists expect the day is not too far distant when it will be possible with humans. Then science could, for example, pick out the ideal astronaut, let's say Neil Armstrong, and produce 100 Neil Armstrongs from his own body to form "ideal" teams for space flight. Other uses of the procedure would obviously be numerous.

The moral question, as with so many other newly-discovered scientific possibilities, is: Should mankind go ahead and do something just because it is possible? If so, under what conditions, and with what safeguards? Who will make the decisions? What human, spiritual, psychological, religious values are involved?

Unfortunately, as with so many other modern technical developments from sperm banks to nuclear weapons, too many responsible persons consider such concerns irrelevant, or at least superfluous. Their thought seems to be: Let's try it and think of the consequences later. By that time, enormous and irreparable damage could be done to the bodies, psyches, and social structure of the human race.

For these reasons, moral theologians of all faiths are wrestling publicly and urgently with such questions.

Trans-sexual surgery

We hear so much these days about trans-sexual operations. Is this a moral procedure — to change a man into a woman, or a woman into a man?

Your question allows of no easy or simple answer. But a couple of things will be significant factors in any such operation.

First, let's suppose we are dealing with a reasonably normal person whose male or female identity is well established — emotionally, psychically and physically, both internally and in relationship to others. For such an individual to attempt a sex change, even to whatever slight degree that might be possible, would be a gross abuse of his or her person, and morally wrong.

Few, if any, such cases are that clear cut, however. It is possible for an individual to possess a clear genetic sexual identity (male or female chromosomes) as well as major physical male or female sex characteristics, and still suffer from a quite confused sexual identity. The complicated system of internal secretions (hormones) which interact from one organ or gland to another, is subject to all sorts of imbalance; if this imbalance is extensive enough, it may cause serious difficulties in an individual's ability to function in his or her "proper" sexual relationships.

In light of this, many other factors enter. Certain remarkable surgical procedures are, or soon may be, available to deal with these kinds of pathologies in men or women. For one thing, however, there's room for question in some cases how much "sex change" is really involved. More importantly, procedures are increasingly available to deal with such physical ills by therapy far less drastic and questionable than surgery.

One gets the impression that most of these radical "treatments" have been carried out, up to now, with almost no serious consideration of the moral implications for either the individual or society. And that in itself must be deplored. But it is too soon and too many variables are involved to conclude at this point that every operation labelled a "sex change" is always automatically wrong.

Sins of the flesh

I am reading a book by a rather famous priest. It says that sins of the flesh send more people to hell than any other sins. What does he mean by sins of the flesh, and is he right?

Sometimes sins involving sex are referred to as sins of the flesh. Since God has never told us how many or how few people might be in hell, or why they are there if they are, any guesses on what kinds of sin might most cause the loss of eternal life are nothing more than purely personal conjecture.

I have been reminded by many devotees of the apparitions at Fatima that Mary is supposed to have said something like this in one of her appearances there early in this century. Even should that be true, however, it would remain what is called a private revelation. People may believe it if they wish, but it is not part of any official church teaching.

Face-lift

This is probably one of the strangest questions you've had to answer. I am a long-time secretary but am also a trained singer. I'd like to try out for television, but even if my songs and style are acceptable, my face would never make it. Years of hard work and tension have left their mark.

Would a face-lift be an intolerable vanity? I confess I've already had some plastic surgery and things are better, but there's still room for improvement.

I know this must sound petty and silly, but it's important to me. Among other things, I'd like to use whatever entertaining ability I have in hospitals, nursing homes and other places that cannot afford to hire entertainment. Should I pursue my "impossible dream" or just keep typing and shut up?

It sounds as if a face-lift would surely not be an intolerable vanity for you. By all means go ahead with your dream, if you have the money, the time, and the inclination. It's never too late, or too silly, if it's something you'd really like to try. Good luck!

Contemplating an abortion

I have a friend who is seriously thinking of having an abortion. To me it's murder. But what can I say to prevent it? She says my church shouldn't dictate to her what she can or cannot do.

The whole abortion controversy has become ridden with almost belligerent emotionalism. In my experience, when a situation of real crisis arises in an individual's life, all rational argument is pretty futile. Deep convictions, faith, and the "feel" the individual has for other children and for life are what will determine her decision.

One observation may help. Participation in dozens of discussions, panels, and ordinary bull sessions with people of all shades of opinion on the question has convinced me of one thing: Very few pregnant women, even those strongly pro-abortion, really believe they are not carrying a human baby. They know, regardless of the line they may give themselves, that what is in their womb is not just a blob, a chunk of material that is as disposable as an appendix or gall bladder. It is a baby, already a boy or girl — her child.

Seen in this light, the words of one mother are, to put it mildly, impressive. "Apart from everything else, maybe I'm just too much of a coward to have an abortion," she said. "I know I'd have to live with it till I die.

"I don't mean just the abortion itself; maybe I could get over that. But what will happen later? Five years from now, when I see a little girl all dressed up downtown, or going to school, I will know she could be my daughter.

"Fifteen years from now, when I see a neighbor's boy growing into manhood, I would know mine could be just like that. And 30 years from now, when I see a young mother taking care of her home and children, I'd know she could be mine — if I hadn't ended it all before it got started.

"I know these thoughts would nag me for the rest of my life. And I'm afraid it would drive me crazy."

Maybe the mother who said this is unusually sensitive and perceptive. But we don't really know much about the satisfactions or regrets of women who have had an abortion, five or 25 years later, do we?

Encourage your friend, and pray for her. If she believes in God, urge her to pray before she makes her final decision.

A mother regrets

The Question Box receives numerous questions concerning abortion. Many require answers far too long for this space. Included are questions relating to the personal aftereffects on a mother who has had an abortion.

Better than any reply I could give is the following letter. The mother who wrote it is not unique.

I have written her assuring her of God's forgiving love, but I hope our readers will remember her and others like her in their prayers.

Dear Father Dietzen:

Please, Father, don't throw this letter away. Let me talk to you. I need it, and perhaps if someone else in my situation reads it, she won't do the same thing.

After finding out I was pregnant I panicked because I picture a very insecure future for my children. I panicked because I thought we wouldn't have enough for everyone since now there are times we have just one complete meal.

So after coming back from the supermarket depressed because of the prices and the foods I couldn't get for my children, I decided I couldn't bring one more child into this world and then not be able to offer him a stable future. I know I was a big coward, but I did it thinking that this was the best thing to do for that baby and for the children I already have.

This was the hardest, the most painful decision I have ever taken in my life.

I cried during the "procedure," as it is called by the so-called counselors and doctors. With that child went part of my heart. I thought I would overcome that, but now I know I just tried to fool myself. I can't stop thinking about that 8-week-old baby I aborted.

I can't forget what I have done. It's just too much for one's conscience. Day and night I keep imagining that baby crying, telling me to let him live. I imagine the baby felt as if he was being caught by a "black hole" when the surgical vacuum was taking him out of me. I'm scared to be alone or in the dark.

Believe me, Father, I feel awful. I truly regret what I have done from the bottom of my heart. I ask God to please forgive me, to help me.

Instead of asking for that valium at the clinic when I felt I just couldn't go through it, I wish that I would have had enough faith in God, in the world, and that I would have left that place.

Is it possible that I can be forgiven — here on earth — at least a little bit? I don't dare go to church when there are people there. I pray alone and ask God for forgiveness.

I wish to advise any woman who, in my situation, thinks that abortion is the practical, easiest and most reasonable way to solve any problems. I know by my own experience that once in the clinic everything sounds "secure, simple, fast, confidential, practical, almost painless, etc."

You see so many women in there, all ages, colors and races, that you really believe temporarily that it is something normal to do, that it is the right thing to do. But once everything is done, once one is out of there, then we can't fool our conscience, our principles.

It is impossible to ignore the conscience, to run away from it. It is an eternal nightmare. It is like having always the need to reach that baby, not to let him go. But, no matter how hard we try, we just can't reach him.

Yes, the procedure is fast but the pain and guilt are endless.

Don't think you have to accept abortion to do it. I always thought I wouldn't do such a thing, but I panicked. I didn't have faith. I was desperate and now I am paying the consequences. No matter how much I cry day and night, I will always feel sorrow for what I have done.

Father, I hope you can tell me I can be forgiven, or where to go.

When is embryo human?

I understand that for a long time the church distinguished between an animated (with a soul) fetus and an inanimated (without a soul) fetus. St. Thomas and other theologians held this view. Why did the church change its position so that a fetus is now considered animated at conception?

It is important first of all, in examining Christian teaching and practice, to separate the question about time of animation from that of abortion.

One of the earliest Christian documents we possess, outside the New Testament, is the Didache, commonly called The Teaching of the Apostles. Written somewhere around the year 125, it contains an explicit condemnation of abortion and infanticide.

That condemnation, in one form or another, continued throughout Christian tradition. Not a lot was known about the formation of humans before birth; hence most of the controversies about the time of "ensoulment." But that a human being was developing somehow, and to kill it was wrong, was never disputed by any major theologian or church official.

The question you ask arises solely from the fact that, until modern times, people had very little knowledge about how new life develops in a mother's womb. First of all, they knew nothing of how sperm and ovum unite to form a human cell. All the living material of a new human (or other animal) life was believed to be in the male "seed." Females contributed only the "nest" and the material (blood) on which the seed fed and grew.

Similarly, little was known about stages of growth, especially before quickening (first feeling of movement), which everyone throughout the ages understandably viewed as a crucial stage of fetal development. I repeat, however, that even with this minimal knowledge, deliberate killing of unborn human life at any stage was never considered, from any Christian point of view, a morally responsible act.

The change for the church (and for the rest of the human race) came from the discoveries of biological, genetic and psychological sciences during the past two centuries, especially in recent decades. To speak only of genetics, it is now a scientific certainty that the genetic code (genes, etc.) which identifies each species and each individual for life is present already in the very first cells.

As the axiom goes, from the moment the first cell is formed (for example in the union of the sperm and ovum), until death occurs, the being "becomes what it already is," human. From the beginning, the cells are living and growing. And the life present is obviously not that of a cat or a monkey. It is definitively identifiable as human life. To put it another way, the church now has a clear scientific basis, not available in previous centuries, for its teaching that taking the life of the unborn is evil, and that killing children, born or unborn, is no civilized solution to any problem.

Anyone interested in more details on the history of how abortion has been viewed in the world and in the church will find much interesting and useful information in the excellent book, *Abortion — The Development of the Roman Catholic Perspective,* by John Connery (Loyola University Press).

Douche and abortion after rape

Several years ago in theology class, the priest told us that in case of rape a woman may have an abortion right away. Can you tell me if this is true?

I'm confident the priest didn't use exactly those words. An abortion, in the sense of directly killing or rejecting a human life that is already begun, is never a morally good act no matter how early in the pregnancy it takes place.

Your teacher was probably referring to the possible use of a douche of the vagina or the uterus of the woman who was raped. After sexual intercourse it takes some time for the male seed (sperm) to pass through the vagina and the uterus and enter the Fallopian tubes where it may unite with a female ovum to begin a new human life. Unless and until those two cells join, there is no human cell, and no human life.

Therefore, in the case of rape, for example, a vaginal or

uterine douche may be used to attempt to wash out the male sperm before it has a chance to unite with an ovum. Doctors and theologians generally agree that this might be done up to about an hour after the attack. It is not an abortive measure since no human life is yet present.

While this procedure is morally permissible, its effectiveness is not impressive and impossible to predict. (Some research places it at about 64 percent effective.) As those who have sought efficient contraceptives have discovered through the years, there's a marvelous persistence in the whole process of human generation, even down to the movement of the tiny reproductive cells after intercourse, a persistence that is not easily frustrated.

Another reason that this procedure is quite uncommon today is that many physicians do not hesitate to use another which is abortifacient — that is, it results in an actual abortion. In the normal course, after the sperm and ovum unite in the Fallopian tube, the new human cell begins multiplying and travels down into the uterus. About a week later it attaches itself to the womb where it grows until birth.

One practice after rape today is to give the victim a dose of diethylstilbestrol (sometimes called simply DES). This synthetic female hormone (estrogen) affects the wall of the uterus so that the new life (called a zygote) cannot attach and develop further. It therefore passes on through the mother and is lost. Such a procedure is a type of abortion and is therefore wrong.

Acceptable abortion laws?

I am much opposed to the Supreme Court decision legalizing abortion and am now planning to work with an organization called Right to Life.

However, recently a question came up about approving legislation that would allow an abortion to save the life of the mother. What is the church's position on this?

The position of the church is as it has been, that deliberate killing of an unborn child is always wrong even if it is intended to save the life of the mother.

However, a Catholic could quite properly approve and work for legislation along the lines you mention because in practice (and perhaps even in theory) sinful abortions "to save the mother's life" are not generally likely to occur.

Let me explain what I mean. It is quite possible, for example, that a pregnant mother may be ill with a serious disease that the doctor must treat immediately. It is also possible that the doctor knows that if he does what is needed to heal the mother, she will lose the baby.

An obvious illustration is cancer of the uterus. If in the physician's prudent and good medical judgment that uterus must be taken out before the baby is viable, or the mother will die (or the cancer will likely spread critically), the uterus may be removed. Naturally with such surgery the baby will die.

Some would incorrectly call this "an abortion to save the mother." It is, however, a perfectly moral procedure. Clearly, the baby is not killed, or aborted, in order to save the mother. It dies when the mother is treated as is medically necessary.

Other medical procedures may be less clear cut, but could fall into the same category.

As indicated before, in practice the problem hardly exists today. In the largest hospitals and clinics in the country which handle especially difficult cases, it has been years since doctors have faced a decision whether to save the mother or the child — if indeed they have ever done so in modern times. Medical management of pregnancy problems, to serve both the child and mother, has made enormous progress.

Also, when a perfect law is not politically attainable, one less perfect might save many babies from being aborted, and at least open a door to legal protection for unborn children.

After two abortions

I must have an answer to this. It has been on my mind for so long, and rightly so. I was raised a Catholic and married a Catholic, though he wasn't practicing his faith. My problem is that I had two abortions, which I didn't want but finally had. I know it was very wrong, so I haven't been able to go

to confession or Communion for 25 or 30 years. It's driving me crazy now. What should I do?

Abortion is a very serious offense against God and man, since it is the taking of a human life. I realize you know this, but I want to emphasize that what I say next is not meant to minimize that fact. The first step to forgiveness is an honest acknowledgment of our sin.

I hope you talk with a priest and receive the Sacrament of Penance soon. One of the strange things about sin is that it frequently seems to diminish in size when we're tempted, and then afterward it looms so huge that we fear even God can't forgive or heal the hurt that is done. In a way, that is an even bigger mistake than the sin itself.

God doesn't like the sin and certainly doesn't encourage us to ignore his commands. But he does tell us often in Scripture that he considers the forgiveness of sins the greatest of all his works. In other words, he is quite proud of the fact that no sin, no evil, is beyond the reach of his goodness and his mercy. That is a joyous and basic fact of our Christian faith.

So, he is there, waiting for you simply to run to him and tell him you're back. Read prayerfully the story of the forgiving father (Luke, chapter 15), and then go to confession and receive the Eucharist. You've been away long enough.

Is baby unjust aggressor?

In a recent group discussion on abortion, one member told us that some theologians have attempted to justify abortions on the basis that the child in the womb can be an "unjust aggressor." What does that mean?

It is a common and generally accepted moral principle that when someone is threatening my life (or someone else's) I have every right to take appropriate measures to defend myself. In this case the person who threatens my health or my life is referred to as an "unjust aggressor."

No theologian, at least no one of any standing, has to my

knowledge seriously defended abortions on the basis of such a moral principle.

Even if the principle were accepted in this area of morality, it would apply only in those instances where the child in the womb constituted a direct threat to the life of the mother. In no way could it be used as a general justification for abortion.

Mother or baby?

In my college ethics classes a thousand years ago, I understood that if there were a question of the mother or baby, the mother's life must be sacrificed. Others said that, since the baby is an unjust aggressor, the baby should be sacrificed. Who is right?

While my college and seminary days were somewhat less than a thousand years ago, I doubt that I'm much younger than you. The only thing I remember about that "mother or baby" position is that it is not, was not, and will not be taught by the Catholic Church as even remotely applicable to a medical dilemma during pregnancy — but there have been, and probably always will be, people who think that's what the church believes.

The history of medical science, biology, and moral theology on the subject is long and complicated, but to claim that a baby in the womb is an "unjust aggressor" in any moral sense of the word is out of the question.

Unfortunately, that term has been used sloppily on occasion in reference to other medical procedures possible during a pregnancy, and which might (or certainly will) result in the death of the unborn child. A classic, though somewhat unreal, example, which I pointed out in a previous question, is a pregnant mother with a uterus her doctor feels should be removed immediately. Such surgery would be morally permissible even though a non-viable fetus would surely die in the process.

I say it is a rather unreal example because this situation, as well as all those other "mother or child" problems, rarely if ever exist in modern medicine. Medical skills and routines provide a wide set of options today. After conversing with or listening to hundreds of physicians, including those in the largest obstetrics hospitals in the country, I have yet to find one who feels he has ever had to make a personal final choice to kill either the mother or the child.

There's an old axiom that remains true here: Good moral theology and good medicine go together, with emphasis on the word "good" in both cases. It is wrong and unnecessary to directly take the life of any innocent person, born or unborn.

Help in pregnancy

Your column recently quoted the deeply moving letter of a distressed woman who had had an abortion.

Nearly every major city has at least one emergency counseling center to urge pregnant women to consider alternatives before having an abortion. These may be found in the phone book under such names as Birthright, Alternatives to Abortion, Life-Line, The Society for the Preservation of Human Dignity, Help-Line, Pregnancy Guidance, Problem Pregnancy Help, Pregnancy Counseling, Help Inc., Guidelines, Personal Crisis Service, Alternatives Inc., Choose Life, Birth Choice Inc., Heartbeat, Pregnancy Aid, and Right to Life.

Perhaps it would be helpful if you could, from time to time when you write about this subject, publish some of this information.

Thank you for the suggestion and the information. I would add that the nearest Catholic newspaper, Catholic Social Service agency, and Catholic parish, as well as an increasing number of Protestant congregations and pastors, are also valuable sources for assistance in finding such centers. Look them up in the telephone book, or, if you wish, ask your parish priest how to contact them.

All these groups perform a continuing valuable service to numerous women with problem pregnancies, as you have also by sending your letter.

Aftermath of rape

I carry a heavy burden and am so ashamed I don't find it fair to tell my parish priest. When I was young I was raped and had so much fear of my parents I never told them even though I didn't realize what had happened to me.

A few years later when I was 18, I married and had one child. Then my husband went to war and I kind of fell to pieces. I had three illegitimate children, divorced my husband, remarried and had four children by this marriage, or at least it was supposed to be a marriage.

I divorced this man because I was so confused and unsettled. God must have been watching over me because all my children are now grown and all seem to be getting along well.

Since then I have turned a complete flip. I have turned toward God again and feel close to him. I'm a volunteer in my community and really try to love my neighbor.

Father, do you feel I am doing the right thing? I really want to be better.

Your letter was a sad one even to read. The tragedies and hurt you have suffered are obviously far more painful than most of us could imagine.

Two things stood out above all, however, in your letter to me. You are truly a good person and in the midst of all that has happened to you, God's love for you has been continuous and enormous.

As you say the rape, along with your inability to share your fright and confusion with anyone, even your parents, is a terrible burden but, to be honest, one you have come through amazingly well.

You do need to talk with someone about it even at this late date — if nothing else simply to get part of the burden off of your own shoulders and see it in perspective. Please find someone in your area — a priest, a friend or even a professional psychologist or psychiatrist to unload on just once.

If you find the right person it will make your heart lighter than it's been for years. And you deserve it.

Abortion and excommunication

I had an abortion 18 years ago and was told that the priest could not give me absolution in the confessional. So I never went back because I could not face that.

The years have passed and it bothers me more every day. I go to Mass all the time but can never bring myself to go to a priest about it because of what I was told. I hope you will be able to help.

I am terribly sorry you have been away from the sacraments all these years. This is especially sad because apparently it resulted, as unfortunately so often happens, from information you received that was almost certainly false.

It is true that, according to our church, anyone who procures a completed abortion (this may include not only the mother, but others directly involved in the act) incurs an automatic excommunication. However, a number of critical conditions must be met before a particular individual incurs that excommunication.

For example, the person must be at least 18 years old, and be aware when the act is committed that such an excommunication is going to be incurred if the act is carried through. Obviously, many people who know that abortion is seriously wrong still do not know that an excommunication is incurred at the same time.

Furthermore, if circumstances surrounding the pregnancy are such as to cause grave fear and confusion in the mind of the woman, or if she is under severe pressure (from family or perhaps close friends), again the excommunication would not be incurred.

Some other conditions are also required but I hope you get the point.

Second, the information you received that the priest was unable to deal with this excommunication in the Sacrament of Penance was almost certainly wrong, even 18 years ago. Even if this excommunication did take place in your circumstances (which as I said is perhaps quite doubtful), a priest in your parish or a neighboring parish can take care of it immediately and finally when you go to confession.

In most parts of the United States, including in your diocese, faculties given to priests by their bishops include authority to remit this type of penalty.

You need not remember all these details. The main point is that you have been away from the sacraments long enough. Please go to a priest and celebrate this Easter as you have been wanting to.

For those interested in checking references, the sections of canon law most relevant here are Canons 1398, 97, 1323 and 1324. Parallel canons in the former code which would have been in effect 18 years ago are worded somewhat differently but are, in practice, basically the same as the 1983 code for this type of penalty.

Can medical care be refused?

A few weeks ago I was diagnosed as having inoperable liver cancer and have been undergoing chemotherapy. Would refusing chemotherapy be the same thing as committing suicide? I read where a member of the Flying Wallendas was diagnosed with cancer, yet refused chemotherapy and was going to let nature take its course.

I personally believe that one should make every attempt possible to extend one's life. If I die I hope doctors would have learned something to help others in the same situation. Refusing any form of chemotherapy would be like a slap in God's face, for he gave doctors the talents to help others.

I admire you greatly for the courageous and thoughtful manner in which you are attempting to meet these painful life decisions. We need to begin, as you already have, by acknowledging our Christian conviction that, while life is a sacred and marvelous gift from God, death for us is not an absolute evil. Since we believe the end of this life is not the end of existence, we do not cling frantically to each additional moment regardless of the cost or consequences to ourselves or others.

Our Christian faith and convictions thus say much about the questions we ask ourselves in times like this. The concerns you have, which are shared by all others in similar circumstances, basically revolve around two words, benefit and burden. What benefits will the therapy, whatever it be, bring to you and to others? You do not mention some important details here. Are you a parent with young children? An older person whose family is grown? What likelihood of success does your team of physicians offer? At best, or at worst, what are the reasonable expectations? All these questions need to enter into your decision. They must be weighed along with the burdens involved.

Today the cost of medical procedures in these areas might easily reach into the hundreds of thousands of dollars. What does this do economically to your family or other loved ones when balanced against the expectations of success? Considering your age and responsibilities, is the sheer pain involved reasonably worth the benefits you might achieve? Consider the other physical and psychological burdens on yourself and those around you. How might your decision affect your chances for anything like a reasonably normal human life?

I recognize that these are heavy, almost brutal, questions. But they are the ones we must deal with when faced as you are with decisions about "extraordinary" ways of regaining or maintaining physical health. I hope all who read this recognize that it barely hints at the complexity and thoroughness with which we must address questions like this. Even should one wish to read up on the subject, most books are far beyond the time and background of the majority of us. There is one recently published book I would recommend highly as a readable and morally solid presentation of the kinds of concerns to be considered in situations like yours. It is "Medical Ethics: A Catholic Guide to Healthcare Decisions," by McCarthy and Caron, published by Liguori Press (Liguori, Mo.). I think you will find it helpful.

Please talk through your questions with others who know your personal and family situation obviously far better than I do.

Penance and Anointing of the Sick

Evolution of private confession

My friends and I have enjoyed a number of group communal penance services in our church. It is so much more meaningful than the private confession we were used to and which I am told was not practiced in the church for a long time.

Can you tell us when our individual type confession was started and by whom?

The history of the sacrament (or sacraments) of forgiveness of sin in our church is far too complicated for the brief and simple answer you are looking for. The following may help.

You are right in believing that private confession as we have it was unknown for a long time. In the early centuries, the process of forgiveness for sins was rather public, required a long time, sometimes even several years, and took place under the direction of the bishop.

The move toward private confession to a priest extended over several centuries, but started for the most part in Ireland about the time of St. Patrick, who died in 461. Monks, most of them not priests, traveled the Irish countryside preaching and baptizing and conducting a simple rite of forgiveness patterned on the type of counseling the monks themselves were accustomed to in their own spiritual lives.

Penitential books began to appear with appropriate penances for various sins and were used by the monks in the penance ceremony.

As Irish monks spread over Europe soon afterward, they took these rituals and books with them and began to use them in all the countries where they settled. But the practice took hold very slowly.

Several bishops and regional church councils roundly condemned what one council, Toledo in Spain, called the "abominable presumption" of "asking a priest to forgive them as often as they wish to sin." They insisted on a return to the ancient and accepted penitential disciplines.

Even as late as the ninth century the practice of private confession apparently was unknown in Rome.

Gradually the idea took hold, however, and bishops moved from condemning the practice to trying to regulate it. By the time of the Fourth Lateran Ecumenical Council (1215), private confession had become pretty much "the" sacrament of forgiveness in the church.

I must add, however briefly, that these changes and developments in the church's understanding and practice of forgiveness of sin should not surprise us. We know it happened with the other sacraments as the people of God lived through the centuries, and could be equally expected in this case.

There is no question that in its understanding of this sacrament, the church is turning from a rather legalistic understanding to one which is more scriptural and liturgical and more centered on conversion of the heart — in other words, more with the focus of the penitential disciplines during the first centuries, but with many insights offered by our experiences of faith in our own age.

What is perfect contrition?

What is an act of perfect contrition? Does it take away mortal sin?

The theological terms, perfect and imperfect contrition, have had differing and sometimes controversial meanings over the past several hundred years. Since the Council of Trent in the 16th century, however, the difference has been placed mainly in the motive of our sorrow for sin. Perfect contrition is sorrow over offenses primarily because of our love for God and for Jesus Christ, and because those sins violated that love. Imperfect contrition, on the other hand, looks more toward ourselves — that our sins are shameful in themselves and cause us to deserve punishment for them.

Obviously, the difference between the two makes more sense in theory than it does in practice. Even imperfect contrition arises from the help of God's grace and has behind it basic elements of faith, hope and love. Otherwise the shame over breaking God's law and the fear of punishment or separation from him would not be there in the first place.

In both cases the sorrow arises, at least in some degree, out of the virtue of charity, and both include a firm turning away from any serious offense against God.

Either of these kinds of contrition is sufficient for receiving the Sacrament of Penance. Understanding the distinction between them in the above traditional manner, however, it is usually understood that perfect contrition is required after a mortal sin in order to re-attain the sharing of divine life that we call sanctifying grace. The Baltimore Catechism puts it succinctly: "A person in mortal sin can regain the state of grace before receiving the Sacrament of Penance by making an act of perfect contrition with the sincere purpose of going to confession."

All the prayers which we call "acts of contrition" reflect sentiments which clearly fall into the category of perfect contrition. They may speak of fear of punishment, but the predominant feelings are those of faith and the awareness of having betrayed the trust of a loving God by acting against his wishes and commands.

Penance after mortal sin?

Is it really necessary to go to confession before receiving Communion if one has committed a mortal sin?

Yes. If someone is certain that he has offended God that seriously, he should receive the Sacrament of Penance before going to Communion, except for emergency situations.

It is true, of course, that such a person reestablishes his or her friendship with God before confession by turning back to him in honest sorrow for the wrong that was done. But going to confession in a case like this is not an empty, superfluous formality.

Any sin, especially more serious sin, injures our relationship not only with God but with our fellow man — and most of all, with our fellow Christians. It may be that the sin involved others directly. At least indirectly, our loss of holiness, our self-centeredness in the sin, and the crippling of our generosity in prayer and other good things we do for others, all in some way affect the human "family" we belong to. It is only fair and just, then, that we first confess our sin and receive the "public" forgiveness for it from the priest who acts in the name of Our Lord and all his people in the Sacrament of Penance.

After that the sharing of the Eucharist in Holy Communion, which is the sign of our mutual friendship with Christ and with each other, makes more genuine sense.

Priest confessors

Why not have mass confessions now? If anyone can give out Communion, anyone can forgive sins.

Ordination to the priesthood is not and has never been a requirement for distributing Communion. It is required in order that one be the church's minister of the Sacrament of Penance.

Can a priest hear confessions everywhere?

A priest-friend of our family told us recently that he could not hear confessions in our church without permission from the bishop. (He is from a neighboring state.)

We didn't have an opportunity to ask him to explain, but that sounds unbelievable. Doesn't a priest have the right to hear confessions anywhere?

Yes, normally he does. According to the Code of Canon Law, if a priest has delegation or permission (technically called "faculties") to administer the Sacrament of Penance in his own diocese, he is able to exercise those faculties anywhere, unless a particular bishop somewhere else specifically denies him those faculties. (CCL 967)

This differs from the former code under which, apart from emergencies, faculties had to be obtained for any diocese in which a priest might happen to be away from his own.

Is ex-priest bound by seal?

If you tell a serious sin to a priest in confession and he leaves the priesthood, could he repeat it to someone? I need to know this.

No. A priest is bound by the seal of confession for life. Even those men who leave the priesthood consider this one of their most sacred obligations, always.

Procedure for Confession

I am returning to the Catholic faith which I love dearly. I know you have face-to-face confession now. What is the procedure? What are the exact words to the priest? Is it still, "Father, I have sinned," and so on?

Most churches today have the opportunity for face-to-face confession as well as the traditional anonymous way. But the option should be entirely yours, depending on what you feel most helpful for you spiritually.

Please don't worry about which words to use. Usually the priest will say a brief prayer before you begin, or read a short passage from the Gospels. Then say whatever you are familiar with. The priest will ask you to fill in the gaps, if any.

The "changes" in the Sacrament of Penance are not so much in procedures as in greater attention to the causes of our sinfulness, and especially to our cooperation with the healing grace of God in committing ourselves to greater holiness of life.

Nearly always the priest will, as much as possible, help you to do that as you receive this sacrament.

Penance: prayer or action?

The last time I went to confession, the priest gave me a penance to do something which I won't explain here. I asked him what prayers I should say and he told me my penance was "the action, not the words." Can you explain this?

It's quite simple. The "penance" requested in the Sacrament of Penance is intended not only to make up for our sins, but to help us remedy the weaknesses that cause our sins and to commit ourselves to a new life. Sometimes the priest may feel that some action — like an act of kindness — will serve that purpose better than "three Our Fathers and three Hail Marys."

The church encourages such penances. In the document outlining the revised ceremony for this sacrament (Rite of Penance, paragraph 18), we are told that the satisfaction or penance imposed should "correspond to the seriousness and the nature of the sins confessed, to the extent possible. This satisfaction may be suitably performed by prayer, by self-denial, especially by service of neighbor and works of mercy through which the social aspect of sin and its forgiveness may be expressed."

You're lucky to have gone to a priest who tried to help you receive the greatest benefit from the Sacrament of Penance in this thoughtful and creative way.

Confession an Easter duty?

In response to a question about the Easter duty, you tell us "The obligation confession during the Easter season is still as it always has been, binding only if it is necessary for an individual to be able to receive the Eucharist."

I refer you to the church canon: "If anyone denies that each of Christ's faithful of both sexes is bound to confess once a year according to the regulation of the great Lateran Council . . . let him be anathema."

How do you explain your answer in the light of this statement?

The best — in fact the only — way for us to discover the proper meaning of a moral or doctrinal statement of the church is to examine what the church itself meant to say at the time, and how it interprets that statement.

So here, in spite of the seeming absolute command of yearly confession, the fact is that, in its sacramental practice and regulations, the church has always, at least as far as I can determine, meant this to apply only where a mortal sin had to be confessed. The context of the Council of Trent's canon, and even more the context of the Fourth Lateran Council statement to which you refer, support this interpretation. Moral theologians, old and new, agree almost without exception.

If you wish a specific example close to home, refer to the Baltimore Catechism No. 3, which was for decades before Vatican II the most official and authoritative expression of beliefs and practices of American Catholics. Question 293 asks: "What is meant by the commandment to confess our sins at least once a year?" The answer: "By the commandment to confess our sins at least once a year is meant that we are strictly obliged to make a good confession within the year, if we have mortal sin to confess." (Baltimore Catechism, St. Joseph Edition)

I trust you realize this is not what the church recommends; it is simply the bare minimum required. If one is in the state of mortal sin, he must receive the Sacrament of Penance within the year. Of course, if one is guilty of serious sin, he would need to go to confession simply to fulfill the other annual sacramental obligation, to receive the Eucharist sometime during the Easter time.

Any Catholic who understands how the Sacrament of Penance heals us in our sinfulness and other weaknesses, and how it strengthens and reconciles us to God and to our fellow members of the church, will normally receive this more than once a year, mortal sin or not.

Confession how often?

Do you have an explanation concerning the need for confession before receiving Communion? I'm confused and I think a lot of Catholics are. Is it every time one goes to Communion? Once a month? Once a year? What is the latest on going to confession to be able to receive Communion?

You really have three questions: Is it necessary always to receive confession before Communion? What does the precept to go to confession once a year really mean? And how often might one properly receive this sacrament?

The practice of receiving the sacrament of penance before each reception of Communion accompanied the great decline in receiving the Eucharist in the late Middle Ages. The high (or low) point of this development came under the influence of the Jansenist heresies beginning in the 16th and 17th centuries.

Under the influence of this severe rigoristic approach to morality and the sacraments, many aspects of Catholic belief and life were bent all out of shape. Among these was the feeling and practice that reception of the Eucharist, even by cloistered nuns and monks, should be limited to a few times a year.

Ordinary folks were encouraged to receive perhaps only once a year, sometimes even less than that. In such confused times it is understandable that people gradually assumed they must go to confession each time before Communion.

This situation prevailed almost into our own century when Pope Pius X (1903-1914) urged early Communion for children and frequent Communion for all. As people began receiving Communion each month (remember the monthly Communion Sundays for the Ladies' Sodality or the Holy Name Society?) or even weekly, the "tradition" of confession before every Communion continued.

The church, in fact, still is wrestling with this same history on the question whether or not confession absolutely must precede first Communion for young children.

This, among others, is a major reason the church today finds it critical to re-evaluate the theology and place of the sacrament of penance in our daily Catholic lives.

How about the obligation "to confess at least once a year"? The church rule on this never has been as absolute as it sounds. Even when this "obligation" first appears (in the year 1215), when already Communion rarely was received by Christians, it is clear that only confession of mortal sins was required once a year.

This, of course, would be necessary to fulfill another requirement of that same council, to receive the Eucharist at least once a year, at Easter time.

Our present canon law (989) continues that tradition. All who have reached the age of reason must confess any serious sins once a year. Obviously this intends to suggest a bare minimum, not the ideal frequency, for receiving the sacrament of penance.

How often should one celebrate reconciliation with God and "with our brothers and sisters who are always harmed by our sins," as the rite of penance puts it?

That same rite, which is the official guide of the church for this sacrament, mentions only Lent, obviously the most appropriate time. Others would be Advent and whatever occasions during the year or in one's life obviously invite us to re-examine the direction of our lives and commit ourselves completely to God.

Why not yes or no?

Someone asked you, "Do you have any explanation concerning the need for confession before receiving Communion? Is it every time one goes to Communion?"

I found your answer confusing and evasive. Why must you answer a simple question with an explanation that goes back to the Middle Ages? I certainly would appreciate having you answer the question in language I can understand such as, "Yes, you must receive confession at least once a month or before Communion, or whatever, or no."

Please try an answer most of us poor Catholics can understand and follow.

I did not respond to the question the way you wish because an honest answer is just not that simple. For one thing, I disagree heartily that "most of us poor Catholics can understand and follow" only simple yes or no rules.

I believe most Catholics and most other Christians increasingly hunger for a deeper personal relationship with God and with Jesus. They are not satisfied any longer with merely "obeying the rules of the club," even in the Sacrament of Penance.

They are aware that no friendship, whether with another person or with God, happens without sincere efforts toward deeper understanding of oneself and the other, and a deep desire for intimacy. Such a relationship, with God or man or woman, does not come about solely by following a set of regulations.

The only purpose of this column is to support people in coming to that kind of intimacy with God. My intention is not merely to provide yes-or-no responses, but to help Catholics understand their faith better so they can live it more deeply.

I felt that, happily, the woman herself wanted more than that; she wanted an explanation.

In my view the simple directive type answer, which unfortunately we Catholics have wanted and received too often in the past, would have been worse than no answer at all. It would have supported many readers and perhaps the woman herself in the serious misconception that simply following regulations, not understanding how the sacraments play an intimate role in building our friendship with God, is the most important thing.

Many Catholics still would like their faith to be summed up in a list of black and white rules. Relationships simply do not grow that way. They demand patience, sincere pursuit of greater understanding and knowledge, prayer, genuine care for the other person and continual reflection.

A mechanical view of our religion which sees our faith obligations, even our sacramental life, as a series of do's and don'ts stunts our spiritual growth and makes a personal, loving friendship with God all but impossible.

Scrupulosity

Two priests have told me recently in confession that I am scrupulous. Both said I should ignore the times I thought I committed a sin and go to Communion anyway. I don't understand how I can do that. I was always taught we have to go to confession before we receive Communion if we have a mortal sin. Can you tell me what to do?

Yes, I can. And I hope you will do it. Follow the directions the priests have given you!

Scrupulosity simply means that for any of several reasons an individual has lost his or her sense of good judgment about what is a sin. A scrupulous person tends to see sin where there is no sin, sometimes interpreting the most innocent action as seriously sinful because of "bad intentions" or wrong evaluation of the seriousness of the action.

A priest is — or should be — prepared to recognize signs of scrupulosity in confession, and to help the individual work through them. In some cases where the problem has developed into a deeper neurosis, he may even suggest professional psychological assistance.

Your best course, in fact your only course, is to go to a priest in whom you have confidence and follow his directions completely, even about Communion. And don't float around looking for a priest who will "really understand" your situation. Chances are that one or both of the priests you mention do understand, and are doing the right thing to help you.

One final word: Don't be discouraged. This kind of difficulty always causes some anxiety and suffering. But there are encouraging signs in your letter that the problem is not yet too deep. If you pray and follow exactly the course I've outlined, you will either solve the difficulty or learn how to live with it peacefully. I hope you do.

Disagrees with answer

My husband has a heated reaction to your answer to the scrupulous lady who worried about what is a sin. Other priests had told her that she should go to Communion no matter what sins she thought she committed. You said she should follow their advice.

We think you should have insisted that one does not go to Communion with a mortal sin, and then approached the possibility that she may be scrupulous.

In the opinion of at least a few priests, the lady in question is a victim of some real scrupulosity. It also came through in her letter to me.

Such persons may be totally incapable of judging the seriousness of any sin or even of judging whether there was a sin at all. It can be highly questionable whether an individual so distraught and emotionally entangled is psychically capable of serious sin. If you recall, two of the requirements for mortal sin are sufficient reflection and full consent of the will.

My response, therefore, described how a scrupulous person may react. The answer obviously does not apply to anyone not afflicted with this emotional problem.

Right to privacy

Our church has fixed a reconciliation room in part of the sacristy. The people were told that the old confessional will no longer be used.

Some of us are disturbed by one of our priests who does not always observe the right of a penitent to go to confession anonymously. He will bounce out to escort one into the room or see the penitent out after confession. It is a bit too much for most of us to take.

Confession has never been a favorite sport of most Catholics. Instead of making it easier, everything is being made more difficult.

You bring up several serious points. First of all a priest who refuses to respect the anonymity of penitents who obviously desire it in their confession unjustly violates a serious and clear right of Catholic people.

Regardless of the priest's personal feelings about what is better in this or in any other matter, he never has a right, whether by edict or intimidation, to impose his feelings on others in contradiction to options legitimately offered by the church. This is particularly true in matters relating to the reception of the sacraments.

How about your priest's remarks concerning the use of old confessionals? It may require time, money, and planning to provide appropriate space for face-to-face reception of the Sacrament of Penance according to the new rite. Priests do have a responsibility, however, to provide such space as soon as the parish is reasonably able to do so. By far the majority of parishes have already done so.

As you indicate, the church's instructions for ministering and receiving the Sacrament of Penance provide that the penitent should have the opportunity to go to confession face-to-face or anonymously, whichever way he or she wishes.

I hope you will try as gently and as honestly as you can to let your priests know your feelings so this sacrament can be for you the healing and helpful experience Our Lord meant it to be.

Penance without serious sin

What does one do when he is sent from the confessional and told not to come back until he has committed a mortal sin? Does that mean we should never go to confession? I know a number of elderly people who are facing this problem. I would like to receive this sacrament more often but I'm confused.

About the only advice I can give to you is to do as the priest says; don't go back — to him — for such a confession. Go to another priest — and there are many of them — who do not have such a rigid view of the nature and purpose of the Sacrament of Penance.

A confession of this nature is usually called a "confession of devotion," that is, only venial sins or previously forgiven sins are told to the priest. Such confessions have been and still are strongly encouraged by the church. The introduction to the new Rite of Penance stresses the value of "confessions of devotion" as having their own kind of healing power. "Those who through daily weakness fall into venial sin draw strength from a repeated celebration of penance to gain the full freedom of the children of God," says this document. Frequent and careful celebration of this sacrament, it continues, "is not a mere ritual repetition or psychological exercise, but a serious striving to perfect the grace of Baptism so that, as we bear in our bodies the death of Jesus Christ, his life may be seen in us ever more clearly." (Paragraph 7)

In other words the Sacrament of Penance is not only for the forgiveness of sins, but for many other spiritual benefits — the growth of purity of heart, a living spirit of sorrow and humility before God, an increased openness of our hearts to the healing power of God for sins of the past, a more intimate sharing in the saving power of the sufferings of Christ, and so on.

As one of the decrees of Vatican Council II puts it, this sacrament "greatly fosters the necessary turning of the heart toward the love of the Father of mercies."

Pope John Paul II, in his exhortation to the whole church on reconciliation and the Sacrament of Penance (1983) explained that Christians come to sacramental penance for other reasons than regaining the grace lost by mortal sin.

Among these reasons, he said, are a need to check one's spiritual progress, sometimes a need for more accurate discernment of one's vocation, a need and desire to escape from spiritual apathy and religious crisis, and often a need for broader spiritual direction which is readily linked with the Sacrament of Penance.

Even the second form of celebration, explains the pope, which unites a communal penance service with the opportunity for individual confession can spiritually assist the Christian whose life reflects not even a hint of mortal sin. He mentions two features here of special importance: the word of God listened to in common, which has a remarkable effect as compared with its individual reading; and a better emphasis on the social character of sin and reconciliation (Apostolic Exhortation on Reconciliation and Penance, no. 32).

Naturally we must never allow such confessions to become mechanical or superficial, or without a true spirit of sorrow. Also, we shouldn't forget that sins can be forgiven in many other ways — prayer, penance, good works, and especially in the Eucharistic Sacrifice, which should always remain the center of our spiritual lives. I'm happy, however, that you see more to the Sacrament of Penance than simply taking away sins. One of the insights that the church has gained more clearly is that this sacrament has as one of its major effects a strengthening of our minds and hearts and wills in developing the virtues that can make our lives more Christian, and in helping us deal with the sinfulness of selfishness, pride, greed and the other things which are the source of our actual sins.

I suggest that when you receive the Sacrament of Penance, you focus attention more on these weaknesses and tendencies toward sinfulness, rather than simply on the actions that you think might be sinful, whether venial or mortal. The forgiving and healing love of God are present in a unique way in the sacrament and I'm glad you are concerned about using it well.

Lacks courage in confession

Here is a serious problem. Is it possible for a person to save his soul if over many years he has received the Blessed Sacrament while in the state of sin, due to embarrassment over sins which were omitted in confession? He makes a perfect Act of Contrition with a promise to straighten out and confess these sins, but at the next confession lacks the courage to tell them.

Then the same problem repeats itself, the same sin is committed and no courage. Is there a chance for repentance for this kind of person?

There's always a chance for repentance and for getting oneself straightened out with God.

Confession of all serious, mortal sins of which a person is aware is surely required in confession. No one can excuse himself from that.

It is possible, however, for an individual to get so mixed up emotionally and so unreasonably frightened by the prospect of confessing the sins, that his personal guilt before God is very questionable. It may reach the point where even the individual himself is incapable of making any decent judgment about his guilt.

My main concern, however, after studying your letter is your own confusion and fear which could be eliminated or alleviated so easily if you would simply go and talk to a priest. I urge you to do that. It doesn't have to be your own parish priest. The city you live in has a dozen or more who would be anxious to help you get out of your dilemma. Please go and talk with one of them soon.

Pregnant, refused absolution

I have a teen-age granddaughter who is unmarried and preg-

nant. This girl regrets her action and went to confession a couple of weeks ago. She went home very upset. After she confessed, the priest refused her absolution, told her she could not receive the sacraments and said she was excommunicated from the Catholic Church.

Did he have the authority to do this? I know there are a lot of changes and maybe I'm too old (75) to adapt.

I know from experience and even more from my mail that priests can do strange things. I have a strong feeling, however, that in this case there is gross misunderstanding somewhere along the line.

Even if the priest reacted perhaps more harshly than he should have, there's nothing in your letter that could remotely bring up the subject of excommunication. The subject is irrelevant to the kind of sins you speak of and would not even arise in the Sacrament of Penance.

My guess is that either your granddaughter mis-read what the priest said, or there is perhaps more to the situation than she has told her family, or than they have wanted to tell you.

If you are still confused, talk it over with a priest — the same priest or another — and explain your concerns. Without violating the confidentiality of the Sacrament of Penance, he might be able to help you or at least ease the hurt caused to your granddaughter and her family.

Only sins are confessed

There is this young married couple, married in church, and one was born and raised Catholic. They both love children and plan to have a family as soon as they feel they are mature enough and their personal circumstances permit.

They have been using the rhythm method but because of the limited period of "safety," they use an artificial method of birth control also. They do not believe in their hearts that this is wrong, but feel they should express their love for one another at other times than just during a short period.

Their problem is that they do not feel like going to confession and confessing this, as they do not feel they are sinning. Must someone go to confession in a case like this? I'm afraid

they are seriously considering leaving the church for another if this is so.

Your letter raises a number of points about which I suspect this couple might need enlightened rethinking, not the least of which is your expression of their reasons for delaying a family; of course, you don't give their ages.

I'll limit myself, however, to answering your direct question. No one is ever required to confess anything that he or she honestly feels is no sin. In fact, when an individual is convinced that what has been done is morally permissible or good, it normally should *not* be mentioned in confession; it might only confuse the priest concerning the penitent's state of conscience.

In forming one's conscience on any serious moral question, the guidance of the church on that particular subject — here, birth control — and on the whole process of reaching practical conclusions in our own conscience, must have a significant influence for Catholic Christians. But when one receives the Sacrament of Penance, it is, among other benefits, of course, for the forgiveness of *sins* — that is, actions which an individual is convinced in his own conscience are wrong but which he goes ahead and does anyway.

Presuming that you reflect this couple's dilemma correctly, they seem to have one of two problems. Perhaps they do not understand confession properly. Or they might not be quite as sure as they say they are that their course of action is right for them, and they feel uneasy enough about it that they feel they should confess it.

Children resist confession?

Perhaps you can advise me on a problem I'm having with my daughter. She received first Communion about two years ago and made her first confession about one and a half years later. Although she receives Communion regularly, she resists confession. I have not made a big issue of it, but am hoping to persuade her to go during Lent.

Must I force her to go if she resists, or should I let it slide for a while?

Yours is a widespread problem these days. We should not be surprised, first of all, at your daughter's confusion since most adult Catholics are still trying to discover just where this sacrament fits into their lives.

No one, not even a parent, should force another to receive any sacrament. That can do no real good either spiritually or psychologically. On the other hand, you should not "let it slide for a while." I think there is a middle way.

Helping your daughter by your own words and actions to understand a few essential things about sin and the Sacrament of Penance is important. One crucial truth forgotten by many who say confession is useless unless one has committed a mortal sin, is that all sin, even slighter sin, is an offense not only against God but against all the church. It weakens and diminishes the holiness of all by lessening one's own holiness and spiritual goodness in it.

When I sin, I injure the body of Christ, and to the degree of my sin, distort the image of Christ existing in all my brothers and sisters. I become part of a sinful church. To be whole, to be honest again, I need not only the "private" telling of my sin to God, I need the church, through its priest, in that living encounter of confession and forgiveness to say to me: "We forgive you. In the shadow of the cross of Christ, let's all undergo a change of heart and try to be again the sign of his loving presence to each other and to the world that we were meant to be."

There are other ways in which our daily faults are forgiven apart from confession — through prayer, good works for others, the Eucharist, and so on. Even most of these, however, relate closely to our ties to our fellow Catholics. But the special encounter with God's forgiving and healing love in the Sacrament of Penance brings him directly into the everyday realities of our guilt, our need for cleansing from sin, and our identity with the death and resurrection of Jesus in a way nothing else does.

These tremendous realities must be thought through and made our own if we expect them to become real to our children. I suggest you use one of the many good books on confession geared for younger people and available from a

Catholic bookstore or through a Catholic catalog you could borrow from your pastor.

I am truly happy you want to help your child become more comfortable with the sacrament of forgiveness. One of the great priests and theologians of our time, Jesuit Father Karl Rahner, spoke once of how many Protestant leaders today recognize the need of regular confession of our sins. He added, "With this situation facing us, would it not be very strange if we began to neglect frequent confession out of carelessness and a desire for comfort in the spiritual life?"

With thoughtful parents like you, maybe that is changing.

Age for "serious" sin?

We are trying as best we can to help our oldest child prepare for his first confession. We haven't received much help. We would really like to know how to help all our children form a good conscience without seeing sin where there isn't any — or at least not anything serious.

If you can help us with this question, it will put some things in focus for us. At what age do you think a child is responsible enough to realize he is committing a mortal sin?

First, you deserve a lot of credit for approaching this task with your child so thoughtfully, and for asking some right and extremely important questions. A correct perspective on this matter can help not only children but most of us adults, too.

No one is guilty of any sin, of course, unless he realizes what he is doing. So what you are really asking is: At what age is a child able to commit a mortal sin?

In practice the answer will differ enormously from person to person. Even theoretically, it might vary widely depending, for example, on exactly what kind of moral perception and spiritual growth is psychologically possible at a given age. But a few things can surely be said. (Note that what follows refers to mortal sin; we are not concerned here with lesser, or venial, sins.)

A mortal sin is, as you know, any action by which a person consciously and with full deliberation and determination turns his whole self away from the friendship and love of God. It contains genuine undertones of eternal commitment because, in itself, the decision is total and permanent even though repentance and conversion may come later.

Now, such a decision demands considerable grasp of one's personal worth and identity, an awareness of one's control over the deepest directions of his loves and commitments, and a fairly profound spiritual perceptiveness. In other words, one must be able to give himself consciously, deeply and fully to God before it can make sense to say he can refuse to give himself to God in committing such a serious sin.

We are talking, then, about something which surely surpasses the moral capability of a normal 7 or 8-year-old. We do not allow even a 12-year-old to marry or to make religious vows. We know he or she is insufficiently developed both psychologically and spiritually for that kind of love or that kind of radical decision on the direction of his or her life.

This tells us much about the answer to your question. Since a child cannot reject (in a serious sin) a love and commitment he has not yet been able to make in the first place, something like the same development and age seems necessary before a person can commit a mortal sin. We are probably talking about somewhere in the middle or late teens or maybe later.

Naturally, one's understanding of mortal sin affects the answer, too. If we insist, for example, that a child can commit a mortal sin at the age of 12 or 14, with all of that age's mental, spiritual and psychological gropings, then it seems we are making mortal sin something considerably less than the catechism and good theology tells us it is. We also threaten to establish a child's whole religious relationship on a rather superficial basis, as if love and friendship with God were something that a person can pop in and out of several times a month.

Threaten with sin?

You have described earlier the conditions for a mortal sin. You said that the psychological requirements for mortal sin are normally probably not present until the middle or late teens and maybe even later than that.

Isn't this just encouraging children to sin?

Isn't a threat that they may sin the thing that often helps them act right? Don't you think if children learn this they would just use it as an out for doing something that is wrong?

If I understand your question correctly (and I'm afraid I do) it reflects an attitude toward sin and conscience that should be unthinkable, but which has been all too prevalent in much of our past religious education.

First, and most important, we have no right to lie to children to make them behave. Particularly we have no right to thus play God and say, in effect: "Even if they haven't committed a serious sin, it's better that they think they have. It will train them to do what is right."

This attitude is, or at least has been, not uncommon among some well-meaning religion teachers. It is, however, a gross injustice to both God and to the individual we're dealing with, and can do irreparable damage to a young person's understanding of his relationship with God.

Of course, if by some mental gymnastics a young person does reflect so fully and completely on the meaning of a serious sin that he consciously figures it is an "out" for him, it would be a good sign he knows what he is doing. The point I made in the previous answer was that until some considerable maturity is attained, a young person psychologically and spiritually cannot adequately comprehend the radical commitments and rejections involved in a mortal sin.

Different rites of penance

I am married, have two children and am 40 years old. My wife is not Catholic but she goes to church with us.

Several years ago a priest nearby had a communal penance service twice a year, before Easter and Christmas. The church was filled every time I went.

This priest has been gone for years and I know a number of people who have not been to confession since he left. As for me, I know there are things I must work on, but I don't feel the need for private confession.

A short time ago I took an adult religion class. Someone asked about the communal penance service and Father said it was not allowed.

This is a shame. As I said, at these services the church was overflowing each time. If this will get people to meditate and examine their consciences and get closer to God, we should not let this happen. Have you any reply?

The church today has three rites for celebrating the sacrament of reconciliation. First is the Rite for Reconciliation of Individual Penitents. This is the one-on-one "private" ritual similar to the one we are traditionally familiar with.

Second is the rite for reconciliation of a number of penitents with individual confession and absolution. This is the form of communal penance service perhaps most familiar to Catholics today. As the ritual for penance indicates, this form shows more clearly the social or ecclesial nature of penance. Everyone listens together to the word of God, examines the conformity of their lives with that word of God and supports one another by prayer together. One or more priests are present so that at some point during this service individual confession and absolution are available.

Third is the rite for reconciliation of a number of penitents with general (not individual) confession of sins and absolution given by the priest to all at one time.

Your letter is not clear about which rite you are speaking of. If it is the third with general absolution, your priest is correct. This form of penance is not allowed as a general rule; it may be used only in emergencies or other clearly defined circumstances.

The second form (worship together with opportunity for private confession) is, I believe, becoming more and more common and enjoys practically all the spiritual advantages of the third rite. Our experience where I am pastor and that of many other parishes is similar to yours; hundreds of people attend these ceremonies, obviously convinced that this method of expressing sinfulness and asking forgiveness fits their personal sense of sin and need for forgiveness and healing. It combines, so to speak, the best (at least most of the best) of both worlds, our need to express personally our sinfulness and desire for forgiveness, and on the other hand our need not only of God's pardon but of "reconciliation with our brothers and sisters who are always harmed by our sins" (Introduction to the Rite of Penance, n. 5).

Finally, I suggest that perhaps you are dismissing the value of individual confession (rite No. 1) too easily. This form has enormous and important spiritual advantages, especially when we realize that the Sacrament of Penance not only looks to forgiveness of the past. It looks particularly to the future, giving us grace to examine the direction of our lives and deal with the pride, selfishness, greed and other sources of sin deep inside us.

A regular and healthy celebration of this rite, along with communal penance services, does much to open our hearts to the healing and creative power of God's presence. (For more on rites for the Sacrament of Penance see page 451 and following.)

General and open confessions

What exactly are the "general and open confessions" some churches have today? Are they new? From what I've heard, I think they would be a wonderful and moving spiritual help if we could have them every month. How could we find out where these take place?

I believe you are speaking of what is more properly called a communal penance service. And it is becoming more popular all the time in many parts of the country.

Basically, a communal penance service is a simple ceremony shared by a group of people and consisting of Scripture readings, songs, prayers, reflections and perhaps a homily on some aspect of God's forgiving love and our conversion to him — and possibly, private confession of one's sins to a priest.

Such a service does not necessarily include personal confession and the Sacrament of Penance, but can be the setting in which that sacrament is received. Group penance ceremonies have become more popular recently with the growing realization that sin is not only a matter between oneself and God, but that it somehow affects the entire Christian family of which one is a part. The covenant between God and his people is in some manner injured when one does wrong, even when the wrong committed seems to be quite private. So it is most proper — in fact, necessary — that sorrow and forgiveness express the fact that one is reconciled not only to God but to one's fellow man and fellow Christians.

For centuries, Christians were much more aware of these "family" ties with other Christians than we are, so common penance services are not new. In fact, private confession as we know it was unheard of for hundreds of years after Jesus died, and only became a common thing in the church after perhaps 1,000 years.

So there's no misunderstanding, it should be noted that public announcement of one's hidden personal sins is not part of any penance ceremony.

Call the parishes in your area for time and places of communal penance services.

Why penance services?

Should we go to confession to gain sanctifying grace, which we were taught we gain from this sacrament, or does the penance service replace going to confession? Our catechism never mentioned penance services.

A communal penance service, which had fallen into disuse in the church long before our catechisms were written, is an increasingly popular rite. It is simply a ceremony in which a group of Catholics (or other Christians) confess their sinfulness before God and each other, reflect on the meaning of their sins with the help of Scripture and meditation, and ask forgiveness for any offenses committed against God and their fellow man.

From the catechism you mention, you will remember that prayer and contrition of this kind can forgive sins. However, this does not mean that such a service (without sacramental absolution) replaces the Sacrament of Penance, which is a very special way of meeting a forgiving God in a spirit of sorrow for our sins and a desire of reconciliation with him. Certain healing, forgiving and sanctifying graces are the fruit of this sacrament, which makes it different and unique among all penance rites.

The Sacrament of Penance is often, but not necessarily, included with the kinds of communal penance services you speak of.

Penance service and sacrament

One parish in our area announced that the communal penance service would "take care of" anyone who desires to receive the Sacrament of Penance. How do you explain that?

A communal penance service, the second method provided for in the Rite of Penance, usually includes the opportunity for private confession of one's sins for those who wish to do so, and private absolution. The other requirements for the Sacrament of Penance can easily be included in the "communal" part of the ceremony.

The announcement you quote probably indicated that the communal service would provide this opportunity.

Generic confession

While my mother and I were discussing the new confession rite, she told me that in her parish during a communal penitential rite people come up in groups, kneel down before the priest one at a time, and he gives them absolution. They do not mention their sins and the same penance is given to everyone.

I'm not saying this is completely wrong. But it could have

disadvantages as well. It gives people an "easy way out" of confessing serious sins if they do not have to tell the priest. It does bring people back to confession who maybe haven't gone in years. People are even coming from other towns to that church. Your thoughts on this will be appreciated.

Your letter brings up some interesting facts about the Sacrament of Penance which may be of increasing significance in communal penance services.

The kind of confession you mention is called a generic confession. The penitent simply says he has sinned without indicating the kind of sin or the number. Such a confession is perfectly legitimate at any time if one is not confessing serious, mortal sins, whether at a communal penance service or not.

This indication of having sinned and that one is sorry need not be made in words. It could be in action — such as your example of kneeling before the priest, which in the context of the penance service obviously means, "Father, I have sinned, and I am sorry." In at least one parish to my knowledge, each penitent who wishes to receive the Sacrament of Penance at a communal service comes and puts his or her hands in the hands of the priest, who then says the words of absolution for each individual.

This method of confessing has some obvious defects along with equally obvious and attractive advantages. Most of all, it limits drastically the helpful and healing interaction that should occur between the priest and penitent in the new Rite of Penance. But such generic confessions are perfectly legitimate any time venial sins are involved.

Generic confession of mortal sins is permissible only in a special emergency situation. These sins should be mentioned later when the first opportunity for private confession presents itself.

As long as these distinctions are somehow made clear, the practice you describe has much to recommend it. Obviously, a lot of people find something in it quite attractive.

Generic confession for me?

You said that a generic confession in which specific sins

were not mentioned should be made only in an emergency if serious (mortal) sins are involved. Many years ago a priest chaplain in a mental hospital where I was hospitalized told me that for the rest of my life, I should confess only by saying I am sorry for all my sins as God sees them, and that I should go to Communion whenever I go to Mass.

Do you think that advice still holds for me?

It surely does still hold for you. The response I gave concerning generic confession dealt with the regular norms for the Sacrament of Penance. Priests are trained, at least in the basics, to discern and help people to deal with special types of personal difficulties relating to this sacrament. The priest who gave you this advice surely did it on solid information he perceived in dealing with your problem. The best and right thing for you to do is to continue to follow that advice.

Denied absolution

What would you say to a mature man who was denied absolution by a priest 15 years ago unless he gave up masturbating and who has been away from the sacraments ever since?

I would say first of all that it is unfortunate and unnecessary that he has been away from the Sacraments of Penance and the Eucharist for so long. You don't say what his present situation is, but whatever it might be, the important and urgent task for him is to find a priest who is compassionate and who is willing to take the time to help him work through whatever problem may remain.

With good will and a desire to do what is right, the grace of the sacraments will help him toward the peace of soul and peace of mind that he is looking for. It will be worth the time and effort to find a priest he can talk to, and then trust the advice and assistance that priest will give.

Afraid of confession

I am married to a Catholic man and gradually have come to realize I would like very much to be a Catholic also.

My problem is that before I knew my husband I had an abortion. I realize this is against the teaching of the Catholic Church. If I become a Catholic, would I have to admit in confession that this is in my past? I hope I would not even have to bring it up.

Please do not let this fear deter you from entering the Catholic Church. Many factors will make this problem much smaller, in fact, than it may look to you right now.

First of all, only serious sins which the individual knew were serious sins at the time they were committed must be mentioned in confession. From your letter it would appear that you perhaps did not realize the enormity of the sin of abortion when you were younger.

In addition, as you learn more about the Catholic faith and specifically more about the Sacrament of Penance, I believe you will find that the fears which seem so huge right now will pretty much fade away. The options open to you about where you go to confession and to whom, the strictest kind of secrecy which binds every priest when he ministers this sacrament, and above all, the healing and forgiveness that comes to us from Jesus and his church, will in the end make things much easier than you could now imagine.

Can't remember my sins

It sure is hard to remember all your sins when you go to confession. When you can't remember them all, how do you tell them to your priest?
I am nine years old and in fourth grade.

First of all, I congratulate you on your interest in the Sacrament of Penance and your desire to receive that wonderful sacrament in the right way.

It is always important to remember something I'm sure you already know. This sacrament not only forgives sins, it strengthens us to live good Christian and Catholic lives. The grace which Jesus gives when we go to confession, therefore, helps us to remember and to want to direct our lives along the lines that Jesus tells us.

One consequence of this is that we should not bother

ourselves too much in trying to remember in detail all the sinful or partially sinful actions that we have done. With your attitude there are surely no serious sins in your life. It's more important that you aim at trying to grow in your trust in God, and your love, in a practical way for God and for those around you — your family, your friends, and, of course, yourself.

I mention these items only to emphasize that the first thing Our Lord wants from us is to be comfortable and happy in our meetings with his forgiving love in the Sacrament of Penance. Beyond that you need to read up on this and other elements of your faith. Your knowledge in these subjects should grow along with your knowledge of other things as you move toward adulthood.

Worrying about past confessions

I spend a lot of time worrying about past confessions, especially those I made as a child or a young teen. As a child my confessions weren't always honest but I did try to straighten things out when I was a teen-ager.

After years I recalled another sin much like the ones I had confessed and repented of. Is it necessary to go back to confession again? I really worked hard trying to clear the slate.

Isn't it strange and unfortunate that the sacrament of forgiveness which Our Lord obviously meant to be a source of peace and appreciation of his mercy turns out sometimes to be an occasion of worry and even fear?

The first and most important thing to remember about the Sacrament of Penance — in fact, about all our relationships with God — is that he looks into our heart and knows what is there. As a Father who loves us without limit, he in fact knows and accepts what is there usually far better than we do ourselves.

It is true that for a good confession we should mention any action of ours which we are sure was a mortal sin. However, God knows we are human; he does not expect us to be computerized data retrieval machines. Our memories slip and sometimes our motives look impossibly mixed-up as we try to evaluate what we have done wrong.

From your letter it seems clear to me that you are like many others who have similar concerns about previous confessions, espcially those that go back many years. I don't think there's any question that you have tried to be honest with your God in your confession and in your sorrow. You are trying to live a good faithful Christian and Catholic life. That is what God sees and that is what is important.

In other words, don't worry about what is past. When you receive the Sacrament of Penance, renew your sorrow for whatever wrongs you may have done in your life, and focus your attention and prayers on the present and the future — which is what this sacrament is all about.

Excused from confession?

Is it possible to be excused from confession if you are 75 years old? And with a speaking and hearing problem? The sin I have trouble with is against purity. I've been told everything by at least seven priests — from "If you waste the seed you are a murderer" to (in a very loud voice) "You do that when you're drunk."
I never married because I thought it was unfair for an alcoholic to marry. I know now that was a larger mistake than our New Orleans Superdome.

I think a major part of your problem is just too many priests. Priests may very legitimately deal with your problem differently, but it's important that you pick one you can talk to, trust him, and be at peace following the guidance he gives you. Drifting from one confessor to another usually brings nothing but more confusion.

As a non-resident of New Orleans (though I confess I have on occasion wished I were), I'm not about to involve myself in the Superdome controversy. I will say only that, whatever mistakes have been made, they are using it. Which is what you must do now with your life — use it! God willing, you have a good number of years ahead of you. I hope you find peace and enjoy them.

"Fifth Step" and confession

In one of your answers you discouraged writing out our sins for confession. Among other comments you suggested, it could be a symptom of or lead to scrupulosity.

Last fall I realized that I had an addiction and joined a 12-step program to help me live my life without the addiction. One of the tools they suggest is writing out my feelings and things I have done wrong; this for me brought a tremendous sense of freedom and helped to get rid of some guilt feelings.

The fifth step of the program involved sharing this information with someone else. In my opinion it would serve as a basis for a really significant reception of the sacrament of reconciliation. I chose to give my fifth step to a lay person, but still feel I may give it to a priest and ask forgiveness in the sacrament of penance. At no time did I feel scrupulous, though I admit it could be a problem with someone else. I just happen to feel strongly that writing is a great help in sorting out feelings, admitting wrongs and understanding myself better. Once that happens I feel I will become a more productive member of the body of Christ.

You make a good and strong point. While Alcoholics Anonymous was the first group to identify the "Twelve Steps," the process has proved effective equally in other types of addiction. The cautions I proposed concerning written confessions are valid generally but the circumstances you describe certainly could be a legitimate and important exception.

I have a number of times talked with individuals as they worked their way through the fourth step ("to make a searching and fearless moral inventory of oneself"), and then assisted them through the fifth step ("to admit to God, to ourselves and to another human being the exact nature of our wrongs"). Sometimes this was done in the context of the sacrament of penance; the occasion became a powerful spiritual sacramental experience for both of us.

I'm sure some people would protest that the sacrament of reconciliation should not become a personal psychological assessment or a therapy session. That is quite true. But neither is it properly a purely clinical recitation of sinful actions and prayer of absolution. The Introduction to the Sacrament of Penance in part proclaims exactly the opposite. In order to fulfill his ministry properly and faithfully, "the confessor should understand the disorders of souls and apply the appropriate remedies to them.

"Discernment of spirits is a deep knowledge of God's action in the hearts of men. It is a gift of the Spirit as well as the fruit of charity." It is one of the skills the confessor should bring to the sacrament. In receiving the repentant sinner and leading him to the light of the truth, a confessor "reveals the heart of the Father and shows the image of Christ the Good Shepherd" (No. 10).

The celebration of this sacrament is "always an act in which the church proclaims its faith, gives thanks to God for the freedom with which Christ has made us free and offers its life as a spiritual sacrifice in praise of God's glory" (No. 7). All this is simply another way of saying that the process of the fifth step frequently may constitute a perfect occasion for the sacrament of penance.

Psychosis about going to confession

For many years I have had a psychotic phobia about going to confession, along with several other phobias. I have undergone treatment for this but am still unable to receive this sacrament.

Several years ago I had an extramarital affair. I told my therapist about it but cannot speak of it to anyone else no matter how hard I try. Because of my inability to confess this to a priest I have stopped going to church. My therapist believes I am forgiven because of my disability.

Am I? I want so much to be a part of the church again but I don't know if I have been forgiven by telling another person. Can I receive Communion again?

We are obliged to confess any mortal sins in the Sacrament of Penance before receiving Communion unless it is just impossible to do so. There are different kinds of impossibility. One kind could be physical, for example, if no priest were available for confession during an unreasonably long period of time. Another could be one you appear to be experiencing. In your case the impossibility is not physical but emotional. I'm assuming, of course, that the information you give is accurate.

You apparently are confident that your therapist is aware of the spiritual seriousness for you of the Sacrament of Penance, and that you are satisfied in your own mind that you suffer from a disorder that goes beyond the usual "fear" of going to confession. (Few people get a large thrill out of telling their sins to someone else, in confession or not.) The type of phobic neurosis you claim to have is quite possible, especially given the usual context of the Sacrament of Penance.

If the above is true for you, as it appears to be, you would not be obliged to receive the Sacrament of Penance before Communion. "No one is obliged to do what is impossible," is a fundamental principle of moral theology.

This seems to apply to you, since it is emotionally impossible for you to do what is required to receive this sacrament. Express your sorrow to God as well and as honestly as you can, and get back to Mass and Communion. You've been away long enough.

Can foreigner go to confession?

A Catholic friend of mine is from a foreign country and does not speak English. She wants to go to Communion, but is hesitant because she cannot go to confession.

Is it all right for her to receive the Eucharist without confession, or what should she do?

Your friend's situation is not uncommon. Many people from foreign countries stay here for long visits with family, or take up residence permanently without being able to carry on a conversation in our language.

It is quite possible for an individual like this to receive the Sacrament of Penance. Confession of sins must be made in some way, but there are other ways than by speech when that is impossible. While specific details may not be expressed so easily in other manners, the penitents can, for example, indicate which obligations or commandments have been violated and by other signs express in some general way their sorrow for their sins and their acknowledgement of having done things for which they wish the forgiveness of God.

It is even possible if the penitent so wishes, for him or her to confess through an interpreter, as long as any abuse or scandal is avoided (CCL 990). In such an instance the interpreter would be seriously bound to secrecy about the confession.

Please help your friend to talk with a priest. Most priests have had experience with this kind of need and can arrange a comfortable and satisfactory way for her to receive the Sacrament of Penance.

Hearing problem in confession

I cannot hear well and have problems with confession. I never know what my penance is; I just leave and say what I always did for years, and add a few more prayers to be sure. I don't know if I'm doing the right thing or not. I only go to confession a few times a year on account of this, and it really upsets me.

It is useless to confide in my parish priest. I am hardly able to understand him when he is standing next to me. This applies to all the priests I go to, even when there are special hearing aids in the confessional. How can I get some help soon?

Priests are always willing to give special assistance to those who cannot hear well in the usual confessional arrangement. Today when face-to-face confessions are much more available, no one who can hear at all need be deprived of an opportunity to hear and be heard satisfactorily in the Sacrament of Penance.

In the meantime, continue your present practice about your penance. What you are doing is quite proper and sufficient.

Getting back to confession

Father, I suppose there are a lot of Catholics out there like me. I used to go to confession at least once a month. Now it's been years, and to tell the truth I miss it. One thing that keeps me away now is, where do I even start examining my conscience? I know there's no way I can remember even half of my sins.

You're right. There are a lot out there like you. It seems to me there are three simple things it would be helpful for you to think about.

It's not necessary, or even desirable, to try to list all sins. Only serious sins need to be confessed. If you're living anything like an honest decent life, as you seem to be, those sins, if there are any, will pop into your mind in a moment. You won't need hours of reflection.

Second, any sins you might forget are forgiven anyway in your general sorrow for all of them. If you feel you forgot something serious, don't worry about it. Mention it the next time you receive the Sacrament of Penance.

Last, and most important, God is not much interested in the past, or how thoroughly you have scraped your soul. He wants your heart, your commitment, your future, your love. All that you have. Please don't wait any longer.

Self-confession?

What is your opinion of self-confession? I have heard of some priests saying you can confess to yourself as long as you don't feel you've committed a mortal sin.

A priest I know tells us we are the ones to judge whether we are worthy of Communion or not — not someone else.

I've never heard the expression "self-confession." From the rest of your question, I assume you mean: Can we have sins forgiven without confessing them in the Sacrament of Penance? The answer to that is definitely yes. The church teaches that any sins which do not completely destroy our friendship with God and the basic direction of our lives toward him, in other words, sins which are not "mortal," can be forgiven many ways — by prayers of contrition, good works, penitential rites such as those at the beginning of Mass, Holy Communion, and so on.

Concerning your second point, the individual involved is the only one who can possibly make the final judgment about his own worthiness to receive the Eucharist in Communion. The Gospels and the teaching of the church should certainly be a major factor in the formation of our conscience and of our evaluation of our actions. But the Council of Trent simply reflected traditional Christian practice when it said that, to be worthy to receive Communion, one should not be *conscious*, or *aware*, of any unforgiven serious sin.

Birth control and Communion

Is birth control a sin that must be confessed before one can receive Communion, or can one receive, and confess it at the next confession?

One of the main requirements for receiving Holy Communion is that the individual not be aware of any unrepented serious offense against God, or in other words that he be in the "state of grace." This simply means that he be in a state of mind and soul that fits into what Holy Communion signifies — a closeness to God, a desire for a deeper union with him, and a willingness to accept God's healing for the effects of whatever wrong he has done.

This includes going to confession before Communion. But in fact a person returns to God's friendship after a serious sin before he actually confesses it — through a genuine Act of Contrition and a renewed acceptance of God's love which is offered to us when we turn back to him. Therefore, for a serious enough reason, one may receive Communion before confession after a mortal sin. The sin should be confessed, however, at the next opportunity.

A sin that might be committed in the category you mention is no different in this regard than any other deliberate refusal to obey what one sees as God's law.

Communion before confession

I blame the priests for much of our loss of morals. When you give the opinion that it is okay to go to Communion after a genuine Act of Contrition, and that one need not confess a sin against birth control until the next confession, there is something very wrong with the Catholic Church.

If you look again at the answer given, you will note it says that "for a serious enough reason" a Catholic may receive Communion before confession after a mortal sin. Apart from being traditional Catholic theology, this is also the official law of the Catholic Church concerning the reception of Holy Communion.

Canon 916 of the Code of Canon Law says that confession should precede Communion if someone is aware of having committed a grave sin unless there is a serious reason (what type of reason is not further spelled out) and there is no appropriate opportunity to go to confession. (The Latin is, "nisi adsit gravis ratio et deficiat opportunitas confitendi.") As indicated before, this implies true sorrow, "perfect contrition," for whatever sin was committed, and the intention of confessing the sin at the next opportunity.

If your point is that a mortal sin which might be committed in the area of birth control is so horrendous that it does not fall under these basic rules for any other serious sin, you would find it difficult to support your opinion. I do not agree with it.

Parents approved abortion

Father, I have a very big burden on my shoulders and I need help. A short time ago my husband and I agreed with our 15-year-old daughter when she had an abortion.

Father, she still sucks her thumb, and even now I don't think she realizes what we have done. I still think we did the right thing.

God says that sinners who are truly sorry will be forgiven, but the thought of going to confession scares me. Having our priest tell me I can no longer go to the sacraments is more than I can face. I am a convert, but my husband who was born a Catholic, feels this is what will happen. What should I do?

Your family obviously has suffered terribly with this experience, but the hope you are looking for is surely there if you will prayerfully follow a couple of suggestions.

First, try to be sincerely honest with yourself. What you did was very wrong. But considering the enormous pressures you were under, no one except God can possibly judge how guilty you may have been for what you did.

However, after writing three full pages defending yourself for doing the right thing, you conclude by saying how much you need God's forgiveness for your actions. You knew, for example, that loving institutions and people were available to help your daughter through the experience with much less trauma than could result from an abortion, if only you would let them.

This leads us to your first and most important step to hope and healing. When we sin at all seriously, it is generally impossible to unravel and analyze all the good, bad and doubtful motives that influenced us. In fact it is generally not even healthy to try to do so. Certainly God does not expect or want this.

We open our hearts to his forgiving love, as did the prodigal son, simply by humbly and trustingly acknowledging our sinfulness to him and telling him we are back.

As I said, this is the big part of the job. Once you do this, with the grace of God, 90 percent of your journey back is completed.

As for your other question, please don't stay away from the Sacrament of Penance any longer. Your husband is mistaken in what he expects the priest to say. Nothing will stand any more in the way of your receiving the Eucharist and the other sacraments.

Sacraments for criminals

Can a murderer, rapist, or a robber who is not Roman Catholic, be converted to Catholicism and receive all the sacraments after living a sinful life for 10 or 20 years?

No question about it: Of course he can. It is hard to believe that some Catholics or other Christians may be surprised at this considering the times Jesus insisted that he came "not to call the just, but to call the sinner to repentance."

If one has to be perfect, or sinless, to become or remain a Catholic, we are all in deep trouble. In fact, if we are to have the spirit of Christ, our best efforts at charity, patience, and acceptance should be directed to those who have (at least as far as our human eyes can see) the most to overcome, and who have the most difficult struggle to become what God is calling us to in this pilgrimage on earth.

No one of us has any right to act otherwise than Christ himself, who was overjoyed and went out of his way to lend a healing word when a sinner showed he was ready to try to find his way back. I suggest you reread chapter 15 of St. Luke's Gospel.

Anointing of the sick

I recently attended a church ceremony in which a friend of mine received what we used to call Extreme Unction. Several people received the sacrament, including some who were young and didn't look sick at all.

Isn't it necessary to be "in danger of death" to have this sacrament? And what is the proper name for it? I've heard it called several things.

This sacrament for the sick is one that has undergone significant development during the past 50 years. The Con stitution on the Liturgy of Vatican Council II recognized this development when it said, "Extreme Unction, which may more properly be called the Anointing of the Sick (its official name today), is a sacrament not only for those who are in danger of death."

Thus, the sacrament is for the sick, but by no means only for the dying. In a scriptural passage which forms one of the main bases for the Anointing of the Sick, St. James says: "Is anyone sick among you? Let him ask for the elders of the church. They will pray over him, and anoint him in the Name of the Lord." (James 5,14)

According to our new rite for Anointing of the Sick, then, an individual need not be in danger of death, but "dangerously ill" either from sickness or advanced age. In other words, older people are considered eligible for the sacrament simply because of the general infirmities of old age, even if they are suffering from no serious specific disease. Moreover, the illness need not be physical. Guidelines on this sacrament issued by the American bishops note, "Sickness is more than a medical phenomenon. Sickness is a crisis situation in the life of a Christian as regards his salvation, his life with Christ in the community of the church." Anointing of the Sick may be administered, then, to people suffering from various kinds of spiritual or emotional crises.

The official directions concerning this sacrament mention several specific circumstances in which people should be anointed — such as old age, before serious surgery, and sick children.

All this simply means that there could be many explanations for the situation you encountered. People no longer need to be dying, or even look sick, to receive the sacrament of the Anointing of the Sick.

Reasons for anointing

Recently a serious back problem forced me to have an extremely dangerous operation. It could have left me crippled for the rest of my life. I asked the chaplain in the hospital to give me the sacrament of the sick. It would have given me a great deal of comfort because I was very frightened.

The chaplain said he would not give it to me because it is given only in danger of death, and as long as I was in the state of grace I didn't need it. Could you explain this? It is not the way I understood this sacrament.

Nor do I understand the reason for his refusal.

The introduction to the church's "Rite of Anointing and Pastoral Care of the Sick" lists the following as among those who may and should receive the sacrament of the sick:

— those who are dangerously ill due to sickness or old age;

— those who have already been anointed but are now suffering from a different illness, or if the danger becomes more serious in the same illness;

— those who are to undergo surgery because of a serious illness (which seems to have been the case with you);

— old people who are weak from age, even if there is no dangerous illness present; and

— sick children, if they have sufficient use of reason to be comforted by this sacrament.

Can lay people administer anointing?

I understand that a lay person can baptize and administer last rites when a priest cannot be located.

If this is true, can you please explain the procedure to me so that I will be prepared in the future?

In emergency situations a lay person can administer the Sacrament of Baptism. When this occurs, the simplest elements of the rite are used. Water is poured over the person and the words are said, "I baptize you in the name of the Father and of the Son and of the Holy Spirit."

If by last rites you mean the sacrament of the Anointing of the Sick, only a priest can administer this sacrament. Obviously, however, any lay person may, and should, assist someone who is seriously injured, or ill and possibly dying, by helping the individual to pray with acts of faith and hope and love of God. This should be done, in fact, even when one is simply visiting another who is seriously ill. Sometimes hearing another person pray can be extremely consoling to a seriously sick person who does not have the physical or mental strength to accompany that prayer.

I'm happy you are trying to prepare yourself for this kind of opportunity.

Anointing and Viaticum

I appreciate your answer explaining the present understanding of the Anointing of the Sick.

A question was prompted by a priest's remark recently that this sacrament is not the sacrament of the dying. Does this mean that one who is dying should not receive this sacrament? I can hardly believe that. What did the priest mean?

One who is dying can and should most certainly receive the sacrament of the Anointing of the Sick. Such an individual needs all the spiritual and physical benefits this sacrament can give.

The priest might have meant two things. First, he perhaps was making the point that the sacrament of the Anointing of the Sick is not only for the dying, or those who are in danger of imminent death, as some formerly believed. As I explained, it is only necessary that the individual be "dangerously ill," even though there may be no real danger of death.

He might also have meant that the real sacrament of the dying is not the Anointing of the Sick, but rather the Eucharist, which is also perfectly correct. Christian tradition, in fact, gives a special name to Communion when it is received by the dying. We call it "Viaticum" — literally, something which is to be with us and help us "on the journey" through death into eternity.

We should, therefore, be certain that our friends or relatives have every opportunity to receive Communion whenever possible as they approach death.

The Sacrament of the Anointing of the Sick may be repeated if the individual recovers and then gets sick again or if, in the same illness, the danger becomes more serious. Under no circumstances, however, would this sacrament be administered every day.

Ecumenism

Does belief make a difference?

Since Vatican Council II we have heard reference to the "people of God" and talk about the Christian churches.

Does this refer to the various Christian denominations? And if it does, does it mean that we now believe that "one religious denomination is as good as another?"

The book of Revelation refers to the seven churches in Asia. Would this be considered the same as the present-day parishes or dioceses? Or is it in reference to the inclusion of Baptist, Presbyterian, and other Christian churches?

You're really asking three questions. First, in Vatican Council II and many times since then, documents of our church refer to other Christian denominations as "churches." By this is meant that they are, as is obvious, members of the family of believers in Jesus Christ and true Christian communities.

The second is too complicated to discuss in detail here. Very briefly, all Christian churches agree in many major areas of belief about Jesus, God, and his "church" on earth. Individual Christians must follow their consciences as they understand what God asks of them in their relationship to him.

However it is overly simple to jump to the conclusion that "one denomination is as good as another," since many denominations differ significantly in major points of doctrine. Catholics, for example, (along with Anglicans and most Lutherans, at least) believe in the real Presence of Jesus in the Eucharist. Other Christians may not believe this and we presume they are following the light of their own conscience in rejecting that belief.

However, it would be foolish and thoroughly irrational to hold that it really doesn't make any difference whether one believes it or not, or whether it is true or not. If Jesus is not present in the Eucharist as we believe, we are (even in good faith) believing that what is only bread is really God.

On the other hand, if Jesus is truly present in the Eucharist and there to be offered and received as the great sign and means of the unity of his people on earth, then those who reject that belief (again, even though in good faith) are missing one of the most beautiful elements of our Christian life on earth.

While there is, therefore, only one God and one Lord, we need to take care that tolerance and acceptance of others, particularly Christians, regardless of our difference of beliefs, do not turn into a position that "it doesn't make any difference what you believe as long as you believe something" — which, if God and religion have any rational meaning at all, is total nonsense.

Finally, the churches in the book of Revelation, which of course was written centuries before Protestant denominations began as we know them, did refer, as you suggest, to the local churches, akin to our present-day diocese or parish. In fact, by the time this book was written most local churches were apparently already under the responsibility of an "Episkopos" (overseer), as our dioceses are under the responsibility of a bishop.

Are only Catholics saved?

I am 14 years old, not Catholic, but I have two questions. First, I attend a Catholic church often, although my mother does not recommend it. I desperately want to receive Holy Communion. Is this possible?

Second, I read somewhere that you have to be Catholic to be saved. Is this true?

My response to your second question is easy. No, you do

not have to be Catholic to be saved. Your first question is more difficult and I can't possibly give you a final answer.

I don't want to encourage you to go against your mother's wishes or commands. She is, after all, primarily responsible for you and, I assume, cares for you very much. Her concerns undoubtedly reflect what she feels is best for you.

On the other hand, you are not an infant or a small child. You are approaching adulthood and are gradually assuming full reponsibility for your life and your decisions. If, then, you feel honestly attracted to something in the beliefs and worship of the Catholic Church, I feel you should at least do a little inquiring about it.

The details you give in your note are nowhere near enough for me to be more explicit than that. Perhaps you can talk with an adult Catholic friend, or arrange through one of your Catholic school friends to discuss your thinking with a priest.

You want to follow the leads of your own thoughts and conscience. But you don't want to hurt your parents. I am sure a kind friend or clergyman will be helpful in meeting both of those responsibilities.

I'll say a prayer that everything goes well for you.

Protests name "Roman Catholic"

Whenever I speak of the Catholic Church, a Protestant friend insists that I should identify myself as a "Roman Catholic" since there are other Catholic churches besides ours. Could you comment on why they should want to be identified as "Catholic?"

The use of the word "catholic" ("universal") to identify the Church of Jesus goes back to biblical times. Even today, Protestant communities use the Apostles' Creed in their worship, including the words: "I believe in . . . the holy catholic church." They obviously do not mean the Roman Catholic Church.

Regular attachment of the word "Roman" to the name began around the time of the Reformation, when many reform leaders resented the implication that they were not part of the "catholic" church. Even at that time, however, many Catholics — English Catholics in particular — who remained in union with Rome, didn't like the name "Roman" since it implied that they were somehow on the fringes, or coattails, of the "real" Catholic Church.

There is nothing derogatory, of course, as far as we are concerned about the name Roman Catholic, for several reasons. Obviously, the main reason is the fact that, while it may be only an accident of history, up to now the pope as spiritual head of the church has been identified as the man who is chosen as Bishop of Rome.

Roman Catholics, other Catholics

Is there a difference between a Catholic and a Roman Catholic? What is the meaning of the adjective "Roman"?

The word "catholic" means "universal." It was first applied to the Christians by St. Ignatius of Antioch around the year 100. We Roman Cathlics often tend to consider ourselves "the" Catholic Church of the world.

While we are the largest in numbers, however, there are numerous other Catholic churches, united with the bishop of Rome but distinct churches in themselves. There are the Melkite, for example, the Armenian, Maronite and Ukrainian Catholic churches, and many more. These churches, including the church of Rome, have their roots in the varying styles of liturgy and expressions of faith that developed in different centers of Christianity during its early centuries.

Such churches are not branches of the Roman Catholic Church. They are of equal dignity and rank with the Roman church and with each other. (See, for example, the Vatican II Decree on Eastern Churches, No. 3.) In this context, the designation Roman Catholic simply distinguishes our part of the universal church from other Catholic churches.

Non-Catholic label

Several times I have been told that people of other faiths don't like to be called non-Catholics — and shouldn't be. What can you call them, then? Sometimes its hard to know.

It does present a sticky situation occasionally (as it might if we were referred to as non-Protestants), and there's no easy answer.

Technically, in Catholic documents, the term non-Catholic usually refers to baptized Christians who are not Roman Catholics, though often the name is used for anyone not of our faith, including Hindus and Moslems.

The title "Protestant" would cover most of the Christians in our country who are not Roman Catholic. Large numbers of Anglican or Episcopalian communities, however, consider themselves more Catholic than Protestant, and do not wish to be called Protestant.

In general, I feel the title "non-Catholic" might have an unintentional disparaging ring to it today, but often a substitute isn't always easy to find.

World Council of Churches

I was told recently that the Catholic Church is about ready to join the World Council of Churches. This puzzles me greatly. How could our church become a member of a Protestant organization like this? Is this where ecumenism is leading us?

The World Council of Churches, founded in 1949, is a partnership "of churches which accept our Lord Jesus Christ as God and Savior." Its purpose is to promote Christian unity, and to aid cooperation among the churches in doctrinal research, relief and welfare programs, missionary activities and other common projects.

From the beginning, even though it numbered some Orthodox and Anglican groups among its members, the WCC was primarily Protestant-oriented, dealing mainly with problems that were considered to concern Protestant churches. During the 1960s, however, Pope Paul VI and WCC officials began a close working relationship, especially in areas involving social justice and peace, a relationship that continues under Pope John Paul II.

Consultants and observers from both groups work together, and apparently agree there is no theoretical reason the Roman Catholic Church should not join. The problem with Catholic membership is practical. Membership in the Catholic Church totals more than the entire membership of the churches presently part of the WCC. (In fact, more than half of all the Christians in the world are Catholics.)

A serious question is, therefore: How can a church of this size and scope share membership with the WCC without, in effect, dominating the whole organization? This is why Pope Paul said in 1969, during his visit to WCC headquarters in Geneva, that the time is not ready for a decision on the matter.

WCC leaders generally agree. Dr. Eugene Carson Blake, then secretary general of the organization, said at the time, "How does a church of approximately the size of the total fellowship of the World Council best cooperate with or have relationships with the World Council, which consists of 240 churches in 80 or 90 countries?"

By now, the WCC consists of nearly 300 churches, with 450 million members, in 100 countries.

Eventually it will be the Catholic Church's decision to ask to join. Until an answer to these practical questions is found, however, we'll have to be satisfied with continued informal, but close, collaboration.

Non-Catholics receive Communion?

I realize it is possible for people who are not Catholic to receive Communion in our church. But it seems different priests have different rules. What exactly is required of a person of another faith to participate in the Eucharist at a Catholic Mass? A Methodist couple I know received Communion at the marriage of their son at a Catholic Mass.

Catholic regulations require that five conditions be fulfilled for the administration of the Sacraments of the Eucharist, Penance, and the Anointing of the Sick to non-Catholic Christians. The persons involved must:

1. be in danger of death, or in urgent need (examples: during persecution or imprisonment),

2. be unable to have access to a minister of his own faith,

3. ask for these sacraments on his own initiative,

4. have faith in these sacraments in accord with the belief of the Catholic Church, and

5. be properly disposed — that is, he or she must be aware of no serious offense against God which would be contradictory to that union with him professed in the Eucharist. (Instruction of the Vatican Secretariat for promoting Christian Unity, June 1, 1972. See also CCL 844 nos. 3 and 4.)

However, the bishop of a diocese (or a national conference of bishops) may allow reception of Communion by non-Catholics in certain other "urgent necessities." I know of instances in which bishops have, for example, allowed non-Catholic parents to receive Communion at the marriage of their Catholic son or daughter, non-Catholic spouses to receive at the funeral of the Catholic husbands or wives, non-Catholic graduates to receive with their classmates at a baccalaureate Mass, and so on.

In all such cases, however, only the bishop has the right and responsibility to judge whether inter-Communion should take place. Of course, the conditions concerning faith in the sacraments and proper disposition must always be present.

You ask about Methodist parents receiving Communion at the marriage Mass of their son. From what I've already said, you can see that if the proper conditions were fulfilled and if permission of the bishop was obtained, neither the priest nor the couple did anything wrong. One would assume that the priest would have explained the situation to those parents and the family in order to avoid as far as possible any misunderstanding.

Behind the regulation allowing Communion under certain conditions is the recognition that, while full Christian unity is not present under these conditions, there is still present enough basic communion of faith in Jesus and in the Eucharist to justify sharing Communion when these requirements are fulfilled.

Priests differ on Communion?

Two years ago my daughter married a non-Catholic in the church. She did not want to receive Communion because her husband-to-be wasn't Catholic and most of the wedding party was Protestant. The priest told her they were all Christians, so they could all receive Communion.

How can this be? One priest says it is wrong and another priest says it is all right. How can two duly ordained priests differ so much on such an important rite?

I must say honestly, I don't know. If you have reflected accurately what happened and have not left out some important detail which might be unknown even to you, the priest who told them to receive Communion had no right to do so.

Whatever a priest's individual opinions may be, I believe Catholic people have a right to be guided by the official practices of the church. A priest may disagree with those regulations, and in important issues there is certainly ample room for dissent and protest. In a matter such as you experienced, however, it seems to me that lay people have a legitimate expectation that priests will direct them according to the teachings and rules of the church, not according to their own personal dissenting views — at least unless they make clear that the position they present is their own and not the church's.

Eucharist and "one faith"

I cannot understand how Holy Communion can be given to Protestants even in the special cases when the church says this is permitted. Isn't Communion supposed to be a sign of

unity? If we are not united, isn't it a sin to act as if we were?

This question particularly involves one of the conditions required before Protestants may receive Communion in the Catholic Church: that they "have a faith in the sacrament in conformity with that of the church."

There are many different levels and degrees of Christian unity. I'm sure, for example, that you disagree on some very important religious attitudes with many people you are at the Communion table with each week. Yet you would probably say that you agree on the "basics."

What are these basic Christian beliefs? Certainly the most fundamental are a belief in God the Creator and in his redeeming love for mankind; in Jesus, the incarnate Son of God, as our Savior and Lord; that by his death, resurrection, and glorification with the Heavenly Father, Jesus has united us with himself and with each other in a way that transcends all hope and power without him; that we are reborn into this eternal life with him through baptism; that we celebrate and keep alive this redemptive act of Jesus by offering and eating the Eucharist as he commanded at the Last Supper; that in this Eucharist it is truly himself — his body and blood — that is our offering and our food; and that we are destined through faith, hope, and mutual love to be together with Christ, our brother, in eternal life.

All Protestants hold most of these truths as sacredly as we do and many Protestants believe *all* of them as explicitly and as sincerely as we do. Surely it is quite an array of awesome doctrines to be united about.

There are other considerable beliefs which divide us, mainly in the area of church structure: the nature of the ministerial order, the role of the spiritual head of the church in the person of the Roman Pontiff, other sacraments, and so on. While acknowledging these differences, the Vatican Council and the Holy Father have insisted that it is equally important to acknowledge in word and action, wherever possible, the much greater elements which unite us as all truly "brothers and sisters in Christ."

We must keep in mind that the Eucharist relates in a special way to the Mystery of the Church and is the sacramental sign par excellence of visible unity. Even here the church says we must acknowledge our common faith, especially if that faith includes similar beliefs concerning the Eucharist, and if the other prescribed conditions for inter-Communion are present.

Communion to non-Catholics

I know you have answered questions previously about non-Catholics receiving Communion at Mass, but something bothers me. Why do groups such as Teens Encounter Christ, Cursillo and Marriage Encounter openly allow non-Catholics to receive Communion almost to the point of encouraging them to do so? Why do our pastors and bishops support these groups while they are in open defiance of the church rules on this point?

I include this question only because I have heard such allegations more than once during the past several years. I have looked into them carefully in my own diocese and others. To my knowledge, whatever may have happened in earlier years with some of these groups, none of them hold the positions you suggest.

It is clearly impossible for directors of any programs as large as the ones you mention to be aware of, or control, what all participants do all the time. I do know, however, that most (perhaps all) Cursillo organizations are aware of the problem and attempt to include in the weekend a careful explanation of why non-Catholics who may be making the Cursillo should not receive Communion at Mass. At least I know of no area which encourages the practice or deliberately approves it by silence.

You surely realize that when individuals present themselves to the priest at Communion time, the priest cannot at that point start checking their credentials. So you may well have seen Protestants going to Communion.

It may be — and I know this to be true in some instances — that under the inspiration of the deep Christian experience they share with others during a retreat, for example, and realizing the special place of the Eucharist in symbolizing the bond that exists among Christians, a non-Catholic has received

Communion during Mass. He can hardly be blamed for this "misunderstanding" let alone be condemned for it. If possible, the priest might attempt to explain the matter to him later.

The fact that this kind of action occurs, therefore, does not automatically imply "defiance of church rules." On the part of all concerned it may be simply a question of trying to exercise basic Christian charity and understanding in dealing with the embarrassing division in the family of Christ, a division that sadly separates us even at the table of unity.

Anglican-Catholic Communion?

My elderly Episcopalian friend has not been to church in years. She would like to come to Mass with me if she could receive Communion. I feel this would be perfectly marvelous. Could she do that?

The Catholic Church's policy on interfaith Communion indicates that there may be situations of "urgent necessity" in which a Christian of another faith cannot approach his or her own clergyman for Communion without considerable trouble or expense. It is the bishop's role to decide whether he or she might receive the Eucharist in a Catholic church.

Perhaps you could encourage your friend to go to her own church, and even offer to go with her. If you discover that she finds it personally extremely difficult or impossible to take that route, there is nothing wrong with taking the matter to the bishop and asking his approval. That is precisely what the church urges you to do if you think you can be helpful to another's spiritual life this way.

It would be wise not to make any even tentative commitments until you know for sure.

Can I receive Communion?

I had a great loss in my life last May. My son, who was in college in Los Angeles, was killed playing basketball.

I am a Baptist, but I attend Mass regularly at the parish church near us. All of my young children are Catholics, as was my son who died. He tried so hard to get an education

and to serve God; he also tried to help as many children in our family as possible to attend church and school.

My husband has started to go to Mass with me every Sunday and I'm grateful to God he has made up his mind to do that. My question is: To take Communion at Mass, do you have to be of the Catholic faith? I would really like to go. My heart is heavy and even though I read the Bible, I still don't understand everything.

I am deeply sorry for the hurt you are suffering because of the death of your son. From your letter, it seems that his death was an unusual loss to all your family.

Through your frequent participation at Mass with your husband and children, you have obviously come to recognize to some degree why Communion holds such an important place in the hearts of Catholics. It is the main way in which we, in our worship, unite ourselves to the death and resurrection of Our Lord, which we offer again to the Heavenly Father in every celebration of the Eucharist.

Because of your family's situation and the Catholic practices you already observe, I am prompted to ask: Could you consider becoming a full member of the Catholic faith?

It is true that except for emergency situations only people of the Catholic faith should receive Communion at Mass. I have already discussed these reasons in previous pages.

For now, I would suggest you go to one of the priests you know and honestly talk your situation over with him, if you have not done so already. I am sure you would like to participate and share in the Mass as intimately as possible; he will help you do that.

Communion at funeral

A dear friend and I attended the funeral of another friend in the Catholic Church. My friend is a Lutheran and is very devoted to her church.

At Communion time, this lady went up to receive and the priest gave her Holy Communion. How could she receive in our Catholic Church if she is not a Catholic? I didn't want to question her about it for fear of hurting her feelings.

According to our Catholic teaching and understanding of the meaning of the Eucharist, unless special conditions were present she should not, of course, have received Communion. In fact, many Lutherans are equally strong in their restrictions about their members' reception of Communion in other churches, or about people of other faiths receiving Communion in the Lutheran Church.

Your friend surely did what she did in a true spirit of friendship, reverence and Christian faith. Since the situation is not likely to be repeated and since there seems little chance of misunderstanding by others, I believe you acted prudently in not attempting to correct her.

The priest, of course, had no way of knowing she is not a Catholic. Priests usually must assume that anyone who approaches for Holy Communion is a practicing Catholic.

The Black Rubric

A recent article on the statement by Anglican and Roman Catholic theologians concerning the Holy Eucharist referred to a problem about the Anglican "Black Rubric." What is this Black Rubric?

The Black Rubric is a name sometimes given to a sentence that appeared a long time ago in the Anglican Book of Common Prayer. It held that the practice of kneeling to receive Holy Communion indicated simply reverence and humility, not adoration of the consecrated bread and wine.

This "rubric" was included in the Book of Common Prayer in 1551 by the English Council of State (at that time under extreme anti-Roman Protestant influence) over the protest of the Anglican bishops.

The Black Rubric contradicts official present belief of the Anglican Church concerning the Eucharist. The joint statement to which you probably refer and which was agreed upon by the Anglican and Roman Catholic theologians who had been assigned by their churches to study the Eucharist together, declares that this sacrament "presupposes his (Christ's) true presence, effectually signified by the bread and wine which, in this mystery, become his body and blood."

Communion in a Protestant church

**Your answers concerning the conditions under which a Pro-
testant may receive Communion in a Catholic church are
helpful.**

**How about the other way around? May Catholics now
receive Communion during a worship service in a Protestant
church? If so, do you think they should?**

You may recall that one of the requirements for a Protestant to receive Communion with Catholics, even in the most
urgent situations, is that his faith in the Eucharist (regarding
the true presence of Jesus) must be in harmony with that of
our church. This is because the Eucharistic Sacrifice and sacrament celebrate and signify the oneness of faith of those who
share it.

This same principle answers your new question. Naturally
every ceremony commemorating the Lord's Supper, even in
a Protestant church, has some similarities to our own
Eucharist. All Christian churches at least believe that eating
the bread and drinking the wine is a special way of recalling
the death of Jesus and uniting us to him in faith.

It is our belief as Catholics, however, that the fullest
Eucharistic Celebration — that is, the one in which there is
the true transformation of the wine and bread into the body
and blood of Christ — is possible only when that liturgy is
presided over by a validly ordained priest. This (along with
other differences in faith and doctrine which are relevant
here) means that there will be significant variations of belief
between Catholics and the official positions of most Protestant churches about what is happening at a Eucharistic
Liturgy, and what the Eucharist is.

Thus, a Catholic may not ask for the sacraments, especially the Eucharist, Penance and the Anointing of the Sick except from a minister who has been validly ordained. (Directory
Concerning Ecumenical Matters of the Secretariat for Promoting Christian Unity, May 14, 1967, no. 55. See also CCL
844, no 2.)

It should be noted that such a policy is also a matter of
courtesy and respect for the beliefs of those churches whose
regulations are similar to our own.

Are Protestants heretics?

Why don't we hear the word "heretic" any more? With so many crazy teachings today, I think it's a sign of how far we've come in not knowing what we believe. Our catechism called Protestants heretics. Aren't they any more — or what is the reason?

Also, why all the Protestant hymns at Mass? I once asked a priest years ago why we couldn't sing "A Mighty Fortress is Our God"and he said it was because it was written by a heretic.

First let's clear up that word "heretic." With all respect to your memory, I don't believe any catechism ever called all Protestants heretics. A heretic, by traditional definition of the church, is one who knowingly and obstinately denies some doctrine that he knows is revealed by God, and which is proposed as an article of Catholic faith by the church. Obviously, if you consider that definition carefully, it does not apply to sincere Protestants. In fact, there might be serious question whether, at least today, it applies to anybody.

You ask why the word isn't used much anymore. Beyond the reason just given, I believe the church (which means all of us) realizes these days that this kind of labeling and name-calling accomplishes little toward the cause of truth or charity. In the earliest years of the Protestant revolt from the Catholic faith, there may have been some justification for this either-or drawing of lines. The situation then was different from now in numerous ways.

Protestants and Catholics clearly still differ on certain significant beliefs, generally dealing with the Eucharist and the structure of the church as an institution. These differences may not be ignored or shrugged off. However, both of these groups of Christians finally seem more ready to acknowledge that substantial points of doctrinal agreement between them are more numerous, and just as significant, as points of disagreement. The feeling seems to be, among the leaders and members of the churches involved, that when our larger "enemies" are the common enemies of all Christians, it is of small value to attempt to pinpoint heretics.

As for your other question, what makes a hymn Protestant anyway? If the words are doctrinally and spiritually suitable, and if its music is of appropriate quality (which may be debatable), a song may be used in our worship no matter who wrote it or who used it first.

A Protestant view

I would like to ask prayers for people who call us Protestants heretics. I was born, baptized and raised by strict Methodist parents. We lived by the Ten Commandments and were taught when we got married it was for better or worse until death.

If we hurt or did wrong to someone, we had to go to that person and say we were sorry and make amends.

Six years ago I married into a Catholic family; there are now six grown children. My husband goes to Mass every Sunday and makes his tithe, which he never did before. I go right along with them.

Every time I just about have my mind made up to convert, something like this — hearing that some people consider Protestants heretics — comes up, and it makes my heart sick to think there are such narrow-minded people.

You said it better than I could. Some of us Christians still carry a remnant of the days when a large part of a Protestant's religious identity (at least in my experience) was that he was not Catholic.

Happily we've come to have much more positive ways of identifying ourselves as Christians, Catholic or Protestant. And so we've come to acknowledge openly and often with some surprise how much faith we do have in common.

Don't let such remarks keep you from doing what you think you should. Often questions or statements such as you have heard are just as much a search for an answer as they are a statement of position.

Happy interfaith marriages?

I recently broke an engagement because of religious differences.

My parents were of two different faiths and we children were raised in both churches. I remember the confusion of it all. After I grew up, I chose to go only to the Catholic church. Shortly before we were to be married, my fiance began pressuring me to drop my formal religion and indicated that he would like to return to his former teachings of the Baptist Church. I refused.

After the break, his brother said they were both taught that all Catholics went to hell. He also said his brother wasn't very stable in his religion and was frightened by the possibility of loving someone who may never be "saved."

I guess I want to know if Protestants, especially Baptists, could ever make it in a marriage to a Catholic. Are there differences that would make a miserable marriage?

As you probably do also, I have dozens of friends and co-workers who are in happy interfaith marriages. To my knowledge, however, not one of them would deny that differences in religion place tensions and strains in a marriage that are normally not present when both partners are of the same religion. It is not unusual for these strains to be more than the husband and wife can handle.

Obviously, much depends on the nature and extent of the difference of faith and the degree of conviction with which each party adheres to that faith. It is not possible to draw general conclusions beyond stressing the absolute necessity for the prospective husband and wife to discuss thoroughly and honestly all the aspects of differences in faith that will affect their marriage and their role as parents, and to do this before making any solid plans or commitment to a marriage.

Younger or inexperienced people tend to underestimate the influence of their spiritual backgrounds on their deepest (often unrecognized) desires for themselves, their spouses and their families. If their parents have passed on to them any kind of religious culture at all, then their understanding of God and how he relates to us and we to him, the ways we encounter Jesus and commit ourselves to him and to his people, the place of the church and its caring love for us in our lives, and even whether any of these elements of faith are seriously important or not — all these determine what a prospective spouse expects to give and to receive during the marriage. To ignore these realities and these expectations can be disastrous whatever the difference in religious faith.

Obviously, these differences may occur just as significantly between Protestants of different faiths as between a Catholic and a Protestant. One must admit, particularly today, that even two baptized Catholics may be so at variance in their understanding and practice of their faith that their union might also need to be approached, for all practical purposes, as an interfaith marriage.

To answer your question then, people of differing faiths can have a successful marriage, but only on the condition that their convictions are strong, that the demands of their consciences are clearly known to each other, and that they have each assured themselves that they will be able to pursue a good normal married life without either of them betraying their hopes or their beliefs.

This may sound like a fairly heavy task, but today more than ever such prayerful reflection and honesty is essential to a rich married life.

If you meet someone else and marriage appears as even a remote possibility, please don't wait until you're engaged to begin this kind of discussion. Good luck.

Mass at interfaith marriage?

My fiance and I will be married in November. I am Catholic, and he has no denomination but he attends Mass with me regularly and loves the Catholic Church. We have begun our pre-nuptial instructions. The priest told us that since my fiance is not Catholic, we could not have a Mass.

We are both disappointed about this, but will accept it. However, several people, including a nun, told me that it simply isn't that way anymore, that it had changed with Vatican II. What is the rule now?

Some things obviously have changed since Vatican II, and nuptial Masses are now sometimes allowed at the wedding of a Catholic and non-Catholic.

By no means, however, is a Mass automatically possible at every interfaith marriage. Two major conditions are required.

First the non-Catholic should be a baptized Christian. Normally, only a Christian would understand and believe in the religious significance of the Lord's Supper, and therefore appreciate in some proper way its reenactment in our Eucharistic Celebration.

Second, both partners must desire and freely request that their marriage be celebrated within the Mass. The intent here, of course, is to be sure that the sensibilities of the non-Catholic and his family are honored, and that both partners see the ceremony as a commitment to God and each other in the Sacrament of Marriage. (See *Rite of Marriage*, Introduction, no. 8)

Both requirements also aim at eliminating any use of the Mass as simply a social adornment making the marriage ceremony more ostentatious.

Decisions on this matter should be reached in consultation with the priest performing the wedding, who ultimately is responsible for assuring that all requirements are fulfilled.

Anglican and Roman priests

We have many friends in our community who are members of the Anglican Church. While we go to each others' churches sometimes, we realize we are not supposed to receive communion in these other churches since there is a problem about the recognition of the Anglican priests.

With all the changes in the church, has there been, or will there be, any change in this matter?

The story of the Roman Catholic Church's concern about the Anglican orders (which is the center of your concern) is a long and complicated one. But these are at least the highlights.

The primary official document of the Roman Catholic Church on the subject is a decree, "Apostolicae Curae," of Sept. 18, 1896, in which Pope Leo XIII declared that the defects in the ordination of Anglican bishops and priests are so critical that Anglican orders must be judged invalid.

Very simply, the Holy Father gave two reasons for this judgment. The first was a presumed disagreement about the nature of the Eucharist, especially the relationship of the sacrifice of the Mass to the sacrifice of Christ on Calvary.

The second was an apparent difference of belief about the origin of the order of bishops and priests. Pope Leo had concluded that there was a serious divergence between the Anglican belief and the Roman Catholic position — which is that the commission of bishops and priests derives from the same commission which Jesus gave to his apostles.

Since Vatican Council II, Roman Catholic and Anglican scholars have devoted years to a restudy of these differences, and have found that these differences are perhaps not nearly as great as they seemed at the time of Pope Leo. The Anglican-Roman Catholic International Commission, appointed by Pope Paul VI and the Archbishop of Canterbury, concluded a few years ago that the judgment of Pope Leo XIII should be put "in a new context" for the church today.

It is impossible here to enter into more details about these agreements, but they are expressed in two documents which you can obtain, each treating one of the major differences that I mentioned above. They are titled, "The Agreed Statement on Ministry and Ordination," and "The Agreed Statement on Eucharistic Doctrine." (USCC Publications, 1312 Massachusetts Avenue, N.W, Washington, D.C, 20005.)

Officially the matter is still being weighed. There is no change at this time in the position of the Roman Catholic Church regarding Anglican orders.

Using Catholic churches

Is it permissible for a priest to allow non-Catholics to use a Catholic church for religious services? A parish church was used in our city for several months by Protestants while they were building a new church. I think it's a good idea, but I'm sure surprised and wonder if this is officially allowed.

Normally Catholic churches are definitely reserved for Catholic worship for reasons which should be obvious. It is a building consecrated to the celebration of the sacraments and other most sacred rites of our faith. In addition, the exclusive use of the church for these ceremonies has a teaching purpose: It reminds us of the holiness and special character of what we do and profess there.

However, under certain circumstances it is and always has been allowed to use the church for other appropriate purposes, sometimes even artistic performances. More recently the use of such buildings for other religious ceremonies has been approve much more than in the past.

Present regulations specifically provide that bishops may allow the use of a Catholic church or other buildings by Protestants if they have no place in which to carry out their religious rites properly. The practice now is quite common. The response to the following question provides more background on this policy.

Protestant use of Catholic church

Our Catholic newspaper recenty informed us that a bishop in another diocese had allowed the use of his cathedral church for the consecration of an Episcopalian bishop. This astonished me.

I realize it is a good gesture on the part of the Catholic bishop to create good will and understanding and that in time to come we may all be one in the eyes of God. But, for now, today? How does even a bishop have a right to do something like this?

For those who grew up in what is still quaintly called the "old church," the consecration of an Episcopal bishop in a Roman Catholic cathedral appears strange, to put it at its mildest.

Any Christian who was raised in the Catholic versus Protestant atmosphere that lasted nearly 400 years (and which ended officially only around the time of Vatican Council II) needs to do a lot of serious thinking to understand what the Catholic Church and others are doing today.

For now it is sufficient to admit that on all sides this opposition was fed by much uncharitableness and even much untruth about each other.

Whatever may have been in the past, all Christians, thank God, are taking a new look at the prayer and wish of Jesus that his followers be one and that they be identified by their love for each other.

The Catholic bishop in this case (the late Bishop Joseph A. McNicholas of Springfield, Ill.) acted quite in accord with present regulations of our church, which are made in the spirit of love and reconciliation.

The Ecumenical Directory states explicitly: "If the separated brethren have no place in which to carry out religious rites properly and with dignity, the local ordinary may allow them the use of a Catholic building, cemetery or church." (Directory for Ecumenical Activities, Vatican Secretariat for Christian Unity, May 14, 1967, No. 61.)

Later explanations of this regulation point out that initiatives in sharing these kinds of facilities can be undertaken only with the authority of the bishop of the diocese. It is impossible for any such regulations to be specific to cover all cases. The bishop must make his decision in response to a local need or an emergency.

Again, in all such activities and cooperation, the Catholic Church is attempting to do everything possible to follow the guidance of the Holy Spirit in bringing about eventual Christian unity. It's worth quoting the foundation laid down in the Ecumenical Directory for this kind of cooperation:

"Fraternal charity in the relations of daily life is not enough to foster the restoration of unity among all Christians. It is right and proper that there should also be allowed a certain sharing of spiritual activity and resources — that is, Christians should be able to share that spiritual heritage they have in common in a manner and to a degree permissible and appropriate in their present divided state.

"Some, even very many, of those elements and endowments which together build up and give life to the church herself can exist outside the visible boundaries of the Catholic Church. These elements, which come from Christ and lead to him, rightly belong to the one church of Christ; they can contribute appropriately to our petitions for the grace of unity; they can manifest and strengthen the bonds which still bind Catholics to their separated brethren."

Incidentally, the event you ask about is not a first. In the 1960s, an American archbishop permitted the ordination of an Anglican bishop in the Roman Catholic cathedral because the Anglican cathedral was too small. The archbishop attended the ceremony.

Joining the YMCA

Is it permissible for a Catholic to join the YMCA? I am nearing retirement and am considering taking out a membership, mainly for use of the swimming pool. I remember some opposition to the YMCA many years ago. What is the present position?

Membership in the YMCA was formerly discouraged for Catholics because such membership was much more closely identified with the religious aspects of that organization than it is today. The organization was, of course, founded by a group of Protestant men for religious as well as recreational purposes. Members are encouraged and sometimes expected to share in the Protestant religious activities and worship provided by the YMCA.

In few places, to my knowledge, is this still true of YMCA centers. Under these conditions, many American Catholics, including many priests, hold membership in the YMCA.

Can Catholics join the Rotary Club?

I have found your answers on the Catholic Church and the Masons very enlightening and helpful. What can you tell us about the Odd Fellows? My husband has been invited, and we want to do the right thing.

We also have heard that the church once prohibited membership in the Rotary Club. Is this correct?

The Independent Order of Odd Fellows was one of several organizations — the Knights of Pythias was another — established in the last century, modeled more or less on Freemasonry, but aimed at the working classes. Dues were less, and membership and activities were less restricted and regimented.

While strictly speaking it may be a "secret society," membership in the Odd Fellows has never been, even in the past, as stringently forbidden as membership in Freemasonry itself.

Rotary was founded in Chicago in 1905 to promote a spirit of friendliness, service and honesty among businessmen.

Rotary organizations, of course, have always tried to follow that spirit. Thousands of cities in the United States and numerous foreign countries are proud to have a Rotary club as part of their community life.

In 1929, for reasons never officially given, the Vatican's Sacred Consistorial Congregation declared that priests and bishops should not be members of Rotary. At the time, the apostolic delegate in the United States explained that the ruling did not apply to the United States.

Twenty-one years later, however, on Dec. 20, 1950, the Congregation of the Holy Office reiterated and expanded the ban. Not only were priests forbidden to join; Catholic laymen were warned against affiliating with any Rotary International group.

Again, no reasons were given for these actions. When the 1950 decree was issued, many American priests and bishops held active and influential positions in Rotary. Some were founding members of Rotary clubs.

Certain unofficial explanations were offered in the Vatican newspaper — Rotary was Masonic, "naturalistic" and anti-Catholic — all of which were vigorously proven erroneous by Catholic and other Rotarians. Most likely, Rome's actions against Rotary resulted largely from a book by an Irish priest, Father E. Cahill, S.J., identifying Rotary International (along with the Boy Scouts, Girl Scouts and the Salvation Army, among others) as a form of "White Masonry," secretly controlled by and promoting Freemasonry.

While no official reversal has been forthcoming, the church today clearly has no desire to forbid or discourage membership in Rotary. In 1965, in an address to Rotarians, Pope Paul VI alluded to "possible problems" in the past, but praised the wisdom and ideals which characterize Rotary International.

Once again, many priests and bishops, as well, of course, as thousands of Catholic laymen, share in those activities.

It may be helpful to note, finally, that the church's Code of Canon Law mentions no forbidden organizations explicitly. It simply prohibits membership in an "organization which plots against the church" (Canon 1374), though regulations about membership in Masonic organizations have been dealt with in other official church documents.

Protestant monks and Sisters?

Are there any Protestant groups of Sisters or monks in existence today? I have heard there are, and that they are getting along better than Catholic Sisters. Is this true?

Around the time of the Reformation, monasteries and convents were outlawed in most Protestant areas, especially in England. A few, however, lasted up to the present, though their membership is small.

During the last century, a major revival of the religious life developed in England, with many Anglican-Episcopalian orders of men and women being formed in Europe and the United States. Numerous such communities still flourish.

Since World War II, a remarkable increase of interest and reappraisal of the importance of religious community life for both men and women has occurred in Europe and, on a smaller scale, in this country. Dozens of orders and brotherhoods have been founded by the Lutheran and Reformed churches alone. Nearly all place heavy emphasis on spiritual renewal and the contemplative life. Many have contributed enormously to the ecumenical and liturgical renewals of the past generation.

Catholic officials, including the pope and monastic scholars, acknowledge often how much Catholic spirituality today owes to some of these Protestant orders, especially in understanding the role of religious communities.

Since most Protestant communities are newer and smaller, they frequently can avoid much of the turmoil from which larger, well-known Catholic orders are suffering. All communities, however, both Catholic and Protestant, feel the pinch of the times, admit they have much to learn from each other, and agree that arguments about which is "getting along better" are presumptuous and futile.

Joining non-Catholic ceremonies

We know that the church has changed a lot in matters pertaining to Catholics and Protestants. What are the rules about

the extent we can participate as Catholics in ceremonies of other faiths?

Prayer services involving Catholics and Protestants are fortunately more and more frequent today. These services focus on common interests such as peace, Christian unity, social problems, and similar concerns. In this type of ceremony, Catholics are not only permitted but encouraged to share, whether in a Catholic or Protestant church or other location.

Catholics may also attend official liturgical ceremonies of another faith, on occasion, for any good reason — friendship or relationship with a member of that congregation, duties of public office, or even out of a simple desire to be better informed. "Official" ceremonies are those carried out according to the proper books and rites by the minister — such as the usual Sunday worship, the rite of the Lord's Supper, and so on.

However, participation in (receiving) the sacraments of another church, such as baptism or the Eucharist, is generally not permitted. Theologians of most churches agree with the Catholic position on this matter since Vatican II: "Celebration of the sacraments is an action of the celebrating community, carried out within that community, signifying the oneness of faith, worship and life of the community." (Directory of the Secretariat for Promoting Christian Unity, 1967)

"Catholic" in Apostles' Creed

During a funeral I attended in a Protestant church, the whole congregation prayed the Apostles' Creed just as we say it — including "I believe in the Holy Catholic Church." This surprised me very much. They're not Catholics, so why do they say that?

The word "catholic" (Greek: catholikos) means universal or general. At least by about the year 100, the Christian community was already sometimes referred to as the Catholic Church, meaning that it was for all men, not just for certain classes or certain places.

The Apostles' Creed did not, as was once believed, derive from the apostles themselves. It went through a few minor changes even after its first use, in about the form we have it, around the year 200. So it's not strange that it should include the phrase "Catholic church."

When Protestants use this creed, they mean the words in their stricter original meaning, not in reference to the Roman Catholic Church.

Hanukkah and Christmas

During the past few years around Christmas time, there's been a lot in the papers and on television about the Feast of Hanukkah. Is there any connection between the two feasts?

The eight-day festival of Hanukkah (often called the Festival of Lights) is a commemoration of a joyous event in Jewish history, the rededication of the temple in Jerusalem about 165 B.C. This rededication, described in the Book of Maccabees, followed a period of religious repression and is therefore a particular celebration of religious freedom.

Hanukkah, unlike other major Jewish feasts, is a family affair, celebrated for the most part in the homes rather than in the temples or synagogues. An additional candle is lit on each of the eight days, symbolizing the growth of holiness that should occur during the feast, and gifts are usually exchanged — in some homes on each of the eight days, which, I suppose, gives the Jewish children some kind of an edge over Christians.

The theme and use of light is also very prominent, of course, in the customs and liturgy of Advent and Christmas. Apart from the religious symbolism, however, and the fact that they both occur about the same time of the year, there seems to be no connection between the two celebrations.

Ecumenism and women's ordination

Some years ago the Anglican Church Board approved the ordination of women to the priesthood. This surprised me. I have been interested for a long time in the ecumenical movement and this should set it back a hundred years. Why did they decide to allow this now? Do you think it ends hope for the reunion of the Anglican and Roman Catholic Churches?

No, I certainly do not think it ends the hope of reunion between our two churches. But a couple of assumptions behind your question are, perhaps, more important than the questions themselves.

First, while the reunion of Christians should be a fervent prayer and goal of us all, our first responsibility, in whatever church we are, is to be as faithful as we can be to the traditions and inspirations of the Holy Spirit as we find them in our own particular community. Christian unity, in whatever form it gradually comes about, will be the work of the Spirit, not of our human ingenuity and compromise.

Those most deeply involved and experienced in ecumenical labors have long since learned this truth. Fidelity to what we believe, along with an open charity and humility toward what other Christians have to say to us and with us — these are the tools the Spirit uses to do his work of bringing us together.

Thus, if our Anglican brothers and sisters (or even a significant group of them) honestly feel this is the way for them to go, all things considered, then decide they must — regardless of possible ecumenical repercussions.

As for ending hopes for reunion of our two churches, this would presume that we know what a "united" Christianity will look like. But do we?

Judging from recent papal statements, it appears quite unlikely that the Roman Catholic Church will allow the ordination of women. From past experience we know that, while tradition is a significant theological argument, it is not always a final argument.

Might not the Roman Catholic Church, for instance, preserve its present policy, and still be able to live with a united Christendom in which one branch allows women priests — much as it has for centuries lived with other branches which allow married priests — while it continues to require that its own priests be celibate?

Unthinkable? I'm not so sure. The Holy Spirit has already brought us far along the way to healing the shameful division in the family of Christ, a long way that 40 years ago would have been called ridiculous and impossible.

So let's keep moving, and give him the benefit of the doubt. He just might have something big going that will astound us even more.

Coptic Orthodox and the Eucharist

Are Greek Orthodox or Coptic Orthodox allowed to receive the Eucharist in the Roman Catholic Church? And is it all right for Roman Catholics to receive the Eucharist in these churches?

Our teen-age children recently spent a weekend with friends who are of the Coptic Church and the priest in that church refused to give them Communion. On several occasions the children of this family have visited us and it never occurred to me that they should refrain from taking Communion in our church.

We are all Christians and the consecrated bread of one church becomes the Body of Christ in the same way as in the other church.

By Coptic Orthodox I assume you mean the church sometimes referred to as the Monophysite Coptics, one of the divisions of the ancient patriarchal See of Alexandria.

The division of this group of Christians from the Roman Catholic Church goes back to the Council of Chalcedon (451), which taught that Jesus had two natures, divine and human, not just one nature, which would have meant that Jesus was not really a full member of the human race at all.

If this is the church you mean, then you are right about their belief in the Real Presence. The Roman Catholic Church considers the priesthood and the Eucharist of this church as valid, as it does, of course, the priesthood and Eucharist of the Greek Orthodox.

In time of need, if a priest of his own church is not available, Roman Catholics or members of these Orthodox communions may approach a priest of the other communion for the Sacrament of Penance.

Thus, it is true that in certain circumstances, we Latin Rite Roman Catholics can share the Eucharist with these other non-Roman Catholic communions. Two major considerations always are involved, however.

First, such sharing should only be in case of necessity, or if one of the faithful could not receive Communion in his own church over a long period of time.

Care also should be taken that one respect the practice of that other church about confession before Communion, the Communion fast, and so on.

The second consideration is even more serious. Generally, the regulations of these Eastern communions are more restrictive in this matter than those of the Roman Catholic Church, and the Roman Catholic Church insists that these policies of the other churches be respected and observed.

Among our first concerns, in fact, is the rule that permission for sharing in the reception or administration of the Sacraments of the Eucharist, Penance, or Anointing of the Sick not be extended to Christians of other non-Roman Catholic communions without satisfactory consultations with the authorities of those other communions.

This means that a Roman Catholic should not attempt to receive the sacraments in one of those churches, nor should members of these other churches receive Communion in our rite, unless the spiritual leaders of those churches approve the practice.

As far as our church is concerned, priests and bishops of the Coptic Rite have a perfect right to establish principles for reception of these sacraments by their members or in their churches and we should honor that right and observe it.

This is not the place to discuss again the background for such regulations. I might only repeat that they are partially founded in the realization that the Body of Christ is, among other things, a celebration and proclamation of the unity of faith among those who receive it together.

For reasons which go far back in history, these Eastern churches are generally far more restrictive in applying this doctrine than is today's Roman Catholic Church.

Mass for non-Catholic spouse

My husband died a few weeks ago. Our family wanted a

Mass offered for him. The priest in my own parish refused, but the priest in the neighboring parish readily agreed.

I was really confused. What are the rules about saying a Mass for a deceased non-Catholic? He was a baptized Christian.

Even the former code of church law (which was superseded by the 1983 Code of Canon Law) allowed the private celebration of Mass for a non-Catholic Christian. "Private" in this context was interpreted to mean a Mass that was not announced, for example, in the bulletin.

A Mass offered for a non-Catholic Christian is definitely permitted. In June, 1976, the Vatican Congregation for the Doctrine of the Faith liberalized the law in this matter a good deal following requests in various countries for Catholic priests to celebrate Mass for deceased persons who were baptized in other denominations. This happens particularly, it noted, when the person who has died showed special respect and honor for the Catholic religion, or held public office in the service of the whole community.

Such Masses, private or public (announced in the parish bulletin, for example), not only are permitted. They can be unreservedly encouraged, said the decree, for reasons of patriotism, friendship, gratitude, and so on, provided there is no other prohibition in the way, if the family or friends request it, and if in the judgment of the bishop there is no danger of scandal.

Assuming these two requirements are met, the decision of the priest to offer Masses for your husband was entirely proper.

Priest is Zen Buddhist?

I read in a national magazine recently about a Catholic priest who is also a Zen Buddhist? Unless I'm wrong, Buddhism is a religion that isn't even Christian. Can you tell me how in the world a priest can be one? If this is ecumenism, it's too far out for me.

I suspect the article didn't really say the priest was a Zen Buddhist. It probably said the priest was a follower, or practioner, of Zen, which is an entirely different thing.

The name "Zen" primarily designates a school or "program" of meditation which has proved to be extremely helpful not only to people of the East, but to many Westerners as well. It is quite possible for a person to be a Christian, and a Catholic priest, and practice this highly specialized form of meditation.

Since Zen arose out of Buddhism, it is often identified with that religion, and many Buddhist religious beliefs are, of course, contradictory to Christian faith. What Buddhism teaches about "God," for example, is radically different from the Christian belief in one, personal God. You are right, therefore, in assuming that no one can be a Buddhist in any traditional, religious sense of the word, and at the same time be a Christian.

Rosicrucians

What is the Ancient Mystical Order Rosae Crucis (the Rosicrucians)? What is the church's position about it?

The Ancient Mystical Order Rosae Crucis (AMORC) seems to be a modern form of gnosticism (from the Greek word *gnosis:* knowledge). It has cropped up through the ages in many forms and in many places. We read even in the New Testament of the problems the early church had with the Gnostics.

The type of gnosticism varied, but always the promise was to open up the secrets of the universe through a profound mystical experience. The initiates — those "in the know" — possessed a grasp on man and the world that remained unintelligible to the rest of the human race.

The Order of the Brotherhood of the Rose Cross appeared perhaps 500 years ago, though many of the earliest documents are now known to be hoaxes written much later. As it now exists, the AMORC was organized about 100 years ago. Units (they call them "colleges") are organized in the United States and Europe. Rosicrucian General Statutes identify it as part of Freemasonry.

What doctrines there are in AMORC seem to be a strange mixture of Christian and non-Christian ideas. Many elements are incompatible with Christian faith. There is, for example, a strong pantheistic strain in such movements, holding that all creation, mankind included, is somehow an extension or a "part" of "God." Such doctrines do not appear in so many words, but they are implied throughout the philosophy.

The church has not taken an official position on the Rosicrucians, just as it has not against numerous other quasi-religious groups. It would seem impossible, however, to accept and believe at one and the same time the truths of the Catholic faith and the teachings of the Ancient Mystical Order.

Son in new church

Our son has become a "born again" Christian, who plans to marry in his new church in a few months. Do we as parents go to the ceremony, or stay away.

It used to be wrong to attend such affairs, but now we don't know. Our nephew was in a similar situation recently, and his parents received all kinds of different answers including "absolutely not" and "do as you like." I'm truly confused. Where do we go from here? We love our son and we love our religion, and we want to do what is right.

This kind of situation is always anguishing for a family. I'm afraid my words may not ease your decision as much as you would wish.

First, however, be assured that there is no black-and-white, right-and-wrong answer to your question. It requires weighing several factors and then making as prudent a judgment as you can, all things considered.

It should first of all be some consolation and support for you to note that a Catholic is now obliged to be married before a priest only if he or she has not formally rejected the Catholic faith. (CCL 1108) The church, therefore, recognizes that people may leave the church, not consider themselves Catholic any more, and perhaps even embrace another faith, and should not then be bound to the Catholic form of marriage. Your son certainly appears to be in that situation.

If he is, and if they are otherwise free to marry, his marriage would be a real marriage, even according to church law. While you regret his loss of the Catholic faith, this fact might affect your own acceptance of him, and of his marriage.

One element I am sure you wonder about is the possibility of scandal. What will your action say to your son, and to the rest of your family and friends, about your own attitude toward his leaving his old faith and changing to the new religion? On the other hand, basic charity and your parental love urge that you let him realize you are not ostracizing him from your family, and that you keep lines of communication open to him.

Remember that you have your own convictions too, and you do not have to apologize for them. You have as much right to your beliefs as your son has to his. If you feel that merely going to the wedding would indicate your approval in some way that would compromise your own faith convictions seriously, then you should not go.

However, you may be able to make your position absolutely clear, and still attend the wedding without being misunderstood.

Obviously, the solution you reach will depend on these and other factors — such as the nature of your relationships within your family, who else will know about it or be at the wedding, and your judgment as to how your friends would understand your presence there.

Other children in your family, especially younger ones, are also a consideration. You naturally do not wish to do anything to confuse or mislead them about your faith and what it demands of them and you.

Perhaps today there is less danger than before in the attendance of parents at such affairs because of the widespread confusion and radical religious searching in many of our young people. One wonders on occasion, to put it bluntly, if they ever had any faith to lose — and this through no moral fault on the part of the parents. Emotional and spiritual maturity of the kind required for a genuine, internal faith commitment seems to arrive awfully late for many young people today.

Think and pray about it, decide, and then don't fret over your decision.

Prayer and Devotions

Do prayers affect God?

Could you explain how our prayers affect God's activity in the world? We ask for recovery from illness, help in safe traveling, and to be protected from rainstorms. Are these things in which God meddles — or do we really think we will change his mind? Aren't we asking for a miracle when we pray, if it doesn't happen to be "God's will?"

It isn't so much a matter of changing God's mind as of recognizing that his providence and care for us include his awareness of our prayers, our desires and our longings. We are dealing here with at least two great mysteries. One is the mystery of God's knowledge of all things, which means that nothing ever takes him by surprise or makes him realize something that somehow "slipped his mind."

The other is the mystery of man's free will, which means there is some way men and women work together with God in shaping their individual lives and destinies. Ours is a genuine personal freedom, not just a game of "let's pretend," a freedom which involves above all a personal relationship with God. It includes sharing with him our joys and sorrows, our hopes and disappointments, our wonders and our regrets — all of which is nothing else but prayer.

This is, of course, why Jesus urges us so often to pray fervently and why he prayed so frequently himself. What the heavenly Father plans and what he does depends very much on what we show is important to us in our prayers.

How prayers are answered

A short time ago you answered a question about prayer, how our prayers are answered by God and how he does things for us in the light of our prayers. But doesn't God know what's best for us and won't he do that, if he really loves us, regardless of what we ask for — or for that matter whether we pray at all?

Obviously, God does love all people. Scripture tells us that he views all of his creation as good, and this goes most of all for human beings who are made most like him in their ability to know and to love. Because of that love he always wants what is best for us.

Many elements essential to our relationship to God enter our lives with prayer, not least of which is the deep desire for the things God gives us, which must be in our hearts if we are to be able to receive his gifts.

But did it ever occur to you that what is best may be quite different if we are praying desperately for something than if we are not? We are individuals, all different, even in our deepest relationship with God and the world.

Our humility before God, our trust in him, our conviction in faith and love that something will be good for us, for our children whom we love, or for the people for whom we care very much — all this goes in to determine what is really best for us in God's eyes here and now.

This surely does not mean that we ought always to receive exactly what we want, as we want it, if we pray hard enough. But prayer (and that means above all a habitual prayerful spirit before God) affects us deeply, so that we are truly not the same persons we would be if we did not pray. Therefore, what is best for us will be different, too, in God's eyes as well as our own.

Prayer for deceased son?

A year ago my son was killed instantly in a motorcycle accident. Although he was raised a Catholic he had neglected his religion, at least outwardly, for the past eight years.

Beyond the terrible blow of his death, I am more concerned with his spiritual welfare. Can my prayers, offerings of

Masses, and so forth, bring him God's pardon? I shall continue to pray regardless, but I hope your answer will be able to strengthen my belief in the hereafter.

I am sorry for your hurt. The sudden death of a son or daughter is always a terrible tragedy; yours is even more painful because of the spiritual concerns.

It may be helpful to remember two things. First, as a parent you are at least somewhat aware of the many complicated factors that might today lie behind a young person's neglect of his religious faith and practices.

I do not say, of course, that such neglect is a good thing. By no means, however, does it necessarily or even usually reflect rejection of God. Each person's relationship to God is unique and extremely personal. And it always exists under at least some influence of the faithful love God has for each of us.

Second, we must never forget that in hearing and answering our prayers God is not bound by the limits of time, past or future. The prayers we offer, in addition to whatever intercessory power they have in (whatever to us would seem like) the present moment, can be "answered" by God long before they are actually said.

This may sound complicated but it is an insight of faith that we Christians have always acted upon.

The official prayers of the church at Masses for the dead, for example, repeatedly imply (by praying for "forgiveness" and so on) an extension of that prayer back to that person's time on earth and his or her preparation for death.

In other words, we pray for a happy and holy death long after the person has died, something which logically and faithfully follows from what we believe about God. Thus, at least one of the things you are praying for at this time is that God might grant the grace of essential faith, hope and love in his life and as the time came for him to die.

This to me is one of the most consoling aspects of our faith. It is, among other things, what we mean when we say we believe in the supreme Lordship of God, and in the Communion of Saints.

Praying for good health

I am up in years and in very poor health. No one seems to be able to help much or relieve the pain. I am getting worse every day and pray for the one thing that is very precious to me, my general health.

Someone told me that it is wrong to pray for this; it is simply meant to be that way by God. Is it a sin to ask someone to pray for your health and to pray for that intention yourself?

By no means is it a sin to pray for anything that is good. Certainly one's health is among the most valuable goods of life and it is natural that one should ask one's friends to pray for that health when it is endangered.

Frequently in the Gospels, in fact, God strongly urges us to put pressure on him with our prayers, not because he is reluctant to help us, but because perseverance and urgency in our prayers helps us to realize our dependence upon his help and increases our openness to the good gifts he can give.

Jesus tells us about the man who was asked in the middle of the night for bread. The lady at the door kept knocking so long he finally got up to give her what she wanted. He tells us that that's the way we should deal with our heavenly Father in our own prayers.

I know you can count on the prayers of many of our readers for your good health and for courage to carry with grace and love whatever crosses may be yours.

Praying for one to die

Is it wrong to hope and pray that someone will die? I know it sounds bad, but I think there are times when it is the right thing to do for all concerned.

It is always wrong to wish evil to another. If one desires that another person die from a motive of hatred, so that death is seen as a punishment or suffering, it is obviously wrong and a gross violation of charity.

Death may often be seen, however, from every prudent and Christian viewpoint, as a blessing not only for others but for the individual himself. One common example is that of an individual with a terminal illness, whose condition is cause of enormous pain and suffering not only to the sick person but to his or her loved ones as well.

Another situation (and this appears to be what your letter is speaking of) is that of an elderly person whose senility causes immense suffering and much needless tragedy for others. This may be because of close family relationships, positions of responsibility held by the older individual, or other ties. Often — perhaps most of the time — such a condition is as painful to the individual himself as to those around him and death may once again be seen, from the human and Christian viewpoint, as a true good for all concerned.

After all, we do believe that death is not the ultimate evil or final destruction, but the necessary passage to eternal life. Also, there is always for us Christians the realization that life and death are in God's hands and our thoughts and prayers in these matters imply recognition of his Divine wisdom and providence.

Someone once said it is wrong to wish another to die, but one may rightly wish him to go quickly to his eternal reward. The remark may sound frivolous, but there is more than a kernel of good theology in it.

Pray for someone's love

My boy friend and I will graduate from college next year. I love him and want to marry him, but he wants his freedom to date other girls, which he is doing now.

My question is: Can I pray for help from God in this matter? I know God will not allow a relationship to continue if it is not in my best interests. I do want to marry this boy, but only if he wants to. I just think he needs inspiration.

If your boy friend still wants to date other girls, for heaven's sake don't push. If there is something good between you that might result in marriage, it can only be helped by his (and your) having the experience of knowing and relating to many other friends, male and female, until you're both comfortable and sure about settling down.

Certainly you should pray about it for God's guidance, that things work out best for both of you, and even that your friend eventually decides to marry you. But don't be surprised if each of you does a lot of changing in the meantime. The entire situation may look a lot different a year or two from now.

Sacramentals

Two weeks ago a neighbor showed me an advertisement which she found in a magazine purchased in a supermarket. I was shocked to say the least. It offered for sale a "lucky water cross" suggesting that it could "bring instant money miracles to thousands in need." "Lucky water of Lourdes inside every cross!" it said. Can't anything be done to stop frauds like this? I'm disturbed because people reading this will think it is Catholic teaching. Do you know what can be done about this kind of rot?

As you indicate, such an attitude toward and understanding of sacramentals is entirely alien and contrary to our Catholic faith.

Unfortunately no steps are possible to my knowledge to prevent this sort of thing. Apart from implications made by referring to Lourdes Water, the ad contains no reference to Catholics or Catholic teaching.

Anyone is free to sell "lucky water" if people are foolish enough to buy it, and if the ads contain no outright fraudulent claims, which such merchants usually carefully avoid.

Unfortunately some Catholic organizations and other sources, even if unwillingly, encourage this kind of thinking. They advertise sacramentals, including blessed or holy water, in ways that seem to the average non-Catholic reader no different than the advertisement you protest.

The "spiritual" power these more orthodox advertisements promise may easily be read by others to mean "magical." It is also true that Catholic sources do not offer such items for sale; an offering of some sort, even a specific amount of money, is usually requested. Such subtleties are, however, generally lost on the average American reader.

Ads such as you describe are reprehensible at very least in

the light of our Catholic faith. It is understandable, however, if not defensible, that certain types of entrepreneurs, totally ignorant of our faith, might say to themselves: If Catholics can do it, why can't we?

Stations of the Cross

Do the stations of the cross, as we have them in our churches, actually describe happenings during the passion of Christ? Someone has said they do not, but I heard from a neighbor who recently visited Jerusalem that the 14 stations are marked along the way of the cross there.

The devotion which we know as the Way of the Cross developed during the very late Middle Ages, perhaps the 1200s and the 1300s, both as a form of prayer and as a sort of catechism about the sufferings of Our Lord.

Various Franciscan communities, which already had charge of the holy places in Jerusalem for Latin-Rite Catholics, helped popularize the devotion which went through many forms. Once they included seven falls under the cross. Another variety totalled 43 separate stations. The 14 stations as we know them became fairly stabilized by Pope Clement XII in 1731.

We may, in fact, be experiencing right now another transition in this devotion. Many, if not most, of the books of stations include a sort of 15th station or meditation which in one way or another calls to mind Christ's Resurrection.

At any rate, the markings of the 14 stations along the Via Dolorosa (Sorrowful Way) in old Jerusalem are comparatively recent. The accuracy and even historical validity of some of them are open to considerable question.

Veronica and the sixth station

My husband is not Catholic but is very familiar with the Bible. He questions me about the sixth station of the cross, Veronica wipes the face of Jesus. He says he cannot find that in the Bible. How do you explain this? Did she go by a different name, or what is the explanation?

There is nothing in the Scriptures about Veronica (or anyone else) wiping the face of Jesus or about his leaving the imprint of his face on a cloth.

No one has ever claimed that this part of the stations is based on anything biblical. For that matter, neither are the "three" falls of Jesus on the way to Calvary; nothing is said of them in the gospels.

Somewhere around the 10th century, a cloth bearing an image that was said to be Christ's turned up in Rome. Various explanations were given through the years. Only in the 14th century did some offer the explanation that the image was miraculously imposed on the cloth by a woman who offered it to him during his journey to his crucifixion.

One must understand that the Stations of the Cross, a beautiful devotion to focus our minds on the suffering and death of Jesus and what these mean to us Christians, only appeared about 700 or 800 years ago. Using Scripture, traditions concerning the death of Our Lord, and some legends, the stations went through many variations, at one time totalling more than three dozen separate incidents — or stations. Somewhere along the line, perhaps about 200 years ago, the present 14 stations became generally accepted and observed.

What is the Magnificat?

I am a young Catholic mother and have had no Catholic education except some Sunday school. I have seen references several times to the "Magnificat." Can you explain what that means?

In the first chapter of St. Luke's Gospel we find the story of the visit of Mary, the Mother of Jesus, to her cousin Elizabeth. In response to Elizabeth's greeting, the Gospel places on the lips of Mary a beautiful prayer or hymn which is found frequently in our Catholic liturgy and other devotions.

In Latin, the hymn begins "Magnificat anima mea Dominum." (My soul proclaims the greatness of the Lord.) It is often referred to as the Magnificat.

You speak of yourself as a young mother. You may be too

young to remember that not many years ago Catholic people were much more familiar with Latin terminology. Phrases like Pater Noster (Our Father), Kyrie eleison (Greek for "Lord have mercy") and many others were everyday terms for Catholics. Sometimes Catholic writers — and liturgists — forget there is a whole new generation of Catholics out there like yourself for whom these words and titles are completely unfamiliar.

Novena devotions

When I was younger, about 30 years ago, my parish had novena devotions one night a week. Other churches had similar devotions on other nights.

Do any churches hold novenas like that anymore? If not, why were they discontinued? I used to enjoy them and looked forward to these ceremonies.

I'm not sure anyone knows the answer to that one. Perhaps it's something like asking why, for no apparent reason and with no change in the teaching of the church about when to receive the Sacrament of Penance, people stopped going to confession with anything like the former frequency. No one has the answer to that either.

My opinion is that a major explanation of the decline in extra-liturgical devotions such as these lies in the greatly increased emphasis on Eucharistic Liturgy since Vatican II. Before the liturgical changes of the past two decades, the Mass was viewed far more than it is today as the priest's personal action, and Masses were generally limited to early morning, particularly on weekdays.

Today peoples' devotional lives are far more Eucharist-centered. Many who in former days might have attended novena devotions now participate in evening Masses. The Eucharistic Sacrifice often constitutes an integral part of important afternoon and evening religious gatherings, which was of course impossible before Vatican Council II.

Add to this the emphasis on Scripture as the primary inspiration of Catholic spirituality, and several significant social developments (change in parish structure, reluctance of people to go out at night, and so on) and you probably have most of the explanation why the kinds of devotion you speak of have declined in American Catholic life.

Nine First Fridays

I am still one who likes to make the nine First Fridays, but I don't know anything about where and when these promises were made. What did Christ promise about this devotion?

The practice of the nine First Fridays resulted from certain revelations apparently made by Jesus to St. Margaret Mary Alocoque about 300 years ago. St. Margaret Mary was a French Visitation nun who had a remarkable devotion to the Heart of Jesus as a symbol of God's love for us. At her urging, after these revelations, the great devotion to the Sacred Heart of Jesus was established in the church, including the Feast of the Sacred Heart which we celebrate in June.

According to St. Margaret Mary, Jesus made 12 "promises" to those who honor his Sacred Heart. The last of these was this: "I promise you, in the exceeding mercy of My Heart, that Its all-powerful love will grant to all those who go to Communion on nine First Fridays of the month the final grace of repentance; they shall not die in Its disfavor nor without receiving the Sacraments, My Divine Heart becoming their assured refuge at that last moment."

The practice is, in other words, a sort of novena — a nine-time prayer which Christians have used for centuries as one of the ways of emphasizing the importance of perseverance and trust in our prayer to God.

One must remember that, at the time of these revelations, Holy Communion was rarely received by many Catholics, especially in France, where the severe Jansenist heresy was strongest. Neglect was such that once a year was often considered enough, even for the "most worthy." The weekly, even daily, Communion so common among practicing Catholics today was all but unheard of.

As a private revelation, of course, these promises in no way constitute an obligatory part of Catholic belief or practice. However, devotion to the Heart of Jesus, as the sign of Our Lord's love, is now an important and special part of Catholic tradition. In approving and promoting it, the church indicates that it contains nothing contrary to our faith, and that it may be devoutly believed and practiced.

Holy water

Why does the church use holy water and what are the effects of its use for those of us who believe it combats evil?
I saw a pamphlet which says that the "devil hates holy water" and that we can sprinkle holy water for a blessing to our loved ones who live far away from us. What do you think of these beliefs?

The pamphlet from which you quote contains some questionable comments about the use of holy water, making it sound almost like a spiritual rabbit's foot.

In all uses of sacramentals, including holy water, we must keep straight exactly what a sacramental is in the church's tradition. A blessed medal, picture, or holy water, is simply a material item over which the church has prayed, asking God to accept the prayers of the church for those who reverently use it.

In a sacramental such as holy water, therefore, the devotion, faith and charity of the person using it is augmented and supported by the prayers of the church. There is no magic-like power in the water itself.

Use of holy water in the proper manner can be of great spiritual benefit. It can be a striking reminder of our baptism and of the commitment to Jesus which we made in receiving that sacrament. It can symbolize and strengthen our faith in the forgiving love of God and therefore assist us in a spirit of conversion that brings with it the forgiveness of sins.

Again, all this can be strengthened and enriched immeasurably by the blessing of the church, which carries with it the assurance of the prayers of all our fellow Catholics and Christians. Properly used with these intentions, there is nothing superstitious about holy water or any other sacramental. Unfortunately some over-zealous devotees of certain sacramentals occasionally come close to stepping over the line.

Religious candles

Where did our use of candles at Mass come from, and are

they still required? There seems to be no consistency about the number of them, or even whether there should be any at all?

Christian use of candles was taken over from the Romans who used them on a variety of civic and religious occasions. The practice is, however, part of a much larger human tradition.

The natural symbolism of light has been recognized by nearly every religion since time immemorial. Even pagans lit lamps over tombs expressing belief in some sort of continued existence for the deceased. Light, particularly a living flame, signified life, hope, joy, divinity, courage — in other words, nearly everything that mankind has considered good and beautiful.

Some of this symbolism may be sensed from the fact that the lighted ceremonial candle for evening prayer developed into our paschal candle. These lights were also used in funeral ceremonies, before the tombs of deceased Christians and in front of images of martyrs and other saints. They symbolized then what they still do for us: light (Christ), life, hope, resurrection and faith.

Candles have been used at Mass in some way since the seventh century, and are still required, though regulations concerning them are considerably simpler than in the past.

Care of palms

Please explain the proper usage of the palm we received on Palm Sunday. How long should it be kept, in what way, and how should it be disposed of?

Palms distributed on the Sunday before Easter remind us of Our Lord's death and resurrection and of our share in his passage from death to life. Any reverent way of keeping these palms in our homes with this kind of prayerful and devout intention is perfectly fine. Some people place them behind a crucifix; others place them with a picture that is particularly meaningful; others merely hang them on the wall or keep them on a desk or table.

As anything that is blessed, palms lose their blessing when

they lose their identity. The proper way to dispose of a palm, therefore, is either by burning or breaking it up. The remains may then be thrown away.

Advent customs

What is now the proper arrangement for an Advent wreath? Formerly we used three purple candles (or white candles tied with a purple bow) and one pink.

In recent years I have seen other forms of the Advent wreath, sometimes with all white candles and blue bows. What is proper now?

There is no official form of the Advent wreath. It can be for our homes a beautiful and meaningful symbol of the spirit of Advent, but its arrangement is only a matter of custom.

The observation you make about Advent, however, is significant in light of the developing flavor of the church's observance of this significant time of year.

In times past Advent was seen as somewhat of a mini-Lent; a time of penance and self-denial but with a tinge of joy in the background — perhaps symbolized most by the rose vestments the priest wore at Mass on the third Sunday of Advent and by the rose candle lit on the Advent wreath that day.

As the church's liturgy developed over the past century or so, particularly in the last several decades, the predominant spirit of Advent is one of joyful awaiting and hope. This theme clearly appears in the scripture readings for weekday and Sunday Masses as well as in the other liturgical texts for this season.

The increase during the past few years of the use of blue (symbolizing hope) rather than purple in liturgical color for Advent reflects this same spirit.

Infant of Prague

We have a picture of the Infant Jesus of Prague in our church. I've seen the picture or statue numerous times in homes and churches but no one seems to have any idea where the picture originated. Can you help us out?

The statue of the Infant of Prague has held a special place in the devotion of Catholics in Eastern Europe and elsewhere for nearly 300 years.

Brought to Czechoslovakia from Spain in the 1500s, it represents Jesus as an infant clothed in apparently royal robes and holding a globe with a cross on top in one hand. The other hand is held up in blessing. The original statue of wood and wax is in the Church of Our Lady of Victory in Prague, which is under the care of Carmelite priests and Brothers.

Particularly through their auspices, devotion to the Infant Jesus of Prague has spread throughout the world and many special favors have been attributed to prayers made to Jesus under that title. Since about 1650, the church has attached many special privileges and indulgences to this particular devotion to Our Lord.

Shroud of Turin

We have seen many references recently to the sacred shroud of Turin. But I've seen no mention of any official church position about it. What does the church say about this relic?

The shroud of Turin is a piece of linen cloth about 14 feet long that reveals the imprint of a human body. Nothing was known of it until the seventh century when the claim was made that it is, in fact, the shroud in which Jesus was wrapped at his burial.

Scientific investigation in this century reveals some intriguing characteristics of the shroud that indicate it may well be the shroud of Christ. But conclusive proof of that will likely never be possible.

The church has no official position on the subject. There's no reason it should have. The findings, whatever they are, couldn't affect Catholic belief one way or the other.

He descended into hell?

In the Apostles' Creed we say, "He descended into hell." Would you please explain why we say this? Jesus was the only perfect person on earth. He never sinned. Why would he have to go to hell?

The word "hell" as it is used in the Apostles' Creed does not mean the "hell of the damned," which it usually means in current English.

Our word "hell" comes from an old Teutonic word "hela," which means a hidden, or covered place. In earlier English literature, it was used to describe any kind of pit, dungeon or dark hole.

The use of the word in our English translation of the Creed is unfortunate but has been traditional for so long it will hardly be changed now. The word is a translation from a Latin (also Greek and Hebrew) word which means the "lower regions" — a generic name for the place where people would go after death without regard to a condition of reward or punishment.

We have a similar word (unfortunately also vastly misunderstood) in our Christian tradition. The name "limbo" has been used to designate a possible place or condition for children who die without baptism — in other words, a place that is neither heaven nor hell, but somehow neutral.

Misunderstandings of what the church has and has not taught about limbo are widespread. Nevertheless, limbo would probably be a more appropriate word than hell for the "place where Jesus went" after his death.

Rosary

Is it necessary to say all five decades of the Rosary at the same time?

I sometimes say only a decade each day. Is that all right?

There is no required way to say the Rosary. In fact, different countries, different Catholic cultures, sometimes vary a good deal in the sequence and number of prayers — though all are based on 150 Hail Marys and reflections on the chief events in the life of Christ.

Regular praying of the Rosary, all of it or any part of it, was and still is a powerful prayer and a marvelous way to express one's love for Our Lord and his mother.

The usual form of the Rosary in most English speaking and many other countries is as follows:

The events are divided into the five *Joyful Mysteries*: the Annunciation, the Visitation, the Birth of Our Lord, the Presentation of Jesus in the Temple, and the Finding of Jesus in the Temple.

The five *Sorrowful Mysteries*: the Agony of Jesus in the Garden, the Scourging at the Pillar, the Crowning of Jesus with Thorns, the Carrying of the Cross, and the Crucifixion.

The five *Glorious Mysteries*: the Resurrection of Jesus from the Dead, the Ascension, the Coming of the Holy Spirit upon the Apostles (Pentecost), the Assumption of Mary into Heaven, and the Crowning (Glorification) of Mary in Heaven.

The praying of each "mystery" consists of one Our Father, ten Hail Marys, and one Glory be to the Father. The Rosary usually begins with the Apostles' Creed, three Hail Marys and one Glory be to the Father.

Hail, Holy Queen

Is it true that the prayer "Hail, Holy Queen" has been deleted from the rosary? If so, why?

The "Hail, Holy Queen" was not deleted from the rosary; it was never in any official way part of the rosary. As I said, the prayer we call the rosary has taken many forms. The core seems always to have been 150 Hail Marys (15 decades) in imitation of the 150 Psalms which people who could not read could not share in the liturgy. Another similar prayer of 150 Our Fathers was popular for a time in some parts of the church.

In various times and places additional prayers before, during and after the Hail Marys became common. The "Hail Holy Queen" is one of them.

This particular ending has been widely used in our country in the past decades, but is not universal. Not long ago, for example, I was at the Vatican on an occasion when Pope John Paul II led the rosary. He did not use this prayer at the conclusion.

Another sign of the cross?

A group of us women attended a diocesan workshop at one

of our schools. When times came to pray, the leaders said, "In the name of the Creator, Redeemer and Sanctifier."

When we asked, we were told this is a different way of making the sign of the cross.

Since then I've heard it again. Is this really just another sign of the cross? One priest said he thought we should not use it, but he didn't say why.

The prayer you quote, invoking God under those titles, can be a good one. Obviously there is nothing wrong with it as it stands. A serious problem arises, however, when it is presented as an equivalent or substitute for our traditional Sign of the Cross.

Most Catholics and other Christians know that the mystery of the Holy Trinity, three persons in one God, is the fundamental doctrine of our faith. The fact that there is "within" God an eternal community of existence, a mutual exchange of life and love that is what we call three Persons, is something we would know absolutely nothing about unless Jesus himself had told us. Theologians refer to this inner divine life as God's action "ad intra," on the inside.

This inner life of God — Father, Son and Holy Spirit, to use the Gospel's own words — is the core of all Christian beliefs. Without it all other crucial elements of our spirituality and faith — the incarnation, Eucharist, sacraments, the church as we know it — would be unthinkable.

Since the beginning, Christians have approached this mystery with the utmost reverence and care. It was in the name of the persons of the Trinity that Christians were, and still are, baptized into the faith of Jesus Christ. It is in their name, as in the Sign of the Cross, that all Christian prayer and important action take place.

In light of the centrality and importance of this great mystery, it is highly significant that this "new" sign of the cross is not an explicit invocation of the Trinity at all. True, our creeds sometimes attribute creation to the Father, redemption to the Son and sanctification to the Holy Spirit. (See the Nicene Creed, for example, which nevertheless first stresses the inner Trinitarian life of the Father, Son and Holy Spirit.) But these attributes or titles all involve actions that theology calls "ad extra," outside of God. As such, they are each and all actions of all three Persons, not only of one. In other words, they are not Trinitarian actions but "God" actions.

In fact, one need not even believe in three divine persons to use this prayer. Jehovah Witnesses, for example, reject belief in the Trinity, but staunchly believe that God is their creator, savior and sanctifier.

These differences may not appear significant to many of us; but to equate Creator, Redeemer and Sanctifier with Father, Son and Holy Spirit is theologically and spiritually dangerous, and contrary to Christian and Catholic tradition. It ignores the relational interior activity of God which is central to our faith in the Trinity.

As our bishops recently repeated, we urgently need to study our liturgical texts to eliminate certain expressions which have lost a more general human connotation they once had. Why should we say things like "Christ died for all men," as we often do in our liturgy, when we mean all people, men and women?

Speaking directly of God, however, is something else entirely. The serious pitfalls in this substitute Sign of the Cross, if it is indeed presented as such, indicate again the extreme care and accuracy we must exercise when we begin tampering with traditional terminology about God.

Cursillo

What is a Cursillo? How does it differ from a retreat?

Since it is intended to help one to examine and improve his life as a Christian, a Cursillo has some similarities to a retreat, but it also has many important differences.

Started in Spain 35 or so years ago, its full name is "Cursillo de Christianidad" — literally, a short course in Christianity. It is intended to be just that: a basic discovery of one's beliefs and responsibilities to God and man as a Christian. Thus, an individual makes only one Cursillo in his life, though he or she may be part of a team presenting the program many times.

There are also follow-up meetings (reunions) and regular large gatherings (ultreyas) of those who have made a Cursillo to preserve and develop the spirit of community and mutual support the program is intended to promote.

Another difference is that the 15 talks contained in the three-day program are standard as to subject, but are prepared and written personally by usually five priests and 10 laymen or women who give them.

As anything else, of course, details and quality of the Cursillo programs differ from place to place, depending on leadership personnel, general interest, and other factors.

Pentecostals-Charismatics

What do you think of the Pentecostal movement? Is it all right for a Catholic to belong to one of these groups and attend the prayer meetings?

The increasing interest in and growth of the Pentecostal movement (more commonly called "Charismatic renewal") seems to have paralleled the growing interest of the church and of theology about the work of the Holy Spirit in the church. Certainly at this point there is no evidence that the movement holds any threat to Catholic doctrine or spirituality. In fact, many Catholics and other Christians have found participation a help to their prayer and to their whole religious life.

The convictions on which the Pentecostal movement is based are that there is a great new outpouring of the gifts of the Holy Spirit in this time; that the Holy Spirit shows these gifts and powers in some ways that resemble his activity among the early Christians, and that this outpouring of grace can help a person to a new and holier way of "living in the Spirit." There appears to be nothing in this in any way contrary to Catholic teaching.

Charismatic Movement

How does the Charismatic Movement coincide with the teaching of the Catholic Church and the teaching of Jesus Christ? Many priests and bishops go along with it, while many do not approve of it because it's too emotional.

Jesus said we must become like little children, and little children surely do not become emotional.

I'll pass over your last sentence. You obviously are acquainted with children quite different from the ones I know.

The Charismatic Movement takes its name from the Greek word *charisma*, which means a free gift, a favor. In the church, it has meant a special talent or power given to certain people by God for the service of the rest of the Christian community, the church.

Some of the charisms are for service in the church (governing, for example), others for teaching or preaching, and others for more spectacular purposes such as healing, speaking in tongues, prediction of the future, and so on.

These gifts of the Holy Spirit were especially necessary in the early days of the church when the Christian people had not yet experienced many of the signs of Christ's presence that intervening history has offered. But such charisms can still be useful even today and may be a source of faith and hope to those who experience them and use them well.

They are also important to the institution of the church, with which they will nearly always be in tension, as a reminder that the Holy Spirit "blows where he will" and that his actions are not limited to popes, bishops and others.

Already in the New Testament, St. Paul warned against two main dangers in the charismatic activities in the church. An individual may too easily fool himself about the genuineness of his special gifts, especially the more spectacular ones. Also, every gift is suspect if it does not serve the whole community by aiding the spirit of cooperation, love and mutual support. If the Charismatic Movement or any other movement becomes divisive or elitist, that's the best proof that there is something seriously wrong with it.

One reason that bishops, priests and others differ on their view of charismatics is that they differ on their basic vision of what the church is. Another reason is that charismatic groups themselves differ enormously in their spirit and in their understanding of where they fit into the rest of the Christian community.

Read First Corinthians, chapters 12-14, for St. Paul's comments on charisms. As St. Augustine said once in a homily, God gives different charisms such as healing, tongues, and others, to different people. As different parts of our body have different functions, people in the Church have varying gifts. Whether one has the gift of healing, for example, or any other charism, has nothing to do with personal holiness. All various gifts of the Spirit, working together, make us the living Body of Christ.

Focolare Movement

Our Catholic newspaper quotes a woman in our diocese who spoke of her discovery of the Focolare Movement and how it gave her strength to live what she believed. I've never heard of this group. Is it a retreat program or what?

Focolare is one of several movements or types of spirituality which have done much in this century for lay men and women to deepen and enrich their Christian lives.

The name itself comes from the Italian word for fire and is said to suggest the meaning "carriers of fire." Officially called the Worldwide Focolare Movement (Work of Mary), it began in Italy during World War II when a few young girls, horrified by the destruction and terror of the war, sought a way to bring about the unity on earth for which Jesus prayed.

Through the years, this theme of unity has become the cornerstone of its ideals, with the conviction that the only solid base of unity, the one reality that will last, is God himself. The movement has flourished particularly since Vatican Council II when its ideals were seen to be stressed often in the council fathers' commitment of the church to the cause of political, social and religious harmony and unity among the people of the world.

Focolare has a number of movements or groups within itself. Some single members, called Focolarini, live in separate communities (Focolare Centers). While they work in businesses or other professions as other lay people, they follow the evangelical counsels of poverty, obedience and chastity.

Another group are volunteers who attempt by their lives to transform all of human activity according to the Gospel and the spirit of the movement.

The first official approval of the movement by the church came from Pope John XXIII in 1962. In 1978 Pope Paul VI also encouraged the movement, saying, "Be faithful to your inspiration which is so modern and so fruitful."

Here in the United States, Focolare operates a publishing house and sponsors a monthly magazine, Living City, promoting the activities and spirituality of the movement.

Headquarters are in Rome, but it has national offices in several countries. One of six in North America may be reached at Box 496, New York, N.Y. 10021.

Rapture in prayer

Some Protestant friends of mine tell me about a "rapture" that takes place in their church. I've heard this mentioned a few times by other people also. What is this rapture?

Rapture is simply another word for a condition that Christian mysticism more generally refers to as ecstasy. In certain stages of prayer, it is not uncommon that the individual becomes so absorbed in God and things of heaven that he goes into a form of trance and is quite literally out of touch with the senses of hearing, sight, and so on.

The situation is expressed very well by the word itself. "Ecstasy" comes from a combination of Greek words that literally means "standing outside of" one's self.

While real mystical ecstasy may accompany higher forms of contemplation, some degree of this experience is not at all uncommon in Christian prayer life. When it does accompany or result from genuine prayer, it is always the work of the Holy Spirit leading the soul to a greater union with God.

The experience of people who have written about this, however, proves that it is not always a pleasant one. In fact, the word rapture more commonly identifies the forms of ecstasy that are more violent or painful.

Obviously the church has enormous respect for this kind of manifestation of the work of the Holy Spirit in our movement toward God. It is also aware that the externals of genuine ecstasy can and do often result from purely psychological causes and not necessarily from any religious experience.

Another rapture

I believe you misinterpreted the meaning of rapture. To most

"born again" Christians, rapture means only one thing, and that is the "great snatch" when Christ comes to take us who live, and his church, out of this world "to meet the Lord in the air."

The subject of the rapture is discussed at length today because they feel the signs of the Great Tribulation Period (Seventieth Week of Daniel) are close at hand. I am sure this is the rapture to which your writer referred.

Rapture in our Christian tradition does also embrace the meaning you indicate: the final coming of Christ to take the world to himself and unite mankind together with him to the Heavenly Father. The Catholic Church obviously considers the final coming of Christ the climax and completion of all human history. To be honest, however, it learned centuries ago not to take too seriously the dire predictions that the heavens are about ready to drop, and that the end of the world is just around the corner. It has lived through hundreds of such predictions that have come and gone.

Whether the end of the world comes one year or a hundred thousand years from now doesn't really make that much difference. The more critical concern is whether we individually are prepared for the "end," for the close of our personal pilgrimage on this earth. Our life as Christians must always be guided by faith in the supreme Lordship of Jesus which will come to its perfection when he comes again. How soon that coming will be isn't at all important.

Indulgences

Gaining indulgences was a big thing when I was growing up. I assume indulgences are still valid. Is there some reason the church doesn't talk about them as much any more?

The church is much more careful, and somewhat reluctant in speaking of indulgences today, largely because this area of our faith has been so badly misunderstood and abused in the past.

The traditional teaching about indulgences is based on two ancient Christian truths. First, every sin is not only a disobedience of God's law; it is a violation of the order established by God and a rejection of his love.

As such, complete forgiveness of sin requires not only conversion but a reintegration of that divine order and plan. This process involves pain and cleansing (purgation) either in this life or in some "temporary" condition after death.

Second, as Pope Paul VI pointed out in *The Doctrine of Indulgences* (DI)(1967), which called for reform of the whole indulgence structure, the early church community "was fully convinced that it was pursuing the work of salvation in community."

The doctrine of the Communion of Saints, so prominent in the early church, taught that all children of God in Christ, whether in this life or in eternity, are linked in the Mystical Body of Christ.

In light of this truth, said the Holy Father, the church "undertook various ways of applying the fruits of our Lord's redemption to the individual faithful and of leading them to cooperate in the salvation of their brothers, so the entire body of the church might be prepared" for the fullness of God's Kingdom (DI, 6).

The remission of temporal punishment for already forgiven sins, through prayer, fasting and good works, has been called "indulgence" for hundreds of years, though the principles of faith involved go back to the beginning of Christianity.

Through the years, indulgences have been formally attached by the church to some specific prayers and actions, and may be applied to oneself or to those who have died.

A few things are worth keeping in mind.

1. The number of formally indulgenced prayers and works is now drastically reduced. "The main concern has been to attach greater importance to a Christian way of life and lead souls to cultivate a spirit of prayer and penance and to practice the theological virtues (faith, hope and charity) rather than merely repeat certain formulas and acts" (*Enchiridion of Indulgences,* 1968).

2. "Partial indulgences" are granted using only those words, with no determination of days or years as was common previously. This is among other things to avoid confusion. Contrary to what many Catholics believed, an indulgence of one year, for example, did not mean one year off of purgatory.

(See question on purgatory on page 635.)

3. Plenary (full) indulgences can be gained only once a day with proper conditions fulfilled.

4. Great pains are taken in the documents today, through scriptural and council citations, to keep the understanding of indulgences in harmony with the Gospel and with the teachings of Vatican Council II.

The main point to remember is that in this as in all spiritual practices of the church, "it is hoped that the faithful will be more effectively moved to live holier and more useful lives, thus healing the split between faith which many profess and their daily lives . . . by gathering their humane, domestic, professional, social and technical enterprises into one vital synthesis with religious values" (*Enchiridion*, Observations No. 4, and Vatican II, *Constitution on the Church in the Modern World*).

Personal spiritual growth

What advice would you give to a person who sincerely desires to grow spiritually? Would making a private retreat be a good start?

Our spiritual life and our growth in it is a many-faceted reality. It involves our knowledge and trust in God; our increasing realization of the presence of God in the events of our daily lives and especially in ourselves and in those around us; our spirit of hope and faith in what is offered to us in the Gospel as essential elements of our Christian commitment, and many other things. Growth comes through prayer and reflection and action, and depends greatly on the circumstances of our personal life — about which, incidentally, you mention nothing.

The best step for you at the moment would not necessarily be a retreat, but some thoughtful reflection and consultation with someone in whom you have confidence, possibly a priest you feel you can talk to about your ideals and concerns. He will assist you in evaluating where you are, the expectations you have of yourself, and what expectations others around you may have. Much depends on whether or not you are married, have children, and their ages. Your own age and experiences of life are important factors.

Please think it over in these terms and ask a priest, if you wish, for an appointment so you can talk with him and allow him to offer some thoughts and options for you to follow through on.

Presider for Benediction

Our discussion group was talking about lay people now leading many activities, including prayers in our parish. What about Benediction? Some said a eucharistic minister can officiate at Benediction, others said not. Who is right?

According to the Ritual for Exposition of the Blessed Sacrament, the ordinary minister of this ceremony is a priest or deacon. Before the end of adoration the priest or deacon blesses the people with the sacrament and places it back into the tabernacle.

If there is no deacon or priest, or if they are for some good reason unable to officiate, the following persons may expose and repose the holy Eucharist for public adoration. 1) An acolyte, that is one who has been installed in this role by the church, not simply an altar server. 2) A "special minister of Communion." 3) A member of a religious community or of a lay association of men and women devoted to eucharistic adoration, if this individual has been appointed by the local bishop.

These three groups may open the tabernacle and place the ciborium on the altar or place the host in the monstrance. At the end of adoration time, they replace the blessed sacrament in the tabernacle. They should not, however, give the blessing with the sacrament ("Holy Communion and Worship of the Eucharist Outside Mass" n. 91).

"Pagan" feasts worked for church

You explained why we celebrate the birth of our Lord on Dec. 25. It took the place, you said, of the pagan Roman feast

honoring the birth of the Unconquered Sun at the beginning of spring. It seems to me a strange thing that such a feast as Christmas should substitute for honoring a pagan god. Why would the church do that?

It might appear strange to us, but it would not be to the Christians of the time. First, when the birth of Christ began to be celebrated with a specific feast about 300 years after our Lord's death and resurrection, it was no way near the major celebration it is now. Second, the church in those times often had a much different attitude toward things pagan than we might assume.

In the year 601, for example, Pope Gregory the Great, in his instructions to St. Augustine and other missionaries to England, told them that under no circumstances should temples to idols be destroyed. They should be sprinkled with holy water, and altars should be set up in them. Seeing their temples are not destroyed, he said, the people may be more ready to return to them "to know and adore the true God." Since they have a custom of sacrificing oxen to demons, he added, "let some other solemnity like the dedication of the church or a martyr's feast be substituted on the same day."

They can decorate the churches as they did before, he instructed, even kill and use the animals as food, not in sacrifice but as a way of giving thanks to the Giver of all gifts. (Letter of Gregory to Abbot Mellitus and Augustine) Rather than considering it a danger or scandal, they saw this sort of "ecumenism," as we might call it, as a help to spreading the Gospel and in making their faith attractive to the people they were hoping to convert. Many more feasts and other Catholic traditions than most of us realize are traceable to this strategy of our Christian forebears.

Belief in guardian angels

What can you tell us about guardian angels? When I was a youngster in school (1930s) we were taught the existence of these angels and their mission "to light and guard, to rule and guide" mortals through life on this earth. I have attempted to find more information in your book and others, but there isn't much real solid information. What is the official position of the Catholic Church on guardian angels? Dogma? Just theological opinion? Or what?

I agree with you. The belief in guardian angels is one of the loveliest and most humanly consoling elements of our Christian tradition. This conviction of followers of Jesus that each human person is given an angel to guard him or her and be a spiritual companion through life is but one extension of our conviction that God has a personal, daily, intimate concern for our good and our happiness.

Perhaps one reason you are disappointed in the amount of material available about guardian angels is that there just isn't that much to say, apart from pointing out the evidence for this belief through the centuries. It is an explicit Catholic doctrine, based largely on evidence from the Bible, that angels, bodiless creatures who possess an intelligence and free will beyond that of the human, really exist. That some of these angels are "guardians" of individual persons or groups is not defined Catholic dogma, but has been a continuous, almost instinctive part of the Christian way of thinking practically from the beginning.

Jesus himself, discussing little children, speaks of "their angels" who look upon the face of the Father in heaven (Mt 18:10). Early Christians in Jerusalem, seeing Peter at their door, couldn't believe he had escaped from prison; Luke tells us they thought they were seeing "his angel" instead (Acts 12:15).

Later on, at least from the second century, one theologian or father of the church after another relates this same Christian view. The great Scripture commentator and spiritual writer Origen, who was born about 185, in his commentary on the book of Numbers, writes, "For each of us in the church of God, no matter how small, there is a good angel of the Lord who stands daily before the face of God to rule and move and govern, to correct our actions and intercede for us in our sufferings."

Origen's limiting of guardian angels to those in the church is not shared by the greater part of Christian tradition. The more universal belief is represented by St. Jerome: "What a great dignity of souls, that each person has, from birth, an angel assigned as guardian!"

The word "angel" comes from the Greek word "angelos," messenger. This obviously identifies them with how they relate to us human beings, as ones who so often bring God's power and message to earth. Guardian angels are, in our Christian insights, God's messengers par excellence, his envoys beside us throughout life.

While the doctrine of guardian angels is not an "article of faith," and acceptance of that belief is not an essential of Christian and Catholic life, in my view those who dismiss it are missing a rich and joyful treasure of our Christian heritage. The prayer you quote from, which is several hundred years old, I also learned in the 1930s; I still pray it regularly. A feast in honor of the guardian angels is celebrated on Oct. 2.

Disposing of blessed articles

My husband purchased an old altar from a parish church some time ago. Now he wants to turn it into a bar and the idea upsets me. Isn't that a sacrilege? We're not even supposed to throw away a cruficix or holy pictures. An altar is much more sacred.

An altar should never be put to common use like this. The importance of recognizing the special nature of blessed or consecrated things increases with the closeness they have to the Mass and the Eucharist. Your husband would, I'm sure, agree that it's wrong to take chalices and start using them for beer mugs!

So what to do? When anything is taken apart, melted, or otherwise radically changed, it is no longer considered blessed. Thus, while it would be wrong to use an altar for a bar, it would be perfectly all right to use the materials from an altar for something else, including a bar — as long as common sense is used and any possible scandal or misunderstanding is avoided. After all, it is the altar that is blessed, not the wood and nails.

The same applies to other blessed items you mention. Unless you own a warehouse, there's a limit to how many blessed candles, cruficixes, statues, rosaries and holy pictures one can accumulate over the years. When they no longer have a use, it is entirely proper to break or tear them so that they lose their identity as a candle or picture, and then discard them. Their purpose is to increase our faith and assist our spirit of prayer and devotion. When they have served that purpose and become worn out or are to be replaced, there is no irreverence in disposing of them appropriately.

Saints

Praying to the saints

I am not a Roman Catholic. I've never received a sufficient explanation why Catholics pray to the saints and give them so much tribute. I believe that Jesus Christ is the one Mediator between God and man.

This special relationship with the saints cannot be understood without recalling a fact that the New Testament is full of: All of those who believe in Jesus, who acknowledge him as their Savior and live according to his teachings, form a special, very close family — whether they are living, or are already dead and "with" God, as St. Paul puts it. As Paul also said many times, all true Christians are in some way saints in that they share in the sanctity and love of the Father, along with and in Jesus, with whom they are united by ties of loyalty and love.

The people we usually call "saints," however, are individuals whom the church, their fellow Christians, acknowledge as having lived the Christian life in an especially holy way, and who thereby give great praise to God and an unusual witness to their fellow men. When we pray to them, we do it simply to be glad with them and ask them to add to our prayers their own intercessions to Jesus, and through him to the Heavenly Father, for whom they have proven their love.

One Protestant lady with whom I was speaking about this recently put it perfectly: "Then it's really just asking these holy people to talk to God with us, and for us, for the things we need! That's beautiful, because it's just what we do with people who are close and dear to us here on earth." The pope couldn't have said it better.

Perhaps much of the problem is in the phrase "pray to," which had a much broader meaning in the past. In present English usage, it more often implies the kind of adoration and relationship that belongs uniquely to God. It is particularly important, therefore, to understand precisely what is meant by "praying to" the saints.

Book of saints?

In the church's celebration of feasts of the saints, is there an ABC rotation of feasts as there is for the Sunday Scripture readings? Is there an up-to-date book of saints similar to one I have which is almost 50 years old? Does it relate to our present calendar?

The reason for asking probably will not interest many readers but it is important to me. For some time I have been attempting meditation using a saint each day, and then linking that person's life with the way Christ might have lived in him. Up to now the attempt is feeble, but it has been fruitful for me.

Your question might not be nearly as uninteresting to other Catholics as you seem to believe. I am often deeply impressed by the number of people who are seriously and sincerely attempting to develop and enrich their life of prayer.

The variety of ways through which they do this is also impressive, and yours is not that unusual.

In the recent revision of the church calendar (which takes place every few hundred years just to eliminate a lot of confusion that develops with the addition of new saints), several dates were changed. There is no rotation of these observances from year to year. Each saint's feast is celebrated each year, unless, of course, that feast is superseded by a Sunday or other more solemn feast.

A few books describing the lives of the saints according to the present church calendar are now available. The classic in this field, however, remains Butler's "Lives of the Saints."

The four-volume set covering the entire year is relatively expensive but well worth saving up for. It presents information not only on the major saint of each day (the one whose name appears on Catholic calendars) but on many other perhaps lesser known but equally inspiring holy men and women whose feast falls on the same date. The set may be ordered through almost any book store.

I hope you persevere in your worthwhile effort.

Why Catholics have statues

What light can you throw on why Catholics have statues in their churches and most Protestant churches do not?

Images of Jesus and the saints have been used, as you probably know, for decorational and devotional purposes since the very beginning of Christianity. Today only the most grossly uninformed person gives any credence to the old accusation that Catholics worship these statues or pictures.

Several hundred years ago, the Council of Trent explained the practice perfectly: "The images of Christ, the Virgin Mother of God, and of the other saints are kept and honored in churches not because it is believed that there is any divinity or power in these images, or that anything may be asked of them, or any faith be put in them. The honor shown to them is really being given to the persons whom they represent. Through these images which we kiss, and before which we bow with bared heads, we worship Christ, and not the saints whose likenesses they display."

Even many Catholics do not realize that, since such pictures and statues become intimately connected with what people believe about God and his revelation, the church is very careful about what images are allowed for public veneration. All such pictures or sculptures must be approved by the bishop or other proper authority.

The reasons most Protestant denominations do not allow images in their churches are varied. One is that, early in the Protestant Reformation there was much misunderstanding about the meaning of honoring images of Jesus and the saints, and "no statues" became one of the symbols of protest against the church of Rome.

Perhaps a more significant reason is that many early Protestant leaders, especially of the Calvinist and other Puritan traditions, were extremely austere and considered any sort of display, color, or emotion, such as might be encouraged by statues and pictures, totally out of place in religious worship.

All Saints is for *all* saints

I am a life-long Catholic and always thought the feast of All Saints was to honor all the canonized saints. Recently we were told in a catechumen class that the feast was to honor all the people in heaven, even our parents, who have died. If this is true, it's a beautiful thought, but what is the church's idea?

It is clear from the earliest centuries of Christianity that the intention of this feast was to honor all those who are in heaven with God. It started as a way of honoring those many martyrs whose very existence was perhaps unknown to the church, but whose names were known only to God. By the fifth century, the celebration (on the first Sunday after Pentecost) included non-martyrs as well, and became known as the Sunday of the Nativity of All Saints, nativity meaning the day of death, of birth into eternal life.

As the prayers and preface of the feast of All Saints make obvious, this continues to be the significance of our All Saints celebration. It may help to note that the canonization process as we know it is not very old. Before that, for many hundreds of years, saints became "official" by general acclaim of their holiness among Christian people of their region, or perhaps of the whole church. In some ways the feast reaches even to us who are still alive on earth. St. Paul, in his letters, refers to the Christians to whom he is writing as "saints." The word comes from the Latin "sancti," holy ones.

For him, as for the church in its liturgy even today, those who believe the good news of Christ, who are united in baptism and faith to him, and who work for the coming of his kingdom, are already in some way God's holy ones. (See, for example, Sunday Preface I and Eucharistic Prayer IV.) To that degree at least, the feast of All Saints extends to all who are still on this life's journey, but who are attempting to live faithfully in the life and grace of Christ.

Any poor Catholic saints?

Can a poor Roman Catholic have a chance to become a canonized saint? Such people do not belong to church societies, do not do much volunteer work, do not attend fairs and luncheons because they cannot afford it, and often don't come in contact with the pastor. All a poor Catholic can do is attend Mass on Sundays and holy days, practice the teachings of the church, raise his children to know their faith, and do small kind deeds the best way he can.

So is the Catholic Church fair in picking out canonized saints? God shows no such partiality.

Probably the most striking and happy note about your letter is that you seriously consider becoming a saint. Great for you. You mention the "only" things a poor person can do. Those aren't so insignificant as you seem to believe. Follow through on them and you can't miss.

You have a couple of misconceptions, however, about canonized saints. One is that there are no poor people among them. The list of poor saints is so huge, one wouldn't know where to begin.

It is true that most canonized saints, particularly in the last several hundred years, have been members of Religious orders or people of some prominence in the church. That is partly because the process of canonization is so long and so complex that a fairly large number of people have to be interested in the project, and able to carry it through many years for a successful canonization procedure. It is not all that rare, though, for a relatively unknown man or woman, lay person or Religious, to be officially declared a saint.

More importantly, in canonizing saints, the church in no

way says these are the only holy people, or even the most holy people, in the world. It is entirely likely that among the
saintliest persons are thousands or millions who were completely unknown to all but a few family members and friends,
but whose faith and love and closeness to God will shine
brilliantly throughout eternity.

When the church canonizes anyone, she doesn't declare that
this man or woman was the holiest on earth. She simply says
that the individual led a Christian life of sufficient and evident heroism that we can be sure that person is in heaven,
and that we on earth might in many ways use that saint's life
as a model for our own.

So maybe you will never have a church built in your honor.
Don't let that bother you. To paraphrase an old saying, some
of my best friends are uncanonized saints.

Why pray to the saints?

**My Presbyterian daughter professes to be a devout Chris-
tian. She questioned me when I said I pray to St. Jude. "Why
would you do that when you can go directly to God. After
all, he is all knowing and all powerful," she said. How would
you answer such a query?**

Has your daughter ever asked you to pray for her? Or has
she asked anyone else to join her in prayer for something she
really wanted?

If she has, you could make the same objection to her. Why
not go directly to God?

The long Christian tradition of praying to the saints is simply another facet of our request for prayers from each other.
We know that as God's family we can approach him together
to strengthen our own faith and increase our desire for the
good things that God can give to us.

Our belief in the "communion of saints" which we profess
every Sunday in the Nicene Creed, simply means that the
union of faith and love which the family of Christ enjoys goes
beyond the limits of death. The saints, including our own
relatives and friends who have died and are with God, are
united with us in some mysterious way by God's providence.

Since they are with God, it is only natural and profoundly Christian that we ask their help and prayers for anything important to us, just as we ask the help and prayers of the people who are still with us on earth.

Mary, the mother of God?

I am a Protestant reader of your column. Most things about the Catholic faith, even your dogmas, I can pretty much agree with. But calling Mary the mother of God really turns me off. How can anyone be God's mother?

Your misgivings are understandable. On the face of it, such a title for Mary sounds at least ridiculous, if not blasphemous.

When Catholics speak of Mary as the mother of God, they do not mean that she was God's parent from eternity, but that she was the mother of Jesus when he came to earth. Since Jesus was God from the first moment of his coming in the womb of Mary, she is correctly called God's — that is Jesus' — mother.

Perhaps it will help if you understand when and how that phrase was first officially applied to her. In the early centuries after Christ, a large and powerful Christian sect, called Nestorians, taught that when Jesus was born he was just a man. As he grew up, they said, God sort of "saddled" him somehow, and "used" him to perform the work of our salvation.

The main body of early Christians had come to realize and believe that Jesus was both God and man from the very beginning of his life. They recognized that this Nestorian doctrine was dangerous to the whole theology of salvation. If Jesus was not really God, or was not really and fully human, something essential would be lacking in the saving work of reuniting God and mankind, which we believe was accomplished by Jesus.

The matter came to a head in 431 at the Council of Ephesus, the third Ecumenical Council. After long and often heated discussion, the council decided that the shortest and most direct way to pinpoint the basic belief that Jesus is truly God is to say simply: Mary is the mother of God — not from eternity, of course, but as he comes into this world in his human nature, in the womb of Mary. No one can accept that brief statement without believing that Jesus is both divine and human. He had a *mother* as we did, and therefore he is one of us. And yet the child of that mother was *God*, not by some later fiction, but as he came from her womb.

The Greek title "Theotokos" (God-bearer) was already commonly applied to Mary in Christian worship and devotion long before the Council of Ephesus.

As you can see, the title "Mother of God" came into official Christian doctrine as a vital part of belief about Jesus himself, not primarily as a way to honor Mary. It does, of course, reflect much honor on her to have had such an intimate share in God's plan of salvation.

Mary in our Faith

How can the church urge that we pray to Mary, as the pope recently did when he recommended prayer to her for an increase in vocations to the priesthood and Religious life? Isn't it true that Catholics pray to Mary? I don't believe there is any place in the Bible that says she is divine.

We do not believe Mary is divine. She is a human being who needed the saving graces of her Son just as we do. While the church has always reserved a special dignity and honor for our Blessed Mother, we pray to her in much the same way as we pray to the other saints, or for that matter, in much the same way as we "pray" to any other Christians when we ask them to pray for us. We simply follow a basic human and Christian instinct that there is a bond between us that even transcends death.

Since the earliest decades, Christian people have honored the Virgin Mary as the greatest of the saints because of her pre-eminent fidelity to God and her Son, attested to so often in the New Testament, and because of her intimate relationship with Jesus, who took his human flesh from her.

For us there is, if possible, an even more personal reason. Since he received from her his life as the incarnate Son of God, and since Jesus shares this very life with those who believe in him, she is also *our* mother. The church has, in fact, always recognized those words to John from the cross, "Behold your mother," as addressed to the whole Body of Christ on earth, whom she loves, cares for and prays for as her own child. This is the reason for one of the loveliest titles we have for Mary, calling her our Blessed Mother.

Pope John Paul II echoed this tradition in his 1987 encyclical, *Mother of the Redeemer*, which incidentally is the most biblically and ecumenically oriented document on Mary in the history of the Church. It should be required reading for anyone interested in her place in our faith.

The church, says the Holy Father, "sees Mary maternally present and sharing in the many complicated problems which today beset the lives of individuals, families and nations; she (the church) sees her helping the Christian people in the constant struggles between good and evil, to ensure that it 'does not fall', or if it has fallen 'to rise again.'"

Unfortunately, some religious devotees in their over-enthusiasm, or sometimes serious lack of knowledge of Christian beliefs, lose this Catholic balance. They occasionally use terminology or express ideas at serious odds with Catholic belief. Some go so far as to suggest that if Jesus is "threatening" us or is reluctant to help, we need only go to Mary and she will obtain what he will not.

Suffice it to say here that, though in a very special way, Jesus is Mary's savior as much as he is ours (see Luke 1:47), and that as God he is the source and infinite exemplar of whatever saving love she or any of the rest of us may have. To even imply that she outshines him in mercy or compassion and that if we're really in trouble she will do for us what he will not, only dishonors the Mother of Christ.

As long as we keep this perspective (and our Catholic tradition certainly does), the prayer and honor that we give to Mary can be nothing but a source of joy and pleasure to her Son. Beginning with the Gospels themselves, she has never been in any competition with him, nor has he been with her.

Immaculate Conception in the Bible?

I realize we have Scripture and tradition as a basis for our

beliefs. But when someone not of our faith asks for proof of the Immaculate Conception of the Blessed Virgin Mary from the Bible, what should be our answer?

There is no proof, in the ordinary sense of the word, of the Immaculate Conception in the Bible. But this is not strange; every Christian believes quite a number of things which, even if he does not realize it, cannot be proven from the Bible.

There are some texts from Scripture, however, that may strongly suggest or imply a belief by the earliest Christians in the Immaculate Conception of Mary — that is, that she was sinless, by the saving grace of Jesus, from the time of her conception in the womb of her mother. Certain passages in the first part of St. Luke's Gospel concerning her and her relation to Jesus clearly indicate a conviction of the first Christians that she was an exceptionally holy person who shared in a particularly intimate and total way in the victory of Our Lord over sin, perhaps even to being totally free from any stain of moral imperfection or offense. But these texts are not what one could call proofs.

The more detailed theological implications of Mary's holiness and of her sharing in the work of Jesus as Savior (such as the Immaculate Conception), while hinted at in Scripture, were only gradually clarified and understood by the church through the centuries.

Immaculate Conception and Jesus

I am a confused convert. I thought I knew what the doctrine of the Immaculate Conception was all about. But after some discussion with Protestants, I'm not sure. I'm almost positive I heard a priest in our parish say recently that it had to do with the birth of Jesus. Can you help?

Surely you misunderstood what the priest said. I'm continually amazed at how many Catholics are still confused about this feast and doctrine.

The Immaculate Conception refers to the conception of Mary — that from the first moment of her existence in the womb of her mother she was free from original sin.

Wrong Gospel for December 8?

My question has to do with the liturgy for the feast of the
Immaculate Conception, Dec. 8. The Gospel for that feast
is the story of the Annunciation, when Jesus was conceived
by the Holy Spirit. The Immaculate Conception, at least as
I understand it, celebrates the conception of Mary in the
womb of her mother, St. Anne. Why doesn't the church correct that? I'm only a tiny bit of the church, but am I the only
one with this question?

You ask a very good question. In fact, the Gospel of that
day (Luke 1:26-38) with the dialogue between Mary and the
angel Gabriel at the time of the conception of Jesus, may be
one reason so many Catholics and others are confused about
the Immaculate Conception.

First, there is, of course, no part of the Gospels that goes
back as far as the time of Our Lady's conception and birth.
This is understandable; the New Testament — particularly the
Gospels — is not about her but about her son Jesus. She
comes into the picture only in relation to him.

We would expect, then, that the Gospel of that feast would
be some passage that reflects that relationship, and would also
give an idea about how early Christians, out of whose lives
the Gospels arose, saw her and the special gifts God gave her.
We must always return to the basic truth that, while we honor
Mary as the greatest of the saints and as the recipient of the
holiest gifts of God's grace, these gifts and her consequent
holiness were given by the Father, first of all, in honor and
goodness to his Son, who would become man through her.

Thus it is the clear teaching of the church that all of Mary's
glory, including her sinless conception in the womb of her
mother, came to her through the foreseen merits of Christ,
and to make her a "worthy dwelling for Christ, not on account of her own bodily endowments but because of that
grace which was hers from the beginning." (Pope Pius IX in
his declaration of the dogma of the Immaculate Conception
in 1854.)

Understanding all this, it is clear why the church would have
chosen this particular passage of Luke for Dec. 8. Every word

and phrase overflows with profound, lyrical biblical themes proclaiming the greatness of Our Lord and Mary's sharing, as participant and recipient, in his redemption of the world.

To mention just one example: Gabriel's words to Mary, "The power of the most high will overshadow you," are a clear echo of the overshadowing cloud or light, the "glory of the Lord," which stood over the Ark of the Covenant in the exodus, and later in the temple of Jerusalem. For the Jews this hovering sign marked the presence of God himself. (See, for instance, Exodus 40:35.)

To those of Luke's readers, then, who saw his words in light of this tradition, this new overshadowing revealed a new "Ark of the Covenant" in which — or rather in whom — the Lord God himself was present.

It would be difficult to find a more appropriate gospel passage to celebrate the sinless entering into this world of her who was to become this new Ark of the New Covenant.

Where was Mary born?

On a trip to Greece we were taken to an island where the Blessed Mother was said to have been born. If this is true, how did she come to Bethlehem and Nazareth?

To the best of our knowledge, Mary was born in Jerusalem. While there may be some doubt about that, I know of no tradition that places her birth in the area you indicate.

Perhaps you're thinking of the ancient city of Ephesus which, according to some traditions, was the home of John the Evangelist in his later years. Since Jesus shortly before his death on the cross gave Mary into John's care, this tradition could also place Mary's final days in Ephesus. It is more commonly believed, however, that she spent her last years in or around Jerusalem and died there.

Mary's death?

I was surprised at your answer concerning the place of Mary's birth and death. You said she probably died in the vicinity of Jerusalem.

I thought we believed that Mary did not die, but was taken

up into heaven by God in the Assumption. Do we believe that
Mary died or don't we?

Catholic doctrine says nothing one way or the other about
Mary's death. Christian writers through the centuries have
debated both sides of this question. It has, however, nothing
to do with the doctrine of the Assumption.

When Pope Pius XII defined the doctrine of the Assumption in 1950, he deliberately avoided any attempt at settling
the controversy. He simply said that "at the end of her earthly life" (the official Latin text reads "expleto terrestris vitae
cursu"), Mary was taken body and soul into heaven by God.

Our Lady of Guadalupe

Our liturgy planning group was discussing the feast of Our
Lady of Guadalupe. We always think of this as a Mexican
feast and celebration. Why is it celebrated and so popular in
the United States?

There are at least two good reasons. First, the many U.S.
citizens of Mexican descent and other Spanish-speaking
Americans are understandably and properly proud of their
religious and other customs and feasts. They have helped make
the devotion of Our Lady of Guadalupe popular in our
country.

Second, and probably more important, the feast is as much
ours (the United States and Canada) as it is anyone else's.
When the Blessed Virgin appeared to the Indian Juan Diego
on the hill of Tepeyac near Mexico City, the year was 1521,
nearly 100 years before the pilgrims landed at Plymouth Rock.

At this time, of course, the present boundaries of nations
in the New World did not exist. Thus the event at Guadalupe
and numerous miracles of faith that this shrine has occasioned
during the past 400 years remain spiritually significant not
only for Mexico but for all the Americas.

The Feast of Our Lady of Guadalupe is December 12.

Our Lady of Czestochowa

Since the election of Pope John Paul there have been many

references to a picture of **Our Lady of Czestochowa.** From what I've seen it is not very attractive, but I understand it has an important history in the church. What can you tell me about it?

The shrine of Our Lady of Czestochowa has been for centuries and remains even now the major place of pilgrimage in central Europe and, without question, is one of the most venerable sites in honor of Our Lady in the world.

According to tradition, the image of Mary was painted by St. Luke the Evangelist on a wooden board made by St. Joseph. As with other work attributed in earlier centuries to Luke, however, including the famous image of Mary in the Borghese Chapel of the Basilica of St. Mary Major in Rome, the Czestochowa icon is now believed to have originated sometime during the ninth century in Greece or Italy.

Around the year 1000, it was given to the princess-wife of Vladimir of Kiev and in 1382 was brought to its present location by Prince Opolszyk of Belz in the Ukraine. The prince established a monastery to care for the icon on a hill, Jasna Gora (hill of light), just above the town of Czestochowa. The present basilica which houses the icon was built in the 1600s.

Over the centuries pilgrims, who included numerous members of royalty and religious leaders from throughout Europe and the Middle East, placed precious metals over much of the image. The rest became blackened from the smoke of torches and votive lights around it.

This explains the still darkened features of representations of the icon, though a major restoration in 1925 helped renew many features that had been obscured. The three scars on the Virgin's face apparently resulted from a desecration of the painting by robbers about 50 years after it was brought to Poland.

For centuries and up to the present day, the icon and shrine of Jasna Gora has exercised a political role in Poland far beyond, but obviously closely connected with, its religious significance. After Swedish forces failed to capture the monastery during a bitter siege in 1656, Our Lady of Czestochowa was proclaimed Queen of Poland and is today the great symbol of Polish national pride and of that nation's determination to preserve its freedom and its faith.

Thus, the pilgrimage of Pope John Paul to Jasna Gora during his visit to Poland was considerably more than a religious act, a fact which wasn't missed by either the people or the Communist Polish government.

In a larger but somewhat similar way, the icon is for Poles what the image of Our Lady of Guadalupe has become for many of the poorer people of Mexico, a proud symbol of their Catholic faith and a rallying point against oppression and persecution.

Decline in honor of Mary?

Is the Rosary a thing of the past? This past October, no one had a rosary in his hand at church. Don't you think people are losing their devotion to Our Blessed Mother when they don't say the Rosary?

I agree with you; people are saying the Rosary a lot less now than they did 20 years ago. However, I'm not at all sure that indicates any less love of Mary, or of Our Lord.

We must remember a few things. One is that the Rosary as a popular devotion developed over about 400 years (the 12th to the 16th century) when Catholics were almost completely cut off from any meaningful participation in the liturgy. In fact, the period was one of the low points in seeing the Mass as a community celebration.

Because of this, and because most persons couldn't read anyway, many devotions arose as a substitute for taking a more direct part in the liturgy, especially the Eucharist. The 150 Our Fathers (later 150 Hail Marys) were sometimes called the "poor man's breviary" — they matched the 150 psalms said by clerics or by others who could read.

Interestingly, saying the Rosary together was one of the first ways, in modern times, that Catholics began to do anything together aloud at Mass, and to see the Mass as something more than just another private prayer, which is about the way some spiritual books described it before the present liturgical renewal.

As the Mass and other sacramental ceremonies become

more significant liturgical events in our lives, it is understandable that certain devotions which partially substituted for them will decline in use.

I really don't believe there is a relatively great loss of honor and love for Mary. She will inevitably hold a high place in any religion that believes her son is God. The Rosary has been and still can be a tremendous help to Christian growth. But I wouldn't identify Our Lady's position in the church with how many Rosaries are said every day.

Jehovah Witnesses and Mary

Several weeks ago two Jehovah Witnesses came to my door. Normally I just tell them I'm Catholic and am not interested. But this time one of the women recognized me as a school friend.

One of them asked why we refer to Mary as the mother of God in the Hail Mary, since she is known as the mother of Jesus. I didn't know the answer but told her it was worth checking into.

Yes, I would agree it's worth checking into! In fact, I would hope that most Catholics could give the answer.

We believe Jesus is God, the Second Person of the Blessed Trinity, who came to this earth and became man. Jesus is God (and man); Mary is his mother; therefore, we believe Mary is the mother of God.

Since Jehovah Witnesses do not believe in the Trinity, and in fact reject that doctrine as a pagan superstition, there is no way they could believe that Jesus is God. Obviously, then, there's no way they could accept the belief that Mary is the mother of God.

Private revelations — Fatima

Our local newspaper and some recent books have included information about Fatima, the appearance of the Blessed Mother, and the miracles that were supposed to have happened there. The church I attend tells people that the first Saturday devotion (receiving Communion on the first Saturday of each month, which Mary was supposed to have re-

quested at Fatima for world peace) is only a private devotion. What is the church's teaching about Fatima, and whatever became of the letter that was to be opened in 1960?

First, a few words about private revelations are in order.

God can speak to us in thousands of different ways. Giving special messages to individual men or women to pass on to the rest of us is one of them. In fact, the prophets of the Old Testament and hundreds of Christians since then have filled precisely that role.

The church has enormous respect for the role of prophets. It realizes, however, that individuals can easily fool themselves into thinking that God is giving them private messages in support of their own prejudices. From the evidence of my own mail, I can testify that there is hardly a weird idea possible in the field of religion that someone doesn't believe God has told him to preach.

Some private revelations (Lourdes is perhaps the most famous) the church has officially approved. Some, such as the alleged appearances of Our Lady at Necedah, Wis., in the 1950s, it has officially rejected. About many of them — including alleged apparitions and other manifestations at San Damiano; Canton, Ohio; Woolongong, Australia; Madero, Mexico; Medjugorje, Yugoslavia; Limpias, Spain; Rwanda, and numerous others — the church has either said nothing or made no decision one way or the other.

When the church approves such messages, all it says is that there is nothing in them contrary to Catholic faith or morals, and that following the suggestions in these messages can be helpful in our efforts toward holiness. It is essential to remember that the church never imposes a special belief, or practices contained in these revelations, as obligations for all Catholics. The Mass and sacraments, the teachings of the Gospel, and universally accepted traditional practices of our faith are basic for everyone. Apart from them, no one is obliged to accept or follow anything in private revelation, though a proper respect for the fact that God can speak to us this way is proper for us, as it is for the whole church.

Now about Fatima. Church officials, including popes, have many times indicated acceptance of the fact that the mother of Jesus appeared to the three shepherd children at Fatima, Portugal, during 1917, urging prayer and penance by all Christians for world peace. Surely many people in the decades since then have been inspired to these spiritual good works by the message of Fatima.

Again, however, no Catholic is obliged to observe special practices, devotions or prayers suggested at Fatima, except insofar as they are already contained in the responsibilities we have as Catholic Christians. In that sense, Fatima, and everything connected with it is private revelation.

The letter you speak of was reputedly passed down by one of the shepherd children to be opened in 1960. Rumor had it that the letter threatened that if mankind did not return to God by that year, the sword of God's vengeance would descend upon us.

What happened to the letter, if it ever existed? One wag suggested a few years ago that Pope John lost it. Whatever the answer may be, the church has never put much stock in that kind of spiritual blackmail, with a vengeful God poised above us in wrath and ready to clobber us properly if we don't shape up. Our sins have enough evil consequences on their own without outside help.

The "letter" from Fatima

In your answer about Fatima and the letter that was supposed to be opened in 1960, you said "Whatever the answer may be, the church has never put much stock in that kind of spiritual blackmail, with a vengeful God poised above us in wrath and ready to clobber us properly if we don't shape up."

I think this was an insult and you owe us a retraction.

When I used the term "spiritual blackmail," I was referring not to Fatima, but to the idea of a God who says, "Do what I say or I will destroy you."

I believe Our Lady appeared at Fatima (though it is not part of our Catholic faith that I must believe it). I believe her message that the need of prayer for peace is crucial in our world, but anyone familiar with the various movements relating to Fatima during the past 30 years or so knows that the "message" some are passing on goes far beyond that.

In the late 1950s, I personally viewed a variety of promotional materials, prepared by some Fatima devotees, threatening what God was going to do if we didn't shape up by the deadline — 1960. I have a suspicion (and it's only that; I don't know any more about it than most others) that this may be one reason the "letter" idea was sort of allowed to die. The dire expectations some appeared to have about it threatened to distort the essential, and very needed, message of Fatima.

There is a persistent type of immaturity in Christianity that tends to fall back on threats if love, patience and personal carrying of the cross do not appear to be working quickly enough. Neither the Gospels, nor the church since then, provide foundation for belief in a God who cajoles, but then threatens to "teach us a lesson" by wielding his sword.

Jesus himself explicitly rejects that approach. Our God is a Savior, not an executioner. If our sins lead to hurt, destruction and alienation, it is because the seeds of decay are already present in pride, greed and the other sources of human evil. It is not because of the "wrath of God."

Fatima: adoration of Mary?

I belong to an interdenominational prayer group. I'm amazed at the misconceptions Protestants still have about Catholics, especially about our veneration of the saints.

It would be easy to explain usually, but then there are articles such as the one that came out in a Catholic paper recently about Our Lady of Fatima that confuse Catholics as well. The article said that during one of the apparitions to the children, Mary asked for adoration of herself.

Any Christian knows that the only being we should adore is God. What is the Catholic doctrine on this?

You are right, of course. Whoever wrote or translated the article you saw was guilty of some sloppy use of words.

Christian theology has a specific Latin word (*latria*) to designate the kind of honor or worship due to God alone. Another word (*dulia*) designates the honor given to saints. There are degrees of honor, of course, depending on the dignity of a particular saint.

As the greatest of the saints, Mary receives the highest honor in the church apart from Jesus himself and the Father and the Holy Spirit. But the church never forgets that she is only human, and that as she said in the Magnificat, (Luke 1,47), God is her Savior just as much as he is ours.

Unfortunately, our English language doesn't have words with such clear-cut theological meanings. Dictionaries give some definitions of worship and adoration which might apply to saints, or even special people on this earth, as well as to God.

Generally, however, we try to reserve these words for God, and use others like honor, veneration or devotion when referring to the saints.

Not all writers, even Catholic writers, always carefully respect this distinction. When they happen not to do so, we should recognize it as a slip of the pen, or maybe overenthusiasm, not an attempt to introduce a new doctrine about the mother of God.

Appearances of Mary at Necedah

Your explanation about private revelations and our attitude toward them was helpful. We get confused by so many conflicting reports on different shrines and apparitions.

Can you tell us about the reported appearances of the Blessed Virgin at Necedah, Wisconsin? Does the church still refuse to approve the visions there?

The story of Necedah and the series of rejections of church authority by Mrs. Mary Van Hoof (who claims that the Blessed Virgin Mary appeared to her in 1950) is unfortunate and sad.

Within five years after the alleged appearances of Mary, officials of the LaCrosse, Wisconsin, diocese investigated the situation and concluded that the visions and revelations were without supernatural basis and were false. In 1969 the bishop of that diocese reached the same conclusion after another investigation. In 1975 he was forced to place leaders of the shrine under personal interdict, which means that they could not receive the sacraments.

In the spring of 1979, the Necedah group seems to have made its final break with the church by inviting someone who claimed to be the "Archbishop and Metropolitan of North America, American National Catholic Church, Roman Catholic Ultrajectine" to bless and consecrate the shrine. The alleged archbishop then left a "priest" at the shrine to care for the pilgrims who might come.

Following this event, the bishop of LaCrosse issued a statement including the following: "For the guidance of the faithful, it should be noted that this action on the part of Mrs. Mary Van Hoof and her followers joined in 'For My God and Country, Inc.' definitely establishes that they are no longer affiliated with the Roman Catholic Church and acknowledge this separation by this action of approving the celebration of the Holy Sacrifice of the Mass by an unauthorized person."

Since then the self-proclaimed bishop, who was apparently a Catholic layman, has severed his connection with the shrine, as has another man who claimed to be a priest and bishop, and some others who were associated with the alleged apparitions. Mrs. Van Hoof died in 1984.

Visions at Garabandal

What is the church's position on the apparitions of the Blessed Virgin at Garabandal? I know the church treats these things in a low-key way, but a film I saw on this subject moved me deeply and I'd like to learn more about it.

Garabandal is another of those shrines at which, after extensive investigation by competent religious and scientific authorities, claims of some supernatural activity have proven groundless.

For readers who may be unfamiliar with the background of this question, the town of Garabandal is in the Diocese of Santander in Northern Spain. For several months, beginning in 1961, some children of that area were said to have seen visions of the Virgin Mary.

During these appearances Mary is reported to have repeated much of the message of Fatima — the need for prayers and conversion of life if mankind is not to suffer greatly from disasters imminent in the world.

In March 1967, Bishop Vicente Montis of Santander, Spain, (Garabandal is located in this diocese) reported the following after his own investigation: "There have been no apparitions of the Blessed Virgin, of Michael the Archangel, or of any other celestial person; there have been no messages. All of the reported happenings in that area have a natural explanation."

In spite of the bishop's findings, local devotees continued their activities. The following year, the succeeding bishop of Santander upheld the decision of Bishop Montis, insisting that priests and lay people refrain from visiting a chapel built at Garabandal "in rebellious resistance to the findings of the church" concerning the so-called apparitions.

In December, 1977, the ordinary of the Diocese of Santander, Bishop Del Val, visited the shrine and met with people said to have been involved in the appearances. Afterwards, noting that his predecessors did not admit a supernatural character to the phenomena that took place there, he said, "I am in agreement with these bishops, my predecessors. I was always open in charity and without prejudice, and will always be willing to consider any occurence that takes place here (in Garabandal). But in the six years that I have been bishop of Santander no new phenomenon has taken place."

Bishop Del Val adverted to the suggestion by partisans of this shrine in many parts of the world that a new investigation take place. If the Vatican wishes to do this, he said, he has no objection. He himself, however, had no reason to review the process and saw no reason for a special commission of the Holy See to do so.

I must repeat what I have insisted several times before when speaking about private revelations, which all such apparitions would be. When local church authorities find no evidence of a supernatural character in these appearances, they mean precisely that and nothing more.

Unless explicitly stated otherwise (as it has been in some instances), the church does not mean to deny the fact of the apparitions, nor to forbid Catholics from observing the spiritual advice involved, which most often is simply restressing the need for prayer and penance, which is and always has been an integral part of a good Christian life.

Bayside

Recently I received material advertising some appearances of the Blessed Virgin in Bayside, N.Y. I know this is possible, but some of the information sounds awfully strange to me. What can you tell us about it? Has the church approved this shrine?

Beginning in 1970 and continuing until the present, a lady in Bayside, Veronica Leuken, has claimed a series of visions of Our Lady and Jesus. These supposedly occur during prayer vigils held about twice a month, to which people from surrounding states and cities are invited.

Following the visions, during which the voices of Jesus and Mary sometimes are taped, long quotes are published, running many hundreds of words, of what Jesus and Mary supposedly said.

The rambling "revelations" cover everything from abortion to the imminent catastrophic punishment of the world by God. They are against just about everything from Communion in the hand to lay ministers of the Eucharist, rock music and ecumenism, and even against joining a particular farm cooperative in New Hampshire.

Much is made of numerous so-called miraculous pictures. In one, for example, a scratching of light is interpreted as "the G-clef, which symbolizes the Rosary, is music to heaven's ears." Photographic experts studying many of these photos have said they could be produced naturally in a variety of ways.

Included in the alleged revelations are poems which, though allegedly dictated personally by Mary, or sometimes St. Theresa, are not likely to win any literary prizes.

The vigils and supposed apparitions take place at Flushing Meadows, site of the New York World's Fair just next to Shea Stadium, home of the New York Giants. Several years ago, Mrs. Lueken introduced a system of light signals so the people could better follow the visions: A blue light announces the arrival of Our Lady; a red light announces the arrival of Jesus. Three red flashes of light signify that Jesus or Mary are bestowing their blessing so the pilgrims can make the Sign of the Cross.

During the early years, a favorite theme of the revelations was how bishops and priests were falling into hell because they were not following Pope Paul VI. Eventually, however, it became clear that the Holy Father, too, departed from Mary's teaching as Mrs. Lueken saw it.

This resulted in what must be one of the most bizarre revelations in the history of the church.

On Sept. 27, 1975, according to Mrs. Lueken, Mary revealed that three top Vatican officials (Cardinal Jean Villot, Archbishop Agostino Casaroli and Archbishop Giovanni Benelli), in league with Satan, had drugged the real Pope Paul VI and kept him a prisoner in the Vatican.

The one who appeared in public, according to Mrs. Lueken, was an imposter changed by plastic surgery to look like Pope Paul but who was actually an agent of the devil. The theory was "proven" to Mrs. Lueken's satisfaction by a series of pictures of the real and the fake pope.

Accordingly, Mary told Mrs. Lueken, "You cannot accept now what comes from Rome, for . . . these directions are not written by the pen of Pope Paul VI. They are written" under the direction of Satan.

This fantastic story was actually believed and promoted by thousands of conservative Catholics until Pope Paul died.

Pope John Paul II seems more acceptable to Mary, at least up to now.

In addition to other problems, alleged statements of Mary

sometimes depart significantly from Catholic doctrine. During one of her reprimands about the church, for instance, Mary warned Mrs. Lueken that "all who are baptized a Roman Catholic must die Roman Catholic to enter heaven."

After an investigation of the alleged apparitions in 1973, officials of the Diocese of Brooklyn (where Bayside is located) concluded that no credibility whatsoever could be given to the events there.

The chancellor of the diocese at that time reported: "The conclusion we reached independently was that the Bayside apparition was the result of a lot of imagination after reading a lot about Lourdes and Fatima."

This remains the official position of the Brooklyn Diocese, that nothing miraculous is occurring there and that no credibility can be given to the so-called visions at Bayside.

Devotions to Mary

I am enclosing a booklet on devotion to the Flame of Love of the Immaculate Heart of Mary. After asking permission, I passed it around to two prayer groups. Our spiritual director told us it was all right but said we had to be careful of some devotions.

I have refrained from passing any more leaflets. Do you know of this devotion? Is it all right to share with others?

Some privately advanced devotions to Mary and other saints fall victim to two serious dangers; the booklet you sent is a classic illustration of both. They tread awfully close to outright superstition and they confuse the relationship between the saints — again including Our Lady — and Jesus himself.

Certain specialized forms of prayer have, of course, become accepted by long tradition in the church. Even these, however, must be understood correctly or they can sound as if we believe they involve some sort of magic.

Novenas are a good illustration. Nine days of prayer, as a sign of faith and expression of persevering trust in God's love for us, can be an excellent manner of laying our petitions, praise and thanksgiving before Our Lord. However, we do not attribute anything miraculous or automatic to the number nine.

The particular devotion about which you inquire is one of those which gets so wrapped up in supposedly pious specifics, it becomes hard to distinguish from plain superstition.

We are told, for instance, that "families who keep the holy hour of reconciliation on Thursdays and Fridays will receive a special grace through which I (Mary) will free a member of their family from purgatory within eight days, if only one of them keeps one day of fasting on bread and water."

Those who fast on bread and water on Mondays will, we are told, free the soul of a priest from purgatory. Those who say three Hail Mary's "mindful of my Immaculate Heart's flame of love, will free one soul from purgatory, and those who say one Hail Mary during November will free 10 souls from the place of suffering." (Another thing common to most of these unusual devotions is their eccentric fascination with purgatory.)

There's simply nothing in Catholic tradition or teaching to give basis or credence to this brand of spirituality.

Even more serious and clearly in contradiction to Catholic teaching, is the tendency to compare the mercy and love of Mary with that of Jesus, with Jesus coming out on the short end. Some may remember the queer legend repeated by some promoters of the Rosary that describes Mary using the Rosary to lift through the back window of heaven those whom Jesus had rejected at the front door. On this the instigators of the Flame of Love devotion mince no words.

The cult derives from messages Our Lady allegedly addressed to six Hungarian children several years ago. The revelation includes the following:

"My children, my holy son's hand is prepared to strike down. It is difficult to hold him back. Help me! If you ask my Flame of Love for help, together we can save the world."

Such nonsense would be ludicrous if it were not that some Catholics really take it seriously. The errors, even heresies, in this kind of thinking are so numerous and complex one hardly knows where to begin.

Suffice it to say here that Jesus is Mary's Savior as much as he is ours and that, as God, he is the source and infinite exemplar of whatever saving love she or any of the rest of us may have. To even imply that she outshines him in mercy or compassion and that if we're really in trouble she will do for us what he won't, only dishonors the Mother of Christ.

The Flame of Love pamphlet claims to be printed with permission of a diocese in Hungary. Given the disturbed circumstances of the church in that nation, one cannot know by whom, or under what circumstances, such permission may have been given.

I find it hard to believe that legitimate Catholic authorities anywhere would sanction such a garbling of Catholic teaching and spirituality.

American saints

Can you tell us how many canonized saints there are from the United States?

Four U.S. citizens have now been canonized: Mother Frances Xavier Cabrini, who died in 1917, was the first, in 1946; John Nepomucene Neumann (died in 1860), bishop of Philadelphia, in 1977; Elizabeth Seton (died 1821), in 1975; and Rose Philippine Duchesne (died 1852), in 1988.

Elizabeth Seton is still the only native-born U.S. saint, though she was born in 1774, some years before the actual establishment of the United States.

Is St. Patrick still a saint?

An argument arose in our group when we were talking about St. Patrick's Day as to whether or not St. Patrick is still considered a saint. Some say they read that he is no longer considered as such by the Catholic Church, but the rest of us say that is impossible.

In the past few years a good deal of confused comment has appeared in the press in connection with St. Patrick's Day celebrations, so it's understandable that your group is confused, too. Several years ago, following extensive scientific research in the catacombs and other ancient locations, Catholic Church officials acknowledged serious doubts about the existence of certain early "saints," at least with the names traditionally given them. The mistakes came from misinterpreting inscriptions on tombs, misreading old documents, and so on.

St. Patrick was not one of these. He is among another group of saints whose feast days were dropped from the universal church calendar for automatic observance by Latin Rite Catholics everywhere. Many saints' feasts were eliminated this way, or otherwise de-emphasized, in order that more liturgical attention might be given the seasonal celebrations of the mysteries of Our Lord — Christmas, Lent, Holy Week, Easter and others.

Though not in the general church calendar, however, these feasts can still be celebrated in countries and localities which desire to do so — as St. Patrick's Day is in most parts of the United States on March 17.

St. Gerard

My husband and I want a child badly and someone gave us a prayer to St. Gerard to say for this intention. Who was he, and why is he supposed to be a patron for people like us?

St. Gerard Majella was an Italian lay brother and mystic who died at the age of 29 in 1755. After a childhood filled with an unusual share of mental and physical hardships, and after being rejected by the Capuchin monks because of ill health, he was finally accepted in the Redemptorist novitiate as "a useless lay brother."

So many miracles were attributed to him that even in his lifetime he became known as the wonderworker. Then and after his death, a number of these miracles involved situations which caused him to become the special patron of couples who seemed to be unable to have children. His feast is Oct. 16.

Veneration of relics

Could you give some information about the church's position on relics of the saints. I am puzzled why we do not encourage the veneration of relics. I believe they are special gifts from God. Is there a special prayer one can say, for example, when venerating a relic of our Lord?

The veneration of relics is one of those areas of Christian belief and practice which possess a solid theological and spiritual foundation, but which experience proves also have an almost built-in temptation for misunderstanding and abuse. The answer to your question involves explaining a bit of that experience.

As most Catholics know, veneration of the bodies of the saints, especially martyrs, goes back to the very early church. Sometimes the blood of the martyrs was collected on a cloth to be kept as a reminder to the Christian community of that individual's fidelity and courage in professing the faith. Later the Eucharist was celebrated and churches were built over their tombs.

Already by the 800s and 900s, however, problems began to surface. Possession of bodies of certain saints became a source of prestige for churches and monasteries. When St. Thomas Aquinas died in the Cistercian monastery of Fossa Nuova, it is reported that the monks there decapitated his body to be sure of keeping his remains. The tug of war between the Cistercians and Dominicans for St. Thomas' body continued for decades after his death. Buying and selling, even stealing bodies or parts of bodies of saints became common. Transfer of relics became a major international business. To this day church law explicitly forbids "alienation" or permanent transfer of major relics from one place to another without the pope's permission (Canon 1190).

It's not surprising that this strange sort of dealing with the bodies of saints should be reflected in popular piety of the Middle Ages and beyond. Veneration of relics gave rise to all kinds of feasts, shrines and pilgrimages. Possession of relics even became one of the marks of affluence and power. In 1392, at a royal feast, France's King Charles VI distributed to guests ribs of his holy ancestor St. Louis. Some opposition to these practices was always heard, but even popes eventually became nearly powerless to do anything to discourage them. Mishandling and even the sale of relics became one of the major abuses attacked by leaders of the Protestant Reformation.

In 1563, the Council of Trent offered three positive reasons for venerating the bodies of the saints. They were living members of the body of Christ, they were temples of the Holy Spirit, and are destined to be raised and glorified by him. (Session XXV) These motives obviously remain valid. But experience understandably makes the church continue to be careful, lest this far less central aspect of Catholic devotion again assume an importance and meaning way out of proportion. This concern is evident in several ways. Some carefully controlled options for veneration of relics which were offered in former church law are not even mentioned in the present Code of Canon Law. (This may be due as much simply to the decline of the importance of relics in popular Catholic devotion as to any other reason.)

The church's current norms and grants for indulgences do not include any prayers or actions relating to relics of the saints. In the late Middle Ages it became customary, and then required, to insert a saint's relic in every altar, the old "altar stone." Eventually this almost always turned out to be merely a tiny piece of bone or other body part. This is no longer required. Relics may be placed in altars today only under certain conditions, one of which is that the relic be at least large enough to be recognizable as part of a human body (Rite of Dedicating a Church, n. 5). Veneration of relics then can be a means of praising the goodness of God and of honoring our brothers and sisters who are saints. It is critical, and obviously not always easy, to preserve that focus.

Relics of saints

I have two first-class relics of saints on which I had proper papers. Over the years I have lost the papers. Do I really need them, and if so, how do I go about getting new ones?

In Catholic tradition, a relic is something that has been closely connected with one of the saints during his or her life on earth, for example, a piece of clothing or an item the person used. A first-class relic is generally defined as an actual part of the body, a particle of bone perhaps.

The keeping of such objects as an element of honor to the saints may sound a little bizarre to some modern ears, but it is really much like our human tradition of retaining keepsakes from people who were dear and special to us in this life.

The papers you refer to are called authentications. They are simply official declarations issued by the church agency or religious order responsible for those particular relics that, as far as possible, it is determined that the relics are what they are reported to be.

Usually it is practically impossible to obtain new authentications, but most relics have a small paper identifying them within the case containing the relic itself.

Luther a saint?

I heard recently that the Catholic Church is thinking of canonizing Martin Luther! How is it possible for the church to make a saint out of someone who lived like he did, and who caused such a terrible break from the Catholic Church?

I hardly know where to start this one. First, it may ease your mind to know that, rumors to the contrary, no one, Catholic or Protestant, is pushing to get Martin Luther canonized, to my knowledge.

A bit of explanation why these rumors have even arisen may help respond to the rest of your question. Sources and methods available to modern history scholars have brought about a major re-evaluation of Luther, and of the whole period that began the Protestant Reformation. One fact clear today, for example, is how drastically the harsh, bitter spirit of debate during the early decades of the Reformation affected the accusations and recriminations of both sides. These writings formed the major basis of what Catholics said about Luther (and Lutherans), and what Lutherans said about Catholics, almost up to our own generation.

Among facts widely acknowledged by historians are that much of what has been written about Luther's personal life is unfounded, and that many of his "heretical" teachings (about faith and the Eucharist, for example) are most compatible with Catholic doctrine when they are understood as he understood them, not as some of his early opponents interpreted them.

In addition, the most authoritative historians on the Council of Trent (which started the year before Luther died, and lasted 18 years) tend strongly to the belief that the reforms of that council would never have happened had it not been for the movement set in motion by Luther and some other early reformers. Pope Paul VI had said several times we all have much to repent in the tragic separation between Catholics and Protestants. He referred, in part, to the fact that the church was in many ways in a sorry condition at the time. A sweeping reform was long overdue, but even the heroic efforts of courageous Catholic reformers like St. Bernardine and St. Catherine of Siena had achieved only limited and local results. Something like Luther and his movement was probably inevitable to make the renewal happen.

This is, of course, not to defend everything Luther did and taught. It does, however, put his life, and what he "caused" in a considerably more charitable light. Lutherans themselves do not, I believe, admire him as a saint, nor as the perfect ideal of a Christian, but as a man who reacted with courage and intelligence to a personal and Christian crisis.

Communion of saints

I would like to know more about helping loved ones by praying for them after they have passed on.

So many other religions believe that when someone dies it is too late. Where in the Bible would I find something to back our beliefs about praying for the dead?

From the beginning, Christian people have believed in the

Communion of Saints — a union with those who have died before us as well as those who are presently in the Body of Christ on earth. They understood this to mean that prayers offered to God for those who have died, as well as for those still alive, are proper and effective in God's providence for his people.

As I said, we have evidence that this was true from the earliest decades of the church. But you won't find much, if anything, about it in the Bible.

True, some have seen hints of the validity of this beautiful Christian tradition and belief in a few Scripture passages, such as the reference in the book of Maccabees, that it is a "holy and wholesome thought to pray for the dead." (As one of the deutero-canonical books Maccabees is not traditionally in the Protestant bible.)

However, Christian belief in the Communion of Saints, and other beliefs following from that, are not primarily based on anything in the Scriptures. They come out of the instincts inspired by the Holy Spirit as the church gradually reflected on what Jesus said and did and how those things should affect the way his people live and pray.

Before going any further, it is helpful to remind ourselves of something extremely important in understanding our religion: not until the Protestant Reformation did Christian people begin to expect something to appear in the Bible before it could become valid Christian belief and practice. Even today most Protestants agree that this is not the way to approach or understand our Christian faith. Even those Christians who claim to believe only what is in the Bible actually believe many things that are not there.

Perhaps most obvious of all, where in the Bible does it even say there should be a Bible in the first place? Nowhere in the New Testament do we have a record of Jesus writing anything (except on the ground in the event of the woman caught in adultery) or asking His disciples to write anything. It was simply assumed to make sense, in light of the obvious intentions of Jesus, that some things be put into writing and recognized as normative by the church to lay out the parameters for Christian belief and practice.

Anything contrary to those parameters would be at least

suspect; but not everything was believed to be in those writings. This is the way the church intended the Scriptures when they were identified as our Christian "inspired writings," and this is the way the church understands them even today.

The same goes then for our belief in the Communion of Saints and prayer for the dead. If there is anything that the Resurrection of Jesus and other events related to the Resurrection told the earliest members of our faith, it was that the walls between heaven and earth are not impregnable. In some mysterious way of Divine Providence there is communication between the life of Eternity and the shadows of that life which we share in this world.

There is another, perhaps simpler, way of putting it: All the rest of what Jesus said and did, his relationships with the early Christians and their understanding of their intimacy with him as the Risen Lord, would make no sense at all if there were not such a thing as the Communion of Saints as the church has understood it, and a recognition of that union in our community of prayer with those who have gone before us.

Death and Burial

A fear of eternity

Sometimes it seems that I am the only one who worries and is depressed by eternity and life hereafter. It frightens this man of 73 that we will go on and on after death. My choice would be to just be reunited with our departed family and call it a day. My weary bones say I have been around long enough. Almost every month one of my former schoolmates takes his leave. I'm ready to join them except for the specter of eternity.

Believe me, you are not alone. Something of your experience is shared by everyone, especially as she or he advances in years. Your question is simply your way of expressing one of the major elements in the age-old experience of the human family, the fear of death. It is not so much death itself, but the wonder of what is on the other side that can give one the shivers.

Even Jesus could not explain that fear away and he did not try. However, one of his favorite expressions was, "Don't be afraid." And there is nothing about which he was more emphatic in that statement than about the fear of death.

I believe his entire attitude can be summarized like this: "I can't begin to explain to you what is on the other side of death. I can only tell you, as I have tried to prove, that the heavenly Father loves you and that where you are going will be your home just as it will be mine. Just try to do as I have told you, and then trust me."

That may sound extremely simple, but it really is what we

well might call the last will and testament of Jesus. I urge you to read the Gospel of St. John, chapters 13-17, where Jesus attempts, among other things, to prepare the disciples (and us) not only for his death but also for our own. Everything revolves around his promise that he is going before us to prepare a place for us, that where he is we also will be and that the joy that is his will be ours to the full.

As I have said before, Jesus really does not tell us too much about life after death, probably because he knows we could not understand if he tried.

Only a few great saints have found the experience of death a total joy and, to be honest, sometimes I wonder about them. For the rest of us, what God asks is a calm, grateful acceptance of his will, and trust that the Father will surely answer the moving prayer of Jesus that all his family, all his friends, will be in his company in the glory of eternity.(John 17:24)

That may not be all we would like to know about eternity, but it far surpasses what mankind once dreamed it would ever know.

Funeral Mass passe?

Many Catholics in our area just have a funeral service at a funeral home but do have a priest present. Is there a reason for this? Is there a trend against bringing the deceased person to the church for a funeral Mass?

There surely is no trend in that direction to my knowledge. As pointed out in a previous question, the celebration of the Eucharist in church, with the body of the dead person present, remains the ideal and normal ceremony before burial. It is a profoundly significant act of prayer for the one who has died, and of faith and hope by those who are left behind.

The official rite of burial does provide for a funeral service outside of Mass. I have officiated at such ceremonies on occasion when the desires of the family or other special circumstances seemed to make that form of funeral rite more appropriate. This is surely the explanation for those occasions you have encountered.

Incense at funeral Masses

Please explain the use of incense, especially at funeral Masses. Why does the priest incense the casket?

The use of burning incense in religious ceremonies as a symbol of prayer and worship of God goes back to ancient times. Pagan religious rites included it and it is referred to often in Scripture in connection with Jewish ceremonies in Old Testament worship. (See, for example, Exodus 30:34-38)

At first Christians refused to use incense because of its connection with pagan Roman worship, but later incense became quite common, especially at Mass. It is both a symbol of prayer to God and of honor to holy things — which is why the altar, the people, the body of the deceased at funeral Masses, the Easter candle and other sacred objects are often incensed during our liturgies.

Funeral services for non-Catholic

Can the funeral of a non-Catholic ever be held in a Catholic church?

Under certain circumstances it is possible for funeral services to be conducted for a non-Catholic in a Catholic church.

Priests often officiate at funerals of those not of our faith, especially when the person is a relative or is otherwise close to a member of the Catholic parish, and when the family requests it. Usually these ceremonies are conducted in the funeral home, but there is nothing in general church law that would forbid holding such a service in church. Naturally, the ceremony would rarely, if ever, include the offering of the Eucharist, but it could include any other appropriate Scripture readings and prayers.

The decision on each case would be subject to the discretion of the pastor or perhaps the local bishop.

Why buried without Mass?

A Catholic friend of mine was buried during the past few

days, but there was no Mass. She was taken from the funeral home to the cemetery for something called a committal service, which lasted about 10 minutes.

In our city, Catholics are always taken to church for Mass before burial. Why wasn't she? Is this something new?

In our country, as in most of the rest of the world, the celebration of the Eucharist is nearly always a part (in fact, the central part) of the funeral rite for Catholics. For one reason or another, it occasionally happens that Mass is omitted at that time, and that the funeral proceeds from the mortuary directly to the cemetery. Such a plan is explicitly provided for in the official "Rite of Funerals."

However, whenever the Mass is not part of the burial rite itself, the Eucharistic Celebration for the deceased person should take place without the body, either before or after the funeral.

You are aware, of course, that someone who is known as a Catholic might not have a Catholic burial at all if he has, in some significant way, rejected the church and his membership in it during his lifetime.

Funeral Mass for "former Catholic"

A friend of mine, a former Catholic, died recently. I say "former Catholic" because for years she did not go to Mass. She requested that she not be brought into church after her death. In spite of this there was a funeral Mass for her.

Is this usual practice? Would a person like this always have a funeral Mass?

When a person dies after years of neglect in the practice of his or her faith, every benefit of doubt is given in determining the type of funeral rite that is provided. Often the children of such individuals are aware of situations in the family that color the attitude of the dead person quite differently than the person appeared to outsiders, possibly even to the parish priest.

On the other hand, the church does not feel it has a right to impose religious ceremonies on people who have explicitly and with full consciousness rejected them. It does not presume to judge how that person stands before God, but the position of the church is that it must respect the clear intent and will of the individual as expressed when that person was alive.

It is impossible to evaluate the circumstances of the individual and family you mention. In fact, I would guess that many elements of that person's religious and family life are unknown even to you as a close friend. I assume, as I suggest you do also, that the parish priest on the scene acted with as great a concern as possible for the woman who died and for her family and friends.

Meriting Catholic burial

My former husband, whom I married in the church at a nuptial Mass, died recently. We were divorced 30 years ago and three years later he married a Catholic woman in a Baptist church. He never practiced his faith as far as I know. Recently he became suddenly ill and died in a coma without regaining consciousness.

But how could he be given the last rites and be buried from the Catholic Church? I'm shocked at this.

First of all, there may be much about his last years and days that you do not know. Offhand, I can think of several circumstances that might legitimately explain his burial from the church. Perhaps some of these would be unknown outside of those closest to him in his final hours.

Most important, however, the church gives every benefit of the doubt to one who has been a Catholic and who indicates any desire to be considered a Catholic when he dies.

Catholic burial never implies approval of all an individual's actions; even less does it imply any judgment of him one way or the other. The church simply accepts the person as one of its children, as a brother or sister of Christ, prays for and professes its faith in the loving mercy of God.

You were deeply hurt by the divorce and the wounds obviously are still far from healed. But I hope you don't begrudge him either the church's prayers or your own.

Husband remarried

I am still indignant about the answer you once gave to a

woman who was divorced 30 years ago and whose husband
remarried in the Baptist Church, died in a coma, and was
given the last rites and buried in the Catholic church. You
remarked that circumstances could allow this, but did not say
what they are.

My husband of 21 years insisted on a divorce last year. I
finally agreed. He remarried immediately in a Protestant
church. I continue as a devout Catholic.

Do you mean to tell me that if he continues as he is until
his death, there is **any** circumstance at all which would allow
him to receive the last rites? Why should I, then, continue
to follow my vows and live the rest of my life alone if this
is the case? That does not make any sense at all.

You have been badly and painfully hurt by your husband.
But before and above everything else, please don't let bitterness
begin to rule your life. You will hurt yourself far more than
you will hurt your husband.

The person who asked the recent question had no intimate
knowledge of the final days of her deceased acquaintance.
As I indicated, unless an individual was with that person
almost continually through those final hours, and unless he
or she were privy to all the thoughts and words of the dying
person, he or she might be unaware of circumstances which
could most certainly open the way for Catholic burial.

The individual may have given clear signs of sorrow to one
person or another, or might even have received the last
sacraments, including the Sacrament of Penance, sometime
before death.

Certainly repentance for wrongs that have been committed is possible all the way up to the time of death. Basic charity
demands that we desire this even for our worst enemies.

In granting Christian burial, whenever it is possible to give
an individual the benefit of any doubt the church makes absolutely no pretense of judgment about that individual's soul.
It simply acknowledges that the deceased man or woman is
one of its children and commends it with every possible prayer
at its command to the merciful judgment of God.

As for why you should continue acting in one way when
your husband acts in another, the answer is very simple: You
believe you are doing what is right. When you die, you will

be asked by God to give an accounting not of someone else's life and actions, but of your own.

As I said at first, don't let your anger cloud that fact or diminish the fullness of the life that remains for you to live.

Burial of a non-Catholic

I am a Catholic and my husband is not. Will he be allowed to be buried in a Catholic cemetery? If not, would it be against the laws of the church for me to be buried in a non-Catholic cemetery?

Christians always have shown great concern that the funeral rites and burial of their dead brothers and sisters reflect their beliefs about the sacredness of the human body and the resurrection. Part of this concern moved them to have special areas set aside for their dead, a custom our church has carried on to the present time.

However, its policies are not so strict as to preclude either of the options you suggest. People who are not Catholics (a common example is the spouse of a Catholic, as in your case) may normally be buried in a Catholic cemetery.

Also, Catholics (again a common example may be a spouse, or a convert whose family plot is in another cemetery) may be buried in a non-Catholic cemetery. In the latter case, the grave is blessed at the time of the burial just as it would be in a Catholic cemetery.

Each diocese has its regulations about these things, which may differ slightly from some others. So it's best to ask your parish priest about details.

Mass intention for non-Catholics

My Protestant employer recently passed away. Today one of my Catholic co-workers and I were discussing the appropriateness of having a Mass offered for him and sending a Mass card to the family.

Is it all right to do this? Do the merits of a Mass for the dead apply to those who are not Catholic?

I confess my hesitation for several weeks before including

this question, frankly because of some embarrassment about it appearing in this column. I certainly mean no disrespect to you, nor do I in any way ridicule your concern and your honest question.

That question, after all, results from a mentality which was not of your making, but which we recognize today came out of an era and a mentality that was heavily influenced by the Catholic Church's efforts to preserve its identity and theological positions after the Protestant Reformation.

Having said that, I also must say that your question reveals so many misconceptions about the church and about our faith that I hardly know where to start.

First, the Mass can definitely be offered for the intention of those who are not Catholic. As I explained in the chapter on Ecumenism, it may even be announced publicly if two conditions are fulfilled:

1. The request for the celebration of Mass for the Protestant person should be made by the family, or at least explicitly approved by them. This is simply to assure that the non-Catholic's family will not be offended by something they do not believe in, and perhaps might reject.

2. There should be no scandal resulting either for Catholics or for those of other faiths because of the announced intention of the Mass. (Decree of the Congregation of the Doctrine of the Faith, 1976)

In this position, the church simply recognizes in one of many ways that it has no corner on God's love or on Christ's redeeming grace. Nor does it feel it has any armhold on the directions in which the grace and love of the crucified and risen Christ — celebrated and represented in the Eucharist — will go.

Jesus Christ died for all mankind, as St. Paul and the rest of the New Testament attest time and again. If the Mass, the celebration of the Eucharist is, as we believe it to be, the reoffering of that once-and-for-all sacrifice to the heavenly Father, then every Mass is for all humankind too. No one, nothing of creation, is excluded.

Our belief is reflected frequently in the documents of Vatican Council II. The plan of the Eternal Father "was to dignify mankind with a participation in his own divine life.

He did not abandon them after they had fallen in Adam, but ceaselessly offered them helps to salvation in anticipation of Christ the redeemer."

At the end of time, "all just men from the time of Adam, from Abel, the just one, to the last of the elect, will be gathered together with the Father in the universal church."

This growth and fulfillment "are foretold in the Lord's words concerning his death on the cross: 'And I, if I be lifted up from the earth, will draw all men to myself' (John 12:32)

"As often as the sacrifice of the cross in which 'Christ our passover, has been sacrificed' is celebrated on an altar, the work of our redemption is carried on . . . All men are called to this union with Christ who is the light of the world, from whom we go forth, through whom we live, and toward whom our journey leads us." (Dogmatic Constitution on the Church, paragraphs 2 and 3)

The Catholic Church does not try to force itself or its beliefs on anyone, so it is very conscious of not imposing itself on another even after death. Hence the rule about not violating another human being's conscience, or that of the family, even after he or she has died.

Its own belief, however, is clear: The love of Jesus as shown on the cross and as remembered and renewed in the Eucharist, is as big and as embracing as the world.

Church's position on cremation?

I am a senior citizen and would like to know about crema-tion. How can it be permitted now if the church once did not allow it? What happens to the ashes? I've been thinking about being cremated, but some of my family is against it.

You're not the only one wondering about this. I receive more letters and questions now about cremation than any other subject.

Cremation was formerly forbidden by the church because it was promoted years ago, especially in Europe, by groups who used cremation as an argument against belief in the resur-rection. How could God possibly collect all those ashes and smoke together to make us rise again?

It's been a long time since that argument was raised seriously by anyone. So cremation is no longer forbidden, provided
that the individual involved and his family intend no disrespect
or contempt for the body or for our faith. In fact, the funeral
rite of the church explicitly provides for cremation ceremonies.
(See Introduction to the Rite of Funerals and CCL 1176)

The ashes need not be buried, as long as they are disposed
of in a manner appropriate to the dignity of the human body.

I strongly suggest a few considerations, however, before you
or anyone else decides on cremation. When it speaks of cremation, the church points out its "preference for the custom of
burying the dead in a grave or tomb, as the Lord himself willed
to be buried." There are good reasons for this reminder, at
least in our Western culture.

Fifteen centuries ago, St. Augustine noted that our Christian funeral rites are more for the living than for the dead.
The deceased individual may be unaffected by cremation as
distinct from usual burial, but his friends and relatives still
have many lessons to learn about life and death, the short-
ness of our time on earth, and the priorities in our life that
can become extremely confused in the business of daily living. As Augustine said, our confrontation with death can put
things back into proper focus.

The point being made by the holy bishop was that we need
the reminders that come to us in the presence of the body
of a friend, in the Eucharist we offer, and in the placing of
the body in the grave. All our funeral liturgy, from wake to
burial, beautifully spells out those reminders in the context
of Jesus' own death and resurrection.

Even though cremation is now lawful, we should think of
what we can do for those left behind. At very least, when family is involved, I believe one should discuss the matter
thoroughly with them and make sure they are psychologically and spiritually comfortable with the arrangements. Should
we ever lose contact with those large spiritual realities that
confront us in death and in the liturgies of burial, we would
lose something very precious in our Christian lives.

History of cremation

I still get arguments from fellow Catholics, including a couple of priests, that cremation is not allowed by the church even yet.

Could you be more specific about when the church allows cremation, and how it happened to put such emphasis on ordinary burial in the first place?

It seems generally agreed that the Christian Church adopted the practice of inhumation (burial in a grave as we have traditionally known it) from the ancient Romans, who adopted the custom in order to have more elaborate and demonstrative funerals.

Whenever feasible, this form of burial became common for nearly all Christians, even in those parts of the world such as the Far East where significantly different funeral customs prevailed.

Burial of the dead was so common in Western society that no laws prohibiting cremation were proposed until the late Middle Ages. The most stringent regulations appeared only about 100 years ago, when cremation became rather suddenly more popular in Europe.

The first general legislation banning the burning of bodies as a funeral rite came from the Vatican's Holy Office in May, 1886, noting the anti-religious and Masonic motivation behind the movement. The Code of Canon Law of 1918 continued the ban because cremation was still considered a flagrant rejection of the Christian belief in immortality and the resurrection. That code forbade Christian burial to anyone who ordered that his body be cremated. (Exceptions were always made for times of urgent public crisis, such as epidemics, war, etc.)

In 1926, the church was forced to repeat the warning, noting that, because of the virulent anti-religious motivation of most cremation proponents, its promoters were "enemies of Christianity."

With the decline of the anti-Christian symbolism of cremation, however, regulations have become far less strict. An instruction of the Holy Office in 1963 recognized that there may be many personal reasons for desiring cremation — financial, emotional, hygienic, and others. While it indicates the church's continued preference for inhumation as more traditionally respectful of the human body, it presumes that people who request cremation are doing so in good faith, not out of some irreligious motive. Laws forbidding cremation now apply only when it is clear that cremation "was chosen through a denial of Christian doctrines, or results from a sectarian spirit, or from hatred of the Catholic religion and the church."

The official Rite of Funerals (which took effect June 1, 1970, by decree of Pope Paul VI) says "Christian funeral rites are permitted for those who choose to have their bodies cremated unless it is shown that they have acted for reasons contrary to Christian principles." In other words, cremation with all ordinary Catholic funeral ceremonies is permissible unless someone desires it in order to deny his belief in the resurrection or other Christian truths.

When a body is to be cremated, the funeral Mass may take place with the body present before cremation, or the funeral ceremonies including the Eucharist could be celebrated after the cremation and burial.

The church has no regulations whatsoever about a casket. Religious customs on this matter differ from country to country.

No state in our country has an actual requirement for a casket if the body will be cremated. A few states do require that the body be shipped to the crematory in a "casket or other suitable container."

These are the facts. However, I must repeat what I said previously: Before deciding on cremation (or giving one's body to science or any other out of the ordinary plans for one's funeral), I believe the psychological and religious needs and desires of your family and friends deserve careful consideration. One of your last beautiful gifts to them can be the way you allow your death and burial to help them remember you well, and support them in their own lives.

Funeral Mass after cremation?

Can there be a Mass of Resurrection for people who donate their bodies or some of their organs to science? How about those who choose cremation? I know several people who carry cards offering their organs after death and who also wish to

be cremated. I'm sure they'd expect the ashes to be placed in a Catholic mausoleum.

Regulations of our church specifically indicate that a funeral Mass may be offered for those who give their body, or parts of their body, for scientific research or for transplants. The same goes for those who desire that their body be cremated.

Normally, as you indicate, the ashes would be placed in a Catholic cemetery.

I should repeat what I have urged several times before. Those who contemplate giving their body to science, or who are thinking of cremation, should consult with their family. Family members may be aided much by appropriate funeral and burial rites, and the person involved should consider the needs of their loved ones before making such decisions.

Incidentally, the proper designation for a funeral Mass is the Mass of Christian Burial, not the Mass of Resurrection, even though one hears the latter term frequently today.

Willing one's body to science

In your answer about cremation you said, "Even though cremation is now lawful, we should think of what we can do for those left behind."

This remark prompted a question that has been on my mind for some time. Is it permissible for a practicing Catholic to will his or her body to science? I would like my body used for the betterment of humanity in any way, after I am finished with it. I am also concerned about the effect on my grieving relatives.

It is certainly lawful and can be a great act of charity for one to donate his or her body, or a needed organ, at the time of death. The use of organs and bodies for transplants, education and research is still significant, even though medical schools themselves rely heavily today on models which simulate most major physical structure and functions.

If the decision is made for such a donation, record is kept by the individual or the family and the body is removed for that purpose immediately after death.

In my opinion, you are wise and thoughtful to consider not

only your own feelings but those of your relatives as well. The funeral and burial rite can help them deal with the grief resulting from death, and also help them accept the reality of death — their own as well as yours. I agree that you should discuss your thoughts with them and learn their feelings before you make a decision.

Two of the major national organ procurement programs are The United Network for Organ Sharing (phone 800-446-2726) and the American Council on Transplantation (phone 800-228-4483).

A Uniform Donor Card providing for the gift of part of one's body to a living person who needs it, or all of one's body for education-research, may be obtained from Living Bank, Box 6725, Houston, Texas, 77265. Many states now have donor forms on the back of, or attached to, drivers' licenses. Ask your funeral director.

Can Catholics avoid wakes?

My husband and I oppose wakes for the dead. When we die we'd like our caskets closed, with no wake, and a service at the funeral home by a priest.

Sometime after the funeral, our loved ones would go to Mass and offer it for the one who has died. Would such a funeral arrangement be permitted by the church?

I realize you are simply exploring the idea. Remember, however, that the funeral ceremony is not primarily for the dead, but for those who are left behind. Prayers for the deceased individual and for all the dead are included in the funeral rite. But much more significant is the aid that the funeral liturgy gives to those who are still alive to evaluate their own lives, confront again the priorities of which death reminds us, and allow our grief over the loss of a loved one to be worked out in a Christian context.

All this may not be important to you after you have died. It may be extremely significant to your children, grandchildren, and friends who will be reminded of some important truths by their encounter with the death of one of their loved ones.

I urge you not to make any such preparations without consulting your family. The ritual you wish to avoid may (excuse the expression) leave you cold. It may also be the richest and most valuable final gift you leave to your family.

Dead fetuses

What does the Catholic Church teach should be done with dead fetuses? Some of those who are in favor of liberal abortion also say that even in Catholic hospitals such fetuses are simply thrown away, which proves that Catholics don't really think fetuses are human after all.

Those who think that proper Catholic practice is to discard the fetus are totally wrong. According to the directives followed in Catholic hospitals (and to large degree in many other hospitals), a dead fetus normally is given proper burial regardless of how mature that fetus is, as is "consonant with the dignity of a human body."

I say "normally" because in some instances there may be serious reason against it (for example, the need to use the fetus for laboratory study and observation) or it may even be impossible. Since the fetus is less than an inch long even after four or five weeks, it is entirely possible, for example, for a spontaneous abortion (miscarriage) to have occurred several days before the mother or doctor would be aware of it.

Catholic burial after suicide

May Catholics who are presumed to have committed suicide have the same funeral service as other Catholics? Are they allowed burial in a Catholic cemetery? Are the rules hard and fast or can they vary from parish to parish depending upon the circumstances and the pastor?

In its legislation dealing with funeral rites, the Church lists briefly those who are to be deprived of Catholic funeral rites, unless they give some sign of repentance before death. Among these are "manifest sinners for whom ecclesiastical funeral rites cannot be granted without public scandal to the faithful" (Canon 1184).

People who attempt or commit suicide are not mentioned explicitly; insofar as they are covered at all it would be as part of that group.

Are people who commit suicide open "sinners" whose Christian burial would give scandal to others? Bishops and other pastors always have, and rightly, acted with great awareness of our limitations in knowing what really happened spiritually, and with particular care for the people who are left behind.

It may help to realize the complications involved if we recall the old catechism criteria for a serious sin: (1) a serious matter; (2) sufficient reflection in the mind; and (3) full consent of the will.

There is no question about the first. Taking one's own life is objectively, perhaps more than any other murder, a radical rejection of God's Lordship and of his supreme and absolute authority over all life. Our life is his created gift; we may never play at being God by pretending this life is ours to destroy. Suicide is then an extremely serious matter.

The last two criteria are just as important but are nowhere near as clear as the first.

I have had the sad experience of dealing with suicide many times in my years as a priest. In each instance, circumstances surrounding the death indicated to everyone who knew them that the deceased were hampered mentally or emotionally, often to a highly serious degree, at the time of death.

As I said, the church has always understood that this can be true. Catholic burial is therefore rarely, if ever, refused because of a suicide.

It is worth noting that this presumption may become less valid in our present social atmosphere where suicide is more and more presented as a "rational" way of ending a life that has ceased to be "useful." It also must be said that this kind of suggestion comes generally from groups and literature which openly reject all religion, if they are not in fact openly antagonistic to any belief in God. Insofar as this would be true also for the individual who commits suicide, the church's regulations, of course, would have no relevance.

Obviously the decision concerning Catholic burial of someone who has committed suicide is a matter of judgment. It usually is made at the parish level; it may be decided finally by the bishop. In any case, that judgment is traditionally very lenient.

After all, in offering Christian burial rites the church makes no judgment on the individual's eternal relationship with God. It simply begs God's mercy for the deceased individual and for those who have been hurt by the death.

Suicide in Christian history

I have been recently told that suicide is not sinful. I always believed it was a sin against the fifth commandment, thou shalt not kill. Someone said that suicide was once all right and approved by Catholics. Is this true?

Before responding to your question directly, something needs to be said that many Catholics (indeed other Christians as well) find hard to believe. This is the fact that the moral code taught by the church, and by other Christians, did not fall explicit and full-blown into our laps.

Jesus gave us the two foundational principles for morality, to love God above all things and our neighbor as ourselves. Throughout its 2,000 years, the church has meditated and reflected on those principles as it tried to discern what they mean in the myriad of cultural, personal, social and religious conditions in which Christian men and women find themselves. Each new circumstance helps clarify these applications more fully and with deeper spiritual insight. If we stop to think about it we can understand that this process will inevitably deal with nearly every aspect of human life and action. In at least most instances, certainly in intricate details, it will probably continue as long as the church exists.

The area of morality about which you speak is a good example. During the early Christian centuries, in the time of the great Roman persecutions, killing oneself in the face of imminent torture and death was looked on with great praise. Bishop Eusebius of Caesarea (died in the year 340) provides our best window into the first Christian centuries in his "History of the Church From Christ to Constantine."

While their fellow Christians praised highly those martyrs who endured the horrendous tortures and trials before they finally died, he tells of others who, "unable to face such a trial, and before they were caught and came into the hands of their would-be destroyers, threw themselves down from the roofs of tall houses, regarding death as a prize snatched from the scheming hands of God's enemies." Women were praised for throwing themselves to their death rather than submit to abuse. One woman, about to be apprehended for dishonor and torture, stabbed herself to death. "By deed that spoke more loudly than any words," says Eusebius, "she proclaimed to all men then living or yet to come that the only unconquerable and indestructible possession was a Christian's virtue" (Book XII, XV).

Suicide was not, incidentally, the only area of moral action about which our Christian forebears held ideals less refined than our own. Eusebius describes with obvious approval how, when the persecutions ended and the "enemies of true religion" were captured, these enemies were themselves subjected to "elaborate tortures" and executed. Obviously, none of us today would sanction these barbarous attitudes toward other human beings, though as we are aware they are all too common among Christians even in our own generation. We need urgently, in other words, to be aware that we do not automatically and necessarily enjoy certain options in the way we treat ourselves and others, simply because Christians of another time acted in a particular way.

To be specific, the church's teaching, based on God's lordship over our lives, is that any attempt to take one's own life is objectively seriously sinful. The individual's subjective responsibility, of course, depends on many factors. We have, or should have, learned much as a community of the church about applying Gospel values to human life. Indeed, if history has anything to teach us, it is that even yet we have not learned it all.

Aftermath of suicide

My question is, did you ever feel like a nothing? Like a blank piece of paper? I've been alive for 22 years and I feel like I've never made an impression on the world.

My brother killed himself, and now I cannot. After he died my family was crushed; they'll never be the same. I can't do that to them again. Does God test everyone this way? Is it my imagination or are other people in this world relatively happy? How can I get help?

I'm sorry you did not send your address. It is impossible for me to respond personally to all the mail I receive, but I would have tried to help you any way I could.

Your letter is proof again of how much we need each other on this earth. It also proves how impossible it is for us to judge another person's life, or even in many ways our own.

For better or worse, we are deeply involved with each other. You need desperately to talk to someone who loves you and is concerned about you, to air your feelings of guilt and frustration.

I'm not sure who that might be for you, but please do not rule out your own family too quickly. Too often after a tragedy such as your family has suffered, parents and children alike tend to hide their feelings from each other out of a loving concern not to add their own problems to the emotional hurts already suffered by other members of the family.

Tenderness and thoughtfulness are called for here. But sometimes one member's willingness to expose his or her fears and hurts can help others to do the same, to the mutual support and encouragement of everyone.

Beyond that you might talk with a friend or with a priest in whom you have confidence, your own parish priest or someone else.

Above all, know that there is real hope for you. The feelings of desolation and depression you express are common, even normal in a time of grief and loss such as you and your family experienced.

Good luck, I'll be praying for you. I know that many of the readers of this column will also.

Burial at sea

I am interested in ocean burial. Does the Catholic Church have any objections to this idea?

From the very beginning Christians have taken burials very seriously. The attitude and customs of any people toward their dead says much about their beliefs concerning the meaning of life, respect for their bodies, and life after death.

The Christian church was, and is, no different. Funeral customs always reflect Christians' faith in Christ, their conviction about the dignity of our human person including the body, and, of course, belief in life after death. To this day it even sets aside reserved space to receive the bodies of those who have died.

For these reasons the church strongly discourages any practices that might, in a frivolous way, begin to reflect dishonor on the dead or seem to minimize, if not ridicule, beliefs which are extremely precious to us.

It is within this context that your question must be approached. If a good and valid reason suggests it, there is no rule against burial at sea. Obviously it is done thousands of times in emergency situations, particularly in time of war. This type of burial, therefore, would not be automatically wrong for you.

I would suggest only that you consider your reasons carefully and that you discuss the matter with your parish priest, who would be responsible for carrying out your wishes within the framework of our Catholic liturgy for the dead.

Right to die

Is there any recent church statement about the right to die with dignity — that there is no need to use extraordinary means to keep a dying person alive, etc? I have a teacher who insists the Catholic Church demands that nothing be done in this way, in order to allow a person to die peacefully.

References of the kind you seek are numerous. One of the more recent appears in a letter written Oct. 12, 1970, in the name of Pope Paul VI by the Vatican Secretary of State to the International Federation of Catholic Medical Associations.

Pointing out that a doctor can never kill, the letter noted, however, that he does not have to use all the techniques of survival that modern science offers. "In many cases," it continues, "would it not be useless torture to impose vegetative resuscitation in the final stages of an incurable sickness? The doctor's duty here is rather to ease the suffering, instead of prolonging as long as possible, by any means and in any condition whatsoever, a life no longer fully human, and which is closing to its natural end . . . In this way, too, a doctor must respect life."

The position indicated here is not new; it dates a long way back in Catholic and other Christian moral teaching.

Won't take care of health

I irk my relatives and friends because I won't seek medical help for any illness. They claim it's due to stubbornness. My argument is, I'll go next week if my time is up whether I go to a doctor or not. Am I right or wrong?

Sorry, but you don't give anywhere near enough information for an answer to be very helpful. How serious is your illness? How much help will medical assistance be? How old are you? And what responsibilities to others have you in your present situation?

A father at age 45 with six growing children obviously has a more serious obligation to seek medical advice for a serious illness than does an old man of 80 whose children are all adults.

But however right or wrong your conclusion may be, I can't say much for your argument. By the same logic, you could drive your car recklessly or stop eating, arguing that when your time is up you'll die anyway. Our responsibility is to take reasonable care of our health and protect it as well as we can, whether the dangers to it come from inside or outside.

Living wills and power of attorney

Newspapers in our state print many stories about living wills and other documents people can sign to prepare for a serious illness. The more I think about it, the more concerned I am. Do you think it is wise for a person to have such a "will"?

Living wills are one form of Advance Directives, various methods of determining which types of medical technology and treatment should not be used if a person suffers a critical, perhaps terminal, illness, but is unable to make necessary health care decisions himself or herself.

A living will is a personal document indicating to the physician, family, or health care institution which life-sustaining or life-prolonging treatments should be withdrawn in a terminal illness.

The other most widely discussed Advance Directive is the Durable Power of Attorney for Health Care. This names another person as your substitute to make critical health care decisions if you are unable to make such decisions yourself.

Many states have established additional legal procedures to provide a health care surrogate. In at least one state, if an individual has no living will or Durable Power of Attorney, the hospital or other health care provider must find the highest person on a legal list (guardian, spouse, adult child of the patient, etc.) to serve as substitute decision maker.

It needs to be said that there is no universal agreement on the value, appropriateness or necessity of these Advance Directives. For one thing, the motivation is not always pure and good. Some organizations who are laboring vigorously for permissive euthanasia laws and for physician-assisted suicide, consider living wills, for example, a first step toward their more sinister goals.

The largest concern, in my judgment, is the inevitable confusion and fuzziness about what exactly is being signed away. The person who makes a living will is rejecting some unspecified future treatment in some unspecified future circumstance.

In addition to other obvious difficulties, a legally executed living will might force a good physician, or at least lead him to feel forced, to act against his better medical and human judgment, even one made in consultation with the family of the patient.

Under any such arrangement, the patient and others designated are morally obliged to base their decisions on several fundamental truths. First, all human life is a gift from God that must be treated with respect and reverence in every circumstance.

Second, death is for us not an absolute evil to be frantically delayed as long as possible at all costs. We believe that death is the beginning of eternal life, not the end of existence. And third, each of us has the right and obligation to be in charge of the health care we receive, whether we make the decisions ourselves or arrange for others to make them in our stead.

All these factors need to be prayerfully and carefully pondered in each life-and-death decision.

The complexity of all this is multiplied by the fact that most states now have some legal guidelines to determine who has what rights and obligations in critical health decisions. These legal guidelines differ from state to state.

State Catholic Conferences in many parts of the country have prepared, or are preparing, explanations of these questions in light of moral concerns and individual state laws.

To discover what is or is not possible where you live, and what the consequences of your own advance directives may be, you need to contact an attorney, or perhaps a priest who would be conversant with such matters, or the chancery of your diocese.

Why no flag on casket?

When a casket is brought into church for a funeral Mass, it is covered with a white shroud. In the case of veterans, the

American flag is removed and the white shroud is placed over the casket. Many veterans and veterans' organizations want an exception to this for veterans whose caskets are covered by the American flag. They wish the flag to remain on the casket during the funeral Mass.

Where should our veterans' posts go to have this exception made official so deceased veterans will have the American flag covering their caskets at all times during the funeral process?

The American (or other national) flag may be placed over the casket until the body enters the church, and at the time of burial, when it would be folded and presented to the surviving family. This is what occurred, you may recall, at the funeral liturgy for President John F. Kennedy. There is no provision, however, in our Catholic rituals for replacing the white pall with the flag during the liturgy in church. When the pall is used (it is optional in the funeral liturgy) along with the sprinkling of water, it is a symbol of the water and white cloth used at baptism. It expresses the baptismal faith of the Christian who is being buried and the faith of the others who are present as participants in the liturgy.

As a Christian, the individual who has died owed many loyalties: to God, to his or her spouse and children, to others who rightfully depended upon him or her for love and care, to work and profession; and of course a patriotic commitment to honor and preserve the country's ideals of justice and freedom. One of the primary intentions of our Catholic funeral liturgy is to acknowledge and thank God for this particular Christian's faithful adherence to all these commitments and loyalties.

It is indeed a virtuous and sometimes heroic act to serve one's nation with a good conscience in whatever capacity, including militarily. We honor and express our gratitude for that patriotism by appropriate honors at the time of burial. It would be inappropriate, however, to single out that one aspect of Christian generosity as symbolically the primary focus of the funeral Mass and other burial liturgies. In designing the funeral liturgy, the church attempts to honor and remind us of all the ways we must respond to our Lord's command to love God and neighbor.

Mass of the Angels?

Could you explain the phrase "Mass of the Angels" in relation to funerals? We still find it occasionally in children's obituary notices in our paper. As I understand it, this was a type of funeral Mass for children under a certain age. Is this accurate? Is it still proper terminology?

This way of describing a funeral Mass for a very young child used to be quite common, but was never an accurate designation for any funeral liturgy. It arose, of course, from a widespread folk custom of describing very young children who have died as "angels in heaven." This expression was in some ways understandable, particularly in comparing their childlike innocence to that of the angels.

There was and is, however, no theological or liturgical basis for this way of speaking. All human persons, regardless of age, are distinguished from angelic creatures by the fact that we have a body and soul, and that we are destined to rise body and soul in the resurrection from the dead. The older pre-Vatican II missals designate all burial or commemorative Masses as simply Masses for the Dead. Our present missal is the same, though it does include special prayers for different classes of people (married people, parents, priests and so on), and special Mass prayers for infant children, even those who have died before baptism.

As I have explained at length previously, our church law provides that even children who have not been baptized may be buried with full liturgical rites, including the Eucharist, if the parents intended to baptize the children but had no opportunity (Canon 1183). No distinction is made between children who die before or after birth.

A similar confusion to the one you mention is often evident today, designating the funeral Mass as the Mass of the Resurrection. This, too, is understandable considering the emphasis in our liturgy for the dead on the hope and joy promised us by our sharing in the death and resurrection of Christ. Another common designation, the Mass of Christian Burial, is less confusing. However, the proper liturgical designation is still the Mass for the Dead, or Funeral Mass.

Passive euthanasia

A newspaper referred to what was called "passive euthanasia." The article seemed to say that this kind of euthanasia is morally permissible. If it's mercy killing, it's still wrong isn't it?

Passive euthanasia is a phrase used occasionally today in medical and moral literature to describe a situation in which a person is allowed to die rather than be provided with treatment or medication that would keep him alive. Thus it is opposed to active euthanasia (euthanasia, or mercy killing, in the traditional sense) in which death is brought about by some positive, deliberate action of a physician or other person.

Using the word euthanasia in this double sense can be confusing. There is a huge difference morally between the two. For example, to administer a fatal drug to a suffering person (active euthanasia) may be called "merciful release" or any number of other pleasant sounding names. But it is plain intentional killing of another human being. It has almost always been recognized as seriously wrong by the human race in general, by moral theologians, and — until recently at least — by the medical profession almost without exception.

On the other hand, it is not always morally necessary to use every conceivable means to keep a sick person going a while longer. Treatment which would be extraordinary under the circumstances because of immense cost, extreme pain, little hope for success, or other reasons, need not always be used.

A very old person might know, for example, that his life could be prolonged by several months only by a very expensive and exhausting operation. He would not be obliged to submit to that operation, nor would his doctor be obliged to perform it against the patient's desire.

Obviously, such a decision can be very complicated and difficult to make. What might be extraordinary and therefore not required for an aged grandmother, could be quite different for a younger father who still has a wife and family depending on him for support.

Passive euthanasia, then, is not necessarily mercy killing in the immoral sense. Whether it is right or wrong depends on the circumstances.

Etcetera

Doubting the existence of God

I am 14 years old and have recently been having doubts as to the existence of God and Jesus and all the other characters of the Bible.

I used to be so devoted to God, said my prayers every night and every morning and participated fully at all the Masses. I know that faith is believing in something you cannot see, but I am finding it very hard.

It started one day at Mass when I got to thinking: What if we're all worshiping something that doesn't exist? I started feeling very silly, like I was taking part in something that had no meaning.

Here are some questions I hope you can answer for me. If there is a God, why is there so much bad in the world? Is everything in the Bible true? How do we know ours is the right religion?

Why doesn't Jesus appear on earth every once in a while just to visit? What exactly is the Holy Spirit?

What was Jesus' job on earth? Wouldn't everything still be the same if he would not have come? Couldn't God allow reincarnation?

I will be anxiously awaiting your answer to all my questions.

First, let me tell you that few of the thousands of letters I have received through this column have pleased me nearly as much as yours. You are a prayerful person; you have a lot more faith than at this moment you give yourself credit for, and you are thinking and probing. That's a perfect combination for a potentially full and real Christian life.

Most of the questions you ask (the ones I have listed here are only about a third of them) reflect searches that have intrigued intelligent men and women as long as the human race has existed. It's impossible to respond to all of them, but I do have a few thoughts that may be helpful.

First, anyone who has not seriously asked these questions has not yet begun to live a deliberate adult life. The fact that you are asking them should in itself be kind of thrilling for you.

Second, you are at an age where you begin to question many significant things in life, most of them involved with the numerous emotional, physical and social changes you are experiencing. You are probably either a freshman or sophomore in high school, which means a lot of adjustment there also. So don't be disturbed at finding yourself confronting these large concerns about God and the meaning of life openly and squarely. It is a sign of your developing maturity that you are doing so.

Finally, in this as in other facets of your life, have a lot of confidence and trust in the people who love you, especially your family, close friends who may be a little older, your parish priest and so on. You are smart enough to know that the big questions of life do not have easy one-paragraph (or even one-book) answers. A good bit of study, prayer and the kind of wisdom that comes from thoughtful living help us toward finding those answers and, maybe even more importantly, help us to accept the relationships with God and those around us which make it possible to integrate those answers into our lives.

You may also be consoled by knowing that millions of good faith-filled Catholic men and women have lived through the same process of doubting and wondering that you now are experiencing.

In other words, for one reason or several, you must have enough insight to know that the kind of answers you are looking for are beyond you right now, but you are beginning to find them far more than a lot of other people your age. It is valuable that you keep your inquisitiveness without losing sight of your own very real faith as you go along, and the faith of those others whose lives reflect to you one solid truth: God and his love really do exist.

I realize this doesn't respond to each of your questions. But as one who still enjoys enormously finding fuller and better answers to them, I believe you are on the right track. At this point for you, that's far more important than knowing all the answers.

Unconditional love

Recently priests and other teachers use the term unconditional love. Is that found anywhere in scripture? If so, where? What is meant by the term and why do we seem to hear about it so often in relation to God?

Unconditional love simply means a love that is not subject to any conditions or "ifs." Many relationships we identify as love are conditional ones: I will love you if you do this, or as long as you behave this way or that.

Obviously the most genuine and total love is unconditioned. We are told often, especially in the New Testament, that our love for God must be total and unconditional and that our love for one another must imitate his love for us.

Even in the Old Testament God insists on the totality of his love for us. Particularly after Hosea, and much later in the book of Deuteronomy, the mutual love which God sees as the relationship he desires between himself and his people becomes more and more evident.

By far the most astounding proofs of the enormity and generosity of God's love are in the New Testament, however, particularly in Jesus' words about how God's love for us can be measured only by the love which he has for the father and the father for him from all eternity.

"As the Father has loved me, so I have loved you," he told his disciples. He later prayed "that they may be one as we are one" so that the world would know "that you loved them as you loved me."

That is genuine unconditional love, the measure Jesus gives for our love of one another.

What do we mean by Trinity?

In the Blessed Trinity did God the Son exist in heaven as separate from God the Father before coming to earth? If so, what was his function in heaven? Did God the Holy Spirit exist in heaven separate before being sent to earth? What was his function?

I have been trying to think a lot about the things I believe as a Catholic and these are some that keep coming back. All three Persons must have existed from the beginning. I just don't understand their purpose in heaven. I also don't understand why God the Father waited all those generations before sending the Son. Didn't he know from the beginning of time that people would never be able to keep the old covenant?

You must remember, first of all, that in the Trinity you are dealing with the central mystery of Christianity, something utterly beyond our comprehension. Any human experience or language can only remotely (the theological word is "by analogy") touch that Supreme Reality.

We believe in one God. Many who are not Christians share that belief. It is one that human beings can arrive at from common sense and intelligence. Before Christ, and after, people in fact did reason their way from the world around them to the conclusion that there had to be an intelligent, personal Being who brought it all into existence.

It was only Jesus, however, who let us in on the rest of the story: "within" this one God there exists, from all eternity, a community or interchange of life and love involving the three persons we (following Jesus' own words) call Father, Son and Holy Spirit. This aspect of God's most intimate inner life is what we name the mystery of the Trinity. Without our Lord's telling us we could never have known about it.

What their "function" might be within that divine life we can barely begin to speculate. Our creed, based on Scripture and other Christian tradition, tells us that in some mysterious way the Son is "begotten" by the Father. The Word comes into being by God's infinite knowledge of himself. The Spirit "proceeds from the Father and the Son," from the love between them, a love so complete and perfect that it literally is another person in the one God — the Spirit (sigh, breath) of love between the Son and the Father. And all this from eternity, without beginning, without end. Three Persons, each of them God, identified by Jesus as somehow distinguishable from each other and yet not three Gods but one.

Perhaps it helps to note that Jesus did not let us in on all this just to satisfy our curiosity. As Christians, our spirituality, our prayer life, our holiness begins with the astounding truth that through and in Christ we share intimately in that inner life of God. "As the Father loves me so I love you," said Jesus. He prayed "that they may be one as you, Father, are in me and I in you . . . I in them and you in me that they may be perfectly one." (See Chapters 15 and 17 in the Gospel of John.)

Thus, easier to understand than their eternal "function" with each other may be the function of the divine Persons in our behalf: the Word made flesh revealing the unfathomable life of the Father, with the Spirit, as Paul says, the binding force uniting us to each other and to them in eternal love.

As for the rest of your question, perhaps all we can say here is that God usually seems to adapt his revelation to our human condition. He generally gives us only what we can handle at one time, even if it did take eons, including nearly 2,000 years of "old covenant" to prepare us for the main event. After all, we believe that because of the eternal "present moment" with which God sees all past, present and future, the saving grace of Jesus Christ was already at work in the hearts of the very first human beings. So, at least from this particular viewpoint, what was the hurry?

Where does evil come from?

The creation hymn of Genesis where God creates the world informs us that God surveyed the cosmos and saw "it was very good" (Gn. 1:31). How is it that all creation proceeded (proceeds) from the Creator, and yet is evaluated as both good and evil? It seems that everything that comes from God should be good. Wouldn't all created things be basically good?

Your's is a very perceptive question. It takes us right to the heart of one of the foundational theological statements in this profound revelation story.

First, we need to recall that these Genesis stories were formed within a strongly monotheistic Hebrew people, who lived (as we are now so well aware) among cultures with vastly different beliefs and theologies. One of these differences centered on the problem of evil. Every people in history who wrestled at all with spiritual concerns has asked the question: How do you explain the presence of evil, hurt, alienation in the world?

Every sane human being claims to want only peace, harmony, love and goodness. Yet, put two of us in the same room for long, or two nations on the same earth, and you soon have misunderstanding, viciousness, hatred and killing. How does one explain that?

The most common explanation, outside of "one God" religions like Christianity, Judaism and Mohammedanism, has been some form of dualism. There are out there somewhere, so this belief goes, two powers or gods, one good and one bad, (or sometimes several of each) always struggling with each other for dominance or control. The good god is the source of our happy situations, so we placate him, pray to him and sacrifice to him. The bad god causes all evil, so we placate him, too, in order to minimize his bad intentions toward us.

All this may sound a bit bizarre, but it's true, and in fact is still present in our world. Even many of our own responses to God as Christians carry echoes of this kind of thinking about and relating to God our Father, precisely one of the attitudes toward God which Jesus came to correct with his "good news."

From our knowledge of contemporary religious outlooks at the time the book of Genesis was formed, we know that one of the great purposes of these biblical stories was to place Hebrew belief in their one God against these beliefs of their neighbors. When God, their God, created the world, he didn't fight or hassle with any other god as the pagans believed. He simply said: "Let it be," and it was. Furthermore, when this world came from his creative will it was "good" to its very core, all good, and finally as you say, "very good."

Then where, according to this Hebrew story, did moral evil, human evil, come from? It came not from God, but from us! The one God loved us enough to want us able to respond to that love, and so gave us a free will. We are able to say yes to God, or no. And all our hurt, all our moral evil, comes from the fact that we, all of us, out of a drift toward selfishness and pride deep within, occasionally and to some degree, do say no in our hearts and with our lives.

This is the Genesis lesson about good and evil. The world, every universe and corner of it, comes from the hand of a God who can make nothing bad. In other words, we cannot look outside for someone to blame for our troubles, although we persist in doing that. We cannot say with Flip Wilson, "The devil made me do it."

Adam, which simply means in Hebrew "the man," and his wife turned their backs on the Friend with whom they walked and talked in the cool of the evening. They refused to accept the realities of creation, and thought they could be "like gods" (3:5). As God told Cain after the death of Abel, sin is a demon lurking at your door and you must master it (4:7).

A basilica or a cathedral?

Last summer I toured St. John Episcopal Cathedral in New York city and the guide said it is the largest cathedral in the world, but the second largest church. The largest is St. Peter's in Rome, but it is considered a basilica. What's the difference between a basilica and a cathedral?

A cathedral is the official church of the bishop of any diocese. It derives its name from the bishop's formal presiding chair (Latin: "cathedra") which is always in the cathedral.

The "cathedral" church of the Holy Father as bishop of Rome is not St. Peter's, but the basilica of St. John Lateran, where the popes lived for many centuries before taking up residence in the Vatican. St. Peter's is one of the four major basilicas in Rome, but it is not a cathedral.

A basilica is simply a church that has been so designated because of its historical importance or other special dignity.

Imprimaturs

Most books written by Catholics, and dealing with religious subjects, used to have an "imprimatur". Now I see many which do not. Has there been a change? If so, what does an imprimatur mean today? Which books have them?

A clear change has occurred recently in the church's understanding of an imprimatur. For a long time an imprimatur (Latin for "it may be printed") was given, usually by a local bishop, to declare that the book or pamphlet was free of doctrinal or moral errors. Normally accompanying it was a "nihil obstat" (Latin: "nothing stands in the way"), a statement by someone well-versed in theology meaning basically the same thing. Neither the imprimatur nor the nihil obstat implied agreement with the content or opinions, merely that nothing in the writing contradicted Catholic doctrine.

In recent years the Vatican has changed the understanding of an imprimatur. In 1983 and 1984, for example, in connection with the removal of the imprimatur from a book of introduction to the Catholic faith, the Sacred Congregation for the Doctrine of the Faith (SCDF) made clear that an imprimatur was only required for books not only theologically correct, but having a methodology rendering them suitable as catechetical texts. The imprimatur, in that particular case, should be removed, the SCDF wrote to the archbishop of Newark, N. J., "since even a (theologically) corrected version would not be suitable as a catechetical text." (March 29, 1983)

Early in 1985 the SCDF repeated its special concern for methodology in catechetical texts in granting imprimaturs. This is one reason many recent books dealing with Catholic spirituality, morals and doctrine do not carry an imprimatur.

Another example of this change is the book you are now reading. Since it is not a text formally organized for systematic catechetical instruction, Church officials in several parts of the country recommended that a nihil obstat and imprimatur were not necessary or appropriate. Previous editions, substantially the same as this, did have both.

Much uncertainty remains today over the exact nature of an imprimatur and which books may or must have one.

Writings found by archeologists

Several years ago I read that Jewish archeologists discovered evidence of writings related to Jesus dating from the first century. These were to be released later, but I've heard nothing on the subject since. Have you any knowledge of what these might be?

During the past few decades, archeologists have discovered numerous writings apparently dating from around the time of Our Lord. To my knowledge, however, none of them deal in any explicit way with Jesus and his life, unless they are documents already familiar to historians.

Throughout Christian history, considerable attention and respect was naturally afforded anything that would enlighten us about Christ. Full texts of many documents have been handed down, even though the original or even a very early manuscript had never been found. Certain modern discoveries seem to give us parts of some of these documents, but contain nothing specifically about Jesus that we did not already know.

Some texts of the Dead Sea Scrolls, discovered after World War II in the southern part of the Holy Land, speak of a Teacher of Righteousness. Certain scholars conjectured at first that this teacher might be Jesus, or at least a man closely connected with him. Experts now agree that this is not so. The Teacher of Righteousness, whoever he was, died some decades before Our Lord and apparently had no more connection with him than any of the other holy men living in first century B.C. Palestine.

The church's stand on astrology

Could you clarify the stand of the Catholic Church on belief in and use of astrology? Many of us have become confused about our church's position on it lately.

On this whole subject of astrology, it is helpful to keep a few facts in mind. From ancient times until only about 200 years ago, the study of the influence of stars and planets on human activity was considered a genuine, legitimate science.

Many great names in physics and astronomy, like Copernicus and Galileo, believed in it, taught it, and practiced it by casting horoscopes.

Most political and religious leaders, including some popes, governed much of their activity by horoscopes. Pope Julius II set the day of his coronation according to the advice of the astrologers.

All this was possible, of course, because of the simple, very limited knowledge of the heavens. As the science of astronomy developed in modern times — particularly after the invention of the telescope — the discovery of thousands of new planets, stars and other materials in space caused the total collapse of astrology as a true science. The entire supposed "system" fell apart.

During this time, the church officially opposed astrology because of two dangers. If the stars governed all mankind's actions, free will would be meaningless. Also, some claimed that the power of Satan and other evil spirits was behind this heavenly influence and that astrology was therefore the devil's way of infiltrating human life.

These concerns remain at the base of whatever reservations the church has about astrology and of its warning that it can involve sinful superstition.

In spite of the array of inconsistencies and contradictions contained in astrology, lots of people are getting rich because it still fascinates millions. Maybe they're only curious. Or maybe they're just anxious to discover somewhere "out there" the cause of their problems.

A Catholic position on humanism?

A friend of mine in college says that humanism is the most beautiful answer to all human relations. Someone else said, however, that it is pure existentialism, and that both of these are un-Christian and un-Catholic.

This came up in our study club, and we had quite a violent argument about the meaning of existentialism, and for that matter, humanism. Is there a Catholic position on humanism? And what does it really mean?

An adequate answer to your question would require at least a book. Both existentialism and humanism have a rainbow of meanings, some of which are compatible with Christian beliefs and some are not. Fundamentally, however, existentialism may be described as a form of humanism, so let's limit ourselves to that second word and its meaning.

Humanism is basically the belief or philosophy that the greatest good of man is the perfection of himself as a human being. All good, all morality, according to this idea, is simply what will make a man or woman more perfectly human, more able to be whole in his knowing and loving and feeling.

Put that way, there is nothing un-Christian about humanism; it is solid Catholic doctrine. As Pope Paul said in his encyclical, "The Development of Peoples," in all the church's labors for truth and justice "what must be aimed at is complete humanism... the integral development of the whole man and of all men."

St. Irenaeus, I believe, was the first to say, "The glory of God is man fully alive."

This is echoed in the Vatican Council II decree, "The Church in the Modern World," in which hope is seen for mankind because "we are witnesses of the birth of a new humanism, one in which man is defined first of all by his responsibility toward his brothers and toward history." (No. 55)

This kind of humanism, therefore, is not only permissible, it is essential if mankind is to develop on this earth in a healthy manner.

Some brands of humanism, of course, in the past as well as today, view the works and goals of mankind in total disregard of any relationship to his Creator, to his Savior, to a life beyond this world. This view of man obviously is opposed to Christian beliefs, and often has been explicitly condemned by Catholic and other Christian authorities.

Shalom

We recently received as a gift a plaque for our home with the world "shalom" on it. We've seen it often even in church, but don't know what it means. Can you tell us?

"Shalom" is the Hebrew word for peace. At least this is

the way it is usually translated; but there really is no English word that carries its rich meaning. The word basically means completeness or wholeness, a situation in which everything is there that should be there and in proper order and balance. It could refer to an individual or a group.

Shalom is considered one of God's greatest gifts and the word was (and still is) used commonly among Jews as a greeting or expression of good wishes. It would have been the word Jesus used at the Last Supper: Shalom (peace) I give to you, my shalom I leave with you. Or when he greeted his apostles on the evening of the Resurrection: Shalom — peace be with you.

"Pagan" feast?

Why do so many Catholic theologians today try to make us believe that our great Christian feasts are really just pagan feasts that the church took over? Now I read (in an article on Lent) that Easter is connected with pagan celebrations and that the name of the feast is from a pagan god.

The reasons for celebrating our major feasts when we do are many and varied. In general, however, it is true that many of them have at least an indirect connection with pre-Christian feasts celebrated about the same time of the year — feasts centering around the harvest, the rebirth of the sun at the winter solstice (now Dec. 21, but Dec. 25 in the old Julian calender), the renewal of nature in spring, and so on.

Our Easter is, of course, directly related to the Jewish feast of Passover which Our Lord and his disciples celebrated shortly before his death. In turn, Passover, which is a joyful festival of freedom and hope, was most probably celebrated in the spring not only because it was naturally appropriate, but particularly as the Jewish version of similar spring feasts celebrated by the pagans all around them, and in which they were forbidden to participate.

The name Easter may have come to the Christian liturgy by way of an old German word for dawn, "eostarum." However, from the time of St. Bede, the renowned sixth century church historian, the more popular explanation is that the word comes from the name of the Anglo-Saxon goddess of spring, Eastre.

Who can distribute ashes?

We moved to another and smaller parish several months ago. On Ash Wednesday we were surprised to find lay people giving out ashes. We always had priests give them. Isn't there some rule that says only priests should do this? The lay people were some of those who usually help give Communion.

Most Catholics would be as surprised as you, since few parishes have used lay ministers for bestowal of ashes up to now. But the practice you experienced could be perfectly legitimate and quite in accord with the church's liturgical regulations.

In a response to the American Bishops' Committee on the Liturgy, dated Jan. 30, 1975, the secretary of the pope's Congregation for Sacraments and Divine Worship indicated that "Extraordinary (eucharistic) ministers cannot bless the ashes but may assist the celebrant in their imposition, and even, if there is no priest and the ashes are already blessed, impose them himself."

Deacons also may assist in giving ashes, even though they are not mentioned explicitly in this response. In fact, the response would provide also for other lay persons to help distribute the ashes if there is real pastoral need.

Most pastors are somewhat reluctant to ask their special eucharistic ministers to assist with the ashes, partly I suppose, out of concern for the sensibilities of their parishioners who, as you, would find it startling.

But it is allowed. Possibly the explanation in your case is the fact that you are now in a smaller parish; if there are fewer priests than in your previous parish (perhaps only one), it may be necessary for your pastor to utilize the assistance of lay ministers more often.

Our experience of this need will doubtless increase with the greatly decreasing number of priests during the next several years.

Date of Easter

The dates for Lent and Easter change all the time. Who determines when these feasts will be celebrated each year?

Though there is some divergence in parts of the Christian world, our celebration of Easter is on the first Sunday after the first full moon following the vernal equinox. The vernal equinox, which we ordinarily refer to as the first day of spring, is on or about March 21.

The dates for Lent, Ascension and Pentecost are determined by counting backward or forward from the date of Easter.

Sacred Triduum

Could you please tell us when Lent officially ends now? Is it after the Holy Saturday Vigil Mass?

Lent now ends on Holy Thursday. Those of us whose memories go back several decades will recall that for a long time Lent ended at noon on Holy Saturday. This happened because the great liturgies of Holy Thursday and Holy Saturday were all twisted out of shape and were celebrated in the morning of those days.

Before this, the long tradition of the church was that the Sacred Triduum (literally the sacred "three days") formed a separate holy time between Lent and the beginning of the Easter season.

Now, of course, the Mass celebrating the institution of the Eucharist takes place on Holy Thursday night and the Easter Vigil is back where it traditionally belongs during the night between Holy Saturday and Easter Sunday.

Thus the "General Norms for the Liturgical Year and Calendar" promulgated by Pope Paul VI in 1969, after defining the purposes of Lent, state: "Lent lasts from Ash Wednesday to the Mass of the Lord's Supper exclusive" (No. 28).

In other words Lent ends before the Mass on Holy Thursday evening.

The Easter Triduum itself begins with the evening Mass on Holy Thursday, reaches its high point in the Easter Vigil and closes with evening prayer on Easter Sunday (No. 19).

These norms are now included in the Roman Missal (Sacramentary) and are reflected in the celebration sections of this and other liturgical books.

The Easter Vigil

Our parish put a lot of emphasis on Holy Saturday this year, so much so that it seemed to overshadow Easter Sunday. Is Holy Saturday a more important day in the church than Easter? If so, why? Easter Sunday has always been such an important day.

To understand my response, it is essential to realize that any Catholic born before the 1950s grew up during a period when the church's Holy Week liturgy had deteriorated almost beyond recognition. We are now beginning to get back to what it always should have been.

Easter was the earliest feast celebrated in the church, for obvious reasons. The main, often the only, celebration of this feast was during Holy Saturday night, the night of the Resurrection, what we now know as the Easter Vigil Liturgy.

The night, with the lighting of the Easter candle and other lamps, the reading of the scriptural stories of God's revelation of his love, the baptism of new Christians and celebration of the Eucharist, was the perfect way to enter the joy of Easter. All these elements remain part of the Easter Vigil ceremonies.

As time went on, and for a variety of reasons, this (and many other) magnificent liturgical treasures of our church became all but totally lost. For the Easter Vigil, the absolute low point came during the past few hundred years, including the first half of this century.

Prompted partly by the fact that Masses could not be offered after noon, the entire glorious ritual of the celebration of the Easter Vigil was compressed into an hour or two early Holy Saturday morning, the priest reciting all the scripture readings and blessings by himself in Latin, and then a simple Mass, much like any other weekday Mass of the year.

With no exaggeration, it was a tragic caricature of what once was and now is gradually becoming again the highest point of our Christian liturgy, the supreme act of worship of the year. In that situation, with the Easter Vigil gone, the Sunday morning Masses were, of course, the only Easter Masses.

Starting some years before Vatican Council II, the church

realized the time had come to restore the Holy Week liturgies, with the Easter Vigil as the top priority. Once again this central celebration of Our Lord's resurrection is taking its place as the focal liturgy of the year; all others either lead up to it or are built upon it.

I hope you can see, then, that the Easter Vigil Service is not a "Holy Saturday Mass." It is the Easter Mass and celebration par excellence.

At our rectory we are sometimes amused or saddened by people who ask, "Does the Easter Vigil Mass count for Easter Sunday?" The answer is, as I explained, that the Easter Vigil celebration is the first and main Eucharist of the entire Easter season. All others, including those on Easter Sunday morning, simply continue the celebration that begins on that holy night.

I hope you take the opportunity to share in that liturgy next Easter. If your parish does it at all well, you'll begin to realize what the church has been missing for too many centuries.

Feast of Christ the King

The Feast of Christ the King was formerly celebrated on the last Sunday in October. Now it is the Sunday before Advent. When was this change made, and why?

The change of date for the Feast of the Kingship of Christ was part of the reconstruction of the missal and the church year after Vatican Council II.

The very end of the church's year of Sunday celebrations was chosen as the most appropriate since this feast celebrates the fact that Jesus is the Lord of the world and of all human history, and at the end of time the Father will make that title perfect and complete in the second coming and final victory of Jesus over sin and death.

Since the final Sunday of the liturgical year wraps up the long series of remembrances and celebrations for God's saving work in the world, and since our liturgy focuses attention in a special way at that time on the end of the world, there couldn't be a more fitting time to observe our recognition of Jesus as King and Ruler of the World.

INRI — IHS

What do the letters INRI stand for on the top of the crucifix? Sometimes the letters are IHS. I have been told that means "I have suffered." Is this true?

The Gospel of John (19:19) tells us that Pilate placed an inscription on the cross of Jesus which read, "Jesus of Nazareth the king of the Jews." The other Gospels have a similar passage.

The letters you indicate are an abbreviation for those words, which in Latin would be "Iesus Nazarenus Rex Iudaeorum."

The symbol IHS is the first three letters, "iota," "eta" and "sigma," of the name of Jesus in Greek. This symbol was used long before the English language developed, so it could not have been an abbreviation for English words.

Do theologians believe in hell?

What does the church think hell is like? Have things changed about that too? Is it true that some theologians don't believe in hell anymore?

Many popular conceptions about hell — that it is a place of bizarre and excruciating torture by fire or whatever other means — have never been taught as doctrine by the church. Check any old catechism and see.

The Bible uses much symbolic language in both the Old and New Testaments about punishment for sin, but picturesque details are not and never were part of the Christian dogma about hell.

Many misconceptions of the past few hundred years result from the fertile and frequently overworked imaginations of medieval artists who gave us some unimaginably lurid pictures of the devil and his kingdom.

The church still teaches, as it always has, that human beings can by their deliberate choice turn themselves off from God and say no to his invitation to friendship and life by a radical selfishness which effectively closes them off from others and from God himself. This alienation from divine love, especially if it should be eternal in its consequences, would bear its own form of regret, pain and unfulfillment.

Artists and poets occasionally run wild in depicting how horrible such a separation might be. But the Christian and Catholic Church has never claimed to know or teach who, if any, are in this tragic situation or what the specifics of their condition might be.

Regarding the last part of your question, I know of no theologian of any stature who doesn't believe that eternal alienation from God is possible. A number might ask, however, considering the power and evident universal intention of the saving work of Jesus in bringing the redemptive mercy of God to the world, whether anyone has in fact so conclusively and totally rejected God's love as to "lose his soul."

Again, we simply don't know.

If the one who is loved is free to answer yes — in other words, free to love — he must be free to say no as well. Indeed, that no must be respected as well as the yes, or the whole invitation to love is meaningless.

To thus say no to God in a final and total way without any later return to him, is to choose separation from him — to choose hell.

Has any human being in history every made such a choice? We simply have no way of knowing. The deepest souls of even those who seem most evil in the history of our human experience are known only to God.

There seem to be indications that certain people may have made such a choice. But we also have strong hints in Scripture that the power of the love and prayer of Christ is stronger than any human tendencies toward evil, and in the end is victorious.

Do we still believe in purgatory?

My question concerns purgatory, which we hardly ever hear about any more. I always thought it was a place, and that a certain amount of time was to be spent in purgatory by those who still have punishment due for sin. How can the Catholic doctrine of purgatory be reconciled with the concept that the afterlife is outside of time and space? What, if anything, are we to believe?

Purgatory has certainly not gone by the wayside. It is still very much a part of our faith, as every sacrifice of the Mass and every other prayer for the dead attests.

Perhaps one reason less is said about it today is that we have a lot of collected debris about purgatory to clear out of our minds. The hoary pictures of torture, pain, and a scourging God — which made of purgatory a kind of mini-hell — may literally scare the devil out of someone, but they're totally irrelevant to the doctrine of purgatory.

These gory images grew up around the idea of purgatory through the Middle Ages and later into the Renaissance.

At least two things are clear in the Catholic tradition concerning purgatory: First, the church teaches that there is some condition or circumstance after death by which any temporal punishment remaining for sins committed during life is satisfied, and that by our prayers and good works on earth we can assist those who are "in purgatory." This is simply an application of our belief in the communion of saints, which unites all who are joined in Christ, whether still on earth or in the next world. This much is taught by the church as revealed truth from God. It is, of course, something about which we would know nothing if he did not tell us.

Second, it is equally clear that the official teachings of the councils and other sources of Catholic belief have no intention of answering details about purgatory — whether it is a state or condition on one hand, or a "place" on the other. Or whether "time" is involved or not. Since the world after death would not seem to have hours or days or locations in our sense of those words, it seems quite unlikely that purgatory involves place or time as we usually think of them. It is very possible that, in the burst of awareness of the reality of God and creation that might occur immediately after death, the pain that comes from our knowledge of our sins and short-comings might be so acute and intense that an entire purgatory — or cleansing, which is what the word purgatory means — could occur in an instant.

While such an explanation seems to square with what we might suspect about the threshold of eternity, we simply don't know for sure. The church hasn't attempted officially to satisfy our curiosity about such questions — and probably couldn't if it tried.

Anything to do in heaven?

This may be a childish question. If it is ignore it.

If we are to live in heaven always and forever, wouldn't it get awfully boring? If there is no work and no play, what would we do? Just hang around? I'd really like to know.

You're not the only one. This profound, frustrating question has intrigued Catholic and other Christian theologians for centuries.

The final truth is we just don't know. Scripture and other Christian traditions tell us a number of things about life after death, but they do not fill in many details. We know first of all that we will rise to a new life. We also know that this being which will exist in eternity will be ourself — each of us with full consciousness of our identity from before death and with our full human nature, body and soul.

Furthermore, from the evidence of Jesus after his own resurrection, we know that this human nature will be dramatically different; our mental and physical capacities will go far beyond our experience in this life.

One thing is sure. Confronted with the unveiled infinite reality of God, with all the potential of creative love that is — in our limited human way of speaking — barely scratched by all the creation we know, and with the highly elevated spiritual and physical powers we will have to know and love that divine nature, I really don't think we'll have a problem of boredom.

We can only walk so close to that great reality of heaven before we are confronted with the simple fact that we are dealing here with a mystery hidden deeply in the heart of God. No theologian has ever gotten far beyond St. Paul's declaration, "Eye has not seen, ear has not heard, nor has it entered into the heart of man what God has prepared for those who love him."

I suppose we just have to trust in God that Paul knew what he was talking about.

Of heaven and hell

My husband and I were talking about heaven and hell. He

believes that God created Lucifer not as an angel of light, but as Satan to test mankind.

He also does not believe in hell, but believes that all souls go eventually to heaven since God is all loving and all knowing. Can you tell us the church's teaching on this?

It is our traditional Catholic and Christian belief that all angels — the non-material, intelligent, spiritual beings created by God — were created in a state of supernatural friendship with God.

Certainly it is clear from Scripture, as well as from the tradition of Christianity, that creation, including any angels, was good as it came from the hand of the Creator. As the story in Genesis tells us, God looked at the whole of his creative work and "saw it was good." Nothing truly evil could come from a God who is unlimited goodness.

Hell, as we Christians understand it, is a condition of eternal separation from God. Since we believe that all goodness and beauty is only a reflection of God's own goodness, and that only he can fulfill the longings of our heart for total happiness, separation from him forever would be the worst imaginable suffering for any human being. Is such a hell possible? We know it must be.

God's very creation of us was an act of love. In his continual creative love, he not only invites us to love him in return, but his love (as all love does in its own degree) enables us, energizes us, to respond to that love by our own growth in goodness, holiness and a loving relationship with him.

However, not even God can force love. At some point, no matter how urgent the invitation or how strong the attractiveness of the lover may be, the one who is calling another to love reaches a point at which he must say: "Now the answer is up to you. Is it yes or no?"

Will dogs be in heaven?

Our family dog, which was loved by all of us, died recently. Now the children are asking whether dogs go to heaven and whether they will have him there. I want them to have peace of mind and also know God loves them. Any suggestions?

Isn't it amazing how children often go to the heart of a theological question more quickly than adults?

Of course, when we get down to it, we don't really know. I wouldn't be at all surprised to see dogs — and trees and flowers — in heaven.

Anyway, my favorite answer to a question like that is: Heaven is a place where we will all be perfectly happy. When we get there, if we really think we need a dog to be perfectly happy, I'm sure God will see that we have one.

I don't believe anyone could argue with that.

What will heaven be like?

In your answer to a mother whose children wondered whether they would have their dog in heaven, you said you would not be surprised to see dogs and trees and flowers in heaven.

I thought heaven was just being with God. Will we need more than God to make us happy? I think your answer is misleading.

I think you're leaving out an important truth of our faith, that we will share in the resurrection of the body.

We know very little about what our bodies will be like in their exalted condition after the resurrection. We do know, however, that they will be our bodies — like Christ's, with eyes, ears, mouth, touch and other senses that are part of our human nature.

If the resurrection means anything, these senses and organs will not be atrophied and useless. Our eyes will see, our ears will hear, our tongue will taste. As Jesus apparently tried to prove to the disciples after he rose from the dead, to deny these things would be to deny the resurrection.

Yet, apart from the human nature of Jesus, God is pure spirit. What then would there be in heaven to hear, feel, taste and touch? True, the essence of heaven is our presence with God. Is it possible, however, that God might even then reveal himself to us in ways similar to, if immeasurably beyond, the ways he reveals himself to us here on earth?

After all, even in heaven our minds and wills will still be

created minds and wills; we will never know and love him as he knows and loves himself, with one eternally perfect act of comprehension and union.

How then will God reveal himself to us? One thing we do know. Having taken our human nature, he has a tremendous respect for it. It is our best Christian guess that he will use it, all of it, even in heaven.

If this sounds strange, perhaps one reason might be that we do not respect and reverence our human nature as much as God does. More than one saint (and theologian) has suggested that one of the great surprises of heaven may be in how many respects it resembles our life on earth, trees, flowers, smiles — and maybe even dogs.

Membership in the Knights of Columbus

I would like to know if a man can be a member of the Knights of Columbus if he is divorced. Doesn't it matter any more if a Knight is divorced and even living with someone else?

The Knights of Columbus fraternity clearly intends and desires that its members be Catholic men who are living their religion faithfully in every way. It is not always easy, however, to assure this is happening, especially when the matter is one of personal private conscience.

Your basic question is: Who may be a member of the Knights of Columbus? The regulations of that organization state: "Only practical Catholics in union with the Holy Spirit shall be eligible to and entitled to continue membership in the order." Another rule asserts that any member who fails to remain a practical Catholic in union with the Holy Spirit shall automatically forfeit membership in the Knights.

There was a time in the history of the K of C when those who were known not to have fulfilled their Easter obligation or who were divorced and remarried were promptly expelled, generally with the consent of the local pastor or chaplain.

After receiving your letter I asked a spokesman for the Supreme Council of the Knights of Columbus to describe their policy today. He correctly noted that the Catholic attitude has changed considerably in the past two decades, at least in that the church no longer excommunicates those who obtain a divorce and remarry. In fact it encourages them to continue the practice of their faith as best they can.

"This more compassionate and hopeful view also has been adopted by most of the Knights of Columbus councils," he said. "There is more concern about bringing the individual back to church and to the sacraments so he indeed will be a practicing Catholic, rather than in rejecting him from our society. One possible exception to the policy would be a case of serious scandal."

I do know that national K of C officials have given much consideration to the problem in the past 10 or 15 years. They have concluded that it is difficult, if not impossible, to find a hard and fast rule which would govern every case and still be fair to everyone.

Consequently, they have left implementation of any penalties to the local grand knight and the chaplain.

As my friend at the supreme headquarters put it: "If this seems to be a rather complex response to the question it is because we are dealing with a very complex situation. We are aware of the issue and our concern is to help rather than harm all involved."

Knights of Columbus auxiliaries

In your column several weeks ago you informed us that the Knights of Columbus now permit a man who is divorced and remarried out of the church to retain his membership. You quoted a Knights official as saying, "There is more concern about bringing the individual back to church and the sacraments so he indeed will be a practicing Catholic, rather than in rejecting him for our society."

According to the rules of our Knights auxiliary a member who is divorced and remarried is automatically expelled. It seems to me she needs the fellowship as much as he does.

Who makes membership rules for the Knights auxiliary? How can they be amended or brought up to date?

The Knights of Columbus has no official national or international auxiliary. Some years ago the Knights' Supreme

Council discussed the advisability of establishing a national auxiliary but decided against it.

Auxiliaries exist in several states and local councils. Some national organizations of women such as the Daughters of Isabella, the Columbiettes and the Catholic Daughters of the Americas, retain a more or less loose connection with the Knights.

The Catholic Daughters of the Americas, for example, the largest of such women's organizations in the United States and other American countries, were founded by the Knights in 1903. But for a long time it has been a separate organization.

According to their national New York office, a woman who is divorced and remarried outside the laws of the Catholic Church is ineligible to remain a member.

Rules of membership for Knights auxiliaries are made at the state and local levels. If you feel regulations for your organization need to be re-evaluated, direct your suggestions to your state or local officers.

Help for mentally handicapped

I have two grandchildren who are seriously mentally handicapped. Fortunately we have good friends and much help from people in our city, but I am interested in contacting and perhaps helping others in this situation.

Is there a national organization or group that I could write to for information?

I'm sure you are aware that literally hundreds of organizations exist for such care on local levels. Two national groups that would be helpful, however, are:

The National Apostolate With Mentally Retarded Persons, founded just about 13 years ago, is headquartered at Trinity College in Washington (P.O. Box 4588, Washington, D.C., 20017). In addition to a periodical, the NAMRP Journal, they can provide you with an enormous amount of information on facilities and programs for the mentally handicapped.

Another group which supports programs for mentally handicapped children is the Order of the Alhambra. They are associated with the Knights of Columbus and may be reached at 4200 Leeds Ave., Baltimore, Md., 21229.

Volunteering to help the needy

Does the Catholic Church have a group of missionaries or volunteers working in poor countries?

I feel like God is asking me to put aside my worldly ways and help out. How can I get more information?

In my view, the best places to start are with two agencies which have remarkable and enviable records for helping serve serious needs in other countries. They are the Catholic Relief Services and the Catholic Medical Mission Board.

You're probably familiar with CRS at least through the collection taken up around the nation each year for its work. In addition to emergency, disaster-type assistance, it also attempts to initiate long-term developments in deprived regions of the world.

CRS maintains offices or local representation in about 70 countries, so it needs a small army of volunteers (and paid workers) of all kinds — skilled and unskilled, professional and nonprofessional. You can get more information from their headquarters at 209 W. Fayette St., Baltimore, Md., 21201.

The medical mission board, as its name indicates, is more specialized. It provides medical supplies and offers medical and paramedical personnel for hospitals, clinics and dispensaries in many countries. Not all workers need training specifically in medical care, however.

You may write to the director of the Catholic Medical Mission Board at 10 W. 17th Street, New York, N.Y. 10011.

Please follow up on your desire to help. You certainly are needed somewhere. If you get stuck let me know and we'll continue looking.

Index of forbidden books

I am a convert of several years to the Catholic faith. A few days ago a friend (Catholic all his life) mentioned something I never heard of before, the Index of Forbidden Books. Is there such a list of forbidden books? What does that mean?

Almost from the beginning, the Catholic Church recognized that what people read has enormous potential influence, for good or bad, on their faith.

For example, this is one reason Christian people were always so careful that translations and copies of the Sacred Scriptures were as accurate as humanly possible. Among the most colorful documents we possess from early Christian centuries are letters that flowed between early theologians and saints arguing over the most appropriate translation of a word in the Bible.

By the fifth century this concern was already shown toward other writings and what later became the index of Prohibited Books came into existence.

This was simply a list of books relating to religion, Christian religion particularly, that members of the church were not to read without sufficient preparation and background.

The index continued, in one fashion or another, up to our time. Gradually, particularly in this century, this sort of prohibition against printing, selling or reading certain books was greatly mitigated and now is repealed altogether. The new (1983) Code of Canon Law contains no provision for such a prohibition of books.

Approval by proper church authorities is still required for certain types of publications either before or after they are printed. These include mainly editions of the Bible, liturgical and devotional books and books intended to be used as texts for religious instruction (see CCL 824-828). These provisions are considerably less restrictive than the previous church law. The church, of course, retains the same concerns for the integrity of our faith as in the past. The shift is toward a different understanding of the purpose of church law.

As the Canon Law Society of America explains: "The purpose of this legislation has partially changed, from a rather paternalistic attempt to protect the faith and morals of the people by safeguarding them from harmful religious publications, to a more restrained and positive effort to assure that those writings which express the church's prayers and beliefs do so accurately" ("The Code of Canon Law: A Text and Commentary").

Ku Klux Klan

A friend of mine from one of the southern states claims that some Catholics are members of the Ku Klux Klan. I thought this was an anti-Catholic group and that Catholics were forbidden to belong to it.

The KKK did form a large part of the wave of anti-Catholic bigotry which lasted through several decades of the last century in our country. It was one of four or five major "native American" organizations which sprang up after the economic panic of 1819, and along with the large immigration of mainly Catholic Europeans.

There have been two major Ku Klux Klan (the name derives from the Greek word "kyklos", circle) organizations. The first, formed immediately after the Civil War, was an extremist white supremacy organization which at one time involved most of the whites in the South. Through terror, lynching, torture and other cruelties, the klan "protected" white people, and opposed all reconstruction efforts of federal and local governments. This klan finally disbanded about 1877.

The second organization began during and after World War I, inspired by the economic, political and social breakdown, and the growing anti-radicalism and nationalism of that period. It was simply an anti-black, anti-Catholic, anti-Jew, anti-foreign movement which by the mid-20s boasted nearly five million members, and in some areas, enormous political power.

No one has attempted to explain how Christian beliefs and practices can co-exist with the policies and activities of the klan.

Devil worship

Is it possible for someone to be possessed by the devil? Is there a rite of exorcism performed by the priest in such a case? What about the so-called Black Masses? Have they actually been said, or is it a horrible creation by a fiction writer?

The Black Mass is no fiction. For centuries up to and including the present time, a central liturgical ceremony of many

Satanists, or devil worshipers, has been a parody of the Sacrifice of the Mass. Often an attempt is made to obtain and desecrate a consecrated Host from a true Mass in these sacrilegious services.

The question about possession is harder to answer. The belief in angels and demons ("fallen angels") is consistent in Christianity since the time of Christ, and existed before that in the Old Testament. The exact nature of these beings, however, is uncertain; there is very little in official church doctrine about them, though it is common teaching that they are intelligent personal beings.

Partly because of this need for much more theological study about the good and bad angels, many problems remain unanswered about diabolic possession — that is, the physical control of a human being's body by a devil or demon. One thing is certainly true: With the advancement of knowledge about psychological and nervous disorders, many strange happenings once attributed to diabolical possession are known to have other possible, very natural, explanations. In addition, our present awareness of the genuine possibility of mental telepathy (transfer of thoughts from one mind to another) and even telekinesis (mental transfer of physical energy) makes the detection of true possession very difficult.

The rite of exorcism is a series of prayers, blessings and commands used by a priest or bishop to drive out the evil spirit in a case of possession. This official ceremony is rarely used today and may be performed only with the permission of the bishop. An effective exorcism is considered by some theologians as perhaps the only absolute proof of true diabolic possession.

Diabolical obsession

A review of the book, "The Exorcist," mentioned diabolical obsession. Is it the same thing as possession?

No. Possession means control or near control of a person's body, as it were, from the inside by an evil spirit.

Obsession is the term traditionally used for a phenomenon experienced by many persons through the centuries. The individual is violently molested physically in circumstances that seem to point to evil spirits as the cause. It is, therefore, more of an external than an internal influence, but it is far more than a "temptation" in the ordinary sense of the word.

Origin of Species

Our study club is thinking of discussing the book "Origin of Species" by Charles Darwin. What do you think of this book? Someone said that we, as Catholics, should not read it.

Darwin's book is naturally of importance in the history of modern science. He was a brilliant observer and had a phenomenal capacity for putting his findings together in a creative way.

The sciences which deal with the development of life on earth have made enormous strides since *Origin of Species,* however, and have corrected many of Darwin's theories. I believe certain other books in the field would be more enjoyable and helpful, unless you're interested in the historical approach.

Some people tried to use Darwin's findings in an antireligious manner, but the book's approach is quite scientific. It's not the usual bedtime reading, though, so be prepared to work if you choose to read it.

Gregorian calendar

A religious tract someone gave me has a lot of insulting things to say about the Catholic Church, especially about the pope. Most of them are ridiculous and I know the answers. One thing I never heard about, though. It says that several hundred years ago one pope (Gregory XIII) foisted the whole new calendar on the world simply out of spite against the Protestants, and to make a feeble attempt to save the declining prestige of the papacy. What about this?

If your reading of this tract is accurate, the resurrection of this old controversy is almost eerie, somewhat like charging that Columbus' claim that the earth is round was simple religious propaganda.

Back in the first century before Christ, Julius Caesar revised the calendar to correct serious errors in the system. Several centuries later, it became obvious that this Julian calendar also had serious defects. The solar year had been computed at 11 minutes and 14 seconds too long. This perhaps doesn't sound like much, but it means a full day every 128 years. By the time of Pope Gregory XIII (who became pope in 1572), the "legal" calendar lagged 10 or 11 days behind true sun time and caused considerable confusion and difficulty politically, religiously, and, of course, scientifically.

Numerous efforts at reform stretching back nearly 200-300 years had flopped. So Gregory determined the time had come to act. After long consultation by an international commission with universities and scientists throughout the western world, our present calendar (with leap years, etc.) was developed — including the complete elimination of 10 days in October, 1582. Oct. 5 became Oct. 15.

Most European nations accepted the new calendar at once, but many Protestant governments refused, particularly in Germany and England. Some labeled the new arrangement the work of Satan, claiming the pope was preparing a blood bath of Protestants, and even that the end of the world was imminent because of Gregory's fooling around with Mother Nature.

Only the vigorous defense of the new calendar by such renowned scientists as Tycho Brahe and Johann Kepler gradually brought such opponents to acknowledge that the change was necessary and had nothing to do with religious sectarianism.

Today, no civilized person denies that the Gregorian calendar reform constitutes one of the most praiseworthy and important accomplishments in modern history.

Who was "Bloody Mary?"

Who is the Catholic queen that the "Bloody Mary" is supposed to be named after? At least this was what I was told a few nights ago by some drinking buddies.

You're thinking of Queen Mary of England, who ruled from 1553 to 1558. Twenty years before she took the throne, her father, King Henry VIII, formally rejected the Catholic faith and took most of the country with him.

When she became queen, Mary tried to reverse the process and as part of her severe program several hundred "heretics" were burned at the stake, most of them peasants. Burning heretics was a popular idea in those days with both Catholic and Protestant governments. History has often referred to this queen as "Bloody Mary," even though her primary mistake in the eyes of most of her countrymen was simply that she burned the wrong people.

The name was given to the modern drink, of course, because of its color and because of the fact that too much tomato juice can cloud one's mind — as is evident from the kind of discussion you and your drinking buddies get into.

Healing on television

What is the Catholic Church's view on the miracle services performed on television by many ministers? I know that whenever there is an alleged miracle, the Catholic Church expects much proof before the said miracle is claimed authentic.

But is this really necessary if there is simple faith that God can heal and will heal? Why cannot we just accept these healings as the real thing without all the proof?

The Catholic Church surely does believe that miracles of healing are not only possible, but are perhaps much more frequent than many of us suspect. The rite for the Sacrament of the Anointing of the Sick, for example, clearly states the church's prayer and expectations for healings of various kinds as a result of the petitions made by the people of God.

The church is concerned in the matter, however, because true miracles (healing or otherwise) are not simply haphazard, frivolous intrusions by God into nature. As Jesus made clear, miracles are, above all, signs — signs of our Heavenly Father's presence and his approval and "authentication" of the person or truth in whose favor the miracle was performed, and signs of his lordship and supreme power over evil.

This is why he once told the people, "If you do not believe

me, believe the works that I do." In other words, his miracles showed that Jesus was the messenger and Son of God he claimed to be.

As you must be aware, experience has taught us that many things can appear to be miracles when they are not. "Mysterious" cures can often have quite non-miraculous physical or psychological explanations. Certain religious con-men have sometimes staged outright fake "miracles" to establish their religious credentials.

Thus, the church intends no disrespect to God or man when it exercises — and suggests — caution in accepting at face value every apparent miracle that comes along. It has too much belief in God's power to allow supposed exercises of that power to be used as entertaining curiosities or religious gimmicks.

Extra-terrestrial life

With all the talk of UFOs and interspace travel, we wonder if the Catholic faith has anything to say about life on other planets. Could there be? If there is intelligent life somewhere else, would that mean that Jesus Christ would have to die on every planet to save souls?

There's no way, of course, that the church would know any more than anyone else whether or not intelligent life exists in other galaxies or worlds. It hasn't attempted any speculation on the subject and there's no reason it should.

The spiritual condition of any intelligent life that might flourish elsewhere is even more of a mystery. Starting with the possibility of a race of beings that might still be in some sort of original innocence (to use terminology we're familiar with), there's a whole rainbow of conceivable circumstances in which such creatures might live.

I'd be intensely interested in such information, because I believe it could enlarge our appreciation of the vastness of God's love and creative power. I must admit, however, that this is more curiosity than anything else.

Direct teachings of the church about the saving grace of Jesus being necessary for salvation apply only to the members of our human family. Concerning the relationship God might have established between himself and creatures of another world, we cannot make even a respectable guess.

How did we get B.C. and A.D.?

Would you explain how B.C. (time before Christ) and A.D. (time after Christ) is measured? There seems to be a lot of confusion about dates in the Bible and in other things we read from ancient history.

It's no wonder you're confused. Keeping track of times and dates in history is a lot more complicated than most people realize. In Old Testament days, for example, most time keeping was based on a particular ruler or king ("in the 11th year of the reign of King Darius"), or major events such as the Babylonian exile in the sixth century B.C. The religious calendar used by Jews today, supposedly based on the time from the creation of the world, began to be used only about 1,000 years ago. The "date" of creation was computed by adding up all references to years and ages in the Hebrew Bible, especially the book of Genesis.

Early Christians employed a variety of methods. Some used local Greek calendars, some the most common Roman method of dating events from the founding of Rome (using initials U.C., "urbis condita") about 753 B.C. Other Christians counted years from the supposed date of the birth of Abraham; some from the schedule of taxation under Emperor Diocletian in the third century. Our current method of dating events from before or after the birth of Christ came as a byproduct of attempting to settle the bitter controversy between the Eastern and Western churches over the date of Easter.

A Roman monk, Dionysius the Little, began the practice in the sixth century. Many historical sources available to us were unknown in his time; this resulted in his setting the year one of the Christian era six or eight years later than it should have been. Thus the birth of Christ took place, according to our calendar, about 7 B.C. It took centuries for the new way of numbering years to be accepted even in the Christian world. The fact that it took hold at all is greatly due to the renowned early historian St. Bede, who utilized this method of dating in his writing of history. As the saying goes, this is probably more than you wanted to know, but it's about as brief a summary possible of an extremely interesting story.

Believing in dreams

An article in a Catholic magazine recently talked about dreams and said that we should think about our dreams, "befriend" them, and that we would learn things this way. I thought that it was superstition to pay attention to dreams. Is it all right to do what this article suggested?

To think about our dreams and even to learn something from them is surely not sinful. We have ample proof even in the Bible that God has used dreams to help people understand his will for them.

Psychological sciences still cannot tell us very much for sure about where dreams come from, or precisely what makes them happen. It is now widely agreed that reflection on one's dreams, trying to enter into their imagery and moods and understand them, can often contribute much to a person's self-knowledge, his perception of his own emotions, and so on. One author who has written much on the subject of psychology and religion coined the term "befriend a dream" — which is probably where your article picked it up.

Some persons who are responsible for formation in Religious orders and communities have found that such "listening" to one's dreams, and even sharing them very simply and non-judgmentally with another, may be quite helpful to both persons.

Of course, dreams could be used wrongly, for example, if one pretended to tell fortunes from them or if one allowed himself to become obsessed with a fantasy world. But it would be just as wrong not to accept dreams as a very natural, if puzzling, part of life, or to assume that there is automatically something magical, even diabolical, about them.

Can we bless God?

During the Stations of the Cross and other prayers, we say, "We adore Thee, O Christ, and we bless Thee." I can't understand what talent or ability I have to bless Christ. Isn't it wrong to say we bless Christ or God?

In a way it is wrong. The Latin word "benedicere" usually means to bless in the commonly understood sense to communicate life or some other good to another. It also, however, may mean to thank someone, or to acknowledge another's power and goodness. The phrase "Blessed be God," for example, which we find often in the psalms and in the New Testament, is a prayer of praise and recognition of the goodness of God, and of the benefits he has bestowed on us. The phrase carries the same meaning in our prayers.

What does the word 'soul' mean?

I am a constant reader of your column. Can you please give me a definition of "soul"?

Please realize that only a very sketchy definition can be given here. Put very briefly, our soul is the spiritual (non-material) part of our nature that makes us distinctly and specifically human.

Long before Christianity, ancient Greek philosophers, for example, arrived at the knowledge that some important things about us simply cannot be totally explained by brain cells or nerve endings or anything else "material."

There must be something else to explain things like our ability to know and love and laugh, to be happy, to forgive and be forgiven, to reflect and plan and think. For these there must be some "part" of us that has no "parts," something we cannot cut in half, something in other words that cannot be fully explained by physical generation from parent to child but which (as our Christian doctrine puts it) requires a unique creative act of God.

In the tradition of Greek philosophy, which for centuries Christians borrowed from heavily, this immaterial part of us was called the soul. In other traditions such as the Hebrews of the Old Testament and the early Christian writers like St. Paul in the New Testament, the distinction between body and soul was not nearly so neat and exclusive, nor were they separable.

Even then, however, especially among Christians, no one denied that there was a "spirit" part of us which constitutes our real dignity and which, along with our bodies, identifies us as human beings.

Reincarnation

Our study club includes one couple from India. They have no particular religion but talk a lot about reincarnation. They say it is a philosophy and can be a part of any religion. We sure have problems with it, but what is your opinion? Is there any way a Catholic or any Christian could accept this belief?

I've dealt with this subject before in the question column, but the same type of question comes up several times every year.

The word "reincarnation" simply means "coming again in the flesh." According to the teaching of several religions (or philosophies), particularly in the East, all living things from divine beings to plants live in a cycle of deaths and rebirths. When they cease one life they come back in another form, better or worse than before, depending on how well they lived the last time around.

This applies in a significant way to human beings. By the law of what Hindus call "karma," one's earthly life does not cease at death. Individuals return under some form, but are usually not conscious of their previous existence even though they are affected by their failings in that past life. Their present life will determine their future reincarnation.

The process is supposed to lead in some mystical way to a final absorption of all being into "absolute reality" which in the end will prove to be the only reality there is. All else is illusion and fantasy.

Obviously these few sentences cannot do justice to an ancient and intricate belief of a large part of the human race, a belief which enfolds within it many insights about our human condition that may be valid for all of us.

Just as clearly, however, the doctrine of reincarnation runs head-on into Catholic beliefs such as the immortality of the soul and the final resurrection of each of us, the finality of death, and the personal, conscious responsibility we have in cooperation with God's grace for our destiny after death.

In truth, practically every major element of our faith is in serious conflict with a belief in reincarnation.

Why does God allow worry?

If God loves us, why does he allow people to suffer mental torment and worry? Why are hospitals filled with people who are sick or who are physical wrecks because of unbearable inhibitions, guilt, lack of self-confidence, loneliness and frustration? This God must be sadistic rather than loving.

In his providence, God has enabled mankind to grow much through the centuries in its capacity to deal with the evils that plague it, including the ones you mention. The advances in sciences of all sorts make possible our management, if not cure, of so many physical and emotional illnesses that once were mysteries and perhaps bearers of certain early death. Our first responsibility, then, is to avail ourselves as much as we can of the care and cure that can help us cope with and heal our hurts.

Your question obviously goes much deeper than that. It is, in fact, among the oldest that has puzzled mankind. The most perceptive people in history have wrestled with what is called the "Problem of Evil" — why is there suffering and evil in the world, and where does it come from? They've never arrived at a satisfying answer.

For example, among the many theological issues addressed in the creation story of Genesis is that of the origin of evil. About the only answer it could give is that suffering and pain certainly do not come from God, from whose hand all things come as good. Evil arises rather in some mysterious way from inside us, from our disobedience and disorientation from the purpose of our creation.

Even Jesus could not remove suffering and death from our human condition even for himself. For the first time, and for all time, he brought to a pained humanity the promise of meaning, healing and hope in its hurt. But he did not create a new Garden of Eden.

The suffering you abhor would lead us to a sadistic God only if the pain were inflicted by him. It is not. Indeed, God could stop it only by removing our free wills, our opportunity for free choices, which would mean taking away our potential for love. God allows us to hurt ourselves and does all he can to reduce the hurt and ease the pain (which is what Jesus is all about) because he knows that in the end the love that has grown amidst that pain will make it all worthwhile.

Of that Our Lord himself is the supreme proof and assurance.

Display flags in church?

Many churches used to have an American flag and a Catholic Church flag in the sanctuary all the time. It seems to me a nice idea, but I see it less and less, especially in new churches.

One of our priest friends said he did not think it was permitted but was not sure. Since our church was repainted those flags are not there. Are there any rules on this? If so, what are they?

Let's take the two flags separately since the answer is somewhat different for each.

As older Catholics will remember, display of the American flag in churches became widespread around the time of World War II, when it was encouraged to exhibit the flag in public buildings. Even then this custom held only in the United States. Catholics of other nations would consider the display of their national flag in church, at least in the sanctuary, as something wholly inappropriate and foreign to the spirit of the Eucharist which knows no national or other political boundary.

In churches of Italy, for example, one sees no Italian flag — or papal flag either, as I will explain in a moment.

As for official regulations, first of all, the General Instruction on the Roman Missal, which gives primary guidelines for everything relating to the Mass, does not list flags or other national symbols as among accoutrements to be in the sanctuary area for the Eucharist.

Display of such national banners or symbols has never been permitted, in fact, and no secular symbol is to be permanently displayed in the sanctuary without special permission.

In 1982, the bishops Committee on the Liturgy of the United States responded this way to a question similar to yours: "When Catholics assemble for worship, they bring with them their cultural, ethnic and national identities. These traits should not be devalued or denied unless, of course, there is something in them which is truly inimical to the gospel of Christ. Still, the liturgy of the church which is expressed in the various cultures of the people must always reflect a church which is truly Catholic."

They then quote the American bishops' document "Environment and Art in Catholic Worship" (No. 101): "Although the art and decoration of the liturgical space will be that of the local culture, identifying symbols of particular cultures, groups, or nations are not appropriate as permanent parts of the liturgical environment. While such symbols might be used for a particular occasion or holiday, they should not regularly constitute a part of the environment of common prayer." (see BCL Newsletter, Dec. 1982)

Obviously, to display the flag or other symbols of our nation and its ideals at the time of major celebrations or holidays is quite proper and appropriate. As for permanent display, however, though some churches have done it and still do it, there is no authorization and never has been.

As to the other part of your question, there is no such thing as a "Catholic Church flag." The yellow and gold flag with the tiara and keys to which I am sure you refer is the personal flag of the pope, a vestige of the era when the pope was literally "king" of the papal states which once included most of what is now Italy.

Today the papal flag is not even displayed in St. Peter's Basilica in Rome. As far as I can learn, its only official use is when the Swiss Guards march in a group; it is their banner as personal guards for the Holy Father.

The only "flag" or standard of our church is, and always has been, the cross. I'm sure even the Holy Father himself wants to keep it that way.

Crucifix, with corpus

I have seen in non-Catholic churches that their crosses do not display the body of Christ. My friends who attend there give me the reason that they believe Jesus is living. I know that we believe he is living, too. When did the Catholic Church begin using the crucifix?

The practice of portraying the body of the crucified Lord on the cross began relatively recently — if one can call about 700 years ago recently.

During the first 600 years or so after Jesus' death and resurrection, portraying the body of Christ on crosses was very rare. The conviction that the death of Christ was part of the whole paschal, or Easter, event was so deep in the church that the heaviest emphasis was placed on the resurrection.

Particularly in the fifth and sixth centuries, crosses were adorned with precious jewels for the same reason. In fact, even when the body of Christ began to appear more on crosses, it was often the risen living Lord that was shown, rather than the dying or dead Christ that became common later.

Around the 1200s, the passion of Christ became more central in Christian theology and spirituality. Crucifixes graphically showing the suffering Christ became popular and remained so until our own time.

With today's renewed emphasis on the resurrection and its central place in the history of salvation, something like jeweled crosses and crucifixes with the body of the risen Christ are seen more and more, even in our Catholic churches.

River Brethren and Dunkers

We found a reference recently to a group of Protestant denominations which included the "River Brethren" and the "Dunkers." Are there really churches with these names? If so, why do they have such strange titles?

Both sects you mention were among numerous Mennonite and other Swiss or German groups who settled around Lancaster County in Pennsylvania about 250 years ago. Though primarily of European Baptist or Lutheran background, many of the sects became known almost officially by plain, simple names which distinguished them in some way from the rest.

The Dunkers (German Baptist Brethren) were so named because of their method of baptizing. The present Church of the Brethren is descended from this tradition.

One sizeable group of these early settlers were called the United Brethren. Several of their members broke off and began meeting along the Susquehanna River in Lancaster County, thus becoming known as "the brotherhood down by the river" — or River Brethren.

The River Brethren continued as a loosely connected group of churches until the Civil War, when they changed their name to Brethren in Christ. This is still their official title.

Requests from charities

Almost every day we receive donation requests from at least one Catholic organization. From what we read we are beginning to suspect that most of what we give is used up by the fund-raising organizations. We are happy to give but want the bulk of our donations to go to the charitable purpose we intend. Can you help us?

Your concerns are frequently legitimate, in light of the numerous questionable groups presenting themselves today as charitable organizations. Even when the organization involved is a highly reputable Catholic community or association, you still like to know what is being done with your money.

If you have these questions my only suggestion is that you write to them for more information on how donated money is spent. There is nothing wrong in itself, of course, in enlisting the assistance of fund-raising companies. Their techniques and experience can be most helpful and there is no reason to condemn missionary societies for using such companies to assist them in raising the funds they need. It is your money, however, and you have every right to ask how much of this money is being used for the purpose you believe you are offering it.

Carrying our crosses

Jesus says we are to take up our cross and follow him. Where does this cross come from? Is it God's will for you? Is it man's doing? Or just circumstances?

The crosses which burden each of our lives comes usually from three directions. The first and most common are those which result from the normal processes of daily living. These may be physical realities, such as illnesses, material disasters of various kinds and so on.

Or they may be the burdens of the emotional, intellectual and spiritual frailties which cause pain to ourselves and, in sometimes mysterious ways, infect our relationship with each other.

The second source of our crosses is hurt done to us — deliberately or undeliberately — by the sinfulness of others, especially by those closest to us.

The third type of crosses, which I believe are for most people the heaviest, are those which result from our own sinfulness and infidelities, in other words from our own (vague perhaps but nonetheless real) consciousness of having contributed to the lack of harmony and peace in our own and others' hearts and lives.

It is the prevalence and weight of these last crosses which make it necessary for God to insist as often and strongly as he does on the limitless power of his forgiving and healing love. When people deny or doubt that they can ever be forgiven of some particularly hurtful sin, I am convinced that most of the time they really are wondering whether even God can make things right again.

It is, I believe, one of the great acts of faith and one of the great steps toward holiness, to trust that he can and will bring about this healing and wholeness.

To answer your questions, any and all of these may be the crosses Jesus asks us to take up daily and follow him. They may not be the ones we would choose or the ones we think "fit" us.

But they happen to be ours. And in some mysterious way we find they do fit us uniquely, as do the graces we receive to carry them.

Salvation outside of church?

A magazine published by a group using the name of a famous shrine of our Blessed Mother insists that to save your soul you must be a Catholic and quotes Vatican Council II as saying: "Outside the church there is no salvation." The article also says that anyone who is a Catholic must remain a Catholic or be lost forever.

Not many years ago, as I recall, the church condemned the teaching of an American priest, Father Leonard Feeney, for saying the same thing as this article says. Do you have an answer? Is the quotation wrong?

The substance of the quote you give is from the Second Vatican Council (Constitution on the Church, No. 14) and from other Catholic documents. However, one must understand that statement as the church clearly explains it. And, as the church explains it and believes it, the statement absolutely does not mean that those who are not members of the Catholic Church are unsaved or "lost."

The Catholic Church, and by that I mean its members, including its leaders, does believe that the fullest riches of the means intended by Christ for our salvation exist in our church. These include the sacraments and liturgical life, unity of faith, communion in organization, and so on. (One would assume that members of other churches believe something like the same about their church, or they would join another.)

However, it explicitly and very strongly teaches that many essential elements of salvation, including the saving guidance and presence of the Holy Spirit, are also at work in other churches. This goes particularly, of course, for other Christian denominations, but applies to non-Christian religions and even those people struggling to live a good life who do not even know of God or Jesus Christ.

Thus the Catholic Church sees these others as closely related to us in the saving faith in Christ. Baptized Christians who live their faith in the Scripture and in Christ, and who often receive sacraments within their own churches, are "in some real way joined with us in the Holy Spirit, for to them also he gives his gifts and graces, and is thereby at work among them with his sanctifying power. Some indeed he has strengthened to the extent of shedding their blood" as martyrs (Constitution on the Church, No. 15).

Pope John Paul II, incidentally, repeated this thought, nearly word for word, in his recent visit to the Netherlands.

Far from being lost outsiders, the Catholic Church sees all people justified by faith through baptism as "incorporated into Christ. They therefore have a right to be honored by the title of Christian, and are properly regarded as brothers in the Lord by the sons of the Catholic Church" (Decree on Ecumenism, No. 3).

As for non-Christians who have no knowledge of Christ, or perhaps even of God himself in any explicit way, our church believes that they too are under the saving love and care of God. The Constitution on the Church affirms: "Those also can attain to everlasting salvation who through no fault of their own do not know the Gospel of Christ or his church yet sincerely seek God and, moved by grace, strive by their deeds to do his will as it is known to them."

This simply repeats traditional Catholic teaching when it adds: "Divine providence does not deny the help necessary to salvation to those who, without blame on their part, have not yet arrived at an explicit knowledge of God, but who strive to live a good life, thanks to his grace" (No. 16).

You ask whether those who are Catholic must remain Catholic until death or be lost spiritually. Much of what is said above applies here as well. But the Vatican Council refers to that situation explicitly and with extremely careful words.

"Whoever — *knowing that the Catholic Church was made necessary by God through Jesus Christ* — would refuse to enter her or to remain in her could not be saved" (Constitution on the Church, No. 14). The words I emphasized are essential and critical.

Just as many outside the church, so many Catholics — because of lack of training and education or opportunity for true commitment — may have little or no real awareness or belief in what those words say. Ultimately, of course, it is a matter between them and God if they turn away from their Catholic faith.

It cannot be said, however, and the church clearly does not believe that such people have automatically sinned seriously and lost any hope for eternal salvation.

Organ donations

There are two sides to every issue but I feel all alone on this one. My simple belief is that God created us with all the "equipment" we need to live out our life on earth. He gave us multiples of some organs. If one malfunctions the other compensates. When we have only one organ we can sometimes be operated on. When they fail completely, are we not at the end of our human life and allowed to die and go home to our Creator?

I cannot envision someone else's heart (or anything else that God gave them) in my body. Or a transplant bank anxiously awaiting a tragedy so that someone else may live. I am confused. Does the church take a position on organ transplants?

The tradition and present teaching of the Catholic Church thoroughly supports the principle and practice of giving an organ of one's body to another. Many circumstances must be examined carefully to determine whether or not the taking of an organ from one person and giving it to another is the morally proper thing to do. This obviously may become quite complicated, since it deals with questions involving certainty of death, if the giving of the organ depends on the donor's death; physical effects on the donor if the donor is living; degree of hope for a successful transplant; consent, and so on.

Obviously it is impossible to discuss all these circumstances in an adequate way here. I believe, however, that your concern is more spiritual than medical, so perhaps it is sufficient to say simply that this is one application of the charity we owe to others.

A few thoughts may help you see what I mean. For example, one of the highest gifts God gives to us for life on this earth is the gift of time. Without that, all other gifts would be to some degree meaningless. In a sense we could say that the "time of our lives" is even more critical to our lives than a second kidney.

Yet, in the time we offer them, we all give great parts of our lives to others, especially to our loved ones. We in turn receive the gift of parts of other people's lives. Over a lifetime of active love and sacrifice, these gifts may involve not only the time directly spent for us, but perhaps even the shortening of others' lives. In other words, we give our lives to one another all the time. If something that has been ours in life can still do good for someone else, before or after death, why not? Many people have given you part of their lives already. Without these you would not be alive today. If medical science can allow us to extend that gift even to the bodies which God has given for our stewardship, it is something to be grateful for, to use cautiously but generously.

Incidentally, Pope John Paul II repeated this position not long ago, speaking of the shortage of available donors for patients awaiting transplants. It is a matter of Christian generosity, he said, and "no solution will be forthcoming without a renewed sense of human solidarity," based on Christ's example, which can "inspire men and women to make great sacrifices in the service of others" (April 30, 1990).

The Catholic Abraham Lincoln

I am sending an article from what appears to be a fringe "Catholic" publication. It claims that Abraham Lincoln was brought up a Catholic, but fell away from the faith because of the influence of some "secret society." They quote bishops who seemed to have a little knowledge of the facts, and a pioneer priest, Father St. Cyr. My wife, a distant relative of President Lincoln, does not agree. Is there any substantial evidence to support this claim?

Yes, an Abraham Lincoln was Catholic, but the Catholic Lincoln did not become president of the United States. Sources which claim our 16th president was Catholic are confusing him with his cousin who had the same name and who is buried in an obscure pioneer cemetery in central Illinois.

There were in fact at least three Abraham Lincolns. The first, grandfather of the president and of the Catholic Abraham, lived in Virginia. In 1782 he sold his farm, moved the family to Kentucky, and in 1788 was killed by an Indian. This grandfather Abraham had three sons, among them Thomas, father of the president, and Mordecai, who became a convert to Catholicism when he married Mary Mudd, daughter of a prominent Catholic family. Their marriage is on record at Bardstown, Ky.

In 1830, Mordecai moved his family, including his children — Mordecai Jr., the Catholic Abraham, James, Elizabeth, Mary and Martha — to Hancock County in western Illinois (my diocese) where they and other Catholic settlers founded St. Simon the Apostle Chapel. Mordecai Sr. died shortly after the great snow winter of 1830-31. Meanwhile, Mordecai's brother, Thomas, married Nancy Hanks, who gave birth to the future president Feb. 12, 1809, in Hodgenville, Ky. Nancy died later, and the family moved to Illinois.

There is no record that President Lincoln himself ever joined any church, though he was familiar with and fond of the Bible. His wife, Mary Todd, attended Presbyterian services in Springfield, Ill., and in Washington. During the 1830s, the pioneer priest Father Irenaeus St. Cyr offered Mass among the scattered Catholic settlements along the Mississippi Valley from St. Louis north and on to Chicago. Historians have reason to believe that he remembered things rather hazily decades later in his old age. He spoke of President Lincoln's immediate family, but it seems certain that his recollections were rather of the Catholic Lincolns in Hancock County, where he labored as a well-known early missionary.

President Lincoln was a man of faith, but there's no convincing evidence that he was raised Catholic or that his visits to his Catholic cousins altered his position. I have visited more than once the cemetery where the Catholic Abraham is buried, at the site of St. Simon Chapel, which has long since disappeared. For many years now the burial plot has been part of a cow pasture. The tomb of his famous cousin is just a short distance away in Springfield.

Chain letters

What is a good Catholic to do with a letter such as the one I received? It assures all kinds of "good luck" if I make 20 copies and send it to others within 96 hours.

It promises good luck if I do what it says and all kinds of bad luck if I don't. And it gives examples.

The letter says that some man named Gene Welch lost his wife six days after receiving the letter because he failed to send copies to other people. However, before her death he received $7,750,000.

My religious belief tells me to throw these things in the garbage, but can you explain why a Catholic would send such a letter to anyone?

I can't imagine why anyone, Catholic or not, would send such a letter. This particular chain letter, one of many dozens I've received during past years, is typical in that it assumes enough people are sufficiently gullible and ignorant to make the game worthwhile.

Most chain letters, even though they are nearly always one hundred percent superstitious, at least make a pass at something that sounds religious. The letter which you send does not even attempt that, apart from the fact that it is apparently "signed" by St. Jude.

If people are naive and uneducated enough to give any credence to this type of mail, they probably will not be influenced by anything you or I or anyone else says.

Throw such letters away. Only the U.S. Postal Service stands to gain from them.

Parousia, second coming of Christ

What is the church's teaching on when the second coming of Christ will take place? Watching Christian evangelical television, I notice that a lot of emphasis is put on the theory that the events taking place today bring us very close to the end times described in the book of Daniel and Revelation.

They also go on to describe the "rapture of the church," the tribulation period, the defeat of the Antichrist in Armageddon, the second coming of Christ, etc. Is there a Catholic book that addresses itself to this subject?

Yes, there is a good book. It's called the Bible. In it Jesus says very clearly, "You know neither the day nor the hour." According to our Christian tradition, even the rest of the Bible doesn't take us much closer to the answer.

First of all, most of the book of Revelation and a good part of the book of Daniel are made up of a type of literature quite well known during the century or so before and after Christ, called apocalyptic.

Generally, apocalyptic writings were composed of a wide variety of symbols and visions, many of them quite bizarre, supposedly containing veiled occult or divine messages. Often, too, an angel or other messenger would be introduced to explain the message — though the explanations sometimes were hardly more clear than the vision itself.

We find all this both in Daniel and Revelation.

Without being at all flippant, it is no exaggeration that certain groups of Christians have had a field day with all those visions for the past 18 or 19 centuries. In every century, perhaps even every generation, one finds movements which make frightening predictions of the end of the world.

These come from people who, deliberately or not, play on the emotional shakiness of people who are afraid of the times, who are perhaps superficial in their knowledge of their Christian faith, people who are easily convinced that the world has never been so evil — which somehow is supposed to bring about God's vengeance by his burning it to a crisp.

The list of these phenomena from history is almost endless. One example is particularly interesting. Revelation 20:4 speaks of a period of 1,000 years between the first coming of Christ and his return.

If some Christians today are still trying to maneuver that figure to refer to the present time, one can imagine the situation when the actual year 1000 was approaching just a thousand years ago.

Other predictions may have been wrong, said many "prophets" of the day, but now the real year 1000 is definitely approaching. The world, indeed Christianity itself, is in such a mess, they preached, that the final battle in the valley of Mageddo (Armageddon) between the good and the bad (Rev. 16:16) is now clearly near.

Obviously they were wrong, as have been a host of others in the centuries that followed.

To answer your question: The church has no teaching whatsoever about the specific time of the second coming of Christ and the events that might accompany it.

It is, in fact, a curiosity-type concern which even Jesus did not seem especially anxious to address, perhaps because it can more easily distract than help us in our daily Christian living in the world.

As I have mentioned before, the end of the world for which Jesus asked us to prepare carefully and well, is not the day the world burns up, but the day each one of us leaves it.

Jehovah Witnesses

My wife has asked my 10 children to help celebrate my 80th birthday. However, two of the children are Jehovah Witnesses and said they do not celebrate birthdays because they live their lives closely following the example that Jesus left us and according to the Bible. They say that neither Jesus nor any early Christians celebrated birthdays. It was a pagan tradition and one that Christians would have nothing to do with. It was viewed as a pagan tradition at the time of Christ and is to be viewed the same way today.

I know this is hurtful for you, but the information you give is correct. Among numerous differences in belief and practices between Jehovah Witnesses and other denominations is this one. Consistent with this belief, their members do not even celebrate Christmas, partly because it celebrates the birthday of Jesus and also because the date of Christmas was established, apparently in the fourth century, on the day of the winter solstice (according to the old Julian calendar), which was before then a great pagan feast.

INDEX